THE
ALL ENGLAND
LAW REPORTS
ANNUAL REVIEW

1990

London
BUTTERWORTHS
1991

UNITED KINGDOM	Butterworth & Co (Publishers) Ltd, 88 Kingsway, **London** WC2B 6AB and 4 Hill Street, **Edinburgh** EH2 3JZ
AUSTRALIA	Butterworths Pty Ltd, **Sydney, Melbourne, Brisbane, Adelaide, Perth, Canberra** and **Hobart**
CANADA	Butterworths Canada Ltd, **Toronto** and **Vancouver**
IRELAND	Butterworth (Ireland) Ltd, **Dublin**
MALAYSIA	Malayan Law Journal Pte Ltd, **Kuala Lumpur**
NEW ZEALAND	Butterworths of New Zealand Ltd, **Wellington** and **Auckland**
PUERTO RICO	Equity de Puerto Rico Inc, **Hato Rey**
SINGAPORE	Malayan Law Journal Pte Ltd, **Singapore**
USA	Butterworth Legal Publishers, **Austin**, Texas, **Boston**, Massachusetts, **Clearwater**, Florida (D & S Publishers), **Orford**, New Hampshire (Equity Publishing), **St Paul**, Minnesota, **Seattle**, Washington

General Editor
Paul Brown, MA

ISBN 0 406 863 113

Typeset by Phoenix Photosetting, Chatham, Kent
Printed and bound in Great Britain by
Mackays of Chatham PLC, Chatham, Kent

Publishers' Note

This is the ninth All England Law Reports Annual Review and as in previous years it is designed as a companion to the All England Law Reports. A number of academic lawyers has been invited to contribute articles evaluating the decisions of the courts relevant to their particular speciality and reported in that series in 1990. Not all of the cases, of course, fall neatly into one or other of the categories of conventional legal classification. The authors have tried to avoid duplication in their discussion of cases and there is a number of cross-references to be found in the articles. Some cases, however, are examined in more than one article because different aspects are of importance in different contexts. Other cases, not actually reported in the All England, have also been referred to where this has been considered worthwhile.

Amongst the most important decisions of 1990, of course, is the House of Lords judgment in *Murphy v Brentwood District Council*, which 'nails shut the coffin' in which *Anns* has been confined over the last six years. But 1990 was a busy year besides, and the All England reflects developments in the law across almost every subject.

Cases from the 1990 All England Law Reports, Simon's Tax Cases and Butterworths Company Law Cases are printed in bold type in the Table of Cases.

This volume should be cited as All ER Rev 1990.

BUTTERWORTH LAW PUBLISHERS LTD

Contributors

Administrative Law
Keith Davies, JP, MA, LLM
Barrister, Professor of Law,
University of Reading

Arbitration
J E Adams LLB, FCIArb
Solicitor, Director of Training,
Titmuss Sainer & Webb;
Emeritus Professor of Law,
Queen Mary and Westfield College,
University of London

Commercial Law
N E Palmer, BCL, MA
Barrister, Professor of Law,
University of Southampton and
Robert Merkin, LLB, LLM
Professor of Law, University of Sussex

Company Law
D D Prentice, MA, LLB, JD
Barrister, Allen & Overy Professor of
Corporate Law, Fellow of Pembroke College,
Oxford

Contempt of Court
C J Miller, BA, LLM
Barrister, Professor of English Law,
University of Birmingham

Contract
Michael P Furmston, TD, BCL, MA, LLM
Bencher of Gray's Inn,
Professor of Law,
University of Bristol

Criminal Law, Criminal Procedure and Sentencing
G J Bennett, MA
Barrister, Senior Lecturer in Law,
City University and
Brian Hogan, LLB
Barrister, Professor of Common Law,
University of Leeds

Employment Law
Ian Smith, MA, LLB (Cantab)
Barrister, Reader in Law,
University of East Anglia

European Community Law
Christopher Greenwood, MA, LLB
Barrister, Fellow of Magdalene College,
Cambridge

Evidence and *Practice and Procedure*
Adrian A S Zuckerman, LLM, MA
Fellow of University College, Oxford

Extradition and *Prisons*
I M Yeats, BCL, MA
Barrister, Senior Lecturer in Law,
Queen Mary and Westfield College,
University of London

Family Law
S M Cretney, MA, DCL, FBA
Solicitor, Professor of Law,
University of Bristol

Land Law and Trusts
P J Clarke, BCL, MA
Barrister, Fellow of Jesus College,
Oxford

Landlord and Tenant
Philip H Pettit, MA
Barrister, Emeritus Professor of Equity,
Universities of Bristol and Buckingham

Medical Law
Andrew Grubb, MA
Barrister, Senior Lecturer in Law,
King's College,
London

Shipping Law
R P Grime, BA, BCL
BT (Marine) Ltd Professor of Law,
University of Southampton

Solicitors
Brian Harvey, MA, LLM
Solicitor, Professor of Property Law,
University of Birmingham

Sport and the Law
Edward Grayson, MA
Barrister, South Eastern Circuit

Statute Law
Francis Bennion, MA (Oxon)
Barrister, Research Associate of the
University of Oxford Centre for
Socio-Legal Studies, former UK
Parliamentary Counsel

Succession
C H Sherrin, LLM, PhD
Barrister, Reader in Law,
University of Bristol

Taxation
John Tiley, MA, BCL
Professor of the Law of Taxation,
University of Cambridge;
Fellow of Queens' College,
Cambridge

Tort
Alastair Mullis, LLB, LLM
Lecturer in Law, King's College,
London

Town and Country Planning
Paul B Fairest, MA, LLM
Professor of Law,
University of Hull

Contents

Table of Cases

Abbreviations

ACT	Advance Corporation Tax
BCLC	Butterworths Company Law Cases
BTR	British Tax Review
CGTA	Capital Gains Tax Act 1979
CLJ	Cambridge Law Journal
CLR	Commonwealth Law Reports
Conv	The Conveyancer
Cr App R	Criminal Appeal Reports
Crim LR	Criminal Law Review
DLR	Dominion Law Reports
DLT	Development Land Tax
ECR	European Court Reports
EG	Estates Gazette
EHRR	European Human Rights Reports
FA	Finance Act
Fam Law	Family Law
FLR	Family Law Reports
FSR	Fleet Street Reports
ICR	Industrial Cases Reports
ILM	International Legal Materials
ILR	International Law Reports
Imm AR	Immigration Appeals Reports
IRLR	Industrial Relations Law Reports
JP	Justice of the Peace Reports
LGR	Local Government Review
LPA	Law of Property Act 1925
LQR	Law Quarterly Review
LRA	Land Registration Act 1925
LS	Legal Studies
LSG	Law Society Gazette
MLJ	Malayan Law Journal
MLR	Modern Law Review
NLJ	New Law Journal
NLJR	New Law Journal Law Reports
Ox Jo LS	Oxford Journal of Legal Studies
P & CR	Property and Compensation Reports
RTR	Road Traffic Reports
SC	Session Cases
SJ	Solicitors' Journal
STC	Simon's Tax Cases
TA	Income and Corporations Taxes Act 1970 and 1988
TC	Tax Cases
TMA	Tax Management Act 1970

Administrative Law

KEITH DAVIES, JP, MA, LLM
Barrister, Professor of Law, University of Reading

Statutory duty and its breach

1990 was a lean year for administrative law as far as the All England Law
Reports are concerned. The most important decision by far is one which at
first sight has nothing to do with administrative law at all. Directly, it has no
relevance; indirectly, it has a great deal. This, of course, is the decision by the
House of Lords in *Murphy v Brentwood District Council* [1990] 2 All ER 908. Its
importance in tort cannot be considered here, fundamental though that is (for
a detailed discussion of this aspect see the chapter on Tort, pp 303–307, 312,
313 below). Its implications for administrative law are less obvious but more
insidious. They concern the statutory functions of public authorities (see also
the chapter on Statute Law, at pp 250–252 below). The central fact is that the
harm which gave rise to the action arose in the course of the carrying out by
Brentwood Council of its statutory functions of exercising control over
building operations. As in *Anns v Merton London Borough* [1977] 2 All ER 492,
buildings had been put up with defective foundations; clearly the builders
were negligent, but that was not in issue. In *Murphy v Brentwood*, consulting
engineers were involved also. It seems to have been common ground that
they were negligent and that was not in issue either. The council placed
reliance on the engineers, justifiably so because of their established repute:
how, then, might the council be liable?

The Court of Appeal founded the council's alleged liability on their
statutory duty, that is to say a duty imposed directly on them – and not on the
builders or consulting engineers – by statute (the Public Health Act 1936, now
the Building Act 1984). This appears to be *not* vicarious liability in common
law negligence for the default of another, but direct liability for breach of the
statutory duty lying on the council. However, in the House of Lords in *D & F
Estates Ltd v Church Commissioners for England* [1988] 2 All ER 992 (All ER Rev
1988, p 70), Lord Oliver spoke (at 1010) of 'a parallel common law duty in a
local authority stemming from and existing alongside its statutory duties and
conditioned by the purpose of these statutory duties', and *Anns v Merton* was
the source of this view. Moreover, he went on to say that 'it was an essential
part of the rationale of the decision [in *Anns*] in relation to the liability of the
local authority that there was a precisely parallel and co-existing liability in the
builder'. As to that, Lord Wilberforce said in *Anns* (at 504) that:

> 'since it is the duty of the builder . . . to comply with the [Building Regulations]
> . . . an action could be brought against him, in effect, for breach of statutory
> duty, by any person for whose benefit or protection the [Regulations were]
> made.'

Putting all these observations together, we see no less than four 'parallel'
liabilities: (1) common law negligence and (2) breach of statutory duty in
regard to local authorities carrying out their functions when controlling

building work, and (3) and (4) the same in regard to builders carrying out that building work.

The effect of the overruling of *Anns v Merton* by the House of Lords in *Murphy v Brentwood* is that this scheme of multiple and 'parallel' liabilities is drastically reduced. Something remains, but the difficulty lies in knowing for certain how much. Here, the only aspect which there is time to look at is breach of statutory duty, because 'statutory duty' refers to functions imposed by Parliament on local authorities and other public bodies, and that is a matter which is central to administrative law. Lord Oliver (at 936) put the rhetorical question; 'on what principle is liability in tort to be imposed on a local authority for failing to exercise its regulatory powers so as to prevent conduct which, on this hypothesis, is not tortious?' ie there is no such principle, the hypothesis being that the cause of complaint consists in 'defects which, ex hypothesi, have injured nobody'. Lord Jauncey (at 943) held that there is 'no policy reason for imposing such a duty on local authorities'.

This seems to dispose of the common law liability in negligence, both for councils and for builders, but leaves the question of breach of statutory duty still to be considered. Lord Oliver said that:

'neither in *Anns* nor in *Dutton* [[1972] 1 All ER 462] . . . was the liability of the local authority based on the proposition that the Public Health Act 1936 gave rise to an action by a private individual for a breach of statutory duty of the type contemplated in *Cutler v Wandsworth Stadium Ltd* [[1949] 1 All ER 544] . . . a type of claim quite distinct from a claim in negligence . . .'

Perhaps so – but this is not to say that liability cannot be based on that proposition. The issue needs to be examined on its merits.

This question is especially important in the light of the earlier decision of the House of Lords in *Cocks v Thanet District Council* [1982] 3 All ER 1135. There it was said that in cases of alleged breach of statutory duty, liability arises in two stages. The first is a matter of public law; and an action to seek judicial review is the only way to challenge an authority's decision at this point in the game. The second stage is a matter of private law; and an action in tort may then lie on the basis that, if and when the duty has been established, the relevant public authority will become civilly liable if they continue to act in such a way as to be in breach of it. Lord Bridge said in that case that there is a 'dichotomy of functions', comprising 'decision-making functions' at the first stage and 'executive functions' at the second. This analysis was being expressed in the most general terms, though it was being applied in particular in that case only to the Housing (Homeless Persons) Act 1977.

The question of breach of statutory duty cannot be disposed of casually in relation to cases such as *Anns* or *Murphy*. The administrative law principles contained in public law are fundamentally affected independently of how things fall out as regards private law liability in the field of tort. How are we to regard the 'dichotomy' now?

Judicial review

In *Caswell v Dairy Produce Quota Tribunal for England & Wales* [1990] 2 All ER 434, the House of Lords affirmed the decision of the Court of Appeal in this case in 1989 ([1989] 3 All ER 205). The tribunal in question had misled the applicants as to their dairy produce quota by not specifying the correct one – an ultra vires act. But relief in judicial review was refused on the grounds that, though it was justified in principle, to grant it would be prejudicial to good administration (ie other persons' quotas might need to be re-opened). Also, there had been 'undue delay', though not through any fault of the applicants. The interesting question which does not seem to have been raised was whether private law liability for breach of statutory duty could be established. The 'dichotomy' mentioned in *Cocks* must surely be present, between the tribunal's 'decision making' act to fix the relevant quota and the 'executive act' involved in doing it wrongly.

As to fairness and natural justice, involving the 'procedural impropriety' principle, in *R v Harrow LBC, ex p D* [1990] 3 All ER 12, a case similar to *R v Norfolk CC, ex p M* [1989] 3 All ER 359 (All ER Rev 1989, p 6) involved the inclusion of the applicant's name on a register of child abusers. The Court of Appeal approved the decision of Waite J in the *Norfolk* case to order judicial review, but refused it in the *Harrow* case itself because the applicant had been given a chance to make representations before being placed in the register. The injustice of what was done in the *Norfolk* case was absent from the *Harrow* case. For further discussion of both cases, see Family Law, pp 148–150 below.

A case on the 'irrationality' principle was the decision of the Court of Appeal in *R v Greenwich LBC, ex p Lovelace and ex p Fay* [1990] 1 All ER 353. Judicial review was sought by councillors who had disagreed with a policy adopted by the majority party group to which they belonged, because that disagreement led to their removal from the council's housing committee. Was the decision to remove them ultra vires? It was held not. Had it been arbitrary the case would have been different; but this was not so, because:

> 'if a council has a policy in an area which is delegated to a committee the council is entitled to seek that the policy is followed in the committee.' (Per Glidewell LJ, at 362.)

A case on judicial review which goes right to the fundamentals is the decision of the House of Lords in *Hammersmith and Fulham LBC v Secretary of State for the Environment* [1990] 3 All ER 589. This arose in relation to the celebrated 'community charge' or 'poll tax'. Section 100(4) of the Local Government Finance Act 1988 empowers the Secretary of State for the Environment to set a limit to the level at which individual councils can set the charge for their respective areas. What is then specified is the maximum expenditure for each respective local authority for a given financial year. When other sources of income, not fixed by the authority but by the central government, chiefly the revenue support grant and the local authority's allotted share of the non-domestic rate, are deducted from that total, what remains must broadly dictate the level of the poll tax for that authority's area. Activating s 100(4) is known in the trade as 'charge-capping'.

In regard to local authority budgets for 1990–91, the Secretary of State applied this procedure to a number of local authorities, which retaliated by seeking judicial review. The ultra vires conduct alleged consisted in not making a detailed assessment of the budget of each authority affected in order to decide whether or not it was excessively high, in applying a national 'norm' to local authorities' expenditure, and in setting the levels after the authorities had set their budgets so that there was no prior consultation. After judicial review had been refused by the Queen's Bench Divisional Court and the Court of Appeal in turn, a further unsuccessful appeal was made to the House of Lords.

The reason for the failure of the judicial review application was that the decision of the Secretary of State was 'administrative'. To 'cap' a local authority's budget so as to limit the amount of the 'community charge' is essentially a matter of political judgment as to what was the appropriate level of expenditure. In other words, it fell on the side of the boundary line on which policy decisions are lawful, and not on the side on which they are unlawful.

The whole of public law is concerned, in one way or another, with the question of whether a policy decision in any particular case is lawful (intra vires) or not (ultra vires). Questions of policy are distinguished from questions of fact (evidence, inference) and questions of law. It is, however, a question of law – and one of overriding importance – whether a policy decision is or is not lawful. Within the boundary of vires, each person, or body of persons, or institution, that exercises official functions (derived ultimately from the Crown), as distinct from natural functions, is free to take decisions as to policy – ie future action or inaction. Outside the boundary the opposite is true. Were there to be no boundary, the exercise of power would be arbitrary. The freedom which is recognised under this system is ex hypothesi not arbitrary as far as English law is concerned. Even the Crown is governed by this principle: '. . . rex no debet esse sub homine sed sub deo et sub lege, quia lex facit regem' (*De Legibus et Consuetudinibus Angliae*, f 5.b) – the greatest of all the principles we owe to Bracton and (subject to him) Coke.

So the *Hammersmith* case illustrates the operation of this fundamental principle. All the parties were and are official bodies exercising functions under public law; but it was the exercise of one particular function by the Secretary of State which was in issue. His conduct was vindicated in this instance not because it (or he) is above the law and free to exercise power arbitrarily, but because the exercise of power here was within the limits prescribed by law. The Crown in Parliament leglislated to give him powers in this area. The courts interpreted the legislation in accordance with 'settled doctrines' embodying relevant principles. Statutory interpretation is a fundamental part of common law.

This was not one of those cases in which 'non-justiciable' matters such as preservation of national security are in issue (see *Council of Civil Service Unions v Minister for the Civil Service* [1984] 3 All ER 935 (All ER Rev 1984, pp 1–5, 139–140)) or those involving mere 'ministerial' or routine activities of government servants. 'Non-justiciable' activities of either kind are intra vires for practical reasons, not independent of the ultra vires rule. The courts decide what is or is not 'justiciable'. In public law, as in private law, the boundary-lines are what matter most of all, and the common law is the guardian of the boundary-lines. This is the theory of law; whether in practice it is correctly applied is a matter of individual judgment.

When examining the judgments in this case, or any other such case, it is essential to draw the distinctions which truly support the above principle. In the House of Lords the judgment is contained in Lord Bridge's speech, with which his four colleagues concurred; and in it, for example, we read this:

'As explained in the affidavit of [an assistant secretary in the Department of the Environment], the political thinking which underlies the new system is that it will operate to secure that local authorities are properly accountable to their electorate'.

It may be that a judge uttering such words is uttering his own private beliefs, his own 'political thinking'; or it may not. But in his capacity as a judge of the court in question, this possibility does not arise and the task of the court, applying the common law, does not extend to it. The lay public may suppose that the court is endorsing the 'political thinking which underlies the new system'; but what the court is doing is to note, as a finding of fact, that the minister has adopted that 'political thinking' and has tried to give effect to it. 'Political thinking' in the widest possible sense of that expression is 'thinking that underlies policy decisions', which may (as in this case) be 'party political' or (as in other cases) may not. As Lawton LJ said in *Asher v Secretary of State for the Environment* [1974] 2 All ER 156 at 168:

> 'Balancing the advantages and disadvantages of one possible course of action against another and making a decision is what Secretaries of State have to do: it is the very stuff of government and the courts should not interfere save for good reason, and disagreeing with the decision is not in itself a good reason.'

Making decisions is what all public authorities have to do – it is what they are there for. 'Good reason' means that the decision-maker has stepped across the boundary of lawful power: what should be intra vires turns out on examination to ultra vires because of (in Lord Diplock's terminology, which the courts in general have adopted) 'illegality', 'irrationality' or 'procedural impropriety'.

Lord Bridge dealt with various points of factual detail and then returned to points of legal principle. As in almost all cases of this kind, what is at stake is the all-pervading common law doctrine of statutory interpretation. The appellant local authorities, said Lord Bridge, placed much reliance here on:

> 'a familiar line of authority of which the leading case is *Secretary of State for Education and Science v Tameside Metropolitan Borough* [1976] 3 All ER 665, [1977] AC 1014. That case concerned the exercise by the Secretary of State . . . of a power . . . to give directions to a local education authority . . . if he was satisfied that the authority was "proposing to act unreasonably . . . [under the Education Act 1944]". The House held that this did not empower the Secretary of State . . . to substitute his own opinion for that of the local education authority . . . but that he could only give directions if, on the material before him, he was entitled to be satisfied that no reasonable local education authority would act as the authority in question was proposing to act. This was a decision on different statutory language in a wholly different statutory context.'

The words 'entitled to be satisfied that no reasonable . . . authority would act' in the manner stated import an objective test, not a purely subjective one. The act of policy decision-making is a subjective matter, whereas questions of law import objectivity.

Lord Bridge then went on to apply Lord Diplock's triple classification for challenge in public law, and said that the above arguments related to 'illegality' – ie ultra vires in principle. He then turned to 'irrationality' – ultra vires in detail – and 'impropriety' – ultra vires procedure.

As to 'irrationality', he referred to the *locus classicus* of this concept, which is, of course, *Associated Provincial Picture Houses Ltd v Wednesbury Corporation*

[1947] 2 All ER 680, [1948] 1 KB 223 – the *Wednesbury* principle' – as formulated in the judgment of Lord Greene MR (at 682). He also referred to Lord Scarman's application of the principle in *Nottinghamshire CC v Secretary of State for the Environment* [1986] 1 All ER 199 at 202 (see All ER Rev 1986, p 271) – 'If a Minister exercises a power conferred on him by the legislation, the courts can investigate whether he has abused his power' (at 202). This exercise may be valid in principle but invalid in detail (a policy decision 'so unreasonable that no reasonable authority could ever have come to it', in the words of Lord Greene). But as for the instant case:

> 'There is here no suggestion that the Secretary of State acted in bad faith or for an improper motive or that his decision to designate the appellant authority or the maximum amounts to which he had decided to limit their budgets were so absurd that he must have taken leave of his senses. Short of such an extreme challenge, and provided always that the Secretary of State has acted within the four corners of the Act, I do not believe there is any room for attack on the rationality of the Secretary of State's exercise of his powers under [the Act of 1988].'

Finally, as to 'procedural impropriety', Lord Bridge said he did not think it possible:

> 'to imply terms in the statute derived from the doctrine of *audi alteram partem*. But it is unnecessary to consider this point further because, at the only point in the process leading to "capping" at which it might be appropriate to insist that, as a matter of fair procedure, authorities should have the opportunity to be heard in opposition to the Secretary of State's proposed "cap" and to make a reasoned case in support of an alternative and less restrictive maximum for their budget, the Act itself by ss 102(5)(a) and 104 expressly prescribes a procedure precisely to this effect. This procedure was duly followed, and in addition all the authorities [concerned] . . . were given the opportunity to make representations orally . . . [to two junior ministers].

In view of this analysis of the case, it cannot be reasonably denied that the House of Lords has given 'illegality', 'irrationality' and 'procedural impropriety' a good run for their money.

Byelaws

The House of Lords has also pronounced on the subject of byelaws and their validity, in *DPP v Hutchinson* [1990] 2 All ER 836. This case concerned the RAF Greenham Common Byelaws 1985, made under the authority of the Military Lands Act 1892, s 14(1). That Act empowers the Secretary of State for Defence to regulate by means of byelaws the use of land appropriated for military purposes, so long as such byelaws do not 'take away or prejudicially affect any right of common'.

The appellants were convicted for breaches of the byelaws. They had entered the 'protected area' of the Greenham Common military air base 'without authority or permission'. They were not claiming to exercise any rights of common, but claiming to have their convictions overturned because the byelaws were themselves invalid. This invalidity would be on the basis that the byelaws were on their face wider than the enabling Act of 1892 authorised them to be.

This argument succeeded in the House of Lords. The practical purpose of the byelaws was to impose an absolute prohibition on all unauthorised access to the 'protected area'. If they had been drafted in such a way as to preserve the rights of persons entitled to common of pasturage etc, which would be necessary to conform to the requirement laid down by the authorising Act, they would have been radically different; and the current byelaws could not be 'severed' so as to exclude wrongful wording. Therefore, their invalidity could not be cured. That is why the appellants had been wrongly convicted.

This would seem to mark the final triumph of the ladies of Greenham Common.

Note – The decision of the Court of Appeal on 'debt-swap finance' contracts of local authorities, reported as *Hazell v Hammersmith and Fulham LBC* [1990] 3 All ER 33, has in part been reversed (to substantial effect) by the House of Lords in 1991. Comment on this is therefore deferred.

Arbitration

J E ADAMS, LLB, FCIArb
Solicitor, Director of Training, Titmuss Sainer & Webb; Emeritus Professor of Law, Queen Mary and Westfield College, University of London

1990 was to a large extent a year of consolidation in the arbitration field. Work continued on the preparation of the new Arbitration Bill, to be presented in 1991 with the aim of consolidating the existing legislation and stating or re-stating in legislative form some yet to be selected facets of the common law of arbitration. Parliament incorporated the UNCITRAL Model Law into the law of Scotland (by the Law Reform (Miscellaneous Provisions) (Scotland) Act, s 66 operative from 1 January 1991) and the massive Courts and Legal Services Act contained five sections affecting arbitration.

Section 10(3) of the 1950 Act, added in December 1985, is further amended. Where the arbitration agreement provides for each party to appoint an arbitrator who then appoints a third, the party who has appointed now has a choice of remedy if the other does not appoint, for which he will elect by service of notice. The notice will call on the defaulter to nominate and, on failure to comply within seven clear days, either the first party's arbitrator can be designated sole arbitrator or, if the first party so elected, he can ask the court to appoint the second arbitrator.

An Official Referee can be appointed as arbitrator or umpire, provided the Lord Chief Justice releases him to do so 'having regard to the state of official referees' business'. This qualification, given the present congestion of the lists, may restrict the use of this facility, which, with consequential provisions, is contained in a new s 11 inserted in the 1950 Act, to replace the existing section, by s 99 of the 1990 Act. With agreement of the parties, a court may exercise powers given to an arbitrator by any arbitration provisions in a contract which is before the court (s 100 introducing a s 43A into the Supreme Court Act 1981). This puts on a firm footing the practice, particularly, of Official Referees, overthrown by *Northern Region Hospital Authority v Derek Crouch Construction Co Ltd* [1984] 2 All ER 175 (see All ER Rev 1984, pp 18–19).

Next, responding to judicial prompting, nay pleading (see All ER Rev 1988, p 11 citing from *The Antaios* [1984] 3 All ER 229), s 102 of the 1990 Act gives power to an arbitrator to dismiss a claim. The new s 13A inserted in the principal Act by this section requires, obviously enough, that the dispute has been referred to him (which may occasionally call for some further step beyond his mere appointment) followed by inordinate and inexcusable delay by the claimant in pursuing it with one or two results. Either delay must give rise to a substantial risk that it is not possible to have a fair resolution of the issues in the claim or cause serious prejudice, or the risk of it, to the respondent. The formulation involves a number of 'value judgments' and it remains to be seen what use will be made of the new powers. Moreover, it will be interesting to see whether or not the dangers of giving the power to the arbitrator, expressed by the virtually lone voice of Mr Rhiddian Thomas in an article at [1990] JBL 110, will become manifest. Would the new statutory tests have been satisfied in all the cases raising the point since the *Bremer Vulkan* case ([1981] 1 All ER 289) or would some still fall outside it? Incidentally, the power of amendment by statutory instrument contained in sub-s (3) is a device for which the Master of the Rolls argued in *Aden Refinery Co Ltd v Ugland Management Co, 'The Ugland Obo One'* [1986] 3 All ER 737 at 739h–i (All ER Rev 1986, p 13).

Lastly, the High Court loses its power, contained in s 12(6)(*b*), to order discovery and interrogatories in arbitrations. That power will remain with arbitrators, unless removed by the arbitrands, who will need to balance the benefits of discovery against the perceived burdens, especially in the minds of foreign parties in non-domestic arbitrations, which have generated the opposition which has led to this result in s 103, Courts and Legal Services Act 1990. It was recommended by the Departmental Advisory Committee in its Second Report.

The new provisions come into force on dates to be set by Ministerial orders.

The 1990 cases

This mild flurry of legislation has been accompanied by cases on leave to appeal (*Ipswich Borough Council v Fisons plc* [1990] 1 All ER 730), the scope for substantive counterclaims in actions challenging the existence of an arbitration clause (*Metal Scrap Trade Corp Ltd v Kate Shipping Co Ltd, 'The Gladys'* [1990] 1 All ER 397), the status and powers of Official Referees to deal with arbitration appeals (*Tate & Lyle Industries Ltd v Davy McKee (London) Ltd* [1990] 1 All ER 157 and extension of time limits (*Comdel Commodities Ltd v Siporex SpA* [1990] 1 All ER 216, CA, and [1990] 2 All ER 552, HL). With only four cases reported in the All England Reports it is quite fortuitous, but fitting, that they come from disputes in property, shipping, construction and commodities, respectively. In the first three instances the earlier decisions have been discussed in previous Reviews.

The Nema guidelines and property arbitrations

The fact that there had been an appeal from the Vice-Chancellor in the *Ipswich Borough v Fisons* case was noted in All ER Rev 1989 at p 10. The interest in the appeal lies not in the fact that his order was upheld in the outcome but in the reasons for the Court of Appeal's decision. A 1955 agreement for a 99-year lease contained an obligation on the council landlord to offer land for a permanent car park. Part of the land was made available and in 1982 the life of the obligation to offer the balance was extended. When the land was offered in 1986, the landlord contended for a rent subject to review to which the tenant objected. On reference to a third party, he ruled that the terms of the further lease should reflect the practices of 1955, not 1986. Browne-Wilkinson V-C gave the council leave to appeal under s 1(3)(*b*) of the 1979 Act. He did so on the basis of entertaining a real doubt whether the third party had been right in his decision. He thus departed from the *Nema/Antaios* guidelines, following his own previous decision in *Lucas Industries Ltd v Welsh*

Development Agency [1986] 2 All ER 858 (noted in All ER Rev 1986, pp 12–13). The two cases, and others to like effect, seemed to have freed property arbitrations (particularly in rent reviews, which this was not) from what many saw as the unwelcome constraints of the guidelines laid down in the two House of Lords decisions.

The Master of the Rolls, who gave the only judgment, started by pointing out that the Act gave no guidance on granting leave to appeal beyond requiring the appeal substantially to affect the rights of the parties, so that the House of Lords needed to give the lead. It so happened that that was in two shipping cases but, he added, 'it would . . . be a profound error to conclude that their Lordships intended their guidance to be confined to shipping disputes or . . . insurance and commodity trade disputes' (732c). He then stressed the point made in *Aden Refinery Co Ltd v Ugland Management Co, 'The Ugland Obo One'* distinguishing between the prescription of the correct spirit in which to exercise the statutory discretion and the guidelines or illustrations of the resultant approach both of which strands are found in the two House of Lords' decisions.

Next, Lord Donaldson briefly lists the reasons the parties chose to arbitrate rather than litigate, a decision from which, in the context of the 1979 Act, both parties can resile by both agreeing to seek a judicial ruling. If only one wishes to seek that review, it faces 'the parliamentary intention to give greater weight to finality that had been the case prior to the Act' (733b). That intention, the presumption against giving leave, is neither 'irrebuttable' nor of 'constant weight'.

Sir Nicholas Brown-Wilkinson's reasons for departing, in the *Lucas Industries* case, from the guidelines are mentioned, but, so the Master of the Rolls indicates, he had given insufficient stress to the bias for finality, albeit tempered by the particular problems of specific cases. Lord Donaldson explores the factors in the instant case for following the guidelines, it being close to a rent review case where the same factors arise more frequently. The absence of a standard clause is acknowledged but 'there must be groups of claims which bear so strong a family resemblance as not to be readily distinguishable from standard contract clauses' (733h). One respectfully concurs. The prospect of general points of law arising in rent review cases, the Vice-Chancellor's second point, applies in other areas, such as shipping and commodity. The third *Lucas Industries* criterion, the future impact between the parties, 'may not be true of a late [decision] or the last one' (734a). Thus the judgment here effectively undermines the triple basis of the more relaxed test propounded in the earlier property cases.

Nonetheless, although rebutting the presumption for finality requires more than 'being left in real doubt' the requisite degree of suspicion varies. For 'one-off' cases the House of Lords has postulated an obvious case of error; that might apply to a final rent review. Otherwise, the standard terms approach would be appropriate, that is a 'strong' prima facie case of error, strength itself being a variable element. The Master of the Rolls illustrates how this would apply in differing aspects of rent review (734d–g). We shall doubtless see references to these examples in future applications for leave to appeal.

In relation to the particular dispute, Lord Donaldson points out that unresolved details were to be settled by an independent expert, but he had been treated by the parties as an arbitrator determining what the parties had agreed. Mr Crome, the solicitor agreed on by the parties, had given a very detailed ruling (except on matters of valuation). The Vice-Chancellor had applied the wrong test in giving leave to appeal against that award, so the Court of Appeal could exercise a fresh discretion (736c). The Master of the Rolls then gave his reasons for thinking the arbitrator was wrong in law (736c–e). Accordingly, the Court of Appeal dismissed the appeal from the decision to give leave to appeal, albeit for wholly different reasons.

It seems likely the decision will settle, finally, the end of any 'break for freedom' in property arbitrations, which will now have to fit into the established categories, as expounded in this judgment. Those classifications are, nevertheless, so stated that the net result may not be too unpalatable to those affected, at least in rent review disputes if not all property matters.

Counterclaims arising from denial of submission to arbitration

The House of Lords in *'The Gladys'* (*Metal Scrap Trade Corp Ltd v Kate Shipping Co Ltd* [1990] 1 All ER 397) reversed the Court of Appeal's decision ([1988] 3 All ER 32), which was discussed in All ER Rev 1988 at pp 12–14. Maltese sellers of a ship had lodged a counterclaim in an action by Indian buyers for a declaration that there was no jurisdiction for arbitrators to decide a dispute between the parties because there was no arbitration agreement between them. There were two grounds for that plea, namely that the parties had made no agreement but, if they had, it incorporated no arbitration clause. (The buyers' appointment of their arbitrator had been without prejudice to this claim). Steyn J dismissed the application to strike out that counterclaim, the Court of Appeal had reversed him by a majority but the Lords restored his order, Lord Goff dissenting.

The majority's view

Lord Brandon delivered the main speech. He pointed out the dilemma with which the seller's counterclaim faced the buyers. If they did nothing, they risked judgment for the sellers in default; if they pleaded, they took a step in the proceedings which ended their right to a mandatory stay under s 1 of the 1978 Act. The buyers, if a contract containing an arbitration clause was found to exist, still wished to arbitrate.

He reviewed the decisions below, first of Steyn J and then of the majority in the Court of Appeal. In the course of the former he dealt in some detail with *Republic of Liberia v Gulf Oceanic Inc* [1985] 1 Lloyd's Rep 539, a Court of Appeal decision the judge had considered binding on him, and which Parker and Staughton LJJ had mentioned in their judgments. He then postulated three questions. The first question was whether the Court of Appeal could properly substitute its decision for the judge's, and he held it could. The briefness of the initial judgment, usual in the circumstances, may well not have justified substitution. However, treating the *Liberia* case as binding, and treating the buyer's arguments as unmeritorious, were both wrong, and so justified a substitution. The second question was whether the Court of Appeal wrongly exercised its own discretion. He held it had. It was wrong to disallow the counterclaim because leave to serve proceedings out of the jurisdiction (so as to pursue it as a claim) would have been refused. It was wrong to treat the action for the particular declaration as 'some special sacrosanct category of proceeding' not permitting a counterclaim in the usual way. It was wrong to treat the counterclaim as vexatious and an abuse of the process of the court. For these reasons (set out at 409d–h) the Court of Appeal erred and so the final question was how the House should exercise its own discretion.

The interest of each party

Each party, Lord Brandon found, had a legitimate interest which the court's order should protect. The buyers wished to maintain their right to a stay, if the court found there was a contract with an arbitration clause, and so it had to avoid taking a step in the counterclaim proceedings. The sellers wished to be able to pursue their counterclaim if the court found there was a contract but no arbitration clause. A finding of no contract would end both proceedings and arbitration. The Court of Appeal's order to strike out the counterclaim protected the buyers' interest but did not recognise the sellers'. To balance the two interests a different order was needed. The correct solution was to allow the counterclaim to stand, but stay all further proceedings on it, except as to the declaration that a purchase contract had been made, until the decision on the buyer's originating summons. If the decision was contract plus arbitration clause, the stay would continue and the dispute go to arbitration; if the decision was contract without arbitration clause, the stay could be lifted (410e–f). The stay was ordered by reason of the inherent jurisdiction, as it could not be ordered on the wording of the relevant RSC 28, r 7(3) (410g). His Lordship declined to speculate on the effect on an application to lift the stay being met with an issue of forum conveniens, which should be dealt with when, and in the circumstances in which, it was raised (411a).

Lord Bridge delivered a brief speech concurring with Lord Brandon and the Lord Chancellor a briefer one to like effect. Lord Oliver concurred.

The dissent

Lord Goff dissented. The buyers held 'taken the only sensible course' in bringing English proceedings to settle the contract/no contract and arbitration/no arbitration issues (411d) but had found themselves faced with a counterclaim by which the sellers might gain an advantage if there was ultimately held to be no arbitration clause. Because the procedure might be novel, it called for close scrutiny. He agreed the judge had gone wrong in treating the *Liberia* case as binding, and the Court of Appeal had erred in striking out the counterclaim as vexatious, because RSC 28, r 7(1) allowed it. The crucial issue was whether striking out was right because, as provided by r 7(3), a separate action was desirable. He thought it was. The only connection with England was the alleged arbitration clause, and, if it was found not to exist, the proceedings to establish that should not provide a basis for a counterclaim on the merits. So a separate action was indicated.

Staying proceedings on the counterclaim till the two initial questions were answered did not satisfy Lord Goff. He was less sanguine than his brethren on the forum conveniens point (412d). Given that the only basis for the counterclaim was the action to challenge the existence of the disputed arbitration clause, it was ideally the case to require the counterclaim to be by separate action. He differed from his fellow peers in not finding a legitimate interest in the sellers to be protected as the majority decision protected it (412g).

A summing-up

Opinions can vary on the reception to be afforded to the result arrived at. The present writer's sympathy lies, just, with the dissentient view of Lord Goff. That the choice of arbitral venue in a disputed clause in an alleged contract creates a risk of having to litigate there, on a basis of the detailed provisions of the domestic law, when no other basis for jurisdiction exists does disservice to the cause of international arbitration, and to the narrower interests of London as an arbitral centre. Action for a declaration on whether or not an arbitration clause exists may not presently be a special category excluding general counterclaims, but a strong case can be made that they should be.

References to official referee upheld

The appellants in *Tate & Lyle Industries Ltd v Davy McKee (London) Ltd* [1990] 1 All ER 157 failed in their attempt to overthrow the decision of Hirst J [1989] 2 All ER 641 (discussed in All ER Rev 1989 at pp 14–15), upholding the practice, followed since 1986, of referring construction arbitration applications for leave to appeal and appeals to an Official Referee. As below, the appellants did not – perhaps, indeed, could not – attack the practical benefits of the practice, so their arguments were entirely based on the technicalities of the legislation and Rules of the Supreme Court. In a (surprisingly) reserved judgment, Bingham LJ, delivering the judgment of the court, analysed the relevant provisions and concluded, as had the judge below, that the reference was wholly compatible with them. So the practice need not be changed, nor, as might well have happened if the decision had gone the other way, need the Rules be amended.

Extensions of time for late arbitrations: the scope of section 27

The arbitration rules of various trade associations lay down time limits to initiate arbitrations and some include power to extend those limits. Does, or should, that state of affairs preclude exercise of the court's power to grant an extension under s 27, Arbitration Act 1950, and, if not, how should it affect the exercise of the discretion? Those were the issues in *Comdel Commodities Ltd v Siporex Trade SA*; both the Court of Appeal and the House of Lords decisions were reported, at [1990] 1 All ER 216 and [1990] 2 All ER 552, respectively. Earlier first instance decisions had given differing answers so clarification was essential.

Comdel bought cotton seed oil and tallow from Siporex, on contracts incorporating terms and conditions of the Federation of Oil Seeds and Fat Associations, including the FOSFA Rules of Arbitration and Appeal. The relevant time limit for claims was 120 days from the final day for contractual delivery. Payment was to be by irrevocable confirmed transferable letters of credit. This obligation was to be backed up by two performance bonds to 10% of the contract price. Conforming letters of credit were not provided. The buyers' bank declined to pay on the bonds but eventually paid following a court judgment. On the same day, the buyers notified a claim for recovery of those sums (less an allowance for failure to provide the letters of credit) and started arbitration proceedings, well out of time. The arbitrators (or rather their umpire) so held and refused to give extensions provided for in the Rules. Both limbs of the decision were upheld by the FOSFA Board of Appeal. On an application under s 27, the judge held the court had no power to grant an extension where the contract gave the arbitrators such a power; he also dismissed an appeal against the award.

The buyers appealed, on the basis that the time limit applied to disputes arising from the sale and purchase of the goods, but they were claiming to recover part of the payment under the bonds, and that the time limit could not apply to a claim first arising (as had this claim) after expiry of the time limit. They also sought an extension of time by appealing against the refusal to grant one.

Clearly the first substantive appeal turned on the construction of the relevant Rules. The Court of Appeal analysed them and found they did apply the time limit to the arbitration and that the problem of post-expiry claims could be dealt with under s 27. Those elements of the decision will doubtless attract close scrutiny by those concerned with the rules of trade associations, but are not of sufficient general interest to merit discussion here. The appeal to the House of Lords did not challenge this part of the judgment.

The scope of section 27

On the s 27 point, Staughton LJ (2281-g) identified five cases where the issue had arisen, including the first instance decision in the present case. Counting dicta as if they were decisions, the tally was 3-2 that arbitral power to extend did not oust the s 27 power. *Mustill and Boyd* espouses that view and so did the commentary in the *White Book*. Stressing the absence in s 27 of the common saving for expression of a contrary intention, he pointed out that the section was 'designed to override the contract' (229a) and he favoured the construction which did not allow contracting out by including powers to waive time limits in the rules. Nicholls LJ briefly reaches the same conclusion for the same reasons (234b–d) and reviews the earlier decisions (237c–238h) and the statutory history of the section (238i–239c). Weighing up the various considerations and 'after a great deal of hesitation' he reaches the like conclusion to his brethren (240a) on the public policy ground of allowing for the court to intervene to prevent undue hardship, which contractual provisions for extending time limits might not do.

Exercise of the discretion

As to whether the discretion should be here exercised, the three Lords Justice were also of one mind. The existing leading authorities on undue hardship *Liberian Shipping Corp v A King & Sons Ltd, The Pegasus* [1967] 1 All ER 934, [1967] 2 QB 86, *Moscow V/O Exportkhleb v Helmsville Ltd, The Jocelyne* [1977] 2 Lloyd's Rep 121 and *Libra Shipping and Trading Corp Ltd v Northern*

Sales Ltd, The Aspen Trader [1981] 1 Lloyd's Rep 273, indicate that 'undue hardship' should not be construed narrowly. In *The Aspen Trader* the relevant elements are summarised and Staughton LJ cites that part of the judgment which lists them (229h–i), and then examines cases in which some of the tests were applied. He analyses the periods of delay in the present case and the reasons for them. With some hesitation, Staughton LJ criticises the judge's conclusion on the issue of delay (233b–c) and stresses the absence of reasons for the Board of Appeal's refusal of an extension (233d).

Weighing up (1) the size of the claim (over $1M at stake), (2) the delay being understandable, (3) the date when the cause of action accrued, (4) later delay being excusable and (5) absence of prejudice to the seller (233g) he found a refusal of an extension would create undue hardship, and so he granted the extension. Nicholls LJ briefly concurred (234e). Purchas LJ also found the judgment of the judge faulty on the issue of delay and reaches the same conclusion as Staughton LJ for the same reasons (242f). The sellers appealed against the extension of time.

The House of Lords' response

Lord Bridge gave the only substantial speech in the House of Lords, the other Law Lords all concurring. He upholds the Court of Appeal decision. After a short resume of the facts and the earlier competing decisions he turns to the issue 'What is the effect of the section if the language used is given its natural and ordinary meaning?' He answers his question:

> '. . . it is apt to apply both . . . where an arbitration agreement imposes an absolute and immutable time bar and . . . where [it] imposes a time bar but gives the arbitrator a discretion to grant a dispensation from it' (556c).

Nothing in the context required a limited meaning to the word 'barred' in s 27. Part of that context, relied on by the judge, was a passage in the MacKinnon Report which led to the 1934 Act, but Lord Bridge rejects the sellers' argument that it justified the restricted interpretation of the section. In what may come to be cited in future as a general policy statement, he says (at 557e):

> 'When a change in social conditions produces a novel situation, which was not in contemplation . . . when a statute was first enacted, there can be no a priori assumption that the enactment does not apply to the new circumstances.'

The relevant change is the post-1934 growth in powers to extend time limits in trade association rules. The mischief aimed at is the avoidance of undue hardship, and that is so whether or not the arbitrator had power to extend or has refused to exercise discretion to grant further time. So the existence of a power in the Rules does not oust the section.

Exercise of discretion

On the issue of discretion, Lord Bridge repeats Staughton LJ's citation from *The Aspen Trader*. He identifies similar salient factors to those relied on in the Court of Appeal and reaches the same conclusion, differing from the judge below on the issue of delay, with a slight gloss on one of the Lord Justice's reasons. Commenting on the 'great care' with which the Court of Appeal examined the reasons for delay, he concludes 'I can find no fault with the Court of Appeal's exercise of discretion and I would accordingly dismiss the appeal'.

Significance of arbitral decisions on extensions

Before doing so, he offered a criticism of the exercise of its discretion below which is also likely to be cited in the future as a guideline. This relates to the weight to be given to the refusal of extensions by the arbitrators (or umpire) and the appeal board. 'In the absence of reasons the fact they had decided adversely to *Comdel* was not, in my opinion, a circumstance to which the court could properly attach any weight' (561d). He continues:

> 'Even where arbitrators . . . have given reasons . . . the court cannot escape the duty to make its own assessment and should accord to the arbitrator's reasons no greater weight than the court thinks they should properly bear' (561f).

That might still argue for seeking reasons for refusal in the arbitration proceedings.

A welcome result

Given the near absolute nature of performance bonds and the unmeritorious benefit their calling in may confer, the significance of the ability to seek recovery through arbitration is obvious, as was acknowledged in the course of the Court of Appeal judgments. The complexities of establishing the rights and wrongs of alleged breaches in relation to, say, the financial arrangements, may well lead to breach of arbitral time limits which are wholly practical for simpler issues of delivery or non-delivery, conformity with contract and so on. The potential for undue hardship is high. So this vindication of the relieving power in s 27 is welcome. One must spare a thought, however, for the total costs so far expended in this particular dispute, on arbitrations and litigation, to arrive at even that measure of finality so far attained.

Commercial Law

N E PALMER, BCL, MA
Barrister, Professor of Law, University of Southampton

ROBERT MERKIN, LLB, LLM
Professor of Law, University of Sussex

Banking

The House of Lords has reversed the decision of the Court of Appeal in *National Bank of Greece SA v Pinios Shipping Co No 1, The Maira*. The Court of Appeal had held that the bank was not entitled to charge compound interest after demanding repayment of the debt: [1989] 1 All ER 213, All ER Rev 1989, pp 253–255. The House of Lords have now held that such a demand does not automatically terminate the relationship of banker and customer, and does not therefore remove the right to charge compound interest: [1990] 1 All ER 78.

Pinios (the first respondents) were the buyers of a ship. At the time of delivery, 70% of the price was outstanding. This amount was payable by 14 half-yearly instalments, secured by a first preferred mortgage in favour of the shipbuilders. Payment of the first six instalments was guaranteed by the appellant bank. The bank was secured by a second mortgage over the ship and by the personal guarantee of the second respondent, Mr Tsitsilianis.

None of the instalments was paid. The shipbuilders recovered the first two instalments from the bank under the guarantee. The ship was lost at sea and the insurance moneys were insufficient to cover the amount secured to the bank. The bank thereupon demanded repayment of these instalments by the two respondents, together with compound interest. This demand was made in November 1978. The demand was unmet and in due course the bank commenced proceedings, claiming (inter alia) that it was entitled to continue to capitalise interest up to the date of judgment. The respondents conceded that a right to charge compound interest with quarterly rests would continue for as long as the banker–customer relationship lasted, but contended that the 1978 demand brought that relationship to an end.

The Court of Appeal agreed with the respondents. Holding that the relationship of banker and customer ceased with the demand, they allowed the bank only simple interest over the period between demand and judgment. The object of the appeal to the House of Lords was to settle the point of principle rather than to recover funds, since the respondents had evidently run out of money and were no longer represented. Lord Goff of Chieveley felt some disquiet at pronouncing on this point in the absence of the other party, and without any evidence as to the practice of bankers. His Lordship was fortified, however, by the respondents' concession in the lower court that the right to compound interest depended on the survival of the banker–customer relationship, and by the fact that there had been a fuller citation of authority before the House of Lords than before the Court of Appeal.

Derivation of the right

The bank grounded its claim on an alleged term of the banker-customer relationship, such term being implied by virtue of the custom or practice of bankers. In denying the term, the Court of Appeal had delivered the only post-1854 decision known to the House where the right to capitalise interest was rendered conditional on a series of periodic or 'staccato' agreements between banker and customer at the end of each interest period (for earlier examples, see *Ex p Bevan* (1803) 9 Ves 223 at 224, 32 ER 558, per Lord Eldon LC, *Lord Clancarty v Latouche* (1810) 1 Ball & B 420, at 429–430, per Lord Manners LC, and *Eaton v Bell* (1821) 5 B & Ald 34, 106 ER 1106). This fiction had been devised to circumvent the usury laws. Lord Goff believed that, with the repeal of those laws, the fiction itself ceased to serve any useful purpose and should be discarded as the exclusive basis for justifying compound interest.

Former restrictive interpretations of the right to charge compound interest were therefore questionable under modern conditions. In *Fergusson v Fyffe* (1841) 8 Cl & Fin 121 at 139–140, [1835–1842] All ER Rep 48 at 50, Lord Cottenham LC, while accepting that a right to capitalise interest might theoretically arise in one of four ways (express agreement, implied agreement arising from the mode of dealing with former accounts, implied agreement arising from custom, or the existence of a mercantile account for mutual transactions) proceeded to doubt whether the first three methods were permissible in view of the usury laws. But reliance on the old usury cases made Cottenham LC's reasoning suspect to modern eyes. Similar criticism could be levelled at *Crosskill v Bower* (1863) 32 Beav 86, 55 ER 34, where Romilly MR overstated the effect of *Fergusson v Fyffe* by saying that compound interest could not be charged without contract or custom, and that a valid custom could arise only in cases of mercantile accounts for mutual transactions (on the latter point, see *Williamson v Williamson* (1869) LR 7 Eq 542); and cf *Deutsche Bank und Disconto-Gesellschaft v Banque des Marchands de Moscou* (1931) 4 Legal Decisions Affecting Bankers 293 (reported in 1949), where, again, Greer LJ (in particular) derived too much from *Fergusson v Fyffe* by stating that the customer's agreement to pay compound interest will never be implied except in cases of mercantile accounts current for mutual transactions.

The true position was as follows. When the usury laws were repealed, and it was no longer legally offensive to charge compound interest, bankers continued to rely on their normal circumventory practice of a series of 'staccato' agreements. Naturally enough, the courts initially responded by continuing to look for the customer's acquiescence in the capitalisation of interest. In *Crosskill* (at 100, 39) Romilly MR regarded such acquiescence as a necessary ingredient in any implied agreement: in his view, such agreement required both the customer's knowledge that his accounts were being so kept, and his consent to the practice. But there were several reasons why modern courts should refuse to approach the question as one of acquiescence in the narrow sense understood by Romilly MR. The first was the unworkable nature of the rules as to acquiescence under modern banking conditions: these rules presuppose that the customer has knowledge that his accounts are being kept in a particular way, but since *Tai Hing Cotton Mill Ltd v Liu Chong Hing Bank Ltd* [1985] 2 All ER 947, All ER Rev 1985, pp 19, 26, 34, the customer owes no implied obligation to examine his accounts. Moreover, the framing of the requirement seems to presuppose that the customer can unilaterally terminate the agreement: a conclusion which might surprise the modern banking community.

Secondly, the surviving practice of capitalisation rapidly outgrew the legal form in which it originated, and became regarded as part of the established usage of bankers. It thus became assimilated into banking transactions as a matter of course, independently of the literal conditions of acquiescence and irrespective of whether the account was a mercantile account for mutual transactions. Many decisions show that this was the prevailing attitude to compound interest by the second third of this century. As early as *Reddie v Williamson* (1863) 1 M 228 at 236, per Lord Justice Clerk Inglis, it had been said that the parties 'must . . . have had in view' (ie can be taken to have expected) that accounts would be kept in this way, and that the annual charging of compound interest was justified on the 'plain ground of equity' that the interest 'ought then to be paid, and, because it is not paid, the debtor becomes thenceforth debtor in the amount, as a principal sum itself bearing interest'. In *Parr's Banking Co Ltd v Yates* [1898] 2 QB 460 at 466–467, the practice was described by Vaughan Williams LJ as the 'ordinary practice of bankers' and by Rigby LJ as the 'manner usual between banker and customer'; a practice based on the assumed understanding of the parties, and one in which banks so habitually engaged that no ordinary guarantor or customer could object to it. In *Yourell v Hibernian Bank Ltd* [1918] AC 372 at 385, Lord Atkinson called it a 'usual and perfectly legitimate mode of dealing', while in *IRC v Holder* [1931] 2 KB 81 at 98 Romer LJ ascribed it to the 'ordinary usage prevailing' within the banking community rather than to any special agreement between banker and customer. And although some authorities still referred flickeringly to acquiescence, the status of the practice was put beyond doubt by *Paton (Fenton's Trustee) v IRC* [1938] 1 All ER 786 esp at 795, [1938] AC 341 esp at 357. There, Lord Macmillan held it to be a 'well established . . . ordinary usage' of bankers, and one fully consistent with general practice, to charge interest with half-yearly rests to the knowledge of the customer. Shortly afterwards, in *IRC v Oswald* [1945] 1 All ER 641 at 651, 653, [1945] AC 360 at 379, Lord Simonds and Lord Porter spoke variously of the 'custom' or 'practice' of bankers to charge compound interest.

Lord Goff drew attention to several notable points about these authorities. None of them had been cited to the Court of Appeal in the *Deutsche Bank* case, and none of them limited the right of capitalisation of interest to mercantile accounts for mutual transactions. Indeed, in *Parr's Banking Co Ltd v Yates* the principle was applied to a case of an ordinary customer's overdraft, while in *Paton (Fenton's Trustee) v IRC* (at 357, 795) it was expressed by Lord Macmillan to apply to any customer who borrows from his bank. Lord Goff took the view that the 'equity', to which Lord Justice Clerk Inglis referred in *Reddie v Williamson*, required that the practice should not be limited to mercantile accounts for mutual transactions, and should be construed no more narrowly than the interpretation which Lord MacMillan put upon it in *Paton*. It followed that this was a clear case for the imposition of compound interest.

Point of cessation of relationship

Having upheld the practice, Lord Goff held that it does not automatically cease to apply when the banker makes a demand on the customer for repayment of the sum outstanding. The only contrary authority (apart from dicta in *Deutsche Bank*) was *Crosskill v Bower*. But Romilly MR's judgment was undermined by its assumption that the bank's right of capitalisation was confined to ordinary mercantile current accounts, and was generally incompatible with the broad 'equity' stated in *Reddie v Williamson*. In Lord Goff's opinion, the strength of the equity is substantially the same whether the banker has already demanded repayment of the outstanding sum or not. Further, there is no compelling reason why such a demand should by itself extinguish the banker–customer relationship.

Lord Goff declined to set out general criteria for the determination of the relationship, because he did not consider this a suitable case. Instead, he founded his conclusion on the particular facts. In his view (at 90), there was no reason why the present relationship:

> 'should not . . . have continued until repayment of the debt, or judgment, whichever first occurred, with the effect that, so long as the contractual interest was payable, the bank continued to be entitled to capitalise it.'

Lord Goff further remarked that if (as seems to have been the case) the House of Lords accepted in *Yourell v Hibernian Bank Ltd* that the bank's commencement of proceedings against its customer did not disentitle the bank from continuing to capitalise interest, the right to capitalise should equally survive in the instant case, where (i) the only event alleged to have extinguished that right was the demand for repayment, and (ii) the bank claimed the principal sum due with interest thereon as agreed until payment or judgment, in the usual way.

The legitimacy of capitalising at quarterly rests

The respondents' earlier concession that the entitlement to charge compound interest as calculated by the bank was commensurate with the banker–customer relationship made it unnecessary for Lord Goff to decide whether the traditional practice could encompass quarterly (as opposed to annual or half-yearly) rests. He tentatively favoured the view that this was permissible but declined to express a concluded opinion.

Insurance

Accident insurance

It is well established that a person who has suffered injuries at the hands of a tortfeasor is entitled to claim full damages from the tortfeasor without deduction in respect of the proceeds of any private insurance policy covering the loss which the assured has taken out. *McCamley v Cammell Laird Shipbuilders Ltd* [1990] 1 All ER 854 raised the question of whether there has to be an allowance in respect of the proceeds of a personal accident insurance policy taken out, and paid for, by an employer for the benefit of his employees. In the instant case the evidence showed that the injured employee had not been aware of the existence of the policy. The Court of Appeal ruled that the insurance moneys were a benevolent gift by the employer, albeit through the mechanism of an insurance policy, and on that basis no account was to be taken of those proceeds in assessing the employee's damages against the tortfeasor (see also Tort, pp 341–342 below).

Brokers

Two cases, both raising issues of limitation of actions, may briefly be mentioned here. In *Iron Trade Mutual Insurance Co Ltd v J K Buckenham Ltd* [1990] 1 All ER 808 reinsurance contracts were entered into between the plaintiff insurers and Portuguese reinsurers in 1976. The negotiations were conducted by the defendant underwriting agency, which allegedly failed to disclose material facts to the reinsurers. In 1981 the reinsurers failed to pay sums allegedly due under the reinsurance agreements, in 1984 the plaintiffs commenced proceedings against the reinsurers, and in 1987 the reinsurers purported to avoid the agreements on the basis of breach of duty in 1976. The plaintiffs brought actions in contract and tort against the underwriting agency, and were met by a limitation defence on the strength of which the defendant sought to have the action struck out. (See also Practice and Procedure, p 218 and Tort, p 322 below.)

The contract action was plainly time-barred by s 5 of the Limitation Act 1980, as the defendant's alleged breach of contract had occurred in 1976. The main issue was whether the action as framed in tort was similarly time-barred. This depended upon whether the action accrued in 1976, when the defendant allegedly acted negligently, or in 1987, when the effects of any negligence became apparent. On this point Rokison QC followed the cases involving solicitors, and held that damage occurred, so that the action accrued, in 1976, for it was at that point that the policies became voidable. The action was, therefore, time-barred. This approach was approved by Evans J in *Islander Trucking Ltd v Hogg Robinson & Gardner Mountain (Marine) Ltd* [1990] 1 All ER 826, which similarly involved alleged misrepresentation and non-disclosure by brokers prior to the inception of the policy (see pp 218 and 323 below).

Rokison QC further considered the effect of the Latent Damage Act 1986 to the facts of *Iron Trade Mutual* (an issue which did not arise in *Islander Trucking*, as the relevant events had taken place before the Act had come into force). He ruled that the additional three-year discoverability period for negligence actions set out in that Act did not apply to actions in contract. Consequently, the Act could be relied on only as regards the tort action; this left for the full trial a question of fact as to whether the plaintiffs ought to have known of the underwriting agency's breach of duty within three years before the action against it had been commenced.

The Latent Damage Act 1986 would seem to resolve most of the limitation problems raised in actions against brokers. Two comments might, however, be made. First, if the House of Lords should at some future time rule that a broker owes duties only in contract and not in tort, the 1986 Act will not come to the rescue. Secondly, as most insurance contracts are periodic, it is arguable that there is a fresh breach of duty by the broker on each renewal, so that there should not in fact be any limitation problem at all.

Third party rights

The Third Parties (Rights against Insurers) Act 1930 operates where an assured under a liability policy becomes bankrupt or goes into insolvent administration or liquidation. Any person who has a claim against the assured within the terms of the policy is entitled to take over the assured's rights against the insurer by way of statutory assignment or subrogation. The purpose of the 1930 Act is to ensure that the insurance moneys which would, in the absence of insolvency, have been channelled via the assured to the third party claimant, are not diverted for the purpose of meeting the general debts of the assured in the event of insolvency.

The 1930 Act operates only to transfer to the third party the same rights as the assured himself possessed against the insurer. This concept raises a complex problem in the case of P & I Clubs, which traditionally include in their insuring terms a 'pay to be paid' provision, under which the assured member is entitled to be indemnified by the insurer only after the assured has actually paid the third party. The application of the 1930 Act to 'pay to be paid' clauses fell to be determined by the House of Lords in joined appeals *Firma C-Trade SA v Newcastle Protection and Indemnity Association, The Fanti* and *Socony Mobil Oil Co Inc v West of England Ship Owners Mutual Insurance Association (London) Ltd, The Padre Island* [1990] 2 All ER 705 (see also Shipping Law, pp 228–230 below). Sharply different views had been taken in the first instance decisions in these cases.

The facts of *The Fanti* and *The Padre Island* are nearly identical. Shipowners incurred liability to cargo interests, and judgments were obtained. Neither judgment was met, and the shipowners were wound up. Each shipowner belonged to a P & I Club, the rules of which contained a 'pay to be paid' provision. Two questions arose before the House of Lords. First, did the clause prevent any rights being transferred to the third party, thereby preventing the operation of the 1930 Act? Secondly, if this was the case, did the clause fall foul of the provisions of the 1930 Act seeking to prevent contracting-out?

The first question had been answered in the third party's favour by Staughton J at first instance in *The Fanti* [1987] 2 Lloyd's Rep 299. Staughton J had ruled that the 1930 Act transferred to the third party the contingent right to make a claim against the insurer subject to prior payment. The third party would, therefore, in order to comply with the contingency, have to make payment to himself. Staughton J held that this was futile, and that it was possible to disregard the 'pay to be paid' provision. By contrast, in *The Padre Island* [1987] 2 Lloyd's Rep 529, Saville J had taken the view that the assured had no claim until payment had been made, so that there was nothing to transfer to the third party until the assured had made payment to him. Saville J's approach led to the paradoxical situation in which the third party was only able to use the 1930 Act in those cases in which he did not need to use it because he had in any event been fully indemnified. The Court of Appeal nevertheless held that Saville J had been right ([1989] 1 Lloyd's Rep 239), and this was confirmed by the House of Lords. Their Lordships also agreed with the Court of Appeal (the point not having been argued at first instance) that it was impossible to resort to any equitable principle whereby a contract of indemnity could be specifically enforced by ordering payment directly to the third party; irrespective of the vitality of that proposition, it could not survive the express wording of the 'pay to be paid' provisions.

The second issue turned on the wording of s 1(3) of the 1930 Act, which renders ineffective any term in an insurance agreement which seeks to 'avoid the contract or to alter the right of the parties thereunder' in the event of insolvency. Staughton J held that the 'pay to be paid' clause contravened s 1(3), as it had the practical effect of preventing any recovery by the assured on his insolvency. Saville J, disagreeing, held that the 'pay to be paid' clause did not affect the assured's *legal* rights one iota: the right to recover was subject to prior payment whether or not the assured was insolvent. The Court of Appeal here affirmed the approach of Staughton J, but the House of Lords reinstated the narrower view of Saville J, and held that the clause survived s 1(3).

The effect of the speeches in the House of Lords is, therefore, to remove the 1930 Act from the scene in P & I Club cases – a somewhat unfortunate position. 'Pay to be paid' provisions are not, however, found in other forms of insurance, so that the damage is likely to be limited to that context.

Utmost good faith

The long awaited decision of the House of Lords in *Banque Financière de la Cité SA v Westgate Insurance Co Ltd* [1990] 2 All ER 947 proved to be something of a disappointment, as many of the important issues canvassed in the lower courts ultimately did not fall to be decided by their Lordships (see also pp 61–62, 311–312 below). The well-known facts may be recounted briefly. The plaintiff banks had entered into syndicated loan agreement with companies controlled by the loans to be secured by the deposit of gemstones and, by way of fallback guarantee, certain credit insurances. The policies were to be arranged by a firm of brokers via its employee, L. L fraudulently indicated to the banks that the policies were fully in place, when in fact a proportion of the cover had not been arranged, and on the strength of that indication the banks released the loans to B. The fact that L had forged the cover notes was known to an employee of the leading insurers, D, but he did not pass his knowledge on to the insurers or to the banks. L subsequently did manage to achieve full cover. Some months later, B sought further loans from the banks, and the brokers were asked to arrange additional insurance to cover those loans. L once again forged cover notes, and further advances were made by the banks on the strength of them. This time, however, L did not manage to obtain the necessary insurance to match the fraudulent cover notes.

B defaulted on the loans, and the gemstones which he had deposited with the banks proved to be worth far less than their valuation. The banks thereupon sought to claim under their credit policies, and at that point discovered that the additional insurance had for the most part not been placed. The banks asserted that they would not have used L to broke the policies had they been informed of L's original fraud, and claimed that the insurers owed them both a duty of utmost good faith and a common law duty of care, under which L's fraud should have been disclosed to them.

In the House of Lords the case took a surprising turn. The credit policies had contained an exception under which the insurers were not to be liable for any 'claims caused directly or indirectly by fraud . . . by any person'. In the lower courts it had been assumed that L's conduct fell within the fraud exception, so that the banks' inability to recover from the insurers had stemmed from L's undisclosed fraud. It was argued before, and accepted by, the House of Lords, that the fraud exception did not extend to fraud by the banks' own brokers but referred only to fraud by the borrower, B. This meant that the banks' claim under their policies was doomed to failure because of B's fraud: L's fraud had not, on that basis, caused the banks any loss so that any breach of duty in failing to disclose it was irrelevant.

That reasoning was enough to dispose of the case. Their Lordships did, however, make fragmented comments on the possibility that an insurer owes a duty of utmost good faith to its assureds (for the negligence aspects of the case, see Tort, pp 311–312 below). There was unanimity that the insurers had owed the banks a duty of utmost good faith, as had been held in the lower courts. The scope of the duty, a crucial issue, was not discussed in any detail. Only Lords Bridge and Jauncey chose to mention the point all: Lord Bridge was not prepared to dissent from the Court of Appeal's view that the duty extended to facts which affected recoverability under the policy, whereas Lord Jauncey expressly confined the insurer's duty to those facts which directly affect the risk insured under the policy.

The question of remedies was taken up by Lord Templeman, who approved the view of the Court of Appeal that damages were not awardable for breach of the duty of utmost good faith, so that the most the banks could have achieved would have been rescission of the insurance contracts. This finding deprives, for the most part, the insurer's duty of utmost good faith of any practical significance.

It is worth drawing attention to Lord Jauncey's obiter comment on the vexed issue of the existence of a post-contractual duty of utmost good faith. In his Lordship's view, such a duty exists only in exceptional cases; the examples which he gave – failure to disclose the entry of a vessel into a war zone, and the making of a fraudulent claim – reflect precisely the decided cases on this matter. It thus remains unclear whether an insurer does in any circumstances owe a continuing duty of utmost good faith to its assureds.

Intellectual property

Copyright

A long-standing and undignified struggle between two national newspaper groups resulted in interesting points of copyright law being raised before Sir Nicholas Browne-Wilkinson V-C in *Express Newspapers plc v News (UK) Ltd* [1990] 3 All ER 376 (also discussed in Practice and Procedure, pp 214–215 below). A reporter employed by the *Daily Express*, obtained an exclusive interview with Miss Pamella Bordes, whose private life had become something of a media obsession. The *Daily Express* published F's article on 3 April 1989, the article including a number of quotes from Miss Bordes. The first edition of the *Today* newspaper for 3 April also featured a story about Miss Bordes, but the second edition, which appeared after the publication of the *Daily Express* – contained a more sensational piece which used the *Daily Express*'s quotes from Miss Bordes, although there was no attribution of the

Daily Express as the source of the publication of those quotes. The owners of the *Daily Express*, EN, rapidly commenced proceedings for infringement of copyright against the owners of *Today*, NL, and sought summary judgment under RSC Ord 14.

Ten days before the hearing, *Today* published an article about, and containing quotations from, Marina Ogilvy, a member of the Royal Family. The following day, the *Daily Star*, which was a sister newspaper to the *Daily Express* in that it was also owned by EN, produced its own story on Miss Ogilvy, in which it used quotations from her which had appeared in *Today* the previous morning. The only attribution of their source was a statement that Miss Ogilvy had spoken to *Today*.

Shortly after this second skirmish, NL served its defence to EN's action in respect of the Bordes interview, and served a counterclaim against EN in respect of the Ogilvy interview. EN's action was heard first, and EN obtained summary judgment. The instant proceedings concerned NL's counterclaim for summary judgment against EN for copyright infringement, to which EN sought to raise various defences.

Browne-Wilkinson V-C gave summary judgment in NL's favour on its counterclaim. This decision was reached irrespective of the merits of the substantive arguments in the case. In the learned judge's view it was not open to EN, having sought and obtained summary judgment in one set of proceedings, to plead a defence to proceedings brought against it and involving, for all relevant purposes, identical facts. Browne-Wilkinson V-C recognised that he had introduced a novel extension of the doctrine of approbation and reprobation, but nevertheless felt that EN could not be allowed to blow 'hot and cold' in its attitude to copying. The judgment nevertheless contains valuable discussion of the scope of copyright and possible defences to infringement.

The first question was whether NL could claim copyright in the article as a whole, and in particular in the direct quotes obtained from the interviewee. On the more general of these points, the learned judge expressed the view that no liability arises where a newspaper publishes, in its own words, a story which has previously appeared in another newspaper. Interestingly enough, Browne-Wilkinson V-C was apparently of the opinion that the copyright in the story would be infringed by such an act, but that a defence (possibly fair dealing or implied licence) would probably succeed. Once again, therefore, the courts have indicated that copyright extends beyond the words used and to the underlying idea which is expressed by those words.

The more specific issue was whether copyright could be claimed in a direct quote from an interviewee. NL pointed to the decision of the House of Lords in *Walter v Lane* [1900] AC 539, in which it had been held that copyright subsisted in a verbatim report of a speech on the basis that skill and judgment had been exercised by the reporter in taking down the speech and in deciding that it should be published. This case was, however, decided under copyright legislation which did not require that a copyright work be 'original', and EN argued that the originality requirement, which had been introduced in 1911 and retained by subsequent legislation, prevented copyright from attaching to mere verbatim reports. Browne-Wilkinson V-C disagreed: the word 'original', now contained in s 1(1)(a) of the Copyright, Designs and Patents Act 1988 had not altered the authority of *Walter v Lane*, and meant that copyright existed as long as the reporter had exercised skill and judgment in reporting the spoken words. This gave rise to no difficulty on the facts, as the *Today* reporter had plainly exercised skill and judgment in distilling a small number of quotes from a lengthy interview. The ruling, that originality implies not 'inventive originality' but rather 'the production of something in a new form', for the time being settles a debate which had raged in Parliament during the passing of the Copyright, Designs and Patents Bill, and which the legislature ultimately felt was better left to the courts.

A number of defences to infringement were put forward by EN. First, EN argued that the copying was justified by the fair dealing exception set out in s 30(2) of the 1988 Act. This, however, failed for want of 'sufficient acknowledgment' of the author of the *Today* article: the court pointed out that the section requires not merely acknowledgment of the copyright owner (*Today*) but of the actual author (the journalist in question). Secondly, EN sought to rely on a line of cases, typified by *Lion Laboratories v Evans* [1984] 2 All ER 417, which have established a public interest justification for the publication of material in a manner which would otherwise constitute breach of confidence and copyright infringement. This was rejected on two grounds: the information in question was not essential to the public interest, and in any event it had been made public by *Today*.

The most plausible defence raised by EN was that of custom within the newspaper industry, whereby it is accepted that newspapers carry stories first published in rival newspapers with or without attribution as to source. Browne-Wilkinson V-C accepted that proof of such a custom might well be possible.

Broadcasting

Sections 297 to 299 of the Copyright, Designs and Patents Act 1988 seek to protect broadcasters and providers of cable programme services, who charge subscribers for receipt of their broadcasts or cable services, against unauthorised reception. Section 297 makes it a criminal offence for any person dishonestly to receive a broadcast or cable service with intent to avoid payment. Section 298 gives the provider remedies equivalent to those for copyright infringement against any person who 'makes, imports, sells or lets for hire any apparatus or device designed or adapted to enable or assist persons to receive the programmes or other transmissions when they are not entitled to do so'. The question which arose before the Court of Appeal in *BBC Enterprises Ltd v Hi-Tech Xtravision Ltd* [1990] 2 All ER 118 was the meaning of the words 'not entitled to do so' in s 298.

BBC was the provider of satellite television services to Western Europe. In order to confine its broadcasts to paying users (other than in the UK), the broadcasts were encrypted. The decoding machines necessary for receipt of the broadcasts were manufactured by Sat-Tel: these were sold to persons wishing to receive the broadcasts, and a proportion of the selling price was to be paid to BBC. The arrangements between BBC and Sat-Tel were exclusive, but the defendants in the present action, Hi-Tech, discovered a method of producing decoders; the decoders were produced in the UK and marketed outside the UK in Western Europe at prices below those being charged by Sat-Tel. BBC sought an injunction under s 298 to prevent

Hi-Tech from supplying decoders, and in the present proceedings Hi-Tech sought to have the action struck out; the parties agreed, however, to accept the decision in these interlocutory proceedings as determinative of their legal rights. The Court of Appeal was thus required to decide whether persons were 'entitled' to receive satellite broadcasts without having paid to do so.

Scott J at first instance held that a broadcaster had no proprietary right in the waves in the ether and had no proprietary right to prevent persons from watching broadcasts. Recipients were thus entitled to watch BBC programmes whether or not they had paid for them, so that no action lay against Hi-Tech. The Court of Appeal found this approach unpersuasive, and held that a right to confine broadcasts to the paying public – however that right was classified – had been created by s 298 itself. Hi-Tech, perhaps recognising the weakness of this line, relied primarily upon its negative counterpart, namely, that in the absence of any express prohibition on receiving broadcasts such conduct was lawful. The Court of Appeal, in rejecting this argument, noted that its acceptance would render s 298 otiose. This left only the conclusion that the effect of s 298 was to confer upon BBC the right to authorise receipt of its broadcasts, and that such authorisation would follow from the purchase of a decoder from Sat-Tel.

Hi-Tech raised two objections to a finding against it in the instant case. First, and in general terms, it claimed that the decision would create a monopoly to the extent that BBC broadcasts could be received only by persons willing to pay the amount charged by Sat-Tel, whereas Hi-Tech could provide the same service for less. The presumption against monopoly has in recent years proved attractive to the English courts, but was here rejected on the ground that the proper market was for broadcasts as a whole and not simply for BBC broadcasts; persons wishing to watch programmes did not, therefore, have to buy Hi-Tech decoders. Secondly, and more specifically, Hi-Tech pointed out that it had supplied its decoders only outside the UK, and that s 298 should not be given extraterritorial effect. The simple answer to this, adopted by the Court of Appeal, was that the decoders were made in the UK, contrary to the express wording of s 298, even though their use was to be abroad. (See p 262 below for further discussion of this case.)

Sale of goods

Compliance with description and merchantable quality

English courts are characteristically reluctant to attach contractual force to attributions of works of art (see *Luxmoore-May v Messenger May Baverstock* [1990] 1 All ER 1067, discussed in Tort at p 316 below). Some of the reasons were given by Sir Raymond Evershed MR in *Leaf v International Galleries* [1950] 1 All ER 693 at 697: the dramatic controversies and reversals of opinion which issues of authenticity can generate, the problems of restitutio in integrum, and the prospect of costly and inconclusive litigation years after the event. These reservations are occasionally translated into the aphorism that the art world deals in opinions and not in facts. They have now been echoed by the Court of Appeal.

In *Harlingdon & Leinster Enterprises Ltd v Christopher Hull Fine Art Ltd* [1990]

1 All ER 737 (also considered in Contract, pp 59–60, the result was to exonerate the seller of a forged painting from liability to refund the price under s 13(1) of the Sale of Goods Act 1979. This provision, it will be recalled, implies a condition that goods should correspond with any description by which they have been sold. The respondent seller, who was innocent of any intention to deceive, believed that the painting which he sold to the appellant was by Gabriele Munter, because he had seen it attributed to her in an auction catalogue. He referred to it as such in his negotiations with the appellant, which began with a telephone conversation. However, when the appellant came to inspect the picture at his gallery he also made it plain to the appellant that he knew or cared nothing about Munter's work, had insufficient expertise to judge whether the painting was authentic, and had never even heard of Munter previously. The appellant (although also lacking expertise in German expressionist painting) examined the picture carefully and concluded that it was authentic. He agreed to buy it and the seller's invoice again referred to the picture as by Gabriel Munter. When it emerged that the picture was a fake, the appellant sought to recover his price under s 13(1) but failed.

Both Nourse and Slade LJJ held that it was insufficient for the seller merely to have uttered some statement which is capable of qualifying as a description of the goods. The buyer must go further and show that the goods were sold 'by' that description. As Slade LJ remarked (at 751):

> '. . . the fact that a description has been attributed to the goods, either during the course of negotiations or even in the contract (if written) itself, does not necessarily and by itself render the contract one for "sale by description".'

According to Nourse LJ, goods will not be regarded as sold by their description unless the description has exerted a sufficient influence in bringing about the sale to suggest to a reasonable and objective observer that the statement has become an essential term, or condition, of the contract. Without this element of influence, a description cannot be said to be one 'by' which the sale was made.

What, then, does this requirement of influence comprehend? In Nourse LJ's opinion, it is virtually impossible for a statement to be influential in the conclusion of the contract without the buyer's having relied on its truth.

Thus, if the buyer does not believe what the seller says, or has forgotten it by the time he buys the goods, or tests its truth personally and forms his own conclusion, he may lose the protection of s 13(1). Nourse LJ explained this (at 744) as follows:

> 'In theory it is no doubt possible for a description of goods which is not relied on by the buyer to become an essential term of a contract for their sale. But in practice it is very difficult, and perhaps impossible, to think of facts where that would be so. The description must have a sufficient influence in the sale to become an essential term of the contract and the correlative of influence is reliance. Indeed, reliance by the buyer is the natural index of a sale by description . . . For all practical purposes, I would say that there cannot be a contract for the sale of goods by description where it is not within the reasonable contemplation of the parties that the buyer is relying on the description.'

The same result was favoured by Slade LJ, although his reasoning differed slightly from that of Nourse LJ. Slade LJ placed somewhat lighter emphasis on the requirement that the description should have influenced the sale in order to render that a sale by description, and somewhat greater emphasis on the need for a common intention that the description should become an essential term of the contract. He considered (at 751) that a sale could not properly be regarded as a sale by description unless the court could:

'. . . impute to the parties . . . a common intention that it shall be a term of the contract that the goods will correspond with the description. If such an intention cannot properly be imputed to the parties, it cannot be said that the contract is one for the sale of goods *by* description within the ordinary meaning of words.'

Even so, Slade LJ was not prepared to discount the question of reliance entirely, observing that this ingredient may be highly material in establishing the parties' intentions at the time of contracting. The fact that a buyer is unable to demonstrate such reliance may afford 'powerful evidence' tending to negate any common intention that the authenticity of the description should constitute a term of the contract (at 752). In Slade LJ's view, no such common intention could be gathered from the instant facts. An independent observer, invited to express an opinion after the meeting in the seller's gallery as to whether the seller appeared to be undertaking any legal commitment as regards the correctness of the attribution would have replied 'Of course not . . .'. The buyer clearly appreciated that he would have to exercise his own skill and judgment and clearly did so.

In so concluding, both Nourse and Slade LJJ cited an observation by Lord Diplock in *Gill & Duffus SA v Berger & Co Inc* [1984] 1 All ER 438 (discussed in All ER Rev 1984, pp 29–31). Lord Diplock (at 445–446) thought that where a contract of sale takes place after (i) the buyer has inspected a sample and (ii) statements about the goods have been made in the contract documents themselves, and where the buyer's examination of the sample has revealed to him certain characteristics in the goods which are also described in the documents, the parties are unlikely to have intended that the written statements should form part of the description 'by' which the goods were sold. It is not the written statements which have influenced the sale but the buyer's own observation.

Stuart-Smith LJ dissented on this point, confessing that he experienced great difficulty in seeing how reliance could be relevant to a sale by description. Nothing said during the meeting in the gallery cancelled or withdrew the earlier attribution which the seller had made during his telephone conversation with the buyer; a conversation which, while undoubtedly constituting an invitation to treat, was a significant component in the parties' negotiations, and (taken alone) clearly entitled the attribution to be identified as a description for the purposes of s 13(1). Had such cancellation or withdrawal occurred, the ensuing sale might well have been deprived of its character as a sale by description. But, in Stuart-Smith LJ's view (at 748), it would:

'be a serious defect in the law if the effect of a condition implied by statute could be excluded by the vendor's saying that he was not an expert in what was being sold or that the purchaser was more expert than the vendor. That is not the law . . .'.

Nourse and Slade LJJ also rejected the buyer's assertion that the picture was not of merchantable quality within s 14(2) and (6) of the Sale of Goods Act.

The very notion that a counterfeit work of art can be stigmatised as defective within the statutory language, or can be classified as 'merchantable or 'unmerchantable', seems gauche if not indecorous. Such considerations may well have informed the majority's conclusion on this point, although Nourse LJ (at 754–746) was not prepared to follow the trial judge to the point of holding that the concept of merchantable quality extended only to the physical qualities of the thing sold and not to authorship (cf *Buchanan-Jardine v Hamilink* 1983 SLT 149). The buyer argued that the principal purpose for which one dealer commonly buys goods from another is that of resale, and that the present picture, being exposed as a fake, was no longer adequate for that purpose. Nourse LJ (at 745) accepted that the 'defect' in the painting constituted a 'defect in quality' (see *Leaf* (above) at 694, per Denning LJ) and that this defect reduced its notional value from £6,000 to between £50 and £100. He also conceded that the seller's attribution could qualify as a 'description' for the purposes of s 14(6) notwithstanding that the picture had not been sold 'by' that description for the purposes of s 13, although he stressed that a description which fails to qualify as one by which the goods were sold clearly merits less weight in identifying a lack of merchantable quality than one by which the goods were sold. In Nourse LJ's view, none of the foregoing considerations detracted from the quality of the picture as merchantable, because they did not deprive it of its capacity for aesthetic appreciation. 'It could still have been hung on a wall somewhere and been enjoyed for what it was, albeit not for what it might have been.' According to Nourse LJ, this decisively outweighed the value-differential on which the buyer placed so much emphasis. A buyer who spends £6,000 relying on his own misjudgment as to authorship can hardly maintain that that misjudgment alone renders unmerchantable a picture which is otherwise adequate for resale and for aesthetic appreciation. A commercial buyer buying goods for resale does not establish that they are unfit for that purpose merely by showing that they can be resold only at a loss. It may not be wholly surprising, given Nourse LJ's overriding emphasis on aesthetic appreciation, to hear counsel in later cases invoking the value of the work as a conversation piece (enlivened, perhaps, by anecdotes as to the manner in which the buyer was duped) as an ingredient in establishing its merchantability. Whether dealers are likely to exhibit their professional errors in this manner is, of course, another matter.

Slade LJ concurred in this conclusion, remarking simply that the buyer's failure to establish a term as to description within s 13 necessarily precluded endowing the misattribution with contractual force by the 'back door' method of s 14. Stuart-Smith LJ again dissented, contending that a balanced and properly-proportioned evaluation of all the matters listed in s 14(6) pointed squarely in favour of the contention that the picture was not merchantable.

In common with Sir Raymond Evershed in *Leaf*, Nourse LJ considered that there were sound practical and professional reasons for witholding contractual force from attributions of works of art, unless this conclusion was compellingly warranted by some express misrepresentation or term. He remarked (at 746) that the age-old industry in faking works of art, combined with modern technological advances which facilitate counterfeiting, enable almost any attribution to a recognised artist to be brought into question, especially where the provenance of the work is unknown. Such matters are common knowledge in the trade, where codes and conventions (eg the use of the artist's initials in the attribution) indicate gradations of confidence in the attribution. Professional evidence in the present case indicated that dealers do not conventionally rely on fellow-dealers' attributions, the prevailing rule being one of caveat emptor. In private sales, responsibility for attribution is customarily disclaimed, the attribution being asserted to be a mere opinion. In Nourse LJ's view, these considerations should make the courts 'exceedingly wary in giving a seller's attribution any contractual effect'. Any contrary policy could impede the efficient working of the market.

It is worth comparing these remarks with the decision of the Queen's Bench Division in *May v Vincent* (unreported, 11 June 1990). This was a prosecution under s 1(1)(a) of the Trade Descriptions Act 1968 it being alleged that the defendant auctioneer had applied, in the course of a trade or business, a false trade description to a picture which he had auctioned on behalf of the owner. The defendant had produced an auction catalogue, one entry in which described a watercolour by 'J M W Turner, RA'. Mr and Mrs Smith bought the picture for £400, only to discover some two and a half years later that the attribution was false and the painting almost worthless. The defendant argued (inter alia) that the Act should not apply to the art world because that world dealt in opinions, and not in facts. This belief was reflected in a comprehensive disclaimer in the catalogue, which warned bidders (inter alia) that all statements as to origin, authorship, date, age, period and authenticity were statements of opinion and not of fact. The court held that the offence had been committed, that the defendant was not protected by the disclaimer, and that there was nothing in the statutory language which justified exempting art auctioneers, as a matter of principle, from its provisions (the same would appear true of dealers). In so holding, the court implicitly accepted that the attribution of a work of art was a 'trade description' for the purposes of the Act. The assumption is justified, because by s 2(1)(i) 'trade description' includes an indication as to the person who 'manufactured, produced, processed or reconditioned' the goods. Again, these words seem hardly suitable to describe the process of artistic creation, however unquestionable their literal application. It remains to be seen whether *May v Vincent* offers a significant challenge to the philosophy of decisions like *Harlingdon*.

A few final points may be noted. First, Nourse and Stuart-Smith LJJ (at 745, 747) approved Denning LJ's observation in *Leaf* that the term as to authorship was a term as to quality. At first sight, this might indicate support for Denning LJ's further observation in *Leaf* that the parties' mistake as to authorship went merely to quality and not to identity, being therefore insufficient to avoid the contract at common law (see also *Bell v Lever Bros* [1931] All ER Rep 1, per Lord Atkin). In fact, however, Stuart-Smith LJ accompanied his approval of Denning LJ's dictum by remarking that it seemed beyond question that 'the identity of the artist who painted a picture can be a substantial ingredient in the identity of the thing sold'. Secondly, there appears to be a divergence between the views of the majority in *Harlingdon* as to whether s 13, while admittedly requiring the buyer to establish that the relevant description is a term and not a mere representation, automatically elevates any such term to the status of a condition irrespective of the status that would be accorded to it at common law. Nourse LJ (at 744), by requiring the description to have had a sufficient influence in the sale to become an 'essential' term thereof, seemed to consider that s 13(1) did not affect the distinction between conditions and warranties. Slade LJ (at 751) clearly thought otherwise:

> 'The practical effect of s 13(1), as I understand it, is to make it plain (if it needed to be made plain) that in a case where such a common intention can be imputed, the relevant term of the contract will be a condition as opposed to a mere warranty.'

Damages

In *Shearson Lehman Hutton Inc v Maclaine Watson & Co Ltd (No 2)* [1990] 3 All ER 723 (also discussed under Contract at p 67 below), the issue was the current or market price of a large quantity of tin which the sellers had sold to the buyers, and which the buyers had wrongfully refused to accept. Both parties conceded that the applicable provision was s 50(3), Sale of Goods Act 1979, and that there was an available market within the meaning of that provision. Section 50(3) provides as follows:

> 'Where there is an available market for the goods in question the measure of damages is prima facie to be ascertained by the difference between the contract price and the market or current price at the time or times when the goods ought to have been accepted or (if no time was fixed for acceptance) at the time of the refusal to accept.'

A number of preliminary points about this section (some of them common ground, and some contested) were made by Webster J. The general operation of s 50(3) displaced the normal rule that a party claiming damages for breach of contract must take reasonable steps to mitigate his loss. Instead, s 50(3) sets out to remove uncertainty by arbitrarily presuming that, if there is an available market and if the seller can get the current or market price for the goods on the date of the breach, his damages are measurable by reference to that price irrespective of whether it would have been prudent to sell on that date or not. In this way, both parties are protected from loss by virtue of price fluctuations either before or after the date of the breach.

The sellers relied on the statutory objective of certainty as justifying their construction of s 50(3). Put broadly, they contended that so long as a single potential buyer for the goods existed on the day in question there was an available market. The price obtainable within that market must therefore be taken as the base-line for assessing the seller's damages. The buyers (seeking to establish a higher base-line, and thus a lower measure of damages) maintained that proof of an available market required rather more than proof of a single willing purchaser. In their contention, it necessitated: (i) a ready demand for the goods, (ii) the existence of such a demand either immediately upon, or within a reasonable time of, the breach, and (iii) a large enough volume of potential buyers to constitute a 'market' in the normal acceptation of that term. The buyers maintained that a market price computed in this way would reflect the value of the goods, and thus the sellers' loss, far more accurately and realistically than a single 'snap-shot' value taken at the time of breach.

Webster J, having reviewed the authorities, drew a distinction between the situation where a seller actually offers the goods for resale on the appropriate day, and the situation where he does not. If the seller does offer the goods for resale, there is no available market unless there is one actual buyer on that day at a fair price. If the seller makes no actual offer, but there is merely a notional or hypothetical sale for the purposes of s 50(3), there is no available market unless on that day 'there are in the market sufficient traders potentially in touch with each other to evidence a market in which the actual or notional seller could if he wishes sell the goods' (at 730). Webster J pointed out that he was limiting his definition to what was strictly necessary to decide the issue before him, so far as was compatible with demonstrating that no material authority had been overlooked. In his view, the principles stated were consistent with *Garnac Grain Co Inc v H M F Faure & Fairclough Ltd and Bunge Corp* [1967] 2 All ER 353 (a case where the sellers were at fault in wrongfully failing to deliver) and inconsistent with no other authority cited to him.

So far as concerned the determination of the appropriate price in cases where there was an available market but no actual sale, Webster J opted for a pragmatic and broad-brushed solution, which he spelt out (at 727) as follows:

> 'where there is no actual sale, the market price must be a fair market price for the total quantity of goods assuming them to have been sold by a seller on the relevant date; but . . . since it might be unfair to the defendant purchaser to confine the price so established to the price obtainable if an actual sale had to be concluded on that day, it is permissible to take into account the price which would be negotiated within a few days with persons who were members of the market on that day and who could not be taken into account as potential buyers on the day in question only because of difficulties of communication. If account is taken of the price which would have been negotiated after a few days, no account can be taken of any price fluctuations after the date of the breach, ie for that purpose it has to be assumed that the price remained constant during the period of the negotiations.'

In Webster J's view, such a result could be reached by invoking the phrase 'prima facie' in s 50(3). This indicated to him that a court would be relieved from applying the section literally, where the price emerging from a strict application would not represent a fair market price on the day of breach. It enabled the court to arrive at what 'would have been in substance a fair price on that day in all the circumstances' (at 731). This latitude allowed the court to assume, for example, that the seller had been negotiating with alternative potential buyers sufficiently far in advance of the date of the buyer's breach as to arrive at a fair current market price for that date; or that all the potential buyers who constituted the relevant market were actually accessible to the seller on that date. Webster J saw no conflict between such an approach and the admitted principle that questions of mitigation were irrelevant to s 50(3). Nor, in his view, did his approach collide with the general measure of damages prescribed by s 50(2).

Reservation of title

In *Armour v Thyssen Edelstahlwerke AG* [1990] 3 All ER 481 the House of Lords, overruling the Scottish decisions in *Deutz Engines Ltd v Terex Ltd* 1984 SLT 273 and *Emerald Stainless Steel Ltd v South Side Distribution Ltd* 1982 SC

61, held that a straightforward reservation of title clause in a contract for the sale of commodities, purporting to reserve legal property to the seller until all debts owing to the seller from the buyer have been paid, does not amount to an attempt to create a security over those goods and does not fall within s 62(4) of the Sale of Goods Act 1979. The clause will therefore be given effect as an ordinary application of ss 17 and 19(1) of the 1979 Act.

German sellers supplied steel strip to Scottish manufacturers under a contract whereby ownership was to remain with the sellers until all debts and existing balances in favour of the sellers were discharged. At the material time, debts of over £70,000 were owing by the buyers to the sellers, and almost 70,000 kilogrammes of steel strip, supplied by the sellers, were in the buyers' possession. The buyers' receivers argued that the retention of title was ineffective because it constituted an attempt to create a security over the goods. The result, according to the receivers, was that property had passed immediately on delivery to the buyers and that there was nothing for the sellers to retain.

In a short speech, Lord Keith of Kinkel dismissed the defence. There could be no question of the sellers' attempting to create a security because they owed nothing to the buyers. Any creation of security must have been made by the buyers in favour of the sellers, and here the mechanics and terms of the delivery were flatly inconsistent with such creation. The true analysis of a security over movables, as indicated by Gloag and Irvine, *Law of Rights in Security* (1897), p 187, is that the debtor retains the ultimate right in his property while conferring an immediate right on the creditor to apply the secured property in satisfaction of the debt. The debtor, by virtue of his ultimate right, is entitled to any surplus in value where the proceeds of the creditor's sale of the secured property exceed the amount of the debt. The buyers could therefore have created a security over the steel only if they had enjoyed such ultimate right to the goods. This, in Lord Keith's view, required them to have had both ownership and actual or constructive possession of the steel before creating the security. Here, however, the contract delayed the passing of the property to the buyers until all outstanding debts were paid: a far cry from the situation where 'a party in possession of corporeal movables is seeking to create a subordinate right in favour of a creditor while retaining the ultimate right in himself' (at 484). The sellers had both the ultimate right to the steel and the right to any surplus on the resale proceeds. However colloquially the sellers' rights might be regarded as constituting a 'security' for the payment of their debts, the legal position was quite different: they were, and had remained throughout, the owners of the steel. In the words of Lord Jauncey of Tullichettle (at 486):

> 'It is of the essence of a right in security that the debtor possesses in relation to the property a right which he can transfer to the creditor, which right must be retransferred to him on payment of the debt.'

The plain fact was that this case involved a simple application of ss 17 and 19(1) of the Sale of Goods Act 1979. Section 17 states that property under a contract for the sale of specific goods passes when the parties intend it to pass, and s 19(1) entitles the seller under such a contract to reserve a right of disposal of the goods until the conditions imposed under the contract are met.

There was no warrant for the receivers' argument that the word 'conditions' in s 19(1) must be read as excluding all conditions imposed by the seller which amount to rights in security to the goods, and that such rights in security are present where the seller reserves to himself the legal property until debts outstanding are paid:

> 'I am . . . unable to regard a provision reserving title to the seller until payment of a debts due to him by the buyer as amounting to the creation by the buyer of a right in security in favour of the seller. Such a provision does in a sense give the seller security for the unpaid debts of the buyer. But it does so by way of a legitimate retention of title, not by virtue of any right over his own property conferred by the buyer.' (per Lord Keith, at 485).

Here, however, the buyers never acquired any interest other than possession which they were capable of transferring to the sellers.

This decision seems unquestionably correct. But a lingering doubt may survive as to the identity of the party entitled to surplus resale proceeds in future cases. In *Armour*, the House of Lords appear to have thought that, in every case where a seller reserves legal property until payment of debts due from the buyer, the seller who repossesses and resells by virtue of the clause can is entitled to any surplus proceeds. Undoubtedly, that will be the position in the great majority of cases, including *Armour* itself; see also *R V Ward Ltd v Bignall* [1967] 2 All ER 449. But in *Clough Mill Ltd v Martin* [1984] 3 All ER 982, All ER Rev 1984, pp 31–36 (to which Lord Keith referred with general approval) both Robert Goff and Oliver LJJ thought that the position might depend on whether the seller had, by reselling the goods, rescinded the original contract of sale. If he had, the result would be the seller's absolute entitlement to the resale proceeds; if not, the buyer might be entitled to any surplus above the original debt and related costs. The question can still be regarded as open, although the remarks in *Clough Mill* (which were merely obiter) are arguably in conflict with the *Ward* decision, which was not cited by the court in *Clough Mill* (see also s 48(4), Sale of Goods Act 1979). A further question expressly left open in *Armour* concerns the position of a buyer who has paid part of the purchase price before the seller's repossession and resale. In *Clough Mill*, the view was taken that the buyer must be credited with such part payment, for otherwise it would be recoverable by him as money paid on a total failure of consideration. It remains to be seen whether this proposition (which has, on its surface, much to commend it) is upheld by later courts.

Company Law

D D PRENTICE, MA, LLB, JD
Barrister, Allen & Overy Professor of Corporate Law,
Fellow of Pembroke College, Oxford

Introduction

It has been a characteristic of company law over the last five years or so that there has been an explosive growth of reported cases on the topic. This may in part be a result of the publication of specialist reports such as Butterworths Company Law Cases (BCLC) but this cannot be the whole explanation. In fact BCLC was really a response to the need for a specialist set of reports. Obviously, our society may have become more litigious but this somewhat common banality provides little guidance as to why this should have happened. One of the reasons in company law is that the legislation on this topic (and in this I include the Insolvency Act 1986) has more and more involved the courts. For example, such diverse topics as directors' disqualification (Company Directors Disqualification Act 1986), minority shareholder oppression (s 459 of the Companies Act 1985) and administration (Part II of the Insolvency Act 1986) all involve the active participation of the courts. (It is sometimes claimed that judges, because of their training, should not be involved in what are 'commercial' disputes; the courts' record in the above areas would call such simplistic criticisms into question.) In fact, one of the features of company law reform has been the more extended involvement of the courts that these reforms require. For example, it is inevitable that the administration procedure in Part II of the Insolvency Act 1986 will require extended judicial involvement throughout the whole procedure and not merely at the time the petition for an administration order is heard. Also, the novelty of many of the reforms has made it inevitable that there will be resort to the courts to sort out initial interpretative difficulties. This would explain a case such as *Re Jaymar Management Ltd* [1990] BCLC 617, which dealt with a technical point of construction of s 16(1) of the Company Directors Disqualification Act 1986. That section requires a person who intends 'to apply for a disqualification order' to give at least ten days' notice prior to the application to the person against whom the order is to be sought. The question before the court was – *when* is the application made? Is it the date on which the proceedings are issued or the time counsel stands up in court to seek the order? Harman J held that it was the former. Novelty would also explain the *Re M C Bacon Ltd* [1990] BCLC 324 litigation which is to be discussed later (see p 38 below).

There has, of course, been a considerable volume of legislation in the general field of company law. The subject has in fact fragmented into three independent but interrelated subjects – company law, securities legislation and insolvency. Even if the government wants to give the matter a rest, it will not have the option, since Brussels will inevitably produce a steady stream of directives (and the occasional regulation). For example, the Insider Trading

Directive (89/592/EC; OJL 33/30 (1989)) has been agreed and will need to be implemented (see *The Law On Insider Dealing*, DTI, consultative document, 1989) and there is a proposed directive on 'money laundering' which, if adopted, will have considerable implications for the financial services industry – in its present form it is difficult to see how 'off the page' sales of investments could be carried on. One feature of domestic legislation does call for comment. The Companies Act 1989 leaves a number of important items to be implemented by regulation. Examples of these are: s 100 (introducing a new s 410 into the 1985 Act) which permits the Secretary of State to introduce regulations for the registration of notices relating to automatic crystallisation; s 193, introducing a new s 62A into the Financial Services Act 1986, requiring the Secretary of State to define 'private investor' for the purpose of recovery under s 62 of that Act; and s 207, empowering the Secretary of State to introduce regulations for the electronic transfer of securities. All these matters are of considerable importance and they reflect what has been a characteristic of contemporary legislation and that is resort to regulation to flesh out the details of the primary legislation. This is a constitutional development of some importance as secondary legislation seldom receives the parliamentary attention that it deserves. There is, however, the slight advantage that secondary legislation provides an opportunity for those affected by the legislation to be adequately consulted, provided, of course, the opportunity is made use of.

Freezing orders

The question before Peter Gibson J in *Re Lonrho plc (No 4)* [1990] BCLC 151 was whether, in making an order freezing shares pursuant to s 216(1) of the Companies Act 1985, the court had jurisdiction to qualify the operation of the freezing order (which was a final order) with respect to some of the shares covered by the order. The specific question before the court was whether it could exempt shares which the registered holder had charged from the effects of the order so as to permit the chargee to enjoy his proprietary rights. Peter Gibson J held that he had no such jurisdiction. The unfairness which this could cause to an innocent third party is self-evident. It has been rectified by s 135(1)(a) of the Companies Act 1989 which empowers the Secretary of State to make regulations 'for enabling orders to be made in a form protecting the rights of third parties'. He is also empowered to enact regulations for the partial relaxation or removal of restrictions and with respect to the making of interim orders (s 135(1)(b) and (c)). (The effects of *Re Westminster Property Group plc* [1985] BCLC 188 have been reversed by the Companies Act 1989, Sch 19, para 10.)

Preferences

The purpose of s 239 of the Insolvency Act 1986 is to prevent a company which is insolvent or on the brink of insolvency from conferring a benefit on a creditor which is denied to other similarly situated creditors. The section underpins the collective nature of insolvency proceedings. It does not, however, impose on a creditor an obligation to look after the interests of his fellow creditors; the race still goes to the swiftest, something which is clear from the important decision of Millett J in *Re M C Bacon Ltd* [1990] BCLC 324.

In that case, a company in financial difficulties had executed in May 1987 a mortgage in favour of its bank to secure an existing overdraft. At the time the debenture was entered into the judge found that (i) the directors were aware that the company was actually or virtually insolvent, (ii) that if the bank withdrew its support the company would be forced into immediate liquidation and (iii) the directors of the company believed that with the continued support of the bank the company could trade out of its difficulties. It is also clear from the facts of the case that the bank was aware of the serious financial plight of the company. However, as it is the intention of the company that determines whether an improper preference has been given, it is the knowledge of the directors of the company of the company's insolvent state that is of importance. In September 1987 the bank appointed an administrative receiver to enforce its debenture and in the same month a liquidator was appointed in a creditors' voluntary winding up. The liquidator challenged the validity of the bank's debenture on the grounds that it was a preference within s 239, or alternatively, a transaction at an undervalue (see s 238 of the 1986 Act).

Section 239 strikes down in certain circumstances unfair preferences which are broadly defined as acts done by a company which are influenced by a desire to put a creditor in a better position than he would have been in the event of the company going into insolvent liquidation had the act not been done. At the time the act is carried out the company must be insolvent or it must become so as a result of the act. Some feared that this would make it virtually impossible for a company in financial difficulty to provide security to a creditor who was willing to lend it support, without the security being open to challenge as an unfair preference. The interpretation that Millett J placed on the section indicates that this fear is unfounded. In finding that the debenture did not constitute a preference, the judge made the following observations:

(i) Because the language of s 239 was radically different from that of its predecessor (see Bankruptcy Act 1914, s 44(1)), Millett J considered that the old cases could have no relevance in interpreting the new section (at 335). As he pointed out, s 239 involved a 'completely new test'. He highlighted the following major difference (at 335):

> 'It involves at least two radical departures from the old law. It is no longer necessary to establish a *dominant* intention to prefer. It is sufficient that the decision was *influenced* by the requisite desire. This is the first change. The second is that it is no longer necessary to establish an *intention* to prefer. There must be desire to produce the *effect* mentioned in the subsection.' (ie sub-s (5).)

(ii) It is the desire on the part of the company to achieve the effect set out in s 239(5) that constitutes a preference; desire in this context is subjective and as Millett J stated a 'man can choose the lesser of two evils without desiring either' (at 335).

(iii) The mere presence of the desire to achieve the purpose in s 239(5) is not determinative in categorising the transaction as an improper preference, the desire must have actually influenced the decision to enter into the transaction. However, the desire to prefer need not be the decisive or precipitating factor influencing the decision, it merely has to be a factor influencing the company's decision. It is not 'necessary to prove that, if the requisite desire had not been present, the company would not have entered into the transaction' (at 336).

As a consequence of Millett J's interpretation of s 239, it will be possible to provide 'assistance to a company in financial difficulties provided that the company is actuated only by proper commercial considerations' (at 336).

Transactions at an undervalue

In *Re M C Bacon Ltd* (the facts of which are given above) it was also argued that the execution of the security in favour of the bank also constituted a transaction at an undervalue within the meaning of s 238 of the Insolvency Act 1986. Whether such a transaction has taken place requires a comparison to be made between the value of what was received by the company and the consideration provided by the company, and both values must be measurable in money or money's worth. Millett J held that the creation of a security does not deplete the assets of the company and therefore there was no lessening of the company's assets which could constitute the basis of a transaction at an undervalue. What the company lost was the ability 'to apply the proceeds otherwise than in satisfaction of the secured debt' (at 340) but this was not something, according to Millett J, capable of 'valuation in monetary terms' (at 341). Even if the security is enforced, the enforcement could not by itself give rise to a transaction at an undervalue, since the proceeds realised could only be used to satisfy whatever outstanding debt was owed to the creditor. No doubt the creation of security could prejudice other creditors but, while this may constitute a preference, it does not constitute a transaction at an undervalue.

Directors' duties

The House of Lords in *Guinness plc v Saunders* [1990] 1 All ER 652, [1990] BCLC 402 upheld the decision of the Court of Appeal ([1988] 2 All ER 940, [1988] BCLC 607, discussed in All ER Rev 1988, p 34) obliging Mr Ward, a director of Guinness, to return a fee which he had obtained for his professional services, but it did not adopt all of its reasoning. The House of Lords reasoned that the articles of association did not empower a committee of the board to fix the remuneration of a director. This was something that had to be done by the full board and since it had not been so done in the *Guinness* case, Ward was obliged to hand back the fee he had received from Guinness on the grounds that it had not been authorised. Ward also claimed a quantum meruit if his claim to be contractually entitled to the fee failed. As the case was decided on the assumption that Ward had acted in good faith, there was some likelihood that this claim would succeed. But the court rightly rejected it, on the grounds that to allow it would undermine the fiduciary duties of directors. Whatever the scope to the principle that to obtain restitution one must do restitution, it must give way to other legal policies. One such firmly entrenched policy is that directors must adhere to their fiduciary duties and that, prima facie, as fiduciaries they are not, unless it is specifically authorised in accordance with the company's articles of association, entitled to remuneration ([1990] 1 All ER 652 at 667, [1990] BCLC 402 at 420). This starting position is, however, somewhat removed from modern reality.

The disagreement between the House of Lords and the Court of Appeal related to the effect of non-compliance with s 317 of the Companies Act 1985. Fox LJ, giving the judgment of the Court of Appeal, was of the opinion that breach of s 317 had civil as well as criminal consequences, and that such a breach resulted in Ward holding the money he had received as a constructive trustee for the company. This read into s 317 civil consequences which were not spelt out in the section, but both as an approach to the interpretation of statutory proscriptions and as a matter of policy it has much to commend it. It is, however, difficult to reconcile with the decision of the Court of Appeal in *Hely-Hutchinson v Brayhead Ltd* [1967] 3 All ER 98, ('an exceptional Court of Appeal consisting of Lord Denning MR, Lord Wilberforce, and Lord Pearson' per Lord Goff, [1990] 1 All ER 652 at 664, [1990] BCLC 402 at 417), which reached the opposite conclusion. The House of Lords declined to depart from the reasoning in the *Hely-Hutchinson* decision, namely, that s 317 imposes an obligation of disclosure breach of which can lead to criminal sanctions (s 317(7)) but that such a breach does not of itself affect the contract. Where articles of association incorporate a provision along the lines of s 317, non-compliance with this article will normally render the ensuing contract voidable but as a pre-condition to allowing the company to exercise its right of rescission there will have to be restoration to the status quo ante ([1990] 1 All ER 652 at 665, [1990] BCLC 402 at 418). However, having found that there was no contract giving rise to an obligation on the part of Guinness to make payment, there was no contract in existence that needed to be avoided.

In agreed take-over bids, the directors of the respective companies will often enter into an agreement to use their best endeavours to consummate the bid. If there are changes in circumstances between the time when the agreement is entered into and the consummation of the bid, the question arises as to whether the directors are obliged to forge ahead regardless? Or can they change their mind and recommend that the take-over be discontinued? This was the issue before the courts in *John Crowther Group plc v Carpets International plc* [1990] BCLC 460 and *Rackham v Peek Foods Ltd* [1990] BCLC 895. These cases, decided in 1985 and 1977 respectively, held that the directors were not obliged by a best endeavours commitment to give bad advice and if circumstances changed so as to make the bid ill advised they had no obligation to persist with it. In fact, if circumstances change so as to make the take-over an unattractive proposition then the directors come under a duty to disclose the altered circumstances to the shareholders. As was stated by Vinelott J in the *John Crowther* decision:

> 'It seems to me plain beyond question that directors are under a duty to disclose the facts to the shareholders. Indeed a resolution passed in ignorance of them would be worthless. If directors must disclose the facts, then it seems to me they must equally express their honest opinion as to what is in the interests of the company.' (at 465).

The question arises as to whether the directors could go beyond a 'best endeavors' obligation and enter into an agreement to recommend a bid come hell or high water. This is not free from difficulty. Obviously, directors can exercise their discretion so as to commit the company to a binding contract; in fact this is what happens every time directors contract on behalf of a company. But directors cannot abdicate their discretion. If they were to bind their discretion in circumstances where they are ignorant of the type of eventuality that could arise, it is submitted that this would constitute an improper fettering of their duty. Such a fetter would render the agreement impeachable under the decision in *Rolled Steel Products (Holdings) Ltd v British Steel Corpn* [1986] Ch 246. In addition, the directors would not be protected by disclosure to the shareholders because of the operation of s 310 of the Companies Act 1985 (as amended).

Re Welfab Engineers Ltd [1990] BCLC 833 raises the interesting question as to what directors are to do where a company is in financial difficulties. Should they merely abandon hope, and either seek the appointment of a receiver or put the company into liquidation? In *Re Welfab Engineers Ltd* the liquidators alleged in a misfeasance summons (Insolvency Act 1986, s 212) that the directors had been in breach of duty in selling the assets of the company, which was in financial difficulties, particularly as there was a higher offer made than the one that they had accepted. The court held that they had not breached their duty. The propriety of the directors' action in selling the business had to be judged in the light of the alternatives available (receivership and liquidation) and, if the directors made an honest attempt to save the business by selling it as a going concern in circumstances where this would not clearly leave the creditors in a worse position than had they adopted either of the former procedures, then they were not to be faulted.

The normal rule as regards litigation is that a body corporate must appear either by counsel or a solicitor. Whatever the justification for this, it cannot, as is often claimed, be because the company is an artificial entity. All this entails is that a company will have to be represented by an individual but it does not at all compel the conclusion that that individual should be legally qualified. *Arbuthnot Leasing International Ltd v Havelet Leasing Ltd* [1991] 1 All ER 591, [1990] BCLC 802 is a welcome relaxation of the rule requiring a company to be represented by someone legally qualified. Scott J held that pursuant to its inherent power to control its own proceedings, the court could permit a director in appropriate circumstances to become a party to litigation in relation to orders which have been made against a company of which he is a director. See also *Kuwait Asia Bank EC v National Mutual Life Nomineess Ltd* [1990] 3 All ER 404, [1990] BCLC 868 (an appeal to the Privy Council from New Zealand) which deals, inter alia, with the duty which directors may owe creditors but which does not discuss some of the more recent cases on the topic (also considered in Practice and Procedure, at p 213 below).

Winding up – costs

Re M C Bacon Ltd (No 2) [1990] BCLC 607, although dealing with a somewhat technical but important question of costs, nevertheless raises some important issues of principle. In that case, the liquidator had brought an action alleging that a floating charge which the company had given its bank constituted a fraudulent preference and also claiming that the bank was liable to contribute to the company's assets under s 214 of the Insolvency Act 1986.

The action was unsuccessful and costs were awarded against the liquidator. In the present proceedings, the liquidator claimed to be entitled to the bank's costs and his own costs as expenses of the liquidation and thus to be entitled to whatever priority that the Insolvency Rules accord to these costs. (Without going into chapter and verse, such costs rank ahead of preferential creditors and floating charge holders and all other creditors subordinate to these: see Fletcher, *The Law of Insolvency*, ch 23). As a starting point Millett J held, following *Re Barleycorn Enterprises Ltd* [1970] 2 All ER 155, that where the word 'assets' or the phrase the 'company's assets' appeared in ss 115 and 175 of the Insolvency Act 1986, they meant assets subject to a floating charge. This, prima facie, would appear to entitle the liquidator to his expenses of the winding up under s 175(2)(a), which confers on the liquidator the right to be paid his expenses in priority to the holder of a floating charge and also in priority to the preferential creditors. However, such expenses are only payable if they have, inter alia, been incurred in 'preserving, realising or getting in any of the assets of the company' (Insolvency Rules 1986, r 4.218(a)). Millett J held that an action to set aside a charge as a preference could not be held to one which was designed to get in or realise the assets of the company. It was a right vested in the liquidator and, if successful, the assets which were recovered did not belong to the company but were impressed with 'a trust' in favour of the general body of creditors (see *Re Yagerphone Ltd* [1935] Ch 392, [1935] All ER Rep 803). He went on to hold that neither s 238(3) nor s 241(1)(c) conferred on the court powers which were 'intended to be exercised so as to enable a debenture holder to obtain the benefit of the proceedings brought by the liquidator' (at 612).

If the expenses of an action to avoid a transaction as a preference were not 'expenses of the winding up' (s 175(2)(a)) then it was inevitable that the expenses of an action under s 214 could also not be treated as such. The right to bring such an action is vested in the liquidator, it only arises on the insolvent liquidation of the company and, as Millett J pointed out, until an order was made under s 214 there was nothing that could be called an asset of the company (at 613d).

Since the winding up in *Re M C Bacon Ltd (No 2)* was a creditors' voluntary winding up, the liquidator called in aid s 115 of the 1986 Act which provides that all expenses incurred in the winding up shall have priority to all other claims and shall be paid out of 'the assets of the company' (at 612i). Millett J held that this was a priority section and did not by itself determine what expenses were so payable. The section only gave priority to those expenses which were properly so payable and this was not a matter determined by the section. As the expenses were not properly so payable, the section had nothing to bite on.

Re M C Bacon Ltd (No 2) is important not merely because of the point relating to costs. It deals with a much broader, and arguably more important, issue and that is the treatment of assets in a liquidation which have been recovered by the liquidator pursuant to a provision which enables him to upset a pre-insolvency transaction or under s 214. This has not been an issue that has been subjected to any extended principled analysis. It is clear from the judgment of Millett J that, at least as regards the provisions that he had to deal with, ss 214 and 239, the right to seek a remedy under them was not an asset of the company and thus would not, for example, be subject to any charge which the company had created. Also, in so far as they resulted in any enhancement in the assets of the company, this would ensure for the benefit of the unsecured creditors. While this may produce a certain degree of fairness for the unsecured creditors it does have the paradoxical result that these sections will be used with less frequency since secured creditors will normally only be willing to fund litigation if they benefit from recovery.

Registration of charges

Re Curtain Dream plc [1990] BCLC 925 raised once again the question of whether a transaction entered into by a company is a charge and hence registrable under s 395 of the Companies Act 1985, or a transaction which, whatever its characterisation, did not constitute a registrable charge. In this case the other possible classification of the transaction contended for was that it was a sale and resale, with title being retained in the reseller until the goods had been paid for. As is inevitable in these cases, the court had to classify the transaction not by what the parties called it, nor by what they had hoped to achieve, but what as a matter of substantive legal classification the parties had achieved. In *Re Curtain Dream plc*, A agreed to provide B with a general line of credit of £500,000; alongside this facility was a contract of trading whereby B sold its goods to A and A resold them to B but retaining title to the goods until there had been repayment for the goods by B. The court considered that the transaction had to be categorised in the light of both the borrowing facility agreement and the sale and resale. On this basis it was not a sale and resale but rather a loan by A to B secured on the goods allegedly sold by B to A and as such it should have been registered. There were a number of factors which led the court to this conclusion but the most important were the virtual simultaneous execution of the facility and trading agreements and the fact that under the trading agreement A, who had allegedly 'purchased' the goods from B, was under an obligation to re-sell them to B. The transaction, as far as the goods were concerned, was wholly circular. The matter, of course, might have been different had merely an option to re-purchase been accorded to B (see *Manchester, Sheffield and Lincolnshire Railway Co v North Central Wagon Co* (1888) 13 App Cas 554 at 567–568). Once again, this case reflects the fact that we lack a sensible system for classifying what constitutes a personal property security interest.

Auditors' duty of care

The courts continue to restrict the duty of care that auditors owe to those who rely on the accounts of companies. In *Al Saudi Banque v Clark Pixley* [1990] BCLC 46 the court held that the auditors of a company owed no duty of care to banks who relied on the company's published accounts when extending a loan to the company. In *Caparo Industries plc v Dickman* [1990] 1 All ER 568, [1990] BCLC 273 the House of Lords held that no duty of care was owed by auditors to investing members of the public or to shareholders who increased their stake in the company. (The latter case is commented on in greater detail in the chapter on Tort at pp 307–311 below.) Only a few brief comments are called for here. In *Caparo* the House of Lords saw the primary purpose of audited accounts as being to enable those who had a proprietary interests in the company to exercise their proprietary rights in an informed manner. No doubt the auditors owe a duty of care to the company but it will often be difficult to show loss flowing from the breach. The failure by the auditors to detect wrongdoing could no doubt result in the company suffering additional loss but this will not always be the case. For example, if the auditors fail to value accurately the assets of the company then, provided the company does not sell its property before the undervaluation is detected, there will be no loss to the company. There will, however, be a loss to any shareholder who sells before the error is detected as the price of the shares will be affected by the auditors' inaccurate report. It may have been for this reason that Lord Bridge left open the question as to whether or not a shareholder who sells at a price depreciated by the auditor's negligently prepared report could have a claim against the auditor. However, given the way the wind was blowing in *Caparo*, the chances of any such action succeeding are not good. Whatever the outcome of such an action, it is difficult to accept the distinction which Lord Bridge draws between a decision to sell and a decision to purchase (at 288) since in both situations an auditor's inaccurate report will have had an impact on the market value of the securities.

Administration – Part II of the Insolvency Act 1986

The general position is that an administrative receiver is in a better position than the company with respect to current contracts and, although he may not, like a liquidator, disclaim such contracts, he can refuse to abide by them (*Airlines Airspares Ltd v Handley Page Ltd* [1970] 1 All ER 29, [1970] Ch 193). This is, in reality, an issue of priorities and a receiver will not be bound by current contracts where the charge under which he is appointed confers a priority which is superior to that of the unsecured contract claimants. This will normally be the case (see *Edwin Hill & Partners v First National Finance Corporation plc* [1988] 3 All ER 801, [1989] BCLC 89, All ER Rev 1989, p 39). This superior right of the security holder and hence the administrative receiver is subject, of course, to whatever duty of care that the administrative receiver owes to the debtor company and any guarantor of its debts. A question which has arisen is whether or not an administrator appointed under Part II of the Insolvency Act 1986 is in the same position as an administrative receiver. This was one of the issues before Vinelott J in *Astor Chemicals Ltd v Synthetic Technology Ltd* [1990] BCLC 1 and the judge held that he was not. The function of the administrative receiver was, according to the judge, 'to get in the assets of company so far as charged for the benefit of the debenture holder' (at 11) whereas the administrator 'is appointed to manage the affairs of the company and not to realise them for the benefit of one of the creditors' (at 12). Given this difference in function, there was no need to recognise the priority of the security holder and therefore to accord the administrator the same right with respect to current contracts that is accorded to the administrative receiver.

One of the purposes for which an administrator can be appointed is the 'survival of the company, and the whole or any part of its undertaking, as a going concern' (Insolvency Act 1986, s 8(3)(*a*)). In *Re Rowbotham Baxter Ltd* [1990] BCLC 397 Harman J held that a 'hive-down' of the a company's affairs could not fall within this provision since this did not constitute a survival of the company but constituted the survival of the hived down part of the company's business. This places a somewhat narrow restriction on the meaning of the subsection and it is submitted that a preferable interpretation would be to interpret the 'and' in s 8(3)(a) as being disjunctive rather than conjunctive.

Bristol Airport plc v Powdrill [1990] 2 All ER 493, [1990] BCLC 585 is an important case both in terms of general principle and in the light that it throws on the specific provisions relating to administration. In that case two airports had detained aircraft pursuant to s 88 of the Civil Aviation Act 1982 because the company which operated them owed them considerable sums of money for unpaid airport charges. The operating company was placed in administration and the broad question before the court was whether the airports were free without a court order to exercise their rights under s 88 of the 1982 Act against the administrator.

(i) *The general principle* Browne-Wilkinson V-C, who gave the leading judgment of the Court of Appeal, held that one of the principle purposes of Part II was to set up a procedure whereby the affairs of a company could be conducted 'with a view either to restoring the financial health of the company or of enabling the business to be sold as a going concern' (at 592b). To these ends, the administrator had to carry on the business of the company and therefore, as far as was consistent with the language of Part II:

> 'Such continuation of the business by the administrator requires that there should be available to him the right to use the property of the company, free from interference by creditors and others during the usually short period during which such administration continues.' (at 594b–c).

(ii) *Meaning of company's property – s 11(3)(c)* This subsection precludes, inter alia, any action to enforce any security against 'the company's property', and the issue that the court had to address in the *Bristol Airport* case was whether or not the aeroplanes held under chattel leases were the property of the company. The chattel lease is a contract which confers on the lessee certain rights with respect to the leased property and it is clear that the lease of personal property does not have the same characteristics as the lease of real property. However, given the definition of property in the Insolvency Act 1986, s 436, to include things in action, it is reasonably clear that for the purposes of the Act a lessee has a property interest for the purpose of s 11(3)(c).

(iii) *Step to enforce any security – s 11(3)(c)* Browne-Wilkinson V-C, having decided that the right of detention under s 88 of the Civil Aviation Act 1982 constituted security within the meaning of s 248(b) of the 1986 Act, the question then arose as to whether the exercise of that right so as to detain the aircraft constituted the enforcement of the security within s 11(3)(c). Since the statutory right to detain the aircraft was somewhat akin to a lien, the issue before the court was whether or not the exercise by the holder of a possessory lien constituted enforcement of a security for which leave of the court or consent of the administrator was required. Browne-Wilkinson V-C held that the exercise of a possessory lien did constitute enforcement partly on the construction of the 1986 Act but mainly on the grounds that to deprive the administrator of control of property which was subject to a possessory lien would thwart the purpose of administration. The difficulty with this from the point of view of a lien holder is that the surrender of property which is subject to a lien results in the loss of the security and the effect of this would be that the appointment of an administrator could turn a secured into an unsecured creditor. To deal with this, the court held that, in recognising the right of an administrator to make use of the property subject to the lien, the court could nevertheless make an order to protect the rights of the lien holder. Also, if the lien holder exercised his rights of possession but took immediate steps to obtain the leave of the court to do so, this would not constitute contempt of court. Lastly, it had to be kept in mind that the administrator could recognise the rights of a security holder and the administrator could thus agree that a lien holder who gave up possession could nevertheless have a non-possessory lien.

(iv) *No 'other proceedings' – s 11(3)(d)* Browne-Wilkinson V-C held that proceedings meant legal or quasi-legal proceedings and the exercise of a right of detention could not amount to proceedings.

 (v) *The exercise of the discretion to allow the security holder to enforce his security* Lastly, the court had to decide whether the trial judge had been correct in not giving the airports the right to enforce its security and the court held that he was. A factor of some importance was the fact that the airports had allowed the administration to continue without taking steps to enforce its security and had only struck at the eleventh hour. What is clear is that the secured charge holder will have to decide promptly whether or not it wants to enforce its security and if it holds back and fails to do so it will normally not obtain leave under s 11(3)(c).

Section 27 of the 1986 Act provides creditors and members of a company which is in administration with the right to petition the court for relief where the affairs of the company are being conducted in a manner which is unfairly prejudicial to their interests. An unsuccessful attempt to invoke this remedy was made in *Re Charnley Davies Ltd (No 2)* [1990] BCLC 760. In the course of his judgment Millett J held that the case law decided under s 459 of the Companies Act 1985 was relevant to interpreting this section and, in particular, following the cases decided under that section it was neither necessary or sufficient to show that the acts complained of were illegal or infringed the legal rights of the petitioner. He drew a difficult distinction between allegations of misconduct simpliciter and conduct which was unfairly prejudicial. The former might give rise to some right of redress but it would not as such ground an action under s 27. The problem with this type of distinction is that a failure by the administrator to correct his misconduct could quite easily be turned into an allegation that this failure constituted unfairly prejudicial conduct, since there is no a priori reason why an isolated act which is uncorrected cannot constitute unfairly prejudicial conduct.

Because the holder of a floating charge can appoint an administrative receiver and thus prevent the appointment of an administrator (s 9(3)), it is essential for there to be strict compliance with the provisions requiring the holder of a floating charge to be informed that a petition is to be presented for the appointment of an administrator. To this end, the structure of the Insolvency Rules contemplates that there will be a delay between the service of the petition and the hearing (see eg rule 2.7). However, in appropriate circumstances the court can abbreviate the period of notice and in *Re Cavco Floors Ltd* [1990] BCLC 940 the court was willing to make an administration order before a petition was presented where an undertaking was given that a petition would be presented forthwith. The circumstances of that case were exceptional in that the company's bank, which held a floating charge, was unwilling to appoint an administrative receiver and the directors were unwilling to continue trading for fear of personal liability. In the generality of cases, however, the court will insist that the notice provisions in the Insolvency Rules be strictly complied with.

Because of the power given to the holder of a floating charge, but not the holder of a fixed charge, to block the appointment of an administrative receiver, the practice appears to have developed of creating floating charges to exist alongside fixed charges so that the charge holder can block the appointment of an administrator. These charges, referred to as 'fully subordinated floating charges', are expressed to be capable of crystallisation on the presentation of a petition for the appointment of an administrator (see Paget, *Law of Banking* (10th edn) at p 279). In *Re Croftbell Ltd* [1990] BCLC 844 it was argued, unsuccessfully, that this type of device ran contrary to the scheme of Part II of the 1986 Act. The court held that to be able to block the appointment of an administrator, a person merely has to be have the right to appoint an administrative receiver as defined in s 29(2) of the 1986. The motive for acquiring this right does not affect the question as to whether or not it operates to preclude an administrator from being appointed. Also, it is submitted that the fact that the floating charge is over an equity of redemption which may be of little or no value at the time of its creation does not preclude the appointment of an administrative receiver.

Minority oppression

In *Re Sam Weller & Sons Ltd* [1990] BCLC 80, Peter Gibson J declined to follow the decision of Harman J in *Re a Company (No 00370 of 1987), ex p Glossop* [1988] BCLC 570 (see also *Re a Company (No 00789 of 1987), ex p Shooter* [1990] BCLC 384) and held that conduct which affected the rights of all members equally (failure to declare an adequate dividend) could nevertheless be unfairly prejudicial to the interests of the petitioners within the meaning of s 459 of the Companies Act 1989. This matter has now been put beyond doubt by Sch 19, para 11 of the Companies Act 1989. There are a number of features of the *Weller* decision, however, that remain of importance:

(i) The test for determining whether or not conduct is unfairly prejudicial is objective – the impact of the conduct on the interests of the petitioner is what the court examines. The importance of this is that it is not necessary to show an intention to cause prejudice as a necessary condition to obtaining relief under s 459.

(ii) Peter Gibson J emphasised that s 459 refers to 'interests', which is a wider term than 'rights', and it imported the possibility that members could have the same rights but different interests.

(iii) In the *Sam Weller* decision, Peter Gibson J refused to strike out the petition which alleged that the petitioner had been prejudiced by, inter alia, the low dividend policy adopted by the company. Although the court will for obvious reasons be reluctant to find that decisions that fall within the legitimate purview of management can nevertheless give rise to a remedy under s 459, a shareholder has a legitimate expectation that he will obtain a return on his investment and where this is not the case then he should have some means of obtaining relief.

Although s 459 should provide the principle source of relief for minority shareholder oppression, s 122(1)(g) of the Insolvency Act 1986 (winding up on the 'just and equitable' grounds) still has a role to play. This is because the structure of the legislation does not accord primacy to the s 459 remedy but merely denies relief to a petitioner under s 122(1)(g) where the court finds that the petitioner possesses an alternative remedy and is acting unreasonably in seeking to have the company wound up rather than pursuing the alternative remedy: s 125(2) of the 1986 Act is 'directed to imposing a mandatory duty on the court to make a winding-up order with a discretion not to make one if certain conditions are satisfied' (*Vujnovich v Vujnovich* [1990] BCLC 227 at 232). Also, in many cases it may be difficult to raise the issue of the relationship between s 459 and s 122(1)(g) as the petitioner may only claim relief under s 122(1)(g). In *Virdi v Abbey Leisure Ltd, Re Abbey Leisure Ltd* [1990] BCLC 342 the petitioner had sought relief under s 459 and s 122(1)(g) but the matter was dealt with by the trial judge ([1989] BCLC 619) and the Court of Appeal on the basis that the petitioner's primary claim for relief was for a winding-up order. In that case, the business of a company had come to an end. The other directors of the company had offered to purchase the shares of the petitioner and proposed that if there was a failure to agree on the valuation of the shares then this should be carried out in accordance with the pre-emption provisions of the articles. The company and the other directors claimed that the petitioner was acting unreasonably in not pursuing this remedy and that the petition under s 122(1)(g) should accordingly be struck out. In reversing Hoffmann J, the Court of Appeal found that the petitioner was not acting unreasonably within the meaning of s 125(2) in seeking the winding up of the company. There were three reasons for this. First, the petitioner should not have to accept the risk that in an agreed sale where the price was set by a third party his shares might be discounted because they were a minority interest, whereas in a liquidation the value would of necessity be on a pro rata basis. Second, there were various legal claims against and on behalf of the company which could be better dealt with in liquidation. Lastly, to consign the petitioner to his remedy under the articles would fail to give full effect to the reasoning in the *Ebrahimi* case ([1972] 2 All ER 492) that in a winding-up petition on the just and equitable grounds the legal rights of the parties might be subject to equitable considerations. Of these reasons, the first is probably the most important. (See *Re Howie and Crawford's arbitration* [1990] BCLC 686 on the valuation of shares in a private company.) This case also calls into question the principle that Hoffmann J has formulated in number of cases dealing with s 459 relief in which he held that a petitioner should be confined to his remedy under a pre-emptive rights provision in the company's articles of association. The difficulties caused by this line of reasoning were dealt with in last year's review (All ER Rev 1989, pp 47–48). By emphasising the entitlement of a shareholder to have his shares valued on a no-discount basis, the Court of Appeal undermined the Hoffmann J reasoning which fails to protect a shareholder against this type of prejudice.

Given the modern practice of conferring on companies the widest possible objects, it is difficult to imagine when the of loss substratum doctrine would ever be applicable. Accordingly, *Re Perfectair Holdings Ltd* [1990] BCLC 423 is something of an oddity in that the petitioner succeeded in obtaining a winding-up order on the grounds that the substratum of the company had disappeared. There, the members of a quasi-partnership type of company had determined that the company should discontinue its business and that its assets be distributed among its members. To this end the property of the company was sold. A petition was presented for the winding-up of the company on the grounds that the substratum of the company had disappeared; this was resisted, the company arguing that it had commenced litigation and that it should remain in existence so that the litigation could be prosecuted. Scott J granted the winding-up order. He considered that since it was no longer possible for the company to carry on its activities and since the majority had indicated an intention that the company should be wound up, this was an appropriate case for the granting of a winding-up order (see *Galbraith v Merito Shipping Co* 1947 SC 446). As regards the prosecution of the litigation on behalf of the company, this could just as well be carried on by the liquidator as by the directors and it was more appropriate that the liquidator should take the steps to bring the company's activities to an end, a function for which the directors were not appointed.

Contempt of Court

C J MILLER, BA, LLM
Barrister, Professor of English Law, University of Birmingham

The All England Law Reports for 1990 contain a number of cases which are of importance to the development of the law of contempt. They concern such matters as the position of journalists seeking to protect their sources of information, the status of mental health review tribunals and the application of the law of civil contempt to directors or other officers of a company.

Journalists and their sources of information

Journalists have long taken the view that it is essential to protect their sources of information from disclosure. Otherwise, it is believed, 'whistle blowers' would not come forward and corruption and incompetence would go unrevealed. Although neither the common law nor statute has accorded complete protection, a partial protection is to be found in s 10 of the Contempt of Court Act 1981. This provides that:

> 'No court may require a person to disclose, nor is any person guilty of contempt of court for refusing to disclose, the source of information contained in a publication for which he is responsible, unless it be established to the satisfaction of the court that disclosure is necessary in the interests of justice or national security or for the prevention of disorder or crime.'

In *X Ltd v Morgan-Grampian (Publishers) Ltd* [1990] 2 All ER 1, the House of Lords was concerned with the 'interests of justice' exception to the general privilege or immunity accorded by s 10 (also discussed in Practice and Procedure, pp 208–211 and Statute Law, pp 265–266 below). The background was that William Goodwin, a journalist working on a weekly journal called *The Engineer*, had received highly sensitive information about the financial affairs of the plaintiff companies which were seeking to raise additional working capital. There was a strong likelihood that the information had been derived from a draft plan which had been stolen from their premises. Goodwin telephoned the plaintiffs and their bankers to check certain facts, thus triggering off a successful application for an ex parte injunction to restrain the publication of information derived from the draft plan. The plaintiffs also sought an order requiring disclosure of Goodwin's notes of his conversation with the source so as to enable them to take steps to recover the plan. Hoffmann J granted the order (see *Re Goodwin* [1990] 1 All ER 608) and he was upheld by the Court of Appeal ([1990] 1 All ER 616) subject to a variation which gave Goodwin the option of delivering his notes to the court in an envelope which would remain sealed until the final determination of his appeal. Goodwin failed to comply with the order, thus evincing what Lord Bridge was later to describe as 'a plain declaration of his determination to set himself above the law'.

On a subsequent appeal to the House of Lords a number of issues were raised. One was that the wording of s 10 seems to limit its application to cases where the source of information is 'contained in a publication' – a condition which was not present on the facts. Sensibly, the House adopted a purposive interpretation to avoid the anomalies which would otherwise arise. As Lord Lowry put it ([1990] 2 All ER 1 at 17):

'I agree that the provision extends to protect from disclosure the source of information contained in an intended publication. This seems to be a necessary interpretation; otherwise a defendant such as Mr Goodwin would be worse off than if he had already published, with only such limited protection as the common law and a judge's exercise of discretion might afford.'

A similar attitude was adopted, albeit in a different context, in *Re an Inquiry under the Companies Securities (Insider Dealing) Act 1985* [1988] 1 All ER 203, HL (All ER Rev 1988, pp 33, 75, 291).

The second and more substantial point concerned the scope of the 'interest of justice' exception and its application to the facts of the case. As Lord Bridge observed (at 8–9), this was the first time that this part of s 10 had come before the House of Lords for decision. His Lordship began by referring to an observation of Lord Diplock in *Secretary of State for Defence v Guardian Newspapers Ltd* [1984] 3 All ER 601, [1985] AC 339 (discussed at length in All ER Rev 1984, pp 67–70, 157–160) where he had said (at 607):

'The expression "justice", the interests of which are entitled to protection, is not used in a general sense as the antonym of "injustice" but in the technical sense of the administration of justice in the course of legal proceedings in a court of law.'

Lord Bridge and the other members of the House agreed with the first part of this observation but not with the second. To limit the matter to legal proceedings in a court of law was too narrow, since the exercise of legal rights would not always require resort to such proceedings. The point was illustrated by saying (at 9):

'Thus, to take a very obvious example, if an employer of a large staff is suffering grave damage from the activities of an unidentified disloyal servant, it is undoubtedly in the interests of justice that he should be able to identify him in order to terminate his contract of employment, notwithstanding that no legal proceedings may be necessary to achieve that end.'

Lord Oliver made a similar point saying (at 17) that the interest of citizens in exercising their legal rights 'cannot reasonably be confined simply to the area of actual or contemplated proceedings'.

Having adopted this broader and less technical approach, the matter became one of exercising judgment in relation to the balance of competing interests involved. Disclosure could be required only when, in the words of Lord Oliver (at 16), the court:

'is satisfied that one or more of the four enumerated considerations (ie the interests of justice etc) are of such preponderating importance in the individual case that the ban on disclosure imposed by the opening words of the section really needs to be overridden.'

Where any such balancing exercise is required it is helpful to have some guidelines as to the factors which need to be taken into account. The decision provides some guidance on this point. For example, it was seen to be necessary to have regard to the magnitude of damage or potential damage to the party seeking disclosure and to the likelihood of repetition. Lord Bridge added (at 9–10):

> 'On the other side the importance of protecting a source from disclosure in pursuance of the policy underlying the statute will also vary within a wide spectrum. One important factor will be the nature of the information obtained from the source. The greater the legitimate public interest in the information which the source has given to the publisher or intended publisher, the greater will be the importance of protecting the source. But another and perhaps more significant factor which will very much affect the importance of protecting the source will be the manner in which the information was itself obtained by the source. If it appears to the court that the information was obtained legitimately this will enhance the importance of protecting the source. Conversely, if it appears that the information was obtained illegally, this will diminish the importance of protecting the source unless, of course, this factor is counterbalanced by a clear public interest in publication of the information, as in the classic case where the source has acted for the purpose of exposing iniquity.'

Applying such considerations to the circumstances of the case, the House of Lords seems to have had little or no doubt as to the need for disclosure. This was seen as necessary to prevent severe damage to the plaintiff's business whilst the importance of protecting the source was much diminished by the latter's complicity in a gross breach of confidentiality. The fact that Lord Templeman clearly did not regard the decision as a close run thing is apparent from the opening words of his speech (at 13):

> 'My Lords, the publication of the information given by the source to Mr Goodwin would have done no good to anybody but would have been partly inaccurate, partly misleading and wholly injurious to the business of the plaintiffs and the interests of their creditors, shareholders and employees. The article drafted by Mr Goodwin was a mixture of information which was not confidential and had already been made available to the public and information derived from the source which Mr Goodwin had been unable to check and which he ought to have recognised as both confidential and damaging. The use of stolen material by the source was wholly irresponsible and either malicious or designed to forward the career of Mr Goodwin without regard to any damage thereby caused to the plaintiffs. It is necessary for the source to be revealed so that the plaintiffs can take steps to ensure that the source does not remain in the position in which he may by disclosing confidential information cause serious damage to the plaintiffs.'

Obviously, views will differ as to whether the courts in general and the House of Lords in particular accord sufficient importance to the protection of sources. Understandably, many journalists believe that they do not (see, for example, Bernard Levin's polemical article 'In contempt, and with reason' in *The Times*, 7 February 1991). What is undeniable is that most of the reported cases on s 10 of the Contempt of Court Act have led to disclosure being required.

A further aspect of the proceedings in the *Morgan Grampian* case concerned the position of a party in contempt. The background is that there is a general and long-standing rule of uncertain scope whereby a court has a discretion to decline to hear a party who had refused to purge his contempt. For example, in a leading case, (*Hadkinson v Hadkinson* [1952] 2 All ER 567), the Court of

Appeal declined to hear a mother who was in contempt of an earlier order not to take a child out of the jurisdiction.

In proceedings such as those in the present case, the application of this rule may cause difficulty in that the journalist is, of course, maintaining that he is protected against disclosure by s 10. Hence, in order to meet this problem the Court of Appeal had adopted the sensible expedient of allowing William Goodwin to place his notes in a sealed envelope to be opened only if he was unsuccessful in his appeal. When he refused to comply with such an order the Court adopted what Lord Bridge was later to describe (at 12) as 'an incongruous procedure' of declining to hear his counsel in support of his appeal whilst entertaining and dismissing the appeal and giving leave to appeal to the House of Lords. The court heard full argument from counsel for the publishers. The House of Lords found that this was not a proper exercise of the discretion, although a simple refusal to entertain the appeal would have been. In the opinion of Lord Oliver (at 15) the contempt, 'however motivated, is as clearly contumacious as a contempt can well be'. His Lordship added:

> 'Moreover, a litigant who demands to use the machinery of the court whilst at the same time denying its authority over him and who puts his opponent to the expense of resisting an appeal in circumstances in which successful resistance can produce only an academic result may, I think, quite properly be said to be abusing the process of the court.'

In the result, the House concluded that it should, on balance, hear Mr Goodwin's appeal.

On a point of more general application, the House favoured a flexible approach in exercising the discretion such as that favoured by Denning LJ in *Hadkinson*'s case. This is preferable to the alternative of a strict rule which is subject to relatively closely defined exceptions.

As a footnote, one can add that Mr Goodwin continued to maintain his position and that Hoffmann J eventually imposed a fine of £5,000 (see *The Times*, 11 April 1990). One assumes that any such fine would be paid by the publishers and it is unclear whether it would have a significant deterrent effect. On the other hand, the alternative of imprisonment is not an attractive one although it was adopted at the time of the Vassall affair (see *A-G v Mulholland* [1963] 1 All ER 767 and *A-G v Clough* [1963] 1 All ER 420). Ultimately, the only solution is likely to lie in persuading journalists that they should re-examine their position. No-one can seriously argue for total protection in all circumstances. Parliament has recently struck the balance in s 10 of the 1981 Act and it is the role of the judges to interpret and apply this. One can argue (although I do not do so) that they do this without paying sufficient attention to the public interest in a full and informed press – even that they have emasculated the protection which Parliament intended to give. The solution is then to seek to persuade the courts that they are wrong.

Directors and civil contempt

In two recent and interesting cases the courts have been concerned with the liability of directors where a company is in breach of an injunction or undertaking. In the first such case, *Director-General of Fair Trading v Buckland* [1990] 1 All ER 545, Anthony Lincoln J was concerned with the determination of a preliminary issue involving the scope and effect of RSC Ord 45, r 5(1), which provides that:

> 'Where . . . (b) a person disobeys a judgment or order requiring him to abstain from doing an act, then, subject to the provisions of these rules, the judgment or order may be enforced by one or more of the following means . . . (ii) where that person is a body corporate, with the leave of the Court, a writ of sequestration against the property of any director or other officer of the body; (iii) subject to the provisions of the Debtors Act 1869 and 1878, an order of committal against that person or, where that person is a body corporate, against any such officer.'

Companies employing two named directors were allegedly in breach of orders of and undertakings given to the Restrictive Practices Court. Both the directors knew of the orders, but it was not alleged that they had been actively involved in any breach or that there had been any failure to investigate or supervise on their part. As Anthony Lincoln J put it (at 547), 'The argument [for the Director General] seems to amount to this, that the director who knows of the making of an order is by virtue of his office amenable to the contempt jurisdiction'. His Lordship refused to accept that such mere passivity was sufficient and concluded that: 'Resort can be had to r 5 only if he can otherwise be shown to be in contempt under the general law of contempt.' In this context this seems to require something in the nature of an assisting in or procuring of the breach or an intent to interfere with the administration of justice. Although it might be thought that stringent requirements are by no means inappropriate when such a 'draconian and far reaching provision' is involved, textbook writers had not read such a limit into the scope of Ord 45 (see eg Miller, *Contempt of Court* (2nd edn, p 436) and Borrie and Lowe, *Law of Contempt* (2nd edn, p 402)).

In the later case of *A-G for Tuvalu v Philatelic Distribution Corp Ltd* [1990] 2 All ER 216, the requirement was diluted or at least reinterpreted by the Court of Appeal. Here the background was the world of stamp dealing and the apparent willingness of collectors to pay a premium for flawed or 'funny' stamps – although not, of course, when such flaws have been deliberately mass-produced. The appellant, Clive Feigenbaum, operated a stamp business through a number of companies, including PDC. Both the company and he personally had, inter alia, given certain undertakings to the court (Henry J) and contempt proceedings were instituted when, it was alleged, these were broken. Dealing with the position of Feigenbaum in relation to the breach of the undertaking given by the company, Woolf LJ summarised the general position by saying (at 222):

> 'In our view where a company is ordered not to do certain acts or gives an undertaking to like effect and a director of that company is aware of the order or undertaking he is under a duty to take reasonable steps to ensure that the order or undertaking is obeyed, and if he wilfully fails to take those steps and the order or undertaking is breached he can be punished for contempt. We use the word "wilful" to distinguish the situation where the director can reasonably believe some other director or officer is taking those steps.'

Later, he added (at 223): 'There must be some culpable conduct on the part of the director before he will be liable to be subject to an order of committal under Ord 49, r 5; mere inactivity is not sufficient.' Then, having referred to the view expressed by Anthony Lincoln J in the *Buckland* case (see above), he said (at 223):

> 'That remark was, however, made in a case where there was no finding made against the director of culpable conduct and it should not be taken as meaning that it is only where a director has actively participated in the breach of an order or undertaking that Ord 45, r 5 can apply. If there has been a failure to supervise or investigate or wilful blindness on the part of a director of a company his conduct can be regarded as being wilful and Ord 45, r 5 can apply.'

The word 'wilful' is hardly a precise one when used in this or any other context. Indeed, it used to appear in the old pre-1966 version of Ord 45, r 5(1) but was then abandoned – now, it seems, to be reintroduced (by the courts) as the basis of a director's liability for a company's breach. On the facts of the case, the Court of Appeal had no difficulty in agreeing that Feigenbaum was liable to punishment for the company's breach. It was found unnecessary to decide whether he was also in breach of his personal undertakings. A £3,000 fine was upheld, but a three months' committal to prison was set aside.

Mental health review tribunals

In last year's Annual Review a brief reference was made (at p 71) to the decision of the Court of Appeal in *Pickering v Liverpool Daily Post and Echo Newspapers plc* ([1990] 1 All ER 335), holding that a mental health review tribunal is a 'court' for the purposes of s 19 of the Contempt of Court Act 1981. The case went on further appeal to the House of Lords ([1991] 1 All ER 622) which allowed the appeals of the newspapers involved. The House confirmed that such a tribunal is a 'court' and that inflammatory public comment might create a substantial risk of serious prejudice to its proceedings for the purposes of the strict liability rule. However, it also disagreed with other important aspects of the Court of Appeal's decision, most notably in relation to the extent to which it was permissible to report about applications to such tribunals and about the results of their deliberations. In the circumstances it seems preferable to leave more detailed discussion until next year's Review.

Press freedom and wards of court

In previous editions of this Review reference has been made to the tensions which can arise when the news media wishes to report on matters which affect wards of court. A modern example is to be found in *Re L (a minor) (wardship: freedom of publication)* [1988] 1 All ER 418, All ER Rev 1988, pp 79–80) where Mrs Justice Booth was concerned with publicity in relation to a ward whose parents had been killed in the Zeebrugge ferry disaster. Similar issues arose in *Re M and another (minors) (wardship: freedom of publication)* [1990] 1 All ER 205 (discussed in Family Law, p 144 below and see also (1990) 106 LQR 372–5) against the background of children being removed from foster parents following allegations of sexual abuse.

In recent years the courts have developed very wide ranging injunctions enjoining the news media from publishing details which might affect the welfare of wards in such cases. Yet the area remains one of great difficulty since, with the obvious concern for the children involved, it is all too easy to overlook the plight of those who have been wrongly accused and whose children may have been removed without warning or explanation. It was this danger which concerned a respected local newspaper in the present case. The judgment of the Court of Appeal contains interesting discussion both of the limited scope of s 12 of the Administration of Justice Act 1960 and of the way in which injunctions should be drawn. In the result, a more limited injunction was imposed which would allow the news media to comment on the conduct of the local authority without identifying the children involved.

Contract

MICHAEL FURMSTON, TD, BCL, MA, LLM
Bencher of Grays Inn, Professor of Law, University of Bristol

Formation

There have been two extremely interesting cases on formation of contract this year. One is *Blackpool and Fylde Aero Club Ltd v Blackpool Borough Council* [1990] 3 All ER 25, in which the defendants, a council which owned and managed an airport, invited the plaintiffs, together with six other parties, to tender for the concession for operating pleasure flights from the airport. The invitation to tender required tenders to be submitted in the envelope which was provided and stated that the envelope was not to bear any identifying mark and that tenders received after 12 noon on 17 March 1983 would not be considered. The plaintiffs had been successful tenderers for the concession in 1975, 1978 and 1980 and were anxious to tender successfully again. They delivered their tender by hand into the Town Hall letter box at 11.00 am on 17 March 1983 but the letter box was not cleared by the council staff at noon on that day as it was supposed to be. Only two of the other parties invited to tender in fact did so. The plaintiffs' tender was, in fact, larger than either of these tenders and also embraced a wider range of aircraft.

The council excluded the plaintiffs' tender, believing it to have been submitted late and therefore in breach of their standing orders and awarded the contract to the higher bid of the other two tenders. When the error was discovered, the council at first sought to restart the tendering process but the successful tenderer objected to this, arguing that it had a binding contract for the concession. The council therefore decided to adhere to the award and the plaintiffs brought an action both in contract and in tort.

The trial judge held that the plaintiffs succeeded in their contract claim. At first sight this is surprising, since the invitation to tender, as such documents usually do, explicitly stated that the council did not undertake to accept any tender or to accept the highest tender or indeed any tender at all. Neverthless, the Court of Appeal thought that although the council was not under an obligation to accept any tender or to accept the highest tender, that did not mean it was under no obligation at all. It was implicit in the adoption of a well established and well tried system that the council undertook to consider all the tenders submitted before the deadline. Any enquiry of the parties before tendering began as to whether all timely tenders would be considered would have received the classic reply 'of course'.

Perhaps fortunately for the consideration of the question of principle, the parties had agreed to try the issues of liability and quantum of damage separately. In many cases of this kind it would be difficult for a plaintiff to establish any real loss but on the present facts the plaintiff would appear to have lost a real chance of being awarded the concession.

The second case, *Williams v Roffey Bros & Nicholl (Contractors) Ltd* [1990] 1 All ER 512, involved the Court of Appeal in revisiting the classic chestnut of

Stilk v Myrick (1809) 2 Camp 317, 170 ER 1168 which has been familiar to many generations of law students. Much turns on the precise facts of the case which must therefore be set out with some care. The defendants were a firm of building contractors who entered into a contract for the refurbishment of a block of 27 flats. They subcontracted to the plaintiff the carpentry work for a price of £20,000. In retrospect, this was too low a figure, but neither plaintiff nor defendant appears to have realised this at the time. The plaintiff was paid money on account. Some months into the contract, the plaintiff having finished the carpentry in nine of the flats and done preliminary work in all the rest but having received some £16,200 on account, found that he was in financial difficulties. The difficulties were caused partly by the original under-estimate of the cost of doing the work and partly by faulty supervision by the plaintiff of his workmen. The plaintiff and the defendants had a meeting at which the defendants agreed to pay the plaintiff a further £10,300 at a rate of £575 per flat as each flat was completed. The defendants were anxious that the plaintiff should carry on with the work, since if the plaintiff had defaulted and they had had to agree to hire another carpenter there was an excellent chance that the defendants would be late and would have to pay liquidated damages under the main contract. The plaintiff at no stage threatened not to complete the contract.

The plaintiff carried on and finished some eight further flats but only one further payment of £1,500 was made. The plaintiff stopped work and brought an action claiming extra payment. The defendants denied liability.

In several modern cases of this kind the plaintiff has, in effect, threatened to break the contract unless paid more and has been held to be guilty of economic duress. No question of economic duress arose on the facts of the present case, since the plaintiff had never made any threats but had simply thrown himself on the mercy of the defendants. The defendants' argument was that there was no consideration for their promise to pay an extra £575 per flat because the plaintiff was in any event under a clear contractual obligation to finish the work without extra payment. The Court of Appeal held that the plaintiff's action succeeded. Glidewell LJ said:

> 'The present state of the law on this subject can be expressed in the following proposition:
>   (i) If A has entered into a contract with B to do work for, or to supply goods or services to, B in return for payment by B, and
> (ii) At some stage before A has completely performed his obligations under the contract B has reason to doubt whether A will, or will be able to, complete his side of the bargain, and
> (iii) B thereupon promises A an additional payment in return for A's promise to perform his contractual obligations on time, and
> (iv) As a result of giving his promise B obtains in practice a benefit, or obviates a disbenefit, and
>   (v) B's promise is not given as a result of economic duress or fraud on the part of A, then
> (vi) the benefit to B is capable of being consideration for B's promise, so that the promise will be legally binding.'

This statement has been criticised by one distinguished Antipodean critic as 'remote from received learning' – Coote, 3 *Journal of Contract Law* 23 at 24.

It is clear that a contracting party who finds himself in the position in which the defendants did in this case has many good business reasons for thinking that it makes sense to pay more to guarantee performance than to stand on its strict contractual rights. The law of contract does not, of course, say that parties must stand on their contractual rights. So there would seem to be no doubt that if the defendants had actually paid the extra money it could not have been recovered, not having been extracted by economic duress. Traditional analysis, however, has usually required some demonstration of fresh consideration in the shape of something to which the promisor was not previously entitled. Arguably, there are traces in the reasoning of the other judges in the court of such fresh consideration. Russell LJ speaks of:

> 'a need to replace what had hitherto been a haphazard method of payment by a more formalised scheme involving the payment of the specified sum on the completion of each flat.'

Purchas LJ said:

> 'it was further agreed that the sum of £10,300 was to be paid at the rate of £575 per flat on completion of each flat. This arrangement was beneficial to both sides. By completing one flat at a time rather than half completing all the flats the plaintiff was able to receive moneys on account and the defendants were able to direct their other trades to do work in completed flats which otherwise would have been held up until the plaintiff had completed his work.'

(It should be noted that there was no express agreement under the original contract for stage payments though extensive stage payments had in fact been made.) These are the sort of vestigial extra benefits which judges have often relied on in the past in order to discover fresh considerations where they considered that the merits required that the promisor be held to his fresh bargain. On the other hand, it must be frankly stated that there is no hint in the judgments of Russell and Purchas LJJ of significant disagreement from Glidewell LJ. It looks, therefore, as if commentators will have to rewrite the relevant section of their books though it may be doubted whether many cases will actually be decided differently as a result.

Contents of the contract

The facts of the next two cases, or something very like them, have appeared in many examination papers in the past. Teachers of the law of contract will recognise that the typical examinee often has difficulty in classifying what part of the book he should be regurgitating when confronted with such facts. It is interesting to see, therefore, that similar difficulties occur in real life.

In *Harlingdon and Leinster Enterprises Ltd v Christopher Hull Fine Art Ltd* [1990] 1 All ER 737 the defendants were a firm of art dealers owned and controlled by Christopher Hull and carrying on a business from a London gallery. In 1984 Christopher Hull was asked to sell two oil paintings which had been described in a 1980 auction catalogue as being by Gabriele Munter, who was an artist of the German Expressionist School. Christopher Hull had no experience or training which would have enabled him to form an independent judgment as to whether the paintings were indeed by Munter. He got in touch with the plaintiffs, amongst others. The plaintiffs were also art dealers but specialised in the German Expressionist School. Christopher

Hull told the plaintiffs that he had two paintings by Munter for sale and an employee of the plaintiffs visited the defendants' gallery to view the paintings. During the visit, Christopher Hull made it clear that he had not known much about the paintings and was not an expert in them. The plaintiffs' employee agreed to buy one of the paintings for £6,000. The invoice described the painting as being by Munter. In due course it was discovered that the painting was a forgery and the plaintiffs sought to recover their £6,000.

In fact, the plaintiffs formulated their claim on the basis that the contract was one for sale by description within s 13 of the Sale of Goods Act 1979 or that the painting was not of merchantable quality under se 14 of the Sale of Goods Act 1979. For a detailed discussion of these points see Commercial Law at pp 27–32 above. The purpose of the present note is to point out that it does not appear to have been argued that it was an express term of the contract that the painting was by Munter. It is not clear why not, since there was uncontradicted evidence that there had been an oral statement that the painting was by Munter together with a clear statement to that effect on the invoice. The facts are, of course, reminiscent of the well known case of *Leaf v International Galleries* [1950] 1 All ER 693 but there is a critical difference here, which is that the plaintiffs appear to have paid a price appropriate to a genuine Munter, whereas the buyers in *Leaf* do not appear to have paid a price which was remotely appropriate to a genuine Constable. One would have thought that this greatly increased the strength of the argument that the seller's statement that the painting was by Munter was intended to be contractually binding.

In *Leaf* the plaintiff buyer chose to formulate his argument in terms of misrepresentation rather than on the basis that the statement about the painting was a term of the contract. This was clearly related to a view that, if successful, a claim founded in misrepresentation would be more attractive than a claim founded on contractual terms. It seems to be tacitly assumed that in cases of this kind the plaintiff can formulate his claim either on the basis that the statement about the painting is an express term of the contract, or on the basis that it is an implied term (sale by description), or on the basis that the statement is a misrepresentation. There is clearly a latent problem here in the extent to which the plaintiff's freedom to formulate his claim is unlimited. Can a defendant who has sued on one basis claim that the plaintiff's analysis is wrong and that he should be formulating his claim in a different way? The answer seems to be that we don't know, because no defendant has argued in this way; no doubt the forensic difficulties of arguing that one might have been liable if sued on a different basis have deterred any defendants from pursuing their zeal for precise analysis. In our second case, the plaintiff formulated his claim in misrepresentation. Here again, arguments of express or implied terms would also have been possible.

In *Naughton v O'Callaghan* [1990] 3 All ER 191 the plaintiffs bought a thoroughbred yearling colt at the Newmarket sales in September 1981. They paid 26,000 guineas for a horse described in the catalogue as 'Lot 200 a chestnut colt named Fondu'. The colt was described as having a sire called Nomalco, whose dam was Habanna, whose sire in turn was Habitat. Habanna was a good class race horse which had won two races and Habitat was establishing a good reputation as a sire of winners and class horses. Fondu was put into training in Ireland and was entered in three races in 1982, all in Ireland, in which it did not do well. In 1983 Fondu was put into training in England and entered for three races but did badly in these as well. In June or July 1983 the plaintiffs discovered that Fondu was not the son of Habanna at all and that Fondu's dam was Moon Min, whose sire was First Landing and whose dam was Capelet. On the face of it the clear statements in the catalogue as to the pedigree, which are clearly of the greatest importance in the purchase of a potential racehorse, were hopelessly wrong and there would appear to have been a serious breach of contract. However, the evidence was that if the pedigree of Fondu had been correctly stated in the catalogue it would still have commanded a price very close to 26,000 guineas. Of course, by the time Fondu had been raced unsuccessfully six times it was clear that the horse was not worth anything like so much, but this was the result of its lamentable performance on the track and not of its breeding. There was therefore a plausible argument that although the sellers were in breach of contract, the buyers were only entitled to a relatively small sum by way of damages on the basis that damages should be calculated as the difference between the likely sale price of Fondu with correctly stated pedigree and the actual price paid. The plaintiffs sidestepped this difficulty by formulating their claim primarily as one in misrepresentation rather than in contract. This is discussed further below under Remedies, p 64.

Non disclosure

In *Banque Financière de la Cité SA v Westgate Insurance Co Ltd* [1990] 2 All ER 947 the House of Lords affirmed the decision of the Court of Appeal, which was considered in the 1989 Review at p 84, but on significantly different grounds ([1989] 2 All ER 952) (see p 23 above and pp 311–312 below for further discussion). It will be remembered that in this case a Mr Ballestero persuaded syndicates of banks to lend his company many millions of Swiss francs and that these loans were secured, partly, by gemstones (which later turned out to be virtually valueless) and partly by credit insurance policies covering failure by the borrowing companies to repay the loans. These policies were issued by the defendant insurers. The policies contained clauses excluding the insurer's liability in the event of fraud. This meant that the lenders could not recover the money they lent to Mr Ballestero's companies when he disappeared with it because the insurance policies themselves were unenforceable since they did not cover the risk of Mr Ballestero's fraud. However, it also appeared that the policies had been procured by an employee of the insurance broker falsely representing that the full amount of the loan was insured when in fact he had only held a cover note valid for 14 days, and that the insurers had discovered this deception but had not revealed it to the lenders. Both Steyn J ([1987] 2 All ER 923, sub nom *Banque Keyser Ullmann SA v Skandia (UK) Insurance Co Ltd*, All ER Rev 1987, pp 290, 311) and the Court of the Appeal had held that an insurer is just as much under a duty to disclose material facts to the insured as the insured is to the insurer. Steyn J had been willing to award damages for breach of this duty but the Court of Appeal thought that the only remedy for non disclosure was the setting aside of the insurance contract, which on the facts would have been a useless remedy for the insureds, enabling them only to recover their premiums. The Court of Appeal also rejected an alternative line of reasoning that the plaintiffs could recover damages in tort for negligently inflicted economic loss.

The House of Lords did not dissent from the view that the insurer is under a duty to disclose material facts to the insured but at this point their reasoning diverged from that of the lower courts. The essential thrust of the reasoning is that the banks did not lose money because of the fraud of Mr L, the agent of the insurance brokers, but because of the quite independent fraud of Mr Ballestero. Mr L had told lies about having obtained in full the three layers of insurance for the banks at a time when he had not obtained it (though he later did so) but since this insurance would have had a fraud exclusion which would have prevented a claim, and since the loss was caused by the fraud of Mr Ballestero, the banks were no worse off without the insurance than they would have been if they had had it. See p 23 above and pp 218, 311–312 below for further discussion of this case.

Illegality

The colourful facts of *Howard v Shirlstar Container Transport Ltd* [1990] 3 All ER 366 should guarantee it a permanent place in the lecture theatres. The plaintiff was engaged by the defendants to recover two aircraft which they had hired out for private use in Nigeria and which they wished to repossess as hire instalments were overdue. The defendants agreed to pay the plaintiff £25,000 'for successfully removing [each] aircraft . . . from Nigerian air space'. The plaintiff flew to Nigeria and found one of the aircraft. In due course he flew the aircraft out of Nigeria without Air Traffic Control clearance and in breach of Nigerian law. He flew the aircraft to the Ivory Coast where it was impounded and in due course returned to Nigeria, the plaintiff being allowed to proceed back to England. While in the Ivory Coast the plaintiff sent a telex to the defendants stating that he had removed the aircraft and they paid the first half of the £25,000. The plaintiff sued to recover the balance of the fee. The defendants raised two objections. The first, that as a matter of the construction of the contract the aircraft had not been removed since it was still in Nigeria, was quickly rejected by the Court of Appeal. The second, that the plaintiff was seeking to benefit from his own crime, presented much greater difficulty. If the facts so far stated had stood alone there can be no doubt that the plaintiff's action would have failed. However, the plaintiff gave evidence, which was not effectively challenged, that he had received advice, while in Lagos, from the head of the Federal Civil Aviation Department in Nigeria that the lives of himself and his fiancée, who was accompanying him as a wireless operator, were in danger if they stayed in Nigeria any longer. The Court of Appeal took the view that if the plaintiff's primary purpose was to escape from pressing danger, the conscience of the court would not be affronted by allowing him to recover the fee for the successful removal of the aircraft.

Termination

In *Cie Commerciale Sucres et Denrées v Czarnikow Ltd, The Naxos* [1990] 3 All ER 641 the House of Lords, by a majority, reversed a majority judgment of the Court of Appeal, which had affirmed a decision of Gatehouse J in the

Commercial Court, itself reversing the arbitral decision of the Council of the Refined Sugar Association. This diversity of judicial and arbitral opinion reflects the knottiness of the point involved. The buyers in this case agreed to buy 12,000 metric tonnes of white crystal sugar f o b stowed on the Assuc Sugar Contract No 2 form which incorporated the rules relating to contracts of the Refined Sugar Association of London. The delivery provision in the contract was:

> 'to one or more vessels presenting ready to load during May/June 1986, buyer to give seller not less than 14 days notice of vessel(s) expected readiness to load. Such notice to be given on a business day in sellers country prior to 16.00 hours London time to be effected that day.'

Rule 14 of the Rules provides amongst other things that in 'f o b stowed contracts the buyer has the option of taking delivery of the contract quantity in one or more lots during the contract period . . .' and in 'f o b contracts the seller shall have the sugar ready to be delivered to the buyer at any time within the contract period'. On 15 May the buyers gave notice for the *Naxos* to lift the full contract quantity, eta Dunkirk 29/31 May 1986. The vessel presented for loading on 29 May 1986 but no cargo was available. Despite repeated requests no cargo was available by 3 June 1986 and the buyers terminated the contract.

These facts presented two questions. The first was whether the contract, combined with the rules, imposed on the seller an obligation to have the sugar available for loading immediately on arrival at the ship after proper notice at the loading port ready to load. The House of Lords were unanimous that it did. This is essentially a question of construction of contract. The second question is of much more general interest and perhaps also greater difficulty. It is, granted that the seller was in breach of an obligation to have a cargo ready when the ship was ready to load, whether this breach was of a condition thereby giving rise to a right to terminate for breach. This was not a contract in which the obligation had been labelled by the parties as a condition, nor one in which previous decisions had so characterised it. The buyers' argument was that a careful consideration of the commercial structure of the contract required this obligation to be construed as a condition, since it would defeat the valuable rights otherwise given to the buyer if the seller could tender cargo at any time within the delivery period, subject only to the payment of damages. In the view of Lord Ackner, speaking for the majority:

> 'It was therefore essential for the buyers to be able to terminate the contract and buy it elsewhere if, when the notice expired and the vessel arrived, the sellers had not then the sugar ready for delivery.'

In a typically terse judgment Lord Brandon took the opposite view, relying principally on other provisions in the contract as to the effects of delay which did not entitle the innocent party to terminate, though the commercial significance of the provision seemed no less.

Remedies

In *National Bank of Greece SA v Pinios Shipping Co No 1, The Maira* [1989] 1 All ER 213, discussed in All ER Rev 1989 at p 89, the Court of Appeal held that once a bank unequivocally demanded immediate payment of outstanding sums and thereby closed the account, the relationship of customer and banker was replaced by one of creditor and debtor so that compound interest ceased to be payable in the absence of an express or implied agreement or binding custom. This decision has now been reversed by the House of Lords at [1990] 1 All ER 78. The respondents accepted that on the facts of the case the banks were entitled to compound interest from August 1977 until the date of the demand in November 1978 but they argued, and the Court of Appeal agreed, that the bank's entitlement to capitalise interest came to an end with the demand on 13 November 1978 so that they were entitled to simple interest up until the date of judgment on 2 March 1988. It is easy to see that very large sums would turn on this distinction, though only in a theoretical sense, since the respondents were not represented at the appeal, having run out of funds. The absence of an argument from the respondents may no doubt be said in a later case to weaken the authority of the judgment of the House of Lords. It is also important to emphasise that in the case no evidence was led as to the custom and practice of bankers (though this was hardly surprising since the trial judge allowed the respondents to raise this point after evidence in the case had been closed). Nevertheless, the single judgment by Lord Goff contains an elaborate examination of the authorities and seems entirely convincing. There was no reason to treat the banker/customer relationship as coming to an end because the bank had asked for its money back. If one may be permitted to say so, banks often ask for their money back as many customers could testify, but the banker/customer relationship continues, not perhaps unharmed, but nevertheless intact. See also Commercial Law at pp 17–20 above.

The remaining cases all deal with the assessment of damages. The facts of *Naughton v O'Callaghan* [1990] 3 All ER 191 have been set out above. In this case the plaintiff chose to formulate his claim as one of damages for misrepresentation. The plaintiffs successfully argued that because they had bought the horse because of a misrepresentation about its pedigree their decision to keep, train and race it was a natural result of the misrepresentation. If they had known the truth immediately after the purchase they could then have resold the horse and recovered nearly all the price but since they did not know, they kept it until it could only be resold at a much lower price, after performing badly on the track. They were therefore able to recover the difference between the purchase price and Fondu's value at the date of judgment. In addition, they were able to recover the training fees and cost of keeping the horse since, again, they would not have incurred this cost if it had not been for the misrepresentation.

Hussey v Eels [1990] 1 All ER 449 is another case on damages for misrepresentation (and is further discussed under Tort, pp 337–339 below). In this case the defendant had sold a bungalow to the plaintiffs in 1983. In response to one of the routine pre-contract enquiries they had negligently stated that the bungalow was not affected by subsidence. By the time the case had reached the Court of Appeal, liability was accepted and the question was to what damages the plaintiffs were entitled. The plaintiffs had paid £53,250 in February 1984. It was accepted that the cost of repair would be of the order of £17,000, which was the amount claimed by the plaintiffs. Again, by this stage it was accepted that if the plaintiffs had actually spent £17,000 repairing the bungalow they would have been entitled to receive it. However, the plaintiffs had chosen not to do this but instead had spent some considerable time and effort in seeking planning permission, had eventually obtained planning permission to demolish the existing bungalow and build two new bungalows on the site, and had sold the site with the benefit of the planning permission for £78,500 in 1986. The defendants argued that the plaintiffs had now not suffered a loss at all but indeed made a profit and they should therefore recover no damages. The trial judge agreed. This was surely on any view too generous to the defendants since it took no account of the movement in house prices between 1984 and 1986. Unless it could be shown that with £78,500 in 1986 the plaintiffs could have bought a bungalow as good as the one they thought they were buying in 1984 for £53,250 (ignoring for present purposes the plaintiffs' transaction costs) they had certainly suffered some loss. However, the Court of Appeal were clear that to go down this path was too generous to the defendants. The negligence which had caused the damage had not caused the profit. As Mustill LJ said:

'When the plaintiffs unlocked the development value of their land, they did so for their own benefit, and not as part of a continuous transaction of which the purchase of land and bungalow was the inception.'

The most interesting point in *Hayes v James & Charles Dodd* [1990] 2 All ER 815 was not argued as fully as it might have been because relatively little money was at stake on this point. The plaintiffs had bought a property for £65,000 intending to run a motor repair business from it. They had employed the defendant solicitors to act on their behalf in the conveyancing. There were two potential accesses to the property; one at the front, which was narrow and inconvenient, and one at the back, which ran over the land of a third party. Before the contract to purchase the property had been entered into both defendants and plaintiffs were aware of the possibility that there was no right of way over the access at the rear, but the defendants assured the plaintiffs that there was no problem as to this. They were negligent in so doing. Within a few days of the completion the owner of the property at the rear blocked off the access and this effectively made the business non-viable. In due course the plaintiffs closed the business down and sought to dispose of the property. It took them five years in all to do so. The plaintiffs formulated their claim for damages on the basis that they were entitled to be put into the position they would have been in if they had never entered into the transaction at all. This was accepted by both Hirst J and the Court of Appeal. The details of the calculation need not detain us here. The interesting point was whether the plaintiffs were also entitled to recover damages for the distress and vexation arising out of the transaction. As Staughton LJ pointed out, this distress was greatly increased by the decision of the defendants to deny liability for most of the five years between the purchase of the property and the case coming to trial. Staughton LJ said:

'I am not convinced that it is enough to ask whether mental distress was reasonably foreseeable as a consequence, or even whether it should reasonably have been contemplated as not an unlikely result from breach of contract. It seems to me that damages for mental distress in contract are, as a matter of policy, limited to certain classes of case . . . it should not, in my judgment, include any case where the object of the contract was not comfort or pleasure, or the relief of discomfort, but simply carrying on a commercial activity with a view to profit.' (at 824)

Swingcastle Ltd v Gibson [1990] 3 All ER 463 (also discussed in Tort, pp 339–340 below) is another case involving professional negligence. The plaintiff company specialised in making high risk mortgage loans. In 1985 it agreed to make a loan of £10,000 to mortgagors on the basis of a valuation of their house by the defendant surveyor who negligently valued the house at £18,000 on a forced sale with vacant possession. The survey was negligently carried out and it was agreed that if the plaintiffs had known the true value of the property they would not have made an advance at all since it was a matter of policy that they did not make loans on properties where the forced sale valuation was less than £15,000.

The mortgagors fell into arrears with repayments very quickly and in due course the plaintiffs obtained an order for possession and placed the property on the market for sale. The amount recovered by the sale was insufficient to meet the amount outstanding on the mortgage and the plaintiffs sued the defendant for the balance.

The major item which gave rise to dispute was the compensation which the plaintiffs sought for the interest which they had lost as a result of the transaction falling through. Under the terms of the mortgage, the annual percentage rate was 36.51% but in the event of default that rate was increased to 45.619%. Although there was evidence that the plaintiffs would not have entered into the transaction at all but for the negligent valuation, these interest rates do not represent loss which would have been avoided if the transaction had never been entered into, unless it could be shown that the plaintiffs could lend all the money which they could lay their hands on at such fancy rates. This seems intrinsically improbable and certainly the plaintiffs do not appear to have led any evidence to that effect. So the claim for interest must be on the basis that the plaintiffs were entitled to be put into the position they would have been in if the contract of loan had been perfectly carried out. However, the defendant had certainly not acted as a guarantor of the loan or even contracted that his estimate was correct. He had simply guaranteed that he had taken reasonable care in arriving at the figure. It is certainly not self evident that for breach of such an undertaking it is appropriate to award the plaintiffs compensation for loss of the very high interest they would have earned if the transaction had gone through. At least two members of the Court of Appeal clearly entertained doubts as to whether, on principle, it was correct to make such an award but considered that the question was, at least in the Court of Appeal, concluded in favour of the plaintiffs by the earlier decision of that court in *Baxter v F W Gapp & Co Ltd* [1939] 2 All ER 752.

Section 50(3) of the Sale of Goods Act 1979 provides:

> 'Where there is an available market for the goods in question the measure of damages is prima facie to be ascertained by the difference between the contract price and the market or current price at the time or times when the goods ought to have been accepted or (if no time was fixed for acceptance) at the time of the refusal to accept.'

As is well known, the application of this principle does not depend on showing that the seller has actually gone out into the market and sold the goods on the relevant day. The seller is entitled to stay out of the market and to sell at a later date. If he gets a higher price he is not obliged to bring it into the reckoning but, contrariwise, if he gets a lower price he cannot charge this to the buyer as an extra loss. This means that where the prima facie rule applies, questions of mitigation need not be examined. No doubt there may be exceptional cases in which either the seller or the buyer can point to what has actually happened as relevant for determining the loss.

There are a number of cases in which the meaning of 'available market' has been considered. *Shearson Lehman Hutton Inc v Maclaine Watson & Co Ltd (No 2)* [1990] 3 All ER 723 (also discussed at p 32 above) raised, however, what appears to be a wholly new point. In this case the defendants had agreed to buy tin from the plaintiffs and refused to accept delivery. The relevant date for considering damages was 12 March 1986 and the parties agreed that there was an available market for the tin on that date. This is hardly surprising since tin is regularly traded on a daily basis (collapse of the market excepted). However, in this case the amount of tin was 7,555 tonnes at a price of £70,203,130. The judgment does not state expressly what the average annual daily turnover of the market is but it is clearly implicit in the reasoning that if a seller were to attempt to sell a package as big as this on the market on a single day, this would have a strong downward effect on the market price. Webster J held that in order to show that there was an available market it was not necessary to show that there were buyers on the market who would buy a package of this size on the day in question. It would be sufficient for present purposes to show that there were enough buyers in the market to absorb this quantity of tin if put on the market by a discreet seller over a period of a few days. For this purpose Webster J did not apply the price readily available in the market on 12 March for small parcels of tin but relied on expert evidence for what price could have been obtained by a seller putting the tin onto the market over a period of a few days around the 12 March, assuming that the market was in other respects stable. That this is a very impressionistic exercise is shown by the fact that the judge came to the conclusion that the fair market price was somewhere in the range from £3,000 to £4,000 per tonne and that the price which should be adopted for the purpose of calculating damages was £3,400 per tonne.

Limitation

Over the last 30 years many plaintiffs have been met with the argument that whatever the merits of their claim it was barred because they had not started their action sooner, even though at the time when the limitation period was said to have elapsed, the plaintiffs did not know that they had a cause of action. Arguments to this effect have succeeded in the House of Lords in *Cartledge v E Jopling & Sons Ltd* [1963] 1 All ER 341 and in *Pirelli General Cable Works v Oscar Faber & Partners* [1983] 1 All ER 65, (both discussed in All ER Rev 1983, pp 331-332) even though the result was clearly unjust. In both cases it had been said that putting the matter right is primarily a matter for Parliament and not for the courts. However, despite repeated attempts, Parliament has not been able to produce a statute which in this area produces sensible or workable results. The latest word from Parliament is the Latent Damage Act 1986, s 1 which inserts a new s 14A into the Limitation Act 1980. This provides a secondary three-year limitation period 'for any action for damages for negligence where facts relevant to the cause of action were not known at the date of the accrual of the cause of action'. Since 1986 there has been considerable discussion as to whether this section applies where a plaintiff formulates his claim in contract on the theory that there was a contractual duty to take care. In *Iron Trade Mutual Insurance Co Ltd v J K Buckenham Ltd* [1990] 1 All ER 808 Kenneth Rokison QC, sitting as a Deputy High Court Judge, held that s 14 A of the 1980 Act did not apply to actions framed in contract (see p 21 above and pp 218, 322 below for further discussion).

One of the few satisfactory decisions in recent years from the point of view of plaintiffs in this kind of situation is the decision of Olive J (as he then was) in *Midland Bank Trust Co Ltd v Hett Stubbs & Kemp* [1978] 3 All ER 571. It will be remembered that in that case solicitors acting on behalf of the grantee of an option negligently failed to register the option as an estate contract so that the grantor of the option was able to defeat it by selling the property to his wife who knew of the option but was not bound by it because it was not registered. In that case, Oliver J held that the plaintiff had concurrent actions in contract and in tort and that the tort action did not arise until within the limitation period. The Court of Appeal in *Bell v Peter Browne* [1990] 3 All ER 124 refused to follow this case. The plaintiff employed the defendant solicitors to handle his divorce. It was agreed between the plaintiff and his former wife that he would transfer his interest in the matrimonial home to her on the basis that when she eventually sold the house he would receive one sixth of the gross proceeds. The defendant solicitors failed to take any appropriate steps to protect the plaintiff's interest, for instance by taking a declaration of trust or mortgage. The court held that the tort claim arose at the time of the conveyance to the wife and failure to register, and that the contract action arose at the same time and was not an obligation of which there was a continuing breach. It was said that the *Midland Bank* case 'may be distinguishable on its facts'. This appears to be on the basis that in the *Midland Bank* case the solicitor had continued dealings with the client after the failure to register.

Criminal Law, Criminal Procedure and Sentencing

G J BENNETT, MA
Barrister, Senior Lecturer in Law, City University

BRIAN HOGAN, LLB
Barrister, Professor of Common Law, University of Leeds

CRIMINAL LAW

General principles

Mens rea – recklessness

'Unhappily', said Lord Lane CJ in *R v Morrison* (1988) *Times*, 12 November, 'there are now in the law of this country two types of recklessness according to the nature of the crime which is charged'. These two types are commonly referred to as *Cunningham* ([1957] 2 All ER 412) recklessness which articulated a subjective test (did the defendant foresee a risk of harm which he unjustifiably decided to take?) and *Caldwell* ([1981] 1 All ER 961) recklessness which while embracing the subjective test of *Cunningham* added an objective limb to it (was there an obvious – later to become serious and obvious – risk of harm to which the defendant gave no thought?).

No one quarrels with subjective recklessness; the defendant who consciously takes the risk of causing the harm that he does in fact cause is properly within the reach of the criminal law. Objective negligence, however, has its critics and its supporters. Essentially, objective recklessness brings the thoughtlessly stupid within the reach of the criminal law. And it may be worth recording that more than one stern academic critic of objective negligence, faced with the task of disciplining unruly but unthinking students, has been heard to say, 'You know, there may be something to be said for *Caldwell* recklessness after all'.

The Lord Chief Justice in *Morrison* did not say which variant of recklessness he preferred. What was unfortunate to him, it seems, was that we have no precise guidance as to which offences attract *Cunningham* recklessness and which attract *Caldwell* recklessness. The guidance offered by Lord Diplock in *Caldwell* seemed to extend objective recklessness only to cases where 'reckless', or its variants, appeared in a modern statute and appeared also to indicate that the *Cunningham* test was appropriate where 'malicious', or its variants, was used in the definition of the offence. Further guidance was offered by Lord Roskill in *R v Seymour* [1983] 2 All ER 1058 (discussed in All ER Rev 1983, pp 130–131, 138–141), when he indicated that recklessness should be given the *Caldwell* meaning in all offences which involve recklessness 'unless Parliament has otherwise ordained'.

The guidance of neither Lord Diplock nor Lord Roskill has been followed to the letter. Interpreting recklessness as to consent in rape, in the obviously modern context of the Sexual Offences (Amendment) Act 1976, the Court of Appeal in *R v Satnam & Kewal* (1984) 78 Cr App R 149 rejected the *Caldwell* test. And, pretty obviously, it cannot be applied to reckless representations for the purpose of obtaining by deception contrary to s 15 of the Theft Act 1968 because of the overriding requirement to prove dishonesty. So Lord Diplock's guidance has proved in some cases either unacceptable or inappropriate.

Lord Roskill's broader guidance has been considered in relation to common assault. Many teachers referred in their discussions with students to common assault as illustrating the problem to which the Lord Chief Justice referred in *Morrison*. We all know from *R v Venna* [1975] 3 All ER 788, that an assault can be committed recklessly and, while the court in that case evidently had in mind subjective recklessness, it was decided before *Caldwell*. Was it now up for grabs? The Diplock guidance is unhelpful on this but the Roskill guidance seems to favour objective recklessness for assault since Parliament has not 'otherwise ordained', at least if this means that Parliament otherwise ordains only where the definition of the crime contains the magic word 'maliciously'.

In *DPP v K (a minor)* [1990] 1 All ER 331, K, a 15-year-old schoolboy, took a phial of acid from the laboratory to the washroom, as he said, to test its reaction on toilet paper. Hearing footsteps approach he panicked and poured the contents of the phial into the hot air dryer. He intended to return later to wash out the drier but before he could do so another schoolboy used the drier and was burned when the acid was squirted into his face.

The magistrates dismissed charges against K under s 20 (malicious wounding) and s 47 (assault occasioning actual bodily harm) of the Offences against the Person Act 1861, but the prosecutor appealed against the dismissal of the s 47 charge. Directing the justices to convict, the Divisional Court, having referred to *Caldwell* and *Seymour*, held that the 'relevant' recklessness was of the *Caldwell* variety. K was thus guilty if he had created a dangerous situation and had decided to risk it or had given no thought to that risk.

Surprisingly, even astonishingly, the court was not referred to *Venna* and *R v Spratt* (1990) *Times*, 14 May, the Court of Appeal held that *K (a minor)* had been wrongly decided because *Venna* was still binding on the Court of Appeal and the Divisional Court.

In *Spratt*, the defendant had fired an air pistol from his flat and two pellets struck a girl who was playing outside. He pleaded guilty to a s 47 charge on the basis that his conduct was reckless in that he had given no thought to the risk of injuring the girl. Quashing the defendant's conviction on this count, the court said that the history of the interpretation of the 1861 Act showed that in relation to all its offences against the person, and not merely those which contained the word 'maliciously', the mens rea required proof of intention, or recklessness in the sense of foresight of the risk of the harm which ensued. Lord Roskill's broad statement in *Seymour* was obiter and did not cast any doubt on the correctness of *Venna*, a decision which had been approved by Lord Elwyn-Jones LC in *DPP v Majewski* [1976] 2 All ER 142 and by Lord Diplock in *Caldwell* itself.

So *Spratt* was greeted with a sigh of relief by the subjectivists; the Court of Appeal had firmly slammed this door against *Caldwell* recklessness.

Nevertheless, it remains the fact that we have two tests of recklessness and that this is unfortunate because we can never be quite sure where the goalposts will be placed next time. It is perhaps surprising in view of the criticism of *Caldwell* that the House of Lords has not yet been asked to reconsider it in the light of the 1966 Practice Direction on precedent. It must surely be the case that the House would replace the goalposts where they were placed by the Court of Appeal in *Cunningham*. The only losers would be the law teachers who would be deprived of a topic for an examination question. But they will be able to think of others.

Parties to crime

Even though the definition of intention is still somewhat blurred at the edges, it is settled law that murder is a crime of intention only and requires an intention to kill or cause grievous bodily harm: *R v Moloney* [1985] 1 All ER 1025 (All ER Rev 1985, pp 108, 110); *R v Hancock & Shankland* [1986] 1 All ER 641 (All ER Rev 1985, pp 108, 134). But what of a secondary party to murder (or any other crime which requires intentional perpetration by the principal)? Must the secondary party intend (or hope or know) that the principal will intentionally kill or cause grievous bodily harm as part of the agreed enterprise, or is it enough that the secondary party is aware that the principal may intentionally kill or cause grievous bodily harm during the enterprise?

In *Chan Wing-sui v R* [1984] 3 All ER 877 (All ER Rev 1984, p 94), the Privy Council expressed a clear preference for the latter or broader view to the former or narrower view. Since *Chan Wing-sui*, however, the Court of Appeal has agonised about the matter, sometimes preferring the narrower view and sometimes the broader. So far as the Court of Appeal is concerned, *R v Hyde* [1990] 3 All ER 892 appears to settle the matter in favour of the broader view since it was decided after reference to, and careful consideration of, its prior conflicting decisions.

But which view is preferable as a matter of principle? In favour of the narrower view, it may be said that it is harsh to a secondary party that he is guilty of murder if he is aware that (he is merely reckless whether) the principal may intentionally kill or cause grievous bodily harm whereas the principal incurs liability only if he intentionally does so. This conclusion might be said to be inconsistent with the rulings of the House of Lords in *Moloney* and *Hancock* that murder is a crime of intention only.

But *Moloney* and *Hancock* are concerned with the liability of the principal and say nothing of the liability of secondary parties, and it is submitted that the broader view taken in *Chan Wing-sui* and *Hyde* is right in principle. A secondary party must of course intend to aid the principal in the enterprise, a burglary or robbery say, that is expressly or tacitly agreed between them. If the agreement contains a provision, express or tacit, that the principal may intentionally kill or cause grievous bodily harm 'if necessary' or 'if resistance is encountered' or 'if police arrive on the scene' then there is nothing unfair or harsh to the secondary party in holding him liable for murder though he hopes (as no doubt the principal may be hoping) that force will not prove necessary or that their enterprise will not be resisted or that the police will not arrive. The secondary party can be heard to say that killing or causing grievous bodily harm was not part of the agreed enterprise in which case he is not a secondary party to acts of the principal to which he has not agreed. But he can hardly be heard to say that though he agreed to an intentional killing in a certain eventuality, he did not intentionally aid an intentional killing because he hoped that eventuality would not arise.

Conspiracy

Historically, English courts have been reluctant to extend jurisdiction in criminal matters beyond the balliwick of the island fortress. Typical of the Brits of course. After all, it is only the Queen's Peace that matters. So in *R v Keyn* (1876) 2 Ex D 63 the Court for Crown Cases Reserved held that English courts had no jurisdiction to try for manslaughter the German captain of a German ship whose alleged negligence had caused the death of a passenger on a British ship within British territorial waters. The fact that international law (a law which common lawyers instinctively mistrust even when they understand it) would have accorded the exercise of jurisdiction counted for nothing and it was Parliament that had to remedy the situation by the Territorial Waters (Jurisdiction) Act 1878.

There are exceptions. Homicide by a British citizen, treason and piracy are indictable here though no overt act takes place in this country. More recently, statutes implementing international conventions provide for jurisdiction in matters such as genocide and hijacking though no breach of the Queen's Peace is involved. But many crimes, most obviously crimes involving fraud and · drugs, have no international boundary. One country (or a citizen in it) is simply targeted from another. Both might be said to have a legitimate interest in the suppression of the crime. But what is the position at common law?

In *Board of Trade v Owen* [1957] 1 All ER 411, the House of Lords decided that a conspiracy in England to defraud persons abroad was not indictable here unless, possibly, the conspiracy was intended to cause loss to persons in this country or to produce a public mischief here. *Liangsiriprasert v US Government* [1990] 2 All ER 866 (also discussed at p 133 below), PC was concerned with looking down the other end of the telescope. Is a conspiracy entered into abroad to commit a crime in England (the country concerned was for the purpose of extradition proceedings assumed to be Hong Kong where the common law in this respect is equally applicable) indictable in England though no overt act takes place in England? Viewing the matter as one of principle, the Law Commission had taken the view (Law Com Working Paper No 29 (1970), para 96) that a conspiracy abroad to commit a crime in England should be indictable only if some overt act in pursuance of the conspiracy took place here. But the Privy Council rejected this limitation as, indeed, did the Law Commission in its subsequent Report on Jurisdiction over Offences of Fraud and Dishonesty with a Foreign Element (Law Com No 180, para 4.4). Given that crime is established on an international scale, there was nothing in precedent, comity or good sense requiring the performance of some overt act in England. Why should the authorities hold their hand until, say, terrorists who had planned abroad an attack here entered this country to plant their bombs? If a conspiracy could be proved, their extradition should be sought at once to forestal the risk of their slipping through the net and effecting their purpose.

It is difficult to quarrel with this conclusion. If there is a conspiracy to launch a terrorist attack in, or import drugs into, England the threat to the peace is not less potent because the conspiracy is hatched in Brussels rather than Birmingham. Moreover, the exercise of such jurisdiction appears to be entirely in accordance with international law under the so-called protective principle.

Attempt: mens rea

Attempt, it is sometimes said, implies intent. Though the crime attempted is one which may be committed recklessly, recklessness will not suffice for an attempt. So if X throws a stone at Y, realising he may break Z's window but not intending to do so, he may be convicted of criminal damage if he breaks Z's window but is not guilty of attempted criminal damage should the stone strike but fail to damage the window.

It is not entirely clear why this should be so. If it is a crime recklessly to break a window, why should it not be a crime simply because the stone recklessly thrown fails to break the window? The argument can be taken further. If there is a policy which justifies strict liability in the commission of a crime, why does not this policy equally justify a conviction for attempt? It is an offence for X to take a girl under the age of 16 out of the possession of her parents though he reasonably believes her to be over 16, but not an offence for Y in like circumstances to attempt to do so. What rational policy justifies the conviction of X for the complete offence and the acquittal of Y for an attempt to commit the offence?

But however logically attractive it may be to have the same mens rea for an attempt as suffices for the completed offence, this is not the law. 'To decide on what constitutes the mens rea in attempt', wrote J W C Turner (Kenny, *Outlines of Criminal Law* (17th edn) p 91):

> 'has not been a matter of difficulty since it is nothing more than a clear intention to perform the actus reus of some other crime. It should be noted that considerations of . . . "recklessness" have no place in the crime of attempt; still less is it relevant to discuss negligence. For whatever a man attempts to do he must intend to achieve if he is able to do so.'

This restricted view of the mens rea of attempt at least has the virtue of simplicity. But it is a view which has not gone unchallenged. Professor Glanville Williams argues (*Textbook of Criminal Law* (2nd edn) p 408) that while intention as to consequence is always required for attempt, recklessness as to circumstance would have sufficed for attempt at common law. So, he thought, if a man tried to have intercourse with a woman who does not consent, not caring whether or not she was consenting, he would be guilty of attempted rape.

But as to whether this would be the case under the Criminal Attempts Act 1981, Professor Williams confessed that he did not know, though he favoured the view that recklessness as to circumstance should suffice. The issue came before the Court of Appeal in *R v Khan* [1990] 2 All ER 783, where it was held that the trial judge had correctly instructed the jury that the defendant could be convicted of attempted rape if they found that he had tried to have intercourse to which she did not consent not caring whether she consented or not. It had been argued on behalf of the defendant that the words in s 1(1) of the Criminal Attempts Act 'with an intent to commit an offence' required for a conviction for attempt an intention to have intercourse intending it to be non-consensual, but the court rejected this view. Russell LJ said:

> 'The only "intent", giving that word its natural and ordinary meaning, of the rapist is to have sexual intercourse. He commits the offence because of the circumstances in which he manifests that intent, ie when the woman is not consenting and he either knows it or could not care less about the absence of consent.'

The court was far from saying that attempts may be committed recklessly. It acknowledged, citing its prior decision in *R v Millard and Vernon* [1987] Crim LR 393, that a charge of attempting to damage property being reckless whether the property would be damaged would be inept, as would a charge of attempted reckless arson or attempting to cause death by reckless driving since these are all crimes where 'no state of mind other than recklessness is involved in the offence'.

On a narrow view, *Khan* is an authority only on attempted rape but it must go further than rape for, at least implicitly, it recognises the distinction in attempts between consequence or result in the actus reus (to which intention is always required) and circumstances (to which recklessness may suffice). If so it is by no means clear that it cannot be applied to criminal damage. Suppose, for example, that X intentionally destroys Y's property being unsure whether Y has or has not consented and Y in fact has not. Such a case is indistinguishable from *Khan* and a conviction for an attempt must follow.

But the distinction between consequence and circumstance is not always easy to draw. In *DPP v Morgan* [1975] 2 All ER 347 the House of Lords appeared to define the consequence (or 'prohibited act' as it was referred to) in rape as not merely intercourse with a woman but as intercourse with a woman who does not consent. If the latter is indeed the consequence in the actus reus of rape, then on a charge of attempt intention should apply to the whole of the consequence as so defined. *Khan*, however, inferentially treats the woman's consent as a circumstance as to which recklessness suffices.

One other point. In *Khan* the victim did not consent to the intercourse. But suppose that she had, though the defendant did not know this, and had tried to have intercourse not caring whether or not she was consenting. Professor Williams considers this case too (op cit at p 409) and concludes: 'If one can commit a reckless impossible attempt, such a man would be guilty of attempted rape!' It is not entirely clear what function the exclamation mark serves here. Does it convey surprise or incredulity? It should convey neither. On the interpretation placed on the Criminal Attempts Act by the House of Lords in *R v Shivpuri* [1986] 2 All ER 334 (discussed in All ER Rev 1986, p 103) it follows that the defendant is guilty of attempted rape. On the facts-as-he-believed-them-to-be theory the defendant is clearly guilty of attempted rape if he believes that the woman is not consenting even though she consents in fact. It inevitably follows that he is guilty of attempted rape if he thinks there is a risk that the woman is not consenting even though she consents in fact. The former is an illustration of the new concept we now have of the 'thought crime'. The latter is the logical consequence: the 'half-thought crime'. Where will it all end?

Attempt: actus reus

Courts, commentators and commissions have for ages grappled with the problem of defining the actus reus of attempt. Some have espoused a first act theory which would punish as an attempt any act done by the defendant with intent to commit a crime, but this has been generally rejected as too wide. Some have espoused a last act theory which requires that the defendant should have performed the act penultimate to the commission of the crime, but this has been rejected as too narrow. Most now espouse a somewhere-in-between theory but the question is: exactly *where* in between?

The common law distinguished between acts of preparation which were not punishable and acts of attempt which were (sometimes referred to as the on-the-job theory) but this formulation was, perhaps, merely to state the problem and not to resolve it. The Law Commission's solution, embodied in s 1(1) of the Criminal Attempts Act, was to make punishable any 'act which is more than merely preparatory to the commission of the offence' but to this definition they added a novel rider. The rider, contained in s 4(3) is that where 'there is evidence sufficient in law to support a finding that [the defendant] did an act falling within [s 1(1)] the question whether or not his act fell within [s 1(1)] is a question of fact'.

This is, of course, a statement of the somewhere-in-between theory which leaves it to the jury, subject to a ruling by the judge that the defendant's act may be regarded as more than merely preparatory, to determine as a matter of fact whether the act is to be regarded as more than merely preparatory.

The Court of Appeal may therefore intervene if it considers that the trial judge was wrong in law in directing a jury that the defendant's act might be regarded as more than merely preparatory and it was on this ground that a conviction for attempt was quashed in *R v Gullefer* [1990] 3 All ER 882. The defendant had placed a bet on a greyhound and, realising during the race that he had backed a loser, he jumped onto the track and tried to distract the dogs in the hope that the stewards would declare a no race in which event he would be able to recover his stake. He was as unsuccessful in distracting the dogs as he had been in picking the winner; the stewards did not declare a no race and he lost his stake. As if that wasn't punishment enough he was subsequently convicted of attempting to steal from the bookmaker and sentenced to six months' imprisonment.

The defendant appealed. His counsel was minded to argue that whatever crime he had been attempting it was not attempted theft, but he abandoned this argument and submitted that the trial judge was wrong to have ruled that what the defendant had done was more than merely preparatory to committing the offence of theft. The court, and it is submitted respectfully entirely rightly, accepted that submission. It could not be said that when the defendant jumped onto the track that he was in the process of committing theft; he had not gone beyond mere preparation.

The court, having referred in effect to the first act and last act theories, pointed out that the words of the Criminal Attempts Act 'seek to steer a midway course'. The headnote to the case in the All ER report says that the court expressed the view that s 1(1) gives clear guidance as to when an attempt begins. In truth the Lord Chief Justice, delivering the judgment of the court, said that s 1(1) 'perhaps' gives as clear a guidance as possible as to when an attempt begins and it may be that one of these days the Lord Chief Justice will have cause to be grateful for that cautionary 'perhaps'. The actus reus of attempt begins, according to the court in *Gullefer*, when the merely preparatory acts come to an end and the defendant embarks on the crime proper.

But where does that leave us? Assuming a no race had been declared in *Gullefer*, would the defendant have taken a more than merely preparatory step when he set off for the bookmaker's stall, or when he joined the queue of punters waiting for refunds, or would he embark on the crime proper only when he presented his betting paper to the bookmaker?

At this point it is appropriate to consider *R v Jones (Kenneth)* [1990] 3 All ER 886. The defendant, bent on killing his ex-mistress's new lover, acquired a shotgun, shortened the barrel and test-fired it. Some days later he entered the back seat of the victim's car just after the victim had dropped off his daughter at school, told the victim he wanted to sort things out and then produced the loaded shotgun from a bag and pointed it at the victim. There was a struggle during which the victim managed to wrest the gun from the defendant. The defendant was convicted of attempted murder.

Examination of the gun showed that the safety catch was on and the victim was unable to say whether the defendant had placed his finger on the trigger. Nevertheless, the Court of Appeal, upholding the conviction, held, and once more rightly it is respectfully submitted, that the trial judge was right to rule that there was sufficient evidence for the jury's consideration so that it was a matter for them to decide whether in fact the acts were more than merely preparatory.

The court expressed the view that the acts of the defendant in acquiring the shotgun, shortening it and making his way to the school were no more than merely preparatory but 'once he had got into the car, taken out the loaded gun and pointed it at the victim with the intention of killing him' then there was evidence on which the jury could find that his conduct was more than merely preparatory.

Obviously right, but two points arise. The first is what the position would have been if the defendant had got no further than taking the gun from the bag, or no further than getting into the car? It is submitted that taking out the gun would be more than merely preparatory and that getting into the car may fairly be regarded as more than merely preparatory, for he has now embarked on the crime proper just as much as an armed man entering a bank may fairly be said to have embarked on the robbery though some moments may elapse and further acts have to be done by him before the bank staff become aware of his intentions.

The second point concerns the jury's determination. In *Jones* it was open to the jury to take the view that since the defendant had not released the safety catch they did not regard his acts as more than merely preparatory. So it is possible that, on the facts of *Jones*, while the jury at Leicester Crown Court convicted the defendant, a jury at Leeds Crown Court may have acquitted him. This seems, however, to be an inevitable, and unfortunate, consequence of the Criminal Attempts Act.

And just suppose the jury in *Gullefer* had returned to the court where the foreman informs the judge that while some of their number take the view that the defendant's acts were more than merely preparatory even though he had not released the safety catch, others of their number are minded to the view that the safety catch should have been released before the conduct could be regarded as more than merely preparatory. How is the judge to instruct the jury? Must he lamely say – 'Well, that's a matter for you to decide; you'll have to argue it out between yourselves.'? Or does he helpfully say – 'Just toss a coin.'?

Offences against property

Theft

To support a charge of theft it must, of course, be proved that the property was property 'belonging to another' and by s 5(1) of the Theft Act 1968 property belongs to any person having 'possession or control of it, or having in it any proprietary right or interest'. In the usual run of case this must be one of the easier elements in theft for the prosecution to prove but there was nothing very usual about the issue as it arose in *R v Hancock* [1990] 3 All ER 183 (see also p 129 below).

The issue concerned treasure trove, which may be shortly defined as articles of gold or silver hidden by an owner with a view to their subsequent recovery and where neither the owner nor his successors in title are known. Such articles belong to the Crown and may be stolen from the Crown. In *Hancock* the defendant admitted to the police that using a metal detector he had found some ancient coins on a site near Guildford. He said the coins were scattered about, thus suggesting that the coins were dropped there at different times by different people, but he acknowledged that they might have been part of one hoard which had been scattered by subsequent ploughing of the land. The expert evidence was conflicting. That called by the defence was to the effect that the site had been a religious one and the coins had been left by people as sacrifices or votive offerings with no intention to retrieve them. That called by the prosecution suggested there was at least a possibility that the coins had been deposited by someone who intended to retrieve them.

The trial judge directed the jury that the Crown had a proprietary right or interest in the coins on the basis that the Crown had an interest in ascertaining whether or not the coins were treasure trove and that the key issue was whether there was a real possibility that the coins might be found to be treasure trove. The defendant was convicted but the conviction was inevitably quashed. It hardly suffices to prove that there is a real possibility that the goods alleged in the indictment to have been stolen belong to another; the jury must be sure that the goods belong to another before they can convict. Moreover, a claim to a proprietary interest can hardly amount to a proprietary interest; either the coins were treasure trove in which case the Crown had a proprietary interest, or they were not treasure trove and the Crown had no proprietary interest whatsoever.

Perhaps it would have been better for the prosecution to have alleged that the defendant stole the coins from the owner of the land but the court did not think this would provide a sure path to conviction, partly because of the confused state of the authorities on title to things found in or on land and partly because dishonesty might be difficult to establish. The former objection is, with respect, a weak one. The authorities may not be wholly consistent but a landowner surely intends, at the very least, to exclude trespassers from his land and what is in it or on it just as much as he intends to exclude them from whatever is in his house. His intention to exclude gives him a proprietary interest in whatever happens to be in or on his land.

The real mischief in a case like *Hancock*, however, lies not in a gain to the defendant at the expense of the Crown but in the despoliation of historic sites and the loss of possibly priceless artefacts to the nation (the coins in *Hancock* which are now happily in the British Museum were said to be unique). The Ancient Monuments and Archaeological Areas Act 1979 makes it an offence to use a metal detector without the written consent of the Secretary of State in a place which is a scheduled monument or is situated in an area designated to be of archaeological importance, or to remove any object discovered by use of the detector. It does not appear in *Hancock* whether the site had been so designated but, if it had, the way to conviction would not have been obscured by issues of ownership and dishonesty.

Public order offences

Breach of the peace

The Police and Criminal Evidence Act 1984 contains an extensive, though not comprehensive, restatement of powers of arrest. Left out of the Act was any reference to the common law power to arrest for breach of the peace and when asked during the passage of the Bill why this should not be put in a statutory form, Mr Mayhew, on behalf of the government, replied that this was not acceptable because, as he put it, 'the common law basis of the power provides the police with a degree of flexibility, particularly when responding to situations requiring urgent attention which is not readily susceptible to precise statutory formulation'. Reading this in Hansard one might have expected an editorial observation to the effect that civil libertarians in the House threw copies of the Bill of Rights at Mr Mayhew who was lucky to escape with his life. But not a bit of it – his explanation was accepted without comment. The degree of 'flexibility' which the power accords was enriched in *McConnell v Chief Constable of the Greater Manchester Police* [1990] 1 All ER 423. This was a decision by the Civil Division of the Court of Appeal and arose from proceedings brought by the plaintiff for false imprisonment.

The police had been called to private premises, a carpet store, where the plaintiff refused the manager's request to leave. A constable then 'took the plaintiff out of the shop' but when they were outside the plaintiff attempted to re-enter whereupon the constable arrested him on suspicion that his conduct was likely to occasion a breach of the peace. The trial judge had ruled that a breach of the peace could at common law take place on private premises and it was this ruling that was challenged in the Court of Appeal.

It seems astonishing that this point had not come before the courts since 1189 but the court had no real difficulty in holding that a breach of the peace could be committed on private premises. There was no authority against this conclusion and what there was tended to favour it.

Now one thing is clear. It is that the police ought to be able to prevent conduct, even if it has not reached the stage of attempt, where the constable has reasonable grounds for suspecting that the suspect is about to commit an offence and if he does not act at once it may be too late to prevent it. This is clearly so where the conduct will result in physical injury to the person and whether on public or private premises, and, arguably, this power should extend to offences against property or, indeed, any offence. Preventing the commission of a crime is better than punishing its commission. Section 3 of the Criminal Law Act comes close to this by authorising any person to use reasonable force in the prevention of any crime and the section does not even hint at any distinction between crimes on public or private premises. Regrettably, s 3 does not make it clear that an arrest may be a reasonable preventive measure, nor does it specify what consequences follow. Despite Mr Mayhew's faith in the flexibility of the law's response by the ad hoc development of the common law relating to breach of the peace, it would be better to have clear statutory guidance. The wait-and-see development of the common law falls well short of being satisfactory.

Firearms

By s 5(1) of the Firearms Act 1968 it is an offence for a person to possess, without the authority of the Defence Council, any weapon of whatever description designed or adapted for the discharge of any noxious liquid, gas or other thing. The offence is punishable on indictment with imprisonment for five years and/or a fine.

In *R v Bradish* [1990] 1 All ER 460, the defendant, who had been arrested in connection with another matter, was on search found to have in his possession a container of CS gas. At his trial on a charge under s 5(1) the defendant's counsel sought a ruling whether the offence required mens rea or was an offence of absolute liability. On the trial judge ruling that it was an offence of absolute liability the defendant pleaded guilty.

On appeal the defendant's contention that the trial judge was wrong so to rule was rejected and his conviction was affirmed. The offence, in the opinion of the court, had the hallmarks of an offence of absolute liability. There was, as the court admitted, a presumption in favour of mens rea, but this was displaced in the case of the offence under s 5(1) because (a) other offences under the Act provided a defence if the defendant could show he lacked mens rea and s 5(1) did not; (b) there was no general 'half-way house' provision (namely, proof of taking due care) as under the Misuse of Drugs Act; and (c):

> 'the possibilities and consequences of evasion would be too great for effective control, even if the burden of proving lack of guilty knowledge were to be on the accused . . . Just as the Chicago style gangster might plausibly maintain that he believed his violin case to contain a violin, not a sub-machine-gun, so it might be difficult to meet a London lout's assertion that he did not know an unmarked plastic bottle in his possession contained ammonia rather than something to drink.'

Oh dear.

What if the recipient of the violin case or the container had not been 'a Chicago-style gangster' or a 'London lout' but a distinguished professor of law or an even more distinguished High Court judge? Would the case have been decided in the same way if the Lord Chief Justice had been handed by a mischievous professor of law a tin of what to all appearances contained nothing more lethal than a pint of Tetley's bitter only to find that it contained, and was designed to discharge, CS gas?

And what was the point of imposing strict liability? The court says, in effect, that the point of it is that it would be easy for an accused to maintain lyingly but convincingly that his possession was innocent. In other words, there are some issues of fact which we cannot trust the jury to determine correctly. It seems we can trust a jury to follow a complex fraud trial for weeks or months and determine the issue of dishonesty but not whether the defendant believed that a can would discharge beer or CS gas. In any case the issue of knowledge has to be determined as it was by the trial judge by way of a *Newton* hearing. He found that the defendant knew perfectly well that he was in possession of a CS gas canister. Without determining that issue against the defendant there would have been no rational basis for imposing a suspended sentence of imprisonment.

CRIMINAL PROCEDURE

Appeal

The unambiguous message of *R v Pinfold* [1988] 2 All ER 217 (All ER Rev 1988, p 99) was that a defendant normally has only one chance of a hearing when it comes to a criminal appeal. In *R v Shama* [1990] 2 All ER 602 the boot was, so to speak, on the other foot. What if the Court of Appeal itself wishes to have an appeal re-heard?

The difficulty arose because, after full argument on an appeal against conviction for an offence contrary to s 17 of the Theft Act 1968, the court failed to reach a unanimous conclusion. As a result it was directed that the appeal should be relisted for a de novo hearing before another differently constituted division of the court. At the relisted hearing counsel for the appellant took the point that the court so constituted had no jurisdiction to hear the appeal. The point was not decided by the court who in the event referred the matter back to the original court which then disposed of the case. What is left undecided, therefore, is whether a differently constituted court could have heard the appeal afresh. There is no statutory authorisation for such proceedings but Lloyd LJ invoked the authority of the Report of the Interdepartmental Committee on the Court of Criminal Appeal (Cmnd 2755 (1965)) under the chairmanship of Lord Donovan. This refers to the practice of having a case re-argued before a five-judge Court of Appeal, where the majority view prevails, following a hearing before three judges where one member of the court has been for allowing the appeal. That committee considered that this was a measure in favour of the appellant which should not be changed. The court in *Shama* assumed that, even if the practice of relisting before a five-judge court had fallen into disuse, there remained the alternative of relisting before a three-judge court.

It is curious that such a point should have been uncertain and this case does nothing to dispel the uncertainty. It might be said, however, that there is no statutory provision which appears expressly to proscribe such a course. Given that it is a measure for the accused's benefit which Lord Donovan's committee chose to approve, there is something to be said for its adoption or retention. In the absence of any doctrine of desuetude in English law there can be little objection that recourse to this procedure has not been taken recently.

Bail

The offence under s 6(1) of the Bail Act 1976 continues to spawn procedural difficulties as is shown by *Murphy v DPP* [1990] 2 All ER 390.

The facts were not remarkable. After being arrested for three different offences the defendant was on each occasion granted police bail. He failed to surrender to the appropriate magistrates' court on each occasion so that bench warrants were issued. After being arrested, informations were laid against him in respect of his failure to surrender on the previous three occasions. At his trial it was submitted that the magistrates had no jurisdiction because the informations were time-barred under s 127(1) of the Magistrates' Courts Act 1980 which sets a six-months time limit. On the face of it, this was a valid submission. The magistrates, however, rejected it, being of the opinion that there was no time limit applicable to an offence under s 6(1).

The basis for the magistrates' opinion, and the object of critical attention in the present case, was the Divisional Court's decision in *Schiavo v Anderton* [1986] 3 All ER 10 and the *Practice Note* [1987] 1 All ER 128 to which the difficulties of that case quickly gave rise. Assiduous readers of the Review will no doubt recall that your reviewers at the time felt some misgivings about this decision (see All ER Rev 1986, pp 112–114, All ER Rev 1987, p 86).

Parker LJ in *Murphy* takes the opportunity to criticise the case after a careful analysis of the statutory provisions relating both to the Bail Act 1976 and the Contempt of Court Act 1981. In particular, the court makes the point that the wording of the Bail Act 1976 hardly supports the view that a magistrates' court has the power to deal with an offence under s 6(1) as if it were a criminal contempt. Similarly, little support can be gained from s 12 of the Contempt of Court Act 1981, which removed the previous inability of magistrates' courts to deal with contempt, a section somewhat remote from the concerns of bail and s 6(1). Parker LJ prefers the view that an offence under s 6(1) should be dealt with as a summary offence and not as if it were a contempt, a view supported, the court considered, by *R v Harbax Singh* [1979] 1 All ER 524. Nevertheless, it has to be said that Parker LJ's observations on *Schiavo v Anderton* are clearly obiter dicta and in any event it is doubtful if precedent allows the matter to be reconsidered by a later Divisional Court.

The practical result of the case law is therefore that in the event of failure to surrender to the Crown Court the offence will normally be dealt with as if it was a contempt. Where bail has been granted by the police the offence must be dealt with as a summary offence which therefore attracts the operation of the six-months time limit under s 127(1) of the Magistrates' Courts Act 1980. In the case of failure to surrender to a magistrates' court where bail has been granted by the magistrates, the offence will be dealt with as if it was a contempt and accordingly the strictures of s 127 do not apply.

It must be doubted if this rather odd result is really what Parliament intended but it appears to be the inevitable outcome of the court's earlier decision in *Schiavo v Anderton*.

Committal

A point that had given rise to divergent practices in magistrates' courts over the extension of custody time limits was disposed of by the Divisional Court in *R v Governor of Canterbury Prison, ex p Craig* [1990] 2 All ER 654.

The applicant had been charged with serious offences and was remanded in custody for 70 days, the maximum period for which he could be remanded prior to his committal for trial. After the defendant had consented to further remands it became clear that the prosecution would be unable to proceed even on the expiry of the most recent time limit. At this point the Crown Prosecution erred. They had still not served the committal papers nor had they given two days' notice of intention to apply for a further extension of the custody time limit as they were required to do under reg 7(2) of the Prosecution of Offences (Custody Time Limits) Regulations 1987. The prosecution's application for the custody time limit to be extended was successful, although strongly resisted by the defendant, and resulted in the matter coming before the court on a motion for habeas corpus.

Watkins LJ, understandably, took the view that reference in reg 7(4) to the fact that the magistrates can effectively waive the requirements of reg 7(2) on the grounds that it was 'not practicable in all the circumstances for the prosecution to comply' with the notice requirements related to the time when the notice should have been given. It would clearly have been difficult to accept the prosecution's contention that the time for determining whether it was practicable was the date of the application. Given that this was so, and the prosecution had failed to give proper notice, could the court nevertheless extend the custody time limit? The answer was 'yes'. The regulations were said to be directory not mandatory and did not prevent the magistrates exercising their basic statutory power under s 22(3) of the Prosecution of Offences Act 1985 to extend or further extend a time limit. In the event of an abuse by the prosecution they could always decline to exercise their discretion.

The court also took the opportunity to clarify a number of related issues. On the question of when a custody time expires it was stated that all custody periods begin at the close of the day during which the defendant was first remanded and expire at the relevant midnight thereafter. Second, the standard of proof embodied in the requirements that the court be 'satisfied' was said to be on the balance of probabilities. The court observed that this was the standard for determining bail applications and a similar standard should apply to the type of interlocutory question raised in these proceedings. Third, if the prosecution are uncertain whether or not they need to apply for an extension it may be desirable, but not strictly necessary, to give such notice unless there is a high likelihood of an application becoming necessary. Finally, the court remarked on the propriety of using habeas corpus proceedings in this case rather than exercising the more usual right of appeal to the Crown Court given by s 22(7) of the 1985 Act. Although this would ordinarily be the correct course to take, a motion for habeas corpus was justified in this case because of the existence of a number of points of pure law which were of general application and concern and which needed an authoritative decision.

Costs

Ten pounds was all that was nominally at stake in *R v Coventry Magistrates' Court, ex p Director of Public Prosecutions* [1990] 3 All ER 277, but the repercussions of this case could easily exceed £2,000,000. The DPP'S application for judicial review of the magistrates' decision arose out of the procedure under s 12 of the Magistrates' Courts Act 1980 to dispose of guilty pleas in summary offences in the absence of both prosecutor and defendant. In motoring cases, particularly, this must be one of those comparatively rare reforms from which all parties benefit. What no one had apparently made specific provision for was the recovery of the prosecution's modest costs in such matters. A practice had therefore grown up of adding beneath the Statement of Facts a claim for costs under s 18 of the Prosecution of Offences Act 1985. This had caused consternation amongst large numbers of justices' clerks, Yorkshire excepted, who had been refusing to place prosecution cost applications before magistrates in s 12 cases. Their concern was perhaps principally that they were at risk of stepping into the arena and doing the prosecutor's job without any express authority to do so.

The emphatic judgment of Watkins LJ makes clear that this practice is 'grossly improper'. Magistrates' clerks must draw the bench's attention to a prosecution claim for costs so that they can adjudicate upon it. The court did suggest that it might be better if the costs application appeared on a separate form which would certainly make clear that it had nothing to do with the Statement of Facts relating to the offence. Nevertheless, and this is surely correct, it cannot have been Parliament's intention in introducing the s 12 procedure to require that a prosecutor make a personal application for costs in each case. This would clearly significantly defeat the object of the legislation in providing a relatively expeditious and inexpensive mode of trial.

As a rather curious footnote to a case about costs, neither the court clerk nor the justices were represented before the court. This was because no provision exists for meeting their costs, should costs be awarded against them. The court described this situation as 'highly regrettable' and one 'for which a remedy must be found'.

Crown Court

Case stated

After their conviction by a magistrates' court the defendants in *Loade v Director of Public Prosecutions* [1990] 1 All ER 36 appealed to the Crown Court. At the commencement of the appeal counsel for the appellants made a submission that the information was defective. That submission was rejected but the Crown Court agreed to state a case on its ruling for the High Court before proceeding to hear the evidence. Such an unusual decision was influenced by the fact that the hearing before the magistrates had lasted 13 days and the hearing of the evidence in the Crown Court was likely to be prolonged. When the case came before the Divisional Court a preliminary question arose as to whether the court could properly deal with the matter at all. Section 28(1) of the Supreme Court Act 1981 provides for appeals by way of case stated in respect of 'any order, judgment or other decision of the

Crown Court'. Was the ruling of the Crown Court a 'decision' which gave the High Court jurisdiction to hear the appeal?

After a careful scrutiny of the practice of the courts and the legislative history of s 28 of the 1981 Act, the court came to the conclusion that it had no jurisdiction to hear an appeal until the Crown Court had reached a final decision. A 'decision' for the purposes of the section did not include a merely interlocutory decision. Even where the High Court does have jurisdiction to hear an interlocutory appeal from the Crown Court in civil cases, this jurisdiction should be exercised sparingly and only in exceptional circumstances.

The outcome of the ruling in *Loade* brings the Crown Court in line with the position in magistrates' courts. In *Streames v Copping* [1985] 2 All ER 122 (discussed in All ER Rev 1985, p 128) it was similarly decided that a magistrates' court had no jurisdiction to state an 'interlocutory' case to the High Court during a hearing.

Fraud

The Criminal Justice Act 1988 introduced a new procedure for helping to deal with serious and complex cases of fraud. In particular, s 7 of the Act enables a Crown Court judge to order a 'preparatory hearing' for certain specified purposes where it appears to him 'that substantial benefits are likely to accrue.' In *R v Gunawardena* [1990] 2 All ER 477 the defendants made an application at the preparatory hearing for a stay of the proceedings on the grounds that they had been prejudiced by the delay in commencing their trial. The judge dismissed the application with the result that the defendants sought to exercise their right to appeal under s 9(11) to the Court of Appeal, for which leave to appeal was required. The trial judge declined to grant such leave on the grounds that he had no jurisdiction to do so. The Court of Appeal held that he was correct.

The specified purposes in s 7 of the 1987 Act relate to assisting the judge's management of the trial and to identifying and clarifying the issues upon which the jury would be required to give a verdict. The defendant's argument was that s 9 enabled a judge to determine issues on the admissibility of evidence and 'any other question of law relating to the case'. This, it was said, was wide enough to embrace the submissions in the present case or presumably any other matter. On the wording of the provisions this was certainly a possible interpretation. Watkins LJ, however, took the view the Parliament could not possibly have intended:

> 'to allow a preparatory hearing to commence for a certain specified purpose and then permit, once a preparatory hearing for that purpose is in being, argument to range around all manner of issues which cannot be said to relate to any of the specified purposes.'

The result of the Court of Appeal's decision is therefore that the provisions of ss 7 and 9 of the Act are to be considered narrowly with a consequent restriction on the range of submissions which can properly be made at the preparatory hearing.

Magistrates

Bail

See *Murphy v DPP* [1990] 2 All ER 390, in Bail, p 81 above.

Bias

Although concerned with a licensing application, not criminal proceedings, *R v Bath Licensing Justices, ex p Cooper* [1989] 2 All ER 897 was mentioned in last year's Review (All ER Rev 1989, pp 109–110) for its interest in touching upon issues of bias which might surface in any hearing before magistrates. Under the name of *R v Crown Court at Bristol, ex p Cooper* [1990] 2 All ER 193 the Court of Appeal reversed the Divisional Court's decision.

What had weighed with the Divisional Court was the fact that, at the end of the day, there might be at least the appearance of bias if one applied the test in *R v Liverpool City Justices, ex p Topping* [1983] 1 All ER 490 (All ER Rev 1983, pp 160, 202–203). In view of the fact that the same licensing justice had sat on the first application for a licence to sell spirits and then on the appeal to the Crown Court from a second application it is understandable that the applicants should have felt some disquiet. The point, however, which the Court of Appeal stressed was that this was a licensing application, where a somewhat different approach to the issue of the appearance of bias is required. As Farquharson LJ put it ([1990] 2 All ER 198):

'. . . any licensing justice, whether sitting in his own jurisdiction or an appeal, not only will have considerable knowledge, but will be expected to have considerable knowledge of the licensing circumstances, policy and premises in the area for which he is responsible. In that sense the justice does not bring a fresh mind to any appeal on which he sits and is not expected to do so.'

It would not therefore necessarily be a disqualification from hearing an appeal that the justice knew the premises or had heard earlier applications by the same party.

The outcome of the case therefore underlines the distinction between the different approach to the issue of bias in criminal and civil proceedings before magistrates. In the latter, a degree of relaxation in the application of the rules of natural justice is acceptable to the courts in a way that it would not be were the proceedings criminal in nature.

If the only basis for this divergence of approach was the difference between civil and criminal proceedings it is hard to see how it could be justified. The effect of an adverse decision in a licensing application may be worse than a criminal conviction. The applicant in the former may be out of a job. If justice must be seen to be done, it can hardly 'appear to be done' in one and not the other. On the other hand, the point made by both Taylor and Bingham LJJ is that licensing magistrates perform both judicial and administrative functions. Since they are charged with making policy as well as applying it, 'They may properly have regard to that policy when hearing individual applications, so long as they consider fairly the merits of each case' ([1990] 2 All ER 199 a). It is not, of course, unknown for the requirements on natural justice to be relaxed when it has been thought that this was realistically unavoidable. The case of *Franklin v Minister of Town and Country Planning* [1948] AC 87 is a striking example, although it did concern the rather special case of a government minister. A less specialised example would be *Ward v Bradford Corporation* (1971) 70 LGR 27 where the court declined to quash the decision of a board of governors of a teacher training college to expel a student despite the fact that they had themselves instituted the proceedings against the woman. It must surely be the case, however, that such flexibility in applying the principle of *nemo index in sua causa* should be viewed as a jealously guarded exception to normal principle. The rather special position of licensing justices may provide legal colour for deviating from the rule, although it is difficult not to feel considerable sympathy for the applicants in such cases, who may well see things rather differently.

Committal

See *R v Governor of Canterbury Prison, ex p Craig* [1990] 2 All ER 654, in Committal, p 82 above.

Costs

See *R v Coventry Magistrates Court, ex p Director of Public Prosecutions* [1990] 3 All ER 277, in Costs, p 83 above.

Extradition

See the chapter on Extradition, p 132 below.

Summary trial

Two or more defendants are jointly charged with a single offence which is triable either way. The magistrates determine that the case is suitable for summary trial. What if one defendant elects trial on indictment? Must all the defendants then be committed for trial on indictment irrespective of their wishes? The clear answer given in *R v Brentwood Justices, ex p Nicholls* [1990] 3 All ER 516 is 'yes'.

This result certainly seems to flow inevitably from the proper construction of the statutory provisions, namely ss 19, 20, 21 and 25 of the Magistrates' Courts Act 1980. Even if it is not what Parliament meant it seems unavoidably the case that this is what it has said. Nevertheless, the court was acutely aware of the problems this interpretation poses. For example, as Watkins LJ observed (at 520):

> 'suppose out of 20 people charged with affray 19 express a wish to be tried summarily and one expresses the wish to be tried on indictment . . . all must be committed for trial.'

This is bad enough but the court gives another example borrowed from counsel's argument. What if a non-legally aided defendant elects summary trial?:

> 'is he to be put to the expense of going where he does not want to go, namely to the Crown Court to be tried on indictment, dragged there so to speak, by that person or those persons who have elected not to be tried summarily?'

The answer is now that he is. Clearly, these consequences could be characterised as, 'inconvenient, unjust perhaps, time wasting and needlessly expensive'. At the very least the law requires reconsideration if not reform.

There are, however, limits to this decision. It does not affect the fact that where a person is charged with two or more offences the loss of his right to summary trial on the jointly charged offence will not affect his right to elect to have the remaining offence or offences tried summarily.

In fairness to the magistrates who heard the original application it should be said that they came to the same result as the Divisional Court. Their reasoning however was encapsulated in the statement that:

> 'We agree with the prosecution with the age-old custom and practice whatever the words of the statute might say.'

This is, of course, a line of reasoning not open to magistrates' courts.

A *Practice Note* [1990] 3 All ER 979 now gives fairly detailed guidance on the factors to take into account when magistrates have to decide whether or not to commit 'either way' offences to the Crown Court. The Note makes the general point that either way offences should be tried summarily unless the court considers that the case has one or more of the aggravating factors and that its sentencing powers are inadequate. It does not affect the fact that it does only provide guidance and does not impinge on a magistrate's duty to consider each case individually.

Warrant

In *R v Bradford Justices, ex p Wilkinson* [1990] 2 All ER 833 (also discussed in Evidence, p 123 below) the defendant had been charged with a driving offence, his defence being that he was not the driver. On two occasions the relevant witnesses had failed to appear and so the defendant applied to the magistrates for witness warrants to be issued under s 97(3) of the Magistrates' Courts Act 1980. The magistrates declined to do so, being influenced by the need to avoid further delay and also being mindful of the quality of the evidence which a coerced witness was likely to give. The defendant was convicted and applied for judicial review of the magistrate's decision on the grounds that they had not exercised their discretion properly.

Not surprisingly, the Divisional Court considered that the magistrates had been in breach of natural justice. The witnesses were material and went to the critical issue in the defendant's defence. Whether they would have turned out to be credible witnesses was not the point.

On the merits and the law the decision of the Divisional Court would seem, with respect, to be entirely correct. The case is also noteworthy for the willingness of the court to consider such an application at all in view of the fact that there was available to the defendant an appeal to the Crown Court. On this, Rose J observed that where there has been a breach of natural justice in criminal proceedings before magistrates it may be appropriate to grant judicial review even if a right to appeal to the Crown Court exists. No authority to the contrary had been cited to the court.

Trial

Bias

Reference has already been made (p 85 above) to the issue of bias in the rather special context of magistrates acting as licensing justices. *R v Mulvihill* [1990] 1 All ER 436 concerned the rather different circumstances of a Crown Court judge in a trial on indictment.

The defendant was convicted of conspiring to rob various banks and building societies. One of the offences had taken place at a branch of a bank in which the trial judge owned 1,650 shares, a fact which was not disclosed in open court. The defendant appealed on the grounds that, had he known of the judge's shareholding, he would have objected to him conducting the trial.

The well-known case of *Dimes v Grand Junction Canal Proprietors* (1852) 3 HL Cas 759, in which a judgment of none less than the Lord Chancellor was set aside, illustrates the strictness of the rule against bias where the judge could be felt to have a direct pecuniary interest in the outcome of the proceedings. *Mulvihill* was not an example of this category where disqualification was automatic. Rather, it raised the issue of the appearance of bias where, as the court observed, 'the summing up is impeccable, the conduct of the trial is not open to criticism, the summary of the facts is accurate and sufficient, and the decision on the facts was a decision of the jury'. After a review of the authorities the Court of Appeal adopted the test in *R v Liverpool City Justices, ex p Topping*. Applying this test to the facts of the case, the question became whether a reasonable and fair-minded person in the court, knowing the judge held those shares, would have a reasonable suspicion that a fair trial was not possible. The court considered that such a remote interest would not have justified such a suspicion.

The court particularly noted that the function of a Crown Court judge is very different from that of a lay justice who is one of the primary decision makers in summary proceedings. An illustration is the subsequent case of *R v Cambridge JJ, ex p Yardline Ltd and Bird* [1990] Crim LR 733. In that case the defendants were convicted of offences arising out of the demolition of a listed building. A member of the bench which convicted the defendant was a chartered surveyor in a firm which had regularly acted for the District Council who was the prosecutor. This association was enough to quash the convictions on the grounds that there had been a breach of natural justice.

Nevertheless, a difficulty with this decision is that 'reasonable and fair minded' people do not always agree on matters of such delicacy, and one may wonder whether such a test gives proper weight to the feelings of the defendant. Suppose at the beginning of the trial the accused had objected to the judge's interest. Could the judge really have said that the fact that I am a shareholder in the company you conspired to rob does not affect me in the slightest? Perhaps he could. The difficulty might, however, be avoided if an accused had a right to a single peremptory challenge of the trial judge, as exists in some American states. This would avoid a possibly unseemly debate as to the bias of the judge and still give weight to the defendant's not entirely unreasonable concerns.

Conversations in chambers

Two somewhat different cases concerning the outcomes of conversations in a judge's private room at least have one thing in common in that they demonstrate, 'once again how things can go wrong, and how a real sense of injustice may be engendered in the absent client'.

In *R v Smith (Terrence)* [1990] 1 All ER 634 there had been discussion between counsel and judge in the judge's room prior to arraignment. The defendant had intended, it was said, to plead not guilty to the charges. In the light of the advice he received from counsel after the conversation the defendant offered a plea of guilty. The defendant's case was that he had been misled by his own counsel into believing that the judge had given some sort of undertaking that he would receive a suspended sentence in return for a plea of guilty instead of the immediate sentence of imprisonment he actually received. It was one of those cases in which there was an unseemly dispute between judge and counsel as to what had in fact transpired in private. With undisguised reluctance the Court of Appeal allowed the appeal and reduced the sentence, there being in this case no appeal against conviction. Even if there were circumstances when counsel might discuss possible sentencing options with the judge in private, such discussions, it was said, should never take place in the absence of a shorthand note-taker or alternatively a recording device.

The ground rules for how such discussions should be conducted were laid down in *R v Turner* [1970] 2 All ER 281 and refined by a spate of cases in the 1970s. Matters seemed to have settled down, or at least have been kept out of the law reports, until this and several other recent cases, namely *R v Pitman* [1991] 1 All ER 468, *R v Keily* [1990] Crim LR 204 and *R v Agar* [1990] 2 All ER 442 raised the issue again. The case of *Smith* adds nothing to the law in stressing again the need for an accurate recording of what took place between judge and counsel. Indeed there is more than a hint of exasperation at the extent to which nothing new is being said in Russell LJ's observation that:

> 'We find it surprising that, despite frequent observations made in this court discouraging unnecessary visits to the judge's room, they appear to continue up and down the country.'

What the case does, however, suggest is that where a judge does give an indication as to the sentence on a plea of guilty, and if the proceedings are not declared a nullity, the defendant may be entitled, so to speak, to enforce the 'bargain'. In *R v Keily*, matters were taken a step further. An indication at a pre-trial review that a plea of guilty would not attract a sentence of immediate imprisonment was held to bind a different judge who tried the case even though the defendant pleaded not guilty and was convicted by a jury. A judge should not indicate that he would take one course on a plea of guilty and another if the matter was contested. If the defendant had been tried before the first judge, and been found guilty by the jury, he would not have been able to impose an immediate prison sentence. It made no difference, the court said, that the appellant was adventitiously tried by another judge.

R v Agar was rather different, not least because the case was actually disposed of on a point relating to the admissibility of evidence of an informer's identity (see Evidence, p 128 below). The issue of private discussion between judge and counsel arose after the prosecution had confidentially informed defence counsel that one of the parties to the case was a police informant. Counsel then sought a ruling from the judge in the judge's room as to the extent he could cross-examine police witnesses about the fact that 'X' was a police informer. The judge ruled that he could not put any such questions to the police which might elicit the fact that 'X' was an informer who was acting in collusion with the police and in addition ruled that counsel was forbidden to disclose to his client what had transpired in the judge's room.

In this case the Court of Appeal felt more sympathy for the plight of the trial judge who was faced with a delicate issue. Nevertheless, defence counsel was placed by this conversation in a difficult situation with a clear conflict of interest. The information that 'X' was a police informer was clearly relevant, indeed central, to a defence of collusion between 'X' and the police, yet this could not be disclosed under the trial judge's ruling either to the defendant or his solicitor. Accordingly, the court was inclined to think that the appeal in *Agar* would have been allowed on this ground alone. What the case does therefore make clear is that defence counsel cannot be bound by the court to keep confidential information which he has acquired in the judge's room, or elsewhere, which is material to his client's defence.

A helpful review of the case law in this area is to be found in Patrick Curran's article, 'Discussions in the Judge's Private Room' in [1991] Crim LR 79.

Direction to convict

A case on the borderline of procedure and evidence which raises again the issue of if and when a judge may direct a verdict of guilty is *R v Gent* [1990] 1 All ER 364. The Court of Appeal confirmed the approach of the earlier cases, stating:

> '. . . if such a category exists at all, it must be confined to wholly exceptional cases where, for example, there has been something in the nature of a formal admission of guilt. The fact that on the evidence, including the evidence of the defendant himself, only one verdict is possible, does not justify the judge in directing the jury to convict . . . if he maintains his plea, the defendant is entitled to the verdict of a jury, even though in the view of the judge an acquittal would be perverse.'

Despite such ringing endorsements of a defendant's right to have the issue left to the jury, a failure to do so has been of little comfort to the defendant. In all the recent cases since *DPP v Stonehouse* [1977] 2 All ER 909 the proviso to s 2(1) of the 1968 Act has been applied. That, as the court commented, is hardly surprising since it is only in cases where the evidence is overwhelming that judges are tempted to direct a conviction. In this respect *Gent* does break new ground in that the Court of Appeal, exceptionally, failed to apply the proviso. It would probably, however, be dangerous to generalise from this decision. In most cases, doubtless, the proviso will continue to be applied. A complicating feature in this appeal was the exclusion of certain evidence which might have been beneficial to the defence. Nevertheless, the court has shown that, despite a strong case against the defendant and the likelihood of conviction if the matter had been left to the jury it was willing to quash a conviction on a directed verdict of guilty.

Verdict

R v Maxwell [1990] 1 All ER 801 is a case that leaves a lurking sense of unease. The appellant was charged with a serious robbery, his 'defence' being that although he had arranged for the house to be burgled he had not committed robbery because he had not intended any violence to be used against the occupants. In the absence of the jury the defendant offered a plea to burglary but the prosecution declined to apply to amend the indictment. The view of both the prosecution and the trial judge was that the evidence disclosed a carefully planned robbery.

After retiring, the jury asked the judge whether they could substitute a conviction for a lesser offence than robbery. The judge said the answer to their question was no, burglary was not an alternative, and they should concentrate on the charge of robbery. Three and a half hours later the jury convicted of robbery. Not unnaturally, the powerful submission made for the appellant was that the jury were forced to make a wholly artificial choice between convicting of robbery or acquitting him altogether. It was, to borrow the graphic words of Phillimore J in *R v Parrott* (1913) 8 Cr App R 186 at 193 a case of 'neck or nothing'. Both the Court of Appeal and the House of Lords upheld the conviction. The view taken by the House of Lords was that a trial judge was only obliged to leave a lesser alternative verdict to the jury if that was necessary in the interests of justice. Here the principal offence was very grave, justified on the facts and the jury did not need to be distracted by considering offences remote from the real point of the case especially when the alternative of theft was so relatively trifling.

As Professor Smith points out ([1991] Crim LR 66) both the reasoning of the Court of Appeal and the House of Lords is open to similar criticism. When the jury asked if there was a lesser offence they could return against the defendant the answer they were given was 'no'. Yet in law, as any first-year student could have said, the answer is that theft is a clear possible alternative. Robbery is, after all, only an aggravated form of theft. If the jury had simply returned a verdict of guilty of theft could it have been assailed on any basis? Certainly, the evidence against the defendant on the charge of robbery was strong and his defence perhaps implausible but, at least if regarded by the jury as raising a reasonable doubt, it was a defence to robbery. In *R v Gent* yet again much was made of the fact that the defendant is entitled to have the jury deliberate on his guilt. What principle of law then justifies concealing from the jury the fact that they are entitled to return an alternative lesser verdict when they have clearly signalled that they are minded to do so? As for the claim that theft could be regarded as relatively trivial compared to robbery, two points could be made. First, as a matter of principle, if an alternative offence is open to the jury why, as Professor Smith asks, should it matter how trivial it is? Second, on any view of the law, how can theft, even as compared to robbery, be regarded as a 'trivial' offence? In any event, trivial or not, the issue is surely one for a jury, not the Court of Appeal or even the House of Lords.

A point of some practical importance was clarified by the Court of Appeal in *R v Mearns* [1990] 3 All ER 989. On an indictment charging assault occasioning actual bodily harm contrary to s 47 of the Offences Against the Person Act 1861, common assault is not a possible alternative verdict unless a

count charging common assault is included in the indictment. This change
has been brought about by ss 39 and 40 of the Criminal Justice Act 1988.
Under s 39 common assault is now a summary offence. This means that it
comes within the scope of s 40 which makes it a requirement that there be a
specific count of common assault in the indictment if it is to be available as an
alternative.

SENTENCING

R v Davison [1990] 2 All ER 976 is an important decision on s 1(4A) of the
Criminal Justice Act 1982 which restricts a court's ability to impose a
custodial sentence on a young offender. What it particularly makes clear is
that when considering for the purposes of s 1(4A)(*c*) whether the offence for
which he was convicted was so serious that a non-custodial sentence would
not be justified, each offence must be considered separately and the total
number of offences may not be aggregated when considering their
seriousness. It is, however, permissible to aggregate when considering a
custodial sentence under s 1(4A)(*b*) which is concerned with protecting the
public from serious harm from the offender. Further, having decided that a
young offender qualifies for a custodial sentence, the court is required by
s 2(4) of the 1982 Act to state under which of the mutually exclusive
paragraphs in s 1(4A) the offender qualifies.

This case restores the law to where it was after *R v Hassan* (1989) 11 Cr App
R (S) 148, although it does not resolve all the difficulties. What if, as Professor
Thomas speculates ([1990] Crim LR 214), the offender is charged with
conspiracy to commit a number of offences? Would s 1(4A)(*c*) be satisfied
even though the individual offences taken on their own would not be 'so
serious that a non-custodial sentence for it cannot be justified'?

It should also be noted that the proper approach to sentencing in the light of
s 1(4A) has exercised the courts in a considerable number of later cases,
particularly: *R v Rhoades* [1990] Crim LR 274; *R v Scott* [1990] Crim LR 440; *R
v Parry* [1990] Crim LR 444; *R v Mitchell, R v Littler and Dooley* [1990] Crim
LR 659; *R v McCarroll* [1990] Crim L R 660: *R v Furnell* [1991] Crim LR 69.
None of them doubt the correctness of *Davison* but they do give further
guidance to sentencers in such cases.

Employment Law

IAN SMITH MA, LLB (CANTAB)
Barrister, Reader in Law, University of East Anglia

The mixed bag of cases this year is a little less mixed than usual, as five concern various forms of discrimination law, with a heavy emphasis towards the impact of EEC law, leading of course with the landmark pensions-equality decision of the ECJ in *Barber v Guardian Royal Exchange Assurance Group* (also discussed in European Community Law, pp 110–112 below). In addition, *James v Eastleigh Borough Council* is an important pronouncement by the House of Lords on the meaning of direct discrimination. In a different context, *Ashmore v British Coal Corporation* considers an informal test case procedure for multiple equal pay applications, *Post Office v Union of Communication Workers* has significant pointers towards future applications of the complicated strike ballot provisions and *Whitfield v H & R Johnson (Tiles) Ltd* settles a difficult point on statutory safety law. However, in case the reader is becoming unsettled at the thought of so much high principle and wide development, it may be reassuring to read *British Coal Corporation v Cheesbrough*, a fiendishly complicated case on calculating a week's pay for the purposes of a redundancy payment, which should restore his or her faith that employment law retains its feet, if not of clay, at least firmly rooted in terra firma.

Pension schemes and EEC law

In 1990 the ECJ decided *Barber v Guardian Royal Exchange Assurance Group* (Case C-262/88) [1990] 2 All ER 660 and thereby outflanked the government's strategy for trying to sweep at least part of the minefield of equality in pension schemes. In a sense, *Barber* was a case waiting to happen, but that did not lessen the shock waves when it appeared.

As is well known, the fundamental problem of equality in pensions arises from discriminatory pension ages, built into the state scheme and carried over by analogy into private schemes. Great care has been taken in the past to try to ensure that ordinary principles of sex equality do not apply to provisions relating to death or retirement, but such exclusions have been construed more restrictively of late. Moreover, EEC Directive 86/378 requires the adoption of a certain level of equality in occupational pension schemes. The government's strategy to deal with this is contained in the Social Security Act 1989, s 23, Sch 5 which follows the terms of the directive in introducing equality into contractual pension schemes in relation to contents and benefits. However, the government in so doing took full advantage of the exceptions and qualifications in the directive, in two ways: (i) Sch 5 is timed to come into force at the latest dates allowed by the directive (1993, with the actuarial defence to last until 1999); (ii) full advantage is taken of three permitted exceptions from the principle of equality – different entitlements to survivors benefits, the actuarial defence to differential contribution rates and, most vital of all, differential pension ages (retainable until either equality is reached in the state scheme or until a further directive requires equality in private schemes specifically). However, it was always thought possible that this whole legislative scheme could be outflanked if it was ever decided that benefits payable under a private pension scheme constitute pay within the meaning of Art 119 of the Treaty of Rome, thus subjecting such schemes to the normal regime of equality required by that Article. This is what *Barber* has done, potentially leaving the provisions of the Social Security Act 1989 as a historical curiosity.

The irony of the case is that the complainant was in fact a man. He was made redundant at age 52. Under the terms of the pension scheme, in such circumstances a woman would have been entitled to an immediate pension at age 50, but as a man, the complainant was not so entitled until the age of 55 (based on differential pension ages of 62 for a man and 57 for a woman, those ages themselves being based on the state retirement ages of 65 and 60). In his claim for equality, the Court of Appeal sought the opinion of the ECJ, which ruled as follows:

(i) Benefits paid by an employer to a worker in connection with compulsory redundancy are within the scope of Art 119. This follows the general trend of finding that pay is not restricted to contractual payments made during employment, but can also apply to sums payable after termination; a statutory or ex gratia nature of a payment will likewise be irrelevant.

(ii) A pension paid under a contracted-out private occupational scheme also falls within the Article. Although there is statutory intervention in the form of the contracting-out procedure, such schemes remain essentially matters between employer and worker and so within the realm of pay (*Bilka-Kaufhaus GmbH v Weber von Hartz* (Case 170/84) [1986] 2 CMLR 701, ECJ applied and extended). Further, the fact that a scheme may be administered by trustees independent of the employer has no bearing on this characterisation.

(iii) Entitlement only to a deferred pension when a woman of the same age would have been entitled to an immediate pension is therefore contrary to Art 119, even where the sex difference is akin to that in the national statutory pension scheme. Further, the application of the principle of equal pay has to be ensured in respect of each element of remuneration, not on the basis of a comprehensive assessment of the total remuneration paid to workers. This is the heart of the case. The rider added about having to apply equality to each individual element of remuneration is justified by the ECJ on the basis of the transparency principle enunciated in *Handels-og Kontorfunktionaerernes Forbund i Danmark v Dansk Aubejdsgiverforening (acting for Danfoss)* (Case 109/88) [1989] IRLR 532, and is in line with the term-by-term approach (rather than the package of terms approach) adopted by the House of Lords in the context of domestic equal value claims in *Hayward v Cammell Laird Shipbuilders Ltd* [1988] 2 All ER 257 (see All ER Rev 1988, p 113).

(iv) Article 119 can be relied on directly, in the national courts, on this matter. This is a straightforward application of direct effect – as the benefit in question is pay it is within the Article itself and so none of the well-known problems with the supporting directives (especially vertical/horizontal effect, see *Foster v British Gas plc*, below) arise to cloud the issue.

(v) Given the problems which may arise from this judgment (a slight understatement?) the ECJ applied *Defrenne v Sabena* [1981] 1 All ER 122 and held that the effects of the judgment will only flow from the date of judgment and not to any claims to entitlement arising prior to that date (except in relation to any claims already initiated under national law before that date). In spite of this sensible limitation, this decision clearly wrecks the government's timetable for implementation of equality measures by legislation. As such, it constitutes perhaps the best example so far of the problem of direct effect referred to in *Smith & Wood's Industrial Law* (4th edn) at p 410 as legal cladism, ie a legal form of the palaeontological theory of sudden catastrophic change, rather than orderly gradual evolution.

One of the reasons for the decision not to give the case retrospective effect was that all parties could have been reasonably entitled to consider that Art 119 did not apply to occupational pension schemes in the light of Directives 79/7 (equal treatment in social security) and 86/378 (equal treatment in occupational schemes), which aimed to give member states a period of time before having to address the fundamental problem of long-standing differential pension ages. It now appears that that period is not to be enjoyed.

Application of directives to public bodies

Unlike Art 119 on equal pay (above), the supporting directives (particularly 76/207, the Equal Treatment Directive) only have vertical direct effect against the state, and not horizontal direct effect as between private individuals or organisations within the state: *Marshall v Southampton and South West Hampshire Area Health Authority (Teaching)*: Case 152/84, [1986] 2 All ER 584 (see All ER Rev 1986, p 133). This raises the difficult questions of what is the state. *Foster v British Gas plc* Case C-188/89, [1990] 3 All ER 897 concerned the compulsory retirement of a woman at an age earlier than that for a man; the case arose before the law on this was amended (to introduce equal ages, in the light of *Marshall*) by the Sex Discrimination Act 1986 and so the complainant sought to rely instead on the Equal Treatment Directive (76/207). She could only succeed if British Gas (as it was before privatisation) was an emanation of the state. The case went up to the House of Lords, who remitted the matter to the ECJ for a preliminary ruling on this point.

In argument, the UK submitted that this whole question was one for the national courts, but the ECJ ruled against that and held that it had jurisdiction on the preliminary ruling to lay down principles to determine the category of persons against whom the provisions of a directive might be relied on; it was then for the national court to apply those principles to the facts. The court then proceeded to rule that the directive could be relied on against:

> 'a body, whatever its legal form, which had been made responsible pursuant to a measure adopted by a public authority, for providing a public service under the control of that authority and had for that purpose special powers beyond those which result from the normal rules applicable in relations between individuals.' (at p 922).

In spite of the fact that the subject matter of the case is now covered by amended domestic legislation, this ruling is of general significance in any other areas where a party is seeking to rely on the direct effect of a directive, rather than an article of the Treaty. Of particular interest is how it may be applied to the various forms of privatised, ex-public sector organisations. (See European Community Law, p 107 below.)

Application of EEC law on equal pay

The decision of the House of Lords in *Duke v GEC Reliance Ltd* [1988] 1 All ER 626 was considered in All ER Rev 1988 at pp 115, 123–6. One of the points there decided was that since the Sex Discrimination Act 1975 and the Equal Pay Act 1970 had not been passed in order to give effect to the Equal Treatment Directive (76/207), the provisions of these Acts did not have to be construed to give effect to that directive especially where (as here, in the context of the statutory exclusion of provisions in relation to death or retirement) the legislation could not, on its plain wording, bear the construction contended for by the complainant. In *Finnegan v Clowney Youth Training Programme Ltd* [1990] 2 All ER 546 an attempt was made to circumvent that decision in *Duke* on facts very similar to those in that case. The argument was that, although the Sex Discrimination Act 1975 was not passed to implement the directive and so did not have to be interpreted in the light of it, the equivalent provision in Northern Ireland (the Sex Discrimination (Northern Ireland) Order 1976) had in fact been enacted shortly after the directive, and so should be interpreted in the light of it. The House of Lords, however, disagreed; they held that the Order had been intended by Parliament to have the same effect as the Sex Discrimination Act 1975, so that *Duke* applied and the claim failed. (See European Community Law, pp 108–109 below for further discussion of these cases.)

Equal pay claims – tribunal procedure

One normally thinks of employment cases before tribunals as being highly individual, being constantly told that each dismissal case depends on its own facts and that even in redundancy dismissals each individual affected must be considered separately. It is hardly surprising, therefore, that (largely in common with other areas of civil procedure) the Rules of Procedure for industrial tribunals have no express provision for hearing test cases or class actions. However, equal pay litigation (and in particular in equal value cases) is an area where an individual claim for parity may be a tiny tip of a very large iceberg. In other words, a tribunal may face a multitude of cases over one issue and in effect be dealing with a collective dispute over pay levels under the guise of individual actions under the Equal Pay Act 1970. *Ashmore v British Coal Corporation* [1990] 2 All ER 981 shows (a) the possible scale of the problem and (b) a use of the rule on striking out (Rule 12) which can, in effect, produce an informal test case procedure.

The applicant was a canteen worker at a colliery. She was one of 1,500 women canteen workers claiming equal pay with certain male comparators on the ground of like work. At interlocutory hearings, the tribunal chairman to whom these cases had been assigned ordered that 14 representative sample cases should be chosen for a hearing and the others stayed. The sample cases were heard in 1986 (sub nom *Thomas v NCB*) and were rejected on the facts; an appeal to the EAT was dismissed. In *Ashmore* the applicant, whose case had been stayed, sought to have the stay removed and the case relisted. The employers sought to have her case struck out under r 12(2)(*e*) as vexatious. The tribunal chairman accepted that, technically, *Thomas* was not binding on her, but ruled that it would be an abuse of process to seek to relitigate the same issues of fact. He therefore struck out her claim. The EAT dismissed her appeal against that order, and so did the Court of Appeal.

The court rejected her argument that she had an absolute right to have her case litigated (in the absence of a defence of res judicata, or her agreement to be bound by the result of the sample cases). Vexatious under r 12 included cases of abuse of process, and that would be the case where (as here) sample cases have been properly tried on all the relevant evidence. The only exception would be where there was fresh evidence that would entirely change the aspect of the case (*Phosphate Sewage Co Ltd v Molleson* (1879) 4 App Cas 801, per Lord Cairns). That was not the case here.

Thus, the procedure of sample cases backed by this interpretation of r 12 can produce an informal test case procedure, particularly useful in multiple equal pay cases. In this case, it acted against the applicant when the issues had been resolved in favour of the employer. However, it would be equally important in a case where the issues in the sample cases were resolved in favour of the applicants, because it would also be possible to use r 12 to strike out any attempt by the employers to ignore the test ruling and insist on continuing to defend each case in an attempt to wear down the applicants. This is because the striking out rule applies to any originating application *or notice of appearance*. (See also Practice and Procedure, pp 215–217 below.)

Redundancy payments – calculating a week's pay

The calculation of a redundancy payment requires the ascertainment of the amount of a week's pay for the employee in question which (subject to the statutory maximum fixed annually) is then multiplied by a factor dependent on age and length of service. The facts and decision in *British Coal Corpn v Cheesbrough* [1990] 1 All ER 641 show how complicated the fixing of a week's pay can be, especially as the Employment Protection (Consolidation) Act 1978, Sch 14, Part II (which governs the calculation of a week's pay for statutory purposes) goes to considerable lengths to exclude overtime and special overtime payments from the relevant calculations.

The employee had been employed at a colliery for 20 years when he was made redundant. Prior to his dismissal (and during the 12-week period over which his week's pay had to be averaged) he had worked under a complicated payment system; he worked a basic 40-hour week for which he was paid a basic hourly rate plus an incentive bonus (based on shift productivity), but on top of that he worked regular overtime for which he was paid at 50% above basic rate (the overtime premium) but no incentive bonus. It was clear that (under Sch 14, para 5(2)) the overtime premium had to be removed in the statutory calculation, but the incentive bonus proved a problem – if you simply stripped out the premium and divided what was left by the total hours actually worked (as the employers did), then because the incentive bonus was not paid for the overtime hours that produced an anomaly, namely that the more hours overtime he worked, the less became his average hourly wage (because the fixed bonus had to be divided by more hours). To avoid this anomaly, the EAT adopted the calculation method devised by the employee, that is to disregard both the overtime premium and the incentive bonus, work out the week's pay on that basis, and then simply add the incentive bonus back in. However, the Court of Appeal allowed the employers' appeal and the House of Lords by 3-2 upheld that decision – the majority held that a week's pay has to be calculated by the plain wording of Sch 14 (especially para 5), which required the averaging as in fact done by the employers, and that remained so even if, on these complicated facts, it produced the anomaly of which the employee was complaining.

The meaning of discrimination

James v Eastleigh Borough Council [1990] 2 All ER 607 was considered (in the Court of Appeal) in All ER Rev 1989 at p 120 and is, it will be recalled, the 75p *cause célèbre* case. The House of Lords have now reversed the decision of the Court of Appeal by 3-2 and upheld the complaint of direct sex discrimination.

The plaintiff, a man of 61, complained of having to pay 75p to swim in his local authority baths when his wife of the same age was admitted free. This different treatment was because free swimming was given to those over pensionable age, which under the state scheme means 65 for a man, 60 for a woman. The decision of the Court of Appeal caused some consternation in the field of discrimination law, for it was there held that it was not direct discrimination under the Sex Discrimination Act 1975 s(1)(*a*) because the plaintiff's less favourable treatment was not on the ground of sex. This involved a subjective approach, looking at the reason activating the alleged discriminator; here, that reason was to better the lot of pensioners, not to discriminate against men. However, it also involved drawing an extremely difficult line between grounds for discrimination (relevant) and intention to discriminate (clearly held not to be relevant or necessary by the House of Lords in *Equal Opportunities Commission v Birmingham City Council* [1989] 1 All ER 769 (All ER Rev 1989, p 120)).

In the House of Lords, Lords Bridge and Goff (with whom Lord Ackner agreed) held that this subjective approach is wrong, involving an insoluble conundrum over reason, grounds, motive etc, and being in their view directly contrary to the *Equal Opportunities Commission* case (in spite of Browne-Wilkinson V-C's erudite attempt to distinguish that case in the Court of Appeal's decision). Adopting what was termed the causative construction contended for by the EOC (backing Mr James) they held that the correct approach was to ask simply would Mr James, a man of 61, have received the same treatment as his wife but for his sex? The answer here was affirmative and so there was direct discrimination. This is an important clarification of a fundamental point of discrimination law.

Two further points are worth noting from the speeches. The first is that Lord Bridge stated that, although discriminatory pension ages are still used in certain contexts where discrimination is allowed by statute, that is no reason for allowing discrimination generally between the ages of 60 and 65 to go unchallenged. This decision of the House of Lords allows such a challenge and employers may have to be wary of basing non-statutory benefits, concessions etc simply on the state pension age. Further, as *Barber* (above) shows, even the area of the linkage of whole pension schemes to the state pension ages is now under attack. Secondly, and following on from this, Lord Ackner added the comment that in the light of changed and changing work practices between the sexes, there is much to be said for linking benefits to actual age rather than to state pensionable age. Again, the juxtaposition of this case and *Barber* is instructive. The death knell of differential pension ages seems to be tolling.

Racial discrimination – statutory exception

The Race Relations Act 1976 s 41(1)(*b*) establishes an exception in that nothing in (inter alia) Part II of the Act (discrimination in the employment field) renders unlawful any act of discrimination done in pursuance of any instrument made under any enactment by a Minister of the Crown. This poses a problem because it is capable of a wide interpretation (extending not just to cases where the discriminatory act was directly required by the instrument/enactment, but to cases of the exercise of an administrative discretion granted by the instrument/enactment) or a narrow interpretation (restricted to cases where the discriminatory act was directly required). This problem arose in *Hampson v Department of Education and Science* [1990] 2 All ER 513 where an experienced teacher from Hong Kong was refused qualified teacher status under the Education (Teachers) Regulations 1982 because the Secretary of State decided that her training was not equivalent to the English training period. The question arose whether any possible discrimination was within the exception in s 41(1)(*b*). The Court of Appeal ([1990] 2 All ER 25) held that the s 41 defence was made out on the facts, though Balcombe LJ dissented on the ground that on principle the narrow approach should be applied. On further appeal the House of Lords (sitting, curiously, with only four members) allowed the complainant's appeal and held that s 41 did not apply. Giving the unanimous decision, Lord Lowry said that as a matter of principle the narrow interpretation must be applied; to do otherwise would severely limit the application of the Act since many public employers operate their employment policies in some way or other under statutory powers and so to allow them to claim that this brought them under one heading or another of s 41 would be entirely unacceptable. This decision, approving Balcombe LJ's dissenting judgment, is far more satisfactory than that of the majority of the Court of Appeal.

Industrial action – the requirements for strike ballots

The decision of the Court of Appeal in *Post Office v Union of Communication Workers* [1990] 3 All ER 199 is of considerable interest in the law relating to industrial action and strike ballots, not just for the actual decision but because of certain obiter statements in the judgment of Lord Donaldson MR.

Faced with Post Office reorganisations to which they objected, the union in August 1988 balloted its members as to whether they were willing to take industrial action up to and including strike action. A narrow majority voted yes and in October, November and December 1988 there was a series of one-day strikes. No further strikes took place until September/October

1989, by which time the Post Office had decided to bring the legal action for an injunction which was the subject of this case. The Post Office argued that the strike action was illegal (as not complying with the balloting requirements) for two reasons – (a) the wording of the original ballot was defective, (b) the ballot of August 1988 no longer validated the strike action in 1989.

On the first point, the Court of Appeal upheld the Post Office's argument and granted the injunction. The Trade Union Act 1984 s 10(4) (as amended by the Employment Act 1988) provides that the appropriate question to be posed by the ballot is whichever of the questions set out in s 11(4) is applicable to the strike or other industrial action. That subsection has two questions, one for a strike and one for other industrial action; thus where, as here, a union contemplates both types of action it must ask *both* questions, a point made doubly certain by s 10(4A). Thus, the union's single rolled up question did not comply with the balloting requirements and so the strike was unlawful.

That decision made it unnecessary to decide on the second point *but* it is possible that the future importance of this decision may lie more in what was said obiter on this second ground, rather than in the actual decision on the first ground (which certainly establishes an important point but one flowing fairly inevitably from the amended wording of s 10).

On that second point, it is reasonably clear from the Master of the Rolls' judgment that the court would also have found for the Post Office if necessary. Lord Donaldson made three points of considerable significance on the *timing* of the ballot. First, Parliament intended that industrial action should start shortly after the date of the ballot (s 10(3)(*c*)). Secondly, it was implicit from this that once the action began it must continue without substantial interruption if reliance was to continue to be placed on the verdict of the ballot. While *Monsanto plc v TGWU* [1987] 1 All ER 358 (see All ER Rev 1987 at p 107) is fairly liberal in allowing there to be a temporary suspension of action pending negotiations, that was not the case here – on these facts it appeared that the action validated by the August 1988 ballot had effectively ceased by December 1988 when the union changed its tactics. When industrial action resumed in September 1989 it represented entirely new and disconnected action which needed the support of a fresh ballot. Thirdly, Lord Donaldson further pointed out that in any event the balloting provisions (s 11(1)) require the balloting of all those likely to be called out. Where there is a long gap between the ballot and any resumed action there may well have been a significant turnover in the workforce (the Post Office estimated in this case a 30% turnover between August 1988 and January 1990), in which case the ballot will not cover the new employees. The logical result of this would be that, even if it was still the same dispute (point two, above) then, discounting any *de minimis* changes in the workforce, any call for action following a ballot should expressly be limited to those employed by the employer, and given the opportunity of voting, *at the time of the ballot.* Obviously, the longer the gap between the ballot and the action, the more material a complication this would be. Although these remarks are obiter, Lord Donaldson's judgment is of major interest on these points. Point two further clarifies the potential open-endedness of *Monsanto*, but it is probably point three that could cause most problems in the future.

Factories Act – when is a load likely to cause injury?

The Factories Act 1961, s 72 states: 'A person shall not be employed to lift, carry or move any load so heavy as to be likely to cause injury to him.' As with several provisions of the Act relating to safety, this section imposes strict liability, assuming two conditions are satisfied – (1) that the person was employed to lift the load (which may cause problems, for example in cases of employees contravening instructions not to lift something) and (2) that the load was likely to cause injury to him. The decision of the Court of Appeal in *Whitfield v H & R Johnson (Tiles) Ltd* [1990] 3 All ER 426 settles the meaning of the latter. (See also Tort, p 336 below.)

The problem with s 72 is that, unlike some provisions which lay down measurable limits (eg s 29(2)), where a person is working at a place where he is liable to fall more than 2 metres), it adopts effectively a comparative test – what is likely to injure him in the circumstances. While clearly some loads would be dangerous for anyone, an area may exist where a load which could be dangerous for Ronnie Corbett would not be dangerous for Geoff Capes. However, in this case a much more difficult problem arose (though potentially just as important, and raising a classic problem in the law of tort) – what if the employee has a particular weakness that in fact makes (in this case) her more susceptible to load-induced injuries but which is unknown to the employer?

The plaintiff had a congenital back condition, making her vulnerable to back injuries. However (1) this was unknown to the employer and (2) she had in fact been carrying out her work lifting and loading tiles for 11 years without mishap. From April 1984 she was required to move heavier tiles and in December 1984 she suffered a back injury which meant she had to leave the employment. Her action against the employers for common law negligence failed on the ground that the employers did operate a safe system of working. However, she also sought to rely on s 72, arguing that the wording of the section (especially the reference to causing injury to him) was wide enough to cover a plaintiff with a latent condition unknown to the employer (in effect saying that the employer had to take his victim as he found her). It is certainly the case that a statute can impose such a heavy onus on an employer (see eg the Employers' Liability (Defective Equipment) Act 1969) and in the only decision on the point, *Bailey v Rolls Royce (1971) Ltd* [1984] ICR 688 the Court of Appeal had indicated obiter that they supported the present plaintiff's argument. However, in deciding *Whitfield* which raised the point directly, the Court of Appeal declined to apply the dicta in *Bailey*. They held unanimously that s 72 does not cover cases of latent susceptibility, and so the judge had been correct to reject her breach of statutory duty action under the section. The result of the case is that the section remains one of strict liability once it applies, but in order for it to apply injury must be likely; this is defined as meaning that the load has to be likely to injure the particular employee employed to lift or move it, having regard to the weight or the nature of the load, the relevant surrounding circumstances and the particular employee's obvious and known characteristics. However, an unknown susceptibility cannot be taken into account when determining likelihood of injury.

European Community Law

CHRISTOPHER GREENWOOD, MA, LLB
Barrister, Fellow of Magdalene College, Cambridge

Introduction

The Court of Justice of the European Communities continued during 1990 to call into question some long established assumptions of English law. Three decisions are of particular significance. In Case C-213/89, *Factortame Ltd v Secretary of State for Transport (No 2)* [1991] 1 All ER 70 the Court of Justice ruled that Community law required the English courts in an appropriate case to grant an interim injunction effectively suspending the operation of an Act of Parliament where the compatibility of the Act with Community law was the subject of challenge. In Case C-262/88, *Barber v Guardian Royal Exchange* [1990] 2 All ER 660 the Court of Justice held that the Community law principle that men and women should receive equal pay for equal work applied to occupational pensions paid by an employer, a decision with far reaching implications for the British pensions industry (see also discussion in Employment Law, pp 93–94 above). Finally, the decision of the Court in Case 145/88, *Torfaen BC v B & Q plc* [1990] 1 All ER 129 has produced a line of conflicting decisions regarding the application of legislation on Sunday trading.

Relationship of Community law and English law: supremacy and direct effect

The Factortame saga

The background to the complex litigation in *Factortame* is to be found in the EEC's attempt to conserve fish stocks by means of a system of national quotas. This system, embodied in EC Council Regulations 170/83 and 172/83, was an unhappy compromise between principle and pragmatism. The principle, reflected in the EEC Treaty and in earlier Community measures regarding access to fish stocks, was the removal of discrimination on grounds of nationality between citizens of different EC states in all matters related to employment and recognition of the rights of fishing vessels registered anywhere in the Community to fish in any Community waters. The pragmatic consideration was the need for the adoption of conservation measures if Community waters were not to be fished dry. While conservation measures were undoubtedly necessary and the quota system was probably the only practicable measure available at the time, the whole concept of national quotas is difficult to reconcile with the basic principles of Community law.

This difficulty might not have mattered had it not been for the special problems of the Spanish fishing industry. Spain, which had not been a member of the Community when the regulations were adopted, fared badly in the allocation of quotas. As a result, a number of Spanish fishing companies attempted to secure part of the British quota by buying up trawlers already registered as British or by re-registering their existing vessels under the British flag. This practice, known as 'quota-hopping', was comparatively easy, because the principal requirement for registration – that a British ship be British-owned – could be satisfied by establishing a subsidiary company in the United Kingdom.

The United Kingdom took a number of steps to prevent quota-hopping. It introduced requirements regarding the nationality and residence of crew members of British fishing vessels ('the crewing conditions') and requirements that they operate from United Kingdom ports ('the operating conditions'). The government considered, however, that these conditions, which were themselves the subject of proceedings before the Court of Justice (discussed below), were proving too difficult to enforce. It therefore took steps to control the ownership of British fishing vessels. Part II of the Merchant Shipping Act 1988 provided that a fishing vessel would qualify for registration as a British ship only if it was owned by British citizens resident in the United Kingdom or by companies 75% of whose shareholders and directors were British citizens resident in the United Kingdom.

The Merchant Shipping Act gave rise to two separate sets of proceedings. The European Commission brought an enforcement action against the United Kingdom in the Court of Justice (*EC Commission v United Kingdom* Case 246/89R [1989] 3 CMLR 601). The Commission challenged only the nationality requirements in the 1988 Act. The Court has yet to give judgment on the merits in this case but the President of the Court has granted interim measures requiring the suspension of the application of the nationality requirements in respect of fishing vessels already registered as British but owned by nationals of other member states (the order is reported in full at [1989] 3 CMLR 601 and substantial extracts are contained in the speech of Lord Goff in *Factortame (2)*, [1991] 1 All ER 70 at 115–7). This order, which did not affect the other requirements of the Merchant Shipping Act, was issued on 10 October 1989, after the first decision of the House of Lords in *Factortame* (see below). It was given effect by the Merchant Shipping Act 1988 (Amendment) Order 1989 (SI 1989/2006).

The second case, *Factortame v Secretary of State for Transport*, was an action for judicial review in the English courts. The applicants were a number of companies, all of which were substantially Spanish owned and which operated fishing vessels affected by the 1988 Act. They challenged all of the new ownership conditions on the ground that the new conditions violated their rights under Community law, in particular under Arts 52, 58, 221 and 7 of the EEC Treaty. All of these provisions have direct effect and therefore must be enforced by national courts. The United Kingdom countered that the provisions of the 1988 Act were not incompatible with these fundamental provisions of Community law but were intended only to ensure that fishing vessels flying the British flag had a genuine link with the United Kingdom. The government maintained that international law entitled each state to determine the conditions under which a ship might fly its flag and that Community law had not removed that right.

The judicial review proceedings clearly raised important questions of Community law and the Divisional Court ([1989] 2 CMLR 353) requested a preliminary ruling from the Court of Justice under Art 177 of the EEC Treaty in respect of those questions. It was accepted by all parties that there would be a considerable delay before that ruling was given (at the end of 1990 the Court of Justice had yet to rule on the substantive questions referred by the Divisional Court). The applicants argued that if the 1988 Act were applied during that period, their businesses would suffer irreparable harm for which they would receive no compensation even if the Court of Justice subsequently ruled in their favour. The Secretary of State, on the other hand, contended that if the operation of the Act were suspended the will of Parliament would have been thwarted and considerable damage done to the United Kingdom fishing industry when it was by no means clear that the Court of Justice would reject the United Kingdom's defence of the 1988 Act as compatible with Community law.

One might have expected these arguments to have been addressed to the Court of Justice in the context of an application for interim measures similar to those which the court was to grant in the enforcement action already mentioned. However, in contrast to its extensive powers in enforcement actions, the Court of Justice has no power to grant interim measures in a case referred to it by a national court under Art 177. The Divisional Court therefore granted an interim injunction 'disapplying' the relevant provisions of the 1988 Act and restraining the Secretary of State from enforcing them in respect of the applicants until the Court of Justice had given its ruling on the questions referred. The *Factortame* case then went to the House of Lords on the question whether the English courts had jurisdiction to grant interim relief of this kind.

The decision of the House of Lords on this point, *Factortame (1)* [1989] 2 All ER 692, was considered in All ER Review 1989, pp 126–30. The House of Lords accepted that if the Court of Justice were to rule in favour of the applicant companies on the substantive questions referred by the Divisional Court, the applicants' directly effective Community law rights would prevail over the Merchant Shipping Act 1988. This is the most authoritative recognition by an English court to date of the principle of the supremacy of directly effective Community law. The House of Lords held, however, that the courts had no jurisdiction under English law to grant an interim injunction 'disapplying' an Act of Parliament. Nevertheless, the House made a second reference to the Court of Justice requesting a ruling on whether Community law required or empowered national courts to grant interim relief in a case of this kind even though the national court had no such power under national law.

In view of the urgency of the issues raised by the House of Lords, the Court of Justice gave its ruling on these questions before it considered the substantive questions referred by the Divisional Court. In a brief judgment, *Factortame Ltd v Secretary of State for Transport (No 2)* Case C-213/89 [1991] 1 All ER 70, the Court of Justice reaffirmed the principle – by now well established in its case law – that a national court must set aside a rule of national law which prevented directly effective Community law from having full force and effect. The court then held that where a litigant was seeking to assert rights which he claimed to possess under directly effective Community law and the existence of those rights was the subject of a reference to the Court of Justice:

'. . . the full effectiveness of Community law would be . . . impaired if a rule of national law could prevent a court seised of a dispute governed by Community law from granting interim relief in order to ensure the full effectiveness of the judgment to be given on the existence of rights claimed under Community law. It follows that a court which in those circumstances would grant interim relief, if it were not for a rule of national law, is obliged to set aside that rule.' (para 21, p 105).

In short, Community law required the English courts to set aside the rules identified in *Factortame (1)* (namely that there was no jurisdiction to grant interim relief suspending the operation of an Act of Parliament and that the courts could not grant interim injunctions against the Crown) and grant interim relief if the normal criteria for granting such relief were met.

The case then went back to the House of Lords ([1991] 1 All ER 70 at 106) for the House to determine whether it was appropriate to grant interim relief until such time as the Court of Justice should give a ruling on the substantive questions referred by the Divisional Court. The difficulty was that the Court of Justice had not indicated what criteria should be adopted for deciding whether to grant interim relief, clearly considering that this was a matter for national law. That approach was in accord with the principle that, while Community law requires national courts to give effective remedies for the enforcement of Community rights, it does not dictate the nature of those remedies. National courts must not, however, discriminate in such a way that they give less effective protection to rights derived from Community law than they give to rights based on national law. The difficulty is that there were no criteria in English law for the grant of an interim injunction against the Crown to suspend the operation of an Act of Parliament, because prior to the decision of the Court of Justice the English courts had had no jurisdiction to grant such an injunction.

Under English law an interim injunction is a discretionary remedy and the courts have been reluctant to impose limitations upon the exercise of discretion in such cases. Nevertheless, guidelines for the grant of interim relief were laid down by the House of Lords in *American Cyanamid Co v Ethicon Ltd* [1975] 1 All ER 504. Under those guidelines, interim relief may be granted provided that there is a serious question to be tried and the balance of convenience favours the grant of interim relief. That test, however, was devised in the context of commercial proceedings between private parties. The House of Lords had to decide to what extent it was suitable for the different and wholly unfamiliar context of a challenge to an Act of Parliament.

The House decided that the *American Cyanamid* test could not be applied without modification. In particular, their Lordships considered that the 'serious question' part of the test was inappropriate. Lord Goff said (at 120) that:

'. . . the court should not restrain a public authority by interim injunction from enforcing an apparently authentic law unless it is satisfied, having regard to all the circumstances, that the challenge to the validity of the law is, prima facie, so firmly based as to justify so exceptional a course being taken.'

Lord Jauncey (at 123–4) considered that the question of granting interim relief in a case involving a challenge to an Act of Parliament was more closely analogous to a challenge to delegated legislation than to the commercial actions for which the *American Cyanamid* guidelines had been fashioned. He therefore concluded that there was a presumption in favour of the validity of legislation, which required the applicants to show a strong prima facie case that it was invalid before it would be appropriate to grant interim relief.

The House of Lords was unanimous, however, that the applicants had shown a strong prima facie case that the 1988 Act would be held to be contrary to directly effective rules of Community law. In reaching this conclusion, their Lordships were influenced both by the reasoning of the President of the Court of Justice in granting interim measures in the enforcement action (see above) and by the decisions of the Court of Justice in two other cases, *R v Minister of Agriculture Fisheries and Food, ex p Agegate Ltd* Case C-3/87 [1991] 1 All ER 6 and *R v Minister of Agriculture Fisheries and Food, ex p Jaderow Ltd* Case C-216/87 [1991] 1 All ER 41. *Agegate* involved a challenge to the crewing conditions introduced in respect of British fishing vessels before the enactment of the Merchant Shipping Act 1988. In a judgment delivered after the House of Lords' decision in *Factortame (1)* but before the decisions in *Factortame (2)*, the Court of Justice ruled, inter alia, that a requirement that 75% of the crew of a British fishing vessel had to be resident in the United Kingdom was incompatible with Community law. If that was the case with regard to the crew, Lord Bridge reasoned, there was a strong prima facie case that the Court of Justice would reject the residence requirements for shareholders and directors introduced by the 1988 Act. The House of Lords therefore granted an interim injunction restraining the Secretary of State from withholding or withdrawing registration from the applicants' vessels on the grounds introduced by the 1988 Act.

Two features of *Factortame (2)* require comment. First, as a matter of United Kingdom constitutional law the case is of immense significance. The principle that Acts of Parliament are now subordinate to directly effective rules of Community law must now be regarded as clearly established. Not only has the House of Lords accepted that such Community rules must prevail even over subsequent legislation once a conflict between the two has been clearly established, it has accepted that the English courts have a duty to give effective interim protection to Community law rights by preventing the application of statutory provisions when there are strong grounds for suspecting that the application of those provisions will be found to be contrary to Community law. As Sir William Wade has put it, 'Acts of Parliament are now subject to a higher law, and to that extent they now rank as second-tier legislation' (107 LQR (1991) 1 at 3).

This aspect of the case has, not surprisingly, been received with consternation by those who believed that the Westminster Parliament enjoyed unfettered sovereignty. Yet, as Lord Bridge pointed out in *Factortame (2)*:

> 'If the supremacy within the European Community of Community law over the national law of the member states was not always inherent in the EEC Treaty it was certainly well established in the jurisprudence of the Court of Justice long before the United Kingdom joined the Community. Thus, whatever limitation of its sovereignty Parliament accepted when it enacted the European Communities Act 1972 was entirely voluntary.' (at 108)

That the judgments in *Factortame* have taken many by surprise reflects in part the reluctance of the Heath government, which had only a small majority in the House of Commons for membership of the Community, to explain the full implications of membership of the Community for the sovereignty of Parliament.

Secondly, the decision of the Court of Justice in *Factortame (2)* shows the extent to which the court is determined to ensure that national courts provide effective remedies for the enforcement of Community rights. As Advocate General Tesauro said in his opinion, effective interim relief is 'a fundamental and indispensable instrument of any judicial system' (at 94). In proceedings under Art 177 of the EEC Treaty, it is the national court, not the Court of Justice, which controls this aspect of the proceedings. While the Court of Justice has made clear on a number of occasions that Community law does not prescribe wholly novel remedies to be applied by the national courts, it will require those courts to strip away some of the limitations on the employment of remedies which already exist under national law.

The effect of directives in national law

The *Factortame* decisions concerned only those provisions of Community law which have direct effect. Most provisions of the Treaties and of regulations are now regarded as possessing direct effect. The position regarding directives is more complicated. In *Marshall v Southampton and South West Hampshire Area Health Authority* Case 152/84 [1986] 2 All ER 584 (discussed in All ER Rev 1986 at p 136) the Court of Justice held that directives are capable of having direct effect only in proceedings against a member state ('vertical direct effect') and not in proceedings between individuals or companies ('horizontal direct effect'). Even then, directives may only have direct effect after the deadline for their implementation has passed. These principles are now well established but they leave two important questions unanswered:
(a) what constitutes 'the State' for these purposes? and
(b) what effect, if any, do the provisions of a directive have in national law in cases where the directive is not directly effective?

The first question was the subject of a ruling by the Court of Justice in *Foster v British Gas* Case C-188/89 [1990] 3 All ER 897 (also discussed in Employment Law, p 95 above). Like Mrs Marshall, the appellants in *Foster* were women who had been forced to retire when they reached the age of 60, even though their employer, British Gas Corporation ('BGC'), did not require its male employees to retire until 65. In *Marshall* the Court of Justice had ruled that a discriminatory retirement age was contrary to Council Directive 76/207 even where, as here, it reflected the different ages at which men and women qualified for state pensions. The *Marshall* decision, however, also meant that only employees who worked for an arm of 'the State' could rely upon the directive against their employer in proceedings in the national courts.

The issue in *Foster*, therefore, was whether BGC was to be regarded as a part of the state for these purposes. The case arose before BGC was privatised and therefore concerned the status of BGC at the time when it was a statutory corporation, regulated by the Gas Act 1972. Under the 1972 Act BGC had a statutory duty to maintain a supply of gas and a monopoly of gas supply; its board of directors were appointed by the Secretary of State who had power to give BGC directions in relation to matters affecting the national interest and the management of BGC; BGC's annual reports were laid before Parliament.

The Court of Justice was unimpressed by arguments about the distinction between a nationalised industry and a state agency and ruled that the directive might be relied upon in proceedings against:

'. . . a body, whatever its legal form, which has been made responsible, pursuant to a measure adopted by the state, for providing a public service under the control of the state and has for that purpose special powers beyond those which result from the normal rules applicable in relations between individuals.' (at 922)

Although the court did not expressly rule that BGC was such a body (it decided that its function was confined to determining the categories of persons against whom the provisions of a directive might be relied upon, while it was for the national court to determine whether BGC actually fell within that category), it is clear the BGC and, presumably, the other nationalised industries are to be treated as part of the state for the purposes of the vertical direct effect of directives. Considerable uncertainty remains, however, about other entities, such as universities and companies in which the government has a controlling share interest.

The implications of a directive for national law in cases where the directive does not have direct effect has also been the subject of much attention. In *Von Colson and Kammau v Land Nordrhein-Westfalen* Case 14/83 [1984] ECR 1891 the Court of Justice held that even though a directive does not possess horizontal direct effect, Community law requires that national legislation which was passed to give effect to the directive must be interpreted in such a way that it does in fact conform to the directive. That principle was accepted by the House of Lords in *Litster v Forth Dry Dock and Engineering Co Ltd* [1989] 1 All ER 1134 (discussed in All ER Rev 1989, p 130). It is far from clear, however, whether the same duty applies where the national legislation deals with the same subject matter as the directive but was not passed specifically to give effect to the directive. The Court of Justice's pronouncements have been ambiguous on this point (see All ER Rev 1988, pp 124–6 and All ER Rev 1989, pp 130–1, and Curtin 'The Province of Government: Delimiting the Direct Effect of Directives in the Common Law Context' 15 EL Rev (1990) 195).

The House of Lords, however, decided in *Duke v GEC Reliance* [1988] 1 All ER 626 (All ER Rev 1988, pp 123–6) that the English courts were neither required nor entitled to distort the plain meaning of United Kingdom legislation in order to bring it into line with the provisions of a directive which the legislation had not been passed to implement. Since the Sex Discrimination Act 1975 had not been passed in order to give effect to Directive 76/207, Mrs Duke, who had worked for a private sector employer and thus could not rely upon the directive as Mrs Marshall and the appellants in *Foster* had done, failed in her attempt to persuade the House of Lords that it had to read the Act in such a way as to conform with the directive. The House has now reaffirmed this stance in *Finnegan v Clowney Youth Training Programme Ltd* [1990] 2 All ER 546 (see also Employment Law, p 96 above). The facts of *Finnegan* were indistinguishable from those of *Duke*, except that the appellant in *Finnegan* had been employed in Northern Ireland, where the Sex Discrimination Act 1975 did not apply and the case was governed by the Sex Discrimination (Northern Ireland) Order 1976, the terms of which were identical to those of the 1975 Act.

Counsel for Mrs Finnegan sought to distinguish *Duke* by arguing that the true rationale for that decision was that the 1975 Act had been passed before the adoption of the 1976 directive, whereas the directive had already been adopted by the time the Northern Ireland Order was enacted. It was argued that there was a presumption that any legislation (primary or secondary) was intended to comply with all Community laws in existence at the time the legislation was adopted. The House of Lords would have none of it. The 1976 Order was in identical terms to the the 1975 Act and the House held that it would be absurd to presume that the intentions which lay behind the two measures were different. The decision thus reaffirms the broad rationale of *Duke*, namely that the English courts regard the duty to engage in 'constructive' interpretation of national legislation in order to ensure conformity with directives as confined to legislation which was intended to give effect to a directive.

Summary

The House of Lords has now considered the effect of Community law in the United Kingdom six times in the last three years. The position which has so far been reached may be summarised as follows:

1. *Directly effective Community law* prevails over inconsistent United Kingdom legislation, even where that legislation has been enacted by Parliament subsequent to the entry into force of the Community rule (*Factortame (1)*). The only possible exception (left open by the House of Lords in *Factortame (1)* but which would not be acceptable to the Court of Justice) is legislation which expressly provides that it is to override inconsistent Community law.
2. Where an applicant can show a strong prima facie case that an Act of Parliament is contrary to directly effective Community law and a reference is made to the Court of Justice, an English court must grant an *interim injunction* effectively suspending the operation of the Act with regard to the applicant pending the ruling of the Court of Justice, provided that the other criteria for the grant of interim relief are met (*Factortame (2)*).
3. Provisions in the EC Treaties, regulations, decisions and agreements between the Communities and non-member states are, in principle, capable of having both vertical and horizontal direct effect. Directives have only vertical direct effect (*Marshall*) but the range of bodies against which directives can be relied upon is defined in fairly broad terms (*Foster*).
4. The courts have a duty to interpret statutes and delegated legislation which has been adopted to give effect to a directive in such a way as to ensure that it conforms with the directive, even if that result cannot be achieved by ordinary English principles of interpretation (*Litster*).
5. No such duty exists, however, in the case of legislation which was not passed to give effect to a directive, irrespective of whether the legislation was passed before or after the adoption of the directive (*Duke* and *Finnegan*).

Sex discrimination: retirement

In addition to the decisions in *Foster* and *Finnegan* (discussed above), 1990 saw a major decision of the Court of Justice in Case C-262/88 *Barber v Guardian Royal Exchange Assurance Group* [1990] 2 All ER 660 (also discussed in Employment Law, pp 93–94 above). Guardian Royal Exchange operated a contracted-out occupational pension scheme under which the normal pensionable age was 62 for men and 57 for women. In the event of compulsory redundancy, male employees were entitled to an immediate pension if they had attained the age of 55, while female employees became so entitled if they had reached the age of 50. Mr Barber was made redundant at the age of 52. He was paid the statutory redundancy payments and an ex gratia payment but did not qualify for an immediate pension. It was common ground that a woman in Mr Barber's position would have received an immediate pension as well as the statutory redundancy payment and that the total value of those benefits would have been greater than the amount paid to Mr Barber. Mr Barber brought an action for unlawful discrimination in the industrial tribunal, eventually appealing to the Court of Appeal, which referred a series of questions to the Court of Justice.

The court ruled that statutory redundancy payments, ex gratia payments and occupational pensions all fell within the principle of equal pay in Art 119, EEC Treaty. Art 119 simply states that:

> 'Each member state shall . . . ensure and subsequently maintain the application of the principle that men and women should receive equal pay for equal work. For the purpose of this article, "pay" means the ordinary basic or minimum wage or salary and any other consideration, whether in cash or in kind, which the worker receives, directly or indirectly, in respect of his employment from his employer.'

The Court held that this definition of pay embraced redundancy benefits paid on termination of employment. The court rejected an argument by the United Kingdom that statutory redundancy payments formed part of a social security scheme and thus could not be regarded as pay. In the court's view, these payments were made by the employer to the employee because of the employment relationship and therefore constituted pay; the fact that the obligation to make the payments derived from legislation rather than a term in the contract of employment was irrelevant. Similarly, the court held that ex gratia payments on redundancy came within the definition in Art 119, notwithstanding that their payment by the employer was purely voluntary.

Of far greater significance, however, was the court's decision that contracted-out occupational pensions fell within the scope of Art 119. On this subject the court had, in the past, spoken with an uncertain voice. In Case 12/81 *Garland v British Rail Engineering Ltd* [1982] 2 All ER 402 the court had held that certain benefits paid after retirement constituted pay and in Case 69/80 *Worringham v Lloyd's Bank Ltd* [1981] 2 All ER 434 it had rejected as incompatible with Art 119 adjustments in gross pay designed to compensate for differential pension contributions (All ER Rev 1982, pp 115–116). In Case 170/84 *Bilka-Kaufhaus GmbH v Weber von Hartz* [1986] 2 CMLR 701 it had held that a purely contractual pension paid by an employer came within Art 119. On the other hand, in Case 19/81 *Burton v British Railways Board* [1982] 3 All ER 537 (All ER Rev 1982, pp 116–117) the court had rejected an argument that a man who was denied access to a *voluntary* redundancy scheme on account of his age when a female employee of the same age would have been eligible for the scheme had been the victim of a violation of Art 119. Moreover, it is clear that state pensions are excluded from the scope of Art 119 and different ages of entitlement to state pensions remain lawful.

In *Barber* the court took the view that contracted-out occupational pensions had to be regarded as a form of pay, rather than a variation on, or substitute for, the state pension scheme. Contracted-out pensions were the result of an agreement between employer and employee or a unilateral decision by the employer and were financed wholly or in part by the employer. A contracted-out pension might offer benefits considerably in excess of the state scheme. Above all, the pensions paid were moneys received by an employee from the employer (or a pension trust acting on his behalf) because of the employment relationship. Once contracted-out pensions were classed as pay, it followed that men and women had to be accorded equal treatment in respect of them. The court rejected suggestions that in assessing discrimination the national court should look at the totality of benefits provided under the contract of employment and held that the principle of equal treatment had to be applied to each element of the package individually.

The decision in *Barber* should not have come as a great surprise. The court has been steadily extending the notion of pay ever since its first landmark decision on Art 119 in Case 43/75 *Defrenne v Sabena* [1981] 1 All ER 122. It has also been chipping steadily away at discrimination in relation to retirement. Nevertheless, the court was sufficiently concerned about the innovative nature of its decision and the effect which it might have upon long established pension arrangements and legitimate expectations that it decided to limit the temporal effect of its decision. The court decided that:

> 'the direct effect of Art 119 of the Treaty may not be relied on in order to claim entitlement to a pension with effect from a date prior to that of this judgment, except in the case of workers or those claiming under them who have before that date initiated legal proceedings or raised an equivalent claim under the applicable national law.' (at 704)

Three features of the case call for particular comment. First, it is unclear where the decision in *Burton* now stands. The two cases can be reconciled (just) on the basis that *Burton* concerned access to voluntary redundancy whereas *Barber* was about the financial consequences of compulsory redundancy. Yet to do so will leave a position which most employees are likely to find anachronistic. The two decisions do not sit happily together and the Commission, in its submissions in *Barber*, suggested that *Burton* should no longer be relied upon.

Secondly, the decision has to a large extent bypassed the Occupational Pensions Directive, Council Directive 86/378. That directive, the deadline for implementation of which has now passed, was a legislative attempt to clean the Augean stables of the occupational pensions industry. It contained a number of delicate and carefully negotiated political compromises which would have preserved certain aspects of differential treatment of men and women, or at least permitted their gradual removal. However, Community legislation cannot override the EEC Treaty and the provisions of the directive are subordinated to the provisions of Art 119 as that has been interpreted by the court in *Barber*. The result is likely to be considerable uncertainty for the pensions industry and for many employers.

Finally, the court's decision on the temporal application of its ruling is likely to give rise to much future litigation. The court was rightly concerned, as it had been in *Defrenne*, not to overturn decades of employment practice with a flood of claims by those whose contributions had been paid over the years on the basis of the old system which permitted differential treatment of men and women. As the court said,

> '. . . overriding considerations of legal certainty preclude legal situations which have exhausted all their effects in the past from being called in question where that might upset retroactively the financial balance of many contracted out pension schemes.' (at 704)

Does that mean that someone made redundant after the date of the judgment may claim, even though almost all his or her pension contributions had been made before that date? Or is the principle of non-retroactivity to preclude claims based upon contributions made before the date of the judgment? (For consideration of this issue, see the detailed and helpful analysis of *Barber* by Honeyball and Shaw in 16 EL Rev (1991) p 47.)

Free movement of goods

The prohibition on Sunday trading has long been controversial. Following the defeat by the House of Commons of a government proposal to change the law in 1985, a number of shops which were prosecuted for opening on Sundays decided to challenge the compatibility of the Shops Act 1950 with Community law. The shops maintained that their enforced closure on Sundays meant that their total sales, including their sale of goods imported from other EC states, were less than they would otherwise have been. They argued, therefore, that the Shops Act amounted to a measure having an equivalent effect to a quantitative restriction on imports, contrary to Art 30, EEC Treaty. In Case 145/88 *Torfaen Borough Council v B & Q plc* [1990] 1 All ER 129, the Cwmbran Magistrates' Court asked the Court of Justice for a ruling on whether Sunday trading legislation came within Art 30, and, if so, whether there were any grounds on which such legislation might be justified.

The case confronted the Court of Justice with some complex questions about the scope of Art 30. It had long been clear that Art 30 was not confined to measures which overtly discriminated against imports and could apply to measures which had an actual or potential effect of reducing access for imports to a national market. Nevertheless, the United Kingdom and the council argued that the Sunday trading legislation was of such a character that it fell wholly outside the scope of Art 30. The council, in particular, contended that Art 30 was confined to 'trading rules', whereas the Shops Act was an exercise of the state's 'police power'. Both the Commission and Advocate General van Gerven also concluded that the legislation fell outside the scope of Art 30, albeit for somewhat different reasons.

The Advocate General, whose opinion contains an invaluable review of the way in which the case law on free movement of goods has evolved, considered that what mattered was not the nature but the effects of the measure in question. He maintained that a general measure (as opposed to one which applied to specific products) would come within the scope of Art 30 only if it either led to a national market being completely screened off from a category of imports or if it rendered access to that market 'unacceptably difficult, less profitable or less attractive for economic operators from other member states' (at 146). If the rule did not completely screen off the market, it would come within Art 30 'only if it appears from the entire legal and economic context that the economic interweaving of national markets sought by the Treaty is thereby threatened' (at 150). The Advocate General concluded that the Shops Act did not have such effects and thus fell outside Art 30. Alternatively, he maintained, if the Act did fall within Act 30, it could be justified by a mandatory requirement (the category of justifications invented by the Court of Justice in the *Cassis de Dijon* case, *Rewe-Zentral AG v Bundesmonopolverwaltung für Branntwein* Case 120/78 [1979] ECR 649 for measures which were not discriminatory but nevertheless had an effect upon trade). He rejected the suggestion that the Shops Act was necessary to protect the working conditions of shop workers, since that end could have been achieved by less drastic measures, but he accepted that the encouragement of non-working activities (including religious activity) and the promotion of social contact constituted a mandatory requirement which would justify the ban on Sunday trading, so long as that ban did not have effects which went beyond what was necessary to achieve those goals.

The Court of Justice, however, did not discuss these issues. In a judgment of only two pages, the court held that two questions had to be examined: did the legislation pursue an aim which was justified under Community law and did the effects of the legislation exceed what was necessary to achieve that aim? With regard to the first question, the court commented that rules governing the opening hours of retail premises:

> '. . . reflect certain political and economic choices in so far as their purpose is to ensure that working and non-working hours are so arranged as to accord with national or regional socio-cultural characteristics, and that, in the present state of Community law, is a matter for the member states.' (at 156g)

On the second question, the court referred to Art 3 of Commission Directive 70/50 (a measure which it had all but ignored in its earlier case law) as limiting the scope of Art 30 of the Treaty to measures governing the marketing of products 'where the restrictive effect of such measures on the free movement of goods exceeds the effects intrinsic to trade rules.' On that basis, the court replied to the Cwmbran Magistrates' Court that:

> '. . . Art 30 of the Treaty must be interpreted as meaning that the prohibition which it lays down does not apply to national rules prohibiting retailers from opening their premises on Sunday where the restrictive effects on Community trade which may result therefrom do not exceed the effects intrinsic to the rules of that kind.' (at 156j)

This brief judgment is highly unsatisfactory and its rationale far from clear. The court may have intended to adopt an approach similar to that of the Advocate General, in which case its judgment means that legislation on Sunday opening falls entirely outside the scope of Art 30 unless the legislation has effects on Community trade which go beyond what is intrinsic in such legislation. If that was what the court intended (and if it was, then it is the greatest pity the court did not say so) then a general measure, as opposed to one dealing with specific products, has to be subjected to a two stage appraisal:

1. Does it fall within Art 30 at all? In answering this question, it will be necessary to apply a proportionality test to ascertain whether the measure's restrictive effects on trade go beyond what is intrinsic; and, if so,

2. Is the measure justified under the *Cassis de Dijon* mandatory requirements of Art 36 EEC Treaty? This question will also require a proportionality test: is the measure more restrictive than is necessary to achieve the mandatory requirement?

Elaborate though this structure may appear, there are reasons to think that it is what the court meant. The reference to Directive 70/50, the failure to mention mandatory requirements and the interpretation placed on the decision by Advocate General Lenz in the *Quietlynn* case (see below) all point in that direction.

On the other hand, the court may have rejected all the arguments about the scope of Art 30 and simply applied the *Cassis de Dijon* test. In that case, the court seems to have accepted that the protection of 'national or regional socio-cultural characteristics' constitutes a newly identified mandatory requirement and simply left the national court to determine whether the Shops Act was more restrictive that was necessary to achieve that requirement. This is the simpler interpretation of the *Torfaen* judgment and the one accepted by the Divisional Court in *W H Smith Do-It-All Ltd v Peterborough City Council* [1990] 2 CMLR 577. Yet if it is what the court intended, it is regrettable that the court did not make clear that it was deciding the case on a basis quite different from that suggested by the Advocate General, the Commission, the United Kingdom and the borough council.

The delphic nature of the court's judgment has also created problems. The first ominous sign was that both sides in the debate over Sunday trading claimed the judgment as a vindication of their position. The Cwmbran Magistrates' Court decided that the purpose of the Shops Act was 'to safeguard the special nature of the English and Welsh Sunday' and that the effects on Community trade were not excessive. B & Q were thus found guilty of contravening the Act ([1990] 3 CMLR 455). Hoffman J also considered that, in the light of the *Torfaen* decision, the Shops Act was not incompatible with Community law (*Stoke on Trent City Council v B & Q plc* [1990] 3 CMLR 31). Other courts, however, have had more difficulty and a second reference has now been made to the Court of Justice in an attempt to clarify the decision in *Torfaen*.

The Court of Justice gave an altogether clearer judgment in Case C-23/89 *Quietlynn Ltd v Southend-on-Sea Borough Council* [1990] 3 All ER 207. That case involved a challenge to the legislation on licensing of sex shops, under which any shop which sold a significant quantity of 'sex articles' (the judgment is somewhat coy about identifying what items fell into this intriguingly named category) was required to obtain a licence from the local council. Quietlynn, which was prosecuted for operating unlicensed sex shops, argued that the legislation contravened Art 30 of the EEC Treaty, since it restricted the outlets through which sex articles, including those imported from other member states, might be sold.

The court would have none of it. In a terse judgment it pointed out that the legislation did not discriminate between imports and domestic products (although there had been a fascinating discussion before the court of whether imported 'sex articles' had a more conspicuous appearance than their British counterparts), did not prohibit the sale of such articles but merely restricted the outlets through which they could be sold and was not, in any event, intended to regulate trade within the Community. In those circumstance, the licensing system fell wholly outside the scope of Art 30.

In many ways, the legislation on sex shops was similar to that on Sunday trading. Neither statute precluded the sale of any category of imported goods or affected the manner of their marketing, in the way that the packaging and advertising restrictions which have been the subject of so many cases before the court have done. Neither statute was discriminatory or bore more heavily on imports. One restricted the time at which goods could be bought and the other the places from which they could be bought. The same principle should, therefore, have been employed to deal with them. Yet the contrast between *Torfaen* and *Quietlynn* could not be more stark. In the former case, the court's reasoning and, to some extent, the results are obscure. In *Quietlynn*, the court was clear that the legislation did not fall within the scope of Art 30; no question of justification under the mandatory requirements ever arose. Moreover, the court's judgment leaves no room for doubt about the application of Community law to the facts of the case. The ambiguities in *Torfaen* should thus be resolved by reference to the *Quietlynn* judgment.

Cases not reviewed

Space permits only a brief mention of three other cases on Community law reported in 1990. In Case 180/87 *Hamill v EC Commission* [1990] 1 All ER 982, the Commission was held liable to compensate a Commission official for the non-material damage caused him by his arrest in the United Kingdom. Having learnt that the British authorities were investigating Mr Hamill with a view to prosecution, the Commission had provided the British police with information about Mr Hamill's movements at the time the alleged offences had occurred. That, the court held, was no more than the Commission's duty. However, the Commission had violated Mr Hamill's rights when it had warned the British police of his travel arrangements for a forthcoming trip to the United Kingdom and thus facilitated his arrest. Mr Hamill was subsequently aquitted of the charges against him.

The Court of Appeal twice considered the compatibility of RSC Ord 23, which provides for a court to require a plaintiff ordinarily resident outside the jurisdiction to provide security for costs, and Art 7 of the EEC Treaty, which forbids discrimination between nationals of member states on matters within the scope of Community law. The House of Lords Select Committee on the European Communities had questioned whether Ord 23 could still be reconciled with Community law in 1987 (HL Paper (1987–88) No 7). In *De Bry v Fitzgerald* [1990] 1 All ER 560 Lord Donaldson MR called, obiter, for the Supreme Court Practice Committee to give the matter urgent consideration. In *Berkeley Administration v McClelland* [1990] 1 All ER 958, however, the Court of Appeal decided that since Ord 23 was based upon the plaintiff's residence, not his nationality, it is not contrary to Art 7 (see Practice and Procedure, pp 203–204 below for further discussion of both cases).

Evidence

A A S ZUCKERMAN
Fellow of University College, Oxford

Confessions and the observance of the Code of Practice

The Court of Appeal has continued to evolve the notion of fairness with regard to the admissibility of confessions. In *R v Delaney* (1989) 88 Cr App R 338 and *R v Keenan* [1989] 3 All ER 598, discussed in last year's Review at pp 145–146, it was held that breaches of the Code of Practice, especially those concerned with the procedures for recording interviews, could adversely affect the fairness of the trial itself. However, the intimate connection between the fairness of the investigation and that of the trial is not yet fully assimilated by the police. The accused in *R v Canale* [1990] 2 All ER 187, was arrested on suspicion of various offences, including conspiracy to rob. During his first two interviews virtually all the provisions concerning recording, laid down by the Code of Practice for the Detention, Treatment and Questioning of Persons by the Police (Code C), were ignored. No contemporaneous record was made and no reason for the omission was entered in officers' notebooks. The police purported to put things right by holding two further interview of which contemporaneous records were made and in which the accused was said to have repeated admissions made in the first interviews, but even then the Code was not scrupulously followed in all its parts. No better justification was provided for the breaches than that police though that the best way would be not to have contemporaneous records. Lord Lane CJ described this justification as a 'cynical disregard of the rules'.

It is important to recognise that the policy reflected in the new approach adopted by the courts is not merely concerned with the formalities of Code but represents a deeper concern. Before the Police and Criminal Evidence Act 1984 came into effect the courts found themselves in an invidious position when it came to determining the admissibility of contested confessions: they were presented with the uncorroborated and conflicting accounts of the accused and the police and, basically, had to decide whether they were prepared to put their faith in the integrity of the police. Prior to 1985, the courts' forgiveness of wholesale breaches of the Judges' Rules suggested that the courts were content to take police integrity for granted. The gravamen of the change that has since occurred lies in the fact that the courts are no longer willing to accept police integrity at face value and are no longer prepared to adjudicate between conflicting claims as to what happens during interrogation unaided by some reliable contemporaneous record of the events in the police station.

The case under consideration illustrates this point. At the start of the interrogation, the accused, a robust ex-soldier, denied any involvement in the offences. During the unrecorded interviews he somehow changed his mind and confessed. The accused's defence was that although he had made the admissions attributed to him, they were induced by the police and were untrue. The Lord Chief Justice explained that while this defence raised a question of admissibility under ss 76 and 78 of the Police and Criminal Evidence Act 1984, the failure to record the interviews:

> 'deprived the [judge] of the very evidence which would have enabled him to come to a more certain conclusion as to what he should do . . . because he was deprived of that contemporaneous note which should have been made.'

In the absence of a reliable record of the interviews, he concluded, it was not possible for the court to come to a fair and reliable conclusion as to what brought about the accused's *volte-face*. An attempt by the police to rescue the admissibility of the statements made during the later interviews on the ground that these, unlike the earlier ones, were not affected by substantial breaches of the Code failed. The Court of Appeal held that 'the admissibility of those [later] interviews depends in turn on whether the admissions in the first interview were proved to be properly obtained or not. Thus the initial breaches . . . affected the whole series of purported admissions'. This point is very important since it makes it clear that the court sees the criminal process as a continuous entity, the various parts of which are intimately connected with each other. Thus, you cannot say that an interview in which the Code was observed was entirely proper and its fruits wholly pure if it was preceded by an interrogation in which all manner of Code provision was breached. And, by the same token, you cannot pretend that a trial is fair if it was preceded by an investigation which rode rough-shod over the suspect's rights.

Although this new notion of procedural fairness is still in its infancy and not entirely coherent, certain salient features are gaining in clarity. One of these is that the exclusion of confessions obtained in breach of the Code does not depend on whether the breaches were in bad faith. The purpose of the exclusionary jurisdiction is not to punish the police for lapses of discipline but to protect the suspect's procedural rights and ensure that he is not deprive of a fair trial. Thus, a breach that denies the suspect the opportunity of reading, and reacting to, a contemporaneous record of his answers to police questions, may subject him to a serious procedural disadvantage, whether or not the breach was in bad faith; *R v Walsh* [1989] Crim LR 822. Another important feature concerns the scope of the Code's application. Many of the provisions in the Code, such as the recording provisions, apply only to interviews. It has been decided that 'interview' includes any discussion between an officer and a suspect about an alleged crime: *R v Absolam* (1989) 88 Cr App R 332; *R v Matthews* (1990) 91 Cr App R 43. Such a wide definition is highly desirable because it leads to comprehensive application of the Code's safeguards.

However, this policy of comprehensive application has been somewhat cut down in two respects. It has been held that the Code's requirement that the suspect be shown the record of his questioning does not apply to interviews outside the police station: *R v Brezeanu and Francis* [1989] Crim LR 650. More disturbing is the decision in *R v Maguire* (1990) 90 Cr App R 115, that it does not amount to an interview, and therefore outside the purview of the Code, for a police officer to ask questions near the scene of the crime in order to elicit an explanation which might exculpate the suspect. It is difficult to see why the motive of obtaining an exculpatory explanation should relieve the police of the need to work within the Code, as it must always be the object of the police to obtain exculpatory explanations as well as inculpatory ones. Indeed, the police have always claimed that at the investigatory stage they do not act as a prosecutor but as an open minded investigator who is looking as much for information that would clear the suspect as for information that would inculpate him. Moreover, it is not possible to distinguish between an interview designed to obtain inculpatory information and one calculated to obtain exculpatory explanation, as the facts of *Maguire* illustrate. Two officers noticed a juvenile trying to enter a house in suspicious circumstances, gave chase, arrested him and asked him some questions. When he appeared evasive, the suspect was told by the officers not to be 'stupid' and to 'tell the truth', 'for your own good'. It is only on the most unrealistic assumptions that such an interview can be described, as it was by the Court of Appeal, as being for the purpose of affording 'the person arrested the opportunity to give an innocent explanation for his conduct, if one existed'. It does not seem sensible to remove all safeguards where the suspect is in the hands of police officers away from the police station and beyond the reach of the moderating influence of senior officers and established practices. Far from throwing all caution to the winds, the insistence upon the implementation of the Code's procedure should be all the more pressing in circumstances such as took place in this case.

A further respect in which the courts' decisions do not appear to be entirely consistent with the policy of insistence on scrupulous observance of the Code has to do with the presence of a solicitor. In *R v Dunn* (1990) 91 Cr App R 237, the police breached the Code by failing to make a contemporaneous record of an interview, failing to enter the reason for this and failing to show the record to the suspect for confirmation. The suspect denied making an inculpatory statement and the issue concerned exclusion under s 78 of the Police and Criminal Evidence Act 1984. The Court of Appeal upheld the refusal to exclude the statement on the ground that the suspect's solicitor was present, notwithstanding the fact that the solicitor supported the suspect's denial of making the statement in question. It might be argued that here too 'the judge was deprived', in the words of Lord Lane CJ in *Canale*, 'of the very evidence which would have enabled him to come to a more certain conclusion as to what he should do . . . because he was deprived of that contemporaneous note which should have been made'. On the other hand, where a solicitor has been present, the court can have greater confidence in it's ability to ascertain the facts and have fewer qualms about having to choose between two uncorroborated and biased sources.

Refreshing memory

In examination in chief, a party may not suggest to his witness what to say because this may prompt the witness to testify not from his own knowledge but from the suggestion. At times a witness may require help in remembering events that took place long before the trial and he is therefore allowed to refresh his memory from a document recording the events in question. However, here too there lurks a danger that the witness may be induced to assert not that which he remembers but that which the document suggests. To counteract this risk, the rule is that only a document written by, or under the supervision of, the witness while the event was fresh in the witness's memory may be used for this purpose. Where the witness has made a statement before the trial, he would at times be offered the opportunity to read his statement prior to going into the witness box but it is also permissible to show the statements to the witness during his testimony. This last course is desirable where the document contains minute details, such as figures, which the witness cannot be expected to retain in his mind.

It was argued in *R v Da Silva* [1990] 1 All ER 29, that the refreshing of memory in the witness box may be facilitated only by a contemporaneous document. Where the witness's statement was not contemporaneous with the event, it was contended, consultation of the document has to take place before the witness takes the stand; once he has begun to testify, it was too late to let the witness look at the document nor was it allowed to adjourn the trial in order to enable the witness to consult the document. The Court of Appeal declined to subscribe to such pointless rule. Stuart-Smith LJ explained that a trial judge has a discretion to allow a witness, who has begun testifying, to refresh his memory from a statement made near the time of the events in question even though it was not contemporaneous with the events. However, before doing so, the judge must be satisfied that the witness cannot otherwise recall the events, that the statement was made near the time of the event in question and represented the witness's recollection, that the witness had not read it before going into the box and, lastly, that he wishes to consult the document.

The ruling in this case makes sense provided that a document helps the witness to remember here and now what he once knew of the past event. If a present memory is revived in the witness's mind it makes little difference whether the document is contemporaneous or not, whether it was read by the witness before or during his testimony in court or, indeed, whether or not it was made under the witness's supervision. But quite different considerations come into play where it cannot be assumed that a present memory is revived in the witness's mind. It would appear that the court was only concerned with the former type of case because Stuart-Smith LJ said that what 'must be avoided is a witness simply reading his statement when he has no real recollection of the events; but that can be avoided by removing the statement from him once he has read it to refresh his memory'. This last course cannot, however, be taken where the witness is testifying to figures he knew long ago, such as accounts or the registration number of a car he fleetingly observed in the past. In such situations it is not customary to remove the record from the witness, once he has looked at it, and examine his present memory of the figures in question because such examination will only yield that which must in any event be assumed: that there is no present recollection. In these cases the talk about refreshing memory is entirely unrealistic and it is better to deal with these situations as an exception to hearsay, provided the statement contains a contemporaneous and verified statement by the witness and the witness is available to cross-examination on the circumstances surrounding the event and the making of the statement.

Cross-examination on credit

The distinction between relevance to issue and relevance to credit has returned to haunt the practice of cross-examination; this time of a complainant of a sexual offence about her previous sexual experience. The appellant in *R v Funderburk* [1990] 2 All ER 482, was charged with several counts of unlawful sexual intercourse with a 13-year-old girl. The complainant gave a detailed description of the incidents and, although the prosecution did not expressly seek to bring this out, indicated that she had not had sexual intercourse with any other person. The appellant denied the incidents and the defence wished to show that the complainant had had sexual experience such as would enable her to give a plausible description of sexual intercourse. Had the complainant denied this, the defence would have wished to prove an out of court statement by the complainant in which she indicated that she had had intercourse with her boy friends. The trial judge refused to allow the cross-examination and, a fortiori, proof of the previous statement. He ruled that the complainant's virginity was not relevant to the issue of intercourse and that therefore s 4 of the Criminal Procedure Act 1865 disallowed both questions about the complainant's sexual experience and proof of her earlier statement.

Section 4 of the 1865 Act allows a party to adduce proof of a previous inconsistent statement which is 'relative to the Subject Matter of the Indictment' but which the witness denies making. This provision, the Court of Appeal has held, governs only proof of inconsistent statements and does not affect the freedom of the opponent to ask the witness in cross-examination whether she had made a statement inconsistent with her testimony in court. It does not, however, follow from this that defence counsel is free to cross-examine a complainant, such as the girl in this case, without inhibition. A statutory provision inhibits the cross-examination of rape victims. Section 2 of the Sexual Offences (Amendment) Act 1976 prohibits questions about the sexual experience of rape victims, but permission to put such questions may be granted where the questions are necessary in fairness to the accused. Although this provision does not apply to the victims of other sexual offences, Henry J indicated that 'the court will not wish to see the mischief sought to be prevented by that act perpetuated in this context [ie unlawful intercourse trials] and therefore will be astute to see such that cross-examination is not abused or extended unnecessarily'.

The Court of Appeal held that the permissibility of cross-examination on credit turns on whether the questions, in the words of Lawton LJ in *R v Seet-Escott* (1971) 55 Cr App R 316, 320, 'relate to his [the witness's] likely standing . . . with the tribunal which is . . . listening to his evidence'. This is no more than the ordinary test of relevance and allows any questions designed to undermine the witness's credibility. On this test, the Court of Appeal has decided, the defence should have been allowed to question the complainant about her sexual experience because if she had not been a virgin at the time of the alleged offence, as she claimed, she could have used her knowledge to concoct a false but plausible story about intercourse with the appellant. The investigation of the complainant's credibility in this regard was of particular importance since it was admitted that the complainant's mother had a grudge against the appellant. Having concluded that the questions were permissible, the Court of Appeal proceeded to consider whether it would have been permissible for the defence to call evidence of the complainant's admission of previous intercourse in order to rebut her claim of virginity.

Here the court came up not only against s 4 of the 1865 Act but also against the *Hitchcock* rule which forbids contradicting a witness by independent evidence on collateral matters. Collateral matters, for the purpose of this rule, are those that go to credibility rather than to the issue. This distinction makes little sense (for discussion see Zuckerman, *Principles of Criminal Evidence* (1989) p 94) as this case illustrates. The entire case for the prosecution depended on the complainant's evidence and consequently everything hangs on her credibility. Clearly, anything that undermined her credibility also undermined the prosecution's case. Unfortunately, the Court of Appeal did not find the strength to accept that the distinction is unhelpful and to hold that admissibility of an inconsistent statement, or for that matter of independent evidence contradicting the witness's testimony, depends on the probative significance of the proposed evidence. It did, however, come close to this conclusion by saying that in the circumstances of this particular case the difference between relevance to credit and to issue is reduced to vanishing point. Henry J explained that:

> 'the challenge to the loss of virginity was a challenge that not only did the jury deserve to know about on the basis that it might have affected their view on the central question of credit, but was sufficiently closely related to the subject matter of the indictment for justice to require investigation for the basis of such challenge.'

This led Henry J to the conclusion that the inconsistent statement was admissible both under the 1865 Act and at common law. This way of arriving at the conclusion seems unduly complicated. What is closely related to the subject matter is clearly the credibility of the complainant; this factor of credibility does not change its quality into something other than credibility by the close relation. It would have been simpler to say, therefore, that when credibility is so central to the issue, it may be independently rebutted.

The Court of Appeal allowed the appeal against conviction on the charges that wholly depended on the complainant's testimony. At the same time it expressed sympathy for the judge's difficulty in dealing with such a complicated legal issue while on circuit and with no access to library facilities and to the authorities. Yet this is a fairly common question which judges trying cases, whether on circuit or not, should be able to resolve without extensive library researches. Sadly, the Court of Appeal took only meagre steps towards making the task of trial judges more straightforward. It perpetuated the distinction between relevance to credibility and relevance to issue by subscribing to the view that where 'questions go solely to the credibility of the witness or to collateral facts the general rule is that answers given to such questions are final and cannot be contradicted by rebutting evidence'. To that rule it listed no less than seven exceptions, two of which are not even true exceptions as they deal with evidence going to the issue. The other exceptions relate to the following categories: evidence showing bias, evidence showing that the police were prepared to go to improper lengths to secure conviction (which is really no different from bias), previous convictions, and evidence of medical condition affecting the credibility of the witness. Explaining these exceptions Henry J said that 'where it is found that rules designed to promote justice [here the rule about finality of answers on collateral matters] interfere in any given case with justice, then the court must look anxiously to see whether this is an exceptional category of case'. He went on to observe that the above categories of exception are not closed and that it 'is impossible to tell the circumstances in which some problems may arise in the future'.

This immediately raises the question: if the categories are not closed, how is a trial judge to know that he is permitted to allow evidence on a collateral matter when the case in front of him does not fall within one of the exceptions? The answer is implicit in the Court of Appeal's decision. Henry J explained that, as a general rule, evidence on collateral issues is excluded because such evidence might unnecessarily multiply issues and distract the jury's attention from the principal matters in dispute. He went further to observe that the exceptions demonstrate the proposition that 'a general rule designed to serve the interests of justice should not be used where . . . it might defeat them'. However, it would be far more helpful to trial and appeal judges alike if the rule, the exception and the general policy, could be assimilated into a simple, uncomplicated and general rule. This rule could take the following form. A party cross-examining a witness may not call independent evidence to contradict the witness's answers except with the leave of the judge. Such leave will not be given except where the party satisfies the judge, in the words of s 2(2) of the Sexual Offences (Amendment) Act 1976, 'that it would be unfair to that [party] to refuse to allow the evidence to be adduced'. This test is basically one of sufficiency of relevance and trial judges are already familiar with it. Indeed, it is the case that except in relation to rape cases, there is no hard and fast rule that informs the judge which questions to allow and which to disallow in cross-examination. Thus judges have to exercise their judgment in drawing the boundaries of permissible questioning. These boundaries will encompass the matters in dispute both with regard to the final issues and to credibility but they would leave out questions which are not directed to elucidate the matters in dispute but rather to annoy or belittle the witness. The Sexual Offences (Amendment) Act 1976 was passed to protect the sensitivity and privacy of rape victims from unnecessary infringement. But, as this case illustrates, such protection is now extended beyond the narrow scope of the Act in the exercise of judicial discretion. Surely, judges can be similarly encouraged to exercise judgment in situations calling for a decision on which matters a witness may be contradicted. Once they become aware that the decision whether or not to allow proof on an inconsistent statement turns on its probative significance, they will be less dependent on library facilities and, indeed, on learned disquisitions about different kinds of relevance.

Disclosure of confidential information

It is well established that confidentiality is not a bar to adducing evidence in court: *X Ltd v Morgan-Grampian Ltd* [1990] 2 All ER 1, 15 (see pp 50–51 above, pp 208–211, 265–266 below). It is equally well established that the need of an accused person to defend himself against a criminal accusation overrides immunity from disclosure in those instances where confidential information is exempt from production on grounds such as public interest immunity or legal professional privilege: *R v Barton* [1972] 2 All ER 1192. What is not always clear is what should a stranger to the criminal trial do when he is in possession of confidential information that is relevant to the accused's defence. This was the situation in *Re an ex parte originating summons in an adoption application* [1990] 1 All ER 639.

A social worker discovered that adoption files contained a statement that corroborated the defence of a person whose conviction of a serious crime was under appeal. The Adoption Agencies Regulations 1983 impose a duty of confidentiality on persons dealing with such files. Upon the discovery of the information in the adoption files, the responsible authority issued originating summons to notify the court of the matter and seek guidance. Ewbank J decided that the information should be disclosed to the Attorney General who is to determine whether the information should then be passed on to the court or to the accused whose appeal was pending. Following this decision a practice direction has been promulgated requiring that the Attorney General should be notified of applications of this kind so that he may be represented at the hearing (see also Family Law, p 151 below).

It may be observed here that in *R v Ataou* [1988] 2 All ER 321, the accused's solicitor discovered during the trial that he was in possession of statement made by a former client, who was now testifying against the accused, in which the former client made claims which were both inconsistent with his testimony and favourable to the accused. The solicitor passed on the statement to the accused's counsel who sought permission to override the legal privilege in the statement so that the witness may be cross-examined on it. The court gave permission but criticised the solicitor in question for his conduct (for commentary see All ER Rev 1988, p 138). One wonders whether it might not be appropriate for solicitors faced with such a situation to approach the court for guidance. At least in this way the matter will not rest entirely on their conscience.

The right to secure attendance of witnesses

The applicant in *R v Bradford Justices, ex p Wilkinson* [1990] 2 All ER 833 (also discussed at p 87 above) was charged with drunken driving. In his defence he contended that it was not him but another person who drove the car at the material time. When the witnesses he summoned did not turn up, he applied for the issue of witness warrants to compel the attendance of this witnesses. The magistrates refused to issue the warrants on the grounds that coerced witnesses were unlikely to be valuable and it was therefore unjustified to delay the trial any further. The applicant was convicted and sought an order for certiorari which was allowed by the High Court. The court held that the justices were under a duty to grant the warrants since evidence sought by the accused was crucial to his case. Rose J described the course taken by the magistrates as a denial of natural justice.

For the possibility open to an accused person to interview a ward of court see *Re R (minors)* (1991) NLJ, 8 February 164.

Corroboration – perjury

Section 13 of the Perjury Act 1911 is unhappily phrased. It provides that a person shall not be liable for conviction for perjury 'solely upon the evidence of one witness as to the falsity of any statement alleged to be false'. The accused in *R v Peach* [1990] 2 All ER 966, testified before a coroner's jury, called to determine whether certain articles were treasure trove, that the articles were found in his brother's house. Later he told two witnesses that he wished to put the record straight and that the items were found elsewhere. Two questions arose: was there evidence of falsity and was it solely based on the evidence of one witness? The Court of Appeal has decided that the statement made by the accused before the two witnesses was, in effect, a confession and amounted to evidence of falsity and that it was attested to by two witnesses and therefore fulfilled the requirement of s 13.

In view of the poor drafting of the section it is difficult to quarrel with this decision though one point may be made. As a matter of construction it is possible to argue that a 'witness as to falsity' means a witness able to testify as to his knowledge of the falsity. For instance, a witness who testifies that he saw the accused dig out the item in a field will be testifying from his own knowledge that the item was not found in the brother's house, as the accused had sworn before the coroner's jury. The Court of Appeal seems to have rejected this contention on the ground that in 'cases where the only person who knows that the sworn statement was untrue is the defendant himself, he will never be convicted, however often he asserted the untruthfulness of the statement which he has made on oath'. This is doubtless true but the Court of Appeal's ruling will now discourage a witness who has given false testimony to own up because by doing so he will be exposing himself to a prosecution for perjury which, had the above-mentioned argument been accepted, would not have been possible. It is difficult to decide whether it is better to deter persons from discrediting their earlier evidence on oath, as this decision does, or to encourage them to put the record straight with impunity.

Unsworn child evidence

R v Z [1990] 2 All ER 971, is one of the first cases concerning evidence given by a child of tender years to be considered by the Court of Appeal since the procedure of video linked testimony was introduced. The appellant, who had been convicted of incest with his five-year-old daughter, contended that the judge should not have allowed the evidence of such a small child. The Court of Appeal rejected this contention holding that the reluctance of courts in the past to accept the evidence of children of this age was in part due to consideration for the children's feelings. With the new procedure in place, it was felt, children are better protected. It was also felt that the abolition of the corroboration requirement in the proviso to s 38(1) of the Children and Young Persons Act 1938, by s 34(1) of the Criminal Justice Act 1988, was indicative of a greater acceptability of the testimony of young children. It has therefore been held that decisions whether children of young age are possessed of sufficient intelligence to warrant the acceptance of their testimony is best left to the discretion of trial judges.

Hearsay – exceptions

R v Cole [1990] 2 All ER 108, is perhaps the first case in which the Court of Appeal has had an occasion to pronounce on the exceptions to the hearsay rule introduced by the Criminal Justice Act 1988. The accused was charged with assault occasioning actual bodily harm. His defence was that the victim approached him in a threatening way and that he struggled with the victim in order to defended himself. The prosecution case was that the accused hit the victim because the latter, who was a security officer, had tried to restrain the accused's children who had been misbehaving. The victim and other persons present testified but, in addition, the prosecution sought to adduce the statement of another security officer, Luff, who was present and who has since died. This statement was contained in a formal witness statement, incorporating the declaration that the maker was aware that it might be tendered in evidence and that he would be liable for prosecution should he willfully make a false statement. Luff stated that the accused first made to hit him but when he was told by his daughter that he was not the right man the accused then set upon the victim.

The statement was tendered under s 26 of the 1988 Act which lays down the conditions for admitting statements which are admissible by virtue of ss 23 or 24 of the Act but which have been prepared for criminal investigation or proceedings. Section 26 provides that such a statement 'shall not be given in evidence . . . unless it [the court] is of the opinion that the statement ought to be admitted in the interests of justice'. The section then enumerates a number of matters to which the court must have regard in determining admissibility including 'to any risk, having regard in particular to whether it is likely to be possible to controvert the statement if the person making it does not attend to give oral evidence in the proceedings, that its admission or exclusion will result in unfairness to the accused'.

The trial judge decided to admit the statement because, amongst others, the accused was in a position to controvert it by his own evidence and by that of other eye-witnesses which he called at the trial. Counsel for the accused contended that the judge should not have taken into account the accused's opportunity to contradict the statement by his own testimony or that of his witnesses. The judge, so it was contended, should only have considered the possibility open to the accused to controvert the statement by cross-examination of witnesses for the prosecution. The Court of Appeal rejected this argument. The trial judge, it held, may take into account any facility that the accused may have to controvert the hearsay statement, whether by challenging prosecution witnesses, calling witnesses that appear to be available to him and testifying himself. Ralph Gibson LJ explained that:

'the court is not required . . . to assess the possibility of controverting the statement upon the basis that the accused will not give evidence or call witnesses known to be available to him. The decision by the accused whether or not to give evidence or call witnesses is made by him by reference to the admissible evidence put before the court; and the accused has no right . . . for the purposes of this provision, to be treated as having no possibility of controverting the statement because of his right not to give evidence or to call witnesses.'

If a statement of the kind adduced in this case remains uncontradicted, the trial judge would presumably be entitled to tell the jury that while the accused has a right not to testify, the jury may have regard to the fact that the statement remained uncontradicted by the accused. The effective consequence of this decision is, therefore, that wherever an out of court statement containing an account of the accused's own acts or of facts that occurred in his presence is admitted in evidence, the accused will be under considerable pressure to go into the witness box and challenge the hearsay statement. This may not, however, be objectionable seeing that the accused would be in no better position, from this point of view, were the prosecution to call to the maker of the statement to testify. Furthermore, the Court of Appeal emphasised that the ability of the accused to controvert the statement is not the only or even the most important consideration in determining admissibility. The judge must consider the extent of the unfairness to the accused that might arise from the admission of a statement made by a person whom the accused cannot cross-examine. A great deal will therefore turn on the quality of the statement adduced. The quality test, which was explained by Lord Griffiths in relation to a different exception to hearsay in *Scott v R* [1989] 2 All ER 305, 313 (All ER Rev 1989, p 142) applies here too.

While the quality factor is both clear and workable, the same cannot be said about other considerations touched upon in the Court of Appeal's judgment. It was said that the trial judge must 'consider how far any potential unfairness, arising from the inability to cross-examine . . . may be effectively counter-balanced' by appropriate warning of the need to treat with caution an out of court statement and by an explanation of any weakness of such statement. It is difficult to see what this consideration adds to the assessment of quality. As far as warning regarding the absence of cross-examination is concerned, either it is possible to convince juries adequately of the necessity of making allowance for the fact that the maker of the statement has not been cross-examined or it is not; there no middle course here. As far as an explanation of the weaknesses of the statement is concerned, this turns entirely on quality; if the quality is good, ie the statement is clear and unambiguous, the maker had no motive to lie and ample opportunity to observe the facts to which he attested, then a warning may be adequate. But no warning will be adequate where the quality is poor, as where the statement is unclear and the maker could have been motivated by malice. It would therefore seem to follow that the effectiveness of any warning about the risk of relying on hearsay or of any explanation of weakness of hearsay also turns on quality.

Similar obscurity lies behind the fairness test. Ralf Gibson LJ said (at 115) that:

> 'In judging how to achieve the fairness of the trial a balance must on occasion be struck between the interest of the public in enabling the prosecution case to be properly presented and the interest of a particular defendant in not being put in a disadvantageous position, for example by the death or illness of a witness. The public of course also has a direct interest in the proper protection of the individual accused.'

Since the public interest requires both that evidence of guilt should be presented and that the accused should be protected from unreliable evidence, it is difficult to see how the balancing process alluded to in this passage can hinge on anything except the quality of the statement. The existence of a balancing test which adds nothing to the criterion of quality is only likely to confuse, as does the existence of various kinds of overriding discretion to exclude hearsay evidence. According to s 28 of the Criminal Justice Act 1988, the provisions concerning hearsay do no affect 'any power of a court to exclude at its discretion a statement admissible by virtue . . . of this Act'.

This is a reference to the discretion to exclude under s 78 of the Police and Criminal Evidence Act 1984 and to the discretion to exclude at common law. All these discretions are exercisable with a view to ensuring the fairness of the trial. It is not easy to see how a judge who is, in the words of s 26 of the 1988 Act, 'of the opinion that the statement ought to be admitted in the interests of justice', can still arrive at the conclusion that its exclusion is required in order to ensure a fair trial, unless we consider the fairness of the trial to be different from the interests of justice. The Court of Appeal did, however, eschew a further source of confusion. The statement adduced by the prosecution in this case would also have been admissible under s 13(3) of the Criminal Justice Act 1925 which renders admissible, in certain circumstances, depositions used in committal proceedings. The court declined to express an opinion on whether the test for admissibility was essentially different and held that where a statement is admissible both under the 1988 and the 1925 Acts, the prosecution should use the provisions of the more recent provision.

The exception to hearsay which was contained in s 68 of the Police and Criminal Evidence Act 1984 was repealed by the Criminal Justice Act 1988 and replaced by the provisions in Part II of the 1988 Act. Nonetheless, *R v Iqbal* [1990] 3 All ER 787, which deals with the repealed provision, is of some interest. The accused was charged with the unlawful importation of a drugs. His defence was that the drugs were placed in his suitcases without his knowledge. To support this defence he wished to adduce the confessions of the alleged perpetrators of the insertion of the drugs, which were made during police interrogation in Pakistan. These confessed perpetrators jumped bail and were not available for testimony. The main issue in the case was whether the confessions recorded by the Pakistan police represented a 'record' as stipulated by s 68 of the 1984 Act, and was answered in the affirmative by the Court of Appeal. Since the new provisions of the 1988 Act no longer stipulate the necessity of a record, this aspect is of limited interest now. What is, however, important is the extent to which an accused may be able to adduce in evidence the confession of a third person.

A confession by a third party, of the kind adduced in *Iqbal*, could be tendered under s 24 of the Criminal Justice Act 1988. This section renders admissible 'a statement in a document . . . created or received by a person in the course of . . . a paid or unpaid office'. A police officer acting in the execution of his duty is presumably fulfilling a paid office for the purpose of this provision. The section requires that 'the information . . . was supplied by a person . . . who had . . . personal knowledge of the matters dealt with'. A person who confesses to the commission of an offence does possess such knowledge. However, limitations are imposed in respect of statements prepared for criminal investigations or criminal proceedings, such as the confessions in this case. These include, according to s 24(4)(*b*), the need to fulfil the conditions of s 23 by, for example, showing that the person who made the confession is not available to testify. Again, this condition was fulfilled here. A further obstacle is set up by s 26 which provides, as we have already seen, that statements prepared for criminal investigation or proceedings shall not be given in evidence unless the court is satisfied 'that the statement ought to be admitted in the interests of justice'. This requires the court to consider the circumstances of the statement and the risk that it was concocted. The Court of Appeal in *Iqbal* made it clear that it was aware of possible abuse in this regard and it is therefore unlikely that the courts will be easily persuaded to admit the confessions of third persons willy-nilly.

Before leaving the 1988 exceptions, mention should be made of one puzzling provision. Section 24(3) states that the exception 'does not render admissible a confession made by an accused person that would not be admissible under section 76 of the Police and Criminal Evidence Act 1984'. It is difficult to assume that the reference to 'an accused person' is directed to the accused in whose trial the statement is sought to be adduced. This is because, as explained above, a confession is admissible only if its maker is unavailable to testify. At the same time it is difficult to see how the reference can indicate the third party who made the confession; for how could the confessions of the escaped Pakistani prisoners in *Iqbal* be put to the s 76 test in England?

Identity of informers and protection of accused

The rule is that a litigant, including an accused in a criminal trial, is not entitled to ask witnesses to reveal the identity of police informers. However, as an exception to this rule, such information may be sought where it is necessary in order to protect oneself against a criminal charge. In *R v Agar* [1990] 2 All ER 442 (see also p 89 above) the Court of Appeal found that the trial judge paid too much attention to the prohibition and too little attention to the interests of the accused. The latter was being tried for possession of drugs with intent to supply. His defence was that he was set up by X, who was acting in concert with the police, to come to X's house where drugs were planted by the police in order to provide false evidence against the accused. Counsel for the accused was confidentially informed by the prosecution that X was a police informer. Counsel then sought a ruling from the judge in chambers whether he could cross-examine the police witnesses about X's role. The judge ruled that he could not and, furthermore, that he was not to reveal the matter to his client or to his client's solicitor. Mustill LJ explained the reasons for quashing the conviction (at 448):

> 'There was a strong . . . overwhelming public interest in keeping secret the source of information, but . . . there was an even stronger public interest in allowing a defendant to put forward a tenable case in the best light.'

His Lordship also expressed the view that the restriction that the judge had imposed on counsel not to reveal the state of affairs to his client or to the latter's solicitor was an unwarranted and unjust interference with the relationship between counsel and client and with the ability of counsel to pursue his client's case. Mustill LJ went out of his way to warn of the undesirability of conducting discussions behind the accused's back. Indeed, it is only necessary to look at what took place in this case to realise the importance of observing this injunction. When counsel for the accused told the trial judge that he was in difficulty because his client wanted to know what took place in the judge's chambers in his absence, the judge advised counsel, essentially, to fob off the accused with some disingenuous explanation. It is to be hoped that the Court of Appeal's criticism will prevent the recurrence of such unseemly incidents.

Burden and standard of proof

Treasure trove is the property of the Crown. It consists, according to its legal definition, of articles of gold or silver deposited by someone who intended to retrieve it. It follows that gold and silver lost or abandoned do not fall into this category. This presents difficulty in prosecutions for theft of treasure trove consisting of ancient articles because it is often debatable whether the articles found were left with an intention of retrieval or were lost or abandoned. To overcome this problem the prosecution in *R v Hancock* [1990] 3 All ER 183, argued that it need not prove beyond reasonable doubt that ancient articles removed by an accused charged with such theft were in fact treasure trove. The Crown, it was contended, had an intermediary proprietary interest to have the status of articles so found determined by a coroner's jury, and concealment of a finding with the intent of defeating this right amounted to theft. The Court of Appeal rejected this argument, holding that no such proprietary right existed and that the prosecution had to establish, by proof beyond reasonable doubt, that the articles in question were treasure trove and thus capable of being stolen from the Crown. This is clearly right. If a person is to be convicted of theft, his guilt should be established by the usual standard and no relaxation of this principle would be justified simply because it is difficult to establish an intention of retrieval with regard to objects many centuries old. It is true that this decision makes prosecution for theft of treasure trove difficult, but the solution of this difficulty lies in a different direction· in legislation placing all objects of antiquity, and not just gold and silver, under a protective regime which is more coherent and rational than the anachronistic notion of treasure trove. (See pp 77–78 above for further discussion of *Hancock*.)

The Drug Trafficking Offences Act 1986 contains draconian provisions designed to enable the courts to seize property which persons convicted of drug trafficking offences have accumulated in their illicit activities. Once a person has been convicted of a drug trafficking offence, the court sentencing him must adopt the procedure laid out in the 1986 Act for the purpose of determining the extent to which the accused has benefited from drug trafficking and the amount that should be seized from him as part of his sentence. The intricacies of this procedure were considered in *R v Dickens* [1990] 2 All ER 626. Here we need only concern ourselves with points concerning the burden of proof.

The court may order the confiscation of only property and proceeds which were derived from drug trafficking activities. Since confiscation is a penal sanction, the prosecution would normally be expected to prove beyond reasonable doubt that the accused benefited from drug trafficking and the amount of such benefit. However, s 2(2) and 2(3) lightens the prosecution's task by creating certain presumptions, referred to in the section as 'assumptions'. These are, first, under s 2(3)(a):

> 'that any property appearing to the court – (i) to have been held by him [the accused] at any time since his conviction, or (ii) to have been transferred to him at any time [during the six years prior to the charge] . . . was received by him . . . as payment or reward in connection with drug trafficking carried on by him.'

and second, under s 2(3)(b):

'that any expenditure of his since the beginning of that period was met out of payments received by him in connection with drug trafficking carried on by him.'

Thus, the Act creates presumptions that any property received by him or expenditure made by him was derived from the accused's drug transactions. The basic facts of these presumptions are, in the case of the first presumption, that it appears to the court that he held or received property during the relevant period or, in the case of the second presumption, that he made expenditure during the same period. Once the basic facts of these presumptions have been established, the court is to infer the presumed facts, namely, that the property and expenditure in question were derived from drug trafficking. This presumption would be rebutted, as Lord Lane CJ explained in *Dickens* (at 629), if 'the defendant shows on the balance of probabilities that in respect to each item of property and expenditure the assumptions are in his case incorrect'. In other words, the defendant has to show that the property or expenditure in question was not connected with drug trafficking.

It was argued on behalf of the accused that before the presumptions can bite, the prosecution must prove, by the usual criminal standard, that the property was in fact held or received by him or that he made certain expenditure. The Court of Appeal rejected this argument, holding that the expression 'appearing to the court' in s 2(3)(a) of the 1986 Act, in the words of Lord Lane CJ:

'meant that, if there is prima facie evidence that any property has been held by the defendant since his conviction or was transferred to him since the beginning of the relevant period, the judge may make the assumption that it was payment or reward in connection with his drug trafficking.' (at 629, and see 630–1).

This conclusion is objectionable on several grounds. It is a fundamental principle that, in the absence of a clear indication to the contrary, a criminal statute is not intended to impose a burden of persuasion on the accused. This was acknowledged by Lord Lane CJ when he observed that:

'the nature of the penalties which are likely to be imposed make it clear that the standard of proof required is the criminal standard, namely proof so that the judge feels sure or proof beyond reasonable doubt.' (at 929)

It is true that this principle is displaced by the express presumptions created by s 2(2) and 2(3), but, as we have seen, a presumption comes into play only once its basic facts have been proved. The effect of the Court of Appeal's decision is to relieve the prosecution from the burden of establishing the basic facts as well as dispensing with proof of the presumed facts.

There is no express provision to dispense with proof of the basic facts and the wording of the section does not support such a conclusion. It is true that s 2(3)(a) refers to 'any property appearing to the court', but it does not follow from this that the facts may appear to the court without having been proved beyond reasonable doubt. Moreover, the presumption in s 2(3)(b) does not contain these words. It merely states 'that any expenditure of his since the beginning of that period was met out of payments received by him in connection with drug trafficking . . .'. If the only reason for relieving the prosecution of its usual burden in respect of the basic facts of the presumption in s 2(3)(a) hinges on the opening words 'any property appearing to the court', then it must follow that the absence of these words from s 2(3)(b) means that here the prosecution must prove expenditure in the usual way. It is seems absurd to assume that the legislature intended to draw such a distinction and that while the prosecution need only adduce prima facie evidence in relation to property held or transferred to the accused, it must prove beyond reasonable doubt any expenditure made by him. The more reasonable conclusion must be that in respect to both property held and expenditure made by the accused the prosecution bears the same burden and that the presumptions come into play only once the prosecution has established their basic facts by proof beyond reasonable doubt.

In making a case that the accused has benefited from drug trafficking and in establishing the extent of such benefit the prosecution may, in accordance with s 3 of the 1986 Act, tender statements dealing with these matters. However, these statements may be relied upon only if they are accepted by the accused. If they are not accepted, the prosecution must adduce evidence to establish the facts contained in such statements.

Extradition

I M YEATS, BCL, MA
*Barrister, Senior Lecturer in Law, Queen Mary and Westfield College,
University of London*

Mr Lorrain Osman has been in custody in the United Kingdom since December 1985; his efforts to resist surrender to Hong Kong over this exceptional period have contributed a substantial body of case law on the Fugitive Offenders Act 1967 in its last years of life. The latest reported episode is *R v Governor of Pentonville Prison, ex p Osman (No 3)* [1990] 1 All ER 999, in which the Divisional Court dealt with points of procedure and substance. The provisional warrant under which he had initially been arrested was the focus of a number of technical criticisms, including the complaint that the initial misspelling of his name with a surplus final 'e' had led to understandable confusion as to his sex in parts of the provisional warrant. The court was critical of the lack of care taken at Bow Street Magistrates' Court in this and other respects but this did not assist his application for habeas corpus.

Two of the procedural issues deserve to be recorded. In January 1989 the Hong Kong Court of Appeal quashed a warrant which had been issued in the colony in November 1985. The Divisional Court, however, held that this had no bearing on the validity of the provisional warrant issued in London. There was no requirement in s 6(1)(*b*) of the Fugitive Offenders Act 1967 that a warrant issued in the colony or a copy thereof should be produced to the magistrate or even that such a warrant should exist; it followed that the invalidity under Hong Kong law of the only warrant then in existence could not affect the English provisional warrant. The only matters on which the magistrate had to be satisfied were those specified in s 6(1)(*b*) and 6(2). Furthermore, the provisional warrant was not an integral step in the proceedings but a preliminary procedure to get the applicant into custody in order that the substantive issues could be determined in committal proceedings. Therefore, any invalidity in the provisional warrant, if there had been such, would not taint the subsequent proceedings. In any case, when the committal proceedings were themselves properly determined, it would be wrong to grant habeas corpus on the basis that the steps leading up to them were merely technically flawed.

Although it had been agreed at the committal proceedings that all the offences were relevant offences, the court reluctantly permitted argument that that was not true of those framed under s 9(1) of the Hong Kong Prevention of Bribery Ordinance. The court had therefore to consider the construction put by the House of Lords in *Government of Canada v Aronson* [1989] 2 All ER 1025 (All ER Rev 1989, p 157) on s 3(1)(*c*) of the 1967 Act, which provides that an offence is a relevant offence if:

> 'the act or omission constituting the offence, or the equivalent act or omission, would constitute an offence against the law of the United Kingdom if it took place within the United Kingdom.'

Section 9(1) is in these terms:

> 'Any agent who, without lawful authority or reasonable excuse, solicits or accepts any advantage as an inducement to or reward for or otherwise on account of his – (a) doing or forbearing to do, or having done or forborne to do, any act in relation to his principal's affairs or business; or (b) showing or forbearing to show, or having shown or forborne to show, favour or disfavour to any person in relation to his principal's affairs or business, shall be guilty of an offence.'

The equivalent English offence (s 1(1) of the Prevention of Corruption Act 1906), (a) qualifies 'accepts or obtains' with the adjective 'corruptly' and omits 'without lawful authority or reasonable excuse' and (b) does not contain the words 'or otherwise on account of'. Neither of these differences prevented the offence from being relevant. In the view of the Divisional Court, if the accused were convicted in Hong Kong under the Ordinance, it would have been determined that he had acted corruptly as that expression is understood in English law. The latter legislative difference could be resolved by deleting the words 'or otherwise on account of' (or, more precisely, since that was beyond the powers of the Divisional Court, by requiring counsel to undertake that particulars of the bribery charges would be amended before proceedings took place in Hong Kong). The situation is clearly different from that usually envisaged in *Aronson* and comparable cases, where the offence in the requesting state requires proof only of factors A, B and C, whereas the corresponding English offence requires proof of factors A, B, C and D. In *Osman* the offence in the requesting state was committed if A or B or C were established, whereas English law required proof of A or B; the particulars of the charge could therefore be framed so as to constrain the prosecution to establish one of the bases of liability recognised by English law.

Surrender of fugitives to a Commonwealth country or colony will in future be dealt with under the single code established by the Extradition Act 1989. Under that statute an extradition crime means (inter alia):

> 'conduct in the territory of a foreign state, a designated Commonwealth country or a colony which, if it occurred in the United Kingdom, would constitute an offence punishable with imprisonment for a term of 12 months, or any greater punishment, and which, however described in the law of the foreign state, Commonwealth country or colony, is so punishable under that law.' (s 2(1)(a)).

The emphasis has therefore moved from 'the act or omission constituting the crime' under the Commonwealth country's law to the notional happening of the conduct in the United Kingdom, and the need for congruence of the laws of the two states (except as to punishment) is eliminated.

In three cases fugitive criminals have argued that in one way or another the extradition proceedings involved an abuse of process or would be oppressive or unfair. In *Liangsiriprasert v United States Government* [1990] 2 All ER 866 (also discussed at p 72 above) the fugitive and an associate had agreed in Thailand with a United States undercover drug enforcement agent to supply heroin for sale in New York and further agreed to go to Hong Kong to collect their share of the proceeds. This arrangement was suggested by the agent because the parties would in the circumstances be subject to extradition under the United States treaty with Hong Kong but not under the treaty with

Thailand. The Privy Council had no difficulty in rejecting an argument that surrender would be oppressive; the fugitive had travelled voluntarily to Hong Kong and had not been removed forcibly or by some abuse of other procedures. The Privy Council distinguished *R v Bow Street Magistrates, ex p Mackeson* (1981) 75 Cr App R 24 on which the applicant relied and did not refer to the fact that that case (which in any event dealt with the propriety of trying the fugitive in, and not of extraditing him from, the United Kingdom) had been regarded by a later Divisional Court in *R v Plymouth Magistrates' Court, ex p Driver* [1985] 2 All ER 681 (All ER Rev 1985, p 169) as decided per incuriam.

Injustice of a different kind was canvassed by the applicant in *R v Governor of Pentonville Prison, ex p Sinclair* [1990] 2 All ER 789. He had been convicted of, inter alia, mail fraud in the United States in 1976 and was eventually ordered to start serving his sentence in March 1978, but in February of that year he went to Trinidad; he remained there until 1983 when he moved to London and established himself as a foreign exchange dealer. There was an unresolved clash of evidence as to whether he had tried to return to the United States from Trinidad and as to why no steps were taken to secure his return. It was also unclear why the decision taken in 1983 to seek his return from the United Kingdom was not actively implemented until 1987. He therefore alleged that it would now be oppressive to return him to the United States after such a lengthy interval. The Divisional Court held that the magistrate had rightly regarded as irrelevant specific provisions of the extradition treaty with the United States and then considered the general principle. The Extradition Act 1870 does not on its face empower the magistrate or the court to refuse extradition on grounds such as delay and hardship, but such a power has been thought appropriate in more recent legislation, namely s 8(3) of the Fugitive Offenders Act 1967 and s 11(3) of the Extradition Act 1989 which will eventually supersede the 1870 Act. Under that Act the Secretary of State alone had the discretion to avoid injustice to the accused by declining to implement a surrender which the court had held to be permissible. In *Atkinson v United States Government* [1969] 3 All ER 1317, [1971] AC 197 Lord Reid had held that once the magistrate had concluded that there was sufficient evidence to justify committal he had to commit the accused for trial. Section 9 of the Extradition Act, however, requires that the magistrate should determine the matter 'as near as may be' as if he were concerned with domestic committal proceedings. Since 1969, a doctrine of abuse of process has developed in relation to domestic committals (see *R v Derby Crown Court, ex p Brooks* (1984) 80 Cr App R 164) and by virtue of s 9 of the 1870 Act this could be absorbed into extradition committals without doing violence to the reasoning in *Atkinson*. The magistrates' power in domestic proceedings is to refuse to commit for trial where that would be an abuse of process and could therefore avail an applicant for habeas corpus only in cases where he was to be surrendered to stand trial in the requesting state. As Sinclair had already been convicted and was to be surrendered to serve a sentence already imposed, the reasoning derived from the development of domestic practice could not assist him.

The argument as to fairness in *R v Governor of Pentonville Prison, ex p Naghdi* [1990] 1 All ER 257 was directed at the extradition proceedings themselves. The applicant did not dispute that the committal proceedings were conducted fairly and justly or that he had received full information as to the charges before they began; he argued that this information should have been supplied earlier and included in the order to proceed. The Divisional Court was unimpressed and held that the established practice conformed to the statutory requirements and adequately protected the accused.

Family Law

S M CRETNEY, MA, DCL, FBA
Solicitor, Professor of Law, University of Bristol

The family – legal status or state of fact?

The Children Act 1989 is not expected to be brought into force until October 1991, but its implications for the development of family law have been the subject of much discussion and comment in the year under review. Broadly speaking, the Act adopts the philosophy that the welfare of the children is best achieved by partnership rather than coercion, and the Act accordingly promotes a non-interventionist policy: 'children are best looked after within the family' (Introduction to the Children Act 1989, HMSO). But what is a 'family'? The Act – at least for the purpose of defining local authority powers and duties – emphasises factual rather than legal links, so that, for example, 'family' in relation to a child in need is defined as including any 'person with whom he has been living' (s 17(10)).

The concept of the family as a factual rather than a juristic entity is for lawyers comparatively novel, and the case of *Re Collins (decd)* [1990] 2 All ER 47 (see also pp 274–275 below) illustrates the more conventional lawyer's perception of family relationships as being founded on legal status (that is to say, 'the condition of belonging to a class in society to which the law ascribes peculiar rights and duties, capacities and incapacities' *The Amthill Peerage* [1976] 2 All ER 411 at 424). Mrs Collins met her husband – a man with a record of violent crime – in 1978; but she left him because of his violence shortly afterwards. She was given leave to bring divorce proceedings within three years of the marriage on the grounds that the case was one of exceptional hardship or depravity. A decree nisi was granted; but before it had been made absolute, Mrs Collins died. Her husband accordingly became entitled on her intestacy to the whole of her estate; and her children – a son of the marriage and an illegitimate daughter who were left to the care of the local authority – were entitled to nothing. However, in proceedings under the Inheritance (Provision for Family and Dependants) Act 1975 the court held that reasonable financial provision had not been made for the daughter; and that she should accordingly receive for her maintenance £5,000 by way of a lump sum out of a total net estate of some £27,000. But the court refused to make any order in favour of the younger child. This was because he had been adopted a few months before the making of the application under the 1975 Act, and the effect of adoption is that an adopted child is treated in law as the child of the adopters and not as the child of any other person (Adoption Act 1976, s 39). The husband thus remained entitled to the rest of Mrs Collins's estate.

The case is a vivid illustration of the importance of legal status as against factual relationships. An apparently totally unmeritorious person succeeded to a substantial sum of money solely by virtue of the fact that he enjoyed the rights flowing from his status as the deceased's spouse. In contrast, the deceased's child was deprived of any provision because adoption had, as a matter of law, destroyed his legal parentage.

The status of legitimacy

Re Spence (decd) [1990] 2 All ER 827 (see also pp 139, 263, 277 below) provides a further example of the continuing importance of legal status in family matters. The plaintiff was biologically the brother of an intestate who had died in 1985; but both he and the intestate had been born illegitimate. The intestate had died before the coming into force of the relevant provisions of the Family Law Reform Act 1987 (on 4 April 1988), and it was thus still the case that an illegitimate person was treated for the purposes of intestate succession as if he had no siblings. The plaintiff claimed that he had been legitimated by the marriage of his parents in 1934, notwithstanding the fact that the 'marriage' was void because the mother's first husband was then alive and her previous marriage had not been dissolved. His claim was founded on the provision, based on the civil law 'putative marriage' doctrine, under which the child of a void marriage, whenever born, is entitled to be treated as the legitimate child of his parents if at the time of the act of intercourse resulting in the birth (or at the time of the celebration of the marriage if later) both or either of the parties reasonably believed that the marriage was valid: Legitimacy Act 1976, s 1(1). However, the Court of Appeal upheld the decision of Morritt J ([1989] 2 All ER 679) rejecting this claim: a person is not to be regarded as a 'child of a void marriage' unless his parents had entered into the 'marriage' *before* the child's birth. It is true, as Nourse LJ pointed out, that the expression 'child of a void marriage' is an unfortunate one; and it is not easy to see why Parliament should have intended to discriminate against a child whose parent reasonably believes that he or she has contracted a marriage which if valid would legitimate pre-marital children: Legitimacy Act 1976, s 2. But the Court of Appeal demonstrated that the legislation consistently treated children born to the parties to a void marriage differently from – and in some ways (for example, in relation to succession to titles of honour) more favourably than – children born to parents who subsequently contract a valid marriage; and it could not have been intended that a child born before a void marriage should be given greater rights in such respects than a pre-marital child legitimated by a valid marriage.

This particular issue (it should be noted) was tried as a preliminary issue; and, had the plaintiff succeeded, the court would, on trial of the action, no doubt have had to consider the reasonableness or otherwise of the parents' belief in the validity of their marriage. In that respect, however, s 28(2) of the Family Law Reform Act 1987 could have been of assistance to the plaintiff (notwithstanding the fact that the Act does not affect rights under intestacies occurring prior to 4 April 1988): this is because the Act 'declares' for the avoidance of doubt that a mistake of law is capable of being reasonable.

Family property

Status therefore remains important; but ever since the decisions of the House of Lords in *Pettitt v Pettitt* [1969] 2 All ER 385 and in *Gissing v Gissing* [1970] 2

All ER 780 it has been clear that marriage does not as such have any immediate effect on the parties' proprietary rights, which must (per Lord Upjohn, [1969] 2 All ER 385, 405) continue to be judged 'on the general principles applicable in any court of law when considering questions of title to property'. Disputes are therefore to be decided by the principles of law applicable to the settlement of claims between 'those who are not married while making full allowance in view of that relationship'.

To talk of family property law as a discrete subject may therefore be something of a solecism; and it certainly remains true (as Lord Dilhorne pointed out in Gissing v Gissing (at 785)) that the once-fashionable expression 'family assets' has no legal meaning as a method of solving questions of beneficial entitlement. Accordingly, full discussion of the two important House of Lords' decisions in the year under review – Lloyds Bank plc v Rosset [1990] 1 All ER 1111, and Abbey National Building Society v Cann [1990] 1 All ER 1085 – is appropriately to be found in the chapter of this Review dealing with Land Law and Trusts at pp 154–159 below. It should suffice to note here that in terms of legal doctrine neither case directly affects the principles clearly established by Pettitt and Gissing or the refinement of those principles in subsequent cases; and that it can accordingly fairly confidently be stated that a spouse (or other partner) who does not have a legal estate or interest in property may nonetheless in appropriate circumstances assert a claim to an equitable interest therein under the doctrines of implied, resulting or constructive trust. Such a trust – and it now seems that the weight of opinion favours classification as a 'constructive' rather than an 'implied' trust – may be made out if two conditions are satisfied. First, it must be shown that the parties had a common intention that the beneficial interests should be owned concurrently. Secondly, the claimant must be shown to have acted to her detriment in reliance on that common intention. So much is now orthodox property law; but it is right in this chapter to highlight some implications of the two cases – and of Lloyds Bank plc v Rosset in particular – which are of particular significance for family law.

In Lloyds Bank plc v Rosset a wife succeeded in satisfying both the trial judge and the Court of Appeal ([1988] 3 All ER 915, All ER Rev 1988, p 163) that she had the necessary intention, and that she had acted thereon to her detriment. These findings were, in the circumstances, unsurprising: she was a skilled painter and decorator, she had designed a breakfast room and kitchen, she had decorated two of the rooms and prepared one other bedroom and two lavatories, she had arranged insurance and security inspection and the installation of burglar alarms, and she had done a great deal to ensure that the semi-derelict farmhouse should be ready for occupation as the family home by Christmas, ie less than two months after the builders had moved in. But Lord Bridge of Harwich, stating the unanimous opinion of the Law Lords, had no doubt that the courts below had been wrong. He asserted (in this respect, at least, undoubtedly correctly) that what was at issue was not whether there was a common intention that a property be used as a family home, but whether there was a common intention that the ownership be shared. What is much more controversial – and indeed disturbing – is his assertion that the wife's activities before completion 'could not possibly justify' the drawing of any inference that such an intention had been present. This was because Lord Bridge considered that in the circumstances:

'it would seem the most natural thing in the world for any wife, in the absence of her husband abroad, to spend all the time she could spare and to employ any skills she might have, such as the ability to decorate a room, in doing all she could to accelerate progress of the work quite irrespective of any expectation she might have of enjoying a beneficial interest in the property.'

Moreover, even if the wife had been unable to demonstrate such an expectation, Lord Bridge would apparently have doubted whether her contributions were capable of constituting the requisite detriment.

Two comments may be made on this. First, it is tempting to suggest that the finding of the trial judge as to the parties' intention was a finding of fact; and that accordingly it should not have been disturbed – at least in the absence of any misdirection as to the law to be applied – by an appellate tribunal which had not heard the evidence or seen the parties. However, it does seem that Lord Bridge considered that there had been errors of law; and in particular, he apparently considered that excessive weight had been attached by the courts below to intention as to use (rather than ownership). Moreover, he considered that the courts had failed to distinguish between evidence capable of establishing an express agreement (which was admittedly not present in the case) and evidence (such as the making of contributions) based solely on the applicant's conduct. Where there was evidence based on 'express discussions . . . however imperfectly remembered and however imprecise the terms' Lord Bridge was prepared to accept that the contributions could be comparatively insignificant. But where the claim was not based on such discussions, the proper approach was much more restrictive:

'. . . direct contributions to the purchase price by the partner who is not the legal owner, whether initially or by payment of mortgage or instalments, will readily justify the inference necessary to the creation of a constructive trust. But as I read the authorities it is at least extremely doubtful whether anything else will do.'

This aspect of the decision is likely to be controversial and it may be questioned whether the distinction between inferences drawn from 'discussions' and those drawn from a pattern of activity is soundly based in principle, satisfactorily workable in practice, or indeed whether it is consistent with previous authority. More generally, there may well be some – apart from committed feminists – who feel that much of Lord Bridge's opinion is based on assumptions about the role of women in society and of the relationship between husband and wife which may not unfairly be described 'as decades if not generations' out of date: see *Porter v Porter* [1969] 3 All ER 640 at 643, per Sachs LJ.

The consequences of divorce and other matrimonial decrees

In *Re Spence (decd)* Nourse LJ stated that a void marriage is a nullity, 'only an idle ceremony. It achieves no change in the status of the participants. It achieves nothing of substance'. (at 832). This statement highlights one of the many paradoxes of modern family law: on the one hand, it is true that the parties to a void 'marriage' have no reciprocal legal rights or duties; yet if either party is granted a decree of nullity the Matrimonial Causes Act 1973, s 24 (1) empowers the court to exercise its discretion to make financial provision and property adjustment orders in favour of either party notwithstanding the fact that the 'marriage' is and always has been void and has never existed. Perhaps this does no more than reflect the policy – surprising to those brought up in other legal traditions – that English family law gives the court a discretion to adjust financial matters on the breakdown of a marriage whilst denying the parties any comparable rights during the subsistence of the marriage.

Two divorce cases reported in the year under review indicate both the extent of the courts' adjustive powers and also their readiness to use them. The more striking of the two is, perhaps *Gojkovic v Gojkovic* [1990] 2 All ER 84, CA – a 'story of high achievement and, many would think, glorious success' as the trial judge (Ward J) vividly put it. Penniless Yugoslavs, by unrelenting hard work, unlimited self sacrifice and absolute determination built up a fortune of some £4m. Their marriage broke down, and the Court of Appeal upheld property adjustment orders in favour of the wife amounting to some £1.3m. The court (per Russell LJ) declined to lay down guidelines about the appropriate level of provision in cases involving substantial capital assets, apparently on the basis that such guidelines are already to be found in the statutory directives: the court is to have regard to all the circumstances (including those particularised in the statute) and make orders accordingly. The 'wide discretion of the court' (said Butler-Sloss LJ, at 87) 'must not be fettered'. It is, however, particularly relevant to take into account the 'needs' of the applicant; and in this case those needs included the wife's requirements to have a sufficient sum of money to enable her to continue her career as a hotelier. It was also emphasised that the case was one in which the wife had made exceptional contributions to the wealth generated during the relationship ('a contribution greater than that often made by wives after long marriages', in the words of Butler-Sloss LJ, at 88); and she had thereby earned an enhanced share in the matrimonial assets. The court specifically rejected the husband's contention that the basic objective of the legislation was merely to provide self-sufficiency, and that accordingly, as a matter of principle, capital provision should not exceed a sum which would enable that objective to be attained. In particular, the income in 1985 values of £30,000 per annum which formed the basis of the award in *Duxbury v Duxbury* (1985) [1990] 2 All ER 77 did not necessarily represent a luxurious way of life; and it was wrong to think that *Duxbury* established any kind of benchmark or that the case had been intended to embody any principle of law.

Curiously, the word 'Duxbury' had come to be associated amongst practitioners with something not referred to in the Court of Appeal's reported judgments in the case – that is to say the computer programme which calculates the capital sum required, on the basis of varying assumptions about earning capacity, rates of inflation, pension expectations and so on to produce a specified income figure. There is no doubt that such calculations have been found useful in negotiating settlements; but in *Gojkovic* the Court of Appeal (surely correctly) held that such computations do no more than produce figures to which the judge is entitled to have regard. They cannot of themselves determine the outcome of the case which is still heavily (and, as some believe, excessively) dependent on judicial discretion.

Both *Duxbury* and *Gojkovic* reflect the fact that the courts appropriately make large awards in cases in which there are substantial assets; and although

– as the Court of Appeal pointed out in *Gojkovic* – the so-called 'minimal-loss' principle originally embodied in s 25 of the Matrimonial Causes Act 1973 has been replaced, so that the court is no longer required to attempt 'that which was impossible in the vast majority of cases' (per Butler-Sloss LJ at 88), yet the effect of the 'needs' approach as applied in these two cases may be to produce comparable levels of award in the absence of special factors (such as a short marriage).

The hidden cost of divorce – improving procedures

In recent years there has been increasing concern about the cost of divorce proceedings: see for example *Re T (Divorce: Interim Maintenance: Discovery)* [1990] 1 FLR 1 (where the total legal costs were in the region of £1m): *Newton v Newton* [1990] 1 FLR 33 (costs estimated at the 'horrifying figure' of £330,000.); *E v E (Financial Provision)* [1990] Fam Law 297 (costs estimated at £300,000). The dissipation of family assets on valuations of property had become a subject of particular concern, and case law (eg *B v B (Financial Provision)* [1989] 1 FLR 119, *P v P* [1989] 2 FLR 241; *B v B (Discovery: Financial Provision)* [1990] 2 FLR 180) had already established the principle that only those enquiries and valuations necessary to enable the court to perform the balancing exercise required by the legislation need to be made: see *Thyssen-Bornemisza v Thyssen-Bornemisza (No 2)* [1985] FLR 1069 at 1080, per Sir John Arnold P. But this involves steering between the Scylla of avoiding confrontation and dissipation of assets and costs on the one hand and the Charybdis of failing properly to protect clients' interest on the other hand: *Dutfield v Gilbert H Stephens and Sons* [1988] Fam Law 474.

The novelty of *Evans v Evans* [1990] 2 All ER 147 is that Booth J (with the concurrence of the President) sought to give clear guidance both of principle and detail to assist the profession and to minimise the burden on clients. Generally, legal advisers should bear in mind the desirability of reaching a settlement throughout the proceedings. They must, of course, have sufficient knowledge of the financial situation of both parties before advising a client on a proposed settlement (see *Dickinson v Jones Alexander & Co* [1990] Fam Law 137 where a solicitor's negligence in failing to make appropriate enquiries resulted in the wife of a man worth £5m becoming dependent on supplementary benefit, and living in a small house burdened with a mortgage that she could not service). But lawyers must also ask what is likely to be achieved by the making of further enquiry, and bear in mind the increased costs which would be incurred.

The judge gave some specific guidance: for example, enquiries under r 77 of the Matrimonial Causes Rules should as far as possible be contained in one comprehensive questionnaire and not piecemeal; a valuation should be obtained from a valuer jointly instructed by both parties (or failing that, reports should be exchanged and the valuers should discuss their differences); solicitors should together prepare the bundle of documents required at the hearing; a chronology of material facts should be agreed and made available to the court; at all stages of the proceedings clients should be kept informed of the costs incurred, and solicitors should ensure that legally aided clients understand the implications of the legal aid charge. But some of the guidance was more general: affidavit evidence should be confined to relevant facts, and not be prolix or diffuse; professional witnesses should be careful to avoid a partisan approach; and emotive issues which were not material should be avoided.

Debt and the family

On divorce (as Lord Denning put it so vividly in *Hanlon v The Law Society* [1980] 1 All ER 763 at 770) the court hands out the pieces of family property 'without paying any too nice a regard to [the parties' legal or equitable rights] but simply according to what is the fairest provision for the future, for mother and father and the children'. Discussion of beneficial entitlement is thus rarely relevant in the context of matrimonial proceedings; but beneficial entitlement remains important when the issue is whether property is to be made available to satisfy obligations incurred to an outsider (as indeed is evidenced in *Lloyds Bank plc v Rosset*, above.) The cases reveal a certain tension, well illustrated by cases decided in the year under review, between the attitudes reflected in the Matrimonial Causes legislation on the one hand and those embodied in debt enforcement law on the other.

In *Austin-Fell v Austin-Fell* [1990] 2 All ER 455 (also discussed in Land Law and Trusts, p 160 below) a bank recovered judgment in April 1984 for debts owed by the husband, and in September 1985 obtained a charging order on his interest in the matrimonial home. The wife had instituted matrimonial proceedings; and the charging order proceedings were on her application transferred to the Family Division and heard at the same time as her application for ancillary relief. The Registrar considered that adequate security could be provided only by giving the wife the entire beneficial interest in the property; and he accordingly (on the authority of a passage in the judgment of Balcombe LJ in *Harman v Glencross* [1986] 1 All ER 545, All ER Rev 1986, pp 168, 171) directed an outright transfer to the wife of the husband's beneficial interest in the matrimonial home. The bank appealed, contending that it was entitled to security for its debt (although it accepted that the enforcement of that security might have to be postponed in the interests of the family). The Divisional Court held that the Registrar had been wrong in assuming that there should ever be automatic predominance for the claim of the wife (or indeed of the creditor). On the contrary, the court's role was to strike a fair balance between the normal expectations of the creditor on the one hand, and the hardship to the wife and children if a charging order were made on the other; and there could thus be cases in which the wife and children would be compelled, in the interests of doing justice to the claims of the judgment creditor, to accept provision for their security of accommodation which fell below the level of 'adequacy': per Waite J at 461. Hence if, for example, the value of the equity were sufficient to enable wife and children to be re-housed (albeit at a lower standard than they might reasonably have expected had there been no indebtedness) the charging order could properly be made absolute at once. But in the present case the wife's equity was insufficient to re-house her and the children in the same area and it would be wrong to make her leave her mother, her job and the children's schools for the sake of ensuring immediate payment of the debt. In those circumstances, an order that enforcement be postponed for ten years (effectively during the minority of the children) under a *Mesher* type order (see *Mesher v Mesher and Hall* (1973) [1980] 1 All ER 126) represented the fairest balance between the competing claims of the wife and the creditor (which, in this case, happened to be a large financial institution unlikely to suffer undue hardship by having to wait to recover its adequately secured debt with accumulated interest). In essence, the wife's right of occupation was protected; but she was not entitled to be given security to remain permanently in comparable accommodation.

Austin-Fell therefore marks a slight swing of the pendulum against the interests of the family and in favour of the interests of the creditor; but if the debtor has been adjudicated bankrupt, 'family' interests have traditionally been accorded a much lower priority. Case law seemed to establish the principle (robustly stated by Walton J: *Re Bailey* [1977] 2 All ER 26) that a man has an obligation to pay his debts and to pay them promptly, even if this affects his ability to maintain his wife and family. The almost inevitable outcome was an order for sale of the family home. However, in *Re Gorman (a bankrupt), ex p the trustee of the bankrupt v the bankrupt* [1990] 1 All ER 717 the Divisional Court, having decided that the wife had a beneficial interest in the property, adopted a more flexible approach to the question. The court attached considerable weight to the hardship which the bankrupt's wife would suffer if she had to move from a house in which she had lived for many years and in which she had brought up her children. Since she had a negligence claim pending against her former solicitor, the court considered that, in principle, sale of the family home might properly be deferred until that claim had been finally determined. The wife should then have the option of purchasing the trustee's share, together with simple interest on that amount in the meantime (see also Land Law and Trusts, pp 160–163 below).

Re Gorman was decided under the law as it stood prior to the re-codification of the law by the Insolvency Act 1986. Applications for sale are now to be made to the Bankruptcy Court, and the court is to make such order as it thinks just and reasonable having regard to the interests of the bankrupt's creditors, the conduct of the bankrupt's spouse 'so far as contributing to the bankruptcy', the needs and financial resources of the spouse, the needs of any children, and 'all the circumstances of the case other than the needs of the bankrupt'. But where an application for sale is made after the end of the period of one year from the bankruptcy, the court is required to assume, 'unless the circumstances of the case are exceptional', that the interests of the bankrupt's creditors outweigh all other considerations: s 336(4) and (5). This clearly seems to indicate that the bankrupt's spouse should be given a 12-month 'readjustment' period, but that there might nevertheless be cases in which a longer postponement would be appropriate – perhaps, for example, on facts such as those in *Re Gorman* where the trustee's interest seemed well secured. However, in *Re Citro (a bankrupt)* [1990] 3 All ER 952 the Court of Appeal held that the reference to the circumstances of the case being 'exceptional' was intended to apply the same test as had developed in cases under the old law: see per Nourse LJ at 963, and per Bingham LJ at 964. In effect, therefore, if this interpretation survives, bankruptcy law will not reflect the preference which the law increasingly gives to personal over property interests, per Bingham LJ at 965; and it will only be in the most unusual circumstances that a sale will be deferred for any substantial period: see *Re Holliday (a bankrupt)* [1980] 3 All ER 385.

Finally, one striking example of the dominance of procedure over substance in this area of the law should be noted. In the case of a conflict between a judgment creditor and a divorcing spouse, the date when the divorce petition is filed may apparently be of crucial importance to the outcome: if, before divorce proceedings have been started, the creditor has applied to make a charging order absolute it seems that the wife will be left to her rights under s 30 of the Law of Property Act 1925; and the protection afforded to her may be less extensive than would result from the application of the wide discretion enjoyed by the court under the matrimonial legislation: see *Harman v Glencross* (above) per Balcombe LJ at 558.

Children's welfare, paramount most of the time?

In contrast to the complexities of the law governing financial matters, the legal principle governing the resolution of disputes about the upbringing of children is simple to state: the child's welfare is to be considered 'first, last, and all the time', (as Dunn J put it, in relation to the wardship jurisdiction *Re D (a minor) (justices' decision: review)* [1977] 3 All ER 481); and this remained the principle even if its application sometimes required the court to override normal concepts of justice – for example by considering a report on a child which has not been seen by the parents or their lawyers, or by requiring a solicitor to disclose information in his possession as to a child's whereabouts notwithstanding the normal rule of professional secrecy: *Re K (infants)* [1963] 3 All ER 191; *Burton v Earl of Darnley* (1869) LR 8 Eq 576. But a number of recent wardship cases have demonstrated that the court, in carrying out its duties, must consider not only the child's interests but also the rights of outsiders and the public interest: *Re X (a minor) (wardship: jurisdiction)* [1975] 1 All ER 697 (where the court refused to prevent the publication of a book containing 'bizarre salacious scandalous and revolting' allegations about the deceased father of a 14-year-old girl notwithstanding the fact that she would be psychologically damaged if she were to read the book or hear about it). In that case, the interests of the child were not allowed to prevail over the wider interests of freedom of publication; and in the year under review the Court of Appeal has again emphasised (see *Re M and another (minors) (wardship: freedom of publication)* [1990] 1 All ER 205, and at p 55 above) that, since a proper balance has to be struck between protecting the ward and upholding the right of free publication, the welfare of the child cannot be the paramount consideration. In practice, the balance might be struck by allowing publication of the facts and decision in a case, on terms that there be no identification of the children or foster parents or of any material likely to lead to those concerned being identified.

Another well recognised exception to the 'paramountcy' principle reflects general principles of administrative law: the inherent wardship jurisdiction is not to be used to interfere with a comprehensive legislative code: *A v Liverpool City Council* [1981] 2 All ER 385. Thus, in *Re A (an infant)* [1968] 2 All ER 145 the court refused to allow wardship to be used as a means of reviewing decisions properly taken by Immigration Officers to deport illegal immigrants. In the light of this principle it was perhaps surprising that in *Re J S (a minor) (wardship: boy soldier)* [1990] 2 All ER 861 Cazalet J made ex parte an order that the Military Authorities should not arrest a 17-year-old soldier on the ground that he was absent without leave; but at the substantive hearing Hollis J had no doubt that the wardship should be terminated:

> 'however sympathetic one might be towards [the boy] and indeed his parents, and however hopeful one might be that proper medical attention would be given to him.'

The judge's only doubt was whether to discharge the wardship or strike out the originating summons as being misconceived. The balance was struck in favour of the more drastic striking out remedy because the Crown cannot, in the absence of express statutory provision, be impleaded in its own courts and Hollis J considered that accordingly the Secretary of State for Defence was probably correct in asserting that the Crown could not be made a party to wardship proceedings. It was suggested that it would be preferable if someone such as the ward's father were made the defendant, and the Attorney General were then to be invited to represent the interests of the Crown. (This case is also discussed in Statute Law, p 266 below.)

Child abduction

The fact that the English courts regarded welfare as the first and paramount consideration notoriously led to special problems where a child was brought to this country in breach of a foreign court order. In such cases, although the English courts would give careful consideration to any foreign order in deciding whether to assume jurisdiction, whether to order the child's summary return, and whether to make a different order, it could and would still make its own conflicting order if it thought that to do so would best serve the child's interest: national status was merely one of the factors which the judge in exercising his discretion would take into consideration: *J v C* [1969] 1 All ER 788. Kidnapping was indeed to be strongly discouraged; 'but the discouragement must take the form of a swift, realistic and unsentimental assessment of the best interests of the child . . . not the sacrifice of the child's welfare to some other principle of law' such as comity or any other abstraction: see *Re R (minors) (wardship: jurisdiction)* (1981) 2 FLR 416 at 425, per Ormrod LJ.

The Child Abduction and Custody Act 1985 gave effect to two international conventions – the Hague Convention on the Civil Aspects of International Child Abduction and the Council of Europe Convention on the Recognition and Enforcement of Decisions Concerning the Custody of Children and on the Restoration of Custody of Children – which were the outcome of prolonged and careful discussions designed to minimise the increasing problem of cross-border removals and retentions. Both conventions give effect to the general principle that a child's welfare is best served by his being returned to the country of his habitual residence: *Re F (minor: abduction: jurisdiction)* [1990] 3 All ER 97. It is true that they recognise situations in which return may be refused; but the English courts have in a series of cases given a restricted construction to these relevant provisions: see for example *Re A (a minor) (abduction)* [1988] 1 FLR 365 (the fact that a court considers the child's welfare would best be served by his remaining here is not of itself a ground for refusing return under the Hague Convention: per Nourse LJ); and *Re K (a minor) (abduction)* [1990] 1 FLR 387 (although a child's interest would be better served by his staying in this country, the effect of a foreign order requiring his return was not within the stipulated grounds on which return could be refused). But the most striking case in the year under review is perhaps that of *Re F (minor: abduction: jurisdiction)* where the child had been removed from Israel. The case was accordingly covered by neither of the two Conventions since Israel was not a party thereto; but the Court of Appeal held that it should nonetheless decide the issue on principles similar to those embodied in, and developed by, the courts under the Conventions. The Court of Appeal forcefully expressed the view that it was desirable that other countries should speedily ratify the Conventions.

This is not to say that return is virtually automatic in these cases, and that there is little scope for forensic argument. In *C v S (minor: abduction: illegitimate child)* [1990] 2 All ER 961, for example, the House of Lords rejected a father's appeal against decisions refusing to order his child's return to Australia (from whence he had been removed by the mother). The short point was that the child was illegitimate, and that, under the law of Western Australia, in the absence of any court order only the mother had the right to the child's custody. Accordingly, the father had 'no custody rights' relating to the child which had been breached by the removal of the child by the mother. Although the father subsequently obtained an order giving him such rights in Australia, the child had by then ceased to be 'habitually resident' in Australia. This followed from the decision that a very young child in the sole lawful custody of his mother would automatically take the mother's habitual residence; and on the facts, the mother's decision to move to this country had effectively changed her habitual residence.

But what is welfare?

So far, we have been concerned with recognised exceptions to the welfare principle; but two decisions of the Court of Appeal in the period under review – *Re K (a minor) (ward: care and control)* [1990] 3 All ER 795, and *Re J (a minor) (wardship: medical treatment)* [1990] 3 All ER 930 demonstrate some of the difficulties implicit in the application of that principle.

First, can it be in the child's interests to withhold medical treatment potentially capable of saving his life? In *Re B (a minor) (wardship: medical treatment)* (1981) [1990] 3 All ER 927 the Court of Appeal overruled the decision of the judge at first instance which would have respected the wishes of the responsible and caring parents that their handicapped baby be not subjected to life-saving surgery (see also pp 182–188 below); but, in contrast, in *Re C (a minor) (wardship: medical treatment)* [1989] 2 All ER 782 (All ER Rev 1989, pp 168, 200, 206–210) the Court of Appeal accepted that it would be in the interests of a terminally ill child to withhold treatment which could only give her a longer life of pain as an alternative to a shorter life free from pain and ending in death with dignity: see per Lord Donaldson of Lymington MR [1990] 3 All ER 930 at 935.

Similar issues fell to be confronted in *Re J (a minor) (wardship: medical treatment)* (also discussed in Medical Law, pp 182–188 below); but once again the court asserted the same underlying principle: the first and paramount consideration – to be applied by the parents or by the court acting in their place under the wardship jurisdiction – is the well-being, welfare or interests of the child who lacks the capacity to reach a decision: *Re B (a minor) (wardship: sterilisation)* [1987] 2 All ER 206 (All ER 1987, pp 137, 176), per Lord Hailsham LC (at 212).

But how is the court to evaluate what will best serve the child's welfare? In *Re J (a minor) (wardship: medical treatment)* the Court of Appeal specifically rejected submissions to the effect that as a matter of principle it could never be appropriate to withhold consent to life-saving treatment; while two members of the court equally firmly rejected attempts to lay down any all-embracing formulation for determining the circumstances in which a court would decide that the child's interests would best be served by withholding consent to treatment.

One thing, at least, is clear: although the views of the parents should be heeded and weighed (*Re J (a minor) (wardship: medical treatment)* at 943, per Taylor LJ) it is for the court – acting on the evidence and solely on behalf of the child – to take the decision. In this respect *Re B (a minor) (wardship: medical treatment)* an ex tempore judgment of a two-man Court of Appeal given in circumstances of pressing urgency – can be seen to have established an important precedent, and merits its place in the Reports.

Parents best?

The precise formulation of the extent to which a parent is to be entitled to care for a child as against others has long been a matter of difficulty; and – in contrast to the medical cases discussed above – it may be that the Court of Appeal's decision in *Re K (a minor) (ward: care and control)* marks a shift of emphasis towards recognising the weight of a claim based on parentage. The facts were that the mother of an illegitimate child had committed suicide; and an uncle and aunt immediately took the child into their care, and had continued to care for her thereafter. In wardship proceedings the judge rejected the father's application for care and control considering that her interests would best be served by staying with the uncle and aunt. The Court of Appeal reversed his decision. The question was not (said Fox LJ) 'where would the child get the better home?'; rather the question was: 'was it demonstrated that the welfare of the child positively demanded the displacement of the parental right – in this case, the 'right' of the child's father?' The court accepted that the word 'right' was not really accurate in so far as it might connote something in the nature of a property right; but in reaching its decision the court attached weight to the now well-known dictum of Lord Templeman in *Re KD (a minor) (ward: termination of access)* [1988] 1 All ER 577 at 578:

> 'the best person to bring up a child is the natural parent. It matters not whether the parent is wise or foolish, rich or poor, educated or illiterate, provided the child's moral and physical health are not endangered.'

(See All ER Rev 1988, p 154.) But it should be pointed out that *Re KD* was a public law case, where the issue was whether the state should be permitted to intervene in the child's upbringing. In such cases – as is recognised in the Children Act 1989 – there is much to be said for the view that the child's welfare cannot be the sole question, and that a family should only be deprived of the right to bring up its own kin if a child is at risk of significant harm attributable, at least to some extent, to inadequate parenting. But in the context of private law disputes – and particularly disputes between relatives – the decision in Re K may be thought to give excessive weight to the claims of a parent.

No review of merits?

The principle that the courts will not review the exercise by a local authority of a discretion relating to their child care responsibilities has been extended in the year under review to decisions of voluntary adoption agencies: in Re W (a minor) (adoption agency: wardship) [1990] 2 All ER 463 a voluntary adoption agency had exercised the power conferred on it by s 30 of the Adoption Act to require the return of a child from prospective adoption. Sir Stephen Brown P held that, since the adoption process is closely regulated by Parliament, it would be inappropriate to allow decisions taken by voluntary adoption agencies on the merits to be questioned by the High Court in the exercise of its wardship jurisdiction; and the case accordingly fell 'fairly and squarely' within the principles set out by the House of Lords in W v Hertfordshire CC [1985] 2 All ER 301 (All ER Rev 1985, pp 179, 181, 264, 268) and in A v Liverpool City Council [1981] 2 All ER 385.

Judicial review as a protective procedure

Wardship is thus no longer to be seen as an effective protection for those affected by local authority or other agency child care decisions; and, in the year under review, the courts have increasingly referred to the availability of judicial review as a procedure more appropriate than wardship for questioning such decisions. The potential scope for judicial review had already been demonstrated by R v Norfolk County Council, ex p M [1989] 2 All ER 359 in which, apparently for the first time, judicial review was successfully invoked to question a decision taken at a case conference: see All ER Rev 1989, pp 169–70. However, the decision in that case – effectively to black-list a worker on suspicion of sexual abuse without giving him any opportunity to defend himself (or even to know that he had come under suspicion) – was taken in a procedure which was manifestly unfair; and in the year now under review the courts have been more concerned to define – and indeed to restrict – the scope of judicial review as a procedure to be permitted to question the outcome of the case conferences at which so many important decisions affecting children are taken.

In R v Harrow London Borough, ex p D [1990] 3 All ER 12 (also discussed at p 3 above) the mother complained that she had not been permitted to attend the case conference which decided that her child should be placed on a Child Protection Register; and she sought to have the decision quashed in judicial review proceedings. The Court of Appeal was clearly concerned lest the unstructured and informal case conference decision-making process should become over-formalised and legalistic; and although it affirmed that judicial review would be available in an appropriate case, the category of case in which leave should be given was to be defined restrictively. Indeed, according to Butler-Sloss LJ, leave to apply for judicial review should be refused unless the applicant could show that the decision in question was 'utterly unreasonable'. The outcome seems to be that, although case-conference decisions might perhaps be set aside as unfair if, for example, a parent were given no opportunity to comment on allegations relevant to the subject matter of the case conference the scope for alleging that the decision was 'unreasonable' is to be very narrow indeed. The courts seem to be less willing to intervene in case-conference decisions than in the decisions of other administrative bodies; and it seems probable that an applicant will not succeed unless the decision can be shown to be 'outrageous in its defiance of logic or common sense' or to 'verge on the absurd': see *R v Parole Board, ex p Bradley* [1990] 3 All ER 828 at 839. A very clear warning has thus been given against widespread invocation of judicial review in attempts to question the merits of case conference decisions; and specifically it is now clearly established that neither the parent nor anyone else has a right to attend a case conference – even though it may well be that the conference is the most important step in the decision-taking process. The Court of Appeal has thus adopted the policy underlying the decision (considered in All ER Rev 1989 at p 165) that a Guardian ad Litem appointed to act for a child in care proceedings has no right to make oral representations to an adoption panel: *R v North Yorkshire County Council, ex p M (No 2)* [1989] 2 FLR 79. In seeking to justify this restrictive view of the scope of judicial review, the Court of Appeal placed heavy reliance on the fact that in case conference decision-taking the relevant considerations are not limited to those affecting the individual who might be prejudiced or the tribunal or organisation being criticised; and it was central to the court's reasoning that the welfare of the child was of enormous importance in these procedures. The court accepted that the interests of adults vitally affected by the outcome might have to yield to the need to protect the child.

The compromise is obviously a somewhat uneasy one; and the decision is all the more striking because of the current tendency to assert the importance of parental involvement in the taking of decisions relating to children: see, for example, the decision of the European Court of Human Rights in *R v The United Kingdom* [1988] 2 FLR 445 (discussed in All ER Rev 1988, pp 154–55) and note the DHSS guidance ('Working Together' (1988) para 5.45) to the effect that parents

> 'should be informed or consulted at every stage of investigation. Their views should be sought on the issues to be raised prior to a case conference to afford them the opportunity to seek advice and prepare their representations. They should be invited where practicable to attend part, or, if appropriate the whole of case conferences unless in the view of the chairman of the conference their presence will preclude a full and proper consideration of the child's interests.'

But this is to state good practice. The Court of Appeal's decision demonstrates the truism that the courts will not interfere in every case in which some departure from the best practice can be demonstrated; and, indeed, more generally that the courts are reluctant to allow the merits of professional child care decisions to be questioned by judicial process.

However, judicial review remains an appropriate method for seeking redress where more formal decision taking process is flawed; and the procedure came to the rescue of parents and child in the disturbing case of *R v Hampshire County Council, ex p K* [1990] 2 All ER 129. A local authority brought care proceedings in respect of a handicapped and mentally retarded girl on the basis that she had been sexually abused. The authority had two medical reports about the alleged abuse: one concluded that there were no physical symptoms on the child consistent with or indicative of sexual abuse; the second that the child had indeed been the victim of sexual abuse. This latter opinion was also to some extent corroborated by a statement made by the child to a social worker which was capable of being construed as an assertion that her father had abused her. But the authority refused to disclose its medical evidence to the parents: the rules, as Watkins LJ put it, allowed the local authority 'not only to keep its cards face down until the first court hearing but also to be as selective as it liked as to which cards were then to be turned up'. Unhappily (as he went on to say) the authority 'made full use of that apparent tactical advantage'. The parents' application for legal aid to have the court consider the case in wardship proceedings was refused in reliance on the *A v Liverpool City Council* principle. But in due course, the parents were able successfully to bring proceedings seeking judicial review. The Divisional Court held that local authorities had a duty in the direct interests of the child (whose welfare they were under a duty to serve) to be open in the disclosure of all relevant material; that the authority's discretion to authorise or refuse a further medical examination was a discretion which it was bound to exercise judicially, weighing fairly and objectively the risk of possible distress to the child against the risk of injustice to the parents if further examination were refused; and that on the facts the authority had failed to exercise its discretion properly. The authority was at fault and in breach of duty in failing to make voluntary disclosure of the reports; and their failure was compounded by their 'subsequent repeated and seemingly obstinate refusals' to comply with the parents' requests for disclosure. Moreover, by withholding disclosure of the reports, the authority had disabled itself from exercising properly its discretion in relation to whether further medical examination of the child should be permitted. Had the two reports been submitted to an expert, that expert would have been equipped to make a proper judgment as to whether further physical examination was called for or whether the reports as they stood enabled an opinion to be formed. In the result, not only was the local authority's decision flawed, but the hearing before the justices was vitiated by failure to give the disclosure which was necessary to a fair hearing.

The case is a chilling reminder of the fact that the structure of the Children and Young Persons' Act 1969 and of the relevant procedural rules – which, as Watkins LJ pointed out, make no provision for pleading or discovery – are difficult to reconcile with judicial statements that care proceedings are not adversarial: see, for example, *Humberside CC v DPR* [1977] 3 All ER 964, *R v Birmingham Juvenile Court, ex p G and others (minors)* [1989] 3 All ER 336 (All ER Rev 1989, p 164). The court in the *Hampshire* case suggested that those responsible for framing the provisions of the Children Act 1989 and the rules of court to be made thereunder should consider the establishment of procedures which would spell out with clarity the duties of advance disclosure imposed on local authorities who seek orders on grounds of alleged child abuse.

Adoption – a complete break?

Adoption is – as *Re Collins (decd)* (above) vividly demonstrates – legally *sui generis*: an adoption order destroys and creates legal status, and in legal theory the adopted child ceases to be the child of the birth parents and becomes the child of his adoptive parents: Adoption Act 1976, s 39. The drastic and irrevocable effect of an adoption order must be the justification for the many distinctive rules applicable in adoption proceedings – for example, that the child's welfare is not the paramount consideration, and also, for example, the procedural rules designed to ensure confidentiality and thereby to protect the adopting family against unwanted intrusion by the birth parents. But is that confidence ever to be broken? Is the barrier created by adoption ever to be breached? In *Re an ex parte originating summons in an adoption application* [1990] 1 All ER 639 (see also p 123 above) the defence to charges of rape and other sexual offence against the defendant's schoolgirl stepdaughter was that a schoolboy friend had been the perpetrator of the alleged abuse, and that this friend was in fact the father of the girl's (subsequently adopted) child. But the father was convicted – solely on the evidence of his stepdaughter – and sentenced to a long term of imprisonment. The Court of Appeal ordered that blood tests should be performed to establish whether or not he was the father of the adopted child. When the adoption agency consulted their files, it was found that the stepdaughter had, in relation to the adoption proceedings, given an account of what had happened which was quite inconsistent with the evidence she had given at the stepfather's trial, but which tallied with the defence which he had consistently put forward. Ewbank J held that the agency's social worker had properly issued a summons for directions, and that a disclosure of the information to the Attorney General was 'necessary' for the proper exercise of the social worker's duties: see r 53(3), Adoption Rules 1984, SI 265. (Subsequently, a *Practice Note* [1990] 1 All ER 640 was issued, and in future in such cases the Attorney General should first be given the opportunity of being heard.)

That case well illustrates the precautions normally taken in order to preserve the confidentiality of adoption proceedings. However, to some extent in contradiction of the traditional policy of the law, it has in recent years been the policy to encourage greater openness about adoption. To this end, statute (Adoption Act 1976, s 51) now gives an adopted adult a right of access to the original birth certificate and thereby to information which in some cases may enable an adopted person to trace the birth parents. Moreover, this trend to greater openness will be reinforced by means of the Adoption Contact Register to be kept by the Registrar General specifically to facilitate the establishment of contact between adopted persons and their relatives: Children Act 1989, Sch 10, para 21.

But the distressing facts of *R v Registrar General, ex p Smith* [1990] 2 All ER 170 show all too clearly that there are bound to be cases in which disclosure and openness could be exceedingly dangerous. The applicant, a patient in Broadmoor Hospital, had been convicted of 'a most brutal and sadistic murder': he attacked a fellow prisoner, tied his hands and feet with string, and strangled him with the sleeve of his shirt (apparently under the belief that the prisoner was his adoptive mother). Disturbed, unstable and a possible danger to the public, he continued to express hatred for his adoptive parents, apparently believing that they had mistreated him. The Registrar General refused the applicant's request for information which would enable him to trace his birth certificate; and the applicant sought judicial review of that decision, on the basis that the Adoption Act conferred an absolute entitlement to disclosure of the relevant information. The Divisional Court rejected the application, holding that it was entitled to extend the recognised principle of public policy which denies a person the right to profit from his own criminality (see *R v Secretary of State for the Home Department, ex p Puttick* [1981] 1 All ER 776; *R v Chief National Insurance Commissioner, ex p Connor* [1981] 1 All ER 769) to cases involving the evaluation of future conduct – in the present case, the risk of the applicant behaving towards his birth-mother as he had behaved towards the fellow prisoner. The court recognised that this might be a novel head of public policy; but it was 'beyond belief' that Parliament had ever contemplated that an adopted child's right to obtain a birth certificate should be absolute; and novelty could not be an adequate reason for declining to extend the law. The need for such a provision was 'glaringly clear' in the present case.

The risk of contact between the child and his birth parent was also the decisive factor in the decision of Douglas Brown J in *Re F (a minor) (adoption order: injunction)* [1990] 3 All ER 580, where it was held that the provisions of the Adoption Act 1976, s 12 (6) (ie that an adoption order may contain such terms and conditions as the court thinks fit) were broad enough to permit the inclusion in an adoption order of an injunction restraining the schizophrenic birth-father from communicating with the child or with the adoptive parents or from coming within 500 yards of the adoptive parents' house. The judge specifically rejected an argument (founded on the maxim, 'no action, no injunction': *Montgomery v Montgomery* [1964] 2 All ER 22) that the making of an adoption order brought the adoption proceedings to an end and that there could accordingly no longer be any jurisdiction to grant an injunction. The judge considered that there would in any event have been jurisdiction to grant the injunction under s 37 of the Supreme Court Act 1981.

Freeing for adoption – protecting the parents

It has already been pointed out that in adoption the child's welfare is not the sole consideration: the child's birth parents also have rights. The Children Act 1975 (now the Adoption Act 1976) in an attempt to remove some of the obstacles to adoption of 'hard to place' children (and also to minimise the anxiety experienced by adopting parents who knew that the birth parents had the right to withdraw consent at any time up to the hearing of the adoption application) introduced a new procedure whereby a child may be declared to be 'free for adoption'. In effect, under this procedure, the issue of parental agreement is dealt with by the court perhaps even before the child has been placed for adoption and if the court declares the child free for adoption the parental rights and duties vest in the adoption agency pending application for an adoption order.

The draftsman was careful to protect the birth parents and the child against the risk that the adoption plans would break down; and the Act (Adoption Act 1976, s 19(3)) accordingly requires an authority to give notice whenever a child is placed for adoption or ceases to have his home with a person with whom he has been placed for adoption; and the birth parent may apply to the court to revoke the freeing order on the ground that he wishes to resume the parental rights and duties if, at any time more than 12 months after the making of the freeing order the child does not have his home with a person with whom he has been placed for adoption.

In *R v Derbyshire County Council, ex p T* [1990] 1 All ER 792 the child had been placed for adoption, but the prospective adoptive mother then became pregnant. The council decided that the placement should be terminated, but anxious not unnecessarily to disrupt the child's life, it did not take any steps physically to remove the child, preferring to wait until a new adoption was in prospect. The birth-parents were not informed of the breakdown of the initial placement. They subsequently sought judicial review of the decision to make a fresh placement on the basis that they had been denied the opportunity to consider the position prior to the move; and, in particular, they claimed that they had been deprived of the right they might have had to apply for revocation of the freeing order.

The Court of Appeal upheld the parents' case. First of all, the court rejected the argument that a child did not cease to have his home with a person with whom he had been 'placed for adoption' until the child had physically been moved. The question was (per Butler-Sloss LJ, at 796) 'one of status' so that 'one must look to the purpose of the placement' rather than to the child's physical whereabouts. As soon as the council's Adoption Panel decided to terminate the child's original placement, the child – notwithstanding the fact that she remained physically in the same house – ceased to have her home with the person with whom she had been 'placed for adoption'. In the result, the council automatically came under a duty to give notice to the parents; and the duty to give notice was (said Butler-Sloss LJ, at 796) 'crucial to the rights of the former parent . . . [since] without notice by the adoptive agency to the former parent, he or she would be most unlikely to have the opportunity' to exercise the right to apply for revocation of the freeing order.

This decision does, of course, increase the risk that an adoption agency will be deterred from leaving a child in the physical care of applicants with some consequent risk that the child's welfare would be jeopardised by disruption in the move and change over, and by her being 'placed in limbo' (per Butler-Sloss LJ at 798); but the court considered that the adoption agency had the specific duty to give notice, and this did not involve the exercise of any discretion by the court to which the duty to give first consideration to the need to safeguard and promote the welfare of the child throughout childhood (Adoption Act 1976, s 6) could apply.

Land Law and Trusts

P J CLARKE, BCL, MA
Barrister, Fellow of Jesus College, Oxford

Co-ownership and overriding interests

The two leading cases for this year are undoubtedly the decisions of the House of Lords in *Abbey National Building Society v Cann* [1990] 1 All ER 1085 (R J Smith 106 LQR 545, John A Greed 135 NLJ 815, A J Oakley [1990] CLJ 397, Cedric Bell 134 Sol Jo 709), and *Lloyds Bank plc v Rosset* [1990] 1 All ER 1111 (J D Davies, 106 LQR 539, Simon Gardner, 54 MLR 126, Greed, ibid, and at 863, M P Thompson [1990] Conv 314. The two cases were heard one after the other, and the speeches in both were handed down on the same day; the constitution of the House of Lords was identical in both cases. Both are also discussed in Family Law, at pp 138–139 above.

In *Cann*, George Cann ('George') had bought, with the aid of a mortgage, the freehold of the leasehold house in which he lived with his widowed mother and her deceased husband's brother. The property was conveyed into the names of George and his mother. George assured his mother that she would not have to pay any rent any more and that she would always have a roof over her head. She and her brother moved house once; and on this occasion, the house was placed in George's name, and his mother knew that there was a mortgage of £15,000 on the property. In 1984, George was in financial difficulties and it was agreed that the second house would be sold and a smaller, third, house purchased. George applied for and obtained a loan of £25,000 from the Abbey National, even though the purchase price of the new house was considerably smaller than the sale price of its predecessor. George executed both mortgage and transfer documents before completion took place on 13 August 1984. Completion of the purchase took place at about 12.20 pm on that day; at about 11.45 am, the vendor having vacated the property, George and his uncle were at the premises, and the carpet-layers moved in and started work. The Court of Appeal [1989] 2 FLR 265 held that Mrs Cann was aware that the balance of the purchase price was going to be raised on mortgage, and her interest was therefore subordinate to that of the building society. Dillon LJ also took the view that events from 11.45 am to 12.20 pm on 13 August constituted actual occupation of the property by Mrs Cann sufficient for her to acquire an overriding interest under the Land Registration Act 1925 s 70(1)(*g*).

The date of registration

The first issue which logically fell for decision was the date at which the existence of overriding interests fell to be determined under the Land Registration Act. This issue had been considered at length by the Court of Appeal in *Lloyds Bank v Rosset* [1988] 3 All ER 915 (All ER Rev 1988, pp 163–166). The Court of Appeal there held that the date for determining actual occupation was the date of completion of the sale and purchase of the property, rather than date of registration. This was criticised as being difficult to square with the precise wording of the legislation, even though such a result was practically convenient. It was also noted that the Law Commission in their 158th Report (para 2.76) had accepted the date of registration as the correct date, and this was the view in what very little authority there was. The Law Commission had pointed out that inconvenience of the rule and had recommended reform. The decision of the Court of Appeal has now been upheld by the House of Lords, though the reasoning is slightly more restricted. It is common ground amongst their Lordships that there is not a single date – ie completion or transfer – which is correct for all the various rights under s 70(1). This is, perhaps an admission that there is something wrong with either the legislation or the decision: and, indeed, as Lord Oliver pointed out, it might be necessary slightly to rewrite the legislation to achieve a sensible result. Moreover, their Lordships were acutely aware of the practical results of their judgments: Lord Oliver justified the result thus, '. . . it produces a result which is just, convenient and certain, as opposed to one which is capable of leading to manifest injustice and absurdity' (at 1093c). Their Lordships seem to have polarised their analysis around two specific examples within s 70(1): paragraph (g), and paragraph (i) – the paragraph dealing with local land charges. Lord Bridge took the view that the date of completion was the general rule, and paragraph (g) was thus an example; the rest of their Lordships took the opposite view, believing that paragraph (i) was the typical example, and paragraph (g) was the anomaly. This difference is not entirely academic: what if, for example, a vendor creates a short legal lease which is protected under s 70(1)(k) in the gap between completion and registration? If Lord Bridge is right, such a lease will not bind the new purchaser; if the majority are correct, it will. The example is an uncomfortable one, but the scheme of the Land Registration Act is clearly that the moment of *transfer* is the key, and the less it is departed from the better. Section 70(1)(g) is regarded as being an awkward – and, indeed, anomalous paragraph, and it is surely best to limit the alteration of the Act – for that is what it really is – to this one troublesome case. There was an analogy with the rights of occupation in unregistered land: see *Hunt v Luck* [1902] 1 Ch 428, [1900–3] All ER Rep 295; and there was real practical difficulty if an occupier moved in after the mortgagee had advanced his money before the date of registration, always bearing in mind that there would be an inevitable delay between completion and registration and that the movements of occupiers into the premises in that period would almost certainly be entirely beyond the control of the mortgagee.

The decline and fall of the scintilla temporis

Ever since medieval times the mind of the property lawyer has been attuned to the concept of the scintilla temporis – that millisecond of time when a property vests in an individual before he is, in part at least, deprived of it. The idea has a certainly logical attraction: after all, if a person does not have an interest, how can he sell, lease or mortgage it? nemo dat quod non habet. However, although the doctrine has its logical attraction, and although it was accepted by the Court of Appeal in *Church of England Building Society v Piskor*

[1954] 2 All ER 85, it has its problems. In the ordinary house purchase, all the purchaser thinks he is getting is a 'house-mortgaged-to-a-building-society'; likewise, in the area of debentures, the doctrine of scintilla temporis had been rejected: see *Re Connolly Bros Ltd (No 2)* [1912] 2 Ch 25, and *Security Trust Co v Royal Bank of Canada* [1976] 1 All ER 381. There the courts had proceeded on the basis that what the debenture holders were acquiring was the property subject to a mortgage rather than an incumbered property which, for a split second, existed independently of the mortgage and so could thus vest in them. Lord Jauncey perhaps oversimplified the position by stating that 'since no-one could grant what he does not have, it follows that such a purchaser could never grant an interest which was not subject to the limitation on his own interest' ([1990] 1 All ER 1107g); this assumes what he is trying to prove, namely that the fee simple never vested in the purchaser before it was immediately mortgaged. However, reality, as perceived by the judges – and as perceived by the house purchaser and mortgagee – has prevailed over history and logic. There is also, as Oakley points out ([1990] CLJ 400) a difficulty where, as is common, banks and other lenders provide bridging facilities against an undertaking by the purchaser's solicitors to hold the deeds to the lender's order. Such an undertaking does not amount to a mortgage (and, in any event, even informal mortgages by deposit of deeds will not now be effective because of the Law of Property (Miscellaneous Provisions) Act 1989, s 2), and therefore the mortgage must, by definition, postdate the purchase and thus any interests that arise at that time or immediately after-wards. Only a formal mortgage would achieve the desired result of protecting the mortgage: and the practical difficulties of this are obvious.

Occupation: the frantic 40 minutes

The Court of Appeal had split over whether Mrs Cann was in occupation of the new house in the 40 minutes between the departure of the vendors and the completion of the purchase. Dillon LJ found that there was sufficient for actual occupation; the other two judges doubted this. A similar difficulty had occurred in *Rosset* in the Court of Appeal: see All ER Rev 1988, pp 166–167. Lord Oliver in *Cann*, therefore, considered the matter in the round. His first comment, that occupation is a concept which may have different connotations according to the nature and purpose of the property which is claimed to be occupied (at 1101c) is a useful start. Most of the cases have involved those who either live or intend to live in residential property, and although the cases (eg *Strand Securities v Caswell* [1965] 1 All ER 820, *Williams & Glyn's Bank v Boland* [1980] 2 All ER 408 and (in unregistered land) *Kingsnorth Trust Ltd v Tizard* [1986] 2 All ER 54 (All ER Rev 1986, pp 181–183, 190, 195) did not present an entirely coherent picture, some general ideas were emerging. But there is little authority on the situation where what is involved is for example, farmland, or a piece of waste land left at the completion of a residential development and is being used – in one sense or the other – by a non-owner. Second, there was no need for the personal presence of the person claiming to occupy: a caretaker or the representative of a company could occupy on the employer's behalf. That, again, is in accordance with authority: though the anomaly of the daughter in *Strand Securities v Caswell*, where she was neither tenant nor occupier should be noted; and since her occupation was not representative either, what might be perceived as an unjust result was reached. The case itself might be differently decided now: in the 25 years since the decision, the Land Registration Act 1925 s 70(1)(g) has come of age, and it is unlikely that present judges would speak of rights being 'lost' in the welter of registration: *Strand Securities Ltd v Caswell* at 826d, per Lord Denning MR. Third, Lord Oliver referred to the need to involve some degree of permanence and continuity which would rule out 'mere fleeting presence'. He gives the example of a prospective tenant or purchaser who is allowed into the property before completion to measure for furnishings or to plan decorations: here, the purpose is such that the visits are likely to be short. However, Lord Oliver goes on to say that, on the facts of *Cann*, those moving Mrs Cann's belongings had an intention that they would remain there and render the premises suitable for her ultimate and permanent use as a residential occupier. However, he rejects the argument that this made a difference: the acts were 'preparatory' ([1990] 2 All ER at 1101e); therefore she acquired no interest. The issue of what amounted to 'actual occupation' had been considered by the Court of Appeal in *Rosset*, but in view of the decision of the House of Lords that Mrs Rosset had acquired no interest in the property, their Lordships did not consider the question on the facts of that case.

Clearly, the type of occupation and its duration were such in *Cann* that, on a broad view, they were insufficient; but what if the duration had been slightly longer – say four hours or so – and that builders, employed to do a 'rush job' had already pulled down walls to carry out major structural alterations? Is this another area of the law where fine distinctions are going to have to be made? When does work cease to become 'preparatory'? If that word means anything, any would-be occupier will be well advised to make as much mess and cause as much destruction in as short a time as possible. To counter any risk of this, a vendor will refuse to allow the purchaser into the house until he is absolutely certain that completion has taken place. Finally, it is clear that *Cann* will not solve everything: for instance the vexed question in *Rosset* in the Court of Appeal as to whether Mrs Rosset's work in supervising the builders was enough to amount to 'actual occupation' is untouched by what is said. Similarly, the hints in *Kingsnorth Trust v Tizard* and *Rosset* that notice may be relevant in determining whether there is actual occupation are not further considered.

The interest in the house: how a co-occupier can obtain an interest

In *Cann* it was conceded that Mrs Cann had an interest in the property; this was, in the view of the House of Lords in *Rosset* the key issue in that case. Mr and Mrs Rosset wished to buy a house; they decided to buy a semi-derelict farmhouse for £57,000; the property needed at least £13,000 to make it habitable. In November 1982 Mr Rosset received £59,200 from a family trust in Switzerland to enable the farmhouse to be purchased, but the Swiss trustees insisted that the transfer should be into Mr Rosset's name alone. Before completion, the workmen moved in, and Mrs Rosset was in the house for much of the period, organising the workmen and wallpapering some of the rooms. Matrimonial disputes occurred, and Lloyds Bank, the mortgagees, sought possession of the property: were they entitled to vacant possession and to evict Mrs Rosset?

She claimed an overriding interest under the Land Registration Act 1925 s 70(1)(g). The trial judge and the Court of Appeal found that Mrs Rosset did have an interest in the property: see All ER Rev 1988, p 164. The Court of Appeal then considered the time at which Mrs Rosset's interest gelled for the purposes of the section, and the question of whether she was then in actual occupation. The House of Lords found that Mrs Rosset did not have an interest in the property; the other issues therefore did not fall for consideration. The only speech was given by Lord Bridge; and he was clearly hostile to Mrs Rosset's claim. First, he pointed out that Mrs Rosset's claim – which was for half the property – involved an immediate gift to her of half the property which would have cost at least £72,000. Further, if the Rossets had thought about matters, they would have realised that, to achieve this, they would have had to have acted in a way which was a subterfuge to circumvent the Swiss trustees' stipulation. There was clearly no declaration of trust because of the absence of writing under the Law of Property Act 1925, s 53(1). Her case, therefore had to rest on an agreement, reliance and an alteration of position which could give rise either to a constructive trust or to an estoppel. There was, the trial judge found, a common intention that the house was to be renovated as a joint venture and was to become a family home. This was not enough to 'throw any light on their intentions with respect to the beneficial ownership of property' (at 1117b). The judge had also relied very heavily on what Mrs Rosset had done after November 1982; again, Lord Bridge would have none of this; Mrs Rosset wanted to be in the house by Christmas, and in those circumstances:

> 'it would seem the most natural thing in the world for any wife in the absence of her husband abroad, to spend all the time she could spare and to employ any skills she might have such as the ability to decorate a room, in doing all she could to accelerate progress of the work quite irrespective of any expectation she might have of enjoying the property.' (at 1118a)

In short, even if there was a clear intention to make a gift of half, it was doubtful if there was sufficient contribution to support a claim to a constructive trust. Lord Bridge then drew what he regarded as a 'critical distinction' to be borne in mind in analysing the cases: first, irrespective of any inference to be drawn from conduct, was there, normally before the date of acquisition of the property, any 'agreement arrangement or understanding' that the property should be shared beneficially? For this an express discussion between the parties was necessary, even if their recollections were imperfect and the terms imprecise. There should be some support from facts that are reasonably clear. Once this is found, then the party claiming an interest will only have to show an acting to his detriment or a significant alteration of position in reliance on the agreement to give rise to a constructive trust or proprietary estoppel.

If, however, there were no such agreement or arrangement, the courts are relying entirely on the conduct of parties as the basis both of inferring a common intention to share the property beneficially and also as the conduct relied on to give rise to a constructive trust. Direct contributions to the purchase price – either to the deposit or by the payment of mortgage instalments will be enough; but it was doubtful if anything less would do.

Lord Bridge's analysis of the authorities is interesting. *Eves v Eves* [1975] 3

All ER 768 and *Grant v Edwards* [1986] 2 All ER 426, All ER Rev 1986, pp 192–195 were regarded as examples of the first category: in both cases there was an agreement or arrangement: both Mr Eves and Mr Edwards had made excuses to their female partners for not putting their respective houses in joint names; and the later conduct of the ladies in question would not, by itself, have been sufficient to found an interest if there had not been a representation that they would have an interest. *Pettitt v Pettitt* [1969] 2 All ER 385 and *Gissing v Gissing* [1970] 2 All ER 780 were cases in the second category. There is no doubt that this approach is a significant restriction on the development of flexible rules about the informal acquisition of house ownership. What is required is a contribution related to joint ownership rather than merely to joint occupation – a distinction that may well not have been contemplated by any but the most hard-headed of parties. Surely people such as Mrs Rosset are both seeking to have the house ready to occupy and looking towards the production of a joint asset which they – eventually – will profit from. The fact that the occupation is more likely to be the immediate aim is not sufficient by itself to render the longer term aim irrelevant.

Second, there is a clear statement that only direct financial contributions will do: whatever the view of the traditional Chancery lawyer that this is the way trusts should operate, it bears little relation either to the realities of domestic life or, indeed, to some of the earlier authorities, for example *Nixon v Nixon* [1969] 3 All ER 1133 and *Re Cummins (decd)* [1971] 3 All ER 782: in both these cases, a wife had helped in the husband's business and was thereby entitled to a share in the property acquired through those profits. Clearly, cases such as *Burns v Burns* [1984] 1 All ER 244 (All ER Rev 1984, pp 167–169) are approved; but why should not a large, non-monetary, specifically referable, contribution still be regarded as enough? Finally, and somewhat tentatively, it may be asked whether this is not a resulting trust rather than a constructive trust: the parties get back that which is related to what they have put in.

Third, there is now a vital distinction between finding an express 'agreement, arrangement or understanding', even if the latter is clearly contractually incomplete and uncertain, on the one hand; and inferring, from conduct, an implied agreement on the other. Given both the natural unclarity of recollections of the parties, their – perhaps selectively – deceptive memories, conflicts of evidence, and a general unclarity as to why the parties did what they did when they did, this distinction (which we are now told is fundamental) is not going to be easy to draw. And, moreover, if a judge, having heard all the evidence in a case, makes findings of fact which are justified on a selective analysis of the evidence and thus finds an express agreement, there is little left for the claimant party to prove; likewise, if the same judge feels that the claimant is unmeritorious, the same evidence can be used to deny the absence of an express agreement, thus making it – in practice – virtually impossible for the claimant to establish his case. Indeed, it could even be argued that by the emphasis which the House of Lords places on oral evidence as distinct from conduct, it has given the trial judge a greater power to make his decision appeal-proof: conduct is more likely to have been agreed in evidence by both parties as having occurred, and therefore, if ignored by the judge could be more easily appealed; but if a judge states that he has heard the witnesses and which oral evidence he prefers, it will hard for an appellate court to upset the decision.

Finally, it may be noted that constructive trust and estoppel seem now to be regarded as similar. The analogy between the two was noted by Sir Nicolas Browne-Wilkinson V-C in *Grant v Edwards*, though it was not suggested that the two concepts were identical. Clearly, the two concepts are similar and may often overlap: but there is one vital difference, if a matter is characterised as an estoppel, the courts seem to have at their disposal a virtually infinite range of remedies: see, eg *Pascoe v Turner* [1979] 2 All ER 945 where a conveyance of the fee simple was ordered; and this may possibly provide a way for a creative judge to escape from the conceptual strait-jacket into which Lord Bridge appears to have forced him.

The wife and the husband's creditors

The eternal triangle has long been regarded as the husband, the wife and the mistress/paramour. In property law a less exciting, but equally problematic triangle seems to have emerged: the husband, the wife, and the husband's creditors. This issue has been much before the courts, and different attitudes are taken depending upon, for instance, whether the husband is insolvent or not: see, eg *Re Holliday* [1980] 3 All ER 385 and *Re Lowrie* [1981] 3 All ER 353, and now the Insolvency Act 1986 ss 332–336. Two cases in 1990 raise problems within this triangular relationship: in *Re Gorman (a bankrupt)* [1990] 1 All ER 717, the husband was insolvent; in *Austin-Fell v Austin-Fell* [1990] 2 All ER 455 he was not, but a charging order had been made against him. (For further discussion of *Re Gorman* and *Austin-Fell*, see the chapter on Family Law at pp 142–143 above.) The issues in the latter situation were fully ventilated in *Harman v Glencross* [1986] 1 All ER 545 (All ER Rev 1986, pp 184–186).

In that case, Balcombe LJ provided a list of general issues that a court should consider in any case where the tripartite dispute arose (the husband not being bankrupt). The third of these issues was explained in the 1986 Review as follows:

> 'if the circumstances are insufficiently clear to make an immediate charging order absolute, the whole issue should be referred to the Family Division, which would consider all the circumstances of the case. It would be rare indeed that an outright transfer of the husband's share to the wife would be ordered, as this would deprive the judgment creditor's charging order of any effect.' (p 185)

Austin-Fell v Austin-Fell provides an interesting example of the operation of this third guideline. H and W married in 1977 and children were born in 1979 and 1981. The husband's business ran into serious financial difficulties and in 1984 the husband's bank obtained a judgment against him for £7,900 and in 1985 obtained a charging order attached to his half share of the matrimonial home. In 1984 the couple separated. The Registrar who heard the case ordered, in the exercise of his discretion under the Matrimonial Causes Act 1973 s 25(1) and the Charging Orders Act 1979 s 1(5), that the charging order should be set aside and the husband's share in the matrimonial home be transferred to the wife. The husband was earning little money, and the wife, who was a teacher, was working part-time. On appeal to Waite J, the judge held that *Harman v Glencross* involved two features which were not present in the instant case: in *Harman v Glencross*, the charging order was for a sum greater than the husband's interest; here it was only for about one-third of his interest in the house. Second, in *Harman v Glencross* the judgment creditor did not ask for the possibility of a deferred operation of the charge to be considered; it sought either immediate imposition or nothing. Waite J found that, although the idea of affording 'adequate protection' to the wives and children of creditors and thus allowing their interests to prevail over the commercial claims of judgment creditors an attractive and humane one, it did not represent the law. As Fox LJ had pointed out in *Harman v Glencross* (at 562), everything depended on 'striking a fair balance between the normal expectations of the creditor and the hardship to the wife and children if a charging order is not made'. This necessarily implied that situations might arise where the wife and children might thus be expected to accept a provision for their security of accommodation which was not adequate. The judge noted that the bank, as judgment creditor, suffered no peculiar financial hardship, but that did not mean that its claims should be ignored. As a result, the judge found (1) that the bank was justified in expecting a charging order, (2) that an immediate enforcement of the order would make it impossible for the wife and children to be rehoused in the area of the matrimonial home, to which they were both linked because of the children's schooling, the specialist nature of the wife's job and what the judge referred to as 'the indispensable help of her mother', (3) that what the bank was seeking, namely a *Mesher* order with the payment to the bank delayed for ten years, would be ordered.

Again, as in all cases where the eternal triangle referred to above subsists, whatever decision the judge reaches is going to cause hardship; but hardship deferred is better than hardship now, and although in ten years' time, the wife – as the judge realised – might be in real financial difficulties, the children by then would be at a much more mature age and, in any event, the whole of the family's circumstances might have changed. One may merely note that if the husband had been bankrupt, the bank – as a creditor in bankruptcy – would very likely have been in a much better position.

Re Gorman is a significantly more complex case which raises an issue of general principle on the construction of co-ownership documents and which, it is submitted, clarifies helpfully one uncertainty in the law. Gorman and his wife purchased property in 1968 with the aid of a mortgage; the mortgage was entered jointly, and the transfer of the property to Gorman and his wife, though unexecuted by them had a declaration indorsed on it which stated both that the land was 'for their own benefit' and that the survivor could give a receipt for capital moneys that arose. The couple divorced and later Gorman became bankrupt. Gorman's trustee in bankruptcy sought the sale of the property. Three questions fell for decision: (1) what were the beneficial interests in the property? (2) had the joint tenancy – if there was one – been severed? (3) what order, and on what terms, should be made for the sale of the property? The trustee in bankruptcy lost at first instance and appealed to the Chancery Divisional Court. First, the court held that the property was held on a beneficial joint tenancy. The document, which contained the indorsement that a survivor could give a receipt was consistent only with a joint tenancy; however, the fact remained that the parties had not signed the transfer. The Land Registration Act and Rules provided that unless the Registrar was satisfied that the survivor of joint proprietors could give a valid receipt – ie if there was a beneficial joint tenancy – he, the Registrar was obliged to enter a restriction on the register. The Registrar was so satisfied, but as the document had not been signed, a decision of Judge Thomas (sitting as a judge of the High Court) in *Robinson v Robinson* (1976) 241 EG 153 stated that the agreement or declaration was ineffective. The Divisional Court in *Gorman* held that the declaration of trust, although inadmissible as such, was admissible as evidence of the intention of the parties. This seems a common-sense approach: why should the court look at some evidence but ignore others? Certainly, *Robinson v Robinson* does cause difficulties: one group of joint purchasers – those who had not executed the deed or declaration – were being treated differently from others: see All ER Rev 1986, pp 191–192. However, a nagging doubt remains: there are formalities rules concerning the creation or disposition of equitable interests in land. *Goodman v Gallant* [1986] 1 All ER 311 (All ER Rev 1986, pp 190–192) emphasises the primacy of the express declaration of trust; *Gorman* goes further and emphasises the primacy of the informally declared trust. Presumably the argument (although unstated in *Gorman* itself) is that there is an agreement of the parties to which effect is being given through the vehicle of a constructive trust.

As to the second point, the court found that the joint tenancy was severed when Gorman's share vested in his trustee in bankruptcy.

Third, the court considered the basis upon which an order for sale should be made; in so considering, the judges first dealt with the question of what, if any, equitable accounting there should be between the parties. Often complicated inquiries will be necessary, but, in some cases the courts had treated mortgage interest paid by a tenant in common as equivalent to an occupation rent: see, eg *Suttill v Graham* [1977] 3 All ER 1117. Some of the theoretical difficulties to which this course may give rise were considered by the courts in *Dennis v MacDonald* [1981] 2 All ER 632 and [1982] 1 All ER 590 (All ER Rev 1982, pp 172–173); these difficulties were not drawn to the court's attention in *Gorman* itself. The court, however, confirmed that payment of an occupation rent as an equivalent to mortgage instalments was not a rule of law; it was rather a rule of convenience that operated more easily between co-occupiers than between an occupier and a trustee in bankruptcy. On the facts, inquiries would be necessary, in default of the parties' agreement.

This left the final question, that of the timing of the sale, to be considered. The issues were finely balanced: in particular, Mrs Gorman had a negligence claim against the solicitors who had acted for her in her divorce proceedings; against that, Gorman's trustee in bankruptcy and his creditors would suffer hardship if they had to wait for an indefinite period. The normal approach, manifested in *Re Lowrie (a bankrupt)*, was that sale should be ordered, but the court noted that the negligence claim – a factor which had not been present in any other case – complicated the issue. The court, in the end, was prepared to defer sale until after Mrs Gorman's litigation was finally determined, with leave to the trustee in bankruptcy to apply if the litigation were either abandoned or pursued dilatorily. She would be given the option to purchase the trustee's share after the claim had been determined, and interest would be charged from the moment of the hearing until the date when the option was exercised. If Mrs Gorman chose not to take this course, sale would be ordered, though it should be deferred for six months. Again, one sees the court displaying a reasonable flexibility, though it is to be noted, as *Re Lowrie* and the Insolvency Act 1986 ss 332–336 make clear, the discretion to refuse sale at the trustee in bankruptcy's behalf is limited indeed. The comparison between *Gorman* and *Austin-Fell* may be noted; the worse the financial position of the husband vis-à-vis his creditors, the worse the position of his wife.

Tenancy or licence: accommodation for the homeless

In recent years, one of the more regular features of the All England Reports has been a series of cases on the distinction between a lease and a licence: see, eg *Street v Mountford* [1985] 2 All ER 289 (All ER Rev 1985 pp 190–196), *AG Securities v Vaughan* and *Antoniades v Villiers* [1988] 3 All ER 1058 (All ER Rev 1988, pp 172–177, 186–191), and *Aslan v Murphy (Nos 1 and 2)* and *Duke v Wynne* [1989] 3 All ER 130 (All ER Rev 1989, pp 172–176, 184–189).

This year's offering raises a point similar to that dealt with in an earlier case, *Ogwr Borough Council v Dykes* [1989] 2 All ER 880 (All ER Rev 1989, pp 187–189). In *Family Housing Association v Jones* [1990] 1 All ER 385 (Jean Warburton, [1990] Conv 397, and Landlord and Tenant, pp 172–174 below), a council granted possession of freehold premises – which it owned but which it wished, in future, to redevelop – to the plaintiffs for use as temporary accommodation for housing homeless families. The defendant and her son were allowed use of part of such accommodation; the use was stated to be temporary, there was a weekly accommodation charge, the document was referred to as a 'licence' and the plaintiff retained keys to the premises so as to offer support to the defendant, to discuss rehousing problems and to inspect the state of repair of the premises. It was apparently common ground that the defendant paid far less than the market rent (per Slade LJ at 396c). With some reluctance, the Court of Appeal found that a tenancy was thereby created. There was money paid weekly and a weekly tenancy was thereby created; there was a right to occupy the flat (the flat was unsuitable for sharing with others), and the retention of the key was not by itself decisive: the purposes for which the keys were retained was what mattered. Slade LJ mentioned the passage in *Street v Mountford* itself where exclusive occupation might not lead to a tenancy being created: in particular he mentions 'an object of charity': see [1985] 2 All ER at 297 and [1990] 1 All ER at 396a. However, notwithstanding that there was an element of charity or bounty in the arrangement, Slade LJ did not pursue the point. The previous decision in *Ogwr Borough Council v Dykes* was not followed; the reasoning in it, as pointed out in last year's review (All ER Rev 1989, pp 187–189) cannot stand with the later decisions of the House of Lords in *Antoniades v Villiers* and *AG Securities v Vaughan*. What mattered was the existence of exclusive possession; the parties' intentions were, by comparison, unimportant. The court went on to hold that even if there were a licence, it was a licence subject to the Housing Act 1985, s 79(3) and therefore conferred on the occupier the same security of tenure she would have had, had she been a tenant. This, however, did not necessarily mean that she had security against the plaintiff: everything depended on the provisions of the Housing Act under which the accommodation had been provided.

This case shows a clear determination of the court to restrict the exceptions to *Street v Mountford*. This clearly concerned Slade LJ; the plaintiff had limited supplies of housing and the decision to which he was a party inevitably restricted the plaintiff's options in using that stock. As the House of Lords had held in *Eastleigh Borough Council v Walsh* [1985] 2 All ER 112 (All ER Rev 1985, pp 190, 216), providing accommodation for the homeless took the case outside the umbrella of *Street v Mountford*. The net result of the case is to restrict the 'object of charity' exception: here there was a charitable purpose, the payments for use of the premises were low in relation to their worth, and the plaintiff retained a key, inter alia, to offer the defendant and her child support. What more should have been required? Is a person in the defendant's position to be forced publicly to acknowledge that she is a recipient of charity? Or must the providing agency charge no rent? Or must they insist upon some sort of sharing? The decision in *Street v Mountford* is widely regarded as having been motivated by a desire to prevent property owners from circumventing the Rent Acts and thus being able to charge high rents for accommodation which they can they repossess when they wish; here, however, the facts are a far cry from that scenario and the result may be seen as impeding, rather than helping, social justice.

Mortgages

This year there were two important cases on mortgages: *Britannia Building Society v Earl* [1990] 2 All ER 469 (Stuart Bridge [1990] Conv 450, and Landlord and Tenant, pp 177–178 below) (on the mortgagee's right to possess) and *Parker-Tweedale v Dunbar Bank (No 1)* [1990] 2 All ER 577 (Lionel Bently, [1990] Conv 431) (on the mortgagee's duties on sale). It is perhaps a reflection on the current economic climate that it is the mortgagee's enforcement of his rights that is causing difficulties in the courts. In *Britannia Building Society v Earl*, the Building Society mortgagees lent money on mortgage to Earl, the house owner, on the security of his house. The mortgage deed was in standard form and contained a prohibition against letting without the Building Society's consent. In breach of this, the property was let to the Amins, who did not know about the prohibition. The Amins, in due course, became statutory tenants. Earl fell into arrears and the Building Society sought possession both against him and against the Amins. This order was granted, but the Amins appealed to the Court of Appeal; their appeal was dismissed. The Amins, as statutory tenants had a right as against the mortgagor, their landlord, but not as against the mortgagee. Further, the court had no discretion under the Administration of Justice Act 1970, s 36 to defer possession; a statutory tenant did not have an estate or interest in the land and therefore did not derive title under the mortgage: he therefore did not come within the protection of the relevant sections. Indeed, the very nature of the statutory tenant – like a protected tenant – has a status of irremovability which derives from statute, not from the contract with his landlord. However, although the court could have determined the case on this ground, McCowan LJ, giving the main judgment of the court, took the view that s 39 of the 1970 Act applied only to the assignees of the mortgagor and not to tenants at all. This, it may well be argued, is too wide a meaning: the phrase 'Any person deriving title under the original mortgagor' seems entirely apt to cover tenants; after all, in the Law of Property Act 1925, s 78, the phrase 'persons deriving title under him or them' was held apt to cover both yearly tenants: *Smith and Snipeshall Farm v River Douglas Catchment Board*

[1949] 2 All ER 179 and weekly tenants: *Williams v Unit Construction Co Ltd* (1951) 19 Conv (NS) 262. (These cases do not appear to have been cited to the court and, in any event, the context may be different – though certainly not necessarily so.) This argument, however, could not help the Amins: they were statutory tenants and did not derive title from their mortgagor/ landlord. There is, moreover, a fundamental difficulty in the way not only of statutory but also protected tenants if they seek the aid of the court under the Administration of Justice Act 1970, s 36. Section 36, put simply, can only operate where there is a breach of an obligation under the mortgage and the [mortgagor] is able to remedy it; and the obligation on the facts of cases such as *Earl* can only be carried out by the tenant leaving, which renders, of course, the whole exercise nugatory. Section 36 has already had to be amended to cater for one difficulty: see the Administration of Justice Act 1973, s 8, reversing *Halifax Building Society v Clark* [1973] 2 All ER 33; the decision in *Earl* is such as to call for a further reconsideration of the section; should not a tenant who is prepared to pay the rent to the mortgagee at least be given a chance to have a discretion exercised in his favour, rather than be debarred totally from seeking the court's protection?

It has been well established for some time that a mortgagee in exercising his power of sale owes a duty to the mortgagor to obtain a proper price for the mortgaged property at the time when he exercises his power of sale: *Cuckmere Brick Co Ltd v Mutual Finance Ltd* [1971] 2 All ER 633, *Tse Kwong Lam v Won Chit Sen* [1983] 3 All ER 54 (All ER Rev 1983, pp 57–58, 236). *Parker-Tweedale v Dunbar (No 1)* shows the disinclination of the court to extend the benefit of rights created under that duty outside the strict mortgagor-mortgagee relationship. The facts were simple: a beneficiary under a trust complained that mortgagees of trust property had sold at an undervalue; and therefore they owed a duty not only to the mortgagee, but to him as well. In the *Cuckmere Brick* case, Salmon LJ had spoken of the concept of a duty of care, though this language had not been adopted by Cross LJ; and, said the Court of Appeal in *Parker-Tweedale*, this remark did not mean that the tort of negligence had to be imported into the mortgager/mortgagee relationship. This relationship had been long understood and regulated by the rules of equity and there was no need for the tort of negligence – with its seemingly continual shifts and nuances (as to which see pp 306–307) being relevant in this context. Nourse LJ took a most robust view of this; there was, he said, no support either in principle or authority for the view that, even if the mortgagor were a bare trustee of the property, a duty would be owed to the beneficiary. There was also a further point: if the beneficiary was to sue, it had to be because the trustee had in some way failed in his duty. The Court of Appeal, like the trial judge, found that there had been no such breach of duty by the trustee: therefore the action of the beneficiary failed. Sir Michael Kerr, however, took a slightly more cautious view: while agreeing with Nourse LJ he expressly left open the following question: if it could be shown that the beneficiary's claim against a mortgagee/trustee were useless, because the trustee had, for example, either no assets or only trusts assets, would a mortgagee be directly liable, especially if he had notice of the situation?

This case is therefore a restrictive decision: it attempts to confine all matters relating to the mortgagee's remedies into the law of mortgagor/mortgagee as understood and implemented by equity. This approach is in accord with the decision of *China & South Seas Bank Ltd v Tan Soon Gin* [1989] 3 All ER 839 (a case on guarantee/surety); the courts are obviously concerned that, with the continually changing fortunes of the tort of negligence, the duties in an area where they have been long-established should not change – especially when it is not perceived that any injustice has arisen. This may be a problem only with the tort of negligence; after all, issues concerning mortgages have involved economic duress and inequality of bargaining power: see eg *National Westminster Bank v Morgan* [1985] 1 All ER 821 (All ER Rev 1985, p 89), *Alec Lobb (Garages) Ltd v Total Oil GB Ltd* [1985] 1 All ER 303 (All ER Rev 1985, p 87).

Commons

This year's leading case on commons is *Hampshire County Council v Milburn* [1990] 2 All ER 257 (Peter Reeves, [1990] LSG No 29 p 17, and see Statute Law, p 267 below). Since the passing of the Commons Registration Act in 1965, considerable judicial attention has been given to the Act, but no underlying philosophy seems to have emerged: see, eg All ER Rev 1982, pp 181–2, All ER Rev 1984, pp 188–9, All ER Rev 1985, pp 203–4, All ER Rev 1989, p 190. However, the House of Lords, in the *Milburn* case have struck a blow for the public interest in protecting land registered under the Commons Registration Act 1965. The case involved some 365 acres of land which had formerly been part of the waste land of the manors of Hazell and Putham. Waste lands were 'the open, uncultivated and unoccupied lands parcel of the manor or open lands parcel of the manor other than the demesne lands of the manor'. (*A-G v Hanmer* (1858) 27 LJ Ch 837 at 840, per Watson B.) In 1925 the Law of Property Act, s 193 granted rights of access for air and exercise to members of the public over any manorial waste wholly or partly situated within a borough or urban district. The land in question was not in such a district, but, in any event, the Law of Property Act, s 194 provided that any building or work which impedes rights of common is unlawful without the consent of the Minister of Agriculture, which consent may only be given if it is of benefit to the neighbourhood and to the commoners.

The waste land of the manors was registered under the 1965 Act as common land being waste land of a manor not subject to rights of common. In 1981 Sir Anthony Milburn, the Lord of the manors of Pulham and Hazell, conveyed his manorial rights away, but reserved to himself the land in the two parishes 'formerly part of the wastes of the said manors'. His argument was that upon the conveyance away of the manors, the land ceased to be common land and therefore an application to remove it from the Commons Register could be made under the provisions in the Regulations made under the 1965 Act. Lord Templeman, with whom all the other members of the House of Lords agreed, adopted two arguments. First, he declared that, as a matter of policy and principle, to adopt Sir Anthony's argument would make a nonsense both of the reasoning of the Royal Commission on Common Land 1955–58 (Cmnd 462) and of the 1965 Act: many areas of waste land were not subject to rights of common but Parliament, on the Commission's advice, had declared that such land should be registrable as common land. Second, the construction of the phrase 'waste land of a manor' had to be construed. It could mean either 'waste land that had once belonged to a manor' or 'waste land that currently belonged to a manor'. There had been a divergence of judicial opinion over this: in *Re Chewton Common, Christchurch* [1977] 3 All ER 509, Slade J had taken the former view; his view had, however, been disapproved by Stamp LJ in *Box Parish Council v Lacey* [1979] 1 All ER 113; he asked the rhetorical question, '. . . why should Parliament have chosen to make registrability dependent on whether the waste land had at some remote date in the past been the waste land of a manor?' Lord Templeman's speech provided the answer: waste land is valuable for the public interest and should be preserved. A change of ownership should no effect on what is clearly regarded as a public asset.

Notice to complete: time of the essence

Delta Vale Properties Ltd v Mills [1990] 2 All ER 176 raises a short but interesting point on the question of the timing of a notice to complete. The contract incorporated the Law Society's General Conditions of Sale (1984 revision). Condition 23, provided, inter alia, that on the service of a completion notice, it became a term of the contract that the transaction should be completed within 15 working days of service of the notice and that time was of the essence. If, after service of that notice, the time for completion was extended by agreement or implication, a second notice could be served but with the period of seven working days substituted for that of 15 working days. A specific clause in the contract drew attention 'to the consequence which will attend your failure to complete within 28 days after service of this notice' – ie the 15 day notice. Completion was scheduled for 15 May 1986; it did not take place and on 20 May 1986 the vendors served a notice to complete within 15 working days; this was ignored, and on 13 August 1986 the vendors issued a further notice requiring completion within seven working days. Completion did not take place and the vendors purported to rescind the contract. The purchasers sought specific performance: this was granted by the trial judge, who held that the period of 15 days was an exact period, being neither a minimum nor a maximum period. The implication of that was that the vendor could not unilaterally have allowed the purchaser a further period of grace of 28 days. The Court of Appeal rejected this: Slade LJ stated (at 181g) that it was always open to a party to a contract unilaterally to waive a term that was solely for his benefit provided only that he made his intentions clear. A more serious point was whether the notice was ambiguous. The test, following cases such as *Hankey v Clavering* [1942] 2 All ER 311 and *Allam & Co Ltd v Europa Poster Services Ltd* [1968] 1 All ER 826 (cases in the context of notices terminating leases or licences), was that notices 'must be sufficiently clear and unambiguous to leave a reasonable recipient in no reasonable doubt as to how and when they intended to operate'. Construing the notice, badly drafted though it was, the court held that its clear construction was that the notice was indeed a condition 23 notice to complete, but that the vendor would not exercise his rights until after 28 days had elapsed. The notices to complete were thus good and the contract had been rescinded. This decision – and both the Court of Appeal and the House of Lords refused leave to appeal – seems both good sense and good law. There was an ambiguity in the drafting, but the ambiguity was one which could either benefit only the person who was prepared to waive it or which would render any notice invalid. The latter construction would frustrate any reasonable intention the parties would have had: the provisions for notices to complete are there to enable one party to force the other to complete an agreed bargain within a reasonable time after the agreement was supposed to have been completed.

Donatio mortis causa: land

Every so often a case is decided which, although apparently merely a re-affirmation of existing orthodoxy), encourages a judge to provide a judicial rationale for an aspect of the law which seldom falls for consideration. Such a case is *Sen v Headley* [1990] 1 All ER 898 (Jonathan Hill, 53 MLR 542, H B Parry, [1990] Conv 132, Debra Morris, (1990) 4 Trusts Law and Practice 110, C E F Rickett, 134 Sol Jo 678 and see Succession, pp 270–271 below). Whether the rationale is satisfactory will be considered later.

The facts were straightforward: the plaintiff, who had long been close to the deceased, visited the deceased in hospital when the deceased was terminally ill. He told her that his house and its contents were hers and told her that the deeds were in a steel box and that she had the keys to it. After his death, three days later, she visited the house, found the box, and used a key which she believed he must have slipped into her bag, opened the box and took possession of the deeds, the house being unregistered land.

Was there a donatio mortis causa? The rules for establishing such a gift are strict: (1) there must be a clear intention to give, but only if the donor dies, (2) the gift must be made in contemplation of death, and (3) the donor had effectively to part with dominium over the subject matter of the gift: there had to be some clear act towards a transfer of the property. On the evidence, the first two requirements were easily satisfied, but the third raised great difficulties and, indeed, the whole question whether a donatio mortis causa of land was possible fell for consideration.

As a matter of principle, the law of donatio mortis causa rests on a compromise: the necessities for a formal gift are not required; if they were, then there would be no need for special rules: there would be a gift simpliciter. However, there had to be some manifestation to show that dominium has passed: thus, for instance, handing over a savings account book or a book of national savings certificates was held sufficient: see *Darlow v Sparks* [1938] 2 All ER 235. This has proceeded on a cases-by-case basis, but what was handed over amounted to 'the essential indicia or evidence of title, possession or production of which will entitle the possessor to the money or other property purported to be given': ([1990] 1 All ER at 903d). On the death of the donor, even if full legal title had not passed, a trust arose by operation of law which had the effect of vesting the legal and equitable title in the intended donee. The question remains, however, as to what property was capable of passing by donatio mortis causa. *Snell's Equity* (29th edn) lists at pp 383–384 things that may pass and things that may not pass. Even disregarding any question of realty, it is clear from the lists that the law is in a arbitrary state: why should the contents of a bank deposit book be capable of passing, whereas a certificate of building society shares not be capable of passing its contents? Why should a promissory note drawn by a third person pass the value in it whereas a cheque drawn by the donor on his own bankers not pass its subject matter? There may be technical explanations, but the overall impression is not one of immediate clarity.

Conventional wisdom has been that realty cannot be made the subject of a donatio mortis causa: this seems to have been assumed by counsel and by Lord Eldon LC himself in *Duffield v Elwes* (1827) 1 Bli NS 497, [1824–34] All ER Rep 247. (In the locus classicus on donatio mortis causa, *Ward v Turner* (1752) 2 Ves Sen 431, Lord Hardwicke LC was concerned about the impact on the doctrine of the Statute of Frauds, and therefore would not allow land to be the subject matter of a donatio mortis causa. Mummery J felt obliged to follow these authorities – and certain Commonwealth cases which had been cited. He gave three main reasons for his decision. First, judicial caution should be exercised in extending the doctrine of donatio mortis causa. Second, although logic, reason and principle were prayed in aid as justifications for extending the doctrine, precedent and policy – in the shape of the requirements of formality – also had to be considered. In the context of land, delivery of the title deeds inter vivos will not, per se, pass ownership of the land to which they relate; if the gift is to take effect on death, the requirements of the Wills Act must be satisfied. Third, in the case of land, the deceased until his death had the right, as absolute owner, to sell or declare trusts over the property; those who took any such interest would take precedence over the plaintiff's claim. Therefore, stated Mummery J, it was difficult to see how dominium could, in any sense, have been transferred.

The doctrine of donatio mortis causa is equitable; and it was presumably intended to give effect to the wishes of the donor, even though there were some rule of formality which prevented the donor's intention from having been recognised at law. There are, of course, modern analogies: the whole doctrine of estoppel, the constructive trust based on informal agreement and the (recently repealed) doctrine of part performance are all manifestations of the idea that equity will ignore formalities where appropriate. Moreover, land – which is a species of property where formalities are regarded as particularly important – has been the subject of disputes in all these areas. Why, therefore, should donatio mortis causa stand apart from this trend? With respect to Mummery J's third reason – that dominium has not passed – this will almost always be the case with donationes mortis causa: what is being sought is an intention coupled with some physical act rather than with an act which will, by itself, pass ownership. What could be more significant that giving the plaintiff the key (one assumes it was the only key) to his deed-box? Short of giving her the deeds themselves – and on the judge's reasoning even that would not have been enough – what else could have been done? On the facts, it is submitted that, as long as the plaintiff could have clearly made out her case – and there is no room in this area for uncertainties being allowed to subvert the basic formalities rules – the doctrine should have been extended to cover cases of land: the plaintiff was surely a clearer intended beneficiary of the property than was the successful plaintiff in the estoppel case of *Re Basham (decd)* [1987] 1 All ER 405 (All ER Rev 1987, pp 156–158). One cannot criticise a first instance judge, who examined the authorities with great care, for not taking a wider view, but the result of the case is that an already untidy area of the law is looking even untidier. Given that cases on donatio mortis causa in the law reports are rare, little is likely to be done.

Trusts and powers: a footnote

Re Beatty's Will Trusts [1990] 3 All ER 844 is a decision which is primarily of interest to will draughtsman: Hoffman J held that there was no independent rule of law that a testator could not delegate the making of his will to trustees; so to hold would prevent the use of widely-drawn powers of appointment in testamentary documents. The decision of the High Court of Australia in *Tatham v Huxtable* (1950) 81 CLR 639, which held that such an independent rule did exist, was not followed. (This aspect of the case is further considered at pp 269–270 below.)

However, there is also much of interest to the trusts lawyer. Powers of appointment can now be extremely widely drawn: the decision in *McPhail v Doulton* [1970] 2 All ER 228, as applied in *Re Manisty's Settlement* [1973] 2 All ER 1203 and *Re Hay's Settlement Trusts* [1981] 3 All ER 786 indicate that there are few limits to the width of a power, although restrictions are clearly contemplated by Lord Wilberforce in *McPhail v Doulton* itself. Only the somewhat unusual case of *R v District Auditor, ex p West Yorkshire Metropolitan County Council* [1986] RVR 24 (noted by C Harpum, [1986] CLJ 391) seems to impose a restriction.

In *Re Beatty's Will Trusts* the will contained a legacy of £1.5m for the trustees 'to allocate. . . to or among such person or persons. . . as they think fit'; there was a further request that any memorandum of the testatrix which contained requests should be observed. Any part of the legacy that was undisposed of was to fall into residue. Counsel for the intestate successor (who would benefit if the trusts of the will were found void for uncertainty) conceded that the powers given to the trustees would have been valid powers if contained in a settlement. Hoffman J did not analyse if this was a trust power – and if so in what sense – and, because the point had been conceded there was no need for him so to do. However, if the concession was properly made, it would seem to follow that the direction in the will was construed as a power in the hands of trustees – though not necessarily a trust power. The terms of the legacy clearly satisfied the 'is or is not' test: every potential object was clearly within the class. But what of the ability to survey? Was there anything like a class? These issues, because of the concession, did not fall to be considered, but, as the majority of the previously decided cases indicate, width is no bar as such to validity; the idea of uncertainty, save for the *West Yorkshire* case, seems to be regarded as of much less significance.

Holding and Management Ltd v Property Holding and Investment Trust plc [1990] 1 All ER 938 (see also pp 175–176 below) provides useful interpretation both of the Rules of the Supreme Court Ord 62, r 6(2) and of the Trustee Act 1925, s 30(2). Disputes had arisen over repairs to a block of flats between the landlord's agent (who was also the maintenance trustee), the plaintiff in the action, and the tenants, the defendants in the action. The plaintiff issued a summons seeking, inter alia, determination of what scheme of works was appropriate; this issue was settled on the second day of the action in favour of the tenants. The plaintiff sought to recover its costs from the maintenance fund to which all tenants contributed under the terms of the lease; Mervyn Davies J ordered that the maintenance trustee was not entitled to its costs; this was upheld by the Court of Appeal. First, RSC Ord 62, r 6(2) did not apply: the plaintiff was suing qua agent, not qua trustee. Further, it had in any event acted unreasonably in demanding a court decision (which it may be noted, although the court did not apparently rely on this, was conceded by the plaintiff in the defendants' favour). Second, the plaintiffs' argument on the Trustee Act, s 30(2) also failed; although trustees are clearly entitled to all their proper costs incidental to the execution of the trust, the plaintiffs' claim went beyond that: neither the landlord nor the tenants wished for the proposed increase, and so the plaintiffs were striking out on their own, rather than considering what the beneficiaries wished; the costs were therefore improperly, not properly, incurred: see *Re Baron Grimthorpe's Will Trusts* [1958] 1 All ER 765 at 769. This did raise an issue of principle: how far could the beneficiaries control the trustees? *Re Brockbank* [1948] 1 All ER 287 held that beneficiaries could not tell the trustees how to administer the trust as long as it subsisted; but, as the Court of Appeal held ([1990] 1 All ER at 948e) this did not automatically mean that if a trustee incurs costs against the wishes of his beneficiaries, he will always be entitled to an indemnity from the trust. Here, one assumes, the court regarded the litigation as unnecessary and hostile; therefore the trustees were disentitled from recovering. On the facts, this is reasonable enough: but in a more borderline case, what will happen if a majority of beneficiaries indicate their hostility to a course of action by the trustees which might be in the general interests of the trust?

Miscellaneous

The definitive nature of a map purporting to be conclusive of the existence of a highway was considered in *R v Secretary of State for the Environment, ex p Simms* [1990] 3 All ER 490, the Court of Appeal held that the Highways Acts did make definitive maps conclusive evidence of the existence of the rights shown on that map until a review occurred; once, however, new evidence was available, the review procedure could operate and the map be altered.

Hussey v Eels [1990] 1 All ER 449 raises an interesting point on damages available where a purchase of a defective property had been induced by a negligent misrepresentation: the case is more fully considered in the chapters on Contract, pp 64–65 above and Tort, pp 337–339 below.

The complicated case of *Arab Monetary Fund v Hashim (No 2)* [1990] 1 All ER 673 (Hoffman J) states that where a person, being a non-fiduciary, is alleged to be accountable as a constructive trustee, it was sufficient for the person making the allegations to plead in general terms that the non-fiduciary had actual or constructive notice of the fraudulent or dishonest breach of trust in respect of which it was sought to make him accountable; there was no need, providing that some evidence of conduct of which the person alleging the misconduct could plead lack of probity; if there was such evidence, the precise particulars of the allegations could wait until later. (This case is more fully analysed in Practice and Procedure, pp 204–205 below.)

Landlord and Tenant

PHILIP H PETTIT, MA
Barrister, Emeritus Professor of Equity, Universities of Bristol and Buckingham

Tenancy or licence?

The Court of Appeal decision in *Family Housing Association v Jones* [1990] 1 All ER 385, briefly mentioned in All ER Rev 1989 at p 185, is now fully reported. Once again the question was whether an agreement created a tenancy or, as it purported to do, merely a licence. The relevant events took place as long ago as 1984 and 1985 and the relevant Act was the Housing (Homeless Persons) Act 1977, now replaced by the Housing Act 1985. However, the court found it convenient to refer to the provisions of the 1985 Act as the relevant provisions of the two Acts are in all material respects the same, save that s 64, unlike s 8 of the earlier Act, requires written notice to be given by the local housing authority when, on completing inquiries under s 62, it notifies the applicant of its decision on the several relevant questions, eg homelessness and priority need.

The facts were that Mrs Jones, the defendant, applied for housing in September 1984 to the Westminster City Council which first accepted that she might be homeless and have a priority need, and subsequently accepted that this was indeed so. She was given written notice by letter dated 13 February 1985. Mrs Jones claimed that she had been given oral notice on 23 October 1984, conditionally on the production of certain documents, which she produced on 6 November 1984.

The plaintiff association (the FHA) came into the picture because it had been granted by Westminster City Council a licence of various properties to be used as temporary housing accommodation for homeless families referred to them by the council. Mrs Jones was so referred and an agreement was entered into on 5 February 1985 between the FHA and Mrs Jones under which she and her four-year-old son were to occupy the two roomed flat in dispute. The agreement was described as a licence, and stated in terms that it was for temporary accommodation only, was not a secure tenancy, and did not give Mrs Jones exclusive possession. The FHA retained a set of keys and there was evidence that the practice of the FHA was to visit their accommodation to offer support to persons occupying their properties, to discuss their rehousing problems and to inspect the state of repair.

In April 1985 Mrs Jones was offered the tenancy of a flat, which she rejected on various grounds. The council considered that making the offer discharged its statutory obligations and consequently the FHA in due course, on 30 September 1985, served Mrs Jones with a four weeks' notice to terminate her licence. At the same time they served a four weeks' notice to quit if, which they did not admit, Mrs Jones was a tenant. It was not until a year later, on 23 September 1986, that possession proceedings were started in the county court, and the matter did not come to trial for a further two years, on 26 November 1988. The leisurely pace continued with the Court of Appeal giving judgment on 2 November 1989.

In considering whether the agreement created a tenancy or a licence, Balcombe LJ started by referring to Lord Templeman's classic speech in *Street v Mountford* [1985] 2 All ER 289 (dicussed in All ER Rev 1985, pp 190–196) which is, of course, the basis of the modern law on the topic. He next cited from the speech of Lord Oliver in *Antoniades v Villiers* [1988] 3 All ER 1058 (All ER Rev 1988, pp 172, 186), where the House of Lords reversed the Court of Appeal decision, and from the summary of the present position made by Lord Donaldson MR, giving the judgment of the Court of Appeal, in *Aslan v Murphy (Nos 1 & 2)* [1989] 3 All ER 130 at 133 (All ER Rev 1989 pp 173, 185). Applying those decisions to the facts of the case, Mrs Jones had exclusive possession of residential property for an ascertainable period in return for periodical money payments and was therefore a tenant notwithstanding the language of the agreement. The only possible contra-indications were said to be the retention of a key by the FHA and the purposes for which that key was retained. Both Balcombe and Slade LJJ (with whom Farquharson LJ agreed) considered this matter and were of opinion that the retention of a key was not by itself decisive. The limited purposes for which it was retained – to offer support and to inspect the state of repair – were insufficient to sustain an assertion that Mrs Jones had not been granted exclusive possession when all the other circumstances pointed the other way.

In deciding that Mrs Jones had a tenancy the court refused to follow *Ogwr BC v Dykes* [1989] 2 All ER 880 (All ER Rev 1989, pp 175, 187), pointing out that it was decided before, and was irreconcilable with, *AG Securities v Vaughan, Antoniades v Villiers* [1988] 3 All ER 1058. Though *Ogwr BC v Dykes* was distinguishable on the ground that the council there was acting under a statutory duty which was not imposed on the FHA, the court said that even if it could not be distinguished they would be bound not to follow it under the second exception to the rule in *Young v Bristol Aeroplane Co Ltd* [1944] 2 All ER 293. Slade LJ expressed some misgiving over the decision he felt bound to make for he was attracted by the view of Purchas LJ, in *Ogwr BC v Dykes*, that if the context in which the right to exclusive occupation is granted specifically and definitively negatives an intention to create a tenancy, then some other interest appropriate to the intention established by that context would be established. He accepted, however, that the line of authorities beginning with *Street v Mountford* ruled out this approach. Noting that Lord Templeman in *Street v Mountford* had said that there were some special cases where a person in exclusive possession was not a tenant, Slade LJ did not think that the special features of the case before them justified the court in formulating a new exceptional category of case to cover the particular situation. As he pointed out *Eastleigh BC v Walsh* [1985] 2 All ER 112 (All ER Rev 1985, pp 190, 216) is House of Lords authority for the proposition that what would otherwise be a tenancy is not excluded from that category because the arrangement is intended to provide temporary accommodation for a homeless person.

Balcombe LJ also went on to consider what the position would have been if the agreement of 5 February 1985 had created a licence, not a tenancy. In that case, he said, Mrs Jones would, under s 79(3), have had the same security of tenure as if she had been granted a tenancy. However, Balcombe LJ continued, there were two pre-*Street v Mountford* decisions of the Court of

Appeal (*Family Housing Association v Miah* (1982) 5 H L R 94 and *Kensington & Chelsea Royal Borough v Hayden* (1984) 17 HLR 114) which held that a licence did not qualify for protection unless it conferred exclusive possession on the occupant. In the light of *Street v Mountford* and *A G Securities v Vaughan* such 'licences' will in fact create tenancies, and accordingly:

> 'if *Miah*'s case and *Hayden*'s case remain good law, their effect would be to deprive s 79(3) of all operation, save only in respect of licences granted for no consideration. That cannot have been the intention of Parliament'.

Balcombe LJ is doubtless right in stating that the intention of s 79(3) was to prevent a local authority from depriving an occupant of security of tenure by granting a licence instead of a tenancy as was thought to be possible before *Street & Mountford* and *A G Securities v Vaughan*. Again applying the second exception to the rule in *Young v Bristol Aeroplane Co Ltd*, Balcombe LJ said that these House of Lords decisions were irreconcilable with *Miah*'s case and *Hayden*'s case, which they were accordingly bound to refuse to follow. The consequences of this were not spelt out, but would seem to raise the possibility of a licensee without exclusive possession obtaining security of tenure.

In providing accommodation to a homeless person a housing authority may be acting under s 63(1) or s 65(2) of the Act. A tenancy under s 63(1) is intended as a temporary measure pending appropriate inquiries and does not confer security of tenure if determined within 12 months under Sch 1, para 4. However, if a tenancy is granted after notification that the housing authority is satisfied that the applicant has a priority need and has not become homeless intentionally, Sch 1, para 4 does not apply and the tenant has security of tenure. As mentioned earlier, the question of whether due notice had been given by the housing authority had not been determined, and the case was accordingly remitted to the county court to determine whether the tenancy arose under s 63 (1) or s 65 (2).

Repairing obligations

The decision in *Associated British Ports v C H Bailey plc* [1990] 1 All ER 929 will necessitate some re-writing of the textbooks, for in it the House of Lords in effect overruled the long-standing decision of the Court of Appeal in *Sidnell v Wilson* [1966] 1 All ER 681, which both the judge at first instance, and the Court of Appeal, had followed in the instant case, as they were bound to do. As is well known, the Leasehold Property (Repairs) Act 1938, as amended by s 51 of the Landlord and Tenant Act 1954, enables a tenant under a lease (not being a lease of an agricultural holding within the meaning of the Agricultural Holdings Act 1986) for a term of at least seven years with three years or more unexpired, to serve a counter-notice claiming the benefit of the Act, where a notice has been served on him under s 146 of the Law of Property Act 1925 for breach of a repairing covenant. The effect of serving a counter-notice is that the landlord is thereby prohibited from taking any proceedings to forfeit the lease 'otherwise than with the leave of the court'. Sub-section 1(5) provides that leave '. . . shall not be given unless the lessor proves –' any one of five things.

On a literal construction of the subsection the court has no power to grant leave unless one of these five requirements is satisfied. On the facts of the case, the landlords had not proved in accordance with the balance of probabilities in the light of the evidence adduced by the parties that one of the requirements had been met, though they had established a prima facie or arguable case. The landlords' argument was that this was all that they were required to do at this stage, and the rationale behind it was said to be that this would avoid duplication and save time and expense. Otherwise, if the landlords proved one of the requirements was satisfied after a full hearing of the evidence, the same or better evidence would have to be rehearsed in the ensuing forfeiture action if the tenants were to resist forfeiture or seek relief against forfeiture. The strongest case in favour of the landlords' argument was *Sidnell v Wilson*, where the Court of Appeal, reversing the decision of the county court judge, had taken this view, though in that case the tenant had conceded on the appeal that the landlord need only show a prima facie or arguable case of breach by the tenants. Lord Denning MR and Harman LJ referred to a prima facie case, an expression with which Diplock LJ was not entirely happy, preferring the phrase 'arguable case'. However, they all shared the same approach to the section and would not accept that it meant what it said. Lord Templeman cited extracts from all three judgments and we may perhaps refer to a crucial sentence in each citation. Lord Denning MR, after pointing out that the application for leave is only an interlocutory application, said: 'It cannot be supposed that the landlord has to prove his whole case as if it were the trial.' Harman LJ said that the contrary view would 'make two actions flourish where one flourished before', which in his view could not have been meant. And Diplock LJ said: 'Parliament cannot have intended that there should be two trials of the matter.'

In the present case, all the other Law Lords agreed with the speech of Lord Templeman, who held that the words of the section were clear and must prevail. The landlord must at this stage prove that one of the five requirements is satisfied. 'The battle between landlord and tenant must be fought at some stage and Parliament has directed that it shall be fought under the 1938 Act when the landlord seeks leave to pursue his remedies for breach of covenant.' If the landlord fails at this stage, there will be no forfeiture proceedings. If he succeeds, Lord Templeman did not think it necessary or proper that the matter should be fought over again in the forfeiture proceedings, and he did not accept that in practice there would be additional expense and delay. In any event, the words of the 1938 Act require that the landlord shall prove his case at that stage. If he succeeds, the court, in the forfeiture proceedings, has a discretion as to whether it should grant relief under s 146.

The practical consequences in the instant case were that the landlords' application under the 1938 Act was directed to be reheard, with both parties being given leave to adduce further evidence.

Holding & Management Ltd v Property Holding & Investment Trust plc [1990] 1 All ER 938 is worth a brief mention, though it was not primarily concerned with landlord and tenant issues. The case concerned a block of 47 residential flats, each let on a standard form lease for 75 years from March 1972. The plaintiff, called the 'maintenance trustee', was made responsible for the repair, decoration and maintenance of the property out of money provided by the tenants through maintenance contributions payable under the leases.

The appeal to the Court of Appeal raised questions – with which we are not here primarily concerned – as to whether the maintenance trustee was entitled to certain costs out of the maintenance fund. It was held that the proceedings were by nature adversarial between the maintenance trustee and the tenants, and were not a conventional application by a trustee for directions from the court. Accordingly, the first instance judge had been entitled, in his discretion, to refuse the maintenance trustee the costs he sought. Nor could he succeed under RSC Ord 62, r 6(2) because in bringing the action it had not acted as in its capacity as trustee of the maintenance fund, and likewise it was not assisted by s 30(2) of the Trustee Act 1925 because the costs and expenses in question had not been properly incurred.

Two landlord and tenant points arose in the case. First the court had to decide whether work under a proposed scheme constituted 'repair' within the terms of the lease. The court approved dicta of Hoffman J in *Post Office v Aquarius Properties Ltd* [1985] 2 EGLR 105, 107, and Sachs LJ in *Brew Bros Ltd v Snax (Ross) Ltd* [1970] 1 All ER 587 at 602–603, and gave a list of circumstances which might be relevant in a particular case. This provides a useful check-list of factors which should be considered, though the court was careful to point out that it was not comprehensive, and that the weight to be attached to each circumstance will vary from case to case.

Secondly, the maintenance trustee had placed some reliance on a provision in the lease that one of the purposes for which the maintenance fund was to be applied was 'the payment of all legal costs incurred by the maintenance trustee'. This point was dealt with very shortly. The provision only covered legal costs reasonably or properly incurred. The court having already held that the costs in dispute had not been reasonably or properly incurred, this provision could not help the maintenance trustee.

Rent Acts and protection from eviction

The facts in *Rakhit v Carty* [1990] 2 All ER 202 were simple. On 1 October 1987 the defendant entered into a tenancy agreement with the plaintiff landlord for a furnished tenancy of a flat for a term of 364 days at a rent of £450 per month, the equivalent of £5,400 per annum. Unknown to the parties, a rent of £550 per annum had been registered for the flat, then unfurnished, effective from 19 November 1973, at which time the plaintiff landlord had no interest in the premises. That rent was duly registered in the rent register on 12 March 1974 and the register recorded the flat as unfurnished.

When the tenancy came to an end by effluxion of time, the defendant became a statutory tenant, but within days the landlord commenced proceedings for possession under Case 9 on the ground that he reasonably required possession of the flat as a residence for himself. He also claimed arrears of rent and mesne profits. The county court judge made an order for possession, and awarded the landlord £2,710.58 arrears of rent together with mesne profits of £380 per month until possession, the latter figure being that determined by the rent officer in December 1988, the consequential entry in the rent register recording the flat as furnished.

The Court of Appeal could see no ground for interfering with the order for possession, which depended on the factual findings of the county court judge. In relation to the claim for rent and mesne profits the tenant repeated the contention that had failed at first instance, namely that the rent registration on 12 March 1974 limited the rent payable under the agreement of 1 October 1987. Accordingly, there were no arrears of rent but the tenant had in fact overpaid £3,069.82 up to the date of the hearing in respect of which a counterclaim was made.

The county court judge had held himself bound by the decision of the Court of Appeal in *Kent v Millmead Properties Limited* (1982) 44 P & CR 353 (followed in *Cheniston Investments v Waddock* (1988) 2 EGLR 136) where the facts, in all material respects, were indistinguishable. It was now argued that these decisions were made per incuriam, in that they did not take account of s 67(3) of the Rent Act 1977 (as amended by s 60(1) of the Housing Act 1980) which provides for the possibility of an application for the registration of a different rent within the normal two years period where, inter alia, there has been a significant change in the quantity, quality or condition of any furniture provided for use under the tenancy. The Court of Appeal thought it plain that, once a fair rent was registered, it set a limit to the recoverable rent for the demised premises until either they undergo such a change in their structure as to render them no longer the dwelling–house in respect of which a rent has been registered, or there is a cancellation of the registration under s 73, or there is a new registration consequent on a fresh application pursuant to s 67(3). There seems to be a slight slip here in that an ordinary application for a new registration after two years is overlooked. The terms of s 67(3) in the view of the court make it clear that provided the dwelling house remains as the same demised property, the provision of furniture as a term of the tenancy does not affect the recoverable rent unless and until the registered rent is increased under the statutory procedure.

In *Britannia Building Society v Earl* [1990] 2 All ER 469 the facts again were simple. There was a mortgage by the first defendant to the plaintiffs with the usual prohibition against letting without the consent of the plaintiffs. The first defendant let to the second defendants without any consent on a protected tenancy, on the expiry of which the second defendants became statutory tenants. The first defendant fell into arrears with his mortgage payments and the plaintiffs brought proceedings for possession which were not contested by the first defendant. The judge made an order for possession against both the first and second defendants against which the second defendants appealed. (See also Land Law and Trusts, p 164 above.)

The first argument on behalf of the second defendants was that as statutory tenants a possession order could only be made against them under the provisions of s 98 of the Rent Act 1977, irrespective of whether proceedings were brought by the landlord or by the mortgagees as holders of a title paramount. On this point *Dudley and District Benefit Building Society v Emerson* [1949] 2 All ER 252, [1949] Ch 707 is Court of Appeal authority for the proposition that in similar circumstances a contractual tenant who is a protected tenant within the Act is liable to be defeated by the assertion by mortgagees of their paramount title. *Bolton Building Society v Cobb* [1965] 3 All ER 814, [1966] 1 WLR 1 applied this decision in the context of the Protection from Eviction Act 1964. Counsel therefore had to contend that a statutory tenancy is different in kind from a contractual tenancy and that a mortgagee's title paramount puts the mortgagee in no better position than the landlord against a statutory tenant. Some dicta could be found in *Jessamine*

Investment Co v Schwartz [1976] 3 All ER 521, [1978] QB 264 to support this view, but the court was, rightly, not persuaded. To have held the contrary would have led to the absurd result that the second defendants would have had no right to possession as against the plaintiffs while they were contractual tenants, but once they became statutory tenants the plaintiffs would no longer be able to recover possession from them. McCowan LJ (with whose judgment Butler-Sloss LJ agreed) was happy to apply the observation of Templeman LJ in *Quennell v Maltby* [1979] 1 All ER 568, 572, [1979] 1 WLR 318, 323 that in such circumstances the tenant becomes a statutory tenant against the landlord but not as against the mortgagee. Though the point had not been argued there it was, he said, none the less a very persuasive authority.

The alternative ground on which the appeal was brought was that the second defendants were persons in whose favour the court should exercise the discretionary powers given to it by s 36 of the Administration of Justice Act 1970 as being, under the definition in s 39(1), persons 'deriving title under the mortgagor'. On this the court accepted the submissions of counsel for the plaintiffs that s 39(1) only applies to assignment of the property and does not include tenants, and that, even if it did, it does not include statutory tenants who have no estate or interest in the land and accordingly do not derive title at all. A further point was that the very existence of the tenancy was a breach of an obligation arising under the mortgage which, though unknown to the mortgagees when they commenced this action based on arrears, was itself a perfectly good ground for seeking possession. The court, it was argued, can only exercise its powers under s 36 if the breach is capable of being remedied. On the facts it could only be remedied by the departure of the tenant. This point was also accepted by the court.

The House of Lords, in *R v Burke* [1990] 2 All ER 385 unanimously approved the decision of the Court of Appeal in *R v Yuthiwattana* (1984) 80 Cr App R 55 on the construction of s 1(3) of the Protection from Eviction Act 1977. This subsection provides:

> 'If any person with intent to cause the residential occupier of any premises – (a) to give up the occupation of the premises or any part thereof . . . does acts calculated to interfere with the peace or comfort of the residential occupier . . . he shall be guilty of an offence.'

The essential facts were that the landlord had prevented two tenants from using the lavatories nearest to their rooms, though there was another lavatory and bathroom available to them elsewhere in the house but less conveniently situated for them; and had disconnected the front door bells communicating with their rooms. The sole question for consideration was whether these actions by the landlord were 'acts' within s 1(3). It was not contended that the trial judge had been wrong in directing the jury that the landlord's actions did not constitute a breach of contract because (a) although the tenants were entitled to have the use of a bathroom and lavatory somewhere in the building they were not contractually entitled to insist on any particular bathroom or lavatory being kept available, and (b) they were not entitled to require the tenant to maintain a system of door bells. The trial judge, however, went on to direct the jury that this was irrelevant and that provided the acts were done with the purpose or the aim of getting the tenants to leave they should convict. What the appellant now argued was that the actions by the landlord would only constitute 'acts' within the section if the conduct amounted to a breach of the civil law in that it was either a breach of contract or a tort.

Lord Griffiths, who gave the leading speech with which all their Lordships agreed, had no hesitation in rejecting this argument. He referred to the Milner Holland Report which gave rise to the harassment legislation and the social evils which the predecessor of the 1977 Act (Part III of the 1965 Rent Act) was designed to prevent, in effect applying the so-called 'mischief rule' of construction. He also pointed out that an additional ground for rejecting the argument was that harassment is not confined to the landlord and tenant relationship. 'Residential occupier' is defined in s 1 (1) very widely, and not only landlords but 'any person' may be guilty under the Act of harassment. There need be no contractual relationship of any kind between the victim and the harasser. It was accordingly held that there is no need for an act by the defendant to be an actionable civil wrong in order for it to be an offence under s 1(3).

It may be added that s 1 of the 1977 Act has been extended by s 29 of the Housing Act 1988. Section 29(1) amends s 1(3) by substituting the word 'likely' for 'calculated'. This probably does not represent any change in the law for it had been held in *R v AKM (Property Management) Ltd* [1985] Crim LR 600, that 'calculated' meant 'likely' rather than 'intended', but the matter is now put beyond doubt. Section 29(2) inserts new sub-ss 3A, 3B, and 3C as a result of which it is not necessary in the case of the landlord of a residential occupier or his agent to establish the intent referred to s 1(3): it suffices to establish that he knew, or had reasonable cause to believe, that the conduct was likely to have the effect referred to.

Agricultural holdings

In *Bell v McCubbin* [1990] 1 All ER 54 the Court of Appeal held that a notice served by a landlord on a tenant of an agricultural holding to quit a farmhouse which the tenant was subletting for residential purposes so that the landlord could let it for like purposes (not therefore requiring planning permission) was a notice falling within para (*b*) of Case B of Sch 3, Pt 1 to the Agricultural Holdings Act 1986. Accordingly, the consent of the agricultural land tribunal was not required. It had previously been thought that sub-para (*b*) referred only to the fact the Crown is exempt from the need for planning permission (see *Ministry of Agriculture Fisheries & Food v Jenkins* [1963] 2 All ER 147). There is, however, no need to discuss this decision because it was reversed by the Agricultural Holdings (Amendment) Act 1990, which restores the law to the position it had generally been believed to be in before this decision.

The right to buy

In *Dance v Welwyn Hatfield District Council* [1990] 3 All ER 572 the Court of Appeal had to decide whether the plaintiff was entitled to an injunction to enforce his right to buy under Part V of the Housing Act 1985 – a right introduced by the Housing Act 1980. The appropriate procedures had been gone through, culminating in a letter from the defendants' chief legal officer dated 6 August 1987 informing the plaintiffs' solicitors that he had received instructions to proceed with the sale. The plaintiffs then served due notice claiming the right to defer completion until 5 February 1990 (see ss 142 and 140 (3)(c)) and paid a deposit of £150. The defendants' chief legal officer duly acknowledged the deferment of completion by a letter dated 29 October 1987. That letter also stated that there was no planned compulsory purchase of (inter alia) the plaintiffs' property, though the defendants' housing committee had in fact resolved on 15 August 1987 to demolish all the buildings in the area. The plaintiffs were not informed of the defendants' intentions until they received a letter from them dated 7 July 1988, which also said that their deposit would be refunded as soon as possible.

The response of the plaintiffs by letter dated 2 September 1988 was to seek to complete the purchase on 26 September. The defendants refused to complete and in fact served a notice on the plaintiffs seeking possession of the property on ground 10 in Part II of Sch 2 (intention to demolish or reconstruct the building). The consequence was that the plaintiffs issued proceedings claiming an injunction directing the defendants to convey the property to them, a remedy expressly made available by s 138(3) when all the relevant matters in relation to the exercise of the right to buy have been agreed or determined. The defendants contended that the plaintiffs' right to buy ceased to be exercisable if an order was made under s 121(1) requiring the plaintiffs to give up possession of their dwelling house, and they counter-claimed for posession.

The county court judge, against his own inclination, thought that he was bound to hold that the plaintiffs' claim must fail as a result of the earlier Court of Appeal decision in *Enfield London BC v McKeon* [1986] 2 All ER 730, discussed in All ER Rev 1986, p 223. In that case Slade LJ said that the Act:

> 'treats a tenant as purporting to exercise his right to buy at any time and from time to time when he takes steps towards implementation of that right, up to and including completion of the purchase. If, therefore, any of the circumstances set out in [s 121] subsist at any time between the time when he serves his [s 122(1)] notice and completion, his right to buy ceases to be exercisable.'

The Court of Appeal of course accepted that it was bound by the earlier Court of Appeal decision, but held that there was a crucial difference in the facts which enabled the court to reach a different result. In *Enfield London BC v McKeon* the right to buy procedures had not, when the council issued possession proceeds, reached the stage when, for the purposes of s 138, all the relevant matters in relation to the exercise of the right had been agreed or determined. In the present case, however, the defendants' letter of 6 August 1987 was effectively an acknowledgment that all the relevant matters in relation to the exercise of the right had been agreed or determined, and it recognised that the defendants had already come under a duty to convey the freehold to the plaintiffs if and when they were requested to do so. Instead of making a request at the time, the plaintiffs chose to exercise their right to defer completion, but this deferment was brought to an end by the letter of 2 September 1988 requesting completion on 26 September. The defendant came under a duty to convey the freehold and by s 138(3) that duty was enforce able by an injunction. As from 2 September or, at the latest, 26 September the plaintiffs were the equitable owners of the property and must have 'exercised' their right to buy for the purposes of s 121. At this time there was no order of the court obliging them to give up possession – indeed there had been no formal notice requiring them to give up possession and no proceedings had even been commenced. Accordingly, s 121 did not operate to take away the tenants' right to buy and they were entitled to enforce a conveyance to them by an injunction. The fact that under s 122(3) the tenants could withdraw at any time by written notice served on the landlords was held not to detract from this: if the tenants do withdraw, the right to buy will admittedly cease to be enforceable. But that does not mean that it has not already been exercised.

Medical Law

ANDREW GRUBB, MA
Barrister, Senior Lecturer, School of Law, King's College, London

Six medical law cases were reported in the All England Law Reports for 1990. Four of these concern the scope of a doctor's legal duty to his patient: to withhold or withdraw life-sustaining treatment from a handicapped baby (*Re J (a minor) (wardship: medical treatment)* [1990] 3 All ER 930 and *Re B (a minor) (wardship: medical treatment)* (1981) [1990] 3 All ER 927) (both also discussed in Family Law, pp 146–147 above), to respect the confidences of a patient (*W v Egdell* [1990] 1 All ER 835) and to prevent a mentally ill patient from committing suicide (*Knight v Home Office* [1990] 3 All ER 237). The remaining two cases examined the powers of the General Medical Council to regulate the medical profession (*R v General Medical Council, ex p Colman* [1990] 1 All ER 489; *Taylor v General Medical Council* [1990] 2 All ER 263).

Duty to treat handicapped neonates

In *Re J (a minor) (wardship: medical treatment)* [1990] 3 All ER 930 the Court of Appeal was asked to decide, for the second time in the space of 18 months, whether it would be lawful to allow a severely physically and mentally handicapped baby to die (see also *Re C (a minor) (wardship: medical treatment)* [1989] 2 All ER 782; discussed in All ER Rev 1989, pp 206–10 and in Family Law, p 146 above). For the second time, the court held that it would be lawful. Baby J was born prematurely. He suffered severe and irreparable brain damage at the time of birth due to shortage of oxygen and impaired blood supply. His physical and mental handicaps were horrendous. He was epileptic and he was likely to develop severe spastic quadriplegia. He would probably never sit up or hold his head upright. He was blind and deaf and he would be unable to speak. However, he had a normal capacity to suffer pain which would continue during his shortened life-time into perhaps his late teens. Added to all this, Baby J was, as might be expected, currently very ill. He had required artificial ventilation for sometime but subsequently he managed to breath without this assistance. For other reasons Baby J was already a ward of court and in these circumstances the parents and doctors sought guidance from the court as to Baby J's future care. In particular, they sought permission not to re-ventilate the baby should he require it. An expert witness supported the view that re-ventilation would not be in Baby J's best interests but that he should otherwise receive treatment with antibiotics for intervening infections, along with hydration and nutrition. Scott Baker J made an order in accordance with this expert opinion. The Court of Appeal agreed.

The Official Solicitor, who represented Baby J, argued that parents or the court are *never* justified in withholding (or withdrawing) life-sustaining treatment, irrespective of the child's 'quality of life' unless the child is already dying or terminally ill. This 'absolutist' submission, as Lord Donaldson called it, was rejected by the court (Lord Donaldson at 936–7; Balcombe LJ at 942; Taylor LJ at 944–5). It places great weight upon the philosophical doctrine of the 'sanctity of human life' and it found support in the earlier decision of the Court of Appeal in *McKay v Essex AHA* [1982] 2 All ER 771 (All ER Rev 1982, pp 297–300). In *McKay* the court refused to allow a child born disabled to recover damages for its 'wrongful life' due to a doctor's negligent failure to advise the mother of the child's handicap and thereby depriving her of the opportunity to seek an abortion. In part this was justified because it would devalue human life even if impaired and encourage mothers to abort their handicapped children (see All ER Rev 1982, p 301 for further discussion). In *Re J* the court refused to recognise that any such absolute doctrine had a place in the law. The court might not award damages for being born disabled and not being aborted but that did not mean that there was a duty to keep a handicapped child alive in all circumstances. While accepting the relevance of protecting the life of a child or baby when the court is reaching any decision, the Court of Appeal followed the approach adopted in *Re C (a minor) (wardship: medical treatment)* that the court had to assess the child's quality of life.

Quality of life

In *Re J* the Court of Appeal extended its earlier decision in *Re C*, which concerned a 'dying' neonate for whom medical treatment was futile. In such a case death is inevitable and the court is not balancing life against death other than 'a marginally longer life with pain against a marginally shorter life free from pain and ending in death with dignity' (per Lord Donaldson at 935). In *Re J*, on the other hand, the baby was not dying in any immediate sense and the court was faced with balancing life with treatment against death. Nevertheless, the Court of Appeal accepted that the court's approach should be the same. The court, or the parents if the court is not involved, must balance the benefits of treatment against the burdens of the treatment to the baby because 'to preserve life at all costs, whatever the quality of life to be preserved, and however distressing to the ward . . . may not be in the interests of the ward' (per Balcombe LJ at 942). In determining the baby's quality of life, the Court of Appeal was influenced by the fact that the baby's existence would be painful and the benefits of the treatment continuing this painful existence would be minimal. Hence, the judge had been correct to approve the course of non-treatment recommended to the court by the expert. On the facts the burdens of treatment outweighed the benefits. In the words of Taylor LJ, 'the quality of life the child would endure if given the treatment . . . would be intolerable to that child' (at 945).

The court distinguished the earlier case of *Re B (a minor) (wardship: medical treatment)* (1981) [1990] 3 All ER 927 where the court had authorised a surgical procedure upon a newborn baby with Down's Syndrome. In that case, the court had held that the baby's quality of life after the operation to remove an intestinal blockage was not such that non-treatment was in its 'best interests'. In *Re B* the child had a prospect of a life expectancy of between 20 and 30 years. The precise extent of its physical and mental disabilities would be unclear for some time. However, it was not in any pain and its life could not, on the evidence before the court, be described as 'intolerable'. Lord Donaldson pointed out that the only reason why a dispute had arisen in that case was because both the doctors and the judge at first instance had been influenced by the parents' objection to the treatment. Medically, all the evidence was in favour of the operation, and the Court of Appeal had rightly treated the parents' wishes as 'irrelevant, since the duty of decision had passed from them to the court' (at 937). For Lord Donaldson, in *Re B* there was no burden to balance against the benefit of the life-saving treatment.

Limitations

The decision in *Re J* should not be seen as a sanction for widespread non-treatment of handicapped neonates; this was not the court's intention. A number of comments by the judges illustrate the cautious approach which the law will take to these cases. First, all the judges emphasised the strong legal policy in preserving life. Taylor LJ spoke of 'a strong presumption in favour of taking all steps capable of preserving [human life], save in exceptional circumstances' (at 943) and Balcombe LJ spoke of 'a strong predilection in favour of the preservation of life' (at 942). Of course, this does not mean that *Re J* was a unique case. Clearly, it is not. There will be many such cases in the future. What the court is emphasising is that decisions to withhold life-saving treatment should only be made in clear cases. Taylor LJ reaffirmed this when he stated that the court would require a 'high degree of proof' that the child's quality of life justified non-treatment (at 945).

Secondly, *Re J*, like *Re B* before it, concerned withholding or withdrawing life-sustaining treatment so that the child died from the underlying medical condition. In *Re J* Taylor LJ emphasised that the court (and a fortiori, parents) could never authorise anything aimed at terminating life or accelerating death (at 943). Lord Donaldson MR (at 938) also distinguished non-treatment cases from 'active killing':

> 'What doctors and the court have to decide is whether, in the best interests of the child patient, a particular decision as to medical treatment should be taken which *as a side effect* will render death more or less likely. This is not a matter of semantics. It is fundamental. At the other end of the age spectrum, the use of drugs to reduce pain will often be fully justified, notwithstanding that this will hasten the moment of death. What can never be justified is the use of drugs or surgical procedures with the primary purpose of doing so.'

Here, Lord Donaldson draws the important distinction between treatment decisions and decisions to terminate life. In doing so he touches on an old chestnut for the medical lawyer – the doctor who administers drugs to relieve pain knowing that this will also shorten the patient's life. The legality of this has been questioned and it is notoriously difficult to justify its legality (see *R v Bodkin Adams* [1957] Crim LR 365, per Devlin J and the discussion in Kennedy and Grubb, *Medical Law: Text and Materials* (1989) at pp 936–939). Could this be a recognition of the doctrine of 'double effect'? If it is, the legality of the doctor's action rests upon his lack of an intent to kill but this cannot stand in the light of the courts' repeated assertion that a defendant may intend that which it is not his purpose to achieve when he knows for certain it will occur: *R v Moloney* [1985] 1 All ER 1025 (All ER Rev 1985, pp 108–111) and *R v Nedrick* [1986] 3 All ER 1 (All ER Rev 1986, p 107).

Thirdly, the court in *Re J* followed the opinion of the expert put before the court that non-treatment was in the 'best interests' of the baby. However, unlike the earlier case of *Re C*, the court was prepared to examine the reasoning of the expert and did not simply adopt it as they seemed to do in *Re C* (see All ER Rev 1989, p 207). Lord Donaldson noted that the trial judge had not 'abdicated his responsibility' because he had 'reviewed and considered the basis of the doctors' views and recommendations in the greatest detail and with the greatest care' (at 939).

Best interests and substituted judgment

In reaching their decision in *Re J*, two approaches can be seen in the judgments of the Court of Appeal. All three judges considered the 'quality of life' approach advocated by them as a 'fleshing out' of the well-known 'best interests' test which parents and courts must be guided by in making decisions about their children or wards. Hence, Lord Donaldson stated that 'there is a balancing exercise to be performed in assessing the course to be adopted in the best interests of the child' (at 938). Balcombe LJ stated that 'preserving life at all cost . . . may not be in the interests of the child' (at 942). Finally, Taylor LJ spoke of a 'scale of disability and suffering' when the court 'ought to hold that the best interests of the child do not require further endurance to be imposed by positive treatment to prolong its life' (at 945). All this reflects traditional family law (see Lowe and White, *Wards of Court* (2nd edn, 1986) ch 7). The test is objective, requiring the court to adopt the 'standpoint of the reasonable and responsible parent' (per Balcombe LJ at 942).

In *Re J*, however, Lord Donaldson (at 936) and Taylor LJ (at 945) introduced a new test previously unknown in modern English case law; the test of 'substituted judgment'. The essence of this test is that 'the court must decide what its ward would choose, if he were in a position to make a sound judgment' (*Re Weberlist* (1974) 360 NYS 2d 783 at 787 per Ashe J). This must not be confused with a situation which some American cases wrongly describe as an application of 'substituted judgment' where there is 'clear and convincing' evidence of the patient's pre-incompetence wishes (see, for example, *Re Conroy* (1985) 486 A 2d 1209 (NJ Sup Ct) and *Re Westchester County Medical Center* (1988) 531 NE 2d 607 (NY CA)). Substituted judgment requires the decision maker to decide what the incompetent patient would have wanted. The patient has never made a decision; it is the proxy who is doing that. In the other situation, on the other hand, the proxy decision maker knows what the patient actually *did* want; the decision was made by the patient and the proxy is seeking to give effect to it. Properly understood, this is not 'substituted judgment' at all but an example of an advance directive about medical treatment (see, for example, *Malette v Shulman* (1990) 67 DLR 4th) 321 (Ont CA)).

Under the 'substituted judgment' test the court (and presumably the parents in an appropriate case) must strive to make the decision that the child would make if it was able to decide for itself. Applying a 'substituted judgment' test requires the court (or parents) to make a decision from the view point of the child. In a passage from the British Columbia case of *Re S D*

[1983] 3 WWR 618, (1983) 145 DLR (3d) 610, McKenzie J, in a passage approved in Re J, explained the application of the substituted judgment test:

'It is not appropriate for an external decision maker to apply his standards of what constitutes a liveable life . . . The decision can only be made in the context of the disabled person viewing the worthwhileness or otherwise of his life in its own context as a disabled person – and in that context he would not compare his life with that of a person enjoying normal advantages. He would know nothing of a normal person's life having never experienced it.'

In principle, the Court of Appeal's acceptance of the 'substituted judgment' test for proxy or surrogate decision making is a welcome one. The test has a historical basis in English law in cases concerned with the disposition of the estates of incompetent adults (see Re Hinde, ex p Whitbread (a lunatic) (1816) 35 ER 878, 2 Mer 99). The test has been widely adopted in American cases concerned with the treatment of incompetent patients (see Robertson, 'Organ Donation by Incompetents and the Substituted Judgment Doctrine' (1976) 76 Col LR 48). The attraction of the test is that it seeks, as best as can be, to reach the decision that the patient would make. It is not an objective test and does not seek to impose the 'best' decision upon the incompetent patient. It is the next best thing to patients making the decision themselves. It allows the court to have regard to the patient's idiosyncrasies, particular values, preferences and dislikes. It recognises that a patient might not wish treatment which, objectively, would be viewed as in his 'best interests' (see, for example, Re Lucille Boyd (1979) 403 A 2d 744 (DC Cir) – no blood transfusion in view of patient's religious beliefs).

However, the specific application of this test to a handicapped neonate is problematic. It is difficult, if not impossible, to apply the test when an adult patient has never had the competence to express any wishes or values. 'What the incompetent would do if she or he could make the choice is simply a matter of speculation' and has been castigated by, for example, the Canadian Supreme Court as 'sophistry' (Re Eve (1981) 115 DLR (3d) 283 per La Forest J). Consequently, some American courts have rejected its application in such cases and have favoured the objective 'best interests' test because of the meaningless application of a test requiring the proxy to decide what the incompetent would have wanted had he been able to decide (for example, Re John Storar (1981) 420 NE 2d 64 (NY CA). Contrast Superintendent of Belchertown v Saikewicz (1976) 370 NE 417 (Ma SJC)). Equally, the test should not be applied to a handicapped neonate who will never have been competent nor ever have interacted with the world to make the 'substituted judgment' test meaningful when applied to him. When applied in such a case the test becomes a 'best interests' test: what would the child have decided? He would have decided to act in his 'best interests'. What other decision i possible given that the values, wishes and preferences of the child are totally unknown? In effect, both Lord Donaldson and Taylor LJ went through this process in Re J because, in the end, both judges sought to determine where the child's 'best interests' lay, notwithstanding their adoption of the 'substituted judgment' test. The test should be restricted to cases where the patient has achieved a degree of competence or interaction with the world such that their personal equation can be taken into account. Even an older child's limited competence might justify a court having regard to its view o the world providing care is taken not, inadvertently, to treat that child as having the competence to make decisions if that is not the case – 'substituted judgment' must never be confused with an 'advance directive'.

There are two specific dangers of using the 'substituted judgment' test in the case of neonates or young children. First, when parents are making a decision for their child, their judgment of what their child would have wanted may easily be coloured by their own values (perhaps religious) and their preferences. It is all to easy to accept the parents' religious views and then attribute them to the child because the child would (at least until it reached its teens) have followed its parents' religious upbringing. The 'substituted judgment' test would then give such a decision the mark of legitimacy. Under the 'best interests' test the parents of a child could not refuse a blood transfusion solely on the ground of their religious views, for example, as Jehovah Witnesses. Would such a decision be legitimated by using the 'substituted judgment' test on the basis that the child would also have followed their faith? On the face of it, their decision would be lawful but an English court would not countenance such a conclusion.

Secondly, could the 'substituted judgment' test justify non-therapeutic procedures such as organ donation or research involving minimal risk to the child? The legality of parental consent to such procedures has always been questionable because they cannot be said to be 'in the best interests' of the child (see Dworkin, 'Law and Medical Experimentation' (1987) 13 Monash Univ LR 189). However, under a 'substituted judgment' test this difficulty disappears and the question becomes whether the child would consent if it were able to. Certainly, it is arguable that a child might consent to the donation of an organ, such as a kidney, to a very sick brother or sister if that were necessary to save their life. Similarly, a child might consent to some forms of non-therapeutic research out of a sense of altruism, as do some adults. What was legally problematical becomes less so under a 'substituted judgment' test (see, for example, *Strunk v Strunk* (1969) 445 SW 2d 145 (Ky CA) – sibling kidney donation authorised under 'substituted judgment' test). It is far from clear that either of these results is desirable and to permit them by sleight of hand via the 'substituted judgment' test would not be acceptable.

Miscellaneous points

Three final points arise from *Re J*. First, the court perceived the balance of benefits and burdens inherent in an assessment of an incompetent's quality of life in terms of their exposure to pain and suffering. Baby J's life was intolerable in a way that Baby B's was not because he would suffer pain during his life. This is too narrow a view of the 'quality of life' approach. It would constrain a court to authorise treatment in every case where a child (or an adult) was in an irreversible coma and could feel no pain. A patient's quality of life should be seen not only in terms of the burdens of pain caused by and after the treatment but also in terms of the indignity and futility of the treatment (see the strong concurring opinion of Handler J in *Re Conroy*). Unless the court is prepared to do this, the 'cabbage' cases, as the court so inelegantly called them, will cause problems of analysis for a future court. In American jurisdictions such as New Jersey which adopt a 'quality of life' test (at least in part) and limit the permissible burdens which can be considered to pain (see *Re Conroy*) the courts have had to abandon the 'quality of life' approach for adult patients in a Persistent Vegetative State (PVS), who can suffer no pain, in order to authorise the withdrawal of life-sustaining treatment which is futile: (*Re Peters* (1987) 529 A 2d 419 (NJ Sup Ct) – look for 'clear and convincing' evidence of patient's wishes; if not, *Re Jobes* (1987) 529 A 2d 434 (NJ Sup Ct) – act upon the basis of the relatives decision of what the patient would have wanted).

Secondly, the approach of the court in *Re J* should be a guide to courts in the future which are faced with similar situations in relation to incompetent adults. Remarkably, such a case has never been litigated in England, although they are legion in America. A combination of 'advance directives', the 'substituted judgment' test and a 'quality of life' analysis should guide a court in an adult 'right to die' case (see Kennedy and Grubb, op cit, ch 14) even after the emphatic approval in *F v West Berkshire HA* [1989] 2 All ER 545 of the 'best interests' test (discussed at length in All ER Rev 1989, pp 200–206).

Thirdly, the court in *Re J* approached its role in the traditional way of substituting its consent for that of the parents. The court (as would the parents) authorised a medical procedure but could not require it. Doctors cannot be required by parents or the court to carry out a medical procedure (see Lord Donaldson MR at 934). This approach reflects the view that the court in exercising its wardship jurisdiction 'steps into the shoes' of the parents and makes their decision for them. Suppose, therefore, that the doctors in *Re B* had refused to carry out the surgical procedure to correct the baby's intestinal blockage; the court could not have required them to act. And yet, surely, their decision would be unlawful since it would not have been in the 'best interests' of Baby B? Of course, there are difficulties in ordering doctors to act. How can the court supervise its order? The problem is similar to the court's reluctance to order specific performance of a contract for personal services. But this difficulty is usually seen as a factual one. If an order can practically be made and is 'workable' then the court may order specific performance (*Hill v C A Parsons & Co Ltd* [1971] 3 All ER 1345 and most recently, *Robb v Hammersmith & Fulham LBC* [1991] IRLR 72). Surely, the court in exercising its wardship power should similarly be able to order treatment in the ward's 'best interest'? What responsible doctor would ignore such a directive from the court? Such an order could be justified under the court's 'protective' jurisdiction as opposed to its 'custodial' or 'parental' jurisdiction (see, for example, *S v McC (formerly S); W v Official Solicitor* [1970] 3 All ER 107, [1972] AC 24; discussed in Lowe and White, op cit, at pp 157–160).

Duty of confidentiality

In last year's Review, the case of *W v Egdell* [1989] 1 All ER 1089 was discussed at pp 210–11. Subsequently, the Court of Appeal dismissed W's appeal ([1990] 1 All ER 835) and upheld Scott J's view that there had not been a breach of confidence.

W was convicted of the manslaughter on the grounds of diminished responsibility of five people he shot and he was detained at Broadmoor suffering from paranoid schizophrenia. W's solicitor asked Dr Egdell, a consultant psychiatrist, to produce a report on his mental condition with a view to putting it before a Mental Health Review Tribunal, who could order his transfer to a regional secure unit which could, in the future, lead to his release into the community. The report was not favourable, stating that W was dangerous and recommending that he should not be transferred. Dr Egdell drew attention to W's fascination, as a child, with fireworks and, as an adult, with explosives which Dr Egdell described as 'a serious abnormal interest in the making of home made bombs'. As a result of its terms, the report was never used by W's lawyers. Some time later, the Home Secretary referred W's case to a Mental Health Review Tribunal. Dr Egdell discovered that his report was not available and so he sent a copy to the medical director of the hospital where W was detained, who forwarded it to the Home Secretary who, in turn, sent it on to the Mental Health Review Tribunal.

The Court of Appeal unanimously held that Dr Egdell was justified in disclosing his report to the authorities. The court held that the proper approach was to balance the public interest in confidentiality against the public interest in disclosure. This reflects the approach of Lord Goff in *A-G v Guardian Newspapers Ltd (No 2)* [1988] 3 All ER 545 (discussed in All ER Rev 1988, p 55) where he said (at 659):

'. . . although . . . there is a public interest that confidences should be preserved and protected by the law, nevertheless that public interest may be outweighed by some other countervailing public interest which favours disclosure.'

In *W v Egdell* the court held that the need of the authorities to know of W's dangerousness outweighed the public interest in maintaining the confidentiality of medical information. Bingham LJ (at 852–3) put it as follows:

'Where a man has committed multiple killings under the disability of serious mental illness, decisions which may lead directly or indirectly to his release from hospital should not be made unless a responsible authority is properly able to make an informed judgment that the risk of repetition is so small as to be acceptable. A consultant psychiatrist who becomes aware, even in the course of a confidential relationship, of information which leads him, *in exercise of what the court considers a sound professional judgment*, to fear that such decisions may be made on the basis of inadequate information and *with a real risk of consequent danger to the public* is entitled to take *such steps as are reasonable in all the circumstances to communicate the grounds of his concern to the responsible authorities.*' (emphasis added)

A number of points need to be made, since there are some differences of emphasis between the Court of Appeal and the trial judge.

First, the court confirmed that there is a public interest in maintaining the confidentiality of medical information protected by the law. The court rejected Scott J's view that only the patient's private interest was at stake. Although it was never expressed in so many words, it is clear from the approach of the Court of Appeal that the burden of justifying disclosure will fall upon he who claims this public interest is outweighed by some competing public interest. This is important, not least for the symbolism which it represents about the significance of respecting a patient's confidences.

Secondly, the Court of Appeal approached the case as permitting Dr Egdell to inform the authorities. In other words, the law conferred on him a discretion to disclose the confidential information. The court did not decide

that Dr Egdell had a duty to tell the authorities. There was some language to
this effect in Scott J's judgment. Consequently, the court's analysis gives no
support to a possible *Tarasoff*-type action by the relatives of a victim of a
patient who is killed following the patient's release because the defendant
psychiatrist, in breach of duty, had not warned the authorities (see *Tarasoff v
Regents of University of California* (1976) 131 Cal Rptr 14 (Cal S Ct).

Thirdly, the court recognised that the information was confidential but
that the danger to others set up a countervailing public interest. Like the trial
judge, the Court of Appeal found assistance in para 81(g) of the GMC's
guidance to doctors: *Professional Conduct and Discipline: Fitness to Practise*
(April 1987). This allows for disclosure in exceptional circumstances relating
to the investigation by the police of a grave or very serious crime. Strictly, it
is difficult to see why *W*'s case fell within para 81(g). But that is ultimately
unimportant, since the GMC guidelines are not law, nor do they purport to
lay down rigid and exclusive categories where disclosure of confidential
information may be made. Underlying para 81(g) is the element of danger to
the public.

However, it will not be every case of danger to others which will justify
disclosure. The danger must be 'real' (per Bingham LJ at 853) or there must
be a 'grave concern for the safety of the public' (per Stephen Brown P at 846).
A doctor may not act on the basis of a fanciful notion of danger to others
because his belief must be reasonably based. Also, it must always be
remembered that the danger in *W v Egdell* was of at least severe injury and,
perhaps, death to others. Further, the disclosure must be only as extensive as
is necessary reasonably to avoid the potential harm. Disclosure to the
appropriate authorities or, perhaps, the potential victim may be lawful but
any wider disclosure will not be. Finally, it may be that in requiring that the
disclosure be reasonably necessary, it will not be lawful to disclose
information which is available elsewhere or which is not new information
which adds to that currently available. Stephen Brown P spoke of Dr Egdell
possessing 'vital information' because only he knew of W's childhood
obsession with fireworks and things which go bang.

Duty of care to mentally ill patients

In *Knight v Home Office* [1990] 3 All ER 237 a prisoner committed suicide
whilst detained in the hospital wing of Brixton Prison. His estate brought a
negligence action against the Home Office. First, it was alleged that the
Home Office was negligent in not providing sufficient staff to supervise the
prisoner ('primary liability'). Second, it was alleged that the doctors employed
in the prison had negligently recommended a regime whereby the prisoner
was observed every 15 minutes and not a regime whereby he would be under
constant supervision ('vicarious liability').

Primary liability

Pill J accepted that a hospital authority (and hence the Home Office in *Knight*)
had a primary duty to exercise reasonable care in providing sufficient staff of
skill and experience to perform the hospital's functions (following *Wilsher v*

Essex AHA [1986] 3 All ER 801 per Browne-Wilkinson VC at 833–4 and Glidewell LJ at 831, see All ER Rev 1986, pp 314, 318). But, he rejected the claim because there had not been a breach of this primary duty by the Home Office in failing to provide (as the plaintiff claimed should have been) staff to meet the higher staff/patient ratio found in outside psychiatric hospitals. Pill J distinguished between the functions of psychiatric hospitals and prison hospitals. The former exist solely to perform the specialist function of treating mental illness. Prisons, on the other hand, function primarily to detain those sentenced by the courts to terms of imprisonment.

Whilst the latter do have a duty to provide medical facilities for their inmates, to treat their physical and mental conditions, the judge was clearly of the view that it would be unrealistic to expect the more exacting duty imposed upon other institutions. Adapting the words of Mustill LJ in *Wilsher v Essex AHA* (at 813), he said '[t]he duty is tailored to the act and function to be performed' (at 243).

At the core of the Home Office's argument in *Knight*, of course, was the issue of limited available resources. While an outside psychiatric institution may have the resources to provide the higher ratio of staff to patients, the prison service does not. Can such an argument ever operate as a defence to an allegation of negligence? In other words, will a failure to provide that which *objectively* is necessary be justified if there is insufficient resources to provide it? The standard of care imposed by the law in negligence actions is objective applying the standards of the reasonable man. By tradition, the reasonable man test does not take account of the defendant's particular 'personal equation'. The law does not take account of the 'idiosyncrasies' of the defendant (*Glasgow Corporation v Muir* [1943] AC 448 at 457 per Lord MacMillan). Logically, this approach ought to lead the court to disregard the personal financial circumstances of the defendant. However, there are a few instances where the courts have taken account of the defendant's financial position, for example, in determining an occupier's liability to trespassers on his land (*British Railways Board v Herrington* [1972] AC 877) and an occupier's liability to his neighbours for natural hazards on his land (*Goldman v Hargrave* [1967] 1 AC 645 and *Leakey v National Trust* [1980] 1 All ER 17, [1980] QB 485). These are exceptional and, in the latter instance, even aberrational. No doubt an employer who failed to take reasonable precautions (ie objectively viewed) to protect his work force would not excuse himself by pleading financial constraints. A publicly funded institution ought to be in precisely the same position.

This issue has received scant attention in the courts. In *Knight* Pill J stated that:

> '[i]t is not a complete defence for a government department any more than it would be for a private individual or organisation to say that no funds are available for additional safety measures.' (at 243)

Consequently, Pill J observed that a complete failure to provide medical facilities could not be justified on financial grounds any more than could the action of a government department which used unsafe vehicles as a result of inadequate maintenance due to a shortage of cash. Nevertheless, Pill J recognised that the court could not ignore the fact that 'resources available for the public service are limited' (at 243). The danger in this approach is that the courts will be drawn into assessing the proper allocation of scarce resources. In *Wilsher*, Browne-Wilkinson V-C acknowledged the potential danger of this and stated that '[t]hese are questions for Parliament, not for the courts' (at 834). A number of judicial review cases reflect the judges' reluctance to be drawn into resource allocation questions within the National Health Service (*R v Secretary of State for Social Services, ex p Hincks* (unreported, 1980); *Re Walker's Application* (1987) *Times*, 28 November; *R v Central Birmingham HA, ex p Collier* (unreported, 1988) reproduced in Kennedy and Grubb, *Medical Law: Text and Materials* (1989) at pp 387–390). It seems likely, therefore, that the courts will listen to the argument 'we could not afford to do better' notwithstanding the words of Mustill LJ in *Bull v Devon AHA* (unreported, 1989) that the court should not abdicate its duty to impose societal standards even on government funded bodies. Only if there is a failure to provide any service will the argument not be heeded; this may have been what Pill J had in mind in *Knight*. Frankly, however, Mustill LJ's view in *Bull* is more in line with the traditional approach in the law of negligence. The best way for the court not to become embroiled in resource allocation is to ignore any governmental plea of insufficiency of funds.

Vicarious liability

The second claim in *Knight* was also dismissed by the judge. He held that the doctors were not in breach of their duty by not keeping the prisoner under constant watch which would have prevented his suicide. The judge held that the doctors' duty was, applying *Bolam v Friern Hospital Management Committee* [1957] 2 All ER 118 at 121, to 'exercise the ordinary skill of an ordinary competent man exercising that particular art'. An expert gave evidence that in the light of the prisoner's previous behaviour he should have been placed under constant watch. There was a 'fairly high' risk that the prisoner would attempt suicide. Nevertheless, Pill J refused to classify the doctor's decision as negligent even though, as he stated, the doctors' reasons for their decision had to be 'examined by the court to see if they stand up to analysis' (*Hucks v Coles* (1968) 112 SJ 483). There were, on the facts, good reasons for the regime actually adopted, not least the dehumanising effect of constant surveillance and also the danger of suicide was, to an extent, coloured by the benefit of hindsight.

The judge's citation of *Hucks v Coles* is interesting because that case is rarely referred to by the courts. Its significance is that the Court of Appeal held that the court could find a doctor negligent even if he acted in accordance with the practice of the medical profession. This is out of line with the so called *Bolam* test which states that a doctor cannot be negligent if he has complied with *the* or *a* practice accepted by a competent body of medical opinion. The House of Lords has accepted this in cases of alleged negligent diagnosis or treatment (*Maynard v West Midland RHA* [1985] 1 All ER 635, and *Sidaway v Governors of Bethlem Royal Hospital* [1985] 1 All ER 643, see All ER Rev 1985, pp 300–301). Whether *Hucks* challenges the orthodoxy or is a unique case turning on its own facts is contentious (see the discussion in Kennedy and Grubb, op cit at 408–20: it arguably turns on the absence of, or a lacuna in, a professional practice). Pill J's citation is, therefore, even more surprising unless *Knight* is seen as a case where there was no evidence of 'professional practice' and so the doctors' actions were not being judged against the background which underpins the *Bolam* test.

Knight also raised the important question of whether an action in negligence can be brought by a deceased's estate for his suicide. Can a hospital owe a duty of care to prevent another killing himself? Is it important that the deceased was not of sound mind at the time? Could the defences of *volenti non fit injuria* and illegality be successfully raised by the hospital? Because Pill J decided that there was no breach of duty, he did not consider these questions in *Knight* (but see the discussion of *Kirkham v Chief Constable of Greater Manchester* [1990] 3 All ER 246 in Tort, pp 314–315 below).

The General Medical Council

In *R v General Medical Council, ex p Coleman* [1990] 1 All ER 489, the Court of Appeal refused Dr Colman's application for judicial review of a decision of the President of the GMC and GMC policy contained in the 'Blue Book' (*Professional Conduct and Discipline: Fitness to Practise*, April 1987) which prevented medical practitioners advertising in newspapers (for a discussion of the history of GMC regulation of advertising see, Irvine (1991) 17 *Journal of Medical Ethics* 35). Dr Coleman practised holistic medicine outside the NHS and considered it necessary to advertise in order for the public to be aware of his services. His proposed factual advertisement was to state his name, his qualifications, the name of his practice 'Holistic Counselling and Education Centre', his address and telephone number and inviting enquiries for a practice information leaflet. In his application for judicial review he claimed that the GMC's advice and the President's action was ultra vires the powers in s 35 of the Medical Act 1983 'to provide, in such manner as the [GMC] think fit, advice for members of the medical profession on standards of professional conduct or on medical ethics'. Although Dr Coleman lost his case, the GMC subsequently revised its guidance so as to allow limited factual advertising of medical services in newspapers (see 'Blue Book' (1990)). Dr Coleman's case may have contributed to this but, in truth, the real reason for change was the condemnation by the Monopolies and Mergers Commission in March 1989 (Cmnd 582) of the GMC guidelines as operating 'against the public interest' (para 1.7).

Coleman reminds us, as the *Gee* case (*Gee v General Medical Council* [1987] 2 All ER 193) three years ago drew to our attention for the first time, that the functions of the General Medical Council operate in the field of public law and hence remain subject to control through an application for judicial review (discussed in All ER Rev 1987 at p 187). It remains the case, however, that the courts will sparingly interfere with the action of the GMC for two reasons: first, its recognised status and that of its membership and secondly, because it is often dealing with matters of professional judgment and competence which the courts are unlikely to want to 'second-guess' through the procedure for judicial review.

In *Taylor v General Medical Council* [1990] 2 All ER 263 the Privy Council considered the scope of the powers of the Professional Conduct Committee of the GMC to impose sanctions on a doctor found guilty of 'serious professional misconduct' under s 36 of the Medical Act 1983. The appellant was found guilty of 'serious professional misconduct' arising from abuses in prescribing methadone hydrochloride to patients. The PCC suspended his registration for 12 months and indicated that they would review the situation during that time. This they subsequently did, and extended the period for a further 12 months on the same terms. When they imposed a third and final 12 months' suspension on the appellant, he appealed. The Privy Council allowed his appeal because the PCC had extended his suspension for an improper reason. The Privy Council held that a suspension could not be extended simply because the PCC though the original punishment was inadequate. A suspension could only be reviewed and renewed or the punishment changed to erasure if *subsequent events* justified it. This would arise, for example, if further misconduct by the medical practitioner reflecting on his fitness to practise justified the new punishment. In addition, it might be that the PCC had thought that the situation justifying the finding of 'serious professional misconduct' might improve such that, for example, erasure would not be necessary and so they suspend judgment. Subsequently, however, this is not proven to be the case and when the PCC review the case they may impose the more severe penalty they would have otherwise imposed at the initial hearing.

Practice and Procedure

ADRIAN A S ZUCKERMAN, LLM, MA
Fellow of University College, Oxford

Mareva injunctions

In a rare display of restraint in this field the Court of Appeal has decided that, normally, a worldwide Mareva injunction will not be granted in support of a foreign judgment or an arbitration award that is sought to be enforced in this country. The reason given for this in *Rosseel NV v Oriental Commercial and Shipping (UK) Ltd* [1990] 3 All ER 545, was that if a number of subsidiary jurisdictions made 'criss-cross' extraterritorial orders, a great deal of confusion could arise. There is, however, a more fundamental reason for exercising restraint in this respect. At the basis of this procedure lies the idea that Mareva orders are intended to prevent the thwarting of the jurisdiction of our courts by dissipation of assets. Where an English court does not have jurisdiction over the cause, the risk of defeating the jurisdiction does not arise. Of course, an English court is bound by international conventions to enforce foreign judgments against assets located in this country, but its jurisdiction should rarely be exercised to prevent the thwarting of a foreign judgment outside England. It did not escape the Court of Appeal's notice that only last year a worldwide injunction was granted in support of a claim that was proceeding in France. However, *Republic of Haiti v Duvalier* [1989] 1 All ER 456, was distinguished principally on the ground that there the assets had been scattered in other countries by an English solicitor and it was convenient to trace them through him (see All ER Rev 1989, pp 213–215).

Privilege against self-incrimination

Mareva injunctions are particularly helpful in fraud cases, but their efficacy can be impaired the privilege against self-incrimination.

The plaintiffs in *Sociedade Nacional de Combustiveis de Angola v Lundqvist*, [1990] 3 All ER 283, (*Sonagol*), brought an action against the defendant and his company for a large sum of money allegedly converted by the defendant. The plaintiffs obtained a Mareva injunction against the defendants and an order for the disclosure of the location of the defendant's assets and their value. The defendant asked to be excused from answering questions regarding his assets on the ground that his answers could incriminate him.

According to the Civil Evidence Act 1968, s 14(1), a person has a right 'to refuse to answer any question or produce any document or thing if to do so would tend to expose that person to proceedings for an offence' under the law of the United Kingdom. The Court of Appeal accepted that there were reasonable grounds for expecting a prosecution here. But turning away the plaintiffs empty handed because their relief inevitably gave rise to a claim of privilege was clearly unsatisfactory and different avenues of surmounting this obstacle were therefore sought.

Section 31 of the Theft Act 1968 removes the privilege in proceedings for the recovery of property or for an account of dealings with any property. This is subject to a crucial proviso: that answers may not be used 'in proceedings for an offence under this Act'. It was found, however, that the plaintiffs could not avail themselves of this section because the offence with which the defendant was in danger of being charged was conspiracy and this offence was not an 'offence under this [the Theft] Act'. Consequently, were the defendant to give incriminating answers, he would not have the protection of the proviso and the Court of Appeal concluded that he was entitled to assert the privilege. This result exposes a paradox: if the defendant commits theft on his own, he is liable to discovery under s 31 of the Theft Act 1968, but if he perpetrates the theft in concert with others, he is not.

A further way of enforcing disclosure was probed in relation to the defendant's company, which had also been ordered to disclose the defendant's assets. The plaintiffs argued that as a person may not claim privilege on behalf of another, the defendant could not claim privilege on behalf of his company. The argument was rejected and the defendant was allowed the privilege because it was his own compliance, as an officer of the company, with the order and his own answers that tended to incriminate him. The position might have been different, it was felt, had the order to the company been capable of being complied with by another officer. This reasoning is not entirely convincing. In *Garvin v Domus Publishing Ltd* [1989] 2 All ER 344 a refusal by a defendant to disclose a document belonging to a company of which he was an employee, on the grounds that it may lay him open to a charge of forgery, was rejected because one could not claim privilege in a document belonging to another (see All ER Rev 1989, p 220). Furthermore, according to *Tate Access Floors Inc v Boswell* [1990] 3 All ER 303, a person cannot claim privilege on behalf of a company of which he is the sole shareholder on the grounds that it is his alter ego. As Sir Nicolas Browne-Wilkinson V-C explained in last mentioned case:

> 'controlling shareholders cannot, for all the purposes beneficial to them, insist on the separate identity of such corporations but then be heard to say the contrary when discovery is sought against such corporations.' (at 315)

Should we not similarly say that a person who is the sole officer of a company cannot refuse to answer as officer because his answers may incriminate him in his personal capacity?

The plaintiffs in the *Sonagol* case did, however, get some help. Although it was felt that the defendant would risk self-incrimination if he were made to divulge the value of his assets, because a connection could then be made between these and the fraudulent transactions, no such connection could be made if he were only asked to reveal the location of the assets. An order to disclose the location was accordingly made so as to enable the plaintiffs to take steps to safeguard them from dissipation.

It might not always be so easy to circumvent the privilege. In order to support a claim for privilege it is sufficient to show that answers might set in motion a train of inquiry which might lead to incriminating evidence. The nexus between the apprehended prosecution and the answer sought can therefore be indirect and inevitably speculative. It would therefore be relatively easy for a defendant in a fraud case to show that disclosure of the location of his assets might stimulate an inquiry that could help a prosecution against him. In this regard it is difficult to accept Staughton LJ's view that immunity may not be claimed in order to excuse oneself from disclosing the identity of persons who could give evidence against one. If the test is not whether the information disclosed will amount to evidence of crime but whether it could lead to such evidence, immunity must obtain in relation to disclosure of the identity of witnesses to crime.

The effects of the privilege on the ability to seek a remedy for fraud received further illustration in *Tate Access Floors Inc v Boswell*. It was decided that the privilege applies to search and seizure in accordance with an Anton Piller order. Since an Anton Piller order is granted ex parte, a plaintiff seeking such an order must draw the judge's attention to the possibility of the privilege and the order should not be so framed as to infringe it.

These cases draw attention to the fact that the clearer the fraud alleged, the more likely the defendant is to inhibit the plaintiff in seeking redress. While a defendant may be ordered to provide information about assets innocently obtained, he seems to be largely immune from having to make full disclosure about assets that have been gained by criminal conduct. This immunity, it should be noted, is not confined to Mareva proceedings. It is also available in pre-trial discovery and at the trial itself. It is, however, doubtful whether a privilege will be available in proceeding for execution of a judgment given against a defendant for the return of fraudulent gains, where it might be argued that the defendant's answers will not expose him to a fresh danger of prosecution over and above the findings in the judgment.

The unsatisfactory nature of the operation of the privilege was not lost on the Vice Chancellor, who sat in both the 1990 cases and expressed the hope that a provision similar to that of s 31 of the Theft Act 1968 and s 72 of the Supreme Court Act 1981 will now be enacted. However, the privilege against self-incrimination requires a more radical review in so far as it concerns its assertion by persons other than suspects in the police station or accused in criminal trials. In support of the present law it is said that in the absence of a privilege witnesses will be deterred from testifying. The main fear of defendants, such as those concerned in the cases discussed above, arises not so much from the prospect of a criminal prosecution as from the likelihood that their assets will be frozen and that a judgment given against them will be satisfied from these assets. If the rules of discovery give no immunity from disclosing information which is immediately and tangibly harmful to one's present civil case, there is little to be said for granting immunity, because disclosure in today's civil case may help a criminal prosecution at an unknown future date. A similar objection may be directed at the privilege of a witness who is not a party to the civil litigation. A witness who has been involved in crime will wish to avoid testifying altogether rather than have to assert the privilege against self-incrimination, because such assertion draws attention to the fact that he has something to conceal. This must surely be as potent a deterrent to coming forward as the prospect that one's answers may subsequently be used in furtherance of a prosecution. It is therefore difficult to believe that the privilege provides a valuable incentive to volunteer information in a court of law.

Use of information obtained in Mareva and Anton Piller proceedings

The general rule is that information obtained in Mareva, Anton Piller or discovery proceedings may not be used otherwise than for the purpose of the proceedings in which the information was obtained. There has been some uncertainty as to the extent to which information obtained in Mareva proceedings may be used to pursue the defendant's assets abroad, in the absence of special permission by the court (All ER Rev 1989, p 215). It now appears that such information may be used without permission for instituting proceedings abroad designed to give effect to an English order, especially where such proceedings have been expressly authorised: *Tate Access Floors Inc v Boswell* [1990] 3 All ER 303.

The obligation to make full disclosure

The fact that a defendant has been convicted abroad of offences connected with the subject matter of a Mareva injunction is inadmissible as evidence that he committed those offences. However, this fact may, and should, be disclosed in English proceedings if it forms part of the background of those proceedings: *Arab Monetary Fund v Hashim (No 2)* [1990] 1 All ER 673.

The duty to investigate the legal position in another country concerning matters relevant to a Mareva application is not absolute. A party is not in breach of his obligation to make full disclosure if his failure to reveal material facts is due to lack of time to investigate the legal position abroad or otherwise stems from ignorance of a recent change in the legal position: *Tate Access Floors Inc v Boswell*.

There has been a conflict of authority with regard to the correct approach to a claim by a defendant that a material non-disclosure took place at the ex parte stage. Some think that the matter should be investigated fully when the defendant applies to set the order aside. Others wish to discourage lengthy investigations of the rights and wrongs at the interlocutory stage and prefer to leave the matter for the trial: All ER Rev 1988 p 218, All ER Rev 1989, p 219. A compromise seems to be emerging. An investigation of the circumstances in which an ex parte order was obtained should take place at the interlocutory stage only where it is clear that there has been a failure to make a material disclosure and the nature of the alleged failure is so serious as to demand immediate inquiry: *Tate Access Floors Inc v Boswell*.

Interlocutory injunctions

The purpose of an interlocutory injunction is to maintain the status quo pending trial. But even this cannot always be achieved without cost to one or other of the parties. The principle laid down by Lord Diplock in the famous *American Cyanamid Co v Ethicon Ltd* [1975] 1 All ER 504, is that an injunction should not be granted unless otherwise damage is likely to be caused which could not be remedied by money compensation. In situations where not just the consequences of failing to grant an injunction will be uncompensable but also those which will flow from the grant of an injunction, the court must determine the case according to the balance of convenience.

Cambridge Nutrition Ltd v British Broadcasting Corp [1990] 3 All ER 523, gave rise to just such a situation. The plaintiffs alleged an agreement with the BBC whereby the latter undertook not to broadcast a programme about the plaintiffs' low calorie diet before an official report into the subject had been published. If the plaintiffs succeeded in obtaining an injunction to prevent broadcasting pending trial, the BBC would have been deprived of the opportunity to broadcast at the most suitable time for which the programme was devised; a loss which would not be compensable in money. On the other hand, if the broadcast went ahead, the plaintiffs will have irretrievably lost their right that the programme should be postponed and would suffer unjust damage to their reputation which could not be compensated in money terms.

In a situation of this kind the rational course is to prefer the interests of the party who is most likely to be in the right on the merits. But the whole philosophy of interlocutory injunctions is that, at this stage, the court is not concerned to decide the rights and wrongs of the dispute but only to hold a just balance until the matter can be resolved at the trial. Lord Diplock emphasised this point in the *Cyanamid* case and warned against the temptation of trying to determine the respective merits of the parties' claims on what is no more that affidavit evidence at the interlocutory stage. This gave rise to the notion that at the interlocutory stage the only question is whether the plaintiff has an arguable case and that it is no business of the judge to concern himself with the plaintiff's prospects of succeeding on the merits. This notion has never been either absolute or well founded. In the *Cyanamid* case itself Lord Diplock said that the parties' respective chances of success become relevant when the balance of advantage and disadvantage between them is evenly balanced ([1975] 1 All ER at 511). In *NWL Ltd v Woods* [1979] 3 All ER 614, Lord Diplock added that when the grant or refusal of an interlocutory injunction effectively determines the dispute and disposes of the action, the court should take into account the respective merits (see also *Cayne v Global Natural Resources plc* [1984] 1 All ER 225).

The *Cambridge Nutrition* case takes matters a step further. Unlike the position in *NWL Ltd*, the injunction sought by the plaintiffs to restrain broadcasting until after the publication of the official report did not, at least in theory, settle the matter once and for all because there was a possibility that the trial of the dispute could be concluded before the publication of the official report. The Court of Appeal decided that neither the *Cyanamid* case, nor the later exception in *NWL Ltd*, were to be taken as laying down strict rules but only as illustrating a general principle. It held that in determining where the balance of convenience lies, when harm will be caused by the preservation of the status quo as well as by its change, the court is entitled, in special circumstances, to take into account each party's chances of success in the case. The special circumstances in this case were, first, that neither side was interested in, or capable of being satisfactorily compensated by, money damages and, second, that the value and impact of the BBC programme depended on its timing. Kerr LJ went further than the other members of the panel and said that a doubtful contract of the kind claimed by the plaintiffs should not prevail over the right of free speech. The Court of Appeal concluded that as the plaintiffs were unlikely to be able to make out their claim in contract, it was not right to grant an injunction. Notwithstanding the court's emphasis on the special nature of the circumstances it is difficult to see anything outstanding in them other than the fact that a decision either way was capable of resulting in irredeemable loss.

The same may be said about *Lansing Linde Ltd v Kerr* [1991] 1 All ER 418, decided by a different panel of the Court of Appeal. The plaintiffs claimed to have a valid contract restraining the defendant, their ex-employee, from taking up a position with a competitor for 12 months and sought an interlocutory injuction to this effect. Knox J decided that since the trial could not take place within the 12 months period of the restraint, it was necessary to take into account the plaintiffs' chances of success at the trial. Having concluded that their chances were poor, he declined the injunction. On appeal the Court of Appeal approved of this approach. One aspect of this decision deserves special notice. We have seen that if one party could be compensated for his loss in the interim period and the other could not, the interests of the latter should prevail. Here, the loss to the plaintiffs from the defendant's breach of covenant, on the assumption that it proved valid, was difficult to quantify. But the defendant's loss of 12 months' work with his new employers, if the plaintiffs were to be granted an injunction which later proved unjustified, could easily be assessed. The Court of Appeal decided that this factor did not provide a conclusive argument in favour of granting an injunction because the defendant's new employers were only prepared to support his resistance to the plaintiffs' application at the interlocutory stage. Thereafter, he would have to finance litigation from his own resources and he might be unable to seek compensation under the cross-undertaking. It would therefore appear that in striking the balance of convenience the judge has to have regard not only to the respective merits of the parties' claims but also to their ability to pursue litigation.

The relevance of merits to interlocutory injunctions has now received a seal of approval from the House of Lords in *R v Secretary of State for Transport, ex p Factortame Ltd (No 2)* [1991] 1 All ER 70. The applicants sought to restrain the Crown from giving effect to an Act of Parliament which effectively disentitled them to fish under British quotas. It was clear that both parties will suffer uncompensable loss from an unfavourable decision at the interlocutory stage. If it emerges at the end of the day that the law suspended by an interim injunction was in fact valid, harm will have been caused to the public interest and, indeed, to British fishermen whose share of the quotas will have been diminished by the applicants' fishing. Similarly, if an injunction were refused and it turned out that the law was invalid, the applicants will have suffered serious loss for which they will not be entitled to compensation. The balance of convenience posed a serious problem for, as Lord Bridge observe:

> 'the injustices [which each party was likely to suffer from an unfavourable interlocutory decision] are so different in kind that [it is] . . . very difficult to weigh the one against the other.'

He concluded that, in the circumstances:

> 'the most logical course in seeking a decision least likely to occasion injustice is to make the best prediction we can of the final outcome and give to that prediction decisive weight in resolving the interlocutory issue.'

Lord Goff stressed that where a person tries to prevent enforcement of the law, due weight has to be given to the interest of the public in the enforcement of a law that appeared valid on its face. It was therefore for the person challenging the law to show special reason why it should not be enforced pending final determination. However, Lord Goff went out of his way to stress that, although in most cases it was for the person arguing for the suspension of a law to show a strong prima facie case, there was no strict rule to this effect and the courts retained a discretion to issue an interlocutory injunction even where the plaintiff's case was no more than arguable. In the event, the House of Lords granted an interlocutory injunction suspending the Act in question because it was likely that judgment in the Community court would be favourable to the applicants.

An interesting situation on the borderline of between Mareva and an ordinary interlocutory injunctions arose in *Eldan Services Ltd v Chandag Motors Ltd* [1990] 3 All ER 459. The plaintiffs purchased the defendants' business and its stock. The stock was paid for by a postdated cheque drawn by the plaintiffs' solicitors. The plaintiffs claimed that the sum they agreed to pay for the stock was grossly inflated and that they were entitled to pay a much smaller sum for it. They therefore applied for an order restraining the defendants from presenting the postdated cheque or, alternatively, for an order to safeguard the proceeds of the cheque pending the hearing of the action. The application for the first order was rejected by Millett J on the ground that the plaintiffs' claim was in effect for a variation of the contract and there were no good reasons for restraining the defendants from presenting the cheque under the contract as it stood. The alternative order sought by the defendants was in the nature of a Mareva injunction designed to preserve the proceeds, but in the absence of a risk of dissipation Millett J declined to grant it.

Putting a plaintiff to an election between giving a cross-undertaking for an interlocutory injunction or giving up injunctive relief altogether

A plaintiff who seeks an interlocutory injunction has to give a cross-undertaking in damages whereby he undertakes to compensate the defendant for having been prevented from exercising his rights, in the event that the plaintiff fails to make out his claim at the trial. A plaintiff may, however, seek injunctive relief in his principal claim and forego any interim injunction pending trial. Such a plaintiff risks an irreversible change of circumstances but he spares himself the cross-undertaking and its attendant risk. Browne-Wilkinson V-C has indicated in *Blue Town Investments Ltd v Higgs & Hill plc* [1990] 2 All ER 897, that the plaintiff's choice between these two courses is not as free as might have been supposed.

The plaintiffs owned a house adjoining land on which the defendants proposed to carry out a development. There were discussions between the parties concerning the plaintiffs' rights of light, in which the defendants indicated that they were prepared to compensate the plaintiff for the loss of light and the plaintiffs indicated their agreement to negotiate about compensation. Three months later, the defendants started the development work and pursued it for three further months before the plaintiffs protested and sued for an injunction. They refrained from seeking interlocutory relief in order to avoid giving a cross-undertaking. The defendants applied to have the injunctive prayer struck out on the ground that it was vexatious. The defendants argued that the plaintiffs' claim for an injunction placed them in an intolerable position: if they desisted from carrying on with the development pending trial they would incur great financial loss even if the decision went in their favour because they had no cross-undertaking from the plaintiffs; if they persisted and the decision went against them, they would have to pull down what they had built.

Browne-Wilkinson V-C found that the plaintiffs had stood by and allowed the defendants to proceed in the belief that the plaintiffs were prepared to accept compensation and, therefore, the plaintiffs had a slim chance of obtaining injunctive relief at the trial. In these circumstances, he felt, it was vexatious for the plaintiffs to put forward a tenuous claim for injunctive relief without being prepared to compensate the defendants for the loss they would suffer if the plaintiffs' claim failed at the trial. The claim for injunctive relief was accordingly struck out.

However, serious doubt was cast on this decision by Hoffmann J in *Oxy Electric Ltd v Zainuddin* [1990] 2 All ER 902. The plaintiffs had a restrictive covenant limiting building on the defendants' land to factories and offices but the defendants proposed to build a mosque and went ahead in the face of the plaintiffs' objections. When the plaintiffs sued for a permanent injunction, the defendants applied to strike out the claim unless the plaintiffs obtained an interlocutory injunction and gave security by way of a cross-undertaking. Their grounds for doing so were similar to those of the defendants in the *Blue Town Investments* case. As the defendants were contemplating a multi-million development, the plaintiffs were in no position to provide the kind of security appropriate for interlocutory proceedings. It followed that by seeking to force the plaintiffs into an interlocutory situation, the defendants were, in effect, seeking to prevent them from obtaining relief altogether.

Hoffmann J's starting point was the law's policy against denying a citizen access to court when he has a bona fide claim or defence. This policy, he explained, is reflected in Ord 18, r 19, which sets out the various grounds for striking out on grounds of abuse of process. Further, there is no power to require an impecunious plaintiff to give security for costs as a condition to proceeding with his claim. Hoffmann J explained that he could see no distinction of principle between the imposition of a condition designed to protect a defendant against loss of costs and a condition, of the kind sought by the defendants here, designed to protect him against loss caused by the uncertainty arising from being sued.

This last point goes to the heart of the matter. Being faced with a claim for injunction is not the only situation that may create difficulty for a defendant and expose him to a risk of irrecoverable loss. Suppose that the defendant is a developer who is sued for £1m of damages. If he sets aside that sum, in case judgment goes against him, he will be losing a new venture. If he embarks on the new venture and judgment goes against him, he will not have the funds to meet it and will be forced to give up the new venture at great financial loss. Or, to take another possibility, a large financial claim hanging over a defendant's head may cause his bank to withhold credit. If the Vice Chancellor's reasoning is valid, a plaintiff in such situations (supposing his chances of success are slim) may be ordered to desist from his claim unless he is prepared to apply for an injunction to freeze the developer's funds and provide a cross-undertaking. It clearly does not make sense to take this line;

and not just because Mareva injunctions are intended to deal with dissipation calculated to evade judgment.

The Vice Chancellor did not rely on authority in the *Blue Town Investments* case but on an analogy with the position where the plaintiff has registered an estate contract over disputed land. Such registration prevents sale of the land to a third party pending the registration. It has been decided that a court may order the registration to be vacated unless the plaintiff applies for an interim injunction to restrain the owner from disposing of the land and provides a cross-undertaking in damages: *Clearbrook Property Holdings Ltd v Verrier* [1973] 3 All ER 614. The analogy is not altogether convincing, as Hoffmann J pointed out. Registration of an estate contract is a clog on the title and is equivalent to an interlocutory injunction because the owner is not merely deterred from sale by a financial risk, but is effectively prevented from affecting such sale. The situation is quite different in the cases we have been discussing. The defendants were not prevented from continuing with the development. The plaintiffs' claim only made it hazardous for them to do so. If the defendants carry on with the development pending trial and then obtain judgment in their favour, they will have lost nothing. The uncertainty for such defendants is therefore the common and inevitable uncertainty involved in pending claims.

While expressing doubt whether the jurisdiction exercised by the Vice Chancellor existed, Hoffmann J was able to distinguish the case before him from that of *Blue Town Investments* on the ground that in the latter the plaintiffs' chances of success were so slim as to border on abuse of process, whereas the plaintiffs before him had a seriously arguable case. This distinction exposed a paradox in the Vice Chancellor's reasoning: he assessed the plaintiffs' chances of success to be negligible and at the same time he thought that they should seek an interlocutory injunction, when such injunctions are not granted in the absence of a good arguable case.

Litigation is hazardous at the best of times and it is certainly desirable to have a fair system of allocating the burden of the risk but there is no simple way of doing so. If anything, the Vice Chancellor's decision could increase the hazard of litigation to the disadvantage of the poorer litigant. However, it seems unlikely that it would survive the criticism to which it has been subjected.

Security for costs

The effect of the Civil Jurisdiction and Judgments Act 1982 and of the Convention on Jurisdiction and the Enforcement of Judgments in Civil and Commercial Matters on orders of security for costs was considered in two cases.

In *De Bry v Fitzgerald* [1990] 1 All ER 560, it was held that a judge who is asked to order security for costs against a plaintiff under Ord 23, r 1(1)(*a*), on the ground that he was ordinarily resident outside the jurisdiction, should bear in mind that the Convention makes it relatively straightforward to enforce English judgments in EEC countries. Indeed, Dillon LJ went as far as suggesting that a defendant ought to show special circumstances before security for costs would be ordered against an EEC resident under Ord 23, r 1(1)(*a*). Moreover, Lord Donaldson MR expressed the view that consideration should be given to removing from Ord 23, r 1 the foreign residence of the plaintiff as a reason for requiring security and substituting it with consideration of practicability of enforcement.

In *Berkeley Administration Inc v McClelland* [1990] 1 All ER 958, a frontal attack was made against Ord 23, r 1(1)(a) as being discriminatory and therefore inconsistent with Art 7 of the EEC Treaty which forbids 'discrimination on the grounds of nationality'. The Court of Appeal rejected this argument, holding that a differential treatment under the rule is on grounds of residence and not nationality and, further, that under rule 1(1)(a) residence abroad is not per se a reason for requiring security for costs but merely confers jurisdiction to require so. This jurisdiction is exercisable only where there are reasons to believe that the defendant would have a real difficulty in enforcing an order for costs. Staughton LJ was not entirely confident that enforcement of English judgments in other EEC countries is as easy as in England and felt that it was therefore desirable to maintain a discretion to require security from foreign residents.

The principles that emerge from these decisions seem to be as follows. Foreign residence is not sufficient by itself to justify an order for security. The practical difficulties that the defendant may encounter in recovering his costs in a foreign country need to be considered. Provided that due weight is given to this factor and to the fact that English judgments are enforceable in other EEC countries, an order imposing a condition of security for costs is unlikely to be interfered with.

The facility of enforcing English judgments is not confined to EEC countries. The United Kingdom has treaties for that purpose with other countries. In *Thune v London Properties Ltd* [1990] 1 All ER 972, the ease of enforcing a costs order in Norway under such treaty was singled out as a sufficient consideration against making an order of security for judgment, provided due weight is given to other relevant factors. One such relevant factor is the impecuniousity of the plaintiff. Although Bingham LJ went out of his way to stress that the impecuniousity of a personal plaintiff could never, by itself, justify the imposition of security for costs, the financial position of the plaintiff may nevertheless be considered along with other relevant factors in exercising discretion under Ord 23, r 1(1)(a). The Court of Appeal held that since there was a risk, albeit small, that the defendants will not be able to enforce an order for costs, were they to succeed, due to the competing claims of the plaintiffs' creditors, security for costs should be given by the plaintiff. It is suggested that if the financial position of the plaintiff is to become a relevant consideration, so should the parties' chances of success. For it would be unfair to handicap the plaintiff's ability to pursue a well grounded claim by putting financial obstacles in his way (cf *De Bry v Fitzgerald* (at 565)).

Discovery

At a time when we witness a continual, if slow, erosion of the principle that all relevant evidence must be made available to the parties and to the court, it is reassuring to see a reaffirmation of this principle. In *Arab Monetary Fund v Hashim (No 2)* [1990] 1 All ER 673, the defendant was sued by the plaintiffs for embezzlement of funds. In his defence the defendant claimed that certain funds were given to him by Iraqi residents who wished to overcome exchange controls in their country. However, he asked to be excused from disclosing the identity of these third parties on the ground that such disclosure might expose them to serious consequences in Iraq. Hoffmann J explained that:

> 'in a civil action the court does not have a discretion to permit a witness giving evidence at the trial to refuse to disclose relevant and admissible facts which are not covered by any recognised privilege.' (at 681)

Although at the discovery stage the court has a discretion in ordering disclosure, this discretion is very limited. Hence, if disclosure will need to be made at the trial, it would not be right to deny disclosure at the discovery stage and thus deprive one of the parties of the opportunity to prepare to meet that evidence. However, the court could postpone the disclosure until it has become clear that the action is proceeding to trial on issues to which the information sought is relevant. The discretion in ordering disclosure of information that may harm third parties was also considered in *Dubai Bank Ltd v Galadari (No 2)* [1990] 2 All ER 738.

In some situations discovery may be made against a person who is not a party to the proceedings. But there is no provision with regard to the inspection of property in the hands of a third party because Ord 29, r 2, which deals with inspection, is confined to property in the hands of a party to the proceedings. The plaintiff in *Douihech v Findlay* [1990] 3 All ER 118, sought to overcome this obstacle by joining a third party, who was in possession of the relevant property, as defendant solely for the purpose of bringing the latter under Ord 29, r 2. It has been decided that joinder for the purpose of inspection is not permissible. This is clearly right, since otherwise one would have been able to obtain discovery against any stranger by joining the person in possession of a relevant document as defendant.

The question of who is a party, for the purpose of discovery, in representative proceedings was considered in *Ventouris v Mountain, The Italia Express* [1990] 3 All ER 157, where Saville J decided that the court has no power to order discovery against a represented party. The reason given was that Ord 24, r 3(1) empowers the court to order discovery only against parties and that Ord 15, r 13(3), indicates that a represented person is not a party. The question of the liability of represented persons to discovery gives rise to a conflict between two competing considerations. On the one hand, it may be said that by virtue of being represented in the proceedings and bound by their outcome such persons must be considered as parties to all intents and purposes. This argues for discovery. On the other hand, the purpose of representative proceedings is to simplify the litigation. To order discovery against persons represented but not participating in the proceedings would complicate the process and this argues against discovery. On balance, the conclusion reached in this case seems right.

Discovery – legal professional privilege

None of the cases dealing with legal professional privilege decided this year is likely to contribute greatly to the fair and efficient resolution of disputes. *Ventouris v Mountain, The Italia Express* [1990] 3 All ER 157, deals with the vexed question of the position of copies. Last year, the Court of Appeal decided that where an original in the hands of a party was not privileged, a copy thereof could not be privileged either, even if made by a solicitor for the purpose of legal advice or litigation: *Dubai Bank Ltd v Galadari* [1989] 3 All ER 769. It was suggested there, obiter, that where a copy was made from an original that was not in the hands of the party, the copy could be privileged, if made by a solicitor, even if the original is not privileged and may be adduced at the trial. This suggestion, as was explained in All ER Rev 1989, p 148, neither relies on sound authority nor makes good sense. Nonetheless, it has now been adopted, albeit obiter, in *The Italia Express*. The reason given by Saville J was that holding a document obtained in connection with litigation not to be privileged:

> 'would be calculated to diminish or destroy the confidential relationship between solicitor and client, and gravely hamper the proper and effective preparation for the trial by solicitors.'

How these calamities will materialise was not made clear. In the present case the document in question was not a copy but an original obtained from a third party. We may speculate that the judge felt that if the opponent could see the documents, he might be able to gather from them the advice that the solicitor gave to his client. This is a rather far-fetched prospect. First, if the opponent can have access to the original and he happens to know that his adversary also had access to it, he will have the information in any event. Second, and more important, discovery of documents is capable, in the nature of things, to provide some indication of the advice that was given and of the line of argument that is likely to be pursued. Indeed, this is the purpose of disclosure: to inform each party what material evidence the opponent has got, so that each party is able to work out the strength of his opponent's case. If anything, Saville J's ruling is likely to impede this process.

Indeed, to ensure that the opponent is kept in the dark, not only of the contents of the copy but also of its existence and, thereby, of the existence of the original, a list of documents served on the opponent need only claim privilege in the following terms:

> 'Original documents not previously in the possession, custody or power of the party . . . but obtained by (the party's) solicitors from third parties for the purposes of these proceedings.'

Saville J explained that:

> 'It is not necessary to provide a description that enables the asserted identity [of the privileged copy] to be tested which reveals the contents, maker or particular provenance of the document.' (at 160)

Saville J's decision has been overruled by the Court of Appeal: (1991) NLJ, 22 February, 236. It had been held that privilege cannot be claimed for an original document, if the document did not come into existence for the purpose of litigation.

In *Derby & Co Ltd v Weldon (No 7)* [1990] 3 All ER 161, Vinelott J decided that information identifying documents in respect of which privilege is claimed need not be given even where the claim alleges fraud and even if it has been shown that some of the advice was sought in furtherance of the fraudulent design. He also decided that where it is claimed that communications with a legal adviser was in furtherance of fraud, the party seeking to override the immunity need not supply conclusive proof that the communication was for an improper purpose, it is sufficient to make a prima facie case: see also *R v Governor of Pentonville Prison, ex p Osman* [1989] 3 All ER 701 at 730, a point discussed in All ER Rev 1989, p 153. However, if this is so, would it not be sensible, at least where there is a well founded suggestion that some of the communications with legal advisers was in furtherance of fraud, to demand particularisation of privileged documents so that an informed decision may be made on the overriding of the privilege?

The arguments against greater particularisation of privileged documents seem to be of three kinds. The first relies on the risk that if the place and dates of documents were given, the opponent might be in a position to guess their contents. It is most improbable that such guesswork is likely to provide the opponent with any realistic insight into what passed between lawyer and client. The second line of argument is more serious. It is said that particularisation would lead to arguments about the validity of claims for privilege. It is difficult to assess the extent to which there is a real risk of this kind but it seems unlikely that litigants would object to privilege on spurious grounds, when such objections are punishable with costs. At the same time there is no reason for discouraging well grounded objections. Lastly, it is said that solicitors should be trusted and that their claim for privilege should not be questioned. Professional trust and probity should indeed be encouraged, but is may be doubted if the best way of doing so is placing claims to privilege above challenge.

The most disappointing decision this year must be *Derby & Co Ltd v Weldon (No 8)* [1990] 3 All ER 762. In the course of discovery the plaintiffs, due to an oversight, failed to claim privilege in respect of a number of privileged documents and supplied the defendants with copies thereof. When they discovered their mistake, the plaintiffs' solicitors sought an order for the return of all copies and for restraining the defendants from using information derived from the documents in the proceedings or for any other purpose. A number of cases decided over the last few years provided authority for such orders: *Guinness Peat Properties Ltd v Fitzroy Robinson Partnership* [1987] 2 All ER 716 (All ER Rev 1987, p 123); *Goddard v Nationwide Building Society* [1986] 3 All ER 264 (All ER Rev 1986, p 160); *British Coal Corp v Dennis Rye Ltd (No 2)* [1988] 3 All ER 816 (All ER Rev 1988, p 140). However, last year Scott J sought a way of reining in the facility with which parties could, as it were, turn back the clock and pretend that privileged documents which have in fact been seen by the other side were to be treated as if they had never been revealed and thereby ensure that information known to both parties was kept away from the court. In *Webster v James Chapman & Co (a firm)* [1989] 3 All ER 939 (All ER Rev 1989, p 150), he decided that where a party receives disclosure of a privileged document through no fault of his own, he should not be restrained from using it in the proceedings if such restraint would hamper the conduct of his case. The Court of Appeal in *Derby & Co Ltd v Weldon (No 8)* does not seem to have been impressed by this policy.

The Court of Appeal affirmed that the courts have a discretion in the matter, as outlined in *Guinness Peat Properties Ltd v Fitzroy Robinson Partnership*, and reiterated that an injunction would normally be granted against a party who must have realised that the documents were accidentally disclosed and is trying to take advantage of the opponent's mistake. The facts in the case before the Court of Appeal were that the defendants' solicitors were allowed to inspect privileged documents. On reading them they realised that the documents were privileged. Nonetheless, they asked for copies, which were duly provided. The Court of Appeal found that by asking for the copies the defendant's solicitors were trying to take advantage of the mistake made by the plaintiffs' solicitors and that an order restraining any use of the information should be made.

Furthermore, it was decided that the importance of the document to the party who received disclosure is not a relevant consideration in the exercise of discretion in this matter. This aspect of the decision is most disturbing because it gives no weight whatever to the interest in the administration of justice which requires that the court should not turn a blind eye to information that is known to both parties. Suppose that the information accidentally disclosed undermines the whole case of the party entitled to privilege or, as was the position in *Webster v James Chapman & Co (a firm)*, reveals a serious inconsistency: would not the litigant who is prevented from using the information and who loses the case leave the court with a legitimate sense of grievance? And would not public confidence in the reliability and fairness of such judgment be sorely strained? It is not easy to see why the defendants' solicitors should have been castigated for taking advantage of the mistake, when all that they were doing was to use information freely, if negligently, disclosed in order to advance their clients' case and help the ascertainment of truth. Indeed, wherefrom does the court take the jurisdiction to say that because something is confidential, it should not be adduced in court? – confidence as such being no ground for privilege: *X Ltd v Morgan-Grampian Ltd* [1990] 2 All ER 1 at 15).

None of these problems were addressed by the Court of Appeal, let alone satisfactorily resolved. Until this is done, we may maintain a glimmer of hope that not all is lost. In the meantime, the task of solicitors who receive discovery is made more difficult. Having innocently read the documents, were the defendant's solicitors to forget all about them, even if they advanced their client's case? As a result of this decision, solicitors must not only effectively raise claims of privilege for the opponent but also conceal from their client, and possibly even themselves, information that advances the client's case. Solicitors who innocently read privileged documents, and feel that they cannot with clear conscience overlook facts favourable to their client, should perhaps refrain from asking for copies and use the information at the trial. By then it would be too late to obtain an injunction and the situation would be covered by the rule in *Calcraft v Guest* [1898] 1 QB 759, [1895–99] All ER Rep 346. The present state of the law invites such subterfuge.

Discovery – journalistic confidence

X Ltd v Morgan-Grampian (Publishers) Ltd [1990] 2 All ER 1, a case also considered at pp 50–51, 265–266 of this Review, is likely to prove a milestone in the treatment of journalistic confidence. The plaintiffs prepared a financial plan in order to obtain credit from banks. Their plan was stolen and handed over to a journalist who proposed to write an article about the matter. The plaintiffs applied for an injunction restraining the journalist and his publishers from publishing information derived from the stolen plan and requiring them to disclose the identity of the thief or of the source of their information. The judge before whom the matter came found that disclosure would cause severe financial damage to the plaintiffs and granted an injunction. He also ordered disclosure of the identity of the wrongdoer. By the time the matter reached the House of Lords, the issue extended beyond the matters involved in discovery, as we shall see later.

Section 10 of the Contempt of Court Act 1981 provides:

> 'no court may require a person to disclose, nor is any person guilty of contempt of court for refusing to disclose, the source of information contained in a publication for which he is responsible, unless it be established to the satisfaction of the court that disclosure is necessary in the interests of justice or national security of for the prevention of disorder or crime.'

Several points were clarified in relation to the meaning of this provision. As the defendants had been restrained from publishing, the information never appeared in a publication and seemed therefore to be outside the scope of the section. However, the House of Lords decided that this fact did not prevent s 10 from applying as long as the communication in question was received for the purpose of publication. Were it otherwise, journalists would be deprived of their protection if they decided not to publish or if they were prevented from doing so by an injunction.

A further problem of construction arose in relation to the meaning of 'the interests of justice'. In *Secretary of State for Defence v Guardian Newspapers Ltd* [1984] 3 All ER 601 (All ER Rev, pp 67–70, 158–160), Lord Diplock confined this phrase to legal proceedings in a court of law. Such a restriction would have left the plaintiffs' application for disclosure outside the scope of the section because they did not necessarily intend to resort to legal proceedings for the protection of their rights. In *X Ltd*, the House of Lords decided that the Diplock interpretation was too narrow. It is, Lord Bridge explained:

> ' "in the interests of justice", in the sense in which this phrase is used in s 10, that persons should be able to exercise important legal rights and to protect themselves from serious legal wrongs whether or not resort to legal proceedings in a court of law will be necessary to attain these objectives.' ([1990] 2 All ER at 9)

It is enough that the person seeking disclosure wishes to protect his interests by identifying and dismissing an employee who has been causing injury to his business.

Important observations were also made in connection with the balancing process required by s 10 between, on the one hand, the protection of journalistic sources of information and, on the other, the interests of justice. The party seeking disclosure must satisfy the judge that disclosure of the information in question is truly necessary in the interests of one of the matters listed in s 10. Thus, the nature of the right or interest of the party seeking disclosure will be an important factor, because the courts will be reluctant to override the public interest in protecting the source of information for the sake of protecting some minor private interest. On the other side of the scales, the court will consider the extent to which the public has an interest in the information given by the source; the greater the legitimate public interest in the information, the greater will be the importance of protecting the source. Much will also turn on the manner in which the information was obtained by the source; legitimate means will weigh in favour of protection, whereas illegitimate means will argue for disclosure. In mentioning these factors, Lord Bridge was illustrating the nature of the considerations involved in the balancing process rather than attempting to provide an comprehensive list of factors. In the event the House of Lords found that a case for disclosure had been made.

One aspect of the analysis of the judicial function in the balancing process is, however, unsatisfactory. In *Secretary of State for Defence v Guardian Newspapers Ltd* (at 623), Lord Diplock described the balancing exercise as 'a question of fact'. It was suggested in the commentary on that case in All ER Rev 1984, p 159, that it is confusing to describe the question of the necessity of the disclosure as one of fact. There may, of course, be a factual aspect to this question. Thus in *X Ltd* it was a question of fact whether identifying the thief would help the applicants to protect their financial position. But beyond that, the issue concerned the relative importance and weight of the interest of protecting the source as against the interest of protecting the applicant. The relative strength of these interests is not observable in the world or discoverable by empirical investigation and is therefore not a matter of fact. The present House of Lords decision adds confusion in this regard. Lord Bridge said:

> 'Whether the necessity of disclosure . . . is established is a question of fact rather than an issue calling for the exercise of the judge's discretion, but, like many other questions of fact, such as the question whether somebody has acted reasonably in given circumstances, it will call for the exercise of discrimination and sometimes difficult value judgment.' (at 9).

Lord Oliver wrote that the balancing exercise 'involves not so much discretion as a value judgment' but hastened to add that:

> 'the formation of a value judgment may, and, indeed, nearly always will, involve the consideration of factors which will be equally relevant to the exercise of discretion.' (at 16)

Once the balancing exercise has been performed, he went on to say, 'there will . . . theoretically remain a residual discretion which is inherent in the common law position'. This way of looking at things is puzzling. If the factors relevant to the balancing process and to discretion are identical, what is the difference between the two? Is it conceivable that the balancing process will result in affirming disclosure, but the subsequent discretionary stage will reverse the position? Mindful of this, Lord Oliver explained that:

> 'once it has been determined [in the balancing exercise] that the need for disclosure is predominant over the public interest in non-disclosure there is nothing more to be asked.'

In that case, we may ask, why is it still necessary or desirable to distinguish between balancing and discretion?

It might be suggested that by saying that the balancing process does not involve discretion, the House of Lords was merely indicating that this is not the type of decision in which appellate courts refrain from interfering with the judgment of the trial judge, as it is customary to refrain in relation to matters left to the judge's discretion. But if this was the aim, it has certainly been undermined by the description of the question as one of fact, in relation to which appellate courts also rein in their interfering urges. It is possible that the House of Lords meant to indicate that the judge does not have a free hand in the balancing process. It is, however, difficult to see why this message should be necessary. First, as a rule, judges do not have a free hand in the exercise of discretion; a discretionary decision may be reversed if the judge misdirected himself or acted unreasonably. Second, by accepting that the balancing process involves value judgment, the House of Lords has acknowledged that a considerable scope for choice between different solutions does exist.

This discussion of the nature of the balancing exercise can only confuse what is otherwise a clear exposition of the judicial task, which Lord Oliver explained by saying that:

> 'the court is not permitted to require the disclosure of a journalistic source unless it is satisfied that one or more of the four enumerated consideration . . . are of such preponderating importance in the individual case that the ban on disclosure by the opening words of the section really needs to be overridden.'

Discovery of documents referred to in affidavits

Order 24, r 10, which provides for the disclosure of documents to which 'reference is made' in pleadings or affidavits, has given rise to a number of important questions in *Dubai Bank Ltd v Galadari (No 2)* [1990] 2 All ER 738. It was said, obiter, that the rule entitles a party to require his opponent to produce a document even though it is referred to in an affidavit sworn by a deponent who is not a party. A further question concerned the scope of disclosure. According to Ord 24, r 13(1) an order for disclosure may be made only if it 'is necessary either for disposing fairly of the cause or matter or for saving costs'. It was argued that this restriction limits disclosure to situations where the documents are necessary for disposing of the main action and not just for an interlocutory application. This argument has been rejected and the Court of Appeal held that disclosure may be ordered whenever it is necessary for the fair disposal of any stage in the proceedings including interlocutory proceedings.

The problem that exercised most of the attention in the Court of Appeal concerned the meaning of the phrase 'reference . . . made to any document' in r 10. Did it mean documents (or classes of documents) specifically mentioned in an affidavit, or did it extend to documents the existence of which was implied by statements made in the affidavit? If, for instance, an affidavit states that a property was conveyed, does this amount to a reference to the document affecting the conveyance? The Court of Appeal held that only a direct allusion to a document will amount to a reference and entitle a party to seek inspection under r 10. An indirect reference, as for example a reference to a conveyance, will not justify inspection under this rule. Explaining this conclusion, Slade LJ said that if an indirect reference were enough, 'this would oblige the court to enter into a process of inference and conjecture in order to determine whether the document in question even existed' (at 744). This does not mean, he added, that the party on whom an affidavit is served is powerless to obtain discovery of documents implied therein. Such party will have several courses open to him: he would be able to ask for further and better particulars; if the deponent failed to identify his sources of knowledge, the party may object to the affidavit; lastly, the party may seek discovery under Ord 24, r 7. Although these alternative courses are indeed open, it is difficult to see the advantage of forcing the party seeking disclosure to take them, rather than the simpler r 10 route, seeing that he is likely to get to the same destination in any event. Indeed, the existence of different rules for discovery of documents expressly mentioned in an affidavit and for documents impliedly mentioned is itself going to produce fine and uncertain distinctions and procedural complexity. As this very case illustrates.

It was held that the mention of a discretionary trust is a reference to the setting up of the trust and not to the document creating it and that, therefore, no order for disclosure of the trust document can be made. Similarly, the mention of the existence of a bank account was held to refer to a state of affairs and not to the documents in which this state of affairs was recorded. Again, a statement that the accounts were guaranteed was not a reference to the documents incorporating the guarantee. By contrast, it was held that the reference to a facility secured 'with a guarantee' was reference to a document that fell under r 10, and the same went for 'a mandate from the account holders' which was held to be a reference to a document. One may be excused for not finding these distinctions as compelling as the Court of Appeal found them. Would it not be simpler to hold that when an affidavit suggests the existence of a document, as does a reference to a conveyance, a bank account or a trust, it should come within the ambit of r 10?

Summary judgment – interest

Section 17 of the Judgments Act 1938 lays down that every judgment debt carries interest from the time it was entered. The House of Lords decided in *Hunt v R M Douglas (Roofing) Ltd* [1988] 3 All ER 823, that an order for payment of costs to be taxed was a judgment debt and carried interest from the date of the order and not from the later date at which the costs are finally assessed. In passing, a view was expressed (at 833) that the same went for a judgment for damages to be assessed, where interest would be due from the date of judgment and not the later date at which the amount of damages is assessed. The plaintiffs in *Putty v Hopkinson* [1990] 1 All ER 1057, who had been injured in a road accident, were hoping to take the benefit of this view and sought summary judgment on liability which was not disputed. However, the defendants asked the judge to exercise his discretion against entering judgment on liability because this would expose them to interest from the date of judgment even though the extent of their liability remained to be determined. Simon Goldblatt QC reviewed the authorities and concluded that, where no issue concerning liability remains to be determined, there is no discretion to withhold judgment for the plaintiffs on liability. He felt, however, that he did have discretion in the form of the judgment and that it was open to him to give judgment in a form that does not attract interest under s 17 of the 1938 Act. He decided that, first, since at that stage the court could not assess the quantum of damage and, second, since the plaintiffs were not ready for a trial of the quantum, the form of the judgment should be such as not to attract interest. These reasons make little sense. If they carried the weight given to them by the judge, *Hunt v R M Douglas (Roofing) Ltd* would have gone the other way; there, too, the costs could not be assessed at the time of judgment and the winning party was not ready for taxation there and then. The main reason for the judge's decision lay in the fear that if he decided otherwise, defendants would be tempted to keep liability in issue rather than submit to judgment at an early stage. However, if it is feared that a defendant would not balk at protracting the trial of liability in order to avoid paying interest, should it not also be feared that as a consequence of the present ruling a defendant would not balk at protracting the quantum stage in order to earn interest on the sum he would have to pay the plaintiff? Pandering to the proclivity of ruthless or cynical litigants is hardly the way to a fair and just procedure. The courts have already sufficient powers to deal with unscrupulous defences and there is no need to extract a tax from plaintiffs in order to add a carrot to the stick.

Service out of jurisdiction

The new High Court Rules of New Zealand, which came into effect in 1986, dispense with the need to obtain leave for service out of the jurisdiction in certain cases. According to rule 219 these include, inter alia, cases where the claim is in respect of an act that was done in New Zealand and cases where the person out of the jurisdiction is a necessary and proper party. In these situations a statement of claim, and not just a writ, may be served without leave. According to rule 131, a defendant who wishes to dispute the jurisdiction of the court may put in an appearance under protest. However, neither the former nor the latter rule make any reference to a power to dismiss the service abroad on the ground of forum non conveniens or for the reason that the plaintiff has not made out a good arguable case. The Privy Council has decided in *Kuwait Asia Bank EC v National Mutual Life Nominees Ltd* [1990] 3 All ER 404, that the court retained an inherent discretion to decline jurisdiction on both these grounds.

Suitability of forum was considered in *Arab Monetary Fund v Hashim (No 3)* [1990] 1 All ER 685, where it was decided that England provided the most convenient forum notwithstanding that the fraud complained of was committed in Abu Dhabi and Switzerland.

Service within the jurisdiction

When it comes to interpreting the rules governing service there are two schools of thought. The literal school holds that the rules of service must be followed to the letter, even if this results in holding a writ to have been invalidly served, although the defendant has voluntarily and knowingly received it. The liberal school holds that the rules are the servants of the legal process, not its masters, and if a defendant receives a writ knowing what it is, he could not turn around and argue that it was invalidly served. Unfortunately, the former school has had the upper hand in *Kenneth Allison Ltd v A E Limehouse & Co* [1990] 2 All ER 723.

The plaintiffs wished to serve a writ on the defendant firm. The plaintiffs' server went to the firm's office and said he wished to serve a writ. A partner in the firm instructed an employee to accept the writ which was then handed over to the partner. The defendant firm challenged the validity of the service on the ground that it was not served 'on one or more of the partners', as required by Ord 81, r 3(1)(a). Lord Donaldson MR, in a minority, outlined the liberal approach to this situation:

> 'Clearly all these provisions [the rules of service] are necessary if the defendant is unwilling in the event to accept service, but I really do not see why they are needed if he is willing to do so and a fortiori why they should be intended to prevent his giving effect to that willingness in any way which appeals to him. The sole purpose of service of proceedings is to bring them to the attention of the defendant, to give him an opportunity to respond and to fix a time by reference to which time limits can be applied either under the Limitation Acts or in the conduct of litigation. This purpose is equally well served by consensual service of proceedings as by service in one of the modes described in the rules.'
> (at 725)

The majority, consisting of Russell and Farquharson LJJ, subscribed to the literal school. They thought that an agreement to accept service in a way not provided by the rule is valid only where it is part of a contract as described by Ord 10, r 3. Otherwise, service has to be affected exactly as prescribed by the rules and since it was not so affected in this case it was not valid. The justification given for this view was that strict adherence to the rules is necessary in the interest of certainty which, in turn, is essential for the calculation of time limits. It is, however, possible that far from promoting certainty such a strategy may well undermine it, as this very case illustrates (for similar comment see All ER Rev 1986, p 236). In circumstances such as the writ server encountered at the offices of the defendant firm it would be hard to expect a server to act differently, once an employee is instructed to receive the writ from him. The Court of Appeal's interpretation of the rule has therefore the effect of making personal delivery of a writ at a firm's place of business more hazardous then sending it by post under Ord 81, r 3(1)(c) or by substitute service under Ord 65, r 4. This would seem to turn the policy of the rules, which places priority on personal service, on its head. Having reached such a pass, the time seems ripe for the rules committee to consider whether it is satisfactory to have a regime under which the validity of service turns on technical arguments of the kind approved of in this case.

Pleadings

A curious, if somewhat undignified, legal battle was joined by two newspaper publishers in *Express Newspapers plc v News (UK) Ltd* [1990] 3 All ER 376, a case discussed at more length in Commercial Law, pp 24–26 above. The plaintiffs sued the defendants for breach of copyright in that the latter published a story derived from one published by the plaintiffs. The defendants counterclaimed complaining that the plaintiffs were guilty of a similar breach of copyright in relation to different story, first published by the defendants. The plaintiffs obtained summary judgment on their claim before the counterclaim was determined. When the defendants' application for summary judgment on the counterclaim came before a different judge the plaintiffs argued that they had an arguable defence. Sir Nicolas Browne-Wilkinson V-C accepted that the plaintiffs had an arguable defence to the counterclaim based on a custom whereby newspapers impliedly waived their copyright in favour of each other. However, he found that such a defence would be inconsistent with the plaintiffs' own claim in the main action. Applying the principle that a party may not approbate and reprobate at the same time he decided that, having chosen to pursue their case against the defendants, the plaintiffs had accepted the absence of such a custom and he gave judgment for the defendants on their counterclaim. The justice of this conclusion can hardly be faulted.

Abuse of process and issue estoppel

In the absence of a class action procedure the courts are having to improvise in order to avoid multiple and fruitless litigation as happened in *Ashmore v British Coal Corporation* [1990] 2 All ER 981 (also discussed in Employment Law, pp 96–97 above). In 1982 some 1,500 women canteen workers in the employment of British Coal (hereinafter 'the board') claimed that they were being paid less than men doing comparable work. The industrial tribunal ordered the stay of all the actions except seven to be chosen by the women's representatives. These were to be pitted against comparator cases chosen by the board. After a hearing, the women's applications were dismissed on the two grounds. First, that none of the women was doing night work on her own, as did the main comparator, and so failed under the Equal Pay Act 1970, s 1(2)(*a*). Second, that the board had established a defence under s 1(3) that the variation in the rate of pay between the women and the comparator was 'genuinely due to a material factor which is not the difference of sex'. The appellant, Mrs Ashmore, brought proceedings under the Act claiming that she, unlike the women in the representative cases, did the same work as the comparator and worked alone at night. The board successfully applied to have the appellant's application struck out under the Industrial Tribunals Rule of Procedure 1985 as being vexatious. The Court of Appeal upheld this decision because even though the appellant might be able to surmount the hurdle of s 1(2)(*a*), she was bound to be defeated by reason of s 1(3).

Two lines of reasoning led the court to regard the appellant's pursuit of her claim an abuse of process. One was that 'it is not in the interests of justice that the time of the courts or tribunals is taken litigating claims that have effectively been already decided' (at 985); the reason being that it is a waste of time to litigate when the result is a foregone conclusion. This ground may be referred to as the futility ground. The second ground was that it is not in the interests of justice that the appellant should be allowed to invite the tribunal to reach different findings of fact on the same evidence. This may be referred to as the danger of inconsistency. An inconsistency of judgments, Stuart-Smith LJ explained, would undermine confidence in the administration of justice and cause a sense of grievance to those who lost in the representative case. These two grounds are not entirely consistent with each other. While the futility ground relies on the likelihood of reaching the same result as in that earlier trial, the inconsistency ground lays stress on the possibility that a different result will be reached in a subsequent trial. If we leave to one side the issue of the right to be heard, the futility ground is relatively unproblematic. But the same cannot be said for the inconsistency ground. Telling Mrs Ashmore that she is not allowed to proceed because a court may find in her favour offends one's sense of justice, even when it added that it is unfair on the board that she should proceed when the board may no longer be able to muster the same evidence as it did in the representative action.

Indeed, the problematic nature of the inconsistency ground is sadly illustrated by *Hunter v Chief Constable of West Midlands* [1981] 3 All ER 727, which provided the Court of Appeal with support for the futility ground. The case arose from the prosecution of the Birmingham Six. These accused were charged with murders by bombing. At their trial they contended that they were beaten up in order to confess. It was not disputed that they had been beaten, but the prosecution's case was that this took place in prison, after they had confessed to the police. Their arguments were rejected and they were convicted. The prison officers involved were subsequently charged with assault on the suspects but were acquitted. Subsequently, the convicted prisoners brought civil actions against the police for assault. The House of Lords held that it was an abuse of process to bring proceedings amounting to a collateral attack on a decision, reached in previous proceedings, which is adverse to the intending plaintiff. Given that the acquittal of the prison officers had already thrown some doubt on the findings in the Birmingham case, the argument from inconsistency was even at that time somewhat weak. In the light of what has recently transpired about the original convictions, we have even more reason to wonder whether it would really have been an abuse of process to take a look at the convicts' allegations in the civil action. It is to be observed that, even in Mrs Ashmore's case, consistency was not in fact achieved because there had been a case prior to the representative proceedings in which an applicant in a situation similar to that of the appellant did succeed in making out a case of unequal pay. In one respect, Mrs Ashmore's claim to a hearing was stronger than that of the Birmingham Six because she, unlike them, never had an opportunity to present her case in court.

Notwithstanding these misgivings, it would not be right to dismiss the Court of Appeal's concern about multiplicity of litigation and inconsistency as ill founded. It is, however, suggested that these concerns are better addressed within a well though out class action procedure rather than in the context of ad hock tinkering.

In addition to the device of striking out for abuse of process there are other devices for preventing the repeated litigation of identical issues, such as issue estoppel. The connection between these two was considered in *North West Water Ltd v Binnie & Partners* [1990] 3 All ER 547. In an accident that took place in water works carried out by a water authority under the supervision of consultant engineers, several persons were killed or injured. The victims sued the water authority and the consultant engineers. The defendants did not serve pleadings on each other or serve contribution notices, but the water authority argued that the accident was caused by the consultant engineer's negligent design of the works. In the event the consulting engineers were found solely to blame and the victims obtained judgment against them and failed against the water authority. Subsequently, the water authority brought an action against the engineers in tort and contract claiming compensation for damage to the works caused by the engineers' faulty design. Drake J held that it would be an abuse of process for the engineers to relitigate the issue of responsibility since it had already been determined in the earlier action. He further held that in these circumstances the engineers were also prevented by issue estoppel from reopening the question of liability since that issue had already been decided against them in the earlier litigation. This aspect throws into relief the difference between a case of this kind and that of Mrs Ashmore. The consultant engineers had had their day in court and had ample opportunity to advance their case. Moreover, issue estoppel is not an absolute bar, as has been illustrated by *Arnold v National Westminster Bank plc* [1990] 1 All ER 529. The Court of Appeal held that special circumstances, such as the emergence of fresh material or of new developments in the law which showed the issue to have been wrongly decided either in fact or in law, may justify reopening the issue in subsequent proceedings, even between the same parties, if to do so was necessary to work justice between the parties. This rider should also be applied to abuse. If such a test had been considered in Mrs Ashmore's case, it would have been possible to argue that the fact that her circumstances were different from those considered in the representative action and the fact that there were conflicting decisions on the point in issue necessitated a hearing of her claim in order to do justice.

Issue estoppel received further attention in *Crown Estate Commissioners v Dorset County Council* [1990] 1 All ER 19.

Limitation

Under s 33(1) of the Limitation Act 1980 the court has the power to allow an action to proceed after the expiry of the limitation period. In exercising its discretion under this provision the court has to consider, amongst other things, the prejudice that a defendant is likely to suffer from the delay. The question addressed by the House of Lords in *Donovan v Gwentoys Ltd* [1990] 1 All ER 1018, was whether a court is confined to considering the prejudice to the defendant from delay after the lapse of the limitation period or whether it is to have regard to the overall delay from the time that the cause of action arose. It has been decided that all the circumstances must be taken into account, including delay before the expiry of the limitation period. Lord Oliver explained:

> 'The fact that the law permits a plaintiff within prescribed limits to disadvantage a defendant . . . [by delay] does not mean that the defendant is not prejudiced. It merely means that he is not in a position to complain of whatever prejudice he suffers. Once a plaintiff allows the permitted time to elapse, the defendant is no longer subject to that disability, and in a situation in which the court is directed to consider all the circumstances of the case and, to balance the prejudice to the parties, the fact that the claim has, as a result of the plaintiff's failure to use the time allowed to him, become a thoroughly stale claim cannot . . . be irrelevant.'

The logic of this position is unassailable and so is the policy behind it, which is calculated to promote efficiency and avoid delay. It is, however, a pity that last year the House of Lords declined to apply the same policy to inordinate and inexcusable delay in taking or prosecuting proceedings. In this regard, the rule is that the time that has elapsed up to the issue of the writ within the limitation period cannot constitute inordinate delay and cannot be taken into account in determining the risk to fair trial or the prejudice to the defendant; *Department of Transport v Chris Smaller (Transport) Ltd* [1989] 1 All ER 897

(All ER Rev 1989, p 235). There is little sense in having different principles for dealing with what is essentially the same problem: how to protect the defendant from delay caused by the procrastination or deleteriousness of the plaintiff. The principle of the *Donovan* case offers the best solution (see also pp 324–325 below).

Section 24(1) of the Limitation Act 1980 provides that an 'action shall not be brought upon any judgment after the expiration of six years from the date on which the judgment became enforceable'. According to CCR Ord 26, r 17(1) a judgment for the recovery of land is enforceable with a warrant of possession. Such warrant may not be issued without the leave of the court 'where six years or more have elapsed since the date of the judgment'; CCR Ord 26, rr 5(1)(a) and 17(6). It might have been thought that s 24(1) of the Limitation Act 1980 would prevent the issuing of a warrant after the expiration of the six year period but the Court of Appeal has decided otherwise. It held that an application for leave to issue a warrant is not an 'action' for the purpose of that section, thus following an earlier decision which held that the limitation provision is concerned with the substantive right to sue on a judgment and not with the procedural right to issue execution on a judgment. Thus, s 24 bars a substantive action on a judgment but not the process of execution. Whatever the historical validity of such analysis there seems little reason for applying it to local judgments because the effect of an action on a judgment is not so different from execution of judgment to warrant a difference in the application of the limitation period and the need to bring the process of law to an end is present in both.

In two cases this year an identical problem has been considered. A person, 'the insured', employs a broker to take out an insurance with an insurer. The broker negligently, and in breach of contract, fails to disclose material facts to the insurer with the result that when the insured makes a claim on the policy the insurer avoids it. It has been decided that the cause of action accrues, both in contract and in tort, when the insurance is taken out and not when the insurer avoids it, even though the insured does not become aware of the flaw in the policy until he makes a claim on it: *Iron Trade Mutual Insurance Co Ltd v Buckenham Ltd* [1990] 1 All ER 808; *Islander Trucking Ltd v Hogg Robinson & Gardner Mountain (Marine) Ltd* [1990] 1 All ER 826. These decisions, both at first instance, put insured persons acting through brokers in a difficult position (see also Commercial Law, p 21 above and Tort, pp 322–32 below). They may yet have to be reconsidered because while it is true that the insured suffers a harm at the time that the voidable policy is taken out, it is also true that quite a different harm is inflicted on the insured when the policy is actually avoided by the insurer, since up to that time the policy is valid and the insurer may choose to honour it; *Fraser v B N Furman (Productions) Ltd* [1967] 1 WLR 898; *Dunbar v A & B Painters* [1986] 2 Lloyd's Rep 38; cf *Banque Financiere de la Cité SA v Westgate Insurance Co Ltd* [1990] 2 All ER 947.

A party who has been added as a defendant by amendment of the writ under Ord 20, r 1, may seek an order under Ord 16, r 6(2)(a) that he should cease to be a party on the ground that the limitation period has expired. However, a claim that the limitation period has expired is not always self evident, as where it is doubtful when the damage complained of has actually occurred. Does the defendant seeking to be left out of the action have to show that he has an arguable case that the limitation period has elapsed, or does he have to show that he has a conclusive case? The Court of Appeal decided that it is the latter: *Leicester Wholesale Fruit Market Ltd v Grundy* [1990] 1 All ER 442.

Interim payment

Neill LJ has set out in *Schott Kem Ltd v Bentley* [1990] 3 All ER 850, the principles governing orders for interim payment, incorporating in a useful summary the rulings made by the courts over the past few years. As these matters have been discussed in previous surveys of the All ER Review it is not necessary to go into them in any detail. There are, however, two points that deserve mention. Neill LJ rejected the argument that a plaintiff will not be able to obtain interim payment unless he could show real need. Although it is customary in personal injury cases to limit payments to sums for which the plaintiff can show a need, this is because in such cases it might be difficult to enforce orders for the return of the payments. Beyond this type of case, however, the court is free to make orders that are just in view of the considerations mentioned in Ord 29. This is, of course, right since the aim of the rules is not so much to avoid hardship to the plaintiff as to ensure that the plaintiff is spared waiting for payment where his entitlement is not open to dispute. The other matter clarified by Neill LJ concerns the form of orders when two or more defendants are liable and the apportionment between them.

Jurisdiction and forum non conveniens

Two cases deal with the affect of the Civil Jurisdiction and Judgments Act 1982 on the plea of forum non conveniens: *S & W Berisford plc v New Hampshire Insurance Co* [1990] 2 All ER 321; *Arkwright Mutual Insurance Co v Bryanston Insurance Co Ltd* [1990] 2 All ER 335.

Issues concerning stay on the grounds of unsuitability of forum were also considered in *Arab Monetary Fund v Hashim (No 3)* [1990] 1 All ER 685.

Constraints of space do not, unfortunately, allow for commentary on these cases.

Exchange of witness statements

Order 38, r 2A was amended in 1988. The facility for ordering exchange of witness statement is no longer confined to the Chancery and Commercial courts but may be employed in all cases in the High Court. Judge Dorby QC has explained in *Richard Saunders & Partners (a firm) v Eastglen Ltd* [1990] 3 All ER 946, that simultaneous exchange of proofs of oral evidence will be ordered irrespective of whether the evidence is technical or is source material, except where such course is found to be inappropriate. It may, for example, be sensible to refrain from making an order in a fraud case so as to preserve the element of surprise in the examination of witnesses. Similarly, exchange of statements will not be ordered where it is likely to be oppressive or cause delay.

Costs

Taxation

A client who is dissatisfied with his solicitor's bill may obtain an order of taxation as a matter of right, if he applies within one month from the delivery of the bill: Solicitors Act 1974, s 70(1). Once the month has expired, he can obtain an order for taxation as a matter of discretion and on such terms as the court thinks fit under s 70(2) of the 1974 Act. But s 70(4) provides that the power to order taxation 'shall not be exercisable on an application made by the party chargeable with the bill after the expiration of 12 months from the payment of the bill . . .'. The House of Lords has held in *Harrison v Tew* [1990] 1 All ER 321 (see pp 254–255 below) that the 1974 Act constitutes a comprehensive arrangement in this regard and that a court has no power to order taxation after the expiration of the time limit. Thereafter, an aggrieved client is confined to his remedies in contract or may complain of serious professional misconduct. If the client takes the latter course, the burden of proof rests on him to prove misconduct but if he succeeds in doing so, the bill may be referred to the taxing master and a refund could be ordered.

Payment of costs by solicitor

Holden & Co (a firm) v Crown Prosecution Service [1990] 1 All ER 368, was concerned with the court's power to make orders of costs against solicitors in criminal cases but some observations concern civil practice. Order 62, r 11, which empowers the court to order solicitors to pay costs that have been incurred unreasonably or improperly, it was explained, encapsulates the common law rule whereby solicitors may be charged for costs caused by their serious dereliction of duty. The object of such orders is not punitive but is limited to recovering costs actually incurred as a result of misconduct.

Costs on appeal

Where a tenant's application for a new tenancy under the Landlord and Tenant Act 1954 is dismissed, the tenant has a right of appeal under the County Courts Act 1984. By s 64(1) of the 1954 Act, the effect of an appeal is to extend the tenancy until three months after the decision of the appeal. The tenant in *Burgess v Stafford Hotel Ltd* [1990] 3 All ER 222 'played the system' and lodged a groundless appeal to obtain an extension of his tenancy. Even so, the Court of Appeal has decided, there is no justification for ordering the tenant to pay costs on an indemnity basis because a person who takes advantage of a right of appeal cannot be said to be behaving disgracefully or deserving moral condemnation. The landlord's remedy in such a situation is to apply for an order to strike out the notice of appeal (see further discussion of *Burgess v Stafford Hotel Ltd* p 222 below) or for an order of security for costs.

Appeal

Appeal by contemnor

In *X Ltd v Morgan-Grampian (Publishers) Ltd* [1990] 2 All ER 1, discussed above, the judge ordered a journalist to disclose the source of the stolen information that was communicated to him. When he refused, the judge postponed dealing with his contempt pending an appeal. When the matter came before the Court of Appeal, the court gave the journalist the option of either complying with the judge's order and purging the contempt or, alternatively, depositing the material in question in a sealed envelope with the Court of Appeal pending the determination of the appeal against the disclosure order. The journalist refused. The House of Lords decided that where a contemnor not only refuses to comply with an order but also makes it clear that he would continue to defy the court whatever the outcome of the appeal, the court has a discretion to decline to entertain the appeal. This is so not only because a person who flouts the authority of the court has forfeited the right to be heard but also because it would be unfair to the respondent to have to defend on appeal, when the appellant has made it clear that he would not comply even if the respondent was successful.

Applications for leave to appeal

The operation of the new rules in Ord 59 governing applications for leave to appeal was explained in *R G Carter Ltd v Clarke* [1990] 2 All ER 209. Under the old Ord 59, r 14(2), an application for leave from the Court of Appeal was made ex parte and, if the judge was satisfied that the application should be refused, the matter would end there. But if he thought that the application might succeed, he had to adjourn it to enable the proposed respondent to be heard. Under the new r 14(2)–(2B), consideration by the single judge is on the basis of written material and he is empowered to grant or refuse the application or direct it to be considered in open court either ex parte or inter partes. The purpose is to dispose of clear cases, where leave may clearly be granted or withheld, without the need for two hearings. The intention is that only in a minority of cases, requiring argument or further material, would it be necessary to direct that the application be renewed in open court. However, the rules enable the affected party to seek rehearing: where an application has been refused, the applicant may renew his application ex parte in open court; where the application has been granted, other than after a hearing inter partes, the respondent may apply to have the leave reconsidered inter partes in open court. In *R G Carter Ltd v Clarke* the hope was expressed that parties will not unnecessarily waste time and money in renewing applications after an ex parte decision by a single judge. This point received further emphasis from the Master of the Rolls in *The Iran Nabuvat* [1990] 3 All ER 9, where he explained that where a single Lord Justice has found that an appeal is arguable and has given leave:

> 'it is really necessary . . . for anybody seeking reconsideration of that to be able to point fairly and unerringly to a factor which was not drawn to the Lord Justice's attention, because, perhaps, it did not feature in the documents which had been studied, or to the fact that he has overlooked some statutory provision which is decisive, or some authority which is decisive, in the sense that the appeal will inevitably fail.'

Otherwise, he explained, the bias must be in favour of allowing the Full Court to consider the appeal. Litigants who fail to observe these principles may find themselves saddled with costs.

R G Carter Ltd v Clarke presented the Court of Appeal with a conflict between two different policies of non-interference on appeal. The plaintiff applied for summary judgment but the judge gave unconditional leave to defend. The plaintiff's application for leave to appeal against this decision was granted by a single Lord Justice, who considered the grounds of appeal to be arguable. The defendant applied for reconsideration inter partes in open court. Lord Donaldson MR explained that two opposing principles were at work here. Where a judge of first instance has given leave to defend because he thought that the defendant had an arguable defence, the policy is not to interfere with the judge's decision since it is unlikely that two or three judges in the Court of Appeal would consider that there is no such arguable defence. But, as we have just seen, there is also a policy, reflected in Ord 59, r 14(2), that where a single Lord Justice has given leave on the basis that there is an arguable ground of appeal, the Court of Appeal will not interfere with his conclusion for similar reasons. In the conflict between these two policies, it has been decided, the former should prevail because leave to defend does not settle the matter once and for all, whereas a reversal on appeal of the judge's decision to give leave would, in effect, deprive the defendant of his day in court and settle the matter for ever.

Striking out notice of appeal

Order 18, r 19, confers on the court a jurisdiction to strike out pleadings which disclose no reasonable cause, or which are frivolous or vexatious, or which constitute an abuse of the process of the court. But this rule does not apply to a notice of appeal which is not a pleading. The Court of Appeal has decided in *Burgess v Stafford Hotel Ltd* [1990] 3 All ER 222, that the court has an inherent jurisdiction to strike out a notice of appeal on the same grounds. However, Glidewell LJ warned against abuse by respondents of this jurisdiction and said that application for striking out should be made only in clear cases where no extensive inquiries into facts are necessary.

Prisons

I M YEATS, BCL, MA
Barrister, Senior Lecturer in Law, Queen Mary and Westfield College,
University of London

In two cases the Court of Appeal has had to consider the remedies available to prisoners if the circumstances of their imprisonment are illegal, either through a breach of the relevant rules or otherwise. The prisoner may have a public law remedy if the rules have been wrongly applied or if a particular rule, circular or direction is invalid. This may sometimes provide a practical remedy, immediate or long-term, if it brings the illegal conditions of detention to an end or ensures that the situation is not repeated. It may, however, be of no benefit to the individual prisoner if, for instance, the illegality has already ceased or the term of imprisonment has ended. The prisoner retains his civil rights other than those necessarily forfeited by loss of liberty; he can therefore bring a civil action in tort, for instance in battery, negligence or misfeasance in a public office. These however either apply only in narrow circumstances or require proof of actual damage.

Is there, and should there be, a cause of action if the conditions of detention are unlawful but the prisoner suffers no actual damage? It has been accepted in the two recent cases by the Court of Appeal that there is no civil action for a breach of the Prison Rules. A claim in false imprisonment is more problematical. In *Weldon v Home Office* [1990] 3 All ER 672 the prisoner alleged that he had been removed from his cell to a punishment cell and then to a strip cell and kept there overnight unclothed. The Court of Appeal refused to strike out a claim in false imprisonment as the allegations had not been proved to be unarguable, since they were based on interference with residual liberty or the deliberate imposition of intolerable conditions, and sufficiently alleged want of good faith on the part of prison officers (see also pp 326–328 below). In *R v Deputy Governor of Parkhurst Prison, ex p Hague* [1990] 3 All ER 687 the prisoner established (as explained below) that his segregation under r 43 of the Prison Rules 1964 (SI 1964/388) as amended had not been properly carried out. The Court of Appeal rejected a claim in false imprisonment, principally on the ground that there was no evidence of intolerable conditions, but also took a less enthusiastic view of the availability of such a claim at all (see also pp 328–329 below).

False imprisonment is not well suited for the purpose; it is a remedy for the total deprivation of liberty and not for interferences with the plaintiff's freedom to do what he likes. The deprivation of liberty results from the conviction by a competent court and from s 12 of the Prison Act 1952 which allows a convicted person to be 'lawfully confined in any prison'. That section ordinarily provides a defence of lawful justification to any claim in false imprisonment.

There are two ways in which it can be argued that a claim in false imprisonment can be made good. The first is that if the conditions of detention are unlawful, the statutory defence in s 12 is wholly destroyed. The difficulty is that the detention is authorised by the statute, and therefore cannot itself normally be unlawful. It is different from the legality of an arrest where, if the arresting officer neglects some essential procedure or does not have the requisite reasonable belief, the procedure of arrest itself is flawed and ceases to afford a valid defence. In *Hague*, Nicholls LJ (at 709) could:

> 'see no room in principle . . . for the retention of any residual right against the prison authorities. False imprisonment is the wrongful deprivation of a person of his liberty: P is wrongfully detained by D in a particular place (or places). Thus if P is *lawfully* detained by D in a particular place, ex hypothesi the detention cannot constitute wrongful imprisonment by D. But that is precisely what occurs when a person is committed to prison. When a person is committed to prison, the prison authorities may lawfully detain him in any place authorised by statute, viz today, in any prison.'

The cases have, however, recognised an apparent exception to this principle, where the conditions of detention are intolerable or dangerous. This, as Taylor LJ expresses it (at 707), 'can be reconciled with the established definition. Such conditions would negative the statutory defence of lawful detention'. In other words, Parliament did not, by s 12, authorise detention in intolerable conditions; such detention is not detention 'in any prison'. If that is so, it is not clear why the prison authorities should have to have knowledge of the conditions or act in bad faith, for detention in intolerable conditions is either permitted or it is not. In *Weldon*, for the purposes of rejecting a striking out application, it was assumed to be relevant. Taylor LJ was surely right to question this (at 707), since 'to require proof of bad faith would be to alter the tort of false imprisonment and in effect to create a new tort special to prisons and prisoners'.

False imprisonment within imprisonment could in some situations be explained differently, namely that the prison authorities had confined the prisoner more narrowly (and/or for longer) than was justified by the rules normally applied. This cannot often be applicable. The prison authorities must determine where within the prison detention is to be effected; the prisoner cannot choose his cell or have the run of the entire prison. Complaints are normally about treatment or conditions, eg that the prisoner is in a cell by himself. Although the court in *Weldon* perhaps implied that in some circumstances an action could be advanced on this basis (at 681–682), Nicholls LJ in *Hague* thought that the:

> 'feature of the r 43 regime which comes closest to "imprisonment" is the restriction imposed on the prisoner against leaving his cell, as do other prisoners, and associating with them for meals, work or recreation. But, even here, the complaint is about treatment.'

If, however, an action can be maintained on this basis, bad faith might not be irrelevant. It would then make sense to say that there was a defence if the prison officers reasonably believed that the circumstances justified such detention.

It remains to explain why Hague's detention was unlawful. The deputy governor of Parkhurst Prison had arranged for the transfer of Hague, who had been causing trouble there, to Wormwood Scrubs prison. In accordance with prison department circular instruction 10/1974 he made the transfer subject to Hague being segregated under r 43 at Wormwood Scrubs. He also obtained authority from the regional director of the prison service in accordance with the circular for segregation to continue for up to 28 days. Hague obtained a declaration that the circular was contrary to r 43 and invalid in two respects. Rule 43 enabled a governor to regulate and manage his own prison and he could not validly be required to segregate a prisoner by the governor of another institution; further, the circular required the regional director routinely to grant a 28-day extension whereas he should, under r 43, give a reasoned decision as to segregation and as to the appropriate period. Two other grounds of challenge failed. The rules of natural justice do not require a prisoner to be heard before a decision is made under r 43 and he is not entitled in all circumstances to a statement of reasons for his removal from association. In any case Hague did have notice of the reasons.

The final point of interest centres on the remedies. Hague obtained declarations that the circular was invalid but was refused certiorari to quash the decision in his case. In itself it was of no value, since he was no longer detained in Wormwood Scrubs, but he was refused it also on the grounds that he had suffered no injustice, because his removal from association for the full period could validly have been achieved. This raises three difficulties, none of which was fully developed. First, the fact that the same decision would certainly have been reached is not always a reason for refusing a remedy where there has been a breach of natural justice or where there has been neglect of an express procedural requirement. Secondly, if Hague would otherwise have had a valid action for false imprisonment, it would be an injustice to impede that claim by refusing to quash the decision to segregate. Thirdly, it is not clear why the decision had to be quashed and not merely held unlawful before the action in tort could proceed. A court can surely award damages after an unlawful arrest without formally quashing the warrant of or decision to arrest. Why should an unlawful detention raise different problems?

Two other cases in part relating to prisons are referred to elsewhere. For *Knight v Home Office* [1990] 3 All ER 237, see Medical Law, pp 190–193 above and for *R v Parole Board, ex p Bradley* [1990] 3 All ER 828, see Family Law at p 149 above.

Shipping Law

R P GRIME, BA, BCL
BT (Marine) Ltd Professor of Law, University of Southampton

At the beginning of 1991, all the signs are that, in shipping matters, insurance is set fair to be the litigants' flavour of the decade, in replacement of such hardy perennials of the 1980s as Bills of Lading Under Charterparties and Cargo Receivers' Title to Sue. With the imminence of a new Bills of Lading Act (however it may be entitled), perhaps some of the case law problems of the 1980s are to be answered by the statutes of the 1990s. However, either in contradiction of or exception to such a perceived tendency, the All England Law Reports for 1990 offered only one serious marine insurance case. Indeed, compared with last year, our shipping law crop has been generally rather poor.

Direct action against marine liability insurers

Law students of the author's generation remember well the case of *Vandepitte v Preferred Accident Insurance Corporation of New York* [1933] AC 70, in which Alice Vandepitte, injured in a motor accident partly by the negligence of Jean Berry, a minor driving her father's car with his consent, sought to recover compensation for her injuries from the insurance company which had issued a policy to Jean Berry's father – a policy which covered liabilities incurred by any person driving with the consent of the assured. Mrs Vandepitte failed in the Supreme Court of Canada and in the Privy Council. The aforementioned law students, righteously incensed by the idea that, even when the English Parliament had in its wisdom declared that all motorists must insure against third party liabilities, it looked rather as if the obscurantist common law courts might not allow those same third-party accident victims the benefit of that provision, would be (rather wearily) referred to the Third Parties (Rights Against Insurers) Act 1930, passed in the same year as compulsory third-party insurance was statutorily required of motorists. The unspoken assumption seemed to be that we do things better in the Old Country.

But do we? The drafting of the 1930 Act seems to have come straight from a very high (and rather beautiful) ivory tower. It does not say (as similarly intended statutes in some other jurisdictions have said) that an unsatisfied judgment obtained against an insured person may be enforced against the insurer of the liability that gave rise to the judgment. Still more does it not say, as a draftsman from a civilian background might have been tempted to say, that a third-party insurance policy, being a contract for the benefit of another, might properly be enforced as a contract by the intended beneficiary. No, our statute operates by way of statutory assignment.

Section 1(1) provides that 'where under any contract of insurance a person . . . is insured against liabilities to third parties which he may incur, then', if he becomes insolvent (defined with wide-ranging precision) and if he incurs such liability, before or after the insolvency, 'his rights against the insurer

. . . shall . . . be transferred to and vest in the third party to whom the liability was incurred'. No need for any judgment against the insured, nor any action by the third party. Simply insurance, liability and insolvency. The solution has a certain elegance. The question is, does it work? From the first, even in motor insurance it was not regarded as a wholly successful experiment. The position was seen to require strengthening in 1934 by the provisions of s 10 of the Road Traffic Act. Further extended, these can now be found in s 149 of the Road Traffic Act 1972.

In order to deal with an obvious escape route, the 1930 Act then proceeds to prohibit the insertion into policies of provisions designed to deactivate the cover in the event of insolvency. This task is executed in very general terms by s 1(3), which provides that 'insofar as any contract of insurance . . . purports whether directly or indirectly, to avoid the contract or to alter the rights of the parties thereunder upon the happening to the insured of any of the events specified [ie insolvency as defined] the contract shall be of no effect'.

Ships are not motor-cars. Except in connection with oil pollution, third-party liability insurance is not compulsory for shipowners. They do, of course, insure as a matter of good business practice. For historical reasons, with the exception of certain property claims arising out of collisions between ships, shipowners' liabilities are almost invariably insured by 'P & I Clubs', Protection and Indemnity Associations. These are mutual corporations, governed by and representative of the insured 'Members', whose unlimited cover (the 'Rules') extends to most liabilities incidental to the operation of ships. In particular, P & I Club Rules cover cargo claims.

There is nothing in the Third Parties (Rights Against Insurers) Act 1930 to limit its application to the social problem which gave rise to its passage. It applies, therefore, to claims against shipowners. The Clubs have never been enthusiastic about direct action claims, whether under our or another state's statutory provisions, or even through the application of third party beneficiary principles. Their position is clearly maintained. This is done by reliance upon an essential analytic difference in this type of insurance.

A distinction may properly be drawn between the insurance of a *liability* and *indemnity* insurance. In the former, the insurer agrees to underwrite his assured's liabilities, where necessary standing in his shoes, fighting the action on his behalf and meeting the final cost. In the latter, the insurer agrees only to make good any expenses actually incurred by the assured: the policy covers, in traditional language, that which the insured 'shall become liable to pay and shall have paid'. The distinction is one which was recognised in equity. In liability insurance, it was thought that the policy might be specifically enforced (at the suit of the assured) by an order that the insurer pay directly to the third party (see per Pickford LJ in *British Union and National Insurance Co v Rawson* [1916] 2 Ch 476 at 482, relying on *In re Law Guarantee Trust and Accident Society* [1914] 2 Ch 617, dicta referred to by Lord Brandon in the case under review). The rule never applied to indemnities, in the sense described above. There the common law rule stood: the assured must meet the third-party claim and sue for damages on the insurance policy or other indemnity contract (see *Johnston v Salvage Association* (1887) 19 QBD 458, a case on the Sue and Labour Clause in the Hull Policy).

The Clubs most definitely do not behave as liability insurers. They never stand in their Members' shoes. Their foreign 'correspondents' do not act as agents of the Members. The lawyers appointed in respect of litigation involving Members act for the Members, despite their looking to the Club (in a business sense) for the ultimate payment of their fees – a circumstance replete with problems of professional ethics in the USA. Above all, the rule is 'pay to be paid' or 'payment first', that is, the Club cover is expressed to follow actual payment by the Member. It is the Member to whom the third party must look for payment, despite the fact that all concerned (including the Member's bankers) proceed in the happy confidence that the Club will eventually foot the bill.

Does 'pay to be paid' defeat the 1930 Act? If a shipowner goes bankrupt and abandons a voyage, can his Club defeat the claim under s 1(1) of the Act by showing that, since the Member-carrier has never paid the cargo-claim, there is no 'right against the insurer under the contract' to be transferred? The factual circumstance is sadly not uncommon. The issue, however, has taken a long time properly to come to judgment.

In *The Allobrogia* [1979] 1 Lloyd's Rep 190, a case in the Companies Court, a cargo claimant sought to wind up a single-ship company as 'the only means available' to recover unsatisfied judgment debts of the company from the Club in which the ship was entered. The Club resisted the petition but failed to satisfy Slade J that the cargo-owner's claim 'had no reasonable prospect of success'. In the same year, in *The Vainqueur Jose* [1979] 1 Lloyd's Rep 557, Mocatta J held that a Club might properly resist a claim in respect of a Member who 'by an extraordinary mixture of action and inaction' had allowed a cargo-claim to go against him by default, had not given any notice to the Club and had been wound up. The Club's defence might be based on either of two grounds: a failure by the Member to comply with mandatory notice requirements in the Rules or the Member's failure to behave (also as required by the Rules) as a 'prudent uninsured shipowner'. Neither case addressed the central issue: whether 'pay to be paid' meant that there was no 'insured liability' in P & I Club Membership.

The issue was, however, faced in *Firma C-Trade SA v Newcastle Protection and Indemnity Association, The Fanti; Socony Mobil Oil Co Inc v West of England Ship Owners Mutual Insurance Association (London) Ltd, The Padre Island* [1990] 2 All ER 705 (see also Commercial law, pp 22–23 above). Two cases were heard as consolidated appeals by the Court of Appeal and the House of Lords. In *The Fanti* at first instance ([1987] 2 Lloyd's Rep 299), Staughton J had found for the claimants. The effect of s 1(1) of the 1930 Act was to transfer to the cargo-owner the shipowner/Member's contractual right against the Club. That right was distinguishable from a cause of action. It was a contractual right that was subject to the condition that the Member should first pay. After the statutory assignment that condition became a requirement that the assignee/claimant/cargo-owner pay himself. That was either impossible or futile and could be disregarded. In any event, the 'pay to be paid' clause was a term which indirectly affected the rights of the parties on the insolvency of the Member, and was so caught by the prohibition in s 1(3) of the Act. In this latter conclusion, Staughton J relied substantially upon the judgment of Slade J in *The Allobrogia* that the use of the word 'indirectly' in s 1(3) was intended to include provisions which 'had the substantial effect' of altering rights on insolvency, even when those provisions did not mention insolvency in terms, and, to a lesser extent, upon the decision of the Court of Appeal (Lord Denning MR, Diplock and Russell LJJ) in *Joseph v Joseph* [1967] Ch 78, that the word 'purport' (also used in s 1(3)) meant 'has the effect of' rather than 'profess'. He might also have been to some extent affected by the concession by counsel for the Club that 'pay to be paid' was intended 'to ensure, if lawfully possible, that a third party had no direct claim'. The concession was later withdrawn. Historically, it may be true for all that.

The judgment in *The Fanti* was delivered on 24 April. Almost exactly three months later Saville J came to an exactly opposite conclusion in *The Padre Island (No 2)* [1987] 2 Lloyd's Rep 529. The Member at no time had a right to be indemnified. At most he had a contingent right against the Club, which was in no way affected by the insolvency. Thus, the 'pay to be paid' clause had no effect, direct or indirect, upon the insurance contract on the occasion of the Member's insolvency.

The two conflicting cases were delivered to the Court of Appeal ([1989] 1 Lloyd's Rep 239). Bingham LJ gave the leading judgment. He agreed with the first ground adopted by Staughton J. The Member had no cause of action when liability accrued but did have a right subject to the 'condition of prior payment'. The condition, on the statutory assignment, became impossible of performance as it involved payment to oneself, and so was ineffective. However, he did not agree with his second ground. 'Pay to be paid' did not fall foul of s 1(3). It did not have the 'substantial effect' of altering rights on insolvency. At most, it altered the chance of enjoying those rights.

The House of Lords reversed the Court of Appeal. Lord Brandon, displaying what (in another context) a national newspaper once described as his 'rat-trap logic', posed three questions: what rights did the Members have under their contracts against the Club immediately before their insolvency?; did the 'pay to be paid' provision purport, directly or indirectly, to avoid the contracts or alter the rights of the parties on the members' being wound up?; having regard to the answers to the first two questions, what rights against the Club, if any, were transferred on the winding-up?

In answer to the first question, the Member had only a right to indemnity contingent upon the condition precedent of prior payment. 'Pay to be paid' was not caught by s 1(3) because it applied throughout the membership not just on insolvency. What was transferred by the Act was a right subject to a condition which could not be disregarded because it was not part of the intention of the 1930 legislators to place the assignee in a better position than the original assured.

Lord Goff gave a longer speech, to the same effect. He did, however, identify a difficulty with the 'futility' argument which had impressed Staughton J and Bingham LJ. The latter had expressed his position by describing what was transferred as being composed of a 'benefit' (the right to claim) and a 'burden' (the payment to the third party): using the language of property, the transferee, taking the benefit, must take the burden, the discharge of which in his hands was futile. But, pointed out Lord Goff, the 'burden' was not an obligation imposed upon the Member. He did not have to pay the third party. If he did, he might be indemnified. It simply defined his entitlement. His Lordship had a degree more difficulty with the so-called 'equity' argument. It proceeds thus: the common law implied or assumed a prior payment rule, since it allowed only an action for damages after payment to the third party; equity, however, would look to the substance and order payment by the indemnifier to the third party; a contractual condition of prior payment could not be allowed to displace the equity. For Lord Goff that misrepresented the position. Although Clubs may (and in practice often do) make direct payment to claimants, this must not be taken as the performance of any obligation: the Club merely waives 'pay to be paid'. For his part, Lord Brandon doubted whether equity could override the express contractual provision of 'pay to be paid'. Both, in substance, are distinguishing the indemnity provided by P & I Club membership from 'true' liability insurance.

This must, in the end, be the point of principle. It is one well known in those jurisdictions which do not adopt a binding rule of privity of contract. Third party beneficiaries in such jurisdictions may enforce contracts made for their benefit, but a contract to indemnify a person after payment to a third party is not such a contract: it is made for the benefit of the assured, not the third party.

Two practical points might be made. The case law in shipping has been about cargo-claims and insolvent carriers. That such claimants may be left without recourse against the carriers' insurers will not wring many withers. The situation presented to the draughtsmen of the Third Parties (Rights Against Insurers) Act 1930 was different. They were faced with a mounting road-toll and uncompensated injured citizens. What, one wonders, would have been the political reaction in the entirely unlikely situation that the *Herald of Free Enterprise* had been owned by an insolvent, non-paying, owner whose P & I Club resisted payment on the grounds of the 'pay to be paid' clause? Might not legislation swiftly have followed?

Finally, much time and effort is already being spent on finding ways round the decision. In *The Allobrogia*, Slade J perhaps gave a hint. While dealing with the question of whether the 'pay to be paid' provision presented insuperable problems for the petitioners, he said ([1979] 1 Lloyd's Rep at 197):

> 'I am not entirely convinced that it would ex hypothesi be impossible. I am not certain, for example, that with the co-operation of the petitioners and a future liquidator of the company a scheme could not be devised which enabled the liquidator to discharge the company's debt to the petitioners out of borrowed money, which in turn would in due course be repaid directly or indirectly out of the proceeds of the claim against the association. It could, perhaps, be that such a scheme would achieve sufficient compliance with the condition precedent . . . to give rise to a right to recovery from the association.'

Would a liquidator be so entitled? The Club may, of course, have a defence, a counterclaim or a set-off. Would such a scheme operate the Act for the benefit of the claimant? Time, and the courts, will no doubt tell.

Limitation funds and procedural creativity

A short but interesting point was raised in a preliminary proceedings arising out of the terrible *Marchioness* disaster in August 1989. In *The Bowbelle* [1990] 3 All ER 476, the owners of the *Bowbelle*, co-defendants in the action arising out of the collision, sought restriction of those proceedings to the limitation fund established under the Merchant Shipping Act 1979, the statute which introduced the 1976 London Convention on Limitation of Liability for Maritime Claims. In other words, they wished to ensure the secure finality of the constituted fund in respect of all liabilities that might arise from the disaster.

The right to limit (or to seek limitation of) maritime claims belongs to the defendant. It may simply be invoked as a defence, and this may be by far the easiest way of proceeding when there is a single claim arising out of one incident. But limitation proceedings also operate as a kind of localised bankruptcy: that is to say, all claims arising 'on any distinct occasion' are aggregated and satisfied, if necessary being rateably reduced, from the 'fund' calculated in accordance with the regime of limitation in force. Where there may be several claims, therefore, it may be sensible to 'constitute' such a fund. In English law, it has always been possible for the defendant to take limitation proceedings to this end. In some jurisdictions (eg Japan), such a procedure is mandatory. Article 10 of the 1976 Limitation Convention allows for states party to the Convention, by their national law, to adopt such a mandatory rule for the constitution of a limitation fund, but the Merchant Shipping Act 1979 did not do so. However, even in permissive form, the Convention's procedure on the constitution of a limitation fund was introduced and, shades of *The Hollandia* [1982] 3 All ER 1141 (All ER Rev 1982, p 253), has 'the force of law' in the UK (Merchant Shipping Act 1979, s 17(1)).

Article 5 of the 1957 Limitation Convention, the predecessor of the 1976 Convention, addressed the issue of the security of the limitation fund by providing for the release of any arrested ship or of any bail or equivalent security 'if it is established that the shipowner has already given satisfactory bail or other security in a sum equal to the full limit of his liability'. The 1957 Convention was implemented in the UK 'old style': that is to say, instead of its provisions being given 'the force of law' (as was done with the 1976 Convention), they were translated into the form of an English statute, with appropriate terminology, and so enacted. And it is the words of the statute that govern, not the words of the Convention, a fruitful source of confusion and frustration (see, among an embarrassment of material, *The Norwhale* [1975] 2 All ER 501; *The Annie Hay* [1968] 1 All ER 657; *The Alastor* [1981] 1 Lloyd's Rep 501). So Article 5 of the 1957 Convention was enacted by s 5 of the Merchant Shipping (Liability of Shipowners and Others) Act 1958 which begins 'where a ship or other property is arrested in connection with a claim which appears to the Court to be founded on a liability to which a limit is set . . .' The formulation 'appears to the Court' on its face required the court to examine the substance of the matter. So, in *The Wladyslaw Lokietec* [1978] 2 Lloyd's Rep 520, Brandon J held that to obtain protection from further arrest the shipowner had to show that 'there was no serious question to be tried' that he might lose his right to limit through his actual fault or privity. That decision, according to Sheen J in the instant case, 'frustrated the use of s 5'.

It will be recalled that under the 1957 Convention, the right to limit was lost in the event of the 'actual fault or privity' of the shipowner, disproof of which lay with the defendant seeking to limit: under the 1976 Convention, limitation is broken only on proof of 'a personal act or omission committed with intent to cause such loss or recklessly and with knowledge that such loss would probably result', proof of which lies upon the claimant seeking to defeat limitation. So, in any event, the room for the practical operation of the *Wladyslaw Lokietek* would necessarily be considerably limited under the new law. But that is not to the point. Article II of the 1976 Convention allows for the constitution of a fund in any state party 'in which legal proceedings are instituted in respect of claims subject to limitation'. Article 13 provides (a) that any person who has made a claim against the fund is barred from 'exercising any right . . . against any other assets' and (b) that any ship or other property of the defendant who has constituted the fund may be released from arrest at the suit of any who may have a claim against the fund, and must be so released if the fund has been constituted in an appropriate jurisdiction, including the place where the occurrence happened. Both Articles 'have the force of law' in the UK. Sheen J concluded that, in such circumstances, the matter is concluded and 'the Court is not required to investigate the question whether the shipowner has been guilty of conduct barring limitation'.

But although the policy is clear, leaving no room for judicial adjustment, and the owners of the *Bowbelle*, having constituted a fund in England, are entitled to have their assets freed from interference, the availability of an entirely appropriate procedure is far less obvious. There is nothing in the Convention prohibiting future arrests. But the effect of Article 13 is to require the court to order the release of any property that might be arrested. Sheen J appealed to that fertile mother of the common law, common sense:

> 'In these circumstances common sense dictates that there should be some machinery by which warning can be given to would be arresters that they should not arrest any of the ships belonging to the owners of the *Bowbelle*. The current Rules of the Supreme Court have not made provision for this situation. Until such provision is made, shipowners who wish to provide some protection against unnecessary dislocation of trade caused by the arrest of their ships should file in the Admiralty and Commercial Registry a praecipe which must be signed by their solicitor who must undertake to acknowledge service of the writ in any action which may be begun against the owners of the ship in question and state that a limitation fund in respect of damage arising from the relevant incident has been constituted by payment into court of the appropriate amount.
>
> Any person who has a claim arising out of the same incident and who wishes to contend that the conduct of the shipowner bars his right to limitation may nevertheless pursue that allegation but he will not have the security provided by the arrest of the ship.'

The procedure adapted by Sheen J for this purpose is that of the caveat against arrest, under RSC Ord 75, r 6.

Misdelivery and theft in the Court of Appeal

In All ER Review 1989 we noted, at p 266, that the decision of Hirst J in *Cia Portorafti Commerciale SA v Ultramar Panama Inc, The Captain Gregos*, there reviewed, had been unanimously reversed by the Court of Appeal on 14 December 1989. At the time of writing last year's Review, the decision had not been reported. It now has been, at [1990] 3 All ER 967.

The issue before Hirst J had been whether a carrier who allegedly stole the cargo could nonetheless rely upon the one-year time-bar in Art III(6) of the

Hague-Visby Rules. The Article applies the time-bar to 'all liability whatsoever in respect of the goods', a formulation which replaces its application by the Hague Rules to 'all liability in respect of loss or damage'. However, Hirst J, claiming a 'broad and purposive approach', had given a somewhat narrower interpretation than these wide words might have been thought to support: Art III had to be read as a 'package' with the other Rules and was thus to be confined in its operation to the 'risks' as set out in Art II. Since Art II envisaged carriage of the goods to their destination, all misdelivery, honest as well as dishonest, lay outside the time-bar. The 'package' approach derived substantially from dicta of Kerr LJ in *D/S A/S Idaho v Peninsular and Oriental Steam Navigation Co, The Strathnewton* [1983] 1 Lloyd's Rep 219.

The Court of Appeal did not adopt the package approach. Neither Art II (which defines the operational scope of the 'responsibilities and liabilities' and 'rights and immunities' set out elsewhere in the Rules), nor yet the definition of 'carriage of goods' in Art I(*e*), should be read so as to restrict the application of Art III, which establishes (subject to the exceptions set out in Art IV) the duties of the carrier and the shipper. Art II(2) ('the carrier shall properly and carefully load, handle, stow, carry, keep, care for, and discharge the goods carried') was clearly broken by deliberate misdelivery as well as by what happened in the instant case: the carrier sailing away with part of the cargo having made short delivery at the end of the voyage.

The cargo interests, however, were not suing on the bill of lading for a breach of Art III(2). Their action was in tort and furthermore centred on events which had occurred after the carriage (and bailment) had ended. Bingham LJ acceded, with somewhat greater alacrity than that showed by Hirst J in the court below, to the suggestion of Lords Wilberforce and Scarman in *Gatoil International Inc v Arkwright-Boston Manufacturers Mutual Insurance Co* [1985] 1 All ER 129 (noted in All ER Rev 1985 at p 238) that reference might be made to the travaux préparatoires. The Stockholm Conference had evinced a clear intention that 'the time limit would apply even if the conduct alleged . . . did not amount to breaches of the Hague-Visby obligations'. Nor was there anything in the point that the wrong had allegedly been committed after the bailment constituted by the carriage had terminated. Such was the position in *Port Jackson Stevedoring Pty Ltd v Salmond & Spraggon (Australia) Pty Ltd, The New York Star* [1980] 3 All ER 257, and Lord Wilberforce, in delivering the opinion of the Privy Council in that case, had made it clear that even under the Hague Rules formula ('all liability in respect of loss or damage') the time-bar applied to events after the bailment: in the words of Lord Wilberforce ' "all liability" means what it says'. As to the words used in the Hague-Visby formulation ('all liability whatsoever'), Bingham LJ commented (at 973): 'I do not see how any draftsman could use more emphatic language'.

The policy of the short time-bar is clear: that there should be finality of suit. If an exception is to be made in respect of the carrier's fraud or reckless misconduct, it could have, should have, been made expressly. It was not. The policy of the Hague-Visby amendment of Art III(6) was equally clear: that the time-bar should apply to all possible claims, however they might be constructed. The Court of Appeal has affirmed both policies. But having decided the time-bar point in favour of the carrier, a wider question arose for the Court of Appeal, the answering of which Hirst J had mercifully been spared. Should the Hague-Visby Rules apply at all?

Arguably, the cargo-receivers were not parties to the original contract of carriage. Should the Rules nevertheless apply to them? In *The Hollandia* the House of Lords had held that the provision, in s 1(2) of the Carriage of Goods by Sea Act 1971, that the Hague-Visby Rules should 'have the force of law', meant that in the UK they took effect as if they were part of an English statute, and so overrode inappropriate contractual provision. Are the Rules, then, a supra-contractual regime for the carriage of goods by sea? But if that possibility be allowed, what of *The Aliakmon* [1986] 2 All ER 145 (All ER Rev 1986, p 252)? In that case, it will be recalled, the House of Lords decided that a cargo-receiver who, although in possession of a bill of lading, had no action under s 1 of the Bills of Lading Act 1855 because he had no title, could not sue in tort either, and for the same reason, that he had no title. Was that decision misconceived? Might he have sued, in effect, under s 1(2) of the Carriage of Goods by Sea Act and Art III(2) of the Hague-Visby Rules, unembarrassed by his lack of title to the goods?

In *The Aliakmon* the question of whether carriage of goods by sea did provide a non-contractual base of liability, perhaps deriving from the bailment, had been canvassed. It had been decisively rejected both by Lord Donaldson MR in the Court of Appeal ([1985] 2 All ER 44 at 54: All ER Rev 1985, p 243) and by Lord Brandon in the House of Lords ([1986] 2 All ER 145 at 155), Lord Brandon pointing out pithily that if it had been possible for any cargo-receiver to base an action upon the bailment and the terms of carriage then it would have been necessary neither to enact the Bills of Lading Act 1855 nor to decide *Brandt and Co v Liverpool, Brazil and River Plate Steam Navigation Co Ltd* [1924] 1 KB 575.

Fortified by this 'specific disavowal', Bingham LJ (with whom Stocker and Slade LJJ agreed) concluded that cargo-owners who were not parties to a bill of lading could not be met by timebars (or other defences) contained in the Hague-Visby Rules thereby incorporated. He had three reasons. The bill of lading, 'a contractual document', is 'the bedrock upon which this mandatory code is founded'. 'Much of' the language of the Rules 'suggests that the code is intended to govern the relations between the parties to the bill of lading contract'. Thirdly, the doctrine of privity of contract is 'well established' in the UK and 'if the draftsmen of the 1924 and 1971 Acts had intended the respective rules to infringe that principle' they would have said so. The force of these arguments has to be recognised. On the other hand, scholars might cavil at the emphasis given to the historical accident of the use of a bill of lading as 'the bedrock' of the Hague and Hague-Visby Rules. One might also doubt the simple analysis of a bill as a 'contractual document', and, implicitly, no more than that. In the hands of the consignor it is often but part of the contract of affreightment, while the holder in due course sues on it and upon nothing else. And it did, after all, start life as a receipt. But these are subsidiary matters. The conclusions of the Court of Appeal are compelling. As a matter of English law, the Hague-Visby Rules operate as, and within, a contractual regime.

That a conclusion is right is not always satisfying. There are some loose ends and several imperfections. Bingham LJ recognised 'the unattractiveness to carriers of exposure to claims by non-parties to bills not subject to limits in time or amount' and also bewailed the fact that he was 'obliged to resolve this issue without the help which the decisions or opinions of foreign judges and jurists might have given us'. After all, the English doctrine of privity of contract is, if not peculiarly, at least markedly English. It also cannot be satisfactory to a common lawyer that the issue was decided in effect hypothetically, argument not being addressed to the court on the question whether the cargo interests were or were not parties to the contract. Perhaps later proceedings will help resolve some of these matters.

The legal position of a consignor with a contract of affreightment evidenced in a bill of lading containing the Hague-Visby Rules is clear, as is that of the holder of the same bill under s 1 of the Bills of Lading Act, for that Act directs us to treat such a holder 'as if the contract contained in the bill of lading had been made with himself'. Whether such sue in contract or tort, the instant decision means that they must proceed within one year and that their claims are subject to the limits and defences in the Rules. Cargo receivers with other documents, and even *Aliakmon*-type cargo receivers who have bills incorporating the Rules but who for other good reasons cannot take the benefit of s 1 of the Bills of Lading Act 1855, may disregard the time-bars, limits and defences in the Rules. The decision in *The Aliakmon*, of course, means that unless they have title to the cargo they may find it hard to discover a cause of action. But they may.

Much of this may well be dealt with in the Law Commission's new Bills of Lading Act, which is likely, it is understood, to be launched under another, rather less appropriate, title. Romantic casuists, which good common lawyers are trained to be, are rather inclined to think that statutes are all very well, but what a pity it is that the courts missed their opportunities, here as well as in *The Aliakmon*, to do the job themselves.

Solicitors

BRIAN HARVEY, MA, LLM
Solicitor, Professor of Property Law, University of Birmingham

Negligence

Professional men of all descriptions are increasingly having to look at their indemnity insurance cover. Clients who were once reluctant to sue have shed that reluctance. In the law, as in medicine, there is a great deal that can go wrong and the error or omission of a member of staff may subsequently give rise to very heavy liabilities. But if the worst happens, is the client's action framed in contract or tort? And what is the position if the client only discovers the error after more than six years from the date of the transaction in question?

These considerations were discussed by the Court of Appeal in *Bell v Peter Browne & Co (a firm)* [1990] 3 All ER 124. The facts giving rise to the negligence were straightforward. In October 1977 Mr Bell consulted the defendant firm regarding the breakdown of his marriage. The future of the matrimonial home was in issue. This was registered in the joint names of himself and his wife. It was then worth about £12,000 subject to a mortgage of about £8,000. The arrangement appears to have been that the house would not be sold for the time being but the wife should be entitled to live in the house and have it transferred into her sole name. This transfer occurred on 1 September 1988. Arrangements were agreed between the parties' solicitors that the husband's continuing interest in the former matrimonial home would be protected by a trust deed or a mortgage. The interest was quantified as being one sixth of the gross proceeds of sale.

Mr Bell's solicitors neglected to take any steps to protect his share, and no caution was registered at the Land Registry. The parties were divorced in the following year.

In 1986 Mr Bell learned from his former wife that she had sold the property two years earlier for £33,000. That sale took place almost eight years after the house had been transferred into her sole name. She had spent all the proceeds. There was clearly no possibility of making any claim in respect of those proceeds. Mr Bell therefore brought this action against his former solicitors for damages for professional negligence. The writ was issued in August 1987. The trial judge had dismissed Mr Bell's appeal against the order of the deputy District Registrar striking out his statement of claim for damages on the ground that it was frivolous and/or vexatious and an abuse of the process of the court since the action was time barred by virtue of ss 2 and 5 of the Limitation Act 1980, having been commenced more than six years after the date on which the cause of action accrued.

The sole question arising on the appeal was, therefore, whether the action was bound to fail because it was statute-barred.

The Court of Appeal analysed the claim both under contract and in tort. With regard to the contractual claim, steps clearly needed to be taken by

Mr Bell's solicitors at the time of the transfer or shortly afterwards to protect his interest in the matrimonial home. When his solicitors failed to take those steps in 1978 they were in breach of contract. This was so even though the breach, so far as it related to failing to lodge a caution, remained remediable for many years. In fact it could have been remediable until the former wife sold the house some eight years later.

On the face of it, therefore, the six-year limitation period began to run from the date of the breach, here September 1978, and expired long before the writ was issued nearly nine years later. But did it make any difference that the contract with the solicitor continued after the divorce proceedings since the breach of duty did not discharge that contract? The Court of Appeal thought not. The breach occurred in 1978 at the time of the transfer. Failure thereafter to make good the omission did not constitute a further breach. It was simply a case of the initial breach remaining unremedied. Nor would it have made any difference if Mr Bell's solicitors had been asked to remedy their breach of contract subsequently. This renewed failure would not have constituted a fresh breach of contract to enable the six-year limitation period to start running again.

> 'A remediable breach is just as much a breach of contract when it occurs as an irremediable breach, although the practical consequences are likely to be less serious if the breach comes to light in time to take remedial action. Were the law otherwise, in any of these instances, the effect would be to frustrate the purpose of the statutes of limitation, for it would mean that breaches of contract would never become statute-barred unless the innocent party chose to accept the defaulting party's conduct as a repudiation or, perhaps, performance ceased to be possible.' (per Nicholls LJ at 127)

The preceding decision in *Midland Bank Trust Co Ltd v Hett, Stubbs and Kemp (a firm)* [1978] 3 All ER 571, [1979] Ch 384 was distinguishable on its facts (see also p 68 above). There there was a continuous course of dealing. Here the client had no further contact with his former solicitors after the conclusion of the divorce proceedings. This was more than six years before the writ was issued.

What about the claim in tort? The key question here was whether the starting date for a claim based on negligence was different from one based on contract. The Court of Appeal confirmed that a cause of action based on negligence does not accrue until damage is suffered. It is then from that date that the six-year limitation prescribed by s 2 of the Limitation Act 1980 runs. It was, indeed, because of the problems caused by damage not becoming apparent for some time that the Law Reform Committee in their 24th report, Latent Damage, (Cmnd 9390, 1984) made recommendations which led to the Latent Damage Act 1986.

The 1986 Act made amendments to the 1980 Act and the new ss 14a and 14b of the 1980 Act would have been of assistance to Mr Bell but for the fact that his action had already been barred by the 1980 Act before the new sections came into force (see s 4 of the 1986 Act). This was because, whichever way the matter was looked at, the damage occurred when the transfer was executed and handed over. The court found against Mr Bell's argument that until the sale of the house he had no right to receive any part of the proceeds of the sale of the property and therefore had in fact suffered no loss. But following a line of cases including *Forster v Outred & Co (a firm)* [1982] 2 All ER 753 (All ER Rev 1982, pp 266–68), the court proceeded to hold that the damage, though latent, was done at the time of the transfer to the wife:

> 'The failure to see that . . . steps were taken promptly meant that Mr Bell was actually, and not just potentially, worse off than if the solicitor had performed his task competently. The sale in 1986 simply meant that the breach and its consequences were irremediable.' (per Mustill LJ at 136).

There are several short points worth noticing about this decision. Firstly, there must be sympathy with view of Mustill LJ that it is a pity that English law has elected to recognise concurrent rights of action in contract and tort. Professional relationships of this sort are founded on contract and there is a case for regarding such claims as lying in contract only. However, the difficulty here is that this would not dispose of all injuries to clients (or patients) within professional relationships. There would be problems, for instance, arising in medical negligence where there was no actual contract between doctor and patient. It is well established in this area that (in NHS cases) the patient's action lies in tort. In any case, the law now appears well settled in this respect and it would presumably need legislation or a clear House of Lords decision to negate any action in tort where there was also a contract.

Secondly, the position in tort would presumably have been different had the fact occurred so as to bring the plaintiff within the Latent Damage Act 1986. But this Act will not avail those who may become aware of their loss after a period of 15 years. Nevertheless, the 1986 Act will remedy some of the problems now arising. (See pp 321–322 below for further discussion of this aspect.)

Finally, and of particular interest to solicitors rather than common lawyers generally, the Court of Appeal uniformly stressed judicial concern where action was taken against a firm of solicitors for alleged negligence. The judgment of Lord Evershed MR in *Kitchen v Royal Air Forces Association* [1958] 2 All ER 241 at 245 was quoted: 'To some extent inevitably, our system and profession of the law is impugned and its adequacy and competency challenged' in such cases. Here the court was concerned that Mr Bell, who had relied on the defendants' competence as solicitors, had no means of knowing that they had by their negligence left him unprotected. The Court of Appeal regretted that he was denied compensation by an accident of limitation which he could hardly prevent.

Payment of costs personally

Almost every Annual Review, under the title Solicitors, has regrettably included a case involving an appeal against an order that a firm of solicitors pay costs personally. Many of these cases have involved civil proceedings. Here, in five separate cases, the question was whether the court had jurisdiction to order a solicitor acting for a defendant in a criminal trial personally to pay the whole or part of the costs of the prosecution.

It would assist understanding of the Court of Appeal's judgment here if the five cases are differentiated. In case 1, the defendant was charged with possessing a shotgun without a licence, but pleaded that the gun belonged to his brother. The defendant's solicitors, knowing the brother's address, made no attempt to contact him until the first day of the trial. They had been told that he had 'gone to ground' and would therefore be unwilling to attend. In fact the brother had never left his last known address and eventually attended the Crown Court, but after the jury had retired. The result was that the trial judge discharged the jury and ordered a fresh trial. He ordered that the defendant's solicitors pay the costs thrown away. In case 2, involving drug offences, the defendant changed his plea of not guilty to guilty on the morning of the trial with the result that witnesses who had been summoned were not needed. This chain of events was caused because the defendant's solicitors were unable to arrange a conference with the chosen counsel until the morning of the trial. Again, the solicitors involved were asked to pay the costs thrown away. In case 3 the defendant was represented under a Legal Aid certificate. His solicitors had little or no contact with him prior to his trial, considering that a conference was not necessary. When the defendant failed to attend for the trial it had to be adjourned and the trial judge ordered that the solicitors pay the costs thrown away on the ground that they had lost contact with their client and ought to have notified the court of that fact. In case 4 the defendant was charged with dishonestly obtaining a pecuniary advantage by failing to disclose her previous convictions when applying for employment with a security firm. At the trial her counsel sought to exclude certain evidence of a conversation between the police and the defendant regarding her previous convictions and the trial was adjourned to enable the prosecution to obtain a memorandum of convictions. Again, costs were ordered to be paid personally. In case 5 the defendant, charged with robbery and assault, pleaded an alibi in the course of the trial by serving an alibi notice on the prosecution. The trial had to be adjourned for two hours to enable the prosecution to investigate the alibi. Although the alibi had been hinted at in the trial preparations the defendant's solicitor was unable to interview the possible witness. Again costs were ordered to be paid personally.

Lord Lane CJ confirmed that there was undoubtedly jurisdiction in a criminal trial to order the solicitors for the defendant to pay personally the whole or some part of the costs of the prosecution. The Chief Justice drew on a long line of cases, starting with *Myers v Elman* [1939] 4 All ER 484, [1940] AC 282, quoting particularly Lord Wright (at 508–509):

> 'The underlying principle is that the court has a right and a duty to supervise the conduct of its solicitors, and visit with penalties any conduct of a solicitor which is of such a nature as to tend to defeat justice in the very cause in which he is engaged professionally . . .'

The doctrine also contains a punitive element and an element of deterrence. It was, however, necessary to analyse the basis for this jurisdiction. The most obvious guidance appears in Ord 62, r 11:

> '(1) . . . Where it appears to the court that costs have been incurred unreasonably or improperly in any proceedings or have been wasted by failing to conduct proceedings with reasonable competence and expedition, the Court may . . . order . . .'

This present version of the relevant rule omits the words 'other misconduct or default' formerly appearing.

Secondly, there is the Practice Direction of 26 May 1989 (see Practice Note [1989] 2 All ER 604 at 607, All ER Rev 1989, p 272). This reads:

> 'In (General) Regulations 1986 to order that costs improperly incurred be paid by a party to the proceedings the Supreme Court (which includes the Crown Court) may in the exercise of its inherent jurisdiction over officers of the court order a solicitor personally to pay costs thrown away by reason of some improper act or omission on his part or that of his staff.'

With respect to these two authorities, the Court of Appeal concluded that at least so far as criminal cases are concerned, neither of them altered Common Law rules as to the jurisdiction of the court. The function of the Practice Direction was to set out the machinery without purporting to delineate the precise nature of a solicitor's duties or of what in the way of misconduct would render him liable to pay costs personally.

Furthermore, the Court of Appeal, following the House of Lords authority of *Myers v Elman* (above) which they thought was wrongly distinguished in the Court of Appeal decision in *Sinclair-Jones v Kay* [1988] 2 All ER 611 (All ER Rev 1988, p 276), regarded itself as free to hold (1) that there was no distinction between civil and criminal trials and (2) that the recent changes in the Rules of the Supreme Court and the recent Practice Directions had not altered in any way the previous law.

Applying this ruling to the cases before it, the Court of Appeal made distinctions between the various circumstances. In the first case (failure to make contact with a key witness until it was too late for his evidence to be considered), this was regarded as 'involving a serious dereliction of the solicitor's duty to the court' (per Lane LCJ at 376). The firm's appeal against the order for costs was therefore dismissed. In the second case (involving a last-minute change of plea to guilty), the Court of Appeal found itself impressed by the difficulties which the solicitors had had in arranging an earlier conference with the counsel of the defendant's choice, or any other counsel. These difficulties had been explained in a very full affidavit by the firm and the Court of Appeal concluded that if there were an error, this was simply an error of judgment. This firm's appeal was therefore allowed. In the third case, involving the non-attendance of the legally aided defendant, whilst the Court of Appeal stated that it would be a serious dereliction of a solicitor's duty to the court not to notify a defendant that the case was in the warned list and might come on for trial at short notice, on these particular facts it appears that the judge misdirected himself in penalising 'a mere lack of care'. There was no satisfactory evidence as to what had actually happened with regard to warnings to the defendant. The firm's appeal was accordingly allowed.

In the fourth case, involving a problem of evidence as to previous convictions, on closer analysis it appeared that it was at the prosecution's insistence that the trial had to be adjourned and the prosecution had not acted with efficiency. The Court of Appeal went on to say that the cause of the wholly lamentable waste of time and money lay either at the door of defence counsel in taking a wholly untenable point of admissibility, or on the prosecution for failing to foresee the point and not being armed with the necessary certificate of conviction. The firm's appeal was accordingly allowed.

In the last case, involving a potential alibi witness, the court concluded that the solicitors were in breach of their duty to the court in not giving requisite alibi notice by an appropriate date. On a closer analysis it appeared that the solicitor involved, supported in his view by counsel, did not regard himself as being in breach of duty to the court because of what he perceived to be a conflict of duty with his client. This involved 'a genuine mistake as to the law'. In those circumstances the court decided that it was not appropriate that what was in part a penal order should be made and the appeal was again allowed.

The report of the case involves five decisions in each of which the Court of Appeal conducted an extensive post mortem of what had gone wrong. In the event only in the first case was there thought to be a serious dereliction of the solicitor's duty to the court. In each case the trial was before a Crown Court judge. One wonders whether judges, naturally concerned and irritated by unnecessary delays in starting or concluding trials, are not using this partially penal and certainly discreditable (to the firm involved) power rather too freely. Some of the problems arising appear to be directly attributable to the serious under-resourcing of the defence process in many cases. In some of these cases the counsel involved appears to have been at least equally to blame. If orders for costs against solicitors are going to be more frequently used in this way then there should also be parallel sanctions, applicable in the same way by an order in open court, against counsel involved. Although the Court of Appeal was careful here not to be unduly censorious, this has not always been the case in the past and as the administration of justice becomes more complex and more obviously under-resourced, one must sadly predict that these problems will continue.

The solicitor as stakeholder

If a solicitor holds money as stakeholder, may the court exercise its summary jurisdiction over solicitors to compel that stakeholder to pay the stake to one of the parties? This question involves two issues – (1) whether a stakeholder was a principal or an agent for both parties and (2) whether the court's summary jurisdiction over solicitors extended to this type of matter.

The facts, briefly, involved a joint venture agreement between a plaintiff company and another company set up by two partners in the defendant firm of solicitors for the purchase, development and sale of a property. Under the terms of the joint venture agreement the plaintiff company paid £80,000 to the defendant's solicitors to be held by them as stakeholders. This sum was to be deposited in a designated deposit account until either 1 June 1989 or the obtaining of vacant possession and planning permission by 1 December 1989, whichever should be the later in time. In the event of the venture failing the deposit of £80,000 plus interest, but less half the professional fees and expenses incurred in the project, was to be returned to the plaintiff company.

Planning permission was not obtained by 1 December 1989. Accordingly the defendant's solicitors, acting for their company, gave notice to determine the agreement. However, they enclosed a schedule of expenses which amounted to £205,405. Since half of this exceeded the deposit plus accrued interest thereon, the defendant's claimed that nothing was repayable to the plaintiffs and instructed the bank to close the special designated deposit account.

There was then a dispute as to whether the expenses claimed were deductible when claiming the £80,000 plus all accrued interest. The President of the Law Society was then asked by the plaintiffs' solicitors to appoint an arbitrator under the terms of the agreement and to determine what, if any, in the way of professional fees and expenses were deductible. The defendant firm stated that they had been advised by counsel that their company was entitled to retain the full amount of the deposit and interest and that the firm had not acted in any way improperly with regard to the deposit which had been removed from the account. The plaintiffs then issued proceedings seeking an order that a fresh deposit account be opened in joint names containing the original sum plus accrued interest.

The first issue was, therefore, whether the defendant firm had acted properly in taking the action that it had as stakeholder. Counsel for the plaintiffs had argued that the stakeholder was in the position of agent for both parties to the contract and could not part with the money until directed by the parties jointly how to dispose of it (or so directed by a tribunal having jurisdiction to decide the issue). The contrary argument for the defendant firm was that a stakeholder was not permitted to continue to hold the stake once the event had happened on which it is to be payable to one or other of the contracting parties. In cases of doubt the stakeholder should interplead. It was up to the stakeholder to take a view as to which of the two parties the stake should be paid subject, of course, to the risk that if the view taken turned out to be wrong he might be liable to pay the stake over to the other party out of his own resources.

The learned judge (Edward Nugee QC), on the authorities, preferred the second argument, following *Potters v Lopperts* [1973] 1 All ER 658, in which Pennycuick V-C had held that the stakeholder was not accountable for interest earned on a deposit to either party (in the absence of specific agreement) since the monetary deposit paid to a stakeholder was not paid to him as a trustee but on a contractual or quasi-contractual liability. Therefore neither party to the contract of sale where a stakeholder holds the deposit has any proprietary interest in that deposit. Each party has merely a contractual or quasi-contractual personal right of action to recover it from the stakeholder. Previous authorities describing a stakeholder as 'agent for both parties' were disapproved.

In the present case, the facts were not quite as simple as the common case of the deposit paid on a contract for the sale of land. This was because the deposit plus interest was payable to the 'successful' party, but the sum was to be reduced by one half of the professional fees and expenses incurred by the joint venture. Nevertheless, the position was essentially the same as that described above. Accordingly, the only remedy against the stakeholder would be an action in contract or for money had and received. It was not appropriate to make an order that the original sum be replaced in a new designated account.

Did it make any difference that the stakeholders in the present case were the solicitors for one of the parties? Counsel for the plaintiffs suggested that the defendants had acted unfairly and had favoured their own client company. He suggested that if they were going to make any payment in respect of the deposit, they ought to have paid half to each party and left the parties to resolve the dispute about their rights under the arbitration clause. Counsel relied particularly on two recent cases in which the court exercised its summary jurisdiction over solicitors, namely *John Fox (a firm) v Bannister, King and Rigbeys (a firm)* [1987] 1 All ER 737 (All ER Rev 1987, p 235) and *Udall v Capri Lighting Ltd* [1987] 3 All ER 262 (All ER Rev 1987, p 236). In both these cases the Court of Appeal confirmed the court's extraordinary jurisdiction over the solicitors in, for instance, the case of broken undertakings. Here, it was argued, since the defendant firm had undertaken to hold the deposit as stakeholders, they should be ordered to perform that undertaking.

For the defendant firm it was denied that any undertaking had been given. They were not parties to the agreement in question and all they had done was to receive the deposit and pay it into the designated deposit account.

The judge held that the summary jurisdiction over solicitors was exercisable whenever a solicitor had accepted an obligation in his capacity as a solicitor, but this was subject to the safeguard that it should only be exercised in a clear case. The mere fact that the word 'undertaking' had not been used was not in itself conclusive. However, the obligation accepted by the firm was an obligation to act as stakeholder until the relevant event. The fact that the stakeholder was a solicitor did not alter the nature of the stakeholder's obligations. It was not appropriate to impose on the defendant firm obligations which would not be imposed on non-solicitor stakeholders. The learned judge therefore refused to make an order against the defendant firm in the terms demanded.

Sport and the Law

EDWARD GRAYSON, MA
Barrister, South Eastern Circuit

Introduction

Sport and the law during 1990 expanded progressively, naturally and almost inevitably within international as well as domestic dimensions. Towards the end of 1990 preparations were made for four conferences with an international flavour for sport and the law outside the United Kingdom from such disparate sources as the International Rugby Union's Medical Committee in Bermuda; the International Athletic Foundation's conference in Monaco; a New South Wales Bar conference in Switzerland, and a meeting of the Union d'Avocates Internationale in Mexico.

By the end of the year, only the International Rugby Board's Medical Committee in Bermuda – made up of 50 doctors from 14 different countries together with their legal adviser – had occurred. It concluded with formal recommendations to its world governing body to uphold the rule of law on the field (ie in respect of violent and illegal foul play) and off it (for creating a proper penal policy for proven drug offences) in anticipation of the publicised World Cup competition, scheduled for the end of 1991 in the UK. The former was consistent with the Court of Appeal Criminal Division's continued policy, identified below, to uphold immediate custodial sentences for violent playing offenders. The latter was in line with the Canadian Government's Commission of Enquiry into the Use of Drugs and Banned Practices Intended to Increase Athletic Performance, under Mr Justice Dubin, also referred to below.

During the International Athletic Foundation and New South Wales Bar conferences, in early 1991, disclosures emerged on each occasion of the International Court of Arbitration at Lausanne in Switzerland, which has dealt with disputes of a sporting flavour since its creation in 1983 by the International Olympic Committee. The European Court of Justice at Luxembourg adjudicated during 1990 on a dispute between a Belgian professional footballer and his club and national federation with an adjourned reference for a ruling from the court on Arts 3(c) and 48 of the Treaty of Rome, to be explained below. Away from the courts, the world governing bodies belatedly recognised their responsibilities to the rule of law within their respective jurisdictions.

Soccer's world governing body, FIFA, attempted to impose mandatory 'Red Card' penal sanctions for the paradoxically named 'professional foul', eight years after the London-based English Football Association had advocated such a policy. Cricket's international administrators, the ICC, created a supervisory status of referees to oversee umpires in test matches, because umpires, captains and administrators had failed to operate effectively Law 42 of the game, against intimidatory and potentially injurious fast bowling. The International Rugby Board confused itself – and everyone else

– with inconclusive attempts to balance retention of its amateur status with extensive commercial exploitation of the public playing level, in a manner which now makes it easy to understand how and why the Court of Appeal in *Williams v Reason* [1988] 1 All ER 262 (All ER Rev 1988, p 332), set aside and ordered a retrial of the £25,000 libel damages award obtained by the celebrated Welsh international J P R Williams, because the trial judge had failed to direct the jury adequately in respect of the relevant International Rugby Football Union Board's regulations relating to amateur status.

The Union d'Avocates Internationale gathering at Mexico City in mid-1991 was, at the time of writing, structuring a programme to absorb some of the disclosures by the New South Wales Bar of developments 'down under' during 1990. A Common Law Division of the New South Wales Supreme Court awarded damages to a professional rugby league international footballer for personal injuries caused by foul play against not only the offender but also his employer club on the basis of vicarious liability: *Rogers v Bugden and Canterbury Bankston Club* (unreported, 1990). Another judgment there found a plaintiff and defendant soccer litigants each guilty of assault against the other, with a damages award by set-off ultimately in favour of the plaintiff: *Sibley v Milutinovic* (1990) Aust Tort Rep 81-013. Also in New South Wales, the Court of Appeal's affirmation of the $A 121,490 damages award in the claim for civil assault and negligence brought by an injured jockey against another (*Frazer v Johnston*, referred to in the 1989 Annual Review at p 281), has sent shock waves throughout the equine insurance world.

In the United Kingdom, the rules of natural justice hit the headlines when the monopolistic cartel of 92 professional Football League club's management committees, functioning within the overall administration of the Football Association with its 43,000 registered clubs, failed in the Chancery Division to strike out Swindon Town's writ in its ultimately successful battle within an internal domestic FA tribunal to preserve its Second Division Football League status. In the world of horse racing, the Aga Khan threatened – and in early 1991 obtained leave – to resurrect the debatable issue of whether judicial review would be available for alleged tribunal errors (an issue discussed in All ER Rev 1989, pp 284-5). In football, the Hitchin Town Football and Social Club Ltd did manage to obtain a judicial review remedy because it challenged a decision of trustees who hold a substantive office of a public nature and permanent character which has been created by a statutory provision (see s 30(2) of the Supreme Court Act 1981). At a more publicised level of the sport, the Tottenham Hotspur and England international footballer, Paul Gascoigne, failed to satisfy Harman J in the Chancery Division that he possessed a sufficiently identifiable legal reputation to be protected in interlocutory proceedings, and his club failed to satisfy the Stock Exchange that its affairs were sufficiently satisfactorily conducted to prevent a Stock Exchange suspension of dealings in the shares of the holding company, Tottenham Hotspur plc. Gascoigne's England international goalkeeper colleague, Peter Shilton, saw his appeal against a General Commissioners of Income Tax decision, which had been allowed by Morritt J, affirmed by the Court of Appeal: *Shilton v Wilmshurst (Inspector of Taxes)* [1990] STC 55. But it has since been overturned by the House of Lords ([1991] STC 88). Also in the year under review, the promotional arm of their union association, the Professional Footballers' Association (Enterprises) Ltd, failed to overturn the Customs and Excise Commissioners' claim for output VAT on the value of various trophies awarded at an annual Players of the Year celebration (*Customs and Excise Commissioners v Professional Footballers' Association (Enterprises) Ltd* [1990] STC 742). Finally, though by no means least, the Football Spectator's Act 1989, which received the Royal Assent in November 1989, became operative during 1990, by a network of Statutory Instruments; and the repercussions of the Hillsborough disaster continued in July 1990 with Hidden J's test case judgment for the class of persons entitled to recover damages for nervous shock: *Jones v Wright* [1991] 1 All ER 353.

Adapting the common law maxim applied to other areas, the categories of 'Sport and the Law' are never closed. However, each of the cases summarised above can be discussed briefly under one of five broad headings.

Criminal liabilities and penalties

In *R v Davies* [1991] Crim LR 70 the Court of Appeal re-affirmed an immediate custodial sentence of six months for an 'off the ball' blow to an opponent's face during a non-professional soccer match which resulted in a fractured cheek bone and an absence from work for two weeks. As the tip of a deep iceberg it reflected a penal policy which will have occurred at different courts throughout the country at every level.

Thus, in an unreported decision at Inner London Crown Court, Fordham J activated an earlier suspended sentence of three months for an earlier assault by one footballer upon another and imposed an additional three months upon a conviction for breaking an opponent's jaw with a punch during the course of play (*R v Gray*). When imposing the sentence, the judge explained with words which clearly require repetition in the light of sustained misconduct:

'It may be time that the public woke up to this and that this is not tolerated in what is supposed to be a pleasure.'

Civil liability and compensation

Professional football, at rugby league as well as association levels, has an economic as well as a pleasurable element. During the course of a rugby football match at Belmore Oval, Sydney, New South Wales, a professional player's broken jaw resulted in a claim for both compensatory and exemplary damages for assault or negligence against both the opponent and his employer club, as vicariously liable. On 14 December 1990 in a 55-page reserved judgment, Lee J in the Common Law Division of the New South Wales Supreme Court awarded a total of $A 68,154.60, with costs, but no exemplary damages against the employer club: *Rogers v Bugden and Canterbury Bankston Club*. At the time of writing, the possibilities of an appeal by the club were being canvassed.

In an earlier Australian decision, *Sibley v Milutinovic* (1990) Aust Tort Rep 81-013, another plaintiff, who was injured by a punch during a soccer match which fractured his jaw, sued. He received a counterclaim from his alleged offender for a bruised ankle suffered during the plaintiff's tackle, which ultimately resulted in the offensive and offending punch. Consent was raised by each of the parties as a defence. Miles CJ found each party liable to the other in assault. He further held that the onus of proving consent was on the party who alleged it and that the plaintiff had failed to establish that his own behaviour was within the rules of the game. Nevertheless, the ultimate award favoured the plaintiff with damages in excess of $A 8,000.

Finally, from 'down under', the New South Wales Court of Appeal dismissed the appeal by the unsuccessful defendant senior jockey, Malcolm Johnston, who had been held by the trial judge to have negligently caused an apprentice jockey, Glenn Frazer, to fall during a cup race, causing serious injuries. It upheld the $A 121,490 damages award recorded in last year's Review at pp 280-281. Again, at the time of writing, a further appeal to the Australian Supreme was being contemplated.

In the UK, Hidden J's judgment of 31 July 1990 in *Jones v Wright* [1991] 1 All ER 353, extended the class of persons entitled to recover for nervous shock from the Hillsborough disaster to those within classes of relationships – including brothers and sisters of victims – who were not present at the disaster, but had witnesses it on the television screens or video recordings. As a test action, the reserved judgment made it clear that appeals were ultimately to be contemplated.

Association football's universal appeal lends itself inevitably to entanglement with the law off as well as on the field. Paul Gascoigne's unsuccessful claim to injunct publication of a book without his consent was based upon a rejected claim by Harman J to a proprietorial interest in his reputation (*Paul Gascoigne Promotions Ltd v Penguin Books Ltd* (1990) *Times*, 13 October).

R v Brooker, ex p Hitchin Town Football and Social Club Ltd (1990) *Times*, 17 April, resulted in a successful application for judicial review against trustees in relation to a meeting for the purpose of electing new trustees concerned with a dispute over the future of about nine acres of land which was at the time of the judgment occupied by the Hitchin Town Football and Social Club.

The Swindon Town Football Club was required, initially, to use the courts when it was demoted from the First to the Third Division by a draconian decision by the Management Committee of the monopolistic cartel created by the 92 Football League clubs. A striking out application was rejected with costs by Mummery J against the club's writ, based upon the proportionality principle that the punishment was disproportionate to the offence; but before the trial was heard, the club opted for an internal disciplinary tribunal to a Football Association within the League's own rules. This resulted in a reversal of the double demotion to preserve the club's Second Division status (*Swindon Town Football Club v The Football League Ltd* (1990) *Times* 20 June).

For reasons explained here last year and based on the Court of Appeal decision in *Law v National Greyhound Racing Club Ltd* [1983] 3 All ER 300 (All ER Rev 1983, p 175), judicial review remedies are not at present available for complaints against sporting governing bodies. Hence Swindon Town's relief claimed by writ.

Also during 1990, the Aga Khan reacted sensationally to a decision by the Jockey Club which disqualified his filly, Aliysa, from its 1989 Oaks victory for alleged failure to satisfy a drug test after prolonged scientific investigations. He publicly withdrew his extensive string of horses in training from English stables in protest, with threatened procedural remedies against the Jockey Club. In early 1991 Macpherson J granted an ex parte application for a judicial review to seek court orders attacking the disqualification ((1991) *Times*, 28 February). With the financial resources available to the Aga Khan, he is in a position to test the Court of Appeal's decision in law all the way to the House of Lords, if so advised and inclined, in the manner that the Jockey Club was forced to capitulate after the Court of Appeal had reversed the master and judge who had struck out Florence Nagle's writ seeking a women's trainers licence in *Nagle v Fielden* [1966] 1 All ER 689.

Taxation

The victory during 1990 of England's internationally renowned goalkeeper Peter Shilton in the High Court and Court of Appeal, reversing the General Commissioners for his 'golden goodbye' on receiving £75,000 from his departing club, Nottingham Forest, upon his transfer to Southampton (*Shilton v Wilmshurst (Inspector of Taxes)* [1990] STC 55 (recorded in the 1989 Review, pp 283-284)) was reversed by the House of Lords during early 1991: [1991] STC 88. The payment is chargeable to tax under s 181(1) of the Income and Corporation Tax Act 1970 because 'emoluments for employment' embraced all 'emoluments from employment'. It was not limited to emoluments in the course of employment, and thereby the farewell payment from Nottingham Forest was caught by the House of Lords with the same ease that Shilton fielded the shots from opposing strikers. (See Taxation at p 279 below.)

For comparable reasoning in constructing another professional footballer's 'emolument of employment', Vinelott J in the Chancery Division on 7 December 1990 upheld a Special Commissioner's conclusion that an interest free loan to trustees, repayable on demand by Arsenal in respect of payment to its Republic of Ireland international, David O'Leary, was nevertheless chargeable under Schedule E on an arising basis rather than on a remittance basis under Case V of Schedule D: *O'Leary v McKinlay* (1991) *Tax Journal*, 7 March.

His union association also found itself 'offside' with regard to the law when Nolan J held that the supply of trophies to award winners at an annual dinner could be described only as a supply of goods for no consideration if regarded in isolation from the surrounding circumstances, which included a luxuriously structured entertainment associated with a celebratory dinner. He held that to regard the supply in isolation would be to ignore the contractual link between the taxpayer company and the dinner, which included presentation of the trophies, attributing a wholly artificial character to the awards. Accordingly, they were a VAT taxable supply which attracted consideration and were thereby liable to VAT output tax (*Customs and Excise Commissioners v Professional Footballers' Association (Enterprises) Ltd* [1990] STC 742).

Parliament and government

In addition to burdening the sporting world with VAT and other taxes, the British Parliament brought the Football Supporters Act 1989 into force. This will now haunt the world of public professional sport, and particularly association football, with financial obligations towards safety.

The Canadian Government was sufficiently haunted by what became known as 'the Ben Johnson affair', after the athlete had been disqualified from holding Olympic Games honours upon his being positively tested for drugs, that it established a judicial enquiry under Mr Justice Dubin as Commissioner. Its 638-page report, published during 1990, made 70 recommendations that will be a yardstick for good behaviour at all international sporting levels hereafter.

European law

The international level of sporting legal activity surfaced on 13 November 1990 with the publication of the Court of Justice at Luxembourg's 41-page typescript on the dispute between Jean-Marc Bosman, a Belgian professional footballer and his club, Liege, and the Belgian Football Association, relating to issues which the common law and equity considered nearly 30 years ago in *Eastham v Newcastle United Football Club Ltd* [1963] 3 All ER 139. The most significant aspect of the judgment was the final decision that '[a] ruling must be sought from the Court of Justice on whether it is permissible under Articles 3(c) and 48 of the Treaty of Rome', inter alia, to continue the restrictive practices under which professional football, internationally, has been administered since its inception for more than three-quarters of a century. Clearly, a matter for further developments.

Conclusion

This last look into the future from Luxembourg and the number of past and prospective appeals referred to above demonstrate the volatility of this area of law. More significant has been the manner in which commentators at the two European international Sport and Law conferences at Monaco and Switzerland trotted out uncritically, as they do elsewhere, the obiter of the Vice Chancellor, Sir Nicholas Browne-Wilkinson, delivered off-the-cuff in interlocutory proceedings concerning a rush to judgment necessity during the Edinburgh Commonwealth Games, relating to a South African-born swimmer claiming eligibility for England:

> 'Sport would be better served if there was not running litigation at repeated intervals by people seeking to challenge the decisions of the regulating bodies.'
> (*Cowley v Commonwealth Games Federation* (1986) *Times*, 24 July.)

As I wrote in my book, *Sport and the Law* (Butterworths, 1988) at pp 26–27:

> 'Such a fundamental contention contrary to the undoubted facts could have been made only without the time or opportunity or sources essential for an appropriate consideration [of] it.'

The development of sport and the law during 1990, and what can be anticipated hereafter, gives me no reason to modify what I wrote in 1988. In fact, what appears above re-affirms it.

Statute Law

FRANCIS BENNION, MA (OXON)
Barrister, Research Associate of the University of Oxford Centre for Socio-Legal Studies, former UK Parliamentary Counsel

Introductory note

For the convenience of readers this section, like its predecessors in the All ER Annual Review series, conforms to the Code set out in the author's book *Statutory Interpretation* (1984, Supp 1989). A reference to the relevant section of the Code is given after each heading in the notes below.

As previously, attention is drawn in the notes below to examples of statute law principles being overlooked or ignored in cases reported during the year (see notes respectively related to Code ss 14, 125 (potency of the term defined), 125 (number), 125 (powers and duties), 281 and 284).

Civil sanction for disobedience to statute (Code s 14)

Liability in negligence

In *Murphy v Brentwood District Council* [1990] 2 All ER 908 (see also pp 303–307 below) the House of Lords overruled *Anns v Merton London Borough* [1977] 2 All ER 492, [1978] AC 728, Supp pp 6–8. As a result, the position regarding liability in negligence may now be summarised as follows (replacing the passage under the heading Page 41 in Supp pp 6–8).

It may be that, by an anomalous development of case law, negligent contravention of a statute gives rise to liability for the tort of negligence as distinct from the tort of breach of statutory duty. The basis of this liability appears to be that the mere existence of a statutory duty raises a duty of care of the kind postulated by the tort of negligence, and that this is apart from, and additional to, the duty to comply directly with the requirements of the statute.

This liability in negligence has been recognised in a long line of authorities culminating in *Murphy v Brentwood District Council*, which concerned the negligent failure of a local authority to observe building regulation requirements. In it the House of Lords restricted the scope of the alleged liability in negligence by overruling its own previous decision in *Anns v Merton London Borough*. In consequence, if it exists at all the liability is now probably limited to injury to the person or to health.

It is noteworthy that the previous authorities mainly concerned the scope and extent of the liability in negligence, rather than its existence. The obligation would inevitably be anomalous because in principle the existence and scope of liability for breach of a statutory duty should depend on the intention of Parliament as indicated in the statute, rather than on judicial application of an extraneous common law doctrine such as the tort of negligence.

However, the idea that such liability exists had secured such a tenacious hold in the profession that in *Murphy* counsel for the party in whose interest it would have been for the court to hold that the liability does not exist failed to argue the point. Nevertheless, the House was clearly uneasy about its existence. Stating that he expressed no opinion on the point, Lord Mackay of Clashfern LC (at 912, echoed by Lord Oliver at 938) pointed out that Parliament had itself made provision regarding liability of this kind in the Defective Premises Act 1972. He added that for the House in its judicial capacity to create a large new area of responsibility on local authorities in this respect would not be a proper exercise of judicial power. Lord Keith said (at 917):

> 'Not having heard argument on the matter, I prefer to reserve my opinion on whether any duty at all exists. So far as I am aware, there has not yet been any case of claims against a local authority based on injury to person or health through any failure to secure compliance with building byelaws. If and when such a case arises, that question may require further consideration.'

Lord Jauncey (at 938) similarly declined to express a view on whether the duty not to be negligent existed. The speeches in *Murphy* appear to be a clear invitation to challenge in some future case the argument that it does.

Enforcement agencies: administrative agencies (Code s 15)

Delegation by minister

In *Oladehinde v Secretary of State for the Home Department* [1990] 3 All ER 393 the House of Lords recognised what it called the *Carltona* principle regarding delegation by a minister to his officials. This was laid down by Lord Greene MR in *Carltona Ltd v Comrs of Works* [1943] 2 All ER 560 at 563 in the following words:

> 'In the administration of government in this country the functions which are given to ministers (and constitutionally properly given to ministers because they are constitutionally responsible) are functions so multifarious that no minister could ever personally attend to them . . . The duties imposed upon ministers and the powers given to ministers are normally exercised under the authority of the ministers by responsible officials of the department. Public business could not be carried on if that were not the case. Constitutionally, the decision of such an official is, of course, the decision of the minister. The minister is responsible. It is he who must answer before Parliament for anything that his officials have done under his authority, and if for an important matter he selected an official of such junior standing that he could not be expected competently to perform the work, the minister would have to answer for that in Parliament.'

After citing this dictum in the court below, Lord Donaldson MR said:

> 'Lord Greene MR contemplated that, in devolving authority to take decisions on his behalf, the Secretary of State would only be answerable to Parliament, but it is conceded that, at least in recent times, such a course of action would also be susceptible to judicial review.' (*R v Secretary of State for the Home Department, ex p Oladehinde* [1990] 2 All ER 367 at 381).

In Oladehinde the House of Lords recognised that the *Carltona* principle could be displaced by a contrary intention in a particular Act. Lord Griffiths (at 401) found three instances of this in the Immigration Act 1971. For example s 13(5) refers to a certificate 'given by the Secretary of State (and not by a person acting under his authority)'. In a reference to the linguistic canon of construction *expressum facit cessare tacitum* (Code s 388), Lord Griffiths added (at 402): 'Where I find in a statute three explicit limitations on the Secretary of State's power to devolve I should be very slow to read into the statute a further implicit limitation.'

Discretion

In *R v Secretary of State for the Home Department, ex p Oladehinde* [1990] 2 All ER 367 (affirmed, *Oladehinde v Secretary of State for the Home Department* [1990] 3 All ER 393: see previous note) Lord Donaldson MR referred (at 379) to what he called the '*Padfield* approach' to the construction of an enactment conferring a discretion. This was stated by Lord Reid in *Padfield v Minister of Agriculture, Fisheries and Food* [1968] 1 All ER 694 at 699 as follows:

> 'Parliament must have conferred the discretion with the intention that it should be used to promote the policy and objects of the Act; the policy and objects of the Act must be determined by construing the Act as a whole . . . if the Minister, by reason of his having misconstrued the Act or for any other reason, so uses his discretion as to thwart or run counter to the policy and objects of the Act, then our law would be very defective if persons aggrieved were not entitled to the protection of the court.'

Enforcement agencies: adjudicating authorities with appellate jurisdiction (Code s 23)

House of Lords (Code pp 65–67)

For an example of the overruling by the House of Lords of its own previous decision see *Murphy v Brentwood District Council* [1990] 2 All ER 908, described in the note on p 250 above related to Code s 14.

Enforcement agencies: judicial review (Code s 24)

Irrationality

(i) In *Champion v Chief Constable of the Gwent Constabulary* [1990] 1 All ER 116 at 127, Lord Lowry suggested that in the *Wednesbury* test as originally formulated by Lord Greene MR (set out at Code p 69) the words 'acting reasonably' should be inserted after 'authority' in the phrase 'a decision . . . so unreasonable that no reasonable authority could ever have come to it'. This would make clear that a normally reasonable authority may on rare occasions suffer a lapse and act unreasonably. It would avoid the undesirable implication that an authority against whom judicial review is ordered must for that reason be regarded as usually unreasonable in its behaviour.

(ii) In *R v Secretary of State for the Home Department, ex p Brind* [1990] 1 All ER

469 at 480–481 Lord Donaldson MR said that the doctrine of 'proportionality', under which administrative action may be attacked if it is out of proportion to the mischief addressed (using a sledgehammer to crack a nut), is not a separate head of judicial review but an aspect of irrationality. He added:

'. . . acceptance of "proportionality" as a separate ground for seeking judicial review rather than a facet of "irrationality" could easily and speedily lead to courts forgetting the supervisory nature of their jurisdiction and substituting their view of what was appropriate for that of the authority whose duty it was to reach that decision.'

As to this case, which was followed by the Court of Appeal in *R v General Medical Council, ex p Colman* [1990] 1 All ER 489, see also the note on p 260 below related to Code s 134.

Procedural impropriety

(i) Unfairness as a ground for judicial review falls within the category of procedural impropriety: *R v Inland Revenue Commissioners, ex p Taylor (No 2)* [1989] 3 All ER 353 at 357–358 (All ER Rev 1989, pp 289–290 and discussed in Taxation, p 135 below). This category has also been described as the requirement of procedural due process: *R v Governor of Pentonville Prison, ex p Naghdi* [1990] 1 All ER 257 at 260, discussed in Extradition, pp 134–135 above.

(ii) It was held in *R v Board of Inland Revenue, ex p MFK Underwriting Agencies Ltd* [1990] 1 All ER 91, following *Preston v IRC* [1985] 2 All ER 327, [1985] STC 282, that what Bingham LJ (at 110) called 'the valuable developing doctrine of legitimate expectation' is an aspect of the treatment of unfairness, and that where (which was not the case here) a statutory body such as the Inland Revenue abuses its power unfairly, as by defeating the legitimate expectation of taxpayers who had relied on its pronouncements, judicial review will lie despite the availability of statutory appeal procedures.

Enforcement agencies: dynamic processing of legislation by (Code s 26)

Overruling of processing decisions

Even though there exists a long line of authority as to the legal meaning of a term or enactment, a higher court may decide to reverse this where it considers it to be based on defective reasoning. The decision of the Court of Appeal in *Cook v Southend Borough Council* [1990] 1 All ER 243 on enactments giving a right of appeal to a 'person aggrieved' affords an example. A line of cases held that, contrary to its natural meaning, the term was not intended to include a local authority whose decision had been impugned. Woolf LJ (at 254) held that in the key case, *R v London Sessions Appeal Committee, ex p Westminster City Council* [1951] 1 All ER 1032, 2 KB 508, the Divisional Court had taken a 'wrong turning'. He went on:

'As the present case illustrates, the question of who is a "person aggrieved" is still very much alive in many statutory situations. It therefore appears to me to be important for this court to intervene so that in future the decisions in the 1950s will not continue to cause the courts unduly to restrict the right of local authorities to appeal. I have therefore come to the conclusion that *Ex p Westminster City Council* should be regarded as having been wrongly decided and should no longer be followed.'

Decisions arrived at per incuriam

In *Rakhit v Carty* [1990] 2 All ER 202 (see also pp 176–177 above) the Court of Appeal held that its decision in *Kent v Millmead Properties Ltd* (1982) 44 P & CR 353 had been arrived at per incuriam, since it was given in ignorance or forgetfulness of an inconsistent statutory provision, namely the Rent Act 1977, s 67(3). Accordingly, the court declined to follow it even though it had previously followed it in *Cheniston Investments Ltd v Waddock* [1988] 2 EGLR 136.

Act of Parliament: definition (Code s 27)

Control over procedure (Code pp 83–84)

In *Rost v Edwards* [1990] 2 All ER 641 Popplewell J ruled that in the light of authority he was compelled to find that the effect of art 9 of the Bill of Rights (1688) is that whatever was said or done in either House of Parliament could not be enquired into in a court of law, even though the enquiry did not in any sense challenge what had been said or done (see pp 332–333 above).

Act of Parliament: overriding effect of (Code s 32)

Court's inherent jurisdiction

In *Harrison v Tew* [1990] 1 All ER 321 the House of Lords considered the position where an Act of Parliament makes comprehensive provision in an area previously forming part of the court's inherent jurisdiction, but does not expressly state whether or not that jurisdiction is to remain effective. The case concerned the court's inherent jurisdiction to tax the bill of costs submitted by a solicitor (based on the fact that a solicitor is an officer of the court) having regard to the fact that a series of Acts beginning with 3 Jac 1 c 7 (1605) has set up a statutory system for the taxation of solicitors' costs. *Held* The court retains no inherent jurisdiction over solicitors in relation to the taxation of costs since the jurisdiction has by implication been ousted and replaced by this series of enactments, of which the one now current is the Solicitors Act 1974, s 70.

Lord Lowry (at 329) cited Coke's statement that 'it is a maxime in the common law, that a statute made in the affirmative, without any negative expressed or implyed, doth not take away the common law' (2 Co Inst (1817) 200). He held that s 70(4) of the 1974 Act (which states that the power to order taxation *conferred by sub-s (2)* shall not be exercisable after a stated period) is a negative enactment in Coke's sense. Although the italicised words might seem to contradict this, it is to be noted that they are a modern consolidated version of the Solicitors Act 1843, s 41, which imposed a time limit in general words. Taken together, these, said Lord Lowry (at 329) 'were negative enactments which in my clear opinion ousted the inherent jurisdiction to refer a bill for taxation in conflict with what they lay down'. (*Note* – The reference at Supp p 13 to *Symbol Park Lane Ltd v Steggles Palmer (a firm)* [1985] 2 All ER 167 (All ER Rev 1985, pp 236, 250, 255), a decision which is criticised by Lord Lowry (at 328), needs to be read in the light of *Harrison v Tew*.)

Whether Crown bound by Act (Code s 34)

In *Lord Advocate v Dumbarton District Council* [1990] 1 All ER 1 (discussed in Town and Country Planning, pp 348–349 below) the House of Lords reviewed the doctrine of Crown immunity from the operation of Acts of Parliament. The following points emerge from the principal opinion, delivered by Lord Keith:

1. A statute must, in the absence of some particular provision to the contrary, bind the Crown either generally or not at all, since there is no logical room for the view that it binds the Crown when the Crown is acting without any right to do so but not when the Crown does have such right. This view of Lord Keith's was expressly supported by Lord Jauncey, who said (at 18):

   'Any other approach would mean that the applicability of a particular statute to the Crown in any given circumstances could depend not on the terms of the statute but on matters extraneous thereto, namely the relevant common law rights of the Crown at the time.'

2. The conclusion that the provisions of a particular Act do not bind the Crown is not controverted by the fact that a section of the Act states expressly that that section shall not bind the Crown, since such saving provisions are commonly inserted *ex abundanti cautela* and do not support the inference that the Crown was in other respects intended to be bound by the Act.

3. It is desirable that Acts should always state explicitly whether or not the Crown is intended to be bound by any, and if so which, of their provisions. It may be remarked of the last of these points that legislative drafters are unlikely to comply with it. This is because Bills are usually drafted in too much of a hurry to permit the weighing of points such as this, which often have difficult aspects.

Act of Parliament: challenges to Act's validity (Code s 47)

Bill of Rights (Code p 128)

In *Rost v Edwards* [1990] 2 All ER 641 Popplewell J ruled that in the light of authority he was compelled to find that the effect of art 9 of the Bill of Rights (1688) is that whatever was said or done in either House of Parliament could not be enquired into in a court of law, even though the enquiry did not in any sense challenge what had been said or done (see pp 332–333 above).

Delegated legislation: doctrine of ultra vires (Code s 58)

Severance (Code pp 144–145)

In *Director of Public Prosecutions v Hutchinson* [1990] 2 All ER 836 (see also Administrative Law, pp 6–7 above) the House of Lords reversed the decision in the court below ([1989] 1 All ER 1060 (All ER Rev 1989, pp 290–291)). The case concerned byelaws made with respect to common land under the Military Lands Act 1892, s 14(1) (which states that no byelaw made under it shall authorise interference with rights of common). The applicant, who was convicted of an offence under the byelaws, possessed no right of common in respect of the land. The byelaws thus interfered with no rights of common of hers, even though they interfered with rights of common possessed by other persons. *Held* The conviction was unlawful. In so far as they affected the rights of commoners, the byelaws were ultra vires. To treat them as nevertheless valid in relation to non-commoners would be to enforce provisions of a totally different character from those in fact made.

Lord Bridge, with whom three of the other four law lords agreed, said (at 839–840) that the cases where part but not the whole of an item of delegated legislation exceeds the powers under which it was purported to be made, and the valid portion is severable, can be divided into cases of *textual severability* (where the so-called blue-pencil test can be applied) and those of *substantial severability* (where it cannot). Lord Bridge said:

> 'A legislative instrument is textually severable if a clause, a sentence, a phrase or a single word may be disregarded, as exceeding the lawmaker's power, and what remains of the text is still grammatical and coherent. A legislative instrument is substantially severable if the substance of what remains after severance is essentially unchanged in its legislative purpose, operation and effect.'

Grammatical meaning: semantic obscurity and the 'corrected version' (Code s 90)

(i) The Animals Act 1971, s 2(2)(*b*), imposes liability where damage is caused by an animal if 'the likelihood of the damage or of its being severe was due to [certain] characteristics of the animal' and other stated requirements are met. In *Curtis v Betts* [1990] 1 All ER 769 the Court of Appeal held that because this wording was obscure it was necessary to construe the provision with the substitution of the simple phrase 'the damage' for the words 'the likelihood of the damage or of its being severe'. This is a good example of the express statement by the court of construction of what is to be treated as the 'corrected version' of the enactment where the court considers it necessary to apply a rectifying construction (see also Tort, pp 334–335 below). (For the presumption that errors in legislation are to be rectified by the court of construction see Code s 142.)

(ii) For a 'corrected version' found by the House of Lords see the note, related to Code s 142, on *McMonagle v Westminster City Council* [1990] 1 All ER 993 at pp 261–262 below.

(iii) For a case where it is submitted the court found the wrong 'corrected version' see the note on *R v Brentwood Justices, ex p Nicholls* [1990] 3 All ER 516 at pp 258–259 below, related to Code s 125 (also discussed in the chapter on Criminal Procedure, p 86 above).

Filling in the detail: implications (when legitimate) (Code s 109)

Implied ancillary powers

Under the rule in *A-G v Great Eastern Rly Co* (1880) 5 App Cas 473, as stated by Lord Blackburn (at 481), 'those things which are incident to, and may reasonably and properly be done under the main purpose [of an enactment], though they may not be literally within it, would not be prohibited'. Or, as stated by Lord Selborne LC (at 478), 'whatever may fairly be regarded as incidental to, or consequential upon, those things which the Legislature has authorised, ought not (unless expressly prohibited) to be held, by judicial construction, to be ultra vires'.

The rule was considered by the Court of Appeal in *R v Richmond upon Thames London Borough Council, ex p McCarthy & Stone (Developments) Ltd* [1990] 2 All ER 852 when ruling upon the legal meaning of the codification of the rule in relation to local authorities in the Local Government Act 1972, s 111(1). This empowers a local authority 'to do any thing . . . which is calculated to facilitate, or is conducive or incidental to, the discharge of any of their functions'. As to the latter case see further the note at p 267 below related to Code s 334, and the discussion in Town and Country Planning at pp 353–354 below.

Filling in the detail: implications affecting related law (Code s 110)

(i) For a case where the House of Lords acknowledged that Parliament had in legislation recognised profound changes in public perceptions of sexual morality see the description, related to Code s 142, of *McMonagle v Westminster City Council* [1990] 1 All ER 993 at pp 261–262 below.

(ii) In *Kirkham v Chief Constable of the Greater Manchester Police* [1990] 3 All ER 246 the Court of Appeal upheld the decision in the court below ([1989] 3 All ER 882 (All ER Rev 1989 p 292)).

Rules: the commonsense construction rule (Code s 122)

For an example of commonsense construction see the description, related to Code s 142, of the important decision of the House of Lords in *McMonagle v Westminster City Council* [1990] 1 All ER 993 at pp 261–262 below.

Statutory definitions (Code s 125)

Application to ancillary documents

Where an Act contains a definition of a term, there is a presumption that when the term is used in a document issued under, or for the purposes of, the Act its meaning in that document is intended to be that given by the definition, rather than its ordinary meaning. In *Wyre Forest District Council v*

Secretary of State for the Environment [1990] 1 All ER 780 (also discussed at pp 347–348 below) the House of Lords had to decide whether the word 'caravan' as used in a planning application had its ordinary meaning or the wider meaning assigned to it by the Caravan Sites and Control of Development Act 1960, s 29(1). *Held* The latter was the case. Lord Lowry said (at 785):

'. . . if Parliament in a statutory enactment defines its terms (whether by enlarging or by restricting the ordinary meaning of a word or expression), it must intend that, in the absence of a clear indication to the contrary, those terms as defined shall govern what is proposed, authorised or done under or by reference to that enactment.'

Elsewhere, (at 788) Lord Lowry referred to a defined term used in 'a formal document under the planning Acts' as prima facie having the meaning assigned by the statutory definition. The principle clearly applies also to a term as used in a document created for the purposes of an Act where, while not being defined by the Act, the term has a distinct meaning in the Act. Prima facie it would have the same meaning in the document.

Potency of the term defined (Code pp 276–277)

It is pointed out at Code p 276 that the natural meaning of a defined term may have a potency sufficient to override the literal meaning of the statutory definition (see also Supp pp 24–25 and All ER Rev 1989, p 293). Although illustrations of this principle arise frequently in practice, the profession is slow to accept it as a distinct type of interpretative problem. *Esso Petroleum Co Ltd v Ministry of Defence* [1990] 1 All ER 163 furnished one more example. It concerned the definition of 'public revenue dividends' in the Income and Corporation Taxes Act 1970, s 107. Without mentioning the principle, the court held that although the definition of 'dividends' stated that the term included 'interest', and was thus literally wide enough to include interest on damages for a tort committed by a government department, the intrinsic meaning of 'dividends' required the general word 'interest' to be limited to interest on securities.

Number: Interpretation Act 1978, s 6(c) (Code p 284)

The Interpretation Act 1978, s 6(*c*), provides that unless the contrary intention appears words in the singular include the plural. This causes difficulty when the drafter forgets that his enactment drafted in terms of what one person does may not work for plural cases, since the people concerned may choose to do different things (for previous examples of these difficulties see *Bennion on Statute Law* (3rd edn) pp 269–270).

The problem arose once more in *R v Brentwood Justices, ex p Nicholls* [1990] 3 All ER 516, where the Divisional Court had to construe the Magistrates' Courts Act 1980, s 20(3). This says that in certain circumstances the court, after explaining specified matters to 'the accused', shall 'ask him whether he consents to be tried summarily or wishes to be tried by a jury'. The subsection goes on to say that 'if he consents to be tried summarily' the court shall proceed to do this. On the other hand 'if he does not so consent' the court must inquire into the information as examining justices. In *Nicholls* three defendants, Nicholls (the applicant for judicial review), Carr and Willbourne were jointly charged with the one offence of affray. Nicholls and Carr wished to be tried summarily, while Willbourne wished to be tried by jury. Relying on s 6(c), the court held that the effect of Willbourne's wish was that all three must be tried by jury.

The decision is difficult to justify. The drafter of s 20(3) had erred by failing to envisage and provide for the fact that defendants are frequently tried jointly for the same offence. Section 6(c) requires references to 'the accused' to be construed as including two or more accused persons, but the obvious possibility that they might decide in differing ways was not dealt with by the wording of s 20(3). The court was therefore required to arrive at the 'corrected version' of the enactment in accordance with the true intention of Parliament (see Code s 90). It is submitted that this would be more likely to have been to the effect that there should be two separate trials, a summary trial for those defendants who wished it and a jury trial for any who elected for that alternative.

Powers and duties: Interpretation Act 1978, s 12(1) (Code p 284)

The Interpretation Act 1978, s 12(1), says that where an Act confers a power it is implied, unless the contrary intention appears, that the power may be exercised from time to time as occasion requires. To the previous examples of the overlooking of this provision (see Supp p 26) there can be added *R v Immigration Appeal Tribunal, ex p Secretary of State for the Home Department* [1990] 3 All ER 652, which concerned the power to make an application for leave to enter the United Kingdom under the Immigration Act 1971, s 3(1).

Principles: nature of legal policy (Code s 126)

Legal policy, which is an aspect of public policy, is explained at Code pp 285–295. For an example of the emergence of a new head of policy see the note on *R v Registrar General, ex p Smith* [1990] 2 All ER 170 at p 265 below, related to Code s 289 (also discussed in Family Law, pp 151–152 above).

Principles: that law should serve the public interest (Code s 127)

Estoppel per rem judicatem

The House of Lords held in *Thrasyvoulou v Secretary of State for the Environment* [1990] 1 All ER 65 that where an enactment creates a specific jurisdiction for the determination of any issue which establishes the existence of a legal right then, unless the contrary intention appears from the enactment, there is an implication that the principle of res judicata is intended to apply to give finality to that determination even though it is not made by a court.

The House accordingly held that a determination in favour of the appellant in an appeal against an enforcement notice under the Town and Country Planning Act 1971, s 88(2)(b) to (e), that an existing use of a building or land was either permitted or beyond the reach of enforcement proceedings gave rise to an estoppel per rem judicatem. Lord Bridge said (at 70–71):

'The doctrine of res judicata rests on the twin principles which cannot be better expressed than in terms of the two Latin maxims "interest reipublicae ut sit finis litium" and "nemo debet bis vexari pro una et eadem causa". These principles are of such fundamental importance that they cannot be confined in their application to litigation in the private law field. They certainly have their place in the criminal law. In principle they must apply equally to adjudications in the field of public law.'

(For further discussion of *Thrasyvoulou*, see Town and Country Planning at pp 350–351 below.)

Principles: that municipal law should conform to public international law (Code s 134)

European Convention on Human Rights

In *R v Secretary of State for the Home Department, ex p Brind* [1990] 1 All ER 469 the Court of Appeal considered the argument that a directive issued by the Home Secretary to the Independent Broadcasting Authority under the Broadcasting Act 1981, s 29(3), prohibiting the broadcasting of direct statements by representatives of proscribed terrorist organisations in Northern Ireland contravened the provisions of art 10 of the European Convention on Human Rights regarding freedom of speech. *Held* Since there was no ambiguity in the wording of s 29(3), which gave the Home Secretary unfettered power to prohibit the broadcasting of 'any matter or classes of matter', its width was not to be treated as cut down by art 10. Lord Donaldson MR said (at 477):

'. . . you have to look long and hard before you can detect any difference between the English common law and the principles set out in the convention, at least if the convention is viewed through English judicial eyes . . . when the terms of primary legislation are fairly capable of bearing two or more meanings [there is] a presumption that Parliament has legislated in a manner consistent, rather than inconsistent, with the United Kingdom's treaty obligations.'

As to this case, which was followed by the Court of Appeal in *R v General Medical Council, ex p Colman* [1990] 1 All ER 489, see also the note on pp 252–253 above related to Code s 24.

Presumptions: that regard be had to the consequences of a construction (Code s 140)

For an example of consequential construction see the description, related to Code s 142, of the important decision of the House of Lords in *McMonagle v Westminster City Council* [1990] 1 All ER 993 at pp 261–262 below.

Presumptions: that 'absurd' result not intended (Code s 141)

For an example see the description, related to Code s 142, of the important decision of the House of Lords in *McMonagle v Westminster City Council* [1990] 1 All ER 993 at pp 261–262 below.

Presumptions: that errors to be rectified (Code s 142)

Garbled or corrupt text (Code pp 339–342)

In *McMonagle v Westminster City Council* [1990] 1 All ER 993 the House of Lords considered the definition of 'sex encounter establishment' in the Local Government (Miscellaneous Provisions) Act 1982, Sch 3 para 3A. The definition contains four sub-paragraphs, numbered (*a*) to (*d*), which respectively specify four classes of premises in which sexual services of various kinds are provided. Sub-paras (*a*) to (*c*) each expressly limit the services covered by them to those which are 'not unlawful'. Thus sub-para (*c*) says 'premises at which entertainments which are not unlawful are provided by one or more persons who are without clothes or who expose their breasts or genital, urinary or excretory organs during the entertainment'. In *McMonagle* the appellant had been convicted of contravening the Act by operating premises falling within sub-para (*c*) without a licence. He argued that the conviction was bad because the prosecution had failed to prove that the entertainments in question were 'not unlawful'. Applying *Stone v Corp of Yeovil* (1876) 1 CPD 691 (see Code p 375) and *Salmon v Duncombe* (1886) 11 App Cas 627 (see Code p 755), the House held that the words 'which are not unlawful' must be treated as surplusage attributable to the ineptitude of the draftsman. Accordingly it was not necessary for the prosecution to prove that the entertainments were not unlawful.

The only speech delivered was that of Lord Bridge (at 994–998). Since this important decision is relevant to no less than eight sections of the Code (all noted in the appropriate places in this article) in addition to s 142, an extended quotation from Lord Bridge's speech is now given.

'Your Lordships, I believe, find it both startling and unedifying that an appellant . . . should be able to dispute his guilt on the ground that the activity on which his conviction is founded is taken outside the ambit of the enactment under which he is charged by reason only that it proves him guilty of another much graver indictable offence . . .

The social background against which the legislation providing for the licensing of sex establishments must be considered is the product of a revolution in public attitudes to every aspect of sexual morality . . . It is . . . inevitable that in the current climate of opinion prosecutions for public indecency offences have become rare and since any such prosecution will, if the defendant so elects, be tried by jury the standard likely to be applied . . . is in a high degree unpredictable . . . what is immediately striking is the extent to which the language of the new para 3A of Sch 3 in sub-paras (*a*) to (*c*) must necessarily be read as giving express parliamentary sanction to some of the more striking manifestations of the sexual revolution to which I have referred.

. . . reading the words ["which are not unlawful"] in their literal sense as defining an essential feature of an establishment requiring to be licensed, the meaning for which counsel for the appellant has energetically argued, would have the consequence, it seems to me, of substantially frustrating what must have been the primary purpose . . . It seems to me manifestly absurd that the intention of the legislation was to subject to licensing control only those establishments conducted in the least offensive way and to leave those which pander more outrageously to the taste of the voyeur immune from any control or legal restraint save such as might be imposed by the possibility of conviction by a jury of a public indecency offence.

For these reasons I entertain no doubt in my own mind that we should be giving effect to the true intention of the legislature if we could avoid this absurdity by treating the phrase "which is not unlawful". . . as mere surplusage. I recognise that this is a strong course to take in construing a statute and one which imputes an unusual degree of ineptitude to the draftsman.'

The decision is open to the criticism that it is perfectly possible that, as its chosen wording indicates, Parliament really did wish to do no more than plug the loophole that existed because lawful sex entertainments etc were not subject to prosecution, and desired to place these, and these alone, under some form of regulation. This is indeed the most likely construction. The fact that, as Lord Bridge says, jury decisions are unpredictable does not justify the House of Lords in using its judicial power to install an alternative form of legal control over unlawful sex shows.

Errors of meaning (Code pp 342–344)

(i) In *BBC Enterprises Ltd v Hi-Tech Xtravision Ltd* [1990] 2 All ER 118 the Court of Appeal considered an enactment which contained, in relation to persons using a device for unscrambling coded television transmissions, the words 'when they are not entitled to do so'. The enactment was the Copyright, Designs and Patents Act 1988, s 298(2)(a). The problem of construction arose because everyone has the right, subject to compliance with licensing requirements, to receive television transmissions. This is under the principle thus described by Staughton LJ (at 122): 'in this country, at any rate, everything which is not prohibited by law is permitted'. How then could anyone (except infringers of the licensing law) fit the words in question?

The intention of s 298 was clear, namely to give certain rights akin to copyright to persons transmitting coded programmes. The court held that, although the drafter had not stated the precondition in a form corresponding to the underlying legal position, this should not be allowed to stultify the enactment. Applying a dictum of Lord Diplock in *Fothergill v Monarch Airlines Ltd* [1980] 2 All ER 696 at 705, Staughton LJ said (at 123):

> 'Save perhaps in revenue and penal enactments, I consider that the courts should now be very reluctant to hold that Parliament has achieved nothing by the language it has used.'

(*Note* – The dictum of Lord Diplock is given at Code p 423, where the case reference is unfortunately omitted.) (See pp 26–27 above for further discussion of this case.)

(ii) In *Re Spence (decd)* [1990] 2 All ER 827 the Court of Appeal considered the legal meaning of the phrase in s 1(1) of the Legitimacy Act 1976 (a consolidation Act) '[the] child of a void marriage, whenever born'. Nourse LJ said (at 832):

> 'I have been much troubled by [this expression]. A void marriage, both as a matter of language and by definition . . . is a nullity. It is only an idle ceremony. It achieves no change in the status of the participants. It achieves nothing of substance. How then can you sensibly refer to a child of a void marriage?'

The court held that since the words presented 'a real and substantial difficulty or ambiguity' within the meaning of that phrase as used by Lord Wilberforce in *Farrell v Alexander* [1976] 2 All ER 721 at 726 it was entitled to refer to the different wording in the original enactment, the Legitimacy Act 1959, s 2 (see Family Law at p 137 above and Succession at p 277 below for further discussion of *Re Spence*).

(iii) For an example of the drafter misconceiving the legislative project by failing to envisage that more than one person might be involved, see the note on *R v Brentwood Justices, ex p Nicholls* [1990] 3 All ER 516 at pp 258–259 above, related to Code s 125.

(iv) To the reference in Supp p 32 to comments made by the court in *Harrison v Tew* [1987] 3 All ER 865 at 872–873, [1988] 2 WLR 1 at 1011, there should be added a reference to comments made by Lord Lowry on an appeal in that case (*Harrison v Tew* [1990] 1 All ER 321 at 326–330).

(v) The decision in *Box Parish Council v Lacey* [1979] 1 All ER 113, [1980] Ch 109, (see Code p 344, Example 12) was overruled by the House of Lords in *Hampshire County Council v Milburn* [1990] 2 All ER 257. As to the latter case see the note on pp 267–268 below related to Code s 363.

Canons: construction of Act or instrument as a whole (Code s 149)

Every word to be given meaning (Code pp 375–376)

For an exception see the description, related to Code s 142, of the important decision of the House of Lords in *McMonagle v Westminster City Council* [1990] 1 All ER 993 at pp 261–262 above.

Conflicting statements within one instrument (Code pp 377–378)

In *Institute of Patent Agents v Lockwood* [1894] AC 347 at 360 Lord Herschell LC said that where there is a conflict between two sections in the same Act: 'You have to try and reconcile them as best you may. If you cannot, you have to determine which is the leading provision and which the subordinate provision, and which must give way to the other'. This dictum was relied on by the Court of Appeal in *Re Marr and another (bankrupts)* [1990] 2 All ER 880 when deciding between two conflicting provisions of the Insolvency Act 1986.

Nicholls LJ said (at 886) that the so-called rule referred to in *Wood v Riley* (1867) LR 3 CP 26 at 27 that 'the last [provision] must prevail', if it had ever existed, was long since obsolete. He added: 'Such a mechanical approach . . . is altogether out of step with the modern, purposive, approach to the interpretation of statutes and documents'. This overlooks the possibility that there may in rare cases be no means of deciding between conflicting provisions on purposive grounds, when a rule of thumb is needed. It should also be remembered that it used to be the practice, and in the case of private and personal Acts still is, to place saving clauses at the end, with the intent that they should override anything inconsistent in the earlier part of the Act.

Weighing the factors: changes in legal policy (Code s 163)

For a case where the House of Lords acknowledged that Parliament had in legislation recognised profound changes in public perceptions of sexual morality see the note, related to Code s 142, on *McMonagle v Westminster City Council* [1990] 1 All ER 993 at pp 261–262 above.

Application: foreigners and foreign matters outside the territory (Code s 223)

In *BBC Enterprises Ltd v Hi-Tech Xtravision Ltd* [1990] 2 All ER 118 at 121 Staughton LJ said 'Parliament is not assumed, in a criminal enactment, to have intended to regulate conduct outside this country'. As to this case see the note, related to Code 142, on p 262 above.

Pre-enacting history: consolidation Acts (Code s 232)

In *Re Spence (decd)* [1990] 2 All ER 827 the Court of Appeal considered the legal meaning of the phrase in s 1(1) of the Legitimacy Act 1976 (a consolidation Act) '[the] child of a void marriage, whenever born'. The court held that since the words presented 'a real and substantial difficulty or ambiguity' within the meaning of that phrase as used by Lord Wilberforce in *Farrell v Alexander* [1976] 2 All ER 721 at 726 it was entitled to refer to the different wording in the original enactment, the Legitimacy Act 1959, s 2.

Enacting history: committee reports leading up to Bill (Code s 237)

For reliance by the House of Lords on the report of a Royal Commission see the note on *Hampshire County Council v Milburn* [1990] 2 All ER 257 at pp 267–268 below, related to Code s 363.

Enacting history: special restriction on parliamentary materials (Code s 241)

Bill of Rights (Code p 530)

In *Rost v Edwards* [1990] 2 All ER 641 Popplewell J ruled that in the light of authority he was compelled to find that the effect of art 9 of the Bill of Rights (1688) is that whatever was said or done in either House of Parliament could not be enquired into in a court of law, even though the enquiry did not in any sense challenge what had been said or done (see pp 332–333 above).

Unamendable descriptive component of Act: headings (Code s 281)

As Code s 281 says, its headings form part of an Act and may be used as a guide to interpretation. It is therefore surprising to find Harman J, in *Esso Petroleum Co Ltd v Ministry of Defence* [1990] 1 All ER 163 at 166, disdaining the assistance of a crossheading on the ground that 'the construction of an Act cannot be controlled by crossheadings'. While construction may not be *controlled* by a crossheading it can often be assisted by one, and it is the court's duty to take advantage of this aid when arriving at the legal meaning of an enactment. As to this case see also the note on p 258 above related to Code s 125, and the note below related to Code s 284.

Unamendable descriptive component of Act: punctuation (Code s 284)

As stated at Code p 86, both public Bills and private Bills are fully punctuated when introduced into Parliament. As Code s 284 says, its punctuation forms part of an Act, and may be used as a guide to interpretation. It is therefore surprising to find Harman J erroneously stating in *Esso Petroleum Co Ltd v Ministry of Defence* [1990] 1 All ER 163 at 165 that 'commas are not part of the draft of Bills laid before Parliament but are inserted at the Queen's Printer's stage of publication'. As to this case see also the note on p 258 above related to Code s 125, and that above related to Code s 281.

Principle against doubtful penalization: danger to life or health (Code s 289)

The principle that, however plain the wording, the court will reject a construction of an enactment that may endanger life or health is illustrated by *R v Registrar General, ex p Smith* [1990] 2 All ER 170. The Adoption Act 1976, s 51, places what is in terms an absolute duty on the Registrar General to supply an adopted person with information needed to enable him to obtain a copy of his birth certificate. In *Smith* the applicant was a psychotic who it was proved might, if he discovered the identity of his natural mother, do her an injury. *Held* The application would be refused. Watkins LJ said (at 175):

> 'In our very firm view, having regard to the potential menace to the safety in the future of the natural mother of the applicant and possibly others related to him by blood or otherwise, a public policy consideration positively demands that we refuse to grant the relief sought by the applicant. It is, we think, beyond belief that Parliament contemplated that an adopted child's right to obtain a birth certificate should be absolute come what may . . . If what we term to be an appropriate head of public policy is apparently novel and wanting until now of expression being given to it, that is no reason at all to deny it a place in the relevant law.'

Purposive-and-strained construction (Code s 315)

(i) In *X Ltd v Morgan-Grampian (Publishers) Ltd* [1990] 2 All ER 1 (see also Contempt, pp 50–51 above and Practice and Procedure, pp 208–211 above) the House of Lords approved a purposive-and-strained construction of the phrase 'information contained in a publication' in the Contempt of Court Act 1981, s 10 (which cuts down the common law powers of the courts to deal with contempts in relation to sources of information). They widened it to include information communicated and received for the purposes of a publication which has not yet taken place and may never take place. Lord Lowry said (at 17):

'This seems to be a necessary interpretation; otherwise a defendant such as Mr Goodwin [a journalist whose information had not been published] would be worse off than if he had already published . . . '

This example of judicial legislation can perhaps be explained, if not justified, by the fact that here the court is choosing to narrow its own powers even further than Parliament had clearly narrowed them.

(ii) For another example of purposive-and-strained construction see the description, related to Code s 142, of the important decision of the House of Lords in *McMonagle v Westminster City Council* [1990] 1 All ER 993 at pp 261–262 above.

(iii) For a further example of purposive-and-strained construction see the note on p 262 above related to Code s 142 and concerning *BBC Enterprises Ltd v Hi-Tech Xtravision Ltd* [1990] 2 All ER 118.

Construction against 'absurdity': avoiding a futile or pointless result (Code s 324)

Pointless legal proceedings (Code pp 702–703)

The law discourages the bringing of legal proceedings without preliminary attempts to settle the matter informally. In *Sandwell Metropolitan Borough Council v Bujok* [1990] 3 All ER 385 the House of Lords considered the provisions relating to statutory nuisances contained in the Public Health Act 1936, ss 91–99. While constrained by the language to hold that s 99 enabled a private person to prosecute for a statutory nuisance without first giving the offender notice of the nuisance and an opportunity to remedy it, the House resolved a doubt whether such a prosecutor was required by s 99 to be granted his costs by reference to the need to discourage prosecutions of this kind. Lord Griffiths (at 389–390) cited with approval the following dictum of Watkins LJ in the court below:

'In law there is no doubt that [the respondent] was entitled to commence proceedings without giving notice of the state of the dwelling to the local authority. But in every other conceivable way I regard that action as entirely wrong. Endless trouble to many people in courts and local authority offices and much money could be saved by the giving of notice of disrepair which it is to be supposed a local authority would appropriately react to.'

Construction against 'absurdity': avoiding a disproportionate counter-mischief (Code s 326)

For an example see the note on *R v Registrar General, ex p Smith* [1990] 2 All ER 710 at p 265 above, related to Code s 289.

Implied application of rules of constitutional law (Code s 334)

Position of the Crown (Code p 722)

In *Re JS (a minor) (wardship: boy soldier)* [1990] 2 All ER 861 (discussed in Family Law at pp 114–145 above) Hollis J struck out an originating summons making JS, a boy soldier, a ward of court on the ground that the Crown was improperly impleaded and that by the Army Act 1955 control of the body of JS was vested in the military authorities. He applied the following dictum of Russell LJ in *Re A (an infant), Hanif v Secretary of State for Home Affairs* [1968] 2 All ER 145 at 152:

'. . . the judge would have no right to complain of or countermand a lawful posting overseas of a ward who was in the armed forces. The law refers the military control of the ward to the military authorities.'

He also applied a dictum of Denning LJ in the same case (at 662) to the effect that the court will not exercise its wardship jurisdiction 'so as to interfere with the statutory machinery set up by Parliament'.

Taxation only by Parliament (Code pp 724–725)

In *R v Richmond upon Thames London Borough Council, ex p McCarthy & Stone (Developments) Ltd* [1990] 2 All ER 852 the Court of Appeal held that a local authority providing a service in exercise of the power conferred by the Local Government Act 1972, s 111(1), to do anything which is calculated to facilitate, or is conducive or incidental to, the discharge of any of its functions is entitled to make a reasonable charge, and that this does not contravene the provision of the Bill of Rights (1688) restricting the levying of taxation to Parliament. As to this case see further the note at p 257 above related to Code s 109.

Implied application of rules of evidence etc (Code s 341)

Estoppel

As to the implied application of the principle of res judicata see the note on pp 259–260 above related to Code s 127.

Reliance on illegality: *allegans suam turpitudinem non est audiendus* (Code s 345)

Ex turpi causa non oritur actio (Code p 759)

In *Kirkham v Chief Constable of the Greater Manchester Police* [1990] 3 All ER 246 the Court of Appeal held that in view of the abolition of the crime of suicide by the Suicide Act 1961, s 1, the principle *ex turpi causa non oritur actio* did not apply to negate an action for damages in tort where the police negligently allowed a prisoner to commit suicide. For the history of the maxim's application see *Pitts v Hunt* [1990] 3 All ER 344 (discussed at pp 317–319 below).

Canons: ordinary meaning (Code s 363)

Several ordinary meanings (Code pp 799–800)

A phrase may have more than one ordinary meaning because it is capable of being construed in different grammatical senses. In *Hampshire County Council v Milburn* [1990] 2 All ER 257 the House of Lords considered the meaning of the phrase 'waste land of a manor' in the Commons Registration Act 1965, s 22(1)(*b*). They held it could mean either land which is currently waste land of a manor or waste land which was formerly, but is not now, waste land of a manor. As Lord Templeman put it (at 262) 'the word "of" may be either a possessive genitive or a genitive of origin'. In view of the fact that no new manors could be created after the promulgation of the statute of Quia Emptores in 1290, and having in mind the purpose of the 1965 Act as indicated in the Report of the Royal Commission on Common Land 1955–58 (Cmnd 462), the House held it must be given the latter meaning. As to this case see also note (v) on p 263 above related to Code s 142.

Canons: *expressum facit cessare tacitum* (Code s 388)

See the note on *Oladehinde v Secretary of State for the Home Department* [1990] 3 All ER 393 at pp 251–252 above, related to Code s 15.

Succession

C H SHERRIN, LLM, PHD
Barrister, Reader in Law, University of Bristol

Delegation of will making power

The right to make a will is a personal privilege to be exercised with care and circumspection and not lightly to be delegated to others. The clearest exposition of this principle is that of Lord Simonds in *Chichester Diocesan Fund and Board of Finance Inc v Simpson* [1944] 2 All ER 60 at 74:

> 'It is a cardinal rule, common to English and to Scots law, that a man may not delegate his testamentary power: to him the law gives the right to dispose of his estate in favour of ascertained or ascertainable persons. He does not exercise that right if in effect he empowers his executors to say what persons or objects are to be his beneficiaries. To this salutary rule there is a single exception: a testator may validly leave it to his executors to determine what charitable objects shall benefit, so long as charitable and no other objects may benefit.'

But few cardinal rules are more difficult to reconcile with practice, for how can such a rule be reconciled with the recognition of wide ranging testamentary powers of appointment? The dilemma was revisited in *Re Beatty's Will Trusts* [1990] 3 All ER 844 (see also Land Law and Trusts, p 170 above). Hoffman J refused to accept that Lord Simmonds was intending to cast doubts on the validity of testamentary powers of appointment, whether special, general or intermediate. The remarks should be confined to the context of the gift in the case, which was expressed in language so conceptually vague that it would be impossible for the court to say whether any specific application was within the terms of the will or not. But the execution of an otherwise valid power is giving effect to the testator's will and not making a will for a testator who has failed to do so himself. The rule is confined to certainty and merely states that a will which is expressed in language too vague to be enforced cannot be rescued by giving the executor a wide power of choice (at 848). Counsel argued that the rule required that the will should give sufficient guidance either from the nature of the class and from its other terms, to enable one to say that the testator had firmly made a choice and had not left everything to the executers. But this would invalidate powers such as those in *Re Manisty's Settlement* [1973] 2 All ER 1203, where a power given in a settlement to trustees to add any persons when they thought to a class to whom appointments could be made. Hoffman J refused to accept counsel's argument, which embodied a test itself vague and uncertain. It would be impossible at this time to hold invalid wide testamentary powers of appointment as amounting to a delegation of will making powers. There are many cases in the modern law upholding such powers, *Re Abraham's Will Trusts* [1967] 2 All ER 1175, being one such case and the court has declined to overrule cases such as *Re Park* [1932] 1 Ch 580, [1931] All ER Rep 633, and *Re Jones* [1945] Ch 105 on the grounds that they were inconsistent with the delegation principle. The common law rule against testamentary delegation was not merely sleeping, as counsel suggested, but, in the sense of a restriction on the scope of testamentary powers, 'is a chimera, a shadow cast by the rule of certainty, having no independent existence', per Hoffman J at 849. Having taken such a bold stance the resolution of the case was straightforward. Helen Gertrude Beatty had by her will bequeathed her personal estate and a legacy of £1.5m to her trustees to 'allocate among such person or persons as they think fit and to give effect to any memorandum which may be deposited with . . . my will or left among any paper . . . or . . . to any wishes of mine which they shall be aware'. It was held that since the clauses would have been valid powers of appointment if they had been inserted in a settlement and gave effect to the testator's will, rather than permitting the trustees to make a will when she had failed to do so, the distributions made by the trustees under the clauses were valid.

Thus is a spectre laid to rest.

Donatio mortis causa

Sen v Headley [1990] 1 All ER 898 decides an interesting point, novel to English case law, that had been previously the subject of academic debate fuelled by Commonwealth cases. Mummery J decided, consistent with the consensus of opinion, that there could not be a valid donatio mortis causa of realty. (This case is also discussed at pp 168–169 above.)

The facts were that the plaintiff and the deceased had lived together as man and wife for ten years, but had separated many years before the death although remaining on friendly terms. In 1986 the deceased was diagnosed as suffering from cancer and admitted to hospital as inoperable. The plaintiff visited the deceased every day to feed him and keep him company. They discussed what should happen to his house after his death, and he told her that the house and its contents were to be hers and told her that the deeds were to be found in a steel box. The keys to this box were in the possession of the plaintiff, she stating that the deceased must have slipped them into her handbag on one of her visits to him. Shortly after the death she opened the box and took possession of the keys. She claimed after his death that the house was hers on the basis of a valid donatio mortis causa to her. This claim was contested by the next of kin.

The essential conditions for a donatio mortis causa were stated by Mr Justice Farwell in *Re Craven's Estate* [1937] 3 All ER 33, [1937] Ch 423. First there must be a clear intention to give, but only if the donor died, whereas if the donor did not die then the gift was not to take effect and the donor was to have back the subject matter of the gift. The gift must, therefore, be conditional in that sense, either expressly or by inference. Secondly, the gift must be made in contemplation of death, by which was meant not the possibility of death at some time or other, but death within the near future, what may be called death for reason believed to be impending.

If a gift was made in contemplation of death it might be readily inferred from the circumstances that it was on condition that it was to be held only in the event of death (*Re Lillingston (decd)* [1952] 2 All ER 184, 187). Thirdly, the donor must effectively part with dominion over the subject matter of the gift. Mere words of gift were not enough: there must be some clear act taken towards a transfer of the property.

In the instant case it was held that the first two conditions clearly satisfied but the issue centered on the 'parting with the dominium'. What is normally meant by this is that the donor must put it out of his power between the date of gift and the date of death to alter the subject matter of the gift and substitute other property for it, so that the original subject of the gift should remain the subject matter in the event of the death of the donor (per Farwell J in *Re Craven's Estate* at 427–428.) The usual subject matter of a donatio is the manual delivery of a chattel but it has been established that there may be a valid donatio of other forms of property which are not capable of physical delivery, such as choses in action.

Cases such as *Birch v Treasury Solicitor* [1950] 2 All ER 1198 have held that the handing over of the instrument or document, such as a saving's bank book, suffices as the essential indicator or evidence of title to the chose in action. It was argued by counsel for the plaintiff that the same principle could apply by analogy to the title deeds to real property. This was rejected. The doctrine has been confirmed within strict limits and the courts are wary of attempts to use the doctrine in order to make a future disposition on death by informal will or to perfect an immediate unconditional inter vivos gift which equity will not execute.

The only English authority where the question of a donatio mortis causa of land was considered, *Duffield v Elwes* (1827) 1 Bli NS 497, [1824–34] All ER Rep 247, did not assist; delivery of mortgage deeds and a bond constituting an effective donatio of the mortgage security, was clearly distinguishable and did not bear on the main issue. The Commonwealth authorities, *Watts v Public Trustee* (1949) 50 SR (NSW) 130, *Bayliss v Public Trustee* (1988) 12 NSWLR 540, *Cooper v Seversen* (1955) 1 DLR (2d) 161 and *Re Sorensen and Sorensen* (1977) 90 DLR (3d) 26, were against the plaintiff's submission. The text books also were almost unanimous in the view that there could not be a donatio mortis causa of real property.

An alternative argument for the plaintiff was that the delivery of the title deeds raised a trust on the death, arising by operation of law, which was binding on the estate. Such a trust, it was argued, was exempt from the usual formalities required in s 53 of the Law of Property Act 1925 as falling with the exemption in s 53(2) applicable to implied, resulting and constructive trusts.

But Mummery J restated the basic proposition that in relation to dispositions of land and interests in land the policy of the law has for long been to require attendant formalities. These formal and evidentiary requirements for the disposition of land, both inter vivos and testamentary, instil into the court a strong reluctance to allow dispositions of land by informal donatio mortis causa, which is a hybrid of inter vivos and testamentary disposition. A donatio mortis causa is inter vivos to the extent that the words of gift and the delivery or act equivalent to transfer take place while the deceased is still alive. It is testamentary in the sense that the gift is incomplete until the death of the deceased. Only after the donor's death can the donee call on the personal representatives of the donor to perfect the title if necessary (at 90).

Thus, the plaintiff's claim failed and was dismissed.

Formalities of execution

Re White (decd) Barker v Gribble [1990] 3 All ER 1

In 1981 the testator made a valid will appointing the first defendant to be his executor and trustee. In 1984 the testator decided to alter his will and dictated certain alterations to the second defendant, who copied them by hand onto the will. The testator checked the alterations, then wrote 'Alterations to Will dated 14-12-84' and asked two witnesses to sign it. The testator did not sign the will again although the will still bore his signature from the original execution in 1981. Following the testator's death the question arose whether the will in its original or amended form should be admitted to probate. It seems clear that the will in its amended form could not be admitted to probate as an altered will because the alterations did not comply with s 21 of the 1837 Act. The alterations had to meet all the formal requirements under s 9 for the execution of a will and had not been signed by the testator or any other person in his presence and by his direction as required by s 9; dictum of Buckley J in *Re Hay, Kerr v Stinnear* [1904] 1 Ch 317 applied; *Re Dewell's goods* (1853) 1 Ecc & Ad 103 disapproved.

An ingenious argument in favour of formal validity was based on the revised form of s 9. Although the will in its amended form was not signed by the testator, could it be said that when the testator presented the will to the witnesses for them to sign, 'the testator intended by his signature to give effect to the will' within para (*b*) of s 9? On this basis the court was invited to pronounce for the 1984 will, as an original will. But the reference in para (*b*) to 'his signature' refers to the act of signing the will and not merely to the presence on the will of the testator's signature. The act of signing occurred in 1981 and there was no basis on which, by signing the will in 1981, the testator could be said to have intended to give effect to the amended 1984 will, per Andrew Park QC (sitting as a deputy judge of the High Court, at 6). This must be a correct view of the section and the requirements relating to the testators signature had clearly not been met.

Another fatal objection to the argument based on validity of the 1984 document as an original will, was that the witnesses did not sign 'the will' in the sense of attesting the 1984 will; the evidence clearly showed that all they were attesting were the alterations to the 1981 will. The authorities of *Re Martin's goods* (1849) 1 Rob Eccl 712 and *Re Shearn's goods* (1880) 50 LJP 15 establish that where the witnesses (who initialled the manuscript amendments) had not attested the altered will as a whole, but merely the alterations, the will could not be regarded as properly witnessed. Thus it was held that the *Re White* will did not satisfy para (*d*) of s 9. This seems a rather strict view and the conclusion could have been avoided if it had been desired to do so, for surely it could be said that although the witnesses' signatures were referable to the alterations, the intention was to witness the will as altered. If this view had been adopted, then the problem regarding the testator's failure to sign the amended will could have been solved by arguing that he had acknowledged his 1981 signature in 1984. There is a great deal of authority on what constitutes an acknowledgment and one such case, *Daintree v Butcher* (1888) 13 PD 102, was referred to. But there is no authority on the point whether a signature to the original execution can be used again, so to speak, and acknowledged to authenticate alterations. In the cases on acknowledgment it is always a 'new' signature, albeit not made in the presence of the witnesses, which is acknowledged. The legislation does not actually require that it should be a 'new' signature and in principle there seems no reason why an 'old' signature cannot be so acknowledged to validate alterations. Andrew Park QC commented without further discussion of the point that he would be disposed to accept that the condition in para (c) of s 9 was satisfied (at 7). It is to be regretted that there was no further discussion of this point, which is potentially the most interesting in the case. Perhaps the factual evidence of the testator's act, sufficient to constitute an acknowledgment, was missing.

The conclusion was that the will in its original 1981 form was admitted to probate and that the 1984 alterations were invalid.

Will: revocation

In *Re Adams (decd)* [1990] 2 All ER 97 decides an interesting point on s 20 of the Wills Act 1837. The facts were that on 21 September 1976 the testatrix made a will with the assistance of a firm of solicitors. On 4 January 1982 she telephoned her solicitor and instructed him to destroy the will. Her solicitor wrote to the testatrix enclosing the will saying that he thought it better that she should destroy it. The testatrix died on 9 September 1987. Among her possessions was found the 1976 will in which the typescript had been scribbled upon in many places with a blue-black ball point pen and the signatures of the testatrix and the attesting witnesses were particularly heavily scored out. Francis Ferris QC (sitting as a deputy judge of the High Court), having closely examined the will stated that he could not read with his eye what the original writing was, whether it was a further part of the testator's signature or what the signature was. He ruled that the signature, if that is what it was, of the testatrix on the will was no longer apparent. The issue was whether this amounted to a revocation of the will by 'burning, tearing or otherwise destroying' it within s 20 of the Wills Act 1837. The principle stated in *Williams on Wills* (6th edn 1987) p 154) to the effect that where a will is destroyed or found mutilated, in a place in which the testator would naturally put it, there is a presumption that the testator destroyed it with the intention of revoking it, was applied. The facility provided by s 20 of the Wills Act 1837 to, in effect, informally revoke a will by destruction can be regarded as anomalous, but the principle remains entrenched in the law and no attempt at modification was made in the Administration of Justice Act 1982.

There are a number of well-known cases on the phrase 'burning, tearing or otherwise destroying'. In *Hobbs v Knight* (1838) 1 Curt 768, the signature of the testator was cut out, and this was held to amount to a revocation, for it is not necessary to destroy the will completely (applying *Doe d Reed v Harris* (1837) 6 Ad & El 209). Similarly in *Re Morton* (1887) 12 PD 141 where the signatures of the testator and the attesting witnesses had been scratched out with a knife. The limits of such symbolic destruction were drawn in *Cheese v Lovejoy* (1877) 2 PD 251, *Stephens v Taprell* (1840) 2 Curt 458 and *Re Godfrey (decd)* (1893) 69 LT 22. In the latter case the testator's signature had been scratched with a penknife but since it was still possible to read it, there was no revocation. In contrast in *Re Adams* the signatures had not been cut away or otherwise excised or abraded away, nothing had been destroyed; the text had simply been overlaid with substance (ink from a ball point pen) to an extent in which it was illegible or barely legible. The judge thought that it would be wrong to draw a distinction between such a situation and a case where a signature had been physically removed from the document. It was thought that the test of destruction in such cases should be that in s 21 of the Wills Act 1837, namely whether the words or effect of the will before such alteration 'shall not be apparent'. Francis Ferris QC then continued (at 102):

> 'the provision is couched in the negative, but if one turns it into positive form one effect of it is that where the original words are not apparent an unattested alteration will have the effect of revoking them. It seems to me that it would be wrong to apply a different test for the purposes of ascertaining whether there is a revocation of the will in its entirety within the words of s 20 from the test which is applied for the purpose of determining whether there is a revocation of a part of the will within s 21.' (Applying *Hobbs v Knight, Townley v Watson* (1844) 3 Curt 761 and *Ffinch v Combe* [1894] P 191).

Applying that test the will was held to have been revoked. Few would argue with this conclusion. Although the previous cases had seemed to insist on some physical mutilation of the document it is hard to argue that a text is any less 'destroyed' by the sort of complete obliteration that had been effected on the *Adams* will. Certainly, the only reasonable inference to draw from the testator's act was that she had intended thereby to revoke the will; no other explanation of the act is sustainable.

Family provision

It is clear from *Whyte v Ticehurst* [1986] 2 All ER 158 (All ER Rev 1986, p 291) that the Inheritance (Provision for Family and Dependants) Act 1975 does not confer an enforceable right of action which endures for the benefit of the estate of a deceased applicant. Qualified applicants merely have a personal right to apply to the court for financial provision from the estate. In that case, it will be recalled, the widow died before the hearing of her application and it was held that there was no cause of action within the meaning of s 1(1) of the Law Reform (Miscellaneous Provisions) Act 1934 that could survive her death and be enforced by her personal representatives. The personal nature of an application under the Act has been reinforced by *Re Collins (decd)* [1990] 2 All ER 47, to the effect that a child who may have been qualified to claim under the Act ceases to be so qualified if he is subsequently adopted before an application for financial provision is made. The child in that case was a child of the deceased but had been adopted after the death and before the issue of the originating summons making a claim under the Act. The Adoption Act 1976, s 39(2) is clear that an adopted child shall be treated in law as if he were not the child of any person other than the adopters or adopter. An argument was based on s 42(4) of the 1976 Act which states that the general provision does not prejudice any interest vested in possession in the adopted child before the adoption, or any interest expectant (whether immediate or not) upon an interest so vested. The right of the son, it was argued, which applied to him as a son at death, was a chose in action, vested in him and thus could be described as an 'interest expectant'. But this was easily disposed of by Hollings J. The 'interest' was no more than a hope and could not be described as a cause of action nor, a fortiori, as an interest expectant. *Whyte v Ticehurst* was conclusive on this point (at 51). In order to be entitled to claim under the 1975 Act the applicant must be qualified at death and must be so qualified at the time of the application.

Two further points were confirmed by *Re Collins*. First, in considering whether to make an order under s 2(1)(d) of the 1975 Act the court may take into account any wish of the deceased expressed before death, including, if and so far as it is relevant, any unexecuted will of the deceased.

Secondly, the financial resources of an applicant to which the court is to have regard under s 3(1)(e) of the 1975 Act in determining whether to make an order under that Act do not include any receipts of social security benefits: *Re E (decd), E v E* [1966] 2 All ER 44 followed. This is consistent with the established practice in matrimonial cases that a person otherwise liable to maintain a child, or a wife or ex-wife, unless he or she is also in receipt of DSS payments, cannot excuse himself or herself from liability to pay maintenance on the ground that the claimant is in receipt of DSS payments (at 52).

The adopted son received no award under the Act for the reasons set out above, but an adult illegitimate daughter was made an award of £5,000 as a lump sum for her maintenance.

The other interesting feature of *Re Collins* is that although the parties obtained a decree nisi many years ago it was never made absolute and so the husband was entitled on the subsequent death intestate of his wife to her whole estate. Further, he would have had locus standi to make an application under the Act if the estate had been left elsewhere. Surely the law should be changed here to recognise that the decree nisi is the effective termination of the marriage so far as intestate is concerned, and for locus standi under the 1975 Act. (See Family Law, pp 136–137 above for further discussion of this case.)

Nomination under power in pension scheme

The power to appoint a nominee to receive benefits payable under a pension scheme if an employee dies while still in employment is a familiar feature of modern pension schemes. Whether such a nomination is testamentary and so subject to the provisions of the Wills Act 1837 depends, in each case, on the provisions of the individual scheme. In *Re MacInnes* (1935) 1 DLR 401, under the trusts of the scheme the deceased had an absolute beneficial interest in his share of the fund during his lifetime, and it was held that the share of the fund passed under the trusts of the testator's will, rather than to the widow, whom he had designated as his beneficiary under a document signed by him and lodged with the trustees of the scheme. In contrast is the well known decision of Megarry J in *Re Danish Bacon Co Ltd staff pension fund, Christensen v Arnett* [1971] 1 All ER 486. In that case the rules of the scheme provided that the member might, and must if required by the trustees, revocably appoint a beneficiary to receive that which would otherwise become due to his personal representatives on his death in service. One issue raised was whether a nomination signed in the presence of a single witness was effective or whether it was a testamentary disposition which required to be executed in the same way as a will. Megarry J held that the nomination was effective (at 493–494):

'First, although a nomination had certain testamentary characteristics, and not least that of being ambulatory, it took effect as a contractual arrangement and not as a disposition by the deceased. The contributions and interest did not come to the deceased and then pass on from him by force of his will or the nomination: they went directly from the fund to the nominee and formed no part of the estate of the deceased . . . Despite certain testamentary characteristics, the nomination takes effect under the trust deed and rules, and the nominee in no way claims through the deceased. Secondly, there is a vast difference, it was said, between a testamentary paper and a disposition of a testamentary nature. A testamentary paper must satisfy the Wills Act 1837; but a disposition might have certain testamentary characteristics without the paper containing it being a testamentary paper . . . non-statutory nominations are odd creatures, and the cases provide little help on their nature. I do not, however, think that a nomination under the trust deed and rules in the present case requires execution as a will. It seems to me that such a nomination operates by force of the provisions of those rules, and not as a testamentary disposition by the deceased. Further, although the nomination has certain testamentary characteristics, I do not think that these suffice to make the paper on which it is written a testamentary paper. Accordingly, in my judgment the requirements of the Wills Act 1837 have no application.'

This influential decision was applied by Lord Oliver in the Privy Council in *Baird v Baird* [1990] 2 All ER 301. The deceased had nominated, in accordance with the rules of a pension scheme, his brother as beneficiary in the event, which happened, of his death in service. Subsequently, he married but did not vary or revoke his nomination of his brother as his beneficiary. His widow argued that the nomination was a testamentary disposition which was only valid if it was executed with the formalities required for a will, which it was not. The first instance judge ruled in favour of the brother and the widow's appeal was dismissed by both the Court of Appeal of Trinidad and Tobago and by the Privy Council. In the normal case of non-assignable interests such as that in the present case, and a fortiori, where the power of nomination and revocation requires the prior approval of the trustees of a management committee, their Lordships saw no reason to doubt the correctness of Megarry J's decision in the *Danish Bacon Co* case. Essentially, the court thought, a pension scheme of this type was no different from any other inter vivos declaration of trust or settlement containing provisions for the destination of the trust fund after the death of the principal beneficiary. By becoming party to the scheme each employee constitutes himself both a beneficiary and (quoad his contributions to the trust fund from which the benefits are payable) a settlor. He retains no proprietary interests in his contributions but receives instead such rights, including the right to appoint interests in the fund to take effect on the occurrence of specified contingencies, as the trusts of the fund confer on him. Thus, the power to appoint the 'death in employment' benefit is no different from any other power of appointment. As such it is not testamentary in character. This was confirmed in the present case by the fact that the nomination lacked the essential testamentary characteristic of being freely revocable since it could be made and revoked or altered only with the consent of the management committee. (Per Lord Oliver at p 305). *Re Joseph Baxter's Goods* [1903] P 12 and *Re MacInnes* distinguished. *Norris v Norris* (1977) 29 WIR 22 doubted. Accordingly, the nominated brother took the pension benefits. Although this conclusion was no doubt correct on the terms of the particular pension scheme under consideration, it can certainly be argued that in most such cases the member would have preferred his widow to receive the death in service benefit. Where the nomination is made before marriage it is thus essential to review the matter after marriage and to revoke other earlier nominations (with the approval of the trustees) and to make a new one in favour of the wife. Pension schemes should clearly highlight this trap and perhaps provide for the automatic revocation of a prior nomination on the subsequent marriage of the member, with the wife being automatically nominated as the beneficiary if no alternative express provision is made.

Intestacy

Morritt J's judgment in *Re Spence (decd), Spence v Dennis* [1989] 2 All ER 679 was fully noted in last year's Review, at pp 305–307. This decision has now been affirmed by the Court of Appeal, [1990] 2 All ER 827, the court expressing itself as being in complete agreement both with the decision of the first instance judge and with his reasoning. It is accordingly not necessary perhaps to review the case in detail here but the main points can be reaffirmed. The Legitimacy Act 1976, s 1(1) states that a child of a void marriage, whenever born, shall be treated as the legitimate child of his parents if at the time of the act of intercourse resulting in the birth, or at the time of the celebration of the marriage if later, both or either of the parties reasonably believed that the marriage was valid. It was held that this section did not apply to a child who was born before his parents entered into the void marriage. This conclusion was based on the intention of Parliament in enacting s 1(1) that only a child born after a void marriage had taken place was to be treated as being in the same position as if that marriage were valid. The term 'whenever born' in the section denoted that the Act was to have retrospective effect only as regards children born after a void marriage had taken place rather than that it applied to all children of a void marriage regardless of whether they were born before or after the void marriage.

It can be noted that if the facts of *Re Spence* were to recur in respect of a death on or after 4 April 1988, the case would now be governed by s 18 of the Family Law Reform Act 1987.

Practice directions

There have been two practice directions relevant to probate, issued during 1990. The first, [1990] 2 All ER 576 provides for the form of oath where the partners in a firm of solicitors are appointed executors of a will, without being named. The second, [1990] 3 All ER 734, states the manner in which postal applications for copies of wills and grants will be dealt with, without prejudice to the existing practice regarding personal applications or the Principal Registry.

Taxation

JOHN TILEY, MA, BCL
Professor of the Law of Taxation, University of Cambridge;
Fellow, Queens' College, Cambridge

The year 1990 has seen a steady stream of cases developing points of tax law. The year has passed relatively quietly but this is not to say that one can be uniformly happy with the outcome.

Schedule E

Few cases have attracted more criticism and comment this year than *Pepper v Hart* [1990] STC 786 CA affirming the decision of Vinelott J ([1990] STC 6). An employer, a private school (Malvern College), provided an 'in-house' benefit in the form of education for the child of a member of the teaching staff for a fee equal to one fifth of the normal fee. By what is now the Income and Corporation Taxes Act 1988, s 154 and 156, the employee was chargeable to tax on the cost to the employer of providing the benefit. What is meant by 'cost'? The fee paid was more than enough to cover the marginal cost to the school but was substantially less than the average cost found by spreading the entire costs of the school for the year over all the pupils.

There are many meanings of cost. First, there is opportunity cost. Suppose that there was evidence that someone was willing to pay twice the normal fee to get his son into Malvern? In these circumstances the college would have foregone the opportunity of making that sum. It is generally thought that the insistence in s 156(2) on a cost being 'incurred' is sufficient to exclude the concept of an opportunity cost, although it is hard to see why this should be so. Secondly, there is the marginal cost of educating this child, ie the extra cost of providing this service. This is what the taxpayer argued for. On a third view, the school must average the entire cost of its activities for the period in question over all the pupils. This is what the Revenue contended for (successfully). However this cost may itself be a matter of dispute. Suppose that an airline flies an employee across the Atlantic. Should the cost include some or all of the overhead costs and over what period? Thus should one take the marginal cost to the airline of running this flight, so spreading the cost over the number of passengers on this flight (a matter of some interest if, for example, the employee were the only passenger on the flight) or, perhaps, the appropriate proportion of the cost of the entire operations of that month (or year), so perhaps treating the employee as receiving a benefit far higher than the normal fare? These problems are not addressed by this decision. There must be a faint hope that the House of Lords will reverse this decision. If not, perhaps legislation will be forthcoming.

Nicholls LJ said that when such a concise formula as that contained in s 156(2) has to be applied across the entire range of benefits, whether provided in-house or externally, it is hardly a matter of surprise if here and there some odd results, which may not have been foreseen by Parliament, are produced (791h). This has great force; and the anomalies are not all one way (consider, for example, the situation arising if the admission of a teacher's child means that an extra employee has to be taken on – under the marginal cost rule the whole of this cost is to be allocated to the new pupil).

One may also wonder about the intellectual cohesion of the area of law. Until 1976 the Revenue would not charge employees on the value of interest-free loans since it took the view that these benefits had no cost; what is now Income and Corporation Taxes Act 1988, s 160 reverses that position by introducing a scale charge. If *Pepper v Hart* is right it is hard to see why tax could not have been effectually charged before 1976, the calculation being made by reference to the average cost to the employer of funds raised for the business. This might well produce a figure different from the position resulting from s 160 but would certainly have been significant. See also JFAJ (1990) BTR 120 and Dyson (1990) BTR 122.

In the much more straightforward decision in *Glynn v Commissioner of Inland Revenue* [1990] STC 227 the Privy Council held that payment by an employer of the employee's child's school fees direct to school was a taxable perquisite within the Inland Revenue Ordinance (Hong Kong). The case is unsurprising but Lord Templeman uses the occasion to take a leisurely browse through the UK authorities and to tell the Hong Kong courts that they were entitled to find the UK cases helpful.

Shilton v Wilmshurst (Inspector of Taxes) [1990] STC 55 is a Court of Appeal decision which has now been reversed by the House of Lords ([1991] STC 88). Comment on the first instance decision of Morritt J ([1988] STC 868) was made in All ER Rev 1988, p 300. See also the comments of Macdonald and Kerridge in (1990) BTR 313 and 315.

For present purposes it will suffice to note that the case concerned the payment of £75,000 to footballer Peter Shilton on his move from Nottingham Forest to Southampton in 1982, the payment being made by Nottingham Forest to persuade him to move (and so go off their payroll) was held by the House of Lords to be taxable in full under TA 1988, s 19 and not just on the terms applicable to golden handshakes (see also Sport and the Law, pp 245, 248 above).

Next come two cases on share options. *Inland Revenue Commissioners v Burton Group plc* [1990] STC 242 is a positive decision of Vinelott J rejecting some narrow Revenue arguments as to the scope of rules relating to share option schemes. The Revenue had refused to approve amendments to the Burton scheme; Vinelott J upheld the decision of a Special Commissioner allowing the company's appeal against that refusal.

The amendments sought related to the setting of key tasks which had to be met before an employee could acquire shares in the company. If the key tasks were not met, the number of shares to which the employee was entitled might be reduced. The proposed amendments would enable the company to set or vary those key tasks after an option had been granted. The company's trade was a volatile one and a scheme whereby key tasks could only be set before an option was granted would have been unsatisfactory.

The first Revenue objection was that the proposed amendments would not enable an employee to know the terms under which he could acquire the shares before the option agreement had been made. Vinelott J rejected this. The option, when granted, would have been understood by both the company and the employee as conferring rights to the specified shares subject among other conditions to the employee meeting key tasks set by the company and if necessary varied from time to time in a way which provides a fair measure of his performance. That was enough.

He specifically left open the wider argument by counsel for the company that:

> 'an option conferring on the option holder a right to call on the option giver to issue or transfer a given number of shares but under which the option giver had a discretion to reduce the number of shares which the option holder could call for at any time before the option was exercised would be a valid option conferring rights on the option holder to the shares specified in the option as varied from time to time.'

The Revenue's second objection that as the effect of the condition would be only to reduce the shares which the employee would otherwise have the right to acquire, the condition was neither 'essential nor reasonably incidental to the purpose of providing for employees . . . benefits in the nature of rights to acquire shares'. Vinelott J said that one had to look at the scheme as a whole. The uncontradicted evidence was that the condition was designed to ensure that the scheme operated more effectively in its purpose of providing share benefits for employees who contribute to the prosperity of the company.

The second share option case is *Ball (Inspector of Taxes) v Phillips* [1990] STC 675. Here the taxpayer argued that he could not be taxed under what is now TA 1988, s 135 on the grant of an option to acquire shares under an employees' savings related share option scheme. Under s 135(1) tax is due on the exercise of the option and under s 135(2) where the option is exercisable only within the seven years from the grant no other charge arises. His argument was that the right to acquire shares was not a perquisite as it was not capable of being turned to pecuniary account. Hoffman J had little difficulty in rejecting this argument; s 135 was an independent charging provision and liability to tax under that section depended solely on whether its conditions had been satisfied.

Parikh v Sleeman (Inspector of Taxes) [1990] STC 233 is another Court of Appeal decision but it appears unlikely that any further appeal can be made, The appeal was from the decision of Vinelott J at [1988] STC 580 and the judges say little more than that the judge was entirely right in the decision he reached. The taxpayer was a doctor in general practice who, in addition to conducting his practice at his own home and surgery, served under three contracts with three separate hospitals as a clinical officer. Vinelott J said that the commissioners had been entirely justified in concluding that while travelling from home or surgery to hospital or between hospitals, the taxpayer was not travelling in the performance of his duties. Slade LJ said that there was no substance in any of the grounds raised.

Finally under this head one may note two cases which are primarily of administrative importance. *Billows Ltd v Robinson (Inspector of Taxes)* [1990] STC 162 is a decision of Vinelott J from which an appeal is about to be heard. The short question was whether, if a taxpayer's income was insufficient to meet his living expenses, the commissioners were entitled to conclude that the difference represented money and so emoluments received improperly from the company of which he was a directors. Vinelott J held that the commissioners' determination in favour of the Revenue was supported by the evidence.

Figael Ltd v Fox (Inspector of Taxes) [1990] STC 583 is a decision of Mummery J on the scope of the PAYE regulations relating to troncs. Under the PAYE regulations the troncmaster can be regarded as the employer for PAYE purposes in relation to tips rather than the actual employer. Mummery J held that the facts with which he was presented did not come within the terms of the regulation. It was not enough to show that there were organised arrangements for gratuities or service charges to be shared out among two or more employees. There also had to be a troncmaster, who makes the payment by way of the sharing. The provisions of the regulation were neither necessary nor appropriate to deal with the case where payments out of the tronc were made by the very same person who pays the emoluments to the employees in the form of wages.

Schedule D, Case I

In *Commissioner of Inland Revenue v Hang Seng Bank Ltd* [1990] STC 733 the issue was where trading activities were carried on. The taxpayer bank invested its surplus holding of foreign currencies in certificates of deposit. These certificates were not marketable in Hong Kong but only in London or Singapore. Sales were invariably effected before maturity. The funds used and accruing from these transactions were debited and credited to the bank's accounts with other banks overseas.

The Privy Council, reversing the Hong Kong Court, held that the profits did not arise in and were not derived from Hong Kong; therefore they were not liable to profits tax under s 14 of the Ordinance. The judgment consists principally of a discussion of the precise terms of the Hong Kong legislation but Lord Bridge, speaking for the Board, said that in determining where profits arose the broad guiding principle was to find what the taxpayer had done to earn the profits in question. Profits from a service would arise where the service was rendered; profits from the exploitation of property assets where the contracts of purchase and sale had been effected.

Inland Revenue Commissioners v Aken [1990] STC 497 is a case on the taxation of earnings from prostitution. The assessment was raised under Schedule D, Case I but the income was described as 'professional fees' or as 'profits of prostitution'; nothing turns on whether the assessment should have been raised under D II. The taxpayer argued that the profits of prostitution could not be taxed as trading income because prostitution was not a trade. It was submitted that for an activity to be a trade within the Taxes Act it must have all the attributes of trade including the right to enter into enforceable contracts, to advertise, to enter into partnership, to employ people and to rent premises; and since it was illegal for a prostitute to do many of those things her activities could not be treated as constituting a trade. This argument was rejected. The provision of services for reward could properly be called 'trade'. It was not necessary to consider whether, as the Crown said, an illegal trade is still a trade because prostitution is not illegal under English law. Many of the activities which are associated with prostitution are in fact illegal – eg, the keeping of a brothel or letting premises for use as a brothel or soliciting – but those are irrelevant. Counsel for the taxpayer referred to the interesting decision of the Supreme Court in Ireland in *Hayes v Duggan* [1929] 1 IR 406, a case concerning a bookmaker who was assessed for profits derived

from the running of sweepstakes; Parker LJ treated it as one where the very
activity from which the profits were derived was itself prohibited by
Parliament and made a criminal act.

In *Lawson (Inspector of Taxes) v Johnson Matthey plc* [1990] STC 149 Vinelott J
allowed an appeal by the Crown against a decision by the commissioners
which had allowed the taxpayer company (JM) to deduct £50m injected into a
subsidiary which was about to be taken over.

JM carried on the business of refining and marketing precious metals and had
a subsidiary, JMB, which carried on the business of banking. In 1984, a board
meeting of JM concluded, inter alia, that JMB was insolvent and could not
open its doors for business the following day unless further financing, which
JM could not afford to supply, was made available; in consequence JMB
should be wound up. The Bank of England then made a non-negotiable offer
to purchase the issued share capital of JMB for £1 provided JM injected £50m
into JMB (free from any obligation to repay) prior to the sale. JM accepted the
offer on condition that the Bank provided a standby facility of £250m. The
agreement was implemented by the opening of business the following day.

JM contended that the payment was an expense of a revenue nature because
it was made to preserve its trade from collapse as a result of the collapse of
JMB and that it was incurred wholly and exclusively for the purpose of its
own trade and was therefore not precluded by s 74(a) of the Income and
Corporation Taxes Act 1988. The Crown contended that the payment was
non-deductible on three grounds: (i) the payment was made to procure the
disposal of a capital asset which were the JMB shares; (ii) the payment was
made to free JM from a liability of a capital nature relating to JMB's business;
and (iii) the payment was not made wholly and exclusively for purpose of
JM's trade since its purpose was, inter alia, to rescue JMB and to preserve the
businesses and goodwill of other companies in the group.

The commissioners rejected all three of the Crown's arguments, and no
appeal was taken on their decision on points (ii) and (iii). In view of the many
cases in which the Crown succeeds on this argument one should note the
commissioners' findings as summarised by Vinelott J.

> 'As to the third ground they held that if the other companies in the group had
> not existed the taxpayer company would still have paid £50m to preserve its
> own trade. The taxpayer company would not have paid any substantial sum to
> preserve the goodwill and trade of the other companies in the group. They
> contributed profits of only £1m to group profits of over £20m; the other £19m
> was earned by the taxpayer company from its platinum trade. They also held
> that if any part fell to be treated as paid for the preservation of the trade of other
> members of the group 96% of the £50m should nonetheless be apportioned to
> the preservation of the goodwill and trade of the taxpayer company.'

The last sentence reflects an interesting line of thought which one can trace
back to *Copeman v William J Flood & Sons Ltd* [1941] 1 KB 202, 24 TC 53.

On the main point Vinelott J's conclusion was short and simple. The
purpose of the board of the taxpayer company in agreeing to make that
payment was no doubt to preserve the taxpayer company's business. But the
means by which that purpose was achieved, and the only means by which it
could be achieved, was to transfer the shares of JMB to the Bank and as part of
a single transaction or arrangement to pay £50m to JMB and to release JMB

from any obligation to repay it. These two elements could not be severed, the one being treated as the disposal for a nominal consideration of a worthless but not an onerous asset and the other as a payment made to preserve the business of the taxpayer company.

Waylee Investment Ltd v Commissioner of Inland Revenue [1990] STC 780 is a Privy Council decision on the tax position of a bank taking a stake in an important customer to protect the bank's advances. The Privy Council held that a bank, like any other trader, may hold investments as capital assets as well as circulating assets in order to meet the demands of depositors whenever necessary. It was clear that the bank in the instant case never intended that the relevant shares acquired by the taxpayer should be held as part of the bank's circulating assets. No cases were cited in the judgment delivered by Lord Bridge.

Finally, one should just record that there are two cases on the now obsolete stock relief – *Klöckner Ina Industrial Plants Ltd v Bryan* [1990] STC 32 and *Shaw v Samuel Montagu & Co Ltd* [1990] STC 538.

Capital allowances

Barclays Mercantile Industrial Finance Ltd v Melluish (Inspector of Taxes) [1990] STC 314 concerns a matter of declining importance since the taxpayer was seeking a first year allowance. However, there are points of general interest.

In 1982 the taxpayer, B, which carried on the trade of leasing equipment bought a film, called *Greystoke*, for £22m and leased it to another company at a rental which would yield a return of 2.16% on the purchase price after making adjustments for interest, corporation tax and any capital allowance obtained by B for 12 years certain but extendible from year to year thereafter unless terminated. Arrangements were made for the distribution of the film in the United Kingdom and outside. There was also an agreement granting an exclusive licence to the BBC to exhibit the film by television. The film was completed and delivered in 1984. A similar arrangement was made for a second film, called *Krull*. B claimed 100% first year capital allowances in respect of its expenditure on the acquisition of the two films.

Vinelott J, allowing the taxpayer's appeal from the Special Commissioners, held that the taxpayer was not caught by what is now CAA 1990 s 75(1)(c) (which bars a first year allowance if the the sole or main benefit which was expected to accrue from the expenditure was the obtaining of capital allowance). This was because the provision was aimed at artificial transactions designed wholly or primarily at creating a tax allowance. B's main object in acquiring and leasing the films was not to obtain a capital allowance but to make a profit. Given the frequency with which the 'sole or main benefit' formula occurs in the tax legislation this decision will be welcome. The learned judge was helped to this conclusion by his view that it would be perverse to construe s 75(1)(c) as denying a first year allowance in a situation clearly covered by another provision (FA 1972, s 68(5)).

He then held that the fact that the lessees had not expected to make a profit out of the licences was not sufficient by itself to found the conclusion that the distribution agreements were not entered into in the ordinary course of the lessees' businesses. It could not be right to separate the distribution agreements and to categorise them as non-commercial on the ground that considered in isolation they were unlikely to give rise to a profit. This too is welcome.

Finally, he held that the distribution agreements were not 'leases' within the meaning of FA 1980, s 64(2)(a) (now CAA 1990, s 39(2)).

Capital gains tax

There are four decisions to note, each on fairly minor parts of the code. Each, however, raises interesting issues of construction.

Lewis (Inspector of Taxes) v Lady Rook [1990] STC 23 is yet another case on the scope of the exemption for private residence where the property disposed of is a cottage occupied by the taxpayer's servant; the question was whether the cottage could be treated as part of the taxpayer's residence for Capital Gains Tax Act 1979, s 101(1)(a).

The facts were that the taxpayer had bought an estate of 10.5 acres which included a large house, an adjacent coach house and two cottages (formerly an oast-house). The relevant cottage was occupied by a gardener employed by the taxpayer. The inspector accepted that the gardener's occupancy of the cottage was occupation by the taxpayer but said that the cottage did not form part of the taxpayer's dwelling house. The taxpayer was an elderly lady who lived alone in the house, and had relied on the gardener's presence in the cottage: he provided help when she needed it and she could call him by ringing a bell or flashing a light.

The General Commissioners applied an 'entity' test and found that the cottage formed part of the entity which comprised the taxpayer's residence and held that she was entitled to relief. Mervyn Davies J applied the same test and held that there was evidence to support the commissioners' decision and the appeal was therefore dismissed.

The nub of the Revenue's case was that the cottage was 190 yards away from the main house. Mervyn Davies J, like Vinelott J in *Williams v Merrylees* [1987] STC 445 (All ER Rev 1987, p 277) distanced himself from the view of Walton J in *Markey v Saunders* [1987] STC 256 (All ER Rev 1987, p 276); Walton J had spelled out of the earlier decision in *Batey v Wakefield* [1982] 1 All ER 61, [1981] STC 521 two distinct conditions – that the occupation must increase the taxpayer's enjoyment of the main dwellinghouse and that it must be closely adjacent to the main building. Such efforts to gloss the state were rejected by Mervyn Davies J. Instead one must just apply a broad test – one has to look for the entity which in fact constitutes the residence of the taxpayer (see *Batey v Wakefield* [1980] STC 572 at 577, [1981] STC 521 at 524, 55 TC 550 at 556B, 560A):

> 'The "entity" constituting the taxpayer's residence means, to my mind, the totality of the parts of the place where the taxpayer lives which pertain to a whole and so are integral to his or her style of life. On that approach I would not suppose that the whole of the Newlands estate is the relevant entity. On the other hand Newlands House itself and its lawn and its vegetable garden and converted coach house would clearly be within the entity.'

Owen v Elliott (Inspector of Taxes) [1990] STC 469 is a Court of Appeal decision reversing that of Millett J ([1989] STC 44 (All ER Rev 1989, pp 323, 328)) on the interpretation of the Finance Act 1980, s 80(1) which gave a relief from tax for 'residential accommodation'; the taxpayer owned a private hotel accommodating long-term or short-term guests; the hotel was also used by the taxpayer as his main residence for part of year.

By the Finance Act 1980:

> 'Where a gain to which section 101 of the Capital Gains Tax Act 1979 (disposals of private residences) applies accrues to any individual and the dwelling-house in question or any part of it is or has at any time in his period of ownership been wholly or partly let by him as residential accommodation the part of the gain, if any, which, apart from this section would be a chargeable gain by reason of the letting, shall be such a gain only to the extent, if any, to which it exceeds the lesser of [two amounts].'

The General Commissioners rejected the claim and their decision was upheld by Millett J. However, the Court of Appeal reversed these decisions and determined the issue in the taxpayer's favour. The purpose of the section can only emerge from the words of the section. It seemed to Parker LJ to be

> 'just as likely that the purpose behind this section was to encourage home owners to make surplus accommodation available on a bed and breakfast basis as it was that they should provide homes within their own homes for other people.'

This decision does not quite reduce the exercise of interpretation to one of complete sterility since it was accepted that the words could fit the taxpayer's case and it was the Crown which was arguing (unsuccessfully) for a modified interpretation. Whether one is more persuaded by the words of Millett J or by those of the Court of Appeal is largely a matter of taste. If the Revenue had wanted to restrict the section in the way for which they contended they could have drafted the legislation more clearly in 1980. See also the note by Sparkes in (1990) BTR 385.

Smith (Inspector of Taxes) v Schofield (1990) STI 658 is another case on a small matter which could so easily have been clarified when the legislation was drawn up. Instead, Hoffman J was treated to argument based on mathematics.

In 1952 the taxpayer acquired a Chinese cabinet and a French mirror for £250. In 1987 she sold them for £15,800. The gain was be computed on a straightline growth apportionment but how did the indexation allowance fit in. Section 86(4)a of the Finance Act 1982 (as amended by the Finance Act 1985) provides that the indexation allowance should be set against the unindexed gain so as to give the gain for the purposes of the 1979 Act and s 86(2)b defined the unindexed gain as the amount of the gain on the disposal computed in accordance with the 1979 Act. The taxpayer contended that the unindexed gain meant the gain computed after time-apportionment and that accordingly the indexation allowance was to be deducted after the chargeable gain had been determined by time-apportionment. The Crown contended that the unindexed gain meant the whole gain between the date of acquisition and the date of disposal and that accordingly the indexation allowance was to be set against the overall gain leaving a gain which would then be time-apportioned to give the chargeable gain. The Special Commissioner upheld the taxpayer's contention. The Crown appealed and Hoffman J allowed that appeal.

Verbal arguments apart, the key point in the Crown's argument was probably this one, as set out by Hoffman J:

'The Crown produced figures, which were not challenged by the taxpayer, demonstrating mathematically that on the assumption the value of the asset after 1982 kept pace with inflation, any gain which had previously accrued would inevitably be eventually turned into a loss. Inexorably, over time the indexation allowance becomes a larger and larger proportion of the total gain until it exceeds the fraction which (on the taxpayer's construction) is time-apportioned to the period after 1965. The higher the annual rate of inflation, the sooner this position is reached. This would be a bizarre result. It certainly does not give effect to a policy of taxing money gains until 1982 and only real gains thereafter. On the other hand, if the indexation allowance is deducted from the overall gain, both that gain and the time-apportionment are calculated on the common hypothesis that there has been no inflation since March 1982.'

Hoffman J added that the Special Commissioner did not have the benefit of these calculations. Whether it was unfair, said Hoffman J, depended entirely on the observer's point of view. If one treated the taxpayer as having an immutable right to a time-apportionment on the basis of unadjusted values, then of course it was unfair to apply the indexation allowance before that apportionment had been made. But this assumed in favour of the taxpayer what the argument was all about.

Now mathematical examples can prove a great many things and it is unlikely that the Crown's argument avoids all absurdities. It remains to be seen whether this is the last word. However, it does seem odd that when the indexation allowance was brought in this matter was not addressed and that taxpayers were not given a new right to elect for value as at 6 April 1965.

Hirsch (Inspector of Taxes) v Crowthers Cloth Ltd [1990] STC 174 is an interesting case on the interaction of capital gains and capital allowances legislation.

Suppose that an asset costs £5,000 and that the owner takes capital allowances of £3,500. He then sells the asset for £7,000. On sale there will be a balancing charge of £3,500 and, after deducting the £5,000 in the usual way under CGTA 1979, s 32(1) a capital gain of £2,000. What was argued in this case was that the taxpayer could also deduct the £5,000 under s 31(1); so making a net loss of £3,000.

In this case, the sums involved were much bigger, a loss of £375,893 instead of a gain of £170,037:

'It is not suggested that this remarkable result came about as the result of any manipulation of the company's affairs or of any planned and artificial acquisition and disposal. Counsel for the company told me that it came as a surprise to a delighted board of directors when it was revealed by their accountants' tax computation. The Special Commissioner thought that common sense would suggest that there was a chargeable gain. I imagine that no one would wish to challenge that proposition.'

Fortunately, Vinelott J felt able to resist the taxpayer's conclusion. While one may be pleased that the right decision has been reached, the real value of the judgment lies in its intricate explanation of the various provisions in this area.

Interest

Peracha v Miley (Inspector of Taxes) [1990] STC 512 is the Court of Appeal's
dismissal of the taxpayer's appeal from the decision of Vinelott J ([1989] STC
76, discussed in All ER Rev 1989, p 317).

The short question was whether interest accruing on an account at a bank
could be treated as the taxpayer's income for Schedule D, Case III. The
taxpayer had guaranteed loans to a company and, under the terms of a letter
of lien in favour of a bank, had made a sterling deposit with that bank's
London branch as security for the loans and had accepted that his liability
should be as that of a principal debtor. As a result of the creation of the state of
Bangladesh and its separation from Pakistan the bank could no longer
recover the debt from the company. In 1979, in a civil action brought by the
taxpayer to obtain the release of the deposit and accumulated interest, the
court had held that the bank was entitled to retain the deposit as security in
respect of the taxpayer's direct personal liability.

In these circumstances the Court of Appeal held that the case was
indistinguishable from *Dunmore v McGowan (Inspector of Taxes)* [1978] 2 All
ER 85, [1978] STC 217. In that case the crediting of the money to the taxpayer
(the guarantor) in the accounts of the bank relieved him immediately from his
subsisting liability to pay interest on the debt that he had guaranteed; that was
enough. The taxpayer had either to wait until the debt became statute barred
or to redeem the deposit by paying off the debt, bringing proceedings for
redemption against the [bank] if necessary. At first instance, Vinelott J had
felt able to distinguish his own earlier decision in *Macpherson v Bond (Inspector
of Taxes)* [1985] STC 678 (All ER Rev 1985, p 279), on the ground that in that
case there had been no personal liability. Dillon LJ refrained from agreeing
with this.

Minsham Properties Ltd v Price (Inspector of Taxes) [1990] STC 718 is a
decision of Vinelott J on the payment of interest and on the distinction
between yearly interest and short interest.

S, a company whose objects were exclusively charitable, had two wholly-
owned subsidiaries, L and M, the two taxpayer companies. By mid-1983, M,
a property trading company, had a substantial overdraft at a bank. S then paid
two sums totalling £270,000 into M's account at the bank so extinguishing
the overdraft. A loan account was opened in the books of S and M. There was
no written agreement as to the terms on which the loan was made. It was
group policy that all companies with exclusively charitable objects loans
should bear interest at commercial rates, here 15%. In April 1986 computer
entries were made to credit S in M's account with interest for the accounting
periods ended 30 September 1983 and 30 September 1984 'as at 30 September
1984'. A corresponding entry for the accounting period ended 30 September
1985 was made in November 1986. The interest was transferred to an accrual
account before being transferred to S's loan account. The added interest was
described as 'increase in S loan'.

For L to establish its claim for group relief it had to show that the interest
payable on the loan from S to M was not yearly interest; only then would the
interest which accrued during each of those years be deductible in
ascertaining the amount of the loss surrendered. This was rejected by the
commissioner (and by Vinelott J). The commissioner had held that as the

loan was provided by the sole shareholder it seems to him to be essentially a long term commitment in much the same way as the investment in the shares in the company. He could not draw the inference that the loan was like the overdraft it replaced. 'Rather the contrary. True, it could be a short term loan, but I infer and find as a fact that it was not.'

Before Vinelott J, counsel for the taxpayer argued that the commissioner had failed to pay sufficient regard to the fact that M was a property dealing company and that the parties must be taken to have contemplated that M would realise part at least of its trading stock in the near future and that the loan would then be repaid. Vinelott J disagreed – noting that only one disposal was made during the three years in question. As to the the inference that the loan was not a short-term loan, Vinelott J said that this was not only one which the commissioner had been fully entitled to draw but the only inference which he could properly have drawn.

The second question arose in M's appeal – whether the interest so credited was 'paid' by M on 3 April 1986 for the purposes of s[338]. If it was, then even if the interest was yearly interest it was deductible as a charge on M's income for the accounting period to 30 September 1986. No tax had been deducted, since the parties had assumed it was short interest, but nothing turned on this. On the main aspect of the matter Vinelott J began by saying that there could be no doubt that a book entry could constitute payment, but this was not so:

> '[i]f, for instance, under the terms of his loan the creditor has the right to add arrears of interest to principal, an entry in his books showing that the interest has been added to the principal will not amount to payment of the interest.'
> (*Paton (Fenton's Trustee) v IRC* [1938] 1 All ER 786, [1938] AC 341.)

In that case Lord Macmillan had said:

> '. . . what the Income Tax Act requires as the condition of repayment of tax on interest is that the sum due as interest shall have been actually discharged, not merely constructively paid. To warrant repayment of tax there must have been a real payment of tax and a real payment of interest without deduction of tax.'

In the light of this, Vinelott J, after examining the circumstances of the payment, concluded that the entry could not be treated as a payment of the interest. *Paton*'s case could not be distinguished simply on the ground that in that case the entry adding the accrued interest to principal was an entry in the books of the lender whereas here the interest was credited to the loan account in the books of both borrower and lender.

Corporation tax

Blackpool Marton Rotary Club v Martin (Inspector of Taxes) [1990] STC 1 is the Court of Appeal decision on a matter heard earlier by Hoffman J ([1988] STC 823; All ER Rev 1988, pp 310, 320). No appeal was taken against the decision of Hoffman J that the club was not a partnership but was an unincorporated association liable to corporation tax. The sole issue was whether the Inspector, in making an estimated assessment, had used his best judgment as required by Taxes Management Act 1970, s 29(1)(b). The court held that he had.

Falmer Jeans Ltd v Rodin (Inspector of Taxes) [1990] STC 270 is an interesting case on TA 1988, s 343 (company reconstruction without change of ownership). This allows for the carry forward of trading losses to a successor company where that company takes over the trade of another company.

Here the business and undertaking of a manufacturing company (FM) was acquired by its only customer, FJ, the sales company. The purpose of the reorganisation was to reduce the costs involved in maintaining two separate companies. The nature of the operations remained unchanged save that they were now conducted by FJ. For the purpose of management accounts, the manufacturing activities continued to be treated as a separate cost centre and all costs attributable to those activities continued to be separately identified.

The issue in the case was whether FJ had actually to succeed to 'the trade' carried on by FM or whether it was enough that it carried on (virtually) all FM's activities; the evidence was that FJ carried on all the activities of FM except for the sending of invoices to FJ! Millett J held that in order to come within s 343(8) the taxpayer had to show that new company carried not all the activities of the trade but sufficient of them (a) to be capable of being treated as a separate trade and (b) to satisfy the commissioners that, if so treated, that separate trade is the same trade as that formerly carried on by the predecessor.

The whole of the judgment merits close attention whenever the s 343 issue is relevant. He held that the purpose of s 343(8) is:

> 'to carry forward relief in situations not covered by sub-s (1); specifically in situations where (i) the trading activities formerly carried on by the predecessor are carried on by the successor but would be differently described when the successor's trade is described as a whole and (ii) where the profits from those activities are realised in the form of global receipts which do not distinguish between the different activities by which they are earned.'

He held that these facts fell within s 343(8). He had, incidentally, some well merited criticisms of the old cases on successions to a trade and, in particular, *Laycock v Freeman, Hardy and Willis* [1938] 4 All ER 609, 22 TC 288.

J Sainsbury plc v O'Connor (Inspector of Taxes) [1990] STC 516 is an enthralling case on the effect of options on the conditions for group relief. It also contains an extremely clear and invaluable exposition of the effect of various parts of TA 1988, Sch 18.

In 1979, Sainsburys and a Belgian company (X) entered into an agreement (the principal agreement) to establish Homebase as a joint venture. The original idea was that Sainsburys should have 70% and X 30% but as this fell short of the 75% ordinary share capital requirement the deal was structured so that Sainsburys held 75% of the issued share capital of Homebase and X held the remaining 25% but by a further agreement (the option agreement) of the same date, Sainsburys granted to X an option to purchase, and X granted to Sainsburys an option to require X to purchase 5% of the issued share capital of Homebase. The options were not exercisable before the fifth anniversary of the incorporation of Homebase. Neither option was exercised and by a deed dated 9 August 1985 the rights of both parties under the option agreement were formally terminated. Sainsburys claimed group relief in respect of trading losses incurred by Homebase for the years 1980–81 to 1984–85. Those claims were resisted.

The first argument was that the option had the effect of depriving

Sainsburys of beneficial ownership of the critical 5%. In rejecting this argument Millett J explored the meaning of beneficial ownership. Counsel for the Crown had suggested that beneficial ownership involved three things (i) the unfettered right to dispose of the shares; (ii) the right to the beneficial enjoyment of any dividends declared in respect of the shares; and (iii) the ability to reap the benefit of any increase (and the risk of suffering loss from any diminution) in the intrinsic value of the shares. Millett J however said that (i) was not an essential feature of beneficial ownership; that in relation to (ii) what was important was the entitlement to such dividends as might be declared and he rejected what lay behind (iii) ie an assumption that beneficial ownership has anything to do with value or the economic (as opposed to the legal) attributes of ownership.

Millett J distinguished the decision of the Court of Appeal in *Wood Preservation Ltd v Prior* [1969] 1 All ER 364, (1969) 45 TC 112. There a company had agreed to sell shares to a purchaser; the sale was subject to obtaining the agreement of an independent third party to the transfer of rights under a licence to the purchaser; the Court of Appeal held that the effect of the contract was that the vendor was not the beneficial owner of the shares; this was separate from the question whether the purchaser could be described as the beneficial owner. Millett J distinguished it on the basis that there the company had disabled itself from disposing of the shares or enjoying dividends from them because, subject only to the fulfilment of the condition, it had already sold them. Now it is not clear why the condition can be so lightly disregarded unless it is because the condition was one which the purchaser could waive, in which case one is left to consider another day the effect of a true condition precedent to a contract. Moreover, one may wonder whether, if the company had already sold the shares in this way, the purchaser should, after all, be treated as the new beneficial owner so that the case was, after all and despite what was said in the judgments, one in which the issue was which of two people should be treated as the beneficial owner.

Millett J concluded that Sainsbury was still the beneficial owner of the 5% of shares subject to the option. This conclusion seems sensible, the more so since it was accepted that many other conditions in the joint venture contract eg as to not disposing of shares without the consent of the other party, were not enough to deprive the owners of beneficial ownership.

This left the question of the application of what are now TA 1988, s 413(7) and Sch 18. Millett J explained the policy behind these provisions which was to stop schemes which satisfied the basic requirements of group relief while at the same time stripping the 75% shareholding of its normal rights. These schemes succeeded because the beneficial ownership of shares involves the right to the beneficial enjoyment of whatever rights may be attached thereto, but does not require those rights to be commercially significant or commensurate with the holding. What is now s 413(7) imposed two additional requirements for group relief; namely (a) that the taxpayer should be beneficially entitled to not less than 75% of any profits available for distribution to equity holders of the subsidiary company, and (b) that the taxpayer should be beneficially entitled to not less than 75% of the assets of the subsidiary company available for distribution to its equity holders on a winding up. This is supplement by Sch 18. The Crown's case was that, so long as the option agreement was in force, para 5 of that Schedule prevented

Sainsburys from satisfying the additional requirements for group relief introduced by s 413(7).

Millett J began by describing the argument as unpromising because there was only one class of shares in Homebase and Sainsburys' shares carried no special rights to dividends or distributions on a winding up. Thus these facts did not fall within the mischief at which the provisions were aimed. This basic approach colours the whole discussion of Sch 18 which follows and which is far too detailed to comment upon here. To take but one point, he said that this was not an 'arrangement' in respect of shares but only an arrangement in respect of the ownership of shares. The writer finds the whole of this part of Millett J's judgment interesting and cogent, but in view of the reception accorded by the Court of Appeal to the learned judge's decision on the capital gains case of *Owen v Elliott* celebration may be premature.

It remains only to note that the option did not cause the facts to fall within s 410 because the option would not transfer the subsidiary to another group.

Farmer (Inspector of Taxes) v Bankers Trust International Ltd [1990] STC 564 involves a short point relating to the procedures for group relief claims. However, the short point has become a minefield owing to the activities of the judges. The taxpayer company (B) made a claim in respect of losses incurred by two of its subsidiaries, X and Y, for the year ending 31 December 1973; the claim had the effect of accounting for all the taxpayer's profits. The claim was made on 22 December 1975 and was stated to be provisional in that it was subject to agreement on the figures. On 25 February 1976, B sent a letter making a claim relating to a third subsidiary, Z, (with an accounting period ending on 28 February) but to be set against the taxpayer company's profits for 1973; the letter contained no figures. The reason for making the claim, which was explained in the letter, was not to reduce the taxable profits in BTI's hands since these were already covered by the losses by the other two subsidiaries, but to protect the interests of the third subsidiary under an agreement. The question was whether the claims in respect of X and Y could now be withdrawn in 1979. Harman J held that it could not. The claims had been given effect in accordance with the terms of that letter and could not be altered. BTI was tied to the set of priorities it had stated. This decision made it unnecessary to decide whether a valid claim had been made. (There is a particularly interesting comment on this case by Colclough in *The Tax Journal* No 88.)

Procter & Gamble Ltd v Taylerson (Inspector of Taxes) [1990] STC 639 is the Court of Appeal decision on an appeal from the decision of Vinelott J ([1988] STC 854). It concerns the form of claim to be made for the carry back of surplus advance corporation tax to be set against tax payable in earlier years. The taxpayer's appeal was dismissed but for reasons different from those put forward by Vinelott J.

In its accounting period to 30 June 1979, the taxpayer company made large profits and paid large dividends and therefore large amounts of ACT; that ACT exceeded the maximum which could be set against its corporation tax for 1979. In December 1979, the taxpayer company sought to carry back the surplus ACT for 1979 to the previous accounting period. The accounts were finally settled in 1981; the surplus ACT was set off against tax liability for 1978. The time limit for carrying back the surplus was two years from the end of the accounting period. In 1982, the company incurred losses set off the losses against profits for the three preceding years, so eliminating the profits of 1981 and 1980 and reducing those for 1979; this reduced the ACT which could be set off against corporation tax for 1979 so there was an increase in the surplus ACT. In 1984, the taxpayer company sought to carry back the revised surplus ACT to the accounting periods ending 30 June 1978 and 1979.

The Crown argued that the 1984 claim was a new claim and outside the two-year time limit. The Court of Appeal agreed. Dillon LJ said:

> 'When something which, even at the time of the settlement in November 1981 had not been adumbrated at all, and so far as I know was not even expected by the taxpayer company, happened, that is to say losses in the year to 30 June 1982, that was wholly outside the claim which had been made on 21 December 1979. It would have had to be the subject of a further claim but unfortunately for the taxpayer company it was too late for such a further claim to be made because the two-year limitation period had long since expired.'

There is a minor problem here in that things can be unexpected for different reasons and may or may not be connected with circumstances contemplated at the time of the claim. There is much room for hair-splitting as there is also in the slight differences of language in the judgments of Dillon and Balcombe LJJ. Dillon LJ also said that it was not necessary to have the precise figure as long as the basis for working the figure out had been provided.

Vinelott J had held that the taxpayer company could only validly claim to carry back an amount of surplus ACT capable of being ascertained by reference to events which had happened when the claim was made. The judges felt it unnecessary to comment upon this.

Shepherd (Inspector of Taxes) v Law Land plc [1990] STC 795 is a decision on TA 1988, s 410, formerly Finance Act 1973, s 29(1). That provision bars group relief where there are arrangements in existence for the transfer of the company with the loss (or other relevant relief) to another group; the question was whether the arrangements bar group relief for whole of the accounting period during which they existed or merely the part during which the arrangements subsisted. Ferris J held that the latter was the correct construction not least because any other construction would have sat very oddly with s 409. The importance of this case is that the view for which the Revenue argued formed part of SP 5/80.

Law Land was a property and investment company incorporated and resident in the United Kingdom. It owned all the shares in Mercure, a Belgian company resident in the United Kingdom. Both companies made up their accounts to 31 March each year. On 6 January 1983 Law Land granted to an unconnected Belgian company and its subsidiaries (the AG group) a series of options under which the AG group was given the right to acquire all the shares in Mercure. The options lapsed on 11 February 1983. In the year to 31 March 1983, Mercure made a trading loss which it surrendered to Law Land. Law Land claimed group relief in respect of that loss. The claim was refused by the inspector of taxes but upheld by the commissioner and by Ferris J. The judgment is a valuable exercise in statutory construction and, if one may say so, right. There is some discussion of s 413 as well as s 410.

International

There have been several cases on the interpretation of double taxation conventions. The first is *Inland Revenue Commissioners v Commerzbank AG*; *Inland Revenue Commissioners v Banco Do Brasil SA* [1990] STC 285; this case might appear to be of marginal interest because it concerns the 1945 US–UK treaty which was superseded in 1975 but the issues (and the outcome) are intriguing; see Troup (1990) *The Tax Journal* 7.

Interest was paid by United States corporations to London branches of West German and Brazilian banks; these banks were not residents of United States nor United Kingdom. The banks made loans to United States corporations and received interest in respect of those loans. But for the treaty, the interest was liable to United States tax and also fell to be included in the computation of the banks' profits liable to United Kingdom corporation tax. The banks claimed exemption from UK tax under Art 15 of the US–UK treaty, which provided that:

> 'interest paid by a corporation of one Contracting Party shall be exempt from tax by the other Contracting Party except where the recipient is a citizen, resident or corporation of that other Contracting Party. This exemption shall not apply if the corporation paying such dividend or interest is a resident of the other Contracting Party.'

Mummery J held that the banks' claim was right. The natural and ordinary meaning of the words of Art 15 was clear; all interest paid by United States corporations was exempt from United Kingdom tax except where the recipient was a United Kingdom citizen, resident or corporation. The banks were none of those and accordingly they were entitled to the relief claimed.

This seems so straightforward that it is worth paying some attention to the way the Crown put its case. This was that: (i) Art 15 was meant to be reciprocal in effect and therefore should not be interpreted so as to have greater effect in the United Kingdom than in the United States. This carried little weight with the judge who, no doubt mindful of his dealings with the conflict of laws, said that reciprocity was an ideal which might not be achieved. (ii) As the convention, read as a whole, dealt almost exclusively with the right to tax, or waiver of the right to tax, citizens, residents or corporations of a contracting party with a permanent establishment in one or other contracting party, Art 15, in the absence of express words to that effect, should not be interpreted as waiving the right to tax a corporation of a noncontracting party with a permanent establishment in a host country. Most conventions now expressly confine their benefits to residents but the 1946 UK–US treaty did not; on this basis the decision may be construed almost out of existence. (iii) As the convention had to be viewed in the context of the power of one of the contracting parties to enter into double taxation agreements with other countries, a German corporation with a permanent establishment in the United Kingdom, for instance, would be expected to have its rights and obligations dealt with in a convention between the United Kingdom and Germany, and not between the United Kingdom and the United States.

These arguments carry great weight as a commentary on the way treaties have moved to the forefront of tax planning and practice since they were first introduced but whether they will carry the day at the technical level of statutory interpretation, especially in the light of cases such as *Owen v Elliott*, seems doubtful. If the courts accept these arguments they will have to assume or create or at least articulate a set of fundamental rules of international taxation. The writer hopes that they will and feels particulaly uneasy about the rejection of Revenue argument (ii) – but we shall have to wait and see. For a delightfully sceptical view see Avery-Jones, (1990) BTR 388.

Inland Revenue Commissioners v Vas [1990] STC 137 has caused considerable commotion within the academic community – this time as taxpayers. Under the UK-Hungary treaty:

> 'An individual who visits one of the Contracting States for a period not exceeding two years for the purpose of . . . engaging in research at a university . . . in that Contracting State, and who was immediately before that visit a resident of the other Contracting State, shall be exempted from tax by the first-mentioned Contracting State on any remuneration for such . . . research for a period not exceeding two years from the date he first visits that State for such purpose'.

The problem concerns the meaning of the last few words. The taxpayer, a Hungarian national, visited the UK on three separate occasions; on each occasion he was a research associate at the University of Newcastle-upon-Tyne. Immediately prior to each visit, the taxpayer was a resident of Hungary. The first visit was from 21 January 1979 to 22 January 1981, the second from 19 February 1981 to 28 January 1982 and the third (which lasted for two years) from 30 March 1982.

The first visit lasted more than two years so the taxpayer was not entitled to the exemption; so the Special Commissioners held and there was no appeal. The effect was that the exemption was lost retrospectively, notwithstanding that the overstay was only by two days and that he did not take up his appointment until 24 January 1981. This retroactive loss of exemption is almost unique to the UK and turns entirely on what the Revenue say the words mean.

The present appeal concerned the year 1981-82 in relation to both the second and the third visits. Vinelott J held that the taxpayer was not entitled to the exemption in either of these years. The taxpayer could not begin a new exemption with each visit. He had used up his entitlement on the first visit – even though he had not been entitled to the exemption. This is not a happy case but then the court was having to deal with a very untidily drafted provision. Vinelott J did not decide as between the Crown's two views of the words (i) that the period began at the start of the first visit and (ii) that one cumulated periods of visits until one had got a total of two years. He also though it unwise to search for the purpose to be inferred from the context and scheme of a double taxation treaty because treaties represent a compromise between the fiscal demands of those two states and there may be economic consequences and other reasons of policy which lie behind and are not discernible from the terms of a treaty.

Finally, there are two cases on the dividend article of the US-UK treaty. The first is the decision of the Court of Appeal in *Union Texas International Corp v Critchley (Inspector of Taxes)* [1990] STC 305. The court dismissed both the taxpayer's appeal and the Revenue cross appeal for reasons already given by Harman J at first instance. Dillon LJ commented:

'The draughtsmanship of this Convention does not get alpha plus marking but I would hesitate long before holding that it is so inept that the deduction provisions [in Art 10(2)(a)(i) and (ii)] can have no effect.'

The construction is now governed by FA 1989, s 115; the 5% deduction under art 10(2)(a)(i) is now calculated by reference to the aggregate of the amount of the dividend and the tax credit without any allowance for the deduction itself (ie the grossed-up amount). This decision took care of the point that would have been raised in *Getty Oil Co v Steele* [1990] STC 434. Section 115 did not of course deal with the issue of the entitlement of the Crown to make a deduction from the tax credit payment to the American company; here the generally accepted view has prevailed.

Anti-avoidance

The activities of the courts in this area have been extensive and not always predictable, as readers of previous volumes will know. However, any thought that the decision in *Craven v White* [1988] 3 All ER 495, [1988] STC 476 (All ER Rev 1988, p 296) has led to a total retreat from the approach laid down in the earlier cases must be resisted, as the decision of Hoffman J in *Moodie v IRC* [1990] STC 475 shows. This case concerned a variation of a scheme used, successfully, by the taxpayer in *IRC v Plummer* [1979] 3 All ER 775, [1979] STC 793. Hoffman J was not deterred by the fact that the House of Lords had upheld the taxpayer's claim in *Plummer*:

'Although it is clear from the dissenting speech of Viscount Dilhorne that the self-cancelling nature of the scheme was appreciated by the House, no argument was based on the Ramsay principle, which had not yet 'emerged'. Plummer cannot be authority for the proposition that the Ramsay principle does not apply to this scheme when the House never directed its mind to whether it did or not.'

He said:

'In this case, there has been the artificial manufacture of a series of payments under a purported annuity which had been deprived of the essential characteristic of an annuity in the real world because, by other integrated and preplanned transactions, the annual payments were on each occasion precisely cancelled by a release of capital to the taxpayer. In my judgment this was not an annuity or other annual payment within the meaning of s [348].'

This decision has been long expected.

The decision of Vinelott J in *Countess Fitzwilliam v Inland Revenue Commissioners* [1990] STC 65 is more problematic. The decision is important because it considers the application of the new principle to inheritance tax or, more accurately, capital transfer tax. Those taxes have their own 'associated operations' provision in IHTA 1984, s 268 but this did not stop Vinelott J assuming, with little explanation, that the new approach did apply. The scheme involved the exploitation of rules (since repealed) relating to mutual transfers so, to some extent at least, the interest of the case is historical.

The tenth Earl Fitzwilliam died in September 1979 leaving a net estate of £12.4m. The Earl's will created a 23-month discretionary trust in order to use the provisions in what is now IHTA 1984, s 144 by which payments out of the trust would be treated as payment by the Earl under his will rather than out of the trust. The main beneficiaries, and the main characters in what follows, were the widow, Lady Fitzwilliam, (F), then aged 81 years and in poor health, and her daughter, Lady Hastings, (H).

If nothing were done there was an imminent risk of a very heavy charge to capital transfer tax on F's death whether she received payments from the trust or if she took a life interest in residue under the will at the end of the 23 month discretionary period. Following advice from solicitors the following steps were taken with the object of utilising the rules in s 144, the surviving spouse exemption under s 18 and the provisions of FA ss 86 and 87 on mutual transfers of value.

(1) On 20 December 1979 the trustees in exercise of the power of appointment declared that £4m should be held on trust as to both capital and income for F absolutely. This would not give rise to a charge to tax because of s 144 and s 18.

(2) On 9 January 1980 F made a gift to H of £2m net of capital transfer tax; this was a chargeable transfer and would have meant a grossed gift of some £5m; this was more than F possessed.

(3) On 14 January 1980 the trustees appointed £3.8m to be held on trust, subject to the income being paid to F until the earlier of 15 February 1980, or her death, for H as to one moiety absolutely (the vested moiety) and as to the other moiety for a contingent interest (the contingent moiety). Thanks to s 144 and s 18 this would not be a chargeable transfer but there would be charges on the ending of F's interest in the income (by 15 February at the latest) unless something else were done.

(4) On 31 January 1980 F assigned to H for £2m her almost valueless beneficial interest in the income of the contingent moiety.

This would be a chargeable transfer of value of £1.9m under what is now IHTA s 52(1) but under s 52(2) account had to be taken of the £2m paid in exchange so that no tax would be due. At this point H, through her interest in the income just assigned to her, had an interest in possession in both moieties and so the vesting of those portions in her absolutely would not give rise to tax, thanks to s 53(2).

What matters about this stage is that the payment by H to F of £2m not only meant that there was no charge on F, thanks to s 52(2), but also that, thanks to the mutual transfer rules, the original transfer by F at stage (1) was removed from any charge to tax. This came about because it had been provided that when considering the purchase by H of F's interest the normal rule treating F's interest as being worth £1.9m was displaced in favour of the real value of that interest; the effect was that almost all of the £2m paid by H fell to be treated as not being in return for F's interest but as a gift and so as a transfer of value by H to F which triggered the application of the mutual transfer rules.

(5) On 5 February 1980 H made a nominal settlement of £1,000 on trust to pay the income to F until her death or 15 March 1980, whichever occurred first, and subject thereto in trust absolutely for herself. On 7 February 1980 H assigned to the trustees of her settlement her beneficial interest in the vested moiety expectant on the termination of the interest of F in the income thereof to hold as an accretion to the £1,000 and as one

fund therewith for all purposes. The effect of this was to continue F's interest for a further month; when that month ended and the property passed to H it would be exempt under the reverter-to-settlor-exemption in s 53(3).

At this point one may have two reactions. The first is to wonder just what has been achieved. The answer is that £2m has been passed back and forth but that £1.9m which would have been subject to a charge has been paid over to H from the estate without any CTT/IHT charge. The second is to marvel at the complexity of the devices used and of the legislation which these devices exploited; this may in turn give rise to a view that legislation as intricate and delicate as this is not to be lightly interfered with by a simple application of the *Ramsay* principle. In turn one may wonder whether it is not all too good to be true.

The Revenue attack on the scheme began before *Craven v White*. The first argument was that the trustees had by a sequence of associated operations effected a composite transaction whereby out of the estate F received £4m and H £3.8m, those steps being contrived and introduced for no purpose other than the avoidance of the capital transfer tax, which would otherwise have been payable. The second line was that CTT was payable on the termination of F's interest in the vested moiety and the contingent moiety because the reverter-to-settlor exemption did not apply because the settlor was not H but the Earl. The trustees argued that the because s 268 had extended the meaning of 'disposition' to include 'associated operations', the *Ramsay* principle did not apply to capital transfer tax, or that the limitations on the *Ramsay* principle established by the Court of Appeal in *Craven v White* precluded its application to the five steps taken.

The Special Commissioners, without ruling on the alternative contentions in the notice of determination, upheld the notice of determination on the grounds that the *Ramsay* principle (*W T Ramsay Ltd v IRC* [1981] STC 174) did apply to capital transfer tax and did apply to this composite transaction. They held that a client who conferred on his solicitor freedom of action to proceed as he thought appropriate could not plead ignorance of any of the steps taken within the scope of that authority.

Vinelott J rejected the conclusion that F had given her solicitors carte blanche. It followed that one could not conclude that everything that happened was part of an indivisible process in a preordained series of transactions and constituted a single composite transaction.

He also held that it was H rather than the Earl who was was to be treated as the settlor; it was not open to the Crown to claim that the gift to H, to the extent that it was expressed to be a net gift, was a pretence; and in any event such a claim was indistinguishable from a claim that it was a sham, which the commissioners had correctly rejected.

The case requires long and careful reading to enjoy its full flavour but is important for three reasons. First, it contains a discussion of the question whether a conclusion by commissioners that a series of transactions constitutes a single composite transaction is what is sometimes called an inference of fact, and if it is the extent to which the court is entitled in an appeal by way of case stated to review their decision. Members of the House of Lords – and others – had left this unclear. His view was that:

'the correct approach in this type of case, where inferences have to be drawn, is for the commissioners to determine (infer) from their findings of primary fact, the further fact whether there was a single composite transaction in the sense in which I have used that expression, and whether that transaction contains steps which were inserted without any commercial or business purpose apart from a tax advantage; and for the appellate court to interfere with that inference of fact only in a case where it is insupportable on the basis of the primary facts so found.'

The second reason is the assumption that the associated operations provisions did not apply. Vinelott J simply said that the Revenue were right to base their claim on the *Ramsay* principle rather than s 268 because s 268 has a very limited scope. This limited scope depends on whether the provision is given a wide or narrow meaning. The Revenue practice in relation to s 268 is very generous – even channelling operations are safe from its application. However, the Revenue may be wrong in this and it is odd to find this as a reason for not applying *Ramsay*. If the Revenue were later to establish a wider ambit for s 268, would the judges then say that *Ramsay* could not apply? Against this, if the *Ramsay* principle is simply a rule of construction it is hard to see how it can not apply to IHT. Quite how the *Ramsay* principle would – or does – apply when both it and s 268 are applicable to the particular scheme is not considered.

The third reason is Vinelott J's decision that *Ramsay* did not apply because H had not give carte blanche to the solicitors. If this is allowed to stand it gives solicitors (and others) very clear guidance as to how they avoid the application of *Ramsay*. Whether they would be wise to do so remains to be seen. See also Nicol, (1990) BTR 392.

Administration

Cox v Poole General Commissioners and Inland Revenue Commissioners (No 2) [1990] STC 122 raises three short points.

The taxpayer had had penalties assessed against him for failure to make a proper return of income. The present proceedings related to further penalties for continued failure. The taxpayer sought to argue that original notice was invalid. Vinelott J would have none of it. Such points should have been taken at the time of the hearing of the summons on the original failure. In any event the defects of form were trivial in the extreme and covered by TMA 1970, s 114. There was no suggestion that the taxapyer did not receive the notice or had been misled by them.

The second point was whether a return in which in relation to details of earnings he had given the names and addresses of his employers but had not given the amounts of his earnings but had simply stated 'as returned by employers' was adequate for TMA 1970, s 8. Vinelott J held that it was not. An inspector may be content to discover this information for himself but cannot be required by the taxpayer to do so; it is not for the inspector at the hearing of an application to explain his reasons for insisting on strict compliance with a notice given under s 8 of the 1970 Act.

Finally, the taxpayer appealed against the amount of the fine – £500 compared with a possible maximum of £8,300. Vinelott J said that the fine was not excessive – the taxpayer had not taken any further steps to comply with the notices.

Inland Revenue Commissioners v Nuttall [1990] STC 194 is a Court of Appeal decision on the nature of the rights acquired by the Revenue on a back duty agreement. The court held that as an agreement it was a contract and therefore enforceable like any other contract, including an action for money due invoking the summary provedoire under RSC Ord 14. The taxpayer's argument that the common law power had been impliedly abolished by what is now the Taxes Management Act 1970, s 54 was rejected. The court also rejected the argument that the agreement was not valid since it was in respect of a single sum covering three years which included one year for which there had been no assessment. The basis for the decision was that the power was necessary for carrying into execution the legislation relating to inland revenue.

Getty Oil Co v Steele (Inspector of Taxes) [1990] STC 434 concerns a case stated. Vinelott J decided that where there were three separate appeals to the commissioners but the commissioners stated a single case in relation to all the appeals by the taxpayers and a single case in relation to all the cross-appeals by the Crown, the court had jurisdiction to hear all three appeals even though the action number allotted to the case related to only one appeal.

Consolidated Goldfields plc v Inland Revenue Commissioners, Gold Fields Mining and Industrial Ltd v Inland Revenue Commissioners [1990] STC 357 discusses the right of a litigant to require the remission of a case stated for further findings of fact. Scott J said that findings of fact were for the commissioners and they could not be instructed to find facts nor could they be instructed as to the manner in which their findings were to be expressed but that those findings should cover the matters which were relevant to the arguments to be adduced on appeal. Before a case stated could be remitted for additional findings of fact, it must be shown that the desired findings were: (a) material to some tenable argument, (b) at least reasonably open on the evidence that had been adduced, and (c) not inconsistent with the findings already made. The court would not remit the case stated if it was full and fair in that it covered the territory desired to be dealt with by the proposed additional findings, particularly if it appeared that the commissioners had borne those findings in mind. In this case those criteria had not been satisfied.

Rea v Highnam (Inspector of Taxes) [1990] STC 368 concerns a finding by the commissioners that the taxpayer had been guilty of wilful default. Vinelott J said that it was not fair to pick at the language used, one must look at the substance of the finding.

Danquah v Inland Revenue Commissioners [1990] STC 672 also concerns the scope of the commissioners' right to state the case. The taxpayer had applied by way of originating motion for an order pursuant to RSC Ord 56, r 8 directing the commissioners to state a case. When the application came on for hearing, the Crown asked the court to dismiss it on the ground that it was no longer necessary as the case had already been sent to the applicant. The applicant contended that the court could direct the commissioners to state a further case as the case stated did not include all the questions of law which had been raised in the originating motion. This was rejected by Vinelott J. The commissioners were required to set out the facts and their determinations in the case stated and the court would determine any question of law arising on the facts so stated. If the facts and determinations had not been set out adequately or accurately, the court could not direct the commissioners to state a further case and the taxpayer could apply to the court for the case to be remitted to the commissioners for amendment under s 56(7) of the Taxes Management Act 1970. The application was dismissed. This is a rather spartan view of the case stated since it is reasonable to expect that the case stated should set out the questions of law that were put before them.

Adams v Hanson (Inspector of Taxes) [1990] STC 374 is a short case in a familiar vein concerning an estimated assessment on a taxi driver. The commissioners examined the taxpayer's records for one year and found them unreliable. They found the taxpayer's declared income to be inadequate to cover his living expenses and were not convinced that the shortfall had been met by gambling wins; they therefore upheld the assessment. Vinelott J found that they had not erred in law.

In *Inland Revenue Commissioners v Aken* [1990] STC 497, discussed at p 281 above in connection with the question whether the profits of prostitution are taxable, the Court of Appeal held that it was not open to a taxpayer to argue in collection proceedings that the assessment is invalid. The statutory machinery is exclusive machinery for an appeal from a notice of assessment; there is normally no other. Judicial review might be appropriate in cases where, for example, there has been some abuse of power or unfairness, which would justify the intervention of the court (see eg *Preston v IRC* [1985] STC 282).

R v Inland Revenue Commissioners, ex p Taylor (No 2) [1989] 3 All ER 353, [1990] STC 379 is a judicial review decision; It is an (unsuccessful) appeal against a decision by the Divisional Court ([1989] STC 600; All ER Rev 1989, pp 289, 298). The points in the case are long and detailed but amongst them one may note the following. Where an appeal is under way it is permissible for the Board to issue notices under s 20(2); the taxpayer had argued that in such circumstances only the the commissioners seised of the appeal could issue notices (under s 51). Secondly, a client's ordinary right to legal professional privilege, binding in the ordinary way on a legal adviser, did not entitle such legal adviser as a taxpayer to refuse disclosure and there was nothing in the legislation to indicate otherwise. The court also held that, on the facts, the notice was not 'unreasonable or irrational and therefore ultra vires'. Although s 20(2), unlike s 51, did not give a taxpayer an opportunity to challenge the notice before it was issued, the applicant had been given full warning and had ample opportunity to advance an opposition. Strictly, however, the taxpayer's remedy was, in the event of noncompliance followed by penalty proceedings, to resist the penalty proceedings and then attack the giving of the notice.

There are two cases on adjournments. *Gault v Inland Revenue Commissioners* [1990] STC 612 is a Scottish decision. The taxpayer argued in effect that because of the refusal of the commissioners to grant an adjournment he had not been able to present his case. The court held that on the facts there was plainly room for the view that the taxpayer had had more than a sufficient opportunity to prepare himself. Inter alia, negotiations between the Inland Revenue Enquiry Branch and the taxpayer had extended over 18 months; the taxpayer had not co-operated with these inquiries, the taxpayer had consulted his solicitors a considerable while earlier and more than five weeks' written notice of the hearing had been given to him. The court also held that the commissioners were entirely right to refuse to read a letter from the taxpayer handed in after the hearing and before the determination was made. In so far as the letter was put forward as indicating a wish to ask for a fresh hearing of argument from both parties on the question whether there should be an adjournment, the point failed on the evidence; this was plainly not the proper way to make such a request which should have been clearly stated, a copy of the request should have been sent to the Crown.

In *Fletcher v Harvey (Inspector of Taxes)* [1990] STC 711, the tale of the accountant with the broken-down car, the Court of Appeal dismissed the taxpayers' appeal against the decision of Vinelott J ([1989] STC 826; All ER Rev 1989, p 327). The appeals were listed to be heard with the commissioners' other business at 10.00 am. They were called on at 10.50 am. No one was present on behalf of the taxpayers. Their tax affairs were in the hands of S, a certified accountant. On the morning of that day he had set out to attend the hearing in ample time. Unfortunately, his car broke down just after 9.00 am. A telephone message, stating what had happened, failed to reach the inspector. So the commissioners proceeded. There had been a long history of delay, all of which is recounted in the cases stated. The commissioners heard submissions by an inspector of taxes, and received evidence from him. They then made their determination. This was all over and done with by 11.30 am when S, who had arrived in the building at about 11.00 am, made his presence known. The commissioners declined simply to set aside their determination, but they listened to submissions from S. Having heard submissions from him and having heard further submissions from Mr Davis, the commissioners decided that their determination for the first six of the nine tax years should stand, but they reopened their determination for the subsequent three years and adjourned them.

Did the commissioners have jurisdiction to set their determination aside? The TMA 1970 contains no provision corresponding to RSC Ord 35, r 2 (which allows the High Court to set aside the judgment on such terms as it thinks fit when a judgment had been obtained where one party did not appear at the trial). However the Crown accepted that the commissioners had such a jurisdiction, at any rate when an application to set aside a determination is made at the same sitting. The matter was not subject to full argument but Nicholls LJ saw no reason to doubt that in the present case when S arrived the commissioners did have jurisdiction to set aside the determination they had already made.

The second question was whether they were bound to exercise that discretion when S appeared. On this Nicholls LJ, after a long and cogent analysis of the facts which defies precis, concluded that they were not; it was a decision which, in all the circumstances, they were reasonably entitled to reach.

R v Boston General Commissioners, ex p CD Freehouses Co Ltd [1990] STC 186 is another judicial review case. The taxpayers alleged that at the hearing of an appeal against assessments they had been prevented from developing the case as they had wished and from putting in evidence all relevant documents. Kennedy J held that they had totally failed to prove their case.

Lastly, one should note the decision of the Court of Appeal, Criminal Division in *R v Mulligan* [1990] STC 220 in which the court held that there was an offence of cheating the public revenue at common law and therefore there was a common law offence of conspiring to cheat the public revenue. *R v Hudson* [1956] 1 All ER 814, [1956] 2 QB 252 and *R v Redford* [1988] STC 845 applied. In finding the accused guilty the court laid some stress on the fact that certificates and vouchers under the scheme for sub-contractors in the construction industry remained at all times the property of the Revenue.

Miscellaneous

Tither v Inland Revenue Commissioners [1990] STC 416 holds that the Revenue are entitled to refuse the benefit of the MIRAS scheme to a Community official. The official is exempt from liability to UK tax in respect of his emoluments but this does not entitle him to the subsidy either on the ground that refusal is indirect taxation or as offending the principle of non-discrimination. The availability of relief against UK income under s 353 is another matter.

Swithland Investments Ltd v Inland Revenue Commissioner [1990] STC 448 is a case on stamp duty with some interesting, if not particularly novel, things to say about the meaning of the expressions 'reconstruction' and 'amalgamation', expressions which feature also in capital gains and corporation taxes. The judgment of Ferris J contains a very useful summary of the law on these two concepts with plentiful quotations from company law (and tax) cases. For a fuller discussion see Pincher, *The Tax Journal* No 78.

Rignell (Inspector of Taxes) v Andrews [1990] STC 410 is a short case on a short point – whether the term 'wife' includes the expression 'common law wife' so as to entitle the taxpayer to higher personal allowance or, now, the married couple's allowance. The taxpayer said that he had been unable to marry her because she had at all material times suffered from acute agoraphobia which had prevented her from being able to participate in a marriage ceremony with him. Surprisingly, the commissioners agreed with the taxpayer but Ferris J reversed them; for the purpose of the tax reliefs, the term 'wife' was confined to a woman with whom the taxpayer had entered into a relationship of marriage recognised by the civil law of England.

Kildrummy (Jersey) Ltd v Inland Revenue Commissioners [1990] STC 657 is another stamp duty case; a sale and lease back scheme failed because when the parties purported to transfer the lease it was not yet in existence; this conflicted with the principle that a man cannot contract with himself.

Tort

ALASTAIR MULLIS, LLB, LLM
Lecturer in Law, King's College, London

Economic loss

The coffin in which the case of *Anns v Merton London Borough* [1977] 2 All ER 492, had been confined by a series of cases from 1984 to 1990 was finally nailed shut by the House of Lords in *Murphy v Brentwood District Council* [1990] 2 All ER 908 (a case also considered in Administrative Law and Statute Law, at pp 1–2, 250–252 above). The House held that no action in negligence could be brought by the owner or occupier of a defective building against those involved in its construction (including the local authority) unless the building had caused personal injury or damage to property other than the structure itself. Economic loss caused to an owner or occupier was held to be irrecoverable. From a broader perspective the speeches of their Lordships indicate an unwillingness to countenance the recovery of economic loss except in a *Hedley Byrne*-type case. It would now seem to be just a matter of time before the landmark decision of *Junior Books Ltd v Veitchi Co Ltd* [1982] 3 All ER 201 (All ER Rev 1982, pp 301–305), is buried along with *Anns*.

In *Murphy*, the plaintiff had purchased from a construction company a semi-detached house which had been constructed using a concrete raft as foundations. The construction company had submitted plans for the raft foundations to the local council for planning regulation approval. The local authority, after seeking advice from consulting engineers, had approved the plans. Some time after the purchase, the plaintiff had noticed serious cracks in the house. On further investigation the source of the cracks was traced to the raft foundation which was discovered to be defective. The plaintiff was unable to carry out the necessary repairs which would have cost £45,000. Instead, he sold the house subject to the defects for £35,000 less than its market value in sound condition. The plaintiff brought an action against the local authority claiming that it was liable for the negligence of the consulting engineers in recommending approval of the plans. At the trial the judge found as a fact that the plaintiff had suffered an imminent risk to health and safety and, applying *Anns*, the local authority therefore owed a duty of care to the plaintiff. The Court of Appeal ([1990] 2 All ER 269) dismissed the local authority's appeal. The House of Lords allowed the local authority's further appeal. Three strands of argument in their Lordships' judgments combined to reach this result.

First, the House of Lords repeated their preference for a restrictive approach to the recognition of duties of care in negligence. *Anns* reflected – indeed it was the starting point for – an expansive approach to the recognition of new duties in the tort of negligence. This era is now over. In adopting this approach, *Murphy* is merely the most recent statement of the House that Lord Wilberforce's two-stage test is not the panacea it was originally thought to be. The case confirms that the law should develop novel categories of negligence incrementally and by analogy with established categories. In this the case adds nothing new to a now well established trend and requires no further comment.

Secondly, as was the case in *Anns*, the plaintiffs in *Murphy* could only show that the building had suffered damage to itself. They could not show that the defective building had caused any personal injury to an occupier or visitor, nor that it had damaged any other property. What therefore was the nature of the harm suffered by the plaintiffs? The characterisation of the harm is important because of the more restrictive rules for the recovery of economic loss as opposed to personal injury or property damage. This contrast is expressed by Lord Oliver where he states (at 935) that, in cases of physical damage, foreseeability alone will usually suffice for the law to recognise a duty of care between the defendant and the plaintiff. However, in cases of economic loss something more will always be required before the court considers it is 'fair and reasonable' to impose a duty of care. In *Anns*, Lord Wilberforce had characterised structural manifestations caused by an underlying defect in the foundations as 'material, physical damage'. In *Murphy*, the House held that this was incorrect. The damage suffered in this case was simply damage to the building itself. This was not damage that would ordinarily come within the type of damage recoverable as a result of *Donoghue v Stevenson* [1932] AC 562. The relevant property for the purposes of recovery under *Donoghue v Stevenson* is, as Lord Keith points out (at 917), property other than the very property which gave rise to the danger of physical damage concerned. What the plaintiffs were really complaining about was that, as a result of the defendants' negligence, their house had diminished in value. This was pre-eminently economic loss.

In reaching the decision that the loss was economic, the House of Lords rejected two 'escape routes' which the courts had used in previous cases to avoid such a characterisation. First, in *D & F Estates v Church Commissioners for England* [1988] 2 All ER 992 (All ER Rev 1988, p 321), Lords Bridge and Oliver had postulated the notion of a 'complex structure' in order to explain *Anns*. Lord Bridge said (at 1006–7):

> '. . . it may well be arguable that in the case of complex structures . . . one element of the structure should be regarded as distinct from another element so that damage to one part of the structure may qualify to be treated as damage to other "property".'

Hence, a house with defective foundations (X) causing cracks in the upper structure (Y) would be a case where a defect in X has caused damage to other property, ie Y. The application of the 'complex structure' argument allows, therefore, the court to fit the claim in a case like *Murphy* within the conventional analysis of *Donoghue v Stevenson*. The House of Lords rejected this argument. Both Lords Bridge and Oliver, in *Murphy* condemned the argument's artificiality and said that this was not an argument they had advanced with any enthusiasm in *D & F Estates*. Instead, they had advanced it as the only 'logically possible' explanation of *Anns*. Reconsidering the argument as a matter of principle, the House held that it was untenable and should not be used in the future. The House were clearly correct in identifying the fictional nature of the argument. This has always been clear. The attraction of the argument was that it enabled the courts to permit recovery in circumstances where the loss was economic without labelling it as such. It was, in other words, a 'means to an end'. In *Murphy*, it is not the integrity of argument that has changed but the desired 'end'.

The second 'escape route', derived from the case of *Anns* itself, was that where the defective building or product threatens imminent danger to the health or safety of persons occupying it, damages were recoverable to put the building (or product) into a state where it was no longer such a danger. This too was rejected. Whether or not the building was qualitatively defective or dangerously defective should make no difference. In both cases, once the defect is identified it is no longer a danger. The purchaser is left with something of less value than he had originally acquired. The plaintiff's loss is thus economic. As with the complex structure argument, the House of Lords are clearly correct to point out that the loss is economic. It may, however, be questioned whether they are correct to refuse to draw a distinction between qualitatively and dangerously defective buildings or products. This is a distinction which has been drawn in a number of American jurisdictions and it certainly emphasises one of the goals of the tort system: to prevent accidents. To refuse to allow recovery in the case of dangerously defective buildings or products allows the producer to take advantage of the fact that the defect has fortuitously been discovered before it caused any damage. It is surely consistent with the policies of tort law to allow recovery in such a case.

Having classified the plaintiff's claim as a claim for economic loss, and having refused to utilise one of the 'escape routes' open to them, the court had to consider directly the question whether economic loss was recoverable. This might be described as the third strand of their Lordship's arguments. In holding that economic loss was not recoverable in these circumstances, a number of arguments can be identified. First, Lord Bridge was concerned that the imposition of liability in this case would lead to the local authority or builder providing a transmissible warranty of quality of the work. Parliament had, he said, provided something of this nature already by the Defective Premises Act 1972. However, this applied only to certain types of building and was subject to a limitation period. It would, he said, be extraordinary if the common law imposed a similar warranty applicable to all buildings without any of the protections provided for in the Act. In essence, this argument seems to be that Parliament has already taken some steps to protect purchasers and it is not therefore up to the courts to go any further. However, there are – as is obvious from Lord Bridge's speech – several gaps in the Act, for example, only dwelling houses not subject to the National House Builder's scheme are protected and a purchaser will have no remedy where, as is often the case, the builder is insolvent. In such cases should the courts refuse to consider granting a remedy?

A second argument put forward was to ask why should the local authority (financed by the public at large) have to bear the loss caused by the building contractor. Why should not the loss instead be covered by private insurance? As Professor Fleming ((1990) 106 LQR 525) points out, the answer to this is not as clear cut as the House of Lords make it. A number of judges in both England and the Commonwealth have expressed the view that a local authority should bear some responsibility for having failed to prevent a builder's negligence. One reason given is that the local authority can control the activities of the builder and thus on the basis of *Home Office v Dorset Yacht Co Ltd* [1970] 2 All ER 294, should be held liable for any default.

Finally, the court considered that their preferred decision was supported by the American case law. The US Supreme Court case of *East River Steamship Corp v Transamerica Delaval Inc* (1986) 476 US 858 was cited as supporting the view that American law did not give a cause of action where the damage suffered was damage to the product itself. Two comments should be made. First, the *East River Steamship* case was an admiralty case which is in no way binding on state courts developing tort law. Secondly, a number of jurisdictions do allow recovery where there is damage to the product itself, provided the product is dangerously defective and the purchaser is a consumer. Such limited citation of American cases should be avoided because it can mislead.

The discussion in *Murphy* is based on the assumption that a local authority owes a greater duty of care than a builder where the damage caused is economic (for further discussion of the effect of *Murphy* on the liability of local authorities see below). The case of *Department of the Environment v Thomas Bates & Son (New Towns Commission, third party)* [1990] 2 All ER 943, confirms that where a builder's negligence causes economic loss only, this is irrecoverable. In that case, the plaintiffs were the underlessees of a building which had been constructed for the lessees by the defendants. Due to the negligence of the defendants, the building required extensive work to render it capable of supporting the design load of the building. Under the sub-lease the plaintiffs were responsible for part of this cost. They brought an action against the defendants to recover the sums they had paid. The House of Lords held that this loss was not recoverable. The money necessary to put the building into a safe condition was an economic loss which, following *Murphy v Brentwood District Council*, could not be recovered.

In *Parker-Tweedale v Dunbar Bank plc (No 1)* [1990] 2 All ER 577, the Court of Appeal held that a mortgagee owed no duty of care to the beneficiary under a trust of the mortgaged property. The plaintiff and his wife had purchased a house with the aid of a mortgage from the defendant bank. The wife was registered as the sole legal owner of the house which the plaintiff occupied as a licensee. He agreed that he would not assert any equitable claim or overriding interest against the mortgagee, but it was agreed that he would be beneficially entitled to the net proceeds of sale after redemption of the mortgage. The plaintiff subsequently became unable to service the debt and the defendant, having obtained a possession order, instructed estate agents to sell it. An offer obtained by the estate agents was accepted by the defendants after consulting with the wife alone. The plaintiff, who was entitled to the proceeds of sale, brought an action against the defendants, alleging that they were in breach of the duty of care they owed him because they had failed to obtain a proper price for the property. The trial judge dismissed his claim and the plaintiff appealed.

The Court of Appeal, in affirming the trial judge's decision, held that the mortgagee did not owe the plaintiff a duty of care. Whilst the court accepted that a mortgagee owed a duty to the mortgagor to obtain a proper price for the mortgaged property, this duty arose not in the tort of negligence but in equity, as a result of the particular fiduciary relationship between them. Once this was made clear, the court held that it must be readily apparent that the scope of the duty could not be extended so as to include beneficiaries under a trust. The remedy available to the beneficiary was against the trustee and not the mortgagee. In his judgment, Purchas LJ commented that an additional reason for holding that no duty was owed in the tort of negligence was that the loss suffered here was economic and the law has traditionally been very circumspect about imposing a duty of care for such loss. (See Land Law and Trusts at pp 165–166 above for futher discussion of *Parker-Tweedale*.)

False information and advice

The courts considered on several occasions in 1990 the application of the tort of negligence to those giving professional financial advice to, or preparing financial information for, companies. The central problem for the courts was whether liability arose in favour of those who had no contract with the advisers but who suffered financial loss when they relied on the advice or information. The basis of the claim that liability should exist in such cases was the decision of the House of Lords in *Hedley Byrne & Co Ltd v Heller & Partners Ltd* [1963] 2 All ER 575, [1964] AC 465, where the court had accepted that damages could be awarded for economic loss caused by a negligent misstatement. The essence of such an action was generally perceived to be that the defendant had voluntarily assumed responsibility to the plaintiff to ensure that the advice or information given was correct. In *Caparo Industries plc v Dickman* [1990] 1 All ER 568, the House of Lords considered the application of *Hedley Byrne*-type liability to cases where investors foreseeably rely on audited financial reports prepared by accountants (see also Company Law, pp 43–44 above).

The appellants, Touche Ross & Co, were the auditors of Fidelity plc, a manufacturer of electrical equipment. The directors of Fidelity plc issued preliminary results for the financial year ending 31 March 1984. These results were well below expectations and, as a result, the share price suffered a dramatic fall. Early in June, the respondents, Caparo Industries plc, began to purchase shares in Fidelity and they continued to do so after the full audited accounts were published on 12 June. Later in the same year, Caparo made a successful takeover bid for Fidelity.

After the takeover, Caparo brought an action claiming damages for negligent misrepresentation against the auditors. They argued that the auditors were in breach of a duty of care owed to them in that they had negligently certified accounts that indicated a pre-tax profit of £1.3 million when, in fact, there had been a loss of £400,000. Caparo alleged that the duty of care was owed to them both as potential new investors and as existing shareholders who, in reliance upon published audited accounts, might make further purchases of shares.

The case was tried on a preliminary issue of whether or not a duty of care was owed. At first instance, Sir Neil Lawson held that no duty was owed either to existing or potential shareholders. The Court of Appeal, by a majority, partially reversed his decision, and held that a duty of care was owed to existing but not potential shareholders. The auditors appealed against the decision that they owed a duty of care to existing shareholders and Caparo cross-appealed against the decision that no duty of care was owed to them as potential shareholders. The House of Lords unanimously allowed the defendant's appeal and rejected the plaintiff's cross-appeal.

The court held that, in the absence of exceptional circumstances, auditors owe no duty of care to third parties who rely on company accounts. It was accepted that there might be cases where liability could arise, but it was emphasised that these were exceptional and could only be identified after taking all the facts of the individual case into account. The judges emphasised that a case by case approach, based on existing authorities directly relevant to this relatively narrow area of law, was to be preferred to the application of broad principles derived from cases such as *Anns v Merton London Borough*. Their Lordships rejected as unhelpful reference to such elusive concepts as proximity, voluntary assumption of responsibility and relationships equivalent to contract.

Having rejected any broad approach to the question of liability, the court went on to consider what approach should be applied on the facts. First, the judges made clear that the fact that a person may foreseeably rely on the information or advice was insufficient. As Lord Roskill said:

> 'the submission that there is a virtually unlimited and unrestricted duty of care in relation to the performance of an auditor's statutory duty to certify company's accounts, a duty extending to anyone who may use those accounts for any purpose such as investing in the company or lending the company money, seems to me untenable. No doubt it can be said to be foreseeable that those accounts may find their way into the hands of persons who may use them for such purposes or, indeed, other purposes and lose their money as a result. But to impose a liability in these circumstances is to hold, contrary to all recent authorities, that foreseeability alone is sufficient . . .' (at 582)

Secondly, the court referred to a series of authorities, *Cann v Willson* (1888) 39 Ch D 39, *Candler v Crane Christmas & Co Ltd* [1951] 1 All ER 426, *Hedley Byrne* itself and *Smith v Eric S Bush (a firm)* [1989] 2 All ER 514 (All ER Rev 1989, p 333). From these cases, the court identified the salient features required for an action for negligent misstatement. In the words of Lord Bridge, it is necessary that 'the defendant knew that his statement would be communicated to the plaintiff, either as an individual or as a member of an identifiable class, specifically in connection with a particular transaction or transactions of a particular kind' (at 576, see also Lord Oliver at 589 and Lord Jauncey at 607).

Applying this to the facts of the case before them, the House of Lords held that the defendants could not be liable. The purpose of preparing such reports must be considered in the light of ss 235 to 246 of the Companies Act 1985. These sections require that a company appoint auditors to conduct the annual audit and to prepare the annual report. This report is sent to all registered shareholders and a copy sent to Companies House which is to be available for public inspection. The provisions also require that the annual report be available to all shareholders at least 21 days before the general meeting of the company. In the light of these provisions, the court held that the central and primary purpose of the legislation is to furnish existing shareholders with the necessary information so that they can exercise an informed judgment when voting at the annual general meeting. In the words of Lord Jauncey:

'I therefore conclude that the purpose of the annual accounts, so far as the members are concerned, is to enable them to question the past management of the company, to exercise their voting rights, if so advised, and to influence future policy and management. Advice to individual shareholders in relation to present or future investment in the company is no part of the statutory purpose of the preparation and distribution of the accounts' (at 607, see also Lord Oliver at 584 and Lord Bridge 580.)

A number of points should be noticed.

First, although the court appears to introduce a new 'test' of liability, based on knowledge of the class of persons who might rely and the likely purpose of reliance, it is unlikely, in view of the stress laid by the court on the point that different cases must be treated differently, that any general principle framed in terms of these two criteria can be applied across the board in negligent misstatement cases. This is especially so because, to the extent that any general test appears in the speeches delivered in the House of Lords, it is one based on the actual or imputed knowledge of the defendant, a question intricately linked with the issue of foreseeability: the knowledge to be imputed to the defendant must depend on what was foreseeable in the circumstances. If such a test were to be definitive, there would, for example, be no satisfactory grounds for distinguishing *Caparo v Dickman* from *Smith v Eric Bush*. On the one hand in *Smith v Eric Bush*, there was an 'overwhelming probability' (per Lord Griffiths) that the purchaser would rely on the building society valuation. On the other hand in *Caparo*, it was at least strongly arguable that the auditors 'knew' that it was highly probable that the shareholders and possibly even potential investors, as an ascertainable class, would rely on the audited accounts in making investment decisions. The best way to view the conditions is as 'tools or control mechanisms' that can be used to limit liability to the extent dictated by policy considerations. As was the case before *Caparo* much is likely to be left to the court's intuitive view of what is fair and reasonable in the circumstances of each case.

Secondly, much of their Lordships' speeches in *Caparo* are devoted to an attempt to identify Parliament's purpose in laying down the requirement that company reports be audited. Although the House of Lords does not satisfactorily explain the relevance of this consideration, the best explanation appears to be that the judges considered the forensic process ill equipped to assess the effects of the expansion of liability in this type of case and hence looked for guidance from Parliament. As already mentioned, the conclusion reached was that the purpose of the audited accounts was to allow shareholders as a body to exercise informed control of the company. This assumption is questionable since the ability to rely on audited accounts is an essential feature of modern commercial life. Accounts are used not only by existing and potential shareholders but also by a wide range of creditors and individual and corporate investors. Further, the institution of preference shares, expressly referred to by Lord Oliver, stands in the way of the court's analysis. Preference shareholders generally have no voting rights and yet the Companies Act requires that annual reports be sent to them. With respect to these type of shareholders the report cannot have the purpose the House of Lords attributed to it.

Thirdly, although there is no systematic analysis of the policy arguments which justified refusing to impose liability, a number of such arguments can be discerned from the judgments. First, Lord Bridge seemed concerned that those relying on such reports would be able to 'appropriate' for their own purposes the benefit of expert knowledge or advice without having to pay for it. Whilst superficially there may appear to be something in this argument, it is clear that there is a number of instances where the law imposes liability on professionals who render gratuitous services. For example, there seems to be no doubt that if a doctor rendered negligent first aid at a road accident he would be held liable. Such an argument cannot therefore be conclusive.

Finally, Lord Oliver in his judgment refers to the danger of creating 'a liability wholly indefinite in area, duration and amount which opens up a limitless vista of uninsurable risks for the professional man' (at 593). This argument reflects the concern of many professionals about the increasing cost and decreasing availability of professional indemnity insurance. Even if it is accepted that some risks are simply uninsurable, even in today's highly sophisticated insurance markets, there are a number of countervailing considerations which exist. First, declining to put the risk on the auditor entails leaving it on the investor. Is this necessarily justified? The auditor is, after all, the person at fault. Further, there are reasons to believe that the auditor is the person best able to bear the loss. Not only is no insurance cover available against bad investments but also many investors are so called 'small investors' who lack the ability of large accountancy firms to spread their loss and for whom such a loss may be catastrophic. Secondly, even if commercial insurance is not available, this is not the only way that accountants have of protecting themselves. For example, in 1986 the largest accountancy firms set up a mutual insurance company which provides, at market rates, higher levels of cover than those commercially available. Finally, declining to hold auditors liable entails the partial abandonment of tort law as a deterrent to inducing auditors to maintain professionally acceptable standards.

In conclusion, it appears likely that the debate on the extent of auditors' and other professionals' liability will not have ended as a result of *Caparo*. The question of the extent of such liability will only be answered as more cases are brought and the different policy arguments are weighed to assess their relative strengths. Two further cases, decided at first instance, soon after *Caparo* give some indication as to the likely future outcome of such cases.

In *Al-Nakib Investments (Jersey) Ltd v Longcroft* [1990] 3 All ER 321, the plaintiff was a shareholder in CT plc. CT plc had developed a new product which they wished to exploit commercially. They therefore issued a prospectus inviting CT plc shareholders to subscribe for shares in CT plc and a new company, M Ltd, which was incorporated to exploit the new product. The subscription was to be by way of a rights issue. The plaintiff subscribed for 400,000 shares under the rights issue. Subsequently, the plaintiff, in reliance on the prospectus and two interim financial reports, purchased nearly 15 million further shares in the stock market. The plaintiff brought this action alleging that he had purchased the shares in the market relying on statements in the prospectus and interim reports. These statements were untrue and as a result of his reliance the plaintiff had suffered loss. It was agreed that there was a triable issue with regard to the shares subscribed for in the rights issue. As to the remaining purchases made in the market, the defendants argued that the statement of claim should be struck out as disclosing no reasonable cause of action.

Mervyn Davies J agreed and ordered the action to struck out. In so deciding, he fastened onto the 'test' put forward in *Caparo v Dickman* which he said meant that:

> 'a duty of care exists only if X when making his statement knew or ought to have known that Y would rely on it for the purpose of such a transaction as Y did, in fact, enter into' (at 326).

Here, the purpose of the prospectus was to invite subscriptions for shares in M Ltd and CT plc by way of rights issue. It was not, as the plaintiff had contended, intended to be relied upon for subsequent purchases in the market. Therefore, as the plaintiff had made use of the prospectus for a purpose otherwise than for the one for which it was issued, the necessary special relationship was not established.

In *Morgan Crucible Co plc v Hill Samuel Bank Ltd* [1990] 3 All ER 330, the relationship between the two parties might be said to have been even closer. The plaintiff company had announced a take-over bid for another company, FCE. The board of FCE, in an attempt to stave off the advances of the plaintiff company, issued various letters to its shareholders in which they forecast a 38% rise in profits for the next financial year. This statement was made with the express concurrence of the company's bankers and their accountants who confirmed that the forecast was made in accordance with the company's stated accounting policies. As a result of this letter the plaintiffs increased their offer and this new offer was accepted. Subsequently, the plaintiffs brought this action, claiming that the forecast was negligently prepared and grossly overstated FCE's financial position. The writ was issued prior to the decision of the House of Lords in *Caparo* and the statement of claim was based solely on the alleged foreseeability of the economic loss suffered by the plaintiffs. The plaintiffs sought leave to amend their statement of claim to allege that the requirement of proximity was established by the plaintiff's materialisation as a bidder prior to the statements being issued. In reply, the defendants argued that the proposed amendments disclosed no cause of action.

Hoffman J refused leave to amend on the ground that takeover documents were prepared for the guidance of shareholders of the target company and not for the bidder. This decision has been overturned by the Court of Appeal in a decision reported at [1991] 1 All ER 148. This case must therefore be reserved for consideration in the next Review.

In *Banque Financière de la Cité SA v Westgate Insurance* [1990] 2 All ER 947, (see All ER Rev 1987, p 290 and All ER Rev 1989, pp 334–335 and the chapters on Commercial Law and Contract, pp 23, 61–62 above) the plaintiff banks had made loans to B, who had perpetrated a massive fraud on them by pledging security gemstones which turned out to be worthless. The banks had arranged through L, an employee of a reputable insurance broker, certain insurance policies (which contained fraud exemption clauses) to protect themselves in the event of the borrowing companies defaulting on the loans. Unknown to the banks, or L's employers, L had fraudulently represented to the banks that they were fully covered at the time the initial loans were made for the amount they sought. This fraud had subsequently come to the attention of D, an employee of the insurers, but he had failed to report this to the banks. He did not report this to the banks because by the time he discovered the fraud the banks were covered for the amount sought. The banks decided to lend further amounts to B. This was to be covered by another insurance policy of a similar type. L issued a covernote in respect of this which, unknown to D, was false. The borrowing companies defaulted and the gems turned out to be worthless. The banks brought an action against the insurers alleging, inter alia, that the insurers owed them a duty of care. They argued that the insurers were under a duty to disclose to them the fraud being practised on them by L as soon as they, acting through D, became aware of it. The banks claimed that if they had known of L's fraud they would not have lent any further sums to B and so would not have incurred any further losses. At first instance, Steyn J held that a duty of care was owed in these circumstances and that therefore the banks were entitled to recover damages from the insurers. The Court of Appeal allowed an appeal by the insurers.

The House of Lords dismissed the banks' further appeal. First, the House of Lords held that the insurers did not owe the duty claimed to exist by the banks. The essence of the banks' claim was that they were seeking to recover for damages resulting from a failure to speak. To allow such an action would require a considerable extension of existing authorities and would be likely to create substantial practical problems. *Hedley Byrne* liability was premised on a negligent misstatement, not on a failure to state. Here there was no statement and the silence of D could not amount to an assertion that L was trustworthy. The practical problem the court had in mind was that of unreliable or inconclusive evidence, the disclosure of which could involve the informant in criticism or litigation. Giving any content to such a duty would be impossible.

Secondly, the House held that the loss suffered by the banks was not in any event a consequence of any breach of duty on the part of D. Even assuming that the insurers were under a duty to disclose L's dishonesty, a breach of that duty would only have meant that the banks were not fully covered. It would not, as the banks had contended, have caused the loss of the money advanced. This was not recoverable because of B's fraud and the resultant exclusion of the operation of the policies as a result of the fraud exemption clause. Thus, even if the banks had been properly covered they would not have been able to recover under the policies because of the fraud exemption clause. D's failure to disclose L's fraud was not, therefore, a cause of the bank's loss and was consequently irrecoverable.

Exercise of statutory powers

In *Murphy v Brentwood District Council*, the House of Lords were content to assume for the purposes of the decision that the potential liability in tort of a local authority was co-extensive with that of a builder. In the light of the decision reached there was no necessity to draw any distinction between the two. However, some doubt was expressed by the court on the question whether there would be any circumstances in which a successful action could be brought against a local authority. Before concluding that there are no such circumstances, two situations should be considered. First, might a plaintiff succeed in an action against a local authority based on the principle in *Hedley Byrne & Co Ltd v Heller and Partners Ltd*? Secondly, might a plaintiff succeed in such an action based on the principles in *Home Office v Dorset Yacht Co* [1970] 2 All ER 294?

As to the first of these possibilities, support can be found in a number of Commonwealth authorities for allowing an action to succeed against a local authority based on *Hedley Byrne*. In *Sutherland Shire Council v Heyman* (1985) 60 ALR 1, a case cited by the House of Lords in *Murphy* with approval, Mason J specifically draws attention to the situation where a person reasonably relies upon a representation by a local authority as being a case where liability may arise. Indeed, had the owners in the *Sutherland Shire Council* case applied and been granted a certificate by the local authority to the effect that the foundations were stable, Mason J would have held the local authority liable on the basis of the principle in *Hedley Byrne*. Similarly, in the New Zealand case of *Brown v Heathcote County Council* [1986] 1 NZLR 76 (a case subsequently affirmed by the Privy Council at [1987] 1 NZLR 721) the New Zealand Court of Appeal held a local drainage board liable, on the basis of *Hedley Byrne*, when they failed to give an accurate report regarding the susceptibility of land to flooding. In the light of these cases it is suggested that a local authority may be liable for making a negligent misrepresentation upon which a person reasonably relies to his detriment. Problems may arise in such cases as to whether the necessary degree of proximity has been established (see *Caparo v Dickman*) and whether a representation has been made. In *Anns v Merton London Borough* for example, it is difficult to ascertain what, if any, representations were made by the local authority to the plaintiffs. In *Murphy* itself, it seems unlikely that the necessary degree of proximity would be established because it was not the owner but ABC Homes who submitted the plans for approval. If, however, a house owner submits plans to a local authority for an extension and these are passed as complying with local planning regulations there seems to be no reason why the owner should not be able to maintain an action against the local authority if he suffers loss as a result of his reliance on their compliance, for example, by having to rebuild the offending extension. If the courts are willing to accept this line of reasoning, tort law could stage a significant come back in defective building litigation.

The second possibility is to base an action on the principle in *Home Office v Dorset Yacht Co*, that is to say, that the relationship which existed between the authority and the plaintiff was such as to give rise to a positive duty to prevent another person, the builder, from inflicting harm. This possibility was adverted to by Lord Oliver in the *Murphy* case (at 936–7). He held, however, that there was nothing in the Public Health Acts, or the duties imposed upon a local authority under the building regulations, to make him think that Parliament had intended to protect property owners from economic loss. It may be, however, that the answer would have been different had the plaintiff suffered property damage (other than to the building itself) or personal injury. In such a case the courts may be willing to construe the Public Health Acts as imposing liability on local authorities where third parties have built a house in such a way that foreseeable personal injury or property damage is caused. Dismal predictions as to possible liability of local authorities therefore may have to be altered if the courts are presented with cases of either of the above types.

Two cases reported in 1990 illustrate the considerations which courts will take into account in deciding whether a duty of care is owed by the police in respect of performance of their statutory duties. In *Clough v Bussan (West Yorkshire Police Authority, third party)* [1990] 1 All ER 431, the plaintiff was injured when a car in which she was a passenger was struck by the first defendant's car. She brought an action against the first defendant who began third party proceedings against the police authority, alleging that the police had become aware, some time prior to the accident, that certain traffic lights were not functioning. They had not responded as quickly as they should have done to this and as a result this accident had occurred. Consequently, the accident had been caused or contributed to by the negligence of the police. The police authority moved to strike out the action. The registrar refused the application and the police authority appealed.

Kennedy J held that the third party proceedings should be struck out. The judge accepted that part of a policeman's duty was the regulation of road traffic and this may involve dealing with situations such as the present. However, the mere fact that it was part of the duty of the police to reduce the risk in situations such as the present did not mean that they owed those injured as a result of the police's failure to perform their duty, a duty of care. The question whether or not a duty of care existed depended not only on the foreseeability of the likelihood of harm but also on whether or not a relationship of proximity existed and, finally, on considerations of policy (*Yuen Kun-yeu v A-G of Hong Kong* [1987] 2 All ER 705 (All ER Rev 1987, p 285)).

In deciding that no duty of care was owed Kennedy J drew heavily on the considerations mentioned in the House of Lords decision in *Hill v Chief Constable of West Yorkshire* [1988] 2 All ER 238 (All ER Rev 1988, p 326). First, a police officer was entrusted with a wide measure of discretion as to how to discharge his duty. This exercise of this discretion would not generally be considered an appropriate matter to be called into question in a court, involving as it does the court second guessing the police. Secondly, one of the consequences of imposing a duty in any case would be to seek to ensure the observance of higher standards. This could not be said of police activities; 'the general sense of public duty which motivates police forces is unlikely to be appreciably reinforced by the imposition of such liability . . .'. Any duty owed was simply to the public at large and not to individual members of the public. Hence, the only remedy was by an application for judicial review. Whilst the decision was perhaps to be expected, the considerations found compelling by the judge would appear to preclude there ever being a duty of care owed by the police. The following case illustrates that this is not so.

In *Kirkham v Chief Constable of the Greater Manchester Police* [1990] 3 All ER 246, (see All ER Rev 1989, p 338 for a review of the decision at first instance ([1989] 3 All ER 882)) an alcoholic with a long criminal record was transferred from police detention to Risley Remand Centre. The police had been told that he had attempted suicide on a number of occasions in the last year. They failed to fill in a form and send it to the remand centre warning them of the plaintiff's instability. On the day after his arrival at the centre he committed suicide. His wife brought an action for damages claiming for herself (under the Fatal Accident Act 1976) and for the estate (under the Law Reform (Miscellaneous Provisions) Act 1934). Tudor Evans J held that the claim should succeed and on appeal this decision was affirmed by the Court of Appeal.

In considering whether a duty of care was owed, the Court of Appeal accepted that this was a case of an omission to act and that the courts do not generally impose liability for omissions. However, as Lloyd LJ pointed out, there are exceptions to this. Whether or not such a duty to act will be imposed depends upon whether:

> 'having regard to the particular relationship between the parties, the defendant has assumed a responsibility towards the deceased and whether the deceased has relied on that assumption of responsibility.'

Here, he said, the police had assumed responsibility towards the deceased and the deceased would be inferred to have relied on that assumption of responsibility. The conclusion that the police assumed responsibility to the deceased is unexceptional. What is perhaps more difficult is the drawing of the inference that the deceased relied on the police. In what sense is reliance being used here? If it is being used in the sense that all people rely on the police to do their duty, it is difficult to see what this adds to the requirement of assumption of responsibility. If this is not correct, what other sense could be meant? Surely not *Hedley Byrne*-type reliance, where it is the reliance that causes the loss? Farquharson LJ, on the other hand, merely asserts that where:

> 'one person is in the lawful custody of another, whether voluntarily or involuntarily, that person must take all reasonable steps to avoid acts or omissions which he could reasonably foresee would be likely to harm the person for whom he is responsible.'

No discussion of policy, or any grounds for distinguishing this case from *Clough v Bussan* or *Hill v Chief Constable of West Yorkshire* are given. (See Statute Law, p 267 above.)

The case of *Davis v Radcliffe* [1990] 2 All ER 536 was, according to Lord Goff, who delivered the judgment of the Privy Council, in all material respects indistinguishable from *Yuen Kun-yeu v A-G of Hong Kong*. The plaintiffs had deposited £7,000 with an Isle of Man bank which collapsed with a substantial deficit in August 1982. The bank was licensed under the Isle of Man Banking Act 1975 until June 1972 when the licence was revoked. All Isle of Man banks were required to be licensed from year to year in accordance with the provisions of the Act. The Act provided that decisions as to the issuance, refusal or revocation of licenses were to be made by the Finance Board. A broad discretion was given to the Board in the exercise of these powers. The plaintiffs brought an action against the members of the Finance Board claiming damages for the amount they had lost in the collapse. The plaintiffs argued that the Board owed them a duty of care to carry out the licensing and supervision of banks in such a way that depositors' funds were safeguarded. The Board applied to strike out the claim as disclosing no reasonable cause of action.

The Privy Council held that the Finance Board owed no duty of care to the plaintiffs. There were several considerations which pointed to there being no duty of care. First, the functions of the Board were typical functions of modern government to be exercised in the general public interest. The Board was empowered to make decisions which would inevitably take into account factors wider than the individual interests of customers. The very nature of the task the Board was engaged in made it an unsuitable one for the courts to review. Secondly, the law was always slower to impose a duty to act, particularly where that duty was to protect other persons against economic loss. Whilst Lord Goff did not say that in such circumstances a duty of care would never be found to exist, on the facts of the case it was difficult to see that the Board possessed sufficient control over the management of the company to justify the imposition of liability. Thirdly, this would be a duty owed to a potentially unlimited class of persons. Finally, as the Board was in fact a Board of the Isle of Man Parliament it would be unreasonable to impose a duty of care.

Standard of care

The Court of Appeal in *Luxmoore May v Messenger May Baverstock (a firm)* [1990] 1 All ER 1067, considered the standard of care owed by a provincial auctioneers where they undertake to 'research' the value of a painting. The plaintiff owned two small paintings of foxhounds. He invited the defendant auctioneers to look at these paintings with a view to selling them. The defendant's representative, Mrs Z, initially valued them as worth between £30 and £50. She agreed, however, to take them away for 'research'. She showed them to a Mr T who was a consultant engaged by the defendants to vet all paintings and drawings taken in by the defendants. Mr T, who had no formal fine art qualifications but had been a dealer for nine years, confirmed Mrs Z's valuation. The plaintiffs instructed the defendants to sell the paintings. Before the sale, Mrs Z, who still had some doubts about the attribution, took the paintings to Christie's. Nothing favourable was said about the paintings. The paintings were sold at auction for £840. Five months later they were sold in a London auction for £88,000.

The plaintiffs brought an action claiming the difference between the two sale prices. The trial judge held that the auctioneers had been negligent and gave judgment for the plaintiffs for the amount claimed. The Court of Appeal allowed the defendant's appeal. In carrying out the duty the standard of skill expected of a provincial auctioneer was akin to that expected of a general medical practitioner. Thus, applying a passage from the judgment of the Lord President (Clyde) in *Hunter v Hanley* 1955 SC 200 (at 204–205):

> 'the true test for establishing negligence in [the valuation of a painting] is whether [a provincial auctioneer] has been proved to be guilty of such a failure as no [provincial auctioneer] of ordinary skill would be guilty of if acting with ordinary care . . .'

Applying this test to the facts of the case, the court held that the conclusion reached was one which a reasonable provincial auctioneer could, at the time he was asked to carry out the valuation, have reached. The court therefore held that the defendants had not been guilty of negligence.

Knight v Home Office [1990] 3 All ER 237 (see Medical Law, pp 190–193 above), discusses the standard of care owed to a mentally ill patient detained in a prison hospital.

Defences

In *Kirkham v Chief Constable of the Greater Manchester Police* [1990] 3 All ER 246 (the facts of which are set out above), the defendant had also sought to argue that the deceased's voluntary act of suicide meant that his claim was defeated by the defence of volenti non fit injuria or alternatively that a claim arising out of suicide was barred by the maxim 'ex turpi causa non oritur actio', ie the defence of illegality. The Court of Appeal held that the defendant could not rely on either of these defences.

First, all three judges held that the defence of volenti non fit injuria could only succeed where the plaintiff was truly volens. This was treated as a question that could only be answered by having regard to the state of mind of the plaintiff. On the facts, the court was of the opinion that the plaintiff was not of sound mind and he could not therefore be said to have truly waived or abandoned any claim arising out his actions. On the question whether the same answer would have been given had the plaintiff been of sound mind, Farquharson and Lloyd LJJ expressed different opinions. Lloyd LJ took the view that the defendant would have been entitled to rely on the defence of volenti. Farquharson LJ, however, expressed a different opinion. He said (at 254) that 'the defence is inappropriate where the act of the deceased relied on is the very act which the duty cast on the defendant required him to prevent'. The act relied on by the defendant to establish the defence, ie the deceased's suicide, was the very act that the defendant had a duty to prevent. The defence of volenti should not, therefore, be open to the defendant in a case where the deceased is of sound mind. It is suggested that the better view is that of Farquharson LJ. There can be few circumstances where the defendant will be under a duty to prevent another person from injuring themselves. Where such a duty does exist, the defendant should not be allowed to escape liability by showing that the other person did the very thing which he, the defendant, had a duty to stop him doing. The fact that the act was voluntary should not affect the issue.

Secondly, the court held that the question whether or not to allow the defence of ex turpi causa was to be answered by applying the test set out in the judgment of Kerr LJ in *Euro-Diam Ltd v Bathurst* [1988] 2 All ER 23, at 28–29, where he said:

> 'the ex turpi causa defence ultimately rests on a principle of public policy that the courts will not assist a plaintiff who has been guilty of illegal (or immoral) conduct . . . It applies if, in all the circumstances it would be an affront to the public conscience to grant the plaintiff the relief which he seeks . . .'

It did not, according to the judges, matter whether the conduct it was sought to rely on to establish the defence was criminal. Conduct which fell short of criminal but which 'offended public sensibilities' would suffice. However, suicide did not fall within this test. The public attitude to suicide had changed since the time when it was a criminal offence, such that suicide was no longer viewed as something to be condemned. Instead, the general public attitude was one of sympathy. The defence of ex turpi causa therefore failed.

The approach taken to the defence of ex turpi causa was not adopted by the majority of the Court of Appeal in a case decided four months later even though it appears that the case was cited to the court. In *Pitts v Hunt* [1990] 3 All ER 344, the plaintiff had been injured as a result of a motor cycle accident. He had been riding pillion on a friend's motor cycle. Both the plaintiff and his friend had been drinking heavily and on the journey home the motor cyclist had, with the encouragement of the plaintiff, been driving in a reckless fashion deliberately trying to frighten other road users. They were involved in a collision with a car. As a result of the collision the driver of the motor cycle was killed and the plaintiff was severely injured. The driver of the car was absolved of all blame for the accident. The plaintiff brought an action against the personal representatives of the motor cyclist. At the trial, the judge held that the plaintiff's action was barred by the maxim ex turpi causa and public policy. He would further have held that the plaintiff would have been defeated by the defence of volenti non fit injuria but for s 148(3) of the Road Traffic Act 1972 (now s 149 of the Road Traffic Act 1988). Finally, he held that the plaintiff was 100% contributorily negligent.

The Court of Appeal affirmed the decision of the trial judge, albeit that they did not accept all his reasoning. First, the court held that it was impermissible to make a finding that the plaintiff was 100% contributorily negligent. Section 1 of the Law Reform (Contributory Negligence) Act 1945 begins with the premise that a person should suffer damage as a result *partly* of his own fault and *partly* of the fault of any other person. The Act thus requires that the trial judge must apportion blame between the two parties. A finding that someone is 100% contributorily negligent clearly does not do that. (This should be contrasted with the view of Lord Reid in *Imperial Chemical Industries Ltd v Shatwell* [1964] 2 All ER 999, where he said, 'where the plaintiffs own disobedient act is the sole cause of his injury, it does not matter in the result whether one says 100% contributory negligence or volenti non fit injuria . . .'). Both Dillon and Beldam LJJ indicated that the correct apportionment in a case such as the present would have been to hold each equally to blame and thus to reduce the plaintiff's damages by 50%.

Secondly, the court agreed with the trial judge that, but for s 148(3) of the Road Traffic Act 1972, the plaintiff's claim would have been defeated by the defence of volenti. In the light of cases such as *Dann v Hamilton* [1939] 1 All ER 59, this may be considered a rather harsh decision. Nevertheless, the court held that the plaintiff had voluntarily agreed to waive any claim for any injury that might befall him. However, s 148(3) of the 1972 Act provides that:

> 'where a person uses a motor vehicle in circumstances such that . . . there is required to be in force in relation to his use of it . . . a policy of insurance . . . then, if any other person is carried in or upon the vehicle while the user is so using it, any antecedent agreement or understanding between them . . . shall be of no effect so far as it purports or might be held – (a) to negative or restrict any such liability of the user in respect of persons carried in or on the vehicle . . . or, (b) to impose any conditions with respect of the enforcement of any such liability of the user; and the fact that a person so carried has willingly accepted the risk of negligence on the part of the user shall not be treated as negativing any such liability of the user.'

On this wording, the court held that the fact that a person has willingly accepted the risk of the other person's negligence cannot be treated as negativing the liability of that other person.

Finally, the court affirmed the trial judge's decision that the plaintiff's action was barred by the defence ex turpi causa non oritur actio. Two approaches to the question when this maxim will apply can be discerned in the judgment of the Court of Appeal. Beldam LJ, after an extensive review of the cases, held that a pragmatic approach should be taken to the question whether the defence should apply. This involved answering two questions: first, had there had been any illegality of which the court should take note and second, would it be an affront to the public conscience to allow the plaintiff to recover. The courts should, he said citing Bingham LJ in *Saunders v Edwards* [1987] 2 All ER 651, at 665–6 (a case discussed in All ER Rev 1987, p 295), take a fairly robust approach to these questions '[they should not] on the first indication of unlawfulness, draw up [their] skirts and refuse all assistance to the plaintiff'. However, taking account of the policy of Parliament with regard to road traffic cases, which was to take an increasingly dim view of drunk driving, and the fact that the driver himself would not have succeeded in claiming an indemnity under any insurance policy, the plaintiff should be precluded on the grounds of public policy from recovering compensation from him.

Balcombe and Dillon LJJ adopted a different approach. Dillon LJ considered the 'conscience' approach but dismissed it as very difficult to apply. Its application, he said, would be problematical because it would inevitably be affected by emotional factors. Further, appeal to the public conscience would be likely to lead to a graph of illegalities graded according to moral turpitude. Thus, he agreed with Mason J in the Australian case of *Jackson v Harrison* (1978) 138 CLR 438, that such an approach would raise an insoluble problem of formulating criteria to separate cases of serious illegality from those which were not serious. A more satisfactory approach could be discerned, and in this Balcombe LJ agreed, from a number of Australian High Court cases. Both judges referred to the judgments of Mason and Jacobs JJ in *Jackson v Harrison* and Barwick CJ in *Smith v Jenkins* (1970) 119 CLR 397, with approval. There the judges had held that the effect of the defence ex turpi causa was to deny the existence of a duty of care in certain cases of joint illegal enterprises. The defence would only have this effect where, first, the plaintiff's action is directly connected with the joint illegal enterprise and not merely incidental to it. Thus, where two safe breakers are engaged in attempting to open a safe and one is injured by the negligent use of explosives by the other, the defence can apply. However, if on the way to open a safe one of the safe breakers struck the other there would be no defence. In such a case the tortious act is merely incidental to the illegal enterprise. Secondly, the circumstances of the illegal venture must be such that the court cannot (or will not) determine the particular standard of care to be observed. Thus, if a robber is injured due to the negligent driving of his get-away driver the court would be unable (or unwilling) to determine what standard of driving should be expected of a competent get-away driver (see *Ashton v Turner* [1980] 3 All ER 870).

The approach of Balcombe and Dillon LJJ is to be preferred in that it does away with the necessity to have reference to that notoriously difficult and fickle concept 'the public conscience'. Having said that, its application in the present case is surely open to criticism. By applying the defence of ex turpi causa, the court evaded the prohibition, in s 148(3) of the Road Traffic Act 1972, preventing drivers 'contracting out' of their liability, where their negligence injures another person who is being carried in or on a motor vehicle. This can surely not have been intended by Parliament. It is worth noting that in the United States, where a similar principle of joint enterprise liability exists, the courts have refused to hold in passenger/driver cases that the passenger is precluded from suing the driver (see *Williams v Knapp* (1968) 248 Md 506 and *Galloway v Korzekwa* 346 F Supp 1086).

In *Morris v Murray* [1990] 3 All ER 801, the Court of Appeal was asked to consider the application of the defence of volenti non fit injuria to the case of a passenger injured in a flying accident where the pilot was drunk. The plaintiff and the deceased had been drinking in a public house for some hours. The deceased suggested that they go for a joy ride in his light aircraft. The plaintiff agreed to this suggestion and the two of them drove in the plaintiff's car to the aerodrome where the plaintiff assisted in preparing the aircraft for take-off. The aircraft, piloted by the deceased, only managed to get airborne for a few minutes before it crashed. The pilot was killed and the plaintiff suffered severe injuries. An autopsy on the pilot revealed that he had consumed the equivalent of 17 whiskies and that his blood alcohol level was more than three times the legal limit for driving a car. The plaintiff brought an action against the pilot's estate claiming damages for personal injuries. The trial judge awarded £139,000 damages. The pilot's estate appealed, arguing that the plaintiff's action should have been barred because he had voluntarily assumed the risk of injury that occurred.

The Court of Appeal held that the defence of volenti non fit injuria should have succeeded. The court considered, first, whether the volenti defence applies to the tort of negligence at all. Fox LJ said that two situations had to be distinguished. First, there was the situation where a dangerous physical condition has been brought about by the negligence of the defendant and after it has arisen, the plaintiff, fully appreciating its dangerous character, elects to assume the risk. In this type of situation the defence could apply. It can be said here that the plaintiff has waived his right of action. However, the present case did not fall into this category. Instead, this case was an instance of the second type of case. This was the situation where the act of the plaintiff relied on as consent precedes and is claimed to licence in advance a possible subsequent act of negligence. Here, it can be said that the plaintiff has waived the defendant's duty to take care. The plaintiff had argued, relying on dicta from the judgment of Diplock LJ in *Wooldridge v Sumner* [1962] 2 All ER 978, where he had said (at 990) that:

> 'the defence of volenti in the absence of express contract, has no application to negligence simpliciter where the duty of care is based solely on proximity or "neighbourship" in the Atkinian sense.'

ie, that the defence of volenti could have no application to this second type of case. The court rejected the defendant's argument. Stocker LJ held that Diplock LJ's dicta was not intended to apply to a pilot/passenger situation. This is so because a special relationship exists between a pilot and his passenger and it is not a case of negligence simpliciter. Where a passenger is injured in an accident, having consented to being driven by a drunken pilot, the question whether his action will be barred by the defence of volenti will depend upon whether the plaintiff foresaw the risk of injury arising from the relationship. Whether or not the maxim will apply depends, therefore, upon the awareness of the plaintiff of the extent of the potential risk in the light of his knowledge of the activity being pursued and the level of intoxication of the defendant. If the injury that occurs is something that the plaintiff could not have foreseen, the defence can have no application.

Fox LJ also took the view that the volenti doctrine could apply to the tort of negligence. He did not, however, require that the accident arise out of some pre-existing special relationship. For Fox LJ, the application of the defence depended on the extent of the risk, the passenger's knowledge of it and what can be inferred as to his acceptance of it. He agreed with Stocker LJ that a passenger could not be volens in respect of acts of negligence which he had no reason to anticipate.

Whilst the court was correct to conclude that volenti can apply to the tort of negligence, it is suggested that there is a danger that the statements of the judges will be read too widely. It cannot be the case that the mere fact that a passenger foresees a danger of the driver's negligence should enable the defendant to rely on the defence of volenti. Knowledge of the risk cannot give rise to acceptance of it. The courts should be careful to avoid resuscitating ideas rejected by the courts for sound policy reasons over many years.

Secondly, the court considered whether the plaintiff's appreciation of the risk should be ascertained by asking what the plaintiff actually appreciated or what a reasonable man in the position of the plaintiff would have appreciated. The court held that the former approach should be adopted. Thus, had the plaintiff been 'blind drunk' such that he had been incapable of appreciating what was going on, the pilot's estate could not have relied on the defence.

Limitation of actions

Three cases reported in 1990 raise the question of when a cause of action accrues where the plaintiff relies upon the defendant's skill and the defendant exercises that skill carelessly, causing damage to the plaintiff. The general rule, endorsed in all three cases, is that the cause of action accrues when damage is suffered. The courts held that the damage was suffered at the moment when the plaintiffs relied upon the defendants and not, as the plaintiffs had argued, when the loss materialised. As a consequence their actions were time barred.

In *Bell v Peter Browne & Co* [1990] 3 All ER 124 (see also Solicitors, pp 236–238 above), the plaintiff consulted the defendant solicitors to act on his behalf in divorce proceedings. It had been agreed between the plaintiff and his wife that the matrimonial home, which was in their joint names, would be transferred into the sole name of the wife. The plaintiff's interest was to be protected by the defendants through the execution of a trust deed or mortgage. Subsequently, the house was transferred to the wife but the defendants failed to take any steps to protect the plaintiff's interest. Eight years later, the wife sold the property and spent the proceeds. The plaintiff brought an action against the defendants claiming damages for breach of contract and negligence. The defendants pleaded that the actions were time barred.

The Court of Appeal held, albeit with not much enthusiasm, that the claims were time barred. The applicable limitation period was six years (Limitation Act 1980, s 2) and this was to run from the time that damage was suffered. The court held that the plaintiff suffered damage when he parted with his legal estate in the property by conveyance to his wife. At that moment the plaintiff acquired an equitable interest in the proceeds of sale which, if left unprotected, was clearly of less value to him. The judges rejected the plaintiff's argument that the damage did not occur until his wife sold the property. The sale after eight years had the effect of making the breach and its consequences irremediable. It did not alter the fact that damage was suffered at the time of conveyance.

In reaching this decision, the Court of Appeal affirmed two first instance decisions reported earlier in 1990. In *Iron Trade Mutual Insurance Co Ltd v J K Buckenham Ltd* [1990] 1 All ER 808 (also discussed at pp 21, 68, 218 above), plaintiff insurers had engaged the defendant brokers to place marine quota share insurance in respect of their underwriting accounts for the years 1976 to 1981. The quota share reinsurance was placed with a Portuguese company. From 1981 the Portuguese company failed to pay claims made against them, with the result that in 1984 the plaintiffs brought an action against them to recover the sums due. In late 1984 the reinsurers purported to avoid the contracts of reinsurance on the ground, inter alia, that they had been misled by the brokers. In late February 1987 the present action was commenced against the brokers alleging breach of contract and breach of the general duty of care owed to them by the brokers. The defendants sought to have the actions struck out on the ground that they were time barred. The contracts of reinsurance, they said, had all be concluded prior to 11 February 1981 and the writ had not been issued within six years from that date. The plaintiffs, on the other hand, argued that their cause of action did not accrue until the reinsurers avoided the contracts. It was only then they suffered any loss.

Kenneth Rokison QC, sitting as a Deputy Judge of the High Court, held that the cause of action accrued at the time when the contracts of reinsurance were executed and not at the moment when the reinsurer avoided the contract. As he pointed out, 'the plaintiffs desired to obtain valid and effective contracts of reinsurance. They only obtained voidable contracts'. Thus, the plaintiffs suffered an actionable loss at the time of the execution of the contracts of reinsurance. He held, therefore, with regard to the contracts for the years 1976 to 1980, that the plaintiff's actions were time barred.

Further, the plaintiffs had contended that s 14A of the Limitation Act 1980 (as inserted by s 1 of the Latent Damages Act 1986) applied to the 1981 contract. Section 14A provides that the limitation period in any action for damages for negligence, where the facts relevant to the cause of action were not known at the date of accrual, will not expire until three years after the earliest date on which the plaintiff 'had both the knowledge required for bringing an action for damages . . . and a right to bring such an action' (s 14A(5)). The plaintiffs argued that they did not acquire the necessary knowledge for the purposes of the Act until the reinsurers avoided the contract in October 1984. Thus, the action in respect of the 1981 contract was not time barred.

The judge considered that the question of the plaintiff's knowledge before February 1984 was essentially one of fact. The question to be asked he said, was:

'when was the earliest date on which the plaintiffs had knowledge of such facts about the damage as would lead a reasonable person who had suffered such damage to consider it sufficiently serious to justify his instituting proceedings for damages against a defendant who did not dispute liability and who was able to satisfy a judgment?'

In answering this question, the judge held that the burden was on the plaintiff to establish the necessary facts. He concluded that this was not an appropriate question to be decided on an application to strike out but should instead be investigated at the trial.

In *Islander Trucking Ltd (in liquidation) v Hogg Robinson & Gardner Mountain (Marine) Ltd* [1990] 1 All ER 826 (see Practice and Procedure at p 218 above), plaintiffs instructed the defendant insurance brokers in October 1980 to obtain 'goods in transit' insurance on their behalf. The plaintiffs were subsequently faced with claims and sought an indemnity against their liability insurers. However, in January 1985 the insurers avoided the plaintiffs' policy, alleging misrepresentation by the brokers. In October 1986, the plaintiffs commenced an action against the brokers. The brokers argued that they were not liable because they were merely acting as sub-agents for Maltese brokers in obtaining the insurance. In January 1989 leave was obtained to join the head brokers. The head brokers later applied to have the order joining them set aside on the ground that the plaintiffs' action against them accrued in October 1980 when the voidable contract of insurance was effected. As they had not been joined in the action until after the expiration of the six year limitation period, the claim for damages for breach of contract and negligence was time barred under the Limitation Act 1980.

Evans J accepted the head brokers' arguments. The judge followed the decision of Rokison QC in the *Iron Trade Mutual* case in holding that the relevant damage for the purposes of the Limitation Act 1980 was suffered at the time when the contract was entered into. At that moment the plaintiffs acquired a form of property less valuable to them than they were entitled to expect. What they sought was a valid contract of insurance; what they had, in fact, got was a voidable contract. Thus, the limitation period commenced at the time the contract was executed and the action against the head brokers was time barred.

Two points should be made about these three decisions. First, although the actual results in these cases may seem somewhat unjust in the light of the fact that in none of them did the plaintiffs find out that they had suffered any actionable loss until after the expiry of the limitation period, the courts were correct in deciding that the cause of action accrued from the moment the respective contracts were concluded. In each of the cases, the plaintiffs acquired something which had less value than they expected. Their loss was thus economic and clearly was suffered at the time the contracts were entered into. In reaching this conclusion, however, the courts refused to apply the result reached by the House of Lords in *Pirelli General Cable Works Ltd v Oscar Faber & Partners (a firm)* [1983] 1 All ER 65 (All ER Rev 1983, pp 331–332). There the House held that the cause of action in tort for the negligence in the design or workmanship of a building, whether by builder, engineer or architect, accrues not at the time the defective building is completed, or at the time the plaintiff acquires an interest in the building, but instead at the date when physical damage occurs. Application of *Pirelli* to the above cases would have led to the cause of action accruing when the loss actually manifested itself. In refusing to apply *Pirelli*, the courts held its reasoning should be restricted to building cases. However, this is an unsatisfactory rationalisation since there appears to be no good reason why building cases should be treated any differently to other cases. The better view, in the light of the characterisation of *Pirelli* in *Murphy v Brentwood District Council* as a *Hedley Byrne*-type case, is that *Pirelli* is no longer good law. If the House of Lords was correct in *Murphy*, economic loss was suffered in *Pirelli* at the time of reliance by the plaintiff on the professional advisers and the limitation period should have run from that earlier point in time.

Secondly, the injustice of the results in these cases should to a large extent be mitigated in future cases by s 14A of the Limitation Act 1980. This allows an extended limitation period where the plaintiff does not have knowledge of the facts required for bringing the action. Had this provision been in effect at the time these actions arose it is likely that the results would have been different.

In *Donovan v Gwentoys Ltd* [1990] 1 All ER 1018, the House of Lords considered the extent of a court's discretion under s 33(1) of the Limitation Act 1980 to override the prima facie time limit in a personal injury or fatal accidents claim. Section 11 of the 1980 Act provides that in an action for death or personal injury caused by negligence, prima facie, the time limit within which the action must be brought is three years from the date on which the cause of action accrued. The cause of action will normally accrue at the time of the accident. However, the time limit is extended when the person injured is under a disability, for example, a child. Section 28 provides that in such a case the limitation period will not expire until three years from the time the disability ends. These time limits can, however, by virtue of s 33(1), be disapplied where the court considers it would be fair, having regard to the degree to which the plaintiff and defendant would be prejudiced, to allow an action to proceed despite the expiry of the time limit. In considering whether to exercise the discretion, the court is directed by s 33(3) to have regard to 'all the circumstances of the case' as well as to a number of other considerations which are specifically mentioned. (See Practice and Procedure, pp 217–218 above for further discussion of this case.)

In *Donovan v Gwentoys Ltd*, the plaintiff was 16 years old when she was injured in an accident at work. She made no mention of the accident to her employers, preferring to make a claim for industrial injury benefit. Five years later, in April 1984, just prior to the expiry of the time limit under s 28, the plaintiff consulted solicitors about her injury. The solicitors failed to issue a writ until some five months after the expiry of the limitation period. The issue of the writ was the first time the defendants had had any indication from the plaintiff of how the accident was alleged to have occurred. The defendants pleaded that the action was statute barred. In reply, the plaintiffs applied to the court for a direction under s 33(1) that the prima facie time limit should not apply. The trial judge held that in deciding whether or not to exercise the discretion under s 33(1) he was confined, in considering the effect of delay, to the time which elapsed after the limitation period expired. As this was only five months, the defendants would not suffer any serious prejudice in respect of this extra period. He therefore granted the plaintiff's application. The defendants appealed.

In allowing the appeal, the House of Lords held that the trial judge had been wrong to confine himself to a consideration of the effect of the delay in the period which elapsed after the limitation period expired. Although s 33(3)(*b*) of the 1980 Act did require the court to have regard to the length of the delay and the delay mentioned in that section did refer to the delay subsequent to the expiry of the limitation period, the court's discretion was not limited to the matters referred to in s 33(3). The House of Lords made clear that the court was free, in exercising its discretion, to take into account any other matters it considered relevant. Here, the first the defendant knew of the claim was five years after the accident. This, the House said, was clearly a relevant consideration when weighing up the prejudice likely to be caused to the defendant if the limitation period was not applied. Thus, it was wholly appropriate to take into account the date on which the claim was first made against the defendant. Taking account of the fact that this was five years after the accident and the difficulties that would as a result arise with regard to investigating the accident, it would not, according to the House, have been equitable to disapply the limitation period.

False imprisonment

Part 9 of the third volume of the All England Law Reports 1990 contains a veritable feast for tort lawyers interested in false imprisonment. Three cases, one of which was decided in 1985, are reported. In each case the Court of Appeal considered, inter alia, the problem of whether, and if so when, a change in the circumstances of detention may give rise to an action for false imprisonment. The conclusions expressed suggest that the Court of Appeal is by no means unanimous in its approach to this question.

In *Middleweek v Chief Constable of the Merseyside Police* [1990] 3 All ER 662 (decided in 1985) the plaintiff was a solicitor engaged to defend a former police officer. At a bail hearing, a police officer noticed that the solicitor's file contained an internal police document. On being asked where he had got this from the solicitor refused to answer. The officer then arrested him at 10.45 am on suspicion of theft. The solicitor was taken to an interview room where he gave an explanation as to the source of the document. The interview ended at 11.22 am. The arresting officer, having determined that further inquiries were necessary, caused the plaintiff to be searched in accordance with the standard procedure. Certain possessions were taken away from him and he was then locked in a cell while the inquiries were carried out. The plaintiff was eventually released at 1.00 pm. He brought an action against the chief constable and the police officer claiming damages for, inter alia, trespass and false imprisonment. At the trial, held before a judge and jury, the plaintiff argued, on the trespass point, that the search and removal of his possessions was wrongful in that the search and removal was carried out according to standing instructions without regard to the circumstances of the case. As to false imprisonment, he argued that he had been detained for an unreasonably long time and that it was unreasonable to detain him in a cell. The judge, having directed the jury that the arrest was lawful, asked them to consider a number of questions. First, was it reasonable to search the plaintiff and remove his possessions? They answered that it was. Secondly, was the detention unreasonably long? To which the answer given was no. Finally, was it reasonable to detain the plaintiff in a cell? The jury replied that it was not and awarded £500 damages. The chief constable appealed and the plaintiff cross appealed.

As to the cross appeal the plaintiff put forward two arguments. First, that where a search and removal of possessions was carried out according to standing instructions it must, ipso facto, be unlawful. Therefore, the question of the reasonableness of the search should never have been left to the jury. The judge should only have left the issue of the quantum of damages to the jury. Secondly, the judge ought to have directed the jury that the plaintiff should have been released at 11.22 am and, therefore, any detention thereafter was unlawful. The Court of Appeal had little difficulty rejecting both contentions. As to the first, the court held that the fact that a search is carried out according to standing instructions does not mean that it is ipso facto unlawful (or for that matter that it is lawful). The Court of Appeal explained *Lindley v Rutter* [1981] QB 128 as deciding that following standing instructions was not of itself a conclusive answer to a complaint that a search was unlawful. It was not authority for the proposition that a search carried out according to standing instructions was unlawful unless regard was had to the particular circumstances of the case. Every search must be considered on its own facts to determine whether it was justified. This was pre-eminently a jury question and, as the judge had correctly left this issue to the jury, the decision on this point must stand.

The second point on the cross appeal by the plaintiff was also dismissed. To accede to the submissions of counsel for the plaintiff, the court said, would have involved accepting both that the police were not entitled as a matter of law to hold the plaintiff while they made further inquiries and/or that as a matter of law the time spent making those inquiries was excessive. The court was unwilling to accept either of those propositions. Again, the question whether or not the period of detention was excessive was a question of fact to be decided in the light of all the circumstances by the jury.

As to the appeal, the chief constable had argued that once it had been decided that the arrest was lawful and that the period of detention was not unreasonable, detention in a cell could not turn what was a lawful detention into an unlawful one. The judgment of Tudor Evans J in *Williams v Home Office (No 2)* [1981] 1 All ER 1211 was cited in support of this. In *Williams* Tudor Evans J said (at 1227), that there was:

> 'no authority in modern law to support the plaintiff's submission that although a detention may be lawful it can become unlawful if the nature (meaning the conditions) of the imprisonment changes.'

The court, however, refused to accept the absolute nature of this statement. Referring to the decision of the Divisional Court in *R v Commissioner of Police of the Metropolis, ex p Nahar* (1983) *Times* 28 May, the Court of Appeal said that where conditions of detention become so intolerable this may render the detention unlawful so that an action for false imprisonment will lie. On the facts, however, it was not established that the conditions in the police cell fell below a reasonable standard. The question whether it was reasonable to detain the respondent in a cell should not, therefore, have been left to the jury and so the court allowed the chief constable's appeal.

In *Weldon v Home Office* [1990] 3 All ER 672, the plaintiff was a prisoner who had been sentenced to four years' imprisonment. He alleged that prison officers acting without lawful authority had dragged him out of his cell and put him in a segregation cell in the punishment block. He brought an action against the defendants, claiming damages for false imprisonment. The Home

Office applied to strike out the plaintiff's claim. They argued; first, that a prisoner could not claim he had been falsely imprisoned because by definition he was not entitled to his liberty; secondly, s 12(1) of the Prison Act 1952 which provides, 'a prisoner . . . may be lawfully confined in any prison', gives prison officers a complete defence to an action for false imprisonment; and, finally, a change in the conditions of a person lawfully imprisoned cannot transform that lawful imprisonment into unlawful imprisonment. To the extent, therefore, that *Middleweek v Chief Constable of Merseyside Police* held that it could, it was wrongly decided or alternatively it should be confined to the case of a prisoner under arrest.

The Court of Appeal refused to strike out the plaintiff's claim. First, the court considered whether a prisoner might, in the absence of intolerable conditions, have an action for false imprisonment. The court held, without reaching a final conclusion on the matter, that he might be able to. In reaching this decision, two broad principles appear to have been uppermost in the court's mind. First, on the authority of *Raymond v Honey* [1982] 1 All ER 756, a case discussed at length in All ER Rev 1982, pp 232–234, 'a person confined to prison retains all his civil rights, other than those expressly or impliedly taken from him by law' and secondly, the policy of the law is 'jealously to protect personal liberty' (at 677). In the light of these principles the court looked at the Prison Act 1952 and the rules made thereunder. These, the court said, provided the framework within which the prisoner's rights must be considered. Their intention was to see that a prisoner should, subject to any lawful order given to him, enjoy such residual liberty as is left to him. This residual liberty should be just as jealously guarded as the personal liberty of any person. Prima facie therefore, a prisoner could have an action for damages for false imprisonment where this residual liberty is interfered with. However, to be set against this was the need to ensure that life in prison was well ordered. This required that prisoners be required to obey the lawful orders of prison officers. A prison officer acting in pursuit of his lawful authority would therefore have a complete defence (by s 12) to an action for false imprisonment. Where, however, a prison officer was shown to have been acting in bad faith it may be, the court held, that a prisoner would have an action for false imprisonment.

In reaching this rather tentative conclusion the court gave extensive consideration to the authorities. None of these, according to the court, precluded them from reaching the present conclusion. Even *Williams v Home Office (No 2)* – which was one of the main planks of the defendant's application – where Tudor Evans J had said that s 12 would in all cases provide a defence to an action of false imprisonment, had not considered the situation where a prison officer deliberately and in bad faith had deprived a prisoner of his residual liberty. In that situation a prison officer could not rely on s 12.

Secondly, the court accepted that imprisonment in intolerable conditions could turn a lawful imprisonment into an unlawful one. The conditions required for such an action to succeed were, however, expressed differently from those in the *Middleweek* case. In order to base a claim for false imprisonment on intolerable conditions it would be necessary for the plaintiff to show that the defendant had continued the confinement of the prisoner in intolerable circumstances, without reasonable cause, with knowledge that the conditions were intolerable.

Having so defined the scope of the tort of false imprisonment the court refused to allow the application to strike out. Since the allegations of false imprisonment – whether based on interference with residual liberty or intolerable conditions – sufficiently alleged bad faith, they had not been shown to be unarguable and should therefore go to trial. (See also Prisons, pp 223–224 above.)

R v Deputy Governor of Parkhurst Prison, ex p Hague [1990] 3 All ER 687, raised similar issues to the *Weldon* case (and is likewise considered in Prisons, p 223 above). In that case, a prisoner serving 15 years was transferred to another prison's segregation unit after he had twice deliberately gone out on unauthorised exercise and had indicated that he would continue to do so. The prison governor had power to order such a transfer under the prison rules where it was considered desirable in the interests of good order and discipline. The prisoner brought an action claiming, inter alia, damages for false imprisonment. The Divisional Court dismissed the claim.

The Court of Appeal dismissed this part of the prisoner's appeal. In so doing they considered a number of authorities including the *Middleweek* and *Weldon* cases. First, the court considered the statements in *Weldon* to the effect that an imprisonment within imprisonment if done in bad faith by a prison officer, may be actionable. This was regarded as somewhat novel. As Taylor LJ pointed out (at 707) 'bad faith has never been a necessary ingredient in the tort of false imprisonment'. Further, in the absence of intolerable conditions, the authorities all supported the proposition that an action for false imprisonment could not lie because the prison officer would be able to rely on s 12. Without actually saying *Weldon* was wrong on this point, the Court of Appeal clearly signalled its preference for the view that the general position was that a prisoner did not have the right to bring an action for false imprisonment because the prison officer would be able to rely on s 12.

Secondly, the court considered whether intolerable conditions could turn a lawful detention into an unlawful one. They were of the view that it could, but as such conditions were not present in this case the appeal would be dismissed. The judges preferred the approach of the *Middleweek* court to that of the *Weldon* court. Although the court accepted that a claim based on intolerable conditions was not the usual claim for false imprisonment in that the claim was not for the deprivation of liberty to move at will but for the nature of that deprivation, the court felt that a claim based on intolerable conditions could be reconciled with existing authorities. Such intolerable conditions would negative the statutory defence in s 12 of lawful imprisonment. The court justified this by saying that there must be implied into the Prison Act 1952 a term making intolerable conditions unlawful. As to the additional element of bad faith suggested in *Weldon*, requiring this would be to alter the established definition of the tort and in effect would lead to the creation of a new tort special to prisons.

A final point dealt with by the court was whether the prisoner could rely upon the prison rules to rebut a defence of lawful detention. Relying on *Becker v Home Office* [1972] 2 All ER 676 and *Williams v Home Office* the court held that the prison rules are regulatory only and even if they are not observed cannot give rise to a private law claim for damages. Any remedy for breach of the rules should be pursued by way of an application for judicial review.

Where does this leave future claims for damages for false imprisonment brought by those arrested or imprisoned lawfully where there has been some change in their conditions of imprisonment? In the light of the different views expressed by the Court of Appeal it is difficult to predict an answer to this with any degree of certainty. It seems clear that an action for false imprisonment based on intolerable conditions may succeed. How the courts will judge whether the conditions are intolerable is more difficult. *Weldon*'s case rejected reliance upon the European Standard Minimum Rules for the Treatment of Prisoners or reference to the European Convention on Human Rights because neither of these can be directly applied by an English court. Presumably, therefore, the court will make its own estimate of what is, or is not, intolerable. A further complication concerns the question of whether, as required by *Weldon*, the officer must continue the detention with knowledge of the intolerable conditions, or whether it is enough that the conditions are in fact intolerable. The better view, and the one more in line with authority, is that knowledge of the conditions should not be necessary.

As to the more general proposition stated by the court in *Weldon* that bad faith on the part of an officer when exercising a power to imprison within prison would be actionable and the officer would not be able to rely on s 12 as a defence to such an action, this is more problematic. As Taylor LJ pointed out in *ex p Hague* such a proposition is not readily reconcilable with the authorities. However, despite this, it is suggested this view should be adopted. To adopt it would be to give effect to the two cardinal principles relied upon in *Weldon*. To reject it would further remove rights of citizenship in the case of prisoners which should be presumed unless explicitly removed.

The case of *Hill (Gary) v Chief Constable of the South Yorkshire Police* [1990] 1 All ER 1046 raised two points of procedure with regard to an application to strike out in a false imprisonment case. The plaintiff had been arrested for being drunk and disorderly. He was taken to a police station at 2.40 am, where he was detained until 5.15 am when he was charged and released. When he appeared before the magistrates he pleaded guilty to being drunk and disorderly and was fined. The appellant subsequently brought this action claiming damages for assault, wrongful arrest and false imprisonment. He claimed, first, that his arrest was unlawful because the police had failed to inform him of the reason for his arrest, as they were required to do by s 28 of the Police and Criminal Evidence Act 1984, and secondly, the detention was unlawful because the custody officer had failed to charge and release him on bail expeditiously as he was required to do by s 37 of the 1984 Act. The registrar ordered that the action be tried by a jury. The respondents appealed against this order and at the same time applied to have the action struck out on the ground that since the appellant had pleaded guilty to the offence he could not have been wrongfully arrested or detained. The judge allowed the appeal and ordered that the action be struck out. The appellant appealed against the judge's order.

The Court of Appeal allowed the appeal. In a striking out action the court had to be satisfied that the plaintiff's case disclosed no reasonable cause of action. This, the respondents argued, must be the case here because the appellant had subsequently admitted his guilt. Thus, the arrest and detention must have been lawful. The Court of Appeal rejected this argument. The fact that the person arrested is in fact guilty cannot, in and of itself, justify his arrest or detention. Parliament has specifically provided that certain requirements must be satisfied for an arrest and subsequent detention to be lawful. If these are not complied with, regardless of guilt, the accused will be entitled to bring an action for their breach. The court therefore held, in the light of the fact that the lawfulness of arrest and detention was arguable, that the judge had been wrong to strike out the action.

The judges then considered the respondent's further contention that the action should be tried by a judge alone. The court decided that it should not. Where, as here, a court was satisfied that there was a triable issue in respect of false imprisonment then, by virtue of s 66(3) of the County Courts Act 1984 this must be tried by judge and jury.

Libel and slander

Sutcliffe v Pressdram Ltd [1990] 1 All ER 269, was one of a series of libel actions brought by Mrs Sutcliffe, the wife of the 'Yorkshire Ripper'. This action concerned articles published in *Private Eye* in 1981 and 1983 alleging that Mrs Sutcliffe had been prepared to sell her story for £250,000 to the *Daily Mail*. At the trial the jury found that the plaintiff had been libelled and awarded her £600,000 damages. *Private Eye* appealed against the award on the grounds, inter alia, that the judge had misdirected the jury on issues relating to damages and also that the amount awarded by the jury was excessive.

As to the misdirection two substantive arguments were put by counsel for *Private Eye*. First, it was argued that the judge had failed to direct the jury properly on the issue of the publication (in 1989) prior to the trial of further alleged libels. These further libels, the judge said, could be taken into account in considering whether aggravated damages should be awarded. The Court of Appeal rejected *Private Eye*'s argument. The trial judge, Michael Davies J had, the court held, made clear that aggravated damages are awarded because other conduct of the defendant makes the injury to feelings occasioned by the original libels worse. They were not to be awarded in respect of injury to Mrs Sutcliffe's reputation occasioned by the 1989 article.

Secondly, the Court of Appeal accepted that a separate vindicatory award should not be given as an element in an award of damages. However, they held that the trial judge was entitled to direct the jury, as he had done, that when they were considering what sum to award, they must consider whether the amount they contemplated would be enough to demonstrate to others the baselessness of the charge.

The principal ground of the appeal was that the sum awarded in damages was out of all proportion to any injury suffered by Mrs Sutcliffe. Whilst the Court of Appeal agreed that Mrs Sutcliffe had suffered grievously and that a large sum was required to vindicate her reputation they held that the sum awarded could not be justified. In reaching this conclusion all the judges stressed the sanctity of the jury's decision. It would be, they said, only on rare occasions that an appeal court would consider itself entitled to interfere. What were those circumstances? All the judges thought that the authorities pointed to some kind of *Wednesbury* test; 'I do not think that the court should interfere [with the jury's decision] unless it can be shown that no reasonable jury properly directed could reasonably make the award'.

Finally, the judges considered what further guidance could be given to juries by the trial judge. First, they said, adopting a passage from the speech of Lord Hailsham in *Cassell & Co Ltd v Broome* [1972] 1 All ER 801 (at 823–824) that juries should not be given information about awards in personal injury claims. Parliament had entrusted the award of damages in personal injury actions to judges, whereas juries were to decide the issue in cases of libel (s 69, Supreme Court Act 1981). Their respective approaches to the question of damages is different, judges being bound by precedent whereas juries are not. It was thus inappropriate to give them information about awards in personal injury actions. Further, the measure of damage was different in the two types of cases, making comparisons inappropriate.

Secondly, the juries should not be referred to other awards by juries in other libel actions. Such reference would, the court said, serve to confuse rather than assist the jury and would be likely to lead to unseemly and unhelpful over and under bidding.

Thirdly, juries could be given further assistance to help them appreciate the true size of the award they were making. Thus, the judge could properly invite them to consider what the result would be in terms of weekly, monthly or annual income if the money were invested in a building society. In the light of the court's advice as to what further guidance may be given to juries in a libel action, it is interesting to note that Parliament had provided, in s 8 of the Courts and Legal Services Act 1990, that the Rules Committee may make rules of court allowing courts to substitute their own award of damages if they consider that the amount awarded by the jury was excessive. Whether Parliament's apparent loss of faith in a jury's ability to make a reasonable assessment of damages will lead to a greater willingness on the part of courts to set aside jury awards remains to be seen.

In *Telnikoff v Matusevitch* [1990] 3 All ER 865, the Court of Appeal gave extensive consideration to the defence of fair comment in a defamation action. The plaintiff wrote an article for a newspaper criticising the BBC's Russian service for recruiting too many employees from ethnic minorities of the Soviet Union and not enough from people who associate themselves 'ethnically, spiritually or religiously with the Russian people'. The defendant, a Russian Jew, was incensed by this article and wrote a letter which was published in the same newspaper. After quoting a short passage from the article, the defendant complained that the plaintiff was a racist, who was advocating the switching from professional testing to a blood test and the sacking of 'ethnically alien' employees from the Russian service. The plaintiff brought an action for libel, and the defendant pleaded fair comment. At the trial the judge withdrew the case from the jury before the presentation of the defendant's case. He concluded that since any reasonable jury would be bound to uphold the defence of fair comment and as there was no evidence of malice, the plaintiff's action must fail. The plaintiff appealed. In dismissing the appeal, a number of points of importance concerning the defence of fair comment were made.

First, the Court of Appeal rejected the plaintiff's argument that in considering whether the words were fact or comment the court was confined to a consideration of the words themselves without reference to the earlier article. Acceptance of the plaintiff's argument would, as the judges pointed out, lead to several unfortunate consequences, not the least of which would be that any wise critic would be forced to quote the article in full before commenting on it. Where, as here, the earlier article was sufficiently indicated in the subsequent letter and had been published in a newspaper to which there was easy access, there could be no justification for failing to interpret the words in the light of the article. Having reached this conclusion, the court agreed with the trial judge that the jury would have been bound to conclude that the words were comment.

The second issue in the case concerned the approach to be adopted to the question of fairness. The plaintiff argued that no comment could be fair unless it was, first, an opinion which an honest man could hold and, secondly, an opinion which the defendant actually held. The burden of proving the latter point was, according to counsel for the plaintiff, on the defendant. As the case had been withdrawn from the jury prior to the presentation of the defendant's case, he clearly could not have satisfied the requisite burden and thus the trial judge had been wrong to stop the case going to the jury. The Court of Appeal rejected this argument. The test as to whether or not a comment was fair was, according to the court, an objective test and not, as the plaintiff contended, both objective and subjective.

The problem remains, however, as to what is meant by objective in this context. It seems from the speeches of the judges that objectivity does not here require an investigation into whether a reasonable man could hold that opinion. The test instead appears to be whether any fair or honest minded man could hold that opinion. Provided the opinion is within the sphere of reasonableness the comment will be fair even if others would not have held that opinion. As Lord Hailsham has said in a different context:

> 'two reasonable [people] can perfectly reasonably [hold different opinions] on the same set of facts without forfeiting their title to be regarded as reasonable.'
> (*Re W* [1971] 2 All ER 49)

Thirdly, the court considered the test to be adopted on the issue of malice. They held that whilst the issue of malice was one for the jury, the trial judge must first consider whether there was any evidence to go to the jury that the defendant was actuated by malice. Here, agreeing with the trial judge, they said that any evidence on the question of malice could be left to the jury only if it was more consistent with malice than the absence of it. On the facts, none of the evidence satisfied this test and the trial judge was, therefore, correct not to leave the issue of the defendant's malice to the jury.

Finally, an interesting problem concerning the defence of fair comment and its availability to newspapers was raised by Lloyd LJ. Can a newspaper plead fair comment if it publishes a libellous letter where the author has a defence of fair comment, even if the views expressed are not those of the newspaper? Whilst Lloyd LJ expressed no final conclusion on this point it seems clear that he would consider it an undue restriction on freedom of expression if the newspaper could not take the benefit of the defence. Although some authority can be found against this view (see, for example, the decision of the majority in *Cherneskey v Armadale Publishers Ltd* [1979] 1 SCR 1067) it is suggested that Lloyd LJ's view is to be preferred.

In *Rost v Edwards* [1990] 2 All ER 641, Popplewell J considered the meaning of article 9 of the Bill of Rights 1688. This provides that 'the freedom of speech and debates on proceedings in Parliament ought not to be impeached or questioned in any court or place out of Parliament'. The plaintiff argued that in a defamation action he should be entitled to lead factual evidence, on the issue of damages, that he had been de-selected from a House of Commons select committee. In support of this, the plaintiff argued that the prohibition in article 9 that proceedings should not be 'questioned' meant should not be 'questioned critically'. Article 9 was, he said, intended to protect free speech in Parliament and to ensure that proceedings in Parliament were not impugned outside. Whilst Popplewell J was attracted by this argument, he felt himself bound by authority to hold that 'questioned' meant not only to 'question critically' but also to 'examine'. Thus, as questions relating to the composition of select committees were clearly within the meaning of 'proceedings in Parliament', he refused to allow the plaintiff to adduce evidence on this point.

The judge also gave consideration to the meaning of 'proceedings in parliament'. Both the plaintiff and defendant wished to lead evidence as to the criteria relating to the register of members' interests. Whilst Popplewell J recognised that full attention must be given to the requirement of comity between the courts and Parliament, he was of the view that the courts should not be astute to hold that their jurisdiction was ousted, particularly where, as here, no issue as to free speech arose. On the facts he therefore held that evidence could be led as to the requirements for the registration of members' interests. This was a matter ancillary to 'proceedings in Parliament'. If Parliament wished such matters to be covered by privilege it was up to them to do so expressly. This robust approach adopted by Popplewell J is to be welcomed.

Finally, in what was a bumper year for defamation cases, the Court of Appeal in *Beta Construction v Channel Four Television Co Ltd* [1990] 2 All ER 1012, set out a number of factors which may be taken into account in considering whether, under ss 69(1) and 69(3) Supreme Court Act 1981, trial by judge alone ought to be ordered in a libel action. The defendants admitted liability and the only question left was the quantum of damages that should be paid. The trial judge directed that, in the light of the need for a 'prolonged examination of documents or accounts' (s 69(1)(c)) this issue should be dealt with by a judge alone. Whilst conceding that a prolonged examination of documents was required, the plaintiffs argued that the trial judge had been wrong to find that it was not convenient for this examination to be made by a jury.

The Court of Appeal dismissed the appeal and held that in considering whether trial by jury is convenient under s 69(1)(c), a court must direct its attention to the issue of the efficient administration of justice. The question that must be asked is whether trial by jury is consistent with the efficient administration of justice and in deciding this the following circumstances may be relevant.

(1) Will trial by jury involve a 'substantial' prolongation of the trial? The court recognised that inevitably any trial by jury will take longer than a trial by judge. It was not, however, in every case that trial by judge would be ordered. It would be ordered only in cases where the prolongation was likely to be so substantial that the administration of justice would be affected.

(2) Will trial by jury involve significant extra expense?

(3) Are the jury likely to be able to understand the issues on the documents or accounts in order to be able to resolve them satisfactorily. The court

highlighted the particular problems likely to be faced by juries when confronted with accounts or other commercial documents.

(4) Will trial by jury entail significant physical or practical problems? The court seems to have in mind here the problem that documents may be too bulky to be conveniently considered by the jury in the confined spaces of the jury box.

(5) Are there likely to be any special complexities in the documents or accounts?

It is perhaps interesting to speculate whether, in the light of s 8 of the Courts and Legal Services Act 1990 and the criteria to be taken into account under s 69, juries will be of less significance in defamation actions in the future.

Statutory torts

Animals Act 1971

The Court of Appeal in *Curtis v Betts* [1990] 1 All ER 769 considered a number of points relating to the interpretation of s 2(2) of the Animals Act 1971, which imposes strict liability for injuries caused by animals of a non-dangerous breed. The plaintiff, a boy aged ten, was severely bitten by the defendant's bull mastiff dog, Max. The incident took place as the dog was being loaded into the back of the defendant's car. The plaintiff brought an action alleging that the defendants were liable under s 2(2) of the 1971 Act. At the trial the plaintiff claimed that bull mastiffs tended to be aggressive when defending what they regarded as their territory. This was supported in relation to Max by evidence that he used to jump up at the defendant's gate, growling and snarling at passers by. The trial judge found that there had been a breach of s 2(2) and awarded the plaintiff £2,368 damages.

The Court of Appeal dismissed the defendant's appeal. The court recognised that for the keeper of an animal to be liable, where the animal did not belong to a dangerous breed (when strict liability arises under s 2(1) of the Act), all three requirements of s 2(2) had to be satisfied. First, s 2(2)(a) provides, 'the damage [must be] of a kind which the animal . . . was likely to cause or which, if caused by the animal, was likely to be severe'. The court held that the trial judge had been correct to find that, under the first part of s 2(2)(a), the damage was not of a kind that Max was 'likely to cause'. Most of the time Max was a quiet and docile dog. However, with regard to the second part of s 2(2)(a), Max was likely, if he did bite anyone, to cause 'severe injury'. The court rejected the interpretation put on this requirement by North's *The Modern Law of Animals* that the second part of s 2(2)(a) would only be satisfied if the animal had such abnormal characteristics that it was likely that if it did cause damage, the damage would be severe. According to Dr North, therefore, it was necessary to read sub-s (a) in the light of the succeeding requirements of the section dealing with abnormal characteristics. The court adopted a narrow view of s 2(2)(a) as only requiring an answer to the question whether if the particular animal did damage anyone that damage was likely to be severe.

Secondly, s 2(2)(b) provides that:

'the likelihood of the damage or of its being severe must be due to characteristics
of the animal which are not normally found in animals of the same species or are
not normally found except at particular times or in particular circumstances.'

The Court of Appeal, reflecting the observations of the court in the earlier
case of *Cummings v Granger* [1977] 1 All ER 104, was of the opinion that this
was unhappily phrased. The majority (Stuart Smith and Nourse LJJ) took the
view that s 2(2)(b) is concerned with the causation of damage. The damage
must have been caused by either the permanent or temporary characteristics
of the animal. Applying this interpretation to the facts, the majority held that
the damage was caused by Max defending what he regarded as part of his
territory and, as this fell within a characteristic found only in 'particular
circumstances', s 2(2)(b) was satisfied. Slade LJ took a slightly different
approach. He likewise had difficulty with s 2(2)(b) but thought that the
difficulty disappeared if 'due to' was interpreted to mean 'attributable to'.
Thus s 2(2)(b) would be satisfied where, on the particular facts, the likelihood
of damage was attributable to characteristics not normally found in animals
of the same species or to characteristics normally found in animals of the same
species at times or in circumstances corresponding with those in which the
damage actually occurred.

Finally, the court held that s 2(2)(c), which requires that the characteristics
must have been known to the keeper of the animal, was satisfied. On the facts
the defendants knew of Max's territorial tendencies and thus liability was
established. (See also Statute Law, p 256 above.)

Nuclear Installations Act 1965

Merlin v British Nuclear Fuels plc [1990] 3 All ER 711 concerned a claim for
statutory compensation under the Nuclear Installations Act 1965. In 1973 the
plaintiffs purchased a house close to the Sellafield nuclear reprocessing plant.
Four years later, as a result of a public inquiry, the plaintiffs were alerted to
the possibility of radioactive contamination in their home. In October 1981,
as a result of test carried out on the house, they learnt that the level of
radioactive contamination was high enough to warrant concern. The
plaintiffs decided to move but experienced considerable difficulty in selling
the house. The house was eventually sold for a sum considerably below the
initial asking price. The plaintiffs brought an action under the 1965 Act
claiming the financial loss represented by the diminution in value of the house
caused by the level of radioactive contamination. They alleged that the
defendants were in breach of s 7(1)(b)(ii) of the Act which imposed a duty on
the licensee of Sellafield to secure that:

'(b) no ionising radiations emitted . . . (ii) from any waste discharge . . . on or
from any site, cause injury to any person or damage to any property of any
person . . .'

Gatehouse J held that the plaintiffs' action failed. First, the admitted
radioactive contamination of the plaintiffs' house had not caused 'physical
damage' to the house or any of the plaintiffs' personal property. The level of
radioactive contamination required to produce any detectable change in the
molecular structure of the plaintiffs' property would have had to have been

substantially greater than that which was present. Secondly, 'damage to property' in s 7(1)(b)(ii) of the Act was not defined. In interpreting it, the judge accepted that regard could be had to the Vienna Convention on Civil Liability for Nuclear Damage 1963 as the Act of 1965 was enacted to give effect to this convention. The convention defined 'nuclear damage' in Art I(k)(i) as 'loss of life, any personal injury or any loss of or damage to property . . .'. While contracting parties to the convention were free to provide that any other losses could be recovered if they so wished, the judge held that Parliament had not sought to extend the losses recoverable beyond those mentioned in Article I(k)(i) and hence 'damage to property' was to be given a meaning limited to *physical* damage to property. The judge felt that his analysis on this point was fortified by the restrictive approach of the common law to the recovery of pure economic loss. The judge remarked that to allow recovery here would be to allow recovery for economic loss contrary to this trend. Although the result was not surprising – in the light of the general antipathy of the courts to actions for the recovery of economic loss – it might be questioned whether there is any real role for the Act in respect of property damage if claims for damage in cases like the present are not to be entertained. How many cases of damaged cows or sheep could Parliament have expected there to be? The result is that another provision creating strict liability is shorn of its teeth.

Factories Act 1961

In *Whitfield v H & R Johnson (Tiles) Ltd* [1990] 3 All ER 426 (see also Employment Law, p 101 above), the plaintiff, who suffered since birth from a congenital back condition, was injured lifting tiles. She had been doing this work for some months without any ill effects and when she was injured she was doing nothing out of the ordinary scope of her work. The defendants did not know and had no reason to know of the plaintiff's back problem. The plaintiff brought an action against the defendants alleging breach of s 72 of the Factories Act 1961. This provides that, 'a person shall not be employed to lift, carry or move any load so heavy as to be likely to cause injury to him'. The plaintiff argued that in considering whether there has been a breach of s 72 the defendants must take the plaintiff as they found her. The test to be applied, according to the plaintiff, was whether, viewed objectively, it was likely that a person with the plaintiff's condition would sustain injury.

The Court of Appeal rejected the plaintiff's argument. Section 72, they held, was passed to make sure that the weight of the loads employees were asked to lift, carry or move were appropriate to the sex, build and physique, or other *obvious* characteristic, of the employee in question. Where, as here, the load was appropriate to an ordinary employee of the plaintiff's characteristics and the plaintiff had no obvious injuries the defendants were not in breach of s 72.

Damages

Where a person enters into a contract in reliance on a negligent misstatement, the basic principle for the assessment of damages is that he should be put in the position he would have been in had the misrepresentation not been made.

The usual time at which such assessment is made is, according to *McGregor on Damages* (para 1724), the time of contracting. Thus, for example, where the plaintiff enters into a contract for the purchase of shares in reliance on a negligent misrepresentation, damages will be assessed on the basis of the difference in value between the purchase price and the actual value at the time of acquisition. A necessary corrollary of this rule is that any increase in the 'actual value' of the subject matter of the contract due to the intervening act of the plaintiff will not be taken into account in the assessment of damages.

It seems clear, however, that this 'usual rule' is not absolute. In certain situations the courts will consider subsequent increases or decreases in the value of the subject matter. In two cases reported in 1990, the courts considered the question whether increases or decreases in value of the subject matter of the contract should be taken into account in assessing the plaintiff's damages.

In *Hussey v Eels* [1990] 1 All ER 449 (also discussed in Contract, pp 64–65 above), the defendant vendors agreed to sell their bungalow to the plaintiffs for £53,250. In answer to the purchasers' preliminary inquiries the vendors negligently misrepresented to the plaintiffs that the property had not been subject to subsidence. Following completion in February 1984, the plaintiffs discovered there had been subsidence but they could not afford the £17,000 it would cost to stablise the foundations. Instead, they sought, and two and a half years later obtained, planning permission for the demolition of the existing bungalow and the erection of two further buildings. They then sold the bungalow, with planning permission, to property developers for £78,500. The plaintiffs brought an action against the defendant claiming £17,000 in damages for negligent misrepresentation. This constituted the difference in value between what they had paid for the property and what it had actually become worth at the time of completion. The defendants argued that this was not the correct measure of damages because any loss suffered had been wiped out by the profit made on the resale.

In *Naughton v O'Callaghan* [1990] 3 All ER 191, the subject matter of the contract was a thoroughbred yearling called 'Fondu' (see also Contract, pp 60, 64 above). Due to a careless misrepresentation by the auctioneers, the colt was described in the catalogue of sale as having been bred from the 'Habitat' line. In fact, the horse was from the 'Moon Min' line. Had the plaintiff known of this he would not have purchased the animal. Instead, in reliance on the misrepresentation, he paid 26,000 guineas for the horse. The horse was put into training in Ireland and England and was raced for two seasons. It was unplaced in all its six races. The plaintiff then discovered the horse's true pedigree and sought to claim damages for the negligent misrepresentation. By this time, due to its lack of success, the horse was only worth £1,500. The plaintiff therefore claimed as damages the difference between the price paid and its current value. They also claimed the cost of training it over the two years. The defendants argued that damages ought to be assessed as the difference in value between the purchase price (26,000 guineas) and Fondu's actual value at the time of the sale (23,500 guineas).

Both these cases raise the issue whether conduct of the plaintiff, after the time of contract, should be taken into account when assessing damages. In *Hussey v Eels*, where the conduct of the plaintiff had led to an increase in the value of the bungalow, the court held that this should not be taken into account in assessing the damages and allowed the plaintiff to recover the full £17,000 claimed. Conversely, in *Naughton v O'Callaghan*, where the conduct of the plaintiff in racing the horse had led to a decrease in its value, Waller J held this should be taken into account. He thus allowed the plaintiff to recover the difference between the purchase price and its decreased value after two years of racing.

How can the difference in result in the two cases be justified? In *Hussey v Eels* two approaches were considered by the Court of Appeal. First, it was argued that the plaintiffs were under a duty to the defendant to mitigate their loss, the resale had been a performance of that duty and as a result this should be taken into account when assessing damages. Mustill LJ (with whom the other members of the court agreed) rejected this argument on the ground that the plaintiffs could have chosen to mitigate their loss in a number of ways, for example, by living in the bungalow or repairing it. Consequently, they were not under any duty to mitigate by reselling the property. With respect to Mustill LJ this reasoning is fallacious. He suggested that the defendant's argument depended on proof that the plaintiffs were under a *duty* to resell the house in mitigation, which was, of course, not the case. Instead, the defendant's argument acknowledged that a number of different steps in mitigation were open to the plaintiffs. They had, however, chosen to mitigate by reselling the property. As such a step in mitigation was clearly reasonable, this ought to have been taken into account by the court in assessing the damages recoverable.

The second approach considered by the Court of Appeal was whether, looking at the dealings as a whole, the misrepresentation could be said to have led to or caused the gain which subsequently occurred, or whether the misrepresentation should be seen as independent of any subsequent gain. This, it is suggested, is the preferable approach. In *Hussey v Eels* the court held that this issue was primarily one of fact. Did the negligence which caused the damage also cause the profit? Mustill LJ thought not. In one sense, as he pointed out, it was true that there was a causal link between the misrepresentation and the sale two and a half years later, because the sale represented a choice of one of the options with which the plaintiffs had been presented by the defendants' wrongful act. However, he preferred the view that:

> 'the reality of the situation [was] that the plaintiffs bought the house to live in and did live in it for a substantial period . . . when the plaintiffs unlocked the development value of their land they did so for their own benefit and not as part of a continuous transaction of which the purchase of the land and bungalow was the inception.'

In *Naughton v O'Callaghan*, Waller J approached the question in a similar way. The decision to keep the horse and race it, he said, was precisely what the seller would have expected. The subsequent fall in the horse's value was special to the horse and was to be expected if it did not win. Thus, there was a clear, causal link between the subsequent decrease in value of the horse and the misrepresentation.

In considering what is in essence a question of fact, it is suggested that a number of factors may be relevant. First, the nature of the subject matter of the contract. Where the 'thing sold' is a commodity such as shares or corn, in the usual course of events the buyer would be expected to go out and sell the 'commodity' after the misrepresentation is discovered. If the purchaser continues to hold the shares or corn in the expectation that the market will rise, this will break the causal link with the misrepresentation. It is not a decision based on any factor related to the misrepresentation but is, instead, unrelated to it. This is not the same as the situation where the purchaser buys, for example, a horse. There it might be expected that the purchaser would put the horse into training and race it. In such circumstances, if the horse is unsuccessful (or for that matter successful) this should be taken into account in assessing damages.

Secondly, subsequent rises and falls in the market will usually be considered to be at the risk of the purchaser. If, for example in *Naughton v O'Callaghan*, the reason for the decline in the value of 'Fondu' was a fall in the market for such animals, this would be at the risk of the purchaser. In such a case the causal link between the misrepresentation and subsequent decrease in value would be broken.

Finally, the capacity in which the purchaser buys the product may be relevant. Had the purchaser in *Hussey v Eels* been a property developer, it is suggested that the subsequent gain should have been taken into account. There it would have been expected that the purchaser would take the steps taken in that case and thus the misrepresentation should be considered to be the 'cause' of any subsequent gain.

In *Swingcastle v Gibson* [1990] 3 All ER 463 (a case also discussed in Contract, p 66 above), the plaintiff finance company specialised in the making of high risk mortgage loans. In 1985 they agreed to loan £10,000 to mortgagors on the basis of a valuation carried out by the defendants surveyors. The valuation was carelessly made; the surveyors valuing the house at £18,000 when a proper valuation would have been closer to £12,000. It was accepted that had there been an accurate valuation the plaintiffs would not have made the loan, it being their policy not to make loans on properties with a value of less than £15,000. The agreement between the plaintiffs and the mortgagors provided that interest on the loan would be 36.5% per annum, but that in the event of default the rate would be increased to 45.6% per annum. The mortgagors fell into arrears almost immediately. The plaintiffs obtained a possession order and managed to sell the house one year later for £12,000. The plaintiffs brought an action for negligent misstatement. The defendants admitted liability. The issue for the court, therefore, was confined to the measure of damages recoverable.

First, the plaintiffs claimed the difference in value between the amount they lent (£10,000) and what they would have lent (nil) had they known of the misrepresentation, less any amount they recovered on the resale (the unpaid principal). Secondly, they claimed not the unpaid interest at the 'normal' rate of interest until the default date but also unpaid interest at the default rate from the time of default until the time of sale. By the time of the sale the amount owed was nearly £8,000.

The Court of Appeal held that, as to the unpaid principal claimed, this was the proper measure of damages. Two type of cases, they said, had to be distinguished. First, there were those cases where, had the misrepresentation not been made, the plaintiff would still have lent money, albeit a lesser amount. There the measure of damages would be the difference between the amount lent and the amount that the plaintiff would have lent had he known of the misrepresentation. The second type of case, of which *Swingcastle v Gibson* was an example, was where, had the plaintiff known the true state of affairs, he would not have lent money at all. In such cases, although the same test is used by the courts in assessing damages, the amount that would have been lent is nil. The plaintiff is thus able to recover his full loss which he may not be able to do in the first type of case.

The Court of Appeal also allowed the plaintiffs to recover the unpaid interest. The court considered themselves bound by the decision of the Court of Appeal in *Baxter v F W Gapp & Co Ltd* [1939] 2 All ER 752. There it was held that, in addition to the principal sum, the interest payable under the mortgage agreement which had not been paid could also be recovered. A number of points should be noticed.

First, as the defendants argued, to allow the recovery of interest at the mortgage rate was to give the plaintiffs the benefit of the bargain. This is surely wrong in principle. Allowing recovery at the mortgage rate, in the circumstances of this case, had the same effect as if the surveyor had warranted the performance by the borrowers of their mortgage obligation. This is more appropriately the proper subject of a contractual and not tortious claim.

Secondly, in *Baxter v F W Gapp & Co*, it was not surprising that the court awarded the mortgage rate of interest. In that case, there was little or no difference between the mortgage rate and 'ordinary' rates of interest. Here there was a substantial difference. *Baxter v F W Gapp & Co* was, therefore, distinguishable on its facts.

Finally, as Neill LJ himself admitted in *Swingcastle, Baxter v F W Gapp & Co* is not easily reconcilable with principle, allowing as it does the recovery of the loss of the bargain in tort. The Court of Appeal recognised that other approaches could have been taken which would have been more consistent with principle. These were:

(a) The lender could be awarded a sum equivalent to the amount he would have earned by way of interest on another loan if he had had the money available for this purpose. This would require evidence to be led of an unsatisfied demand for loans. If such evidence were forthcoming, interest should be awarded at the standard rate and not the default rate.

(b) The lender could be awarded a sum equivalent to the interest he would have earned if the sum had been placed on deposit.

(c) The lender could be awarded a sum to represent the loss of opportunity to invest the money elsewhere.

Whilst any one of these methods of assessment may not be appropriate for all cases, they do at least have the advantage of being consistent with the general principle of recovery in a tort action. It is to be hoped that the House of Lords will take the earliest opportunity to review this unsatisfactory decision.

In *Murray v Lloyd* [1990] 2 All ER 92, the question of the proper measure of damages when an action is brought in both contract and tort was considered. The plaintiff had engaged a solicitor to advise and act for her in the purchase of a leasehold interest in a house. The lease was for a term of 15 years and was subject to a prohibition against assignment without the prior consent of the landlord, such consent not to be unreasonably withheld. Acting on the solicitor's advice, the house was assigned in the name of the British Virgin

Islands company to avoid United Kingdom income tax. The solicitors advised the plaintiff that assignment to the company would not prevent a later assignment by the company to her. The plaintiff would thus be able to become a statutory tenant under the Rent Act. This was wrong and when the landlord refused his permission for the assignment the plaintiff sued her solicitors alleging negligence and/or breach of an implied contractual term that they would act with due care in advising her. The solicitors admitted negligence but denied that any loss or damage had been suffered by the plaintiff.

John Mummery, sitting as a deputy judge of the High Court, awarded the plaintiff substantial damages. The loss that the plaintiff had suffered, he said, was the opportunity of becoming a statutory tenant. He therefore assessed damages by reference to the cost of acquiring similar rights of occupation on similar terms in similar alternative accommodation.

At first sight, the decision in this case may appear to be inconsistent with the decision of the Court of Appeal in *Esso Petroleum Co Ltd v Mardon* [1976] 2 All ER 5. There a tenant was induced to take a lease of a petrol station by a statement made by the landlord that the future annual turnover could be estimated at 200,000 gallons per annum. The estimate had been carelessly made and the actual turnover was much lower. The landlord was held liable in the tort of negligence and for breach of a collateral warranty. The tenant, however, failed to recover damages for loss of his bargain. The court held that the landlord had not warranted that the turnover would be 200,000 gallons per annum, but instead that the estimate had been carefully prepared. Thus, the court awarded damages assessed on a tortious basis to put the plaintiff in the position he would have been in had the misrepresentation not been made.

Applying *Esso Petroleum v Mardon* to the facts of this case, it would appear that, as the solicitors did not warrant the truth of the advice given but only promised to take reasonable care in advising her, the plaintiff ought to have been put in the position she would have been in had she not taken the lease. Thus, the damages awarded would be the price paid for the lease less its sale value at the time the misrepresentation was made.

It is suggested however, that *Murray v Lloyd* is a different type of case to *Esso Petroleum v Mardon*. In *Murray v Lloyd*, the plaintiff was not arguing, as was the case in the *Esso Petroleum* case, that but for the misrepresentation she would not have entered into the contract. Instead, she argued that, had there been no misrepresentation, she would still have entered into the contract for the lease, but would have done so on terms that the lease was assigned to her. In such circumstances she was correctly allowed to recover damages for the lost opportunity of this, namely the opportunity of becoming a statutory tenant.

Personal injuries

In *McCamley v Cammell Laird Shipbuilders* [1990] 1 All ER 854 (see also Commercial Law, p 20 above), an employee of the defendants was injured due to their negligence. The trial judge awarded the plaintiff £387,000 damages. The defendants appealed against the award on the ground, inter alia, that the trial judge ought to have deducted a sum paid to the plaintiff by the defendants under a personal accident group insurance scheme which paid out a lump sum in the event of an employee being injured, regardless of fault. This policy had been taken out by the defendants, for all their employees and was funded solely by the defendants' requiring no contribution from the employee.

The Court of Appeal held that the insurance moneys were not deductible. In reaching this decision, O'Connor LJ, who delivered the judgment of the court, said that as a general rule gains accruing to the plaintiff as a result of the accident were, prima facie, to be taken into account in assessing the damages payable. There were, however, two well established exceptions to this rule (see Lord Bridge in *Hussain v New Taplow Paper Mills Ltd* [1988] 1 All ER 541, discussed in All ER Rev 1988, p 333). First, there were insurance policies to which the plaintiff had himself contributed. The policy here in issue did not fall within this exception because the plaintiff had made no contribution. Secondly, there was the situation where the plaintiff receives money from the benevolence of a third party. The court held that the sum paid under the policy fell within this exception:

> 'The whole idea of the policy . . . was clearly to make the benefit payable as an act of benevolence whenever a qualifying injury took place.' (at 861c–d)

The sums paid out in respect of injuries were not intended to be in substitution of loss of wages resulting from the accident and were, therefore, not deductible.

Fatal accidents

The Court of Appeal has affirmed ([1990] 2 All ER 69) a decision of Sheen J in *Pidduck v Eastern Scottish Omnibuses Ltd* [1989] 2 All ER 261 (discussed in All ER Rev 1989, p 341) on the issue of deducting pensions paid to a dependant from the damages representing their dependency (recovered under the Fatal Accidents Act 1976). The plaintiff was the widow of a retired Bank of England employee. She brought an action under the Fatal Accidents Act 1976 against the defendants, who had negligently killed her husband. The deceased had, until the time of his death, been receiving a monthly retirement pension from his employers. On his death the widow began to receive from the bank a pension and a widow's allowance which was paid under the same scheme as the deceased's pension had been paid. Whilst the general rule in personal injuries actions is that benefits received as a result of the death must be deducted, under s 4 of the Fatal Accidents Act 'benefits which accrued . . . as a result of the deceased's death' are to be ignored and not to be deducted from any award of damages. The question for the court was, therefore, whether these pensions were 'benefits' within s 4.

Not surprisingly, the Court of Appeal held that the pensions were 'benefits' which 'accrued as a result of [his] death'. What the plaintiff had lost as a result of her husband's death was the financial support he provided from his pension. But the pension and widow's allowance she received on his death were distinct payments or benefits, as they were payable to her directly after his death. Since, therefore, these 'benefits' accrued as a result of her husband's death they would be disregarded in assessing damages.

The *Pidduck* decision seems to highlight the contrasting approach of the courts in personal injury cases and that of Parliament in Fatal Accident cases. Why should it be that dependants are more favourably treated than live plaintiffs? If the answer is that no reason exists, then which is the correct approach as a matter of policy: general deductibility of benefits or non deductibility?

Town and Country Planning

PAUL B FAIREST, MA, LLM
Professor of Law, University of Hull

Introduction

One of the most significant events of 1990 so far as this subject is concerned is not referred to in the All England Law Reports – namely the repeal of the Town and Country Planning Act 1971. Lest, however, jubilation or grief be unconfined, it is only fair to point out that it has been replaced by a pair of new (consolidating) Acts, the Town and Country Planning Act 1990 and the Planning (Listed Buildings and Conservation Areas) Act 1990. The cases decided during the year and reported in the All England Law Reports refer to the 'old' sections in the 'old' Town and Country Planning Act 1971; where practicable, reference will be made (in italics) to the corresponding provisions in the new Acts.

There has been something of an increase in the number of cases reported in the pages of the All England Law Reports during the year, including a number of excursions to the House of Lords.

Planning permission – motives

An interesting and unusual point fell to be considered by Simon Brown J in *R v Exeter City Council, ex p J L Thomas & Co Ltd* [1990] 1 All ER 413.

In brief, the applicants sought to challenge by way of judicial review a grant of planning permission for substantial residential development on a site adjacent to their industrial premises. They contended that the planning permission had been granted in the hope that the incompatibility of the proposed residential use with the applicant's established industrial use would lead to pressure upon the applicants to relocate their industrial activities. This, it was said, was an improper motive which would justify the annulment of the grant of planning permission.

The factual background to the application was as follows. J L Thomas & Co Ltd (Thomas) are tallow and animal feeding meal manufacturers, rendering down animal waste products collected in from abattoirs and slaughterhouses. Their co-applicants, Blight & White Ltd (B & W) are steel fabricators. Thomas's operations are smelly; B & W's are noisy. Thomas operated with Exeter City Council's consent, as theirs was an offensive trade within the meaning of s 107 of the Public Health Act 1936. B & W enjoyed the necessary planning permission for their activities. Both firms operate within the Haven Banks area, the most heavily industrialised part of Exeter.

There is a small amount of residential development in the area, in Cotfield Street, but this development preceded the commencement of operations by Thomas and B & W. The planning permission which gave rise to the present proceedings was a grant of planning permission, to Tutorhome Ltd, for a much larger residential development in the shape of 87 flats and maisonettes together with a shop, on a site about 100 yards from Thomas, and nearer still to B & W. What the applicants feared was that the occupants of the new housing development would foreseeably object to the noise and smells emanating from the premises of the two applicants. There might be nuisance claims which would compel the applicants to relocate.

The applicants' first argument was to the effect that if the City Council wished to force the applicants to relocate, the proper procedure to employ was a discontinuance order under s 51 of the Town and Country Planning Act 1971 (*now s 102 of the Town and Country Planning Act 1990*). If this machinery was employed, there would be an obligation to pay compensation under s 170 (*now s 115, Town and Country Planning Act 1990*).

This argument was summarily rejected by Simon Brown J, who said it was founded on the 'wholly unsustainable premise that a local planning authority are deprived of their s 29 (*now s 70*) power (to grant planning permission) save only if they regard their s 51 (*s 102*) discretion as a duty'.

The second argument was more subtle; it suggested that the council granted the planning permission for an ulterior and improper purpose, namely to procure Thomas's discontinuance of their existing lawful user without the compensation they could expect under s 51 (*s 102*). It was clear on the facts that the council hoped to achieve Thomas's departure consequent on the grant of planning permission. This was, however, a subsidiary aim, as the planning permission was granted out of a genuine desire to see the site developed for residential use in accordance with the planning permission. Relying on *Westminster Bank Ltd v Minister of Housing and Local Government* [1970] 1 All ER 734 and *Hoveringham Gravels Ltd v Secretary of State for the Environment* [1975] 2 All ER 931, Simon Brown J rejected the applicants' argument:

> 'It is in my judgment perfectly proper for a planning authority to wish to encourage residential development in a particular area even if it contains existing industrial users. It is legitimate also for the planning authority to recognise and accept that planning permission for residential development in such an area is likely to give rise to conflicts with those existing users. It is also perfectly proper for the authority to harbour the wider aspiration that the existing users will relocate . . . The one thing that would flaw the authority's decision is if they were concerned to promote rather than minimise the conflict, which I am satisfied is not this case. I conclude therefore that the grant of residential planning permission in these circumstances would not be unlawful even if a substantial part of the authority's motivation was the hope that they might thereby avoid the subsequent payment of s 51 (*s 102*) compensation.' (at 420j–421a)

The authorities relied on by the applicants were distinguished. A dictum in *Newbury DC v Secretary of State for the Environment* [1980] 1 All ER 731 (at 745–6) was regarded as being concerned with the improper use of planning conditions, and the remarks in *Minister of Housing and Local Government v Hartnell* [1965] 1 All ER 490 were concerned with the safeguarding of existing use rights and legitimate expectations. Thomas had no legitimate expectation that other conflicting uses would never be introduced into the vicinity. A final contention was that the council's decision was *Wednesbury* unreasonable, wholly absurd and perverse, given the inescapable conflicts which must result from the introduction of residential use. This was again rejected. The effect of a proposed development on an existing use is a material consideration within s 29 of the Town and Country Planning Act 1971 (*now s 70, Town and Country Planning Act 1990*) (see *Stringer v Minister of Housing and Local Government* [1971] 1 All ER 65), but it certainly does not follow that the interests of the existing user must prevail:

> 'On the contrary, provided only that such interest is properly considered, it is the duty of the planning authority to decide between it and any proposed competing use and to take this decision solely in light of the public interest.' (421h)

It was also noted that Thomas's application was not made promptly, and Simon Brown J properly reminded litigants of the crucial need in cases of this kind for applicants to proceed with the greatest possible urgency, giving, moreover, to those affected the earliest warning of an intention to proceed:

> 'Only rarely is it appropriate to seek judicial review of a s 29 (s 70) permission; rarer still will be the occasion when the court grants relief unless the applicant has proceeded with the greatest possible celerity.' (423a).

Planning permission – material considerations

The fate of County Hall, Westminster was the subject of a leading decision of the House of Lords in *London Residuary Body v Lambeth London Borough Council* [1990] 2 All ER 309. The issue which fell to be decided was the scope of the local planning authority's discretion under s 29 of the Town and Country Planning Act 1971 (*now s 70, Town and Country Planning Act 1990*).

County Hall was formerly the seat of the London County Council, for whom it was originally constructed, with space for offices and function rooms, such as a Council Chamber; it then became the seat of the Greater London Council, until the abolition of that body by s 1 of the Local Government Act 1985. The property of the former Greater London Council became vested in the London Residuary Body (the LRB). The LRB wished to sell County Hall with vacant possession for office accommodation. The view was taken that a change to (non-local authority) office use would be a material change of use, thus necessitating planning permission. LRB applied to Lambeth (the local planning authority) for planning permission; no decision was reached by Lambeth within the stipulated time, so, treating this as a rejection of planning permission as they were entitled to do under s 37 of the Town and Country Planning Act 1971 (*now s 78, Town and Country Planning Act 1990*), they appealed to the Secretary of State. After a public local enquiry under an inspector, the Secretary of State granted permission for general office use, at least in part by relying on the 'presumption in favour of development' as expressed in Circular 14/85, para 3, which states:

> 'There is therefore always a presumption in favour of allowing applications for development, having regard to all material considerations unless that development would cause demonstrable harm to interests of acknowledged importance.'

Appeals were then lodged to the High Court under s 245 (*now s 288, 1990 Act*). At first instance Simon Brown J quashed the Secretary of State's decision to grant planning permission, basically because the reasons were not adequately stated in the decision letter (see 58 P & CR 256). On appeal to the Court of Appeal (Slade, Lloyd, and Stocker LJJ), the decision of Simon Brown J on this point was upheld, but on different grounds. The reasons were adequately stated in the decision letter, it was said; but the reasons were bad in law, because the Secretary of State had not applied the correct test (see 58 P & CR 370). He should, in the view of the Court of Appeal, have applied a 'competing needs' test (which, interestingly, Simon Brown J at first instance would have no truck with). This involved, essentially, weighing against each other the desirability of preserving the existing use and the merits of the proposed new use. Only where these were evenly balanced, in the Court of Appeal's view, would there be any scope for the presumption in favour of development to operate. The House of Lords disagreed; the main speeches (those of Lord Keith and Lord Templeman) clearly reject the approach of the Court of Appeal. After stressing that the amount of weight to be given to any material consideration was a matter for the person or body considering the application, Lord Keith added:

> 'There is no warrant in the authorities for the view that a competing needs test exists in law and falls to be applied as a matter of legal obligation . . . Such a proposition would involve putting an unwarranted gloss on the language . . . of the Act . . . [T]he desirability of preserving an existing use of land is a material consideration, provided there is a reasonable probability that such use will be preserved if permission for the new use is refused. If the Court of Appeal is right, it must follow that the presumption in favour of development can in law only receive effect where other planning considerations for or against a proposed use are evenly balanced. Such a strait-jacket cannot properly be imposed on the Secretary of State. It must be left to him, in the exercise of a reasonable discretion, to form his own judgment whether any planning objections are of sufficient importance to overcome the presumption . . . [I]n the case of many individual planning applications, for example to build a single house somewhere in the country, there is no question of it being possible to prove a need for the development. There may, however, be some planning objection to it which is not of very great weight. In such a situation it must surely be open to the determining authority to decide that the presumption may properly receive effect and to grant planning permission.' (p 314d–315a)

Caravans – statutory meaning

In *Wyre Forest District Council v Secretary of State for the Environment* [1990] 1 All ER 780, the House of Lords considered the question whether the word 'caravan' in a planning permission had to be construed in its ordinary sense or whether it should be construed in the special sense given to the term by s 29(1) of the Caravan Sites and Control of Development Act 1960 (see also Statute Law, pp 257–258 above).

In simple terms, the issue arose in this way. Allen's Caravans (Estates) Ltd claimed that the erection of a chalet structure on land which they occupied was a 'caravan' and thus covered by a planning permission obtained in 1960 by their predecessors in title, Kingsford Holiday Camp Ltd, from Kidderminster Rural District Council, the predecessors of Wyre Forest District Council. Wyre Forest took the view that the chalet was not a 'caravan', and served an enforcement notice requiring its removal. It was common ground that it was not a caravan within the ordinary meaning of the word – so that if the ordinary meaning of the word applied, the enforcement notice was good. It was, however, also common ground that the structure was a 'caravan' in the unusual sense of that term as defined by the Caravan

Sites and Control of Development Act 1960. If that definition was held to apply, then the enforcement notice was bad. The House of Lords, in a single speech delivered by Lord Lowry, held that the definition applicable was that in the 1960 Act.

The terms of the definition in s 29(1) of the 1960 Act are as follows:

> 'In this Part of this Act, unless the context otherwise requires – "caravan" means any structure designed or adapted for human habitation which is capable of being moved from one place to another (whether by being towed, or by being transported on a motor vehicle or trailer) and any motor vehicle so designed or adapted, but does not include – (a) any railway rolling stock which is for the time being on rails forming part of a railway system or (b) any tent . . .'

The litigation revealed a remarkable divergence of judicial opinion. The Secretary of State's inspector and Mr David Widdicombe QC, sitting as a deputy High Court judge, had taken the view that the 1960 Act definition was the correct one to be applied in this context. The Court of Appeal unanimously took the contrary view (see (1989) 87 LGR 464). The House of Lords, as mentioned above, agreed with the first instance judge. In so doing, the House rejected the view, which had found favour in the Court of Appeal, that 'caravan' should be construed in its ordinary popular sense.

Enforcement – Crown immunity

The first pages of the All England Reports for the new decade contained an important decision by the House of Lords on the application of planning and similar legislation to the Crown. In *Lord Advocate v Dumbarton District Council; Lord Advocate v Strathclyde Regional Council* [1990] 1 All ER 1, the House of Lords had to face the fundamental question of the extent of Crown Immunity, in Scotland, from enforcement action under the Town and Country Planning (Scotland) Act 1972 – for present purposes, similar to the Town and Country Planning Act 1971, (now Town and Country Planning Act 1990 – though this, too, does not apply to Scotland – s 337(3)) which applies south of the border – and the Roads (Scotland) Act 1974, which corresponds to some extent to the Highways Act 1980.

In general terms, the House of Lords decided that the English rule – that the Crown was not bound except by express words or by necessary implication – applies to Scotland also. The speech of Lord Keith of Kinkel, in whose judgment the rest of the House of Lords concurred, contains a wealth of detailed learning on the constitutional position of the Crown, both in England and Scotland.

The Ministry of Defence decided to erect an improved security fence at its submarine base at Faslane, Dumbartonshire. Part of the fence ran alongside the A814 road between Helensburgh and Garelochhead. As part of the construction works, the Ministry proposed to close off part of the A814 and to use it as a construction site for the building of the fence. Strathclyde Regional Council, as the roads authority, took the view that its permission would be required for this work, but the Ministry of Defence maintained that no such permission was necessary, because of Crown immunity.

Dumbarton District Council, as local planning authority, also objected to the works, and served on the Property Services Agency, who had taken charge of the works on behalf of the Ministry of Defence, an enforcement notice under s 84 of the Town and Country Planning (Scotland) Act 1972 (which corresponds to s 87 of the Town and Country Planning Act 1971 – *s 172 of the Town and Country Planning Act 1990*), and a stop notice under s 87 of the Town and Country Planning (Scotland) Act 1972 (which corresponds to s 90 of the Town and Country Planning Act 1971 – *s 183 of the Town and Country Planning Act 1990*). It was conceded by the Crown that the works involved amounted to 'development' within the meaning of the Town and Country Planning (Scotland) Act, s 19, which is in similar terms to s 22 of the Town and Country Planning Act 1971 (*s 55, Town and Country Planning Act 1990*).

On behalf of the Secretary of State for Defence, the Lord Advocate presented to the Court of Session separate petitions for judicial review, directed against Strathclyde Regional Council (the roads authority) and Dumbarton District Council (the local planning authority); the Lord Advocate also sought interdicts against enforcement of the notices. First hearings in the two petitions took place before Lord Cullen, who found that the Crown was not bound by the relevant enactments. On reclamation, the First Division (the Lord President, (Lord Emslie), Lord Grieve, and Lord Brand) held that the relevant enactments did bind the Crown. Before the appeal to the House of Lords, the work was completed, and thus the issue became in a sense academic. In view of the importance of the question, however, the House thought that it was important to address the major point of principle. Before the Act of Union in 1707, English law and Scots law had diverged on this point. The general approach of English law had been that Statutes did not bind the Crown, save where expressly provided (see *The King's Case* Case 84 (1604) Jenk 307, 145 ER 224). Scots law had recognised no such principle and held the Crown bound by general words in an Act of Parliament which were capable of applying to it. Some dicta of Scottish courts after the Union had seemed to adhere to the old doctrine (see for example, *Sommerville v Lord Advocate* (1893) 20 R 1050 and *Edinburgh Magistrates v Lord Advocate* 1912 SC 1085). Lord Keith contrasted these dicta with the consistent line of English cases which had followed the approach of *The King's Case*. The present position was regarded as correctly summarised by Diplock LJ (as he then was) when he stated in *BBC v Johns (Inspector of Taxes)* [1964] 1 All ER 923 at 941:

> 'The modern rule of construction of statutes is that the Crown, which today personifies the executive government of the country and is also a party to all the legislation, is not bound by a statute which imposes obligations or restraints on persons or in respect of property, unless the statute says so expressly or by necessary implication.'

It was also noted that in *Ministry of Agriculture Fisheries and Food v Jenkins* [1963] 2 All ER 147, it was held by the Court of Appeal that the Crown was not bound by the provisions of the Town and Country Planning Act 1947. In the Court of Session, the respondents had successfully contended for a more limited version of Lord Diplock's formulation, and had persuaded that court to adopt a test of whether the provision in question would in any event 'divest the Crown of some of its existing rights, interests or privileges'. Lord Keith found himself unconvinced by this interpretation of the authorities. It was preferable, in his view:

'to stick to the simple rule that the Crown is not bound by any statutory provision unless there can somehow be gathered from the terms of the relevant Act an intention to that effect. The Crown can be bound only by express words or by necessary implication. The modern authorities do not, in my opinion, require that any gloss should be placed on that formulation of the principle.' (18a)

In view of this approach, his Lordship held that there was nothing in either the Roads (Scotland) Act 1984 or the Town and Country Planning (Scotland) Act 1972 which was indicative of a Parliamentary intention that the Crown should be bound. So far as the planning Act was concerned, s 253, which had been taken by the Court of Session to support their conclusion that the Crown was bound, was thought by Lord Keith to point to the opposite conclusion, since it provides, in sub-s (1)(b), for the imposition of planning control to interests in Crown lands held otherwise than by or on behalf of the Crown. (The corresponding section in the Town and Country Planning Act 1971 is s 266, and *in the Act of 1990, ss 294–8*.):

'These provisions, read as a whole, make it quite clear that the whole Act proceeds on the assumption that the Crown is not subject to any requirement of planning permission for development carried out by it. It is true that the ordinary contemplation is that any development carried out by the Crown would be carried out on Crown land. It may be doubted whether Parliament could ever have envisaged that the Crown might carry out development anywhere but on Crown land. There would be no need for the Crown to seek planning permission for development on land which it was proposing to acquire in the future, because once it had acquired the land it could carry out the development without planning permission. So I do not consider that there can be any question of a Parliamentary intention that the Crown should be subject to the requirements of planning control in relation to land other than Crown land.' (at 16j–17a)

In addition, the appeal and calling in provisions of the planning Acts, establishing that 'the Crown, in the person of the Secretary of State is the final arbiter on planning control matters'. (17e) strongly suggested that the Crown itself was immune from planning control. It is difficult not to echo Lord Keith's *cri de coeur* at 18(b), that:

'it is most desirable that Acts of Parliament should always state explicitly whether or not the Crown is intended to be bound by any, and if so which, of their provisions.'

Enforcement – issue estoppel

In *Thrasyvoulou v Secretary of State for the Environment* [1988] 2 All ER 781, noted in All ER Review 1988, pp 340–342, the Court of Appeal confirmed the availability of 'issue estoppel' in certain planning contexts. This decision, to which, by the 'leap-frog' procedure, a further case (*Oliver v Secretary of State for the Environment*) was added, has now been confirmed by the House of Lords ([1990] 1 All ER 65).

The only speech in the House of Lords was delivered by Lord Bridge. In the *Thrasyvoulou* case he concentrated on the issue as it was alleged to have arisen in connection with Nos 13 and 15 Wilberforce Road. Here the issue could be summarised thus. In 1981, enforcement notices had been served alleging a breach of planning control in the use of the properties as a hotel, or alternatively as a hostel. In an appeal (the 1982 appeal), Thrasyvoulou contended that the use of these properties as a hotel had originated before 1964, and was thus outside the reach of an enforcement notice (s 87(1), Town and Country Planning Act 1971 – now reproduced in *s 172(4), Town and Country Planning Act 1990*). The inspector determined that the building was used as a hotel, not as a hostel, and that the premises had indeed been used as a guesthouse since 1960. In 1985, the use of the properties not having changed in the meantime, the local planning authority (Hackney London Borough Council) served a further enforcement notice alleging a breach of planning control in the use of the properties as hostels for homeless families. This was thought by Thrasyvoulou to be an attempt to revive an issue which had been decided in his favour by the inspector in the course of the 1982 appeal. He appealed against the 1985 enforcement notice; in these further appeal proceedings (the 1986 appeal) the inspector thought that he was entitled to consider afresh the issues which had been discussed in 1982, as the inspector thought that he was not bound by the decision of the previous inspector in the 1982 appeal.

In *Oliver*'s case, an enforcement notice was served in 1982 alleging a breach of planning control relating to the change of use of a structure standing on land in Hornchurch, which, it was said, was being used for storage purposes without the necessary grant of planning permission in that behalf. The Olivers appealed against this notice on the ground, inter alia, that the use of the structure in question was part of the use of the site as a whole as a transport and storage depot which was an established use of the site, having been commenced before 1964, and was therefore immune from attack by enforcement notice. The case for the local planning authority in that appeal was that although certain buildings on the site had an established use for storage purposes, other parts of the site had an established use of a different character, namely 'ancillary purposes such as the parking of vehicles' – thus, in effect, contending that different parts of the site were to be treated as different planning units. The inspector took the view that there was only one planning unit involved, which had an established use for storage purposes, and thus resolved the issue in favour of the Olivers. In 1986, the local planning authority, there having been no material change in the character of the use before that date, served a further enforcement notice, alleging a material change in the use of the land 'to a use for the purposes of a business of merchants, importers, repackers, and distributors of goods including paper products, textiles, and candles'. An appeal was lodged against this notice, and the inspector in the second appeal found against the Olivers, who appealed to the High Court under s 246 of the Town and Country Planning Act 1971 (*now s 289, Town and Country Planning Act 1990*). Malcolm Spence QC, sitting as a deputy judge of the High Court, took the view that if the question of issue estoppel could arise in planning proceedings (ie if *Thrasyvoulou*, which was then under appeal to the House of Lords, was correctly decided), then an issue estoppel arose against the local planning authority which was fatal to the 1985 enforcement notice. He granted the necessary certificate under s 12(1) of the Administration of Justice Act 1969 to enable an appeal to be brought direct to the House of Lords. Dismissing both appeals, Lord Bridge confirmed the availability of issue estoppel in general terms, regarding the availability of issue estoppel as a principle of statutory interpretation:

> 'The doctrine of res judicata rests on the twin principles which cannot be better expressed than in terms of the two Latin maxims, *interest reipublicae ut sit finis litium* and *nemo debet bis vexari pro una et eadem causa*. These principles are of such fundamental importance that they cannot be confined in their application to litigation in the private law field. They certainly have their place in criminal law. In principle they must equally apply to adjudications in the field of public law. In relation to adjudications subject to a comprehensive self-contained statutory code, the presumption, in my opinion, must be that, where the statute has created a specific jurisdiction for the determination of any issue which establishes the existence of a legal right, the principle of res judicata applies to give finality to that determination unless an intention to exclude that principle can properly be inferred as a matter of construction of the relevant statutory provisions.' (70j–71a)

He added that a refusal of planning permission gave rise to no such estoppel. A decision to withhold planning permission resolves no issue of legal right whatever. It is no more than a decision that in existing circumstances and in the light of existing planning policies the development in question is not one which it would be appropriate to permit. Clearly, in enforcement appeals no issue estoppel could arise where the appeal is on ground (a) in s 88(2) (*now s 174, Town and Country Planning Act 1990*).

In Lord Bridge's view, if issue estoppel in *Thrasyvoulou*'s case operated to resolve the issue in relation to numbers 13 and 15 Wilberforce Road, it was equally effective in the case of the other properties involved, and so he did not find it necessary to discuss the issues arising therein. As he saw it, issue estoppel was most likely to arise in planning appeals when one of grounds (b) to (e) in s 88(2) (*s 174 in the 1990 Act*) is in issue, because then there is a determination of a legal right. In holding issue estoppel to be available – though only where the finding was essential to the decision (see *Young v Secretary of State for the Environment* (1990) *Times*, 26 February) – in the light of the history of the planning legislation (whereunder magistrates were originally given the task of dealing with challenges to enforcement notices), Lord Bridge rejected the argument for the appellants that a statutory body could not be estopped from carrying out its statutory duty. It is clear that an estoppel by representation cannot have this effect – see *Southend-on-Sea Corporation v Hodgson (Wickford) Ltd* [1961] 2 All ER 46; but the rationale underlying the doctrine of res judicata is so different from that which underlies estoppel by representation that these authorities were not regarded as relevant.

In conclusion, it is interesting to note how flexibly the courts are prepared to regard the approach of Lord Scarman in *Pioneer Aggregates (UK) Ltd v Secretary of State for the Environment* [1984] 2 All ER 358, noted in All ER Rev 1984, p 301. In that case, it will be recalled, he enunciated the principle that planning law:

> 'is a field of law in which the courts should not introduce principles or rules derived from private law unless it be expressly authorised by parliament or necessary to give effect to the purpose of the legislation.'

Issue estoppel is clearly not within Lord Scarman's first exception – 'expressly authorised by Parliament'. One is thus forced to the conclusion that it falls within the second exception – the 'necessary to give effect to the purpose of the legislation' rule.

Enforcement – compensation after breach of planning control

Hughes v Doncaster Metropolitan Borough Council [1990] 2 All ER 53 involved an interesting issue as to the payment of compensation for disturbance on compulsory acquisition. Land had been used without planning permission, but enforcement proceedings were time-barred by the provisions of the Town and Country Planning Act 1971, as the use had commenced before 1964.

Did that mean that the use was 'contrary to law' within the meaning of rule 4 in s 5 of the Land Compensation Act 1971? This question, which had not apparently come up in quite that form, divided the Court of Appeal. The majority of the court (Staughton and Mann LJJ) were prepared, in conformity with the decision in *LTSS Print and Supply Services Ltd v Hackney London Borough* [1976] 1 All ER 311, to hold the use to be 'contrary to law', (though, of course, immune from enforcement proceedings). Dillon LJ dissented; finding that the *LTSS* case was inconsistent with the 1968 Act, and, in any event, concerned with a different issue. He thought that Parliament had recognised, in the provisions relating to enforcement notices in the case of change of use development, that 'there was an act of oblivion in respect of breaches of planning control before that date (ie 1964) and . . . it would be quite wrong to regard the use of the . . . land as a use which is "contrary to law"'.

Since Dillon LJ's dissent has now (on 13 December 1990) been approved by the House of Lords – (see *Hughes v Doncaster Metropolitan Borough Council* [1991] 1 All ER 295, allowing the cross-appeal on this point), fuller discussion of the majority decision in the Court of Appeal seems otiose; the decision in the House of Lords will be examined in next year's Review.

Miscellaneous

Two other cases, of some interest to planning lawyers, deserve a brief mention.

Charges for pre-planning consultations

In *R v Richmond upon Thames London Borough Council, ex p McCarthy & Stone (Developments) Ltd* [1990] 2 All ER 852, the Court of Appeal considered the legality of the practice of charging, by a local authority, for pre-application planning consultations. It is a common practice for developers who are minded to submit proposals for development or re-development to seek the informal views of the officers of the planning authority concerned as to the likely acceptability of their suggestions. The process is a useful one, both to the developer and the local planning authority – but, there being no free lunches, a cost is involved. The Court of Appeal has confirmed in this case that a charge (in this case a flat fee of £25) may lawfully be made for such consultations under s 111(1) of the Local Government Act 1972. The legislature had specifically conferred upon local planning authorities neither the duty nor the power to give such pre-application advice, but a charge could be made because such pre-application consultation was 'calculated to facilitate, or was conducive or incidental to' the local planning authority's exercise of its planning functions.

The Rose Theatre and locus standi

In *R v Secretary of State for the Environment, ex p Rose Theatre Trust Co* [1990] 1 All ER 754, Schiemann J, sitting in the High Court, held that the Secretary of State, in declining to schedule as a monument the site of the theatre in Southwark, had not acted improperly. Developers wished to develop the site as an office block, and had obtained planning permission in that behalf. He also held that the Rose Theatre Trust Company had no locus standi to move for judicial review of the Secretary of State's decision.